Champagne

Champagne

Tom Stevenson

Sotheby's Publications

This book is dedicated to my father,
a silver tankard and the 1928 vintage

© 1986 Tom Stevenson

First published 1986 for
Sotheby's Publications by
Philip Wilson Publishers Ltd
26 Litchfield St., London WC2H 9NJ

Available to the USA book trade from
Harper and Row, Publishers, Inc
10 East 53rd Street
New York NY 10022

Exclusive distribution to the wine trade
in the USA:

THE WINE APPRECIATION GUILD
155 Connecticut Street
San Francisco
California 94107
(415) 864-1202

ISBN 0 85667 318 8
Library of Congress Catalog Number 86-050037

Designed by Tim Higgins
Phototypeset in Linotron Sabon by
Tradespools Ltd, Frome
Printed and bound by Alden Press Ltd, Oxford

Contents

Maps

Foreword

IN WRITING THESE FEW WORDS as a preface to a penetrating and meticulously researched analysis of the wine of Champagne, I seek to pay tribute to the author's depth of research of his subject, greatly aided by the painstaking assistance, not only of the Comité Interprofessionnel du Vin de Champagne, but of the Houses and, by no means least, the *récoltants-manipulants*, those devoted disciples of the unique wine. For Champagne is a great wine *per se*, not merely designed to create an atmosphere of jollity at a wedding reception or to splatter on the bow of a ship at launching, but a drink to treasure and to enjoy for its own qualities.

This is a book which will be of interest to the connoisseur, for it deals with the intricate rules and regulations regarding the production and perfecting of the wine, as well as the complicated relationships stabilised by the CIVC between grower and merchant. But it is also of interest to the novice studying viticulture, and it stresses the basic fact that in producing Champagne, quantity invariably takes second place in importance to quality. Champagne is unique. No other wine can replace it.

MAURICE BUCKMASTER
Representative of the Comité Interprofessionnel du Vin de Champagne

Acknowledgements

I would like to thank a great number of people who have assisted me in the production of this book, but I owe so much to so many that I confess I cannot do justice to everyone concerned.

My thanks go to all those who assisted in various aspects of my research and to those who kindly provided me with so many informative and extensive tastings, but two people toiled on my behalf to such a disproportionate degree that it would be unjust not to single them out. Catherine Seydoux-Laffitte and Philippe le Tixerant of the Comité Interprofessionnel du Vin de Champagne (CIVC) between them coordinated my visits to more than fifty Champagne houses. They also bore the brunt of my enquiries and soon came to realise that answering one of my questions merely provoked another ten. I have happy memories, especially of my earliest days in Champagne when Philippe was relatively new to his job and we could both enjoy such novel experiences together. Dear Catherine, who arrived at the CIVC much later and has since departed, was very perceptive of and receptive to the depth and direction of my research and for this I shall always be grateful.

I experienced the greatest possible cooperation at most of the houses I visited, but I have to single out two in particular for the services they supplied while I was resident in Reims. I am extremely grateful to Champagne Piper-Heidsieck for supplying office and secretarial facilities and to Champagne Taittinger for the use of one of its furnished flatlets.

Over the six years it has taken to see this project to its fruition, I wondered more than once whether the book would ever be published. I dare say similar doubts have crossed the minds of others, not the least Philippe's and Catherine's, yet, if they did, it rarely showed and never interfered with their efforts to help me.

My thanks also go to: Monsieur Leroy Champagne Ayala; Jean-Michel Ducellier of Champagne Ayala and Champagne Montebello; Jean-Paul Brice of Champagne Barancourt; Colonel Maurice Buckmaster, Ron Emler, Malcolm McIntyre, Alison Pendree and Debbie Scott of The Champagne Bureau (UK); Xavier Bernard-Bordes of Champagne Besserat de Bellefon and Champagne Salon; James Coffinet and Jean Roland-Billecart of Champagne Billecart-Salmon; Christian Bizot and Arnold d'Hautefeuille of Champagne Bollinger; Pascal Andriveau of Champagne Canard-Duchêne; Pierre Planas of Champagne de Castellane; André Charbaut and René Charbaut of Champagne Charbaut; Jean-Marc Charles Heidsieck of Champagne Charles-Heidsieck; Alain Collery of Champagne Collery; Arnould Bro de Comères and André Lallier of Champagne Deutz: Jean-Charles Duval of Champagne Duval-Leroy; Christian Gallé of Champagne Alfred Gratien; Marcel Mabille of Champagne Germain; Antoine Gosset, the late Claude Gosset and Monsieur J. F. Paillard of Champagne Gosset; Thierry Mantoux of Champagne Henriot; Angela Glass of Champagne Heidsieck & Co Monopole; Pierre Horriot of Champagne Horriot; Jacques Seguillon of Champagne Irroy; Bernard Ivernel of Champagne Ivernel; François-Louis Bernard of Champagne Jacquart; Jean Hervé Chiquet and Yves Heidsieck of Champagne Jacquesson; Henri Krug and Rémi Krug of Champagne Krug; Jean-Baptiste Lanson and Pierre Lanson of Champagne Lanson and Champagne Massé; Mark Kernick, Comte Bernard de la Giraudière and Jean-Marie Loeillot of Champagne Laurent-Perrier; Dominique Foulon of Champagne Mercier and Champagne Moët & Chandon; Yves Benard, Dominique Foulon,

Jean-Paul Medard, Henri Perrier and Gilette Simon of Champagne Moët & Chandon; Monsieur Weremienko of Champagne Mumm; Étienne Prieur of Champagne Napoleon; Bruno Paillard of Champagne Bruno Paillard; Monsieur J. C. Colson of Champagne Palmer; Jean-Claude Fourmon and Jean-Louis Lange of Champagne Joseph Perrier; Michel Budin, Paul Couvreur and Philippe Gassiat of Champagne Perrier-Jouët; Dominique Collard-Philipponnat and Michel Collard of Champagne Philipponnat; Monsieur Dupin and Patrick Misselis of Champagne Piper-Heidsieck; Christian de Billy and Christian Pol Roger of Champagne Pol Roger; Patrick Bertrand, Mme Bezard, Claude Devos and Comte de Nattes of Champagne Pommery; Albert Ricciuti of Champagne Ricciuti-Révolte; Monsieur A. de Mareuil of Champagne Ruinart; Aymar de Baillenx and André Rouzard of Champagne Louis Roederer; Claude Taittinger of Champagne Taittinger and Champagne Irroy; Mme Schilliger and Wanda Wendelle of Champagne Taittinger; Michel Tixier of Champagne Michel Tixier; Paul Bergeot of Champagne de Venoge (formerly of Champagne Besserat de Bellefon and Champagne Salon); Luc Trouillard, formerly of Champagne de Venoge; Comte Louis-Marc d'Harcourt and Comte Alain de Vogüé of Champagne Veuve Clicquot; Joseph Dargent, formerly of the CIVC; André Enders, Jean Philippe Moulin and Jacques Perin of the CIVC; Monsieur G. Fremeaux of Coopérative Mailly-Champagne; Monsieur Fourchet, Rosine Page and Monsieur Pithois of les Grands Champagnes de Reims; Bertran de Belanda of the INAO based in Champagne; Monsieur A. Devletian of the INAO in Paris; Monsieur Baijot and Gaston Burtin of Marne & Champagne; Monsieur R. Delery of the Syndicat de Défense du Cru 'Blanquette de Limoux'; Monsieur Blaque and Roland Chaillon of the Syndicat Général des Vignerons de Champagne; Pierre Maury of UCAVIC; Monsieur Cestia of Union Champagne; Monsieur Duntze and Monsieur Lombard of the Union des Syndicats du Commerce des Vins de Champagne.

The following people deserve mention: Michael Bloom of Abingdon CFE for various translation tasks; John Clevely MW of H. Parrot & Co. Ltd, the UK agent for Veuve Clicquot and Canard Duchêne, for kindly providing an extensive tasting of both ranges in London; the late Colin Fenton MW for his invaluable tasting notes of Champagne Salon and for providing his historical researches on the origin of that fine house; Patrick Forbes of Moët & Chandon (London) for digging around in his attic for his old text book from the Avize School of Viticulture and Oenology to explain some of the statements made in *Champagne* (London, 1967) and, of course, for writing such an excellent book in the first place; Nancy Jarrat, also of Champagne Moët & Chandon (London), for her calm, cool and swift help during last-minute updating; the late Lord Kenilworth of the Ordre des Coteaux de Champagne, UK Chapter; Mark Savage MW of Windrush Wines for further discussions on the construction and ageing potential of Champagne Billecart-Salmon; my brother Bill for a catalogue of frank criticisms which greatly improved the original manuscript; Harry Waugh for his enthusiasm over lunch at the house of Salon, which prompted me to seek out Colin Fenton, thus taking my research much further than I had initially planned; Laurence Webber of Champagne Lanson in London; Michael Hodgson and Arthur Thomason of the Soil Institute at Rotherhamstead Experimental Station; Dr Geoffrey Tresise of the Merseyside County Museum; and Dr P. H. T. Beckett of the Soil Science Laboratory, University of Oxford.

Introduction

THE VICTORIANS CALLED IT 'Fizz', the Edwardians called it 'Bubbly', in the 1960s and '70s it was 'Champers'. Now it is 'Shampoo'. Since the Americans christened Charles-Camille Heidsieck 'Champagne Charlie' and George Leybourne hit the boards with his celebrated 'Champagne Charlie' song, Champagne has been affectionately referred to by some slang-name or other. No other wine can challenge its claim to be the world's most famous wine. 'Champagne with its foaming whirls/As white as Cleopatra's pearls' – Byron's lines are apt, for only Cleopatra and Helen of Troy launched more ships than Champagne.

In 1558 Paulmier described the wines of Aÿ, at that time the most celebrated growth in all Champagne, as 'the ordinary drink of kings and princes'. And the first wine to reach England from Champagne was a shipment of 'vin d'Aÿ'. Sent to Cardinal Wolsey in 1518, it was not sparkling of course, as sparkling wines were unknown during the reign of Henry VIII. When fizzy Champagne first emerged is unclear, but it evidently appeared in England before the renowned Benedictine cellarmaster Dom Pérignon had successfully produced an effervescing wine at the abbey of Hautvillers, and by 1676 had assumed such a fashionable status that Sir George Etherege could write in *The Man of Mode*:

> To the Mall and the Park
> Where we love till 'tis dark,
> Then sparkling Champaign
> Puts an end to their reign;
> It quickly recovers
> Poor languishing lovers,
> Makes us frolick and gay, and drowns all sorrow;
> But, Alas, we relapse again on the morrow.

In the eighteenth century the habit of drinking Champagne spread to Germany, Italy, Holland, Flanders, Switzerland, Denmark, Sweden, Norway and Russia. America took it up soon after George Washington served it to Senator Johnson of South Carolina in 1790. But it was not until the nineteenth century, when Champagne was exported under the *marques* of famous houses, that the entire civilised world began to drink it in quantity. By the mid-century America and England were jointly consuming more Champagne than all other countries put together. For specific houses like Roederer and Veuve Clicquot, Russia was the most lucrative market until the revolution. During the twentieth century Britain has consistently drunk more Champagne than any other country, although this achievement was America's in 1984, and it now looks as if that country, with four times Britain's population, might be set to out-drink the rest of the world.

As it is intended to establish in this book, not every sparkling wine may be called Champagne. Champagne is the product of specific grape varieties, Chardonnay, Pinot Noir and Pinot Meunier, grown in a legally delimited region of northern France. Having undergone two fermentations, the second of which gives it its luxurious sparkle and occurs in the bottle in which it is to be sold, the wine must undergo a maturation before it is allowed to be sold as Champagne. This ageing takes place in deep, dark cellars, often adapted from *crayères*, the vast Gallo-Roman caverns which were hewn out of the solid limestone subsoil to provide building materials for the construction of Reims.

Other good sparkling wines are made throughout the world, but none may be compared to the classic style and breed of Champagne. It did not become a star overnight. The region is situated in a viticultural twilight zone and Champagne's rise to fame and fortune was the result of a long, hard struggle by man and vine against the unfriendly elements of a mean northerly climate. The developments critical to Champagne's pre-eminent position in the world of sparkling wines stretched over more than two centuries.

When Dom Pérignon began his experiments in the seventeenth century, the procedure he used for producing sparkling wine was very crude and one which dated back to the monks of St Hilaire in 1531. Champagne was not invented, by Dom Pérignon or anyone else for that matter: its creation was an evolutionary process, not a revolutionary one. What elevated Champagne into a completely different league was what we call today the *Méthode Champenoise*, a sophistication of the procedure used at St Hilaire, yet a sophistication which took far longer than the single lifetime of Dom Pérignon to achieve. The *Méthode Champenoise* was a two-hundred-year accumulation of various practices: the utilisation of a *liqueur de tirage*, consisting of wine, yeast and sugar, to induce and thereby control the second fermentation and the degree of effervescence it creates; the invention of *remuage* to encourage all of the sediment to fall to the base of the cork, thus achieving a starbright wine through the application of *dégorgement* which removes the sediment; the development of the bottle-holding *pupitre* to increase the efficiency of *remuage*; and the addition of a *liqueur d'expédition* to improve the palatability of young sparkling wines.

When I started writing about Champagne I was aware that there was much to be learned on the subject. After writing this book, I realise how much more there is to be learned.

TOM STEVENSON, *April 1986*

I

Historical Perspective

Champagne with its foaming whirls
As white as Cleopatra's pearls.
Byron, *Don Juan* (1819–24)

The emergence of Champagne and its early wines

BEFORE THE ROMAN CONQUEST, the region we call Champagne was merely part of a fragmented group of Celtic kingdoms known as Gaul, an area of land roughly equivalent to present-day France. Viticulture was then unknown in its cold northern reaches: according to the observations of Dioderus Siculus, a Greek historian of the first century BC, 'the frigid climate of the uncultivated North forbade production of either wine or oil'.

By the first century AD, however, the Romans were cultivating the vine in Northern Gaul. We know from Cato the Censor (234–149 BC), the author of *De agri cultura*, that the various methods of planting, grafting, training and pruning of the vine, which the Romans would have introduced into Champagne, had been in common use throughout the warmer parts of the empire for at least two hundred years. Without a doubt, the Romans had achieved a sophisticated level of vine-growing, training the vines, much as today, in parallel rows, and ensuring proper spacing between each plant. No less than six different methods of pruning were employed, the utilisation of each being dependent upon the variety of grape, type of soil and wind conditions.

Curiously, however, between AD 90 and 97, an imperial order went out to uproot all commercial vineyards throughout Gaul. Issued by Emperor Domitian, the decree also prohibited the extension of vineyards in Italy. It seems a strange edict for an empire so intent on spreading the culture of the vine, but it was one of economy and rationalisation, in an endeavour to effect a balance between the overproduction of wine and the shortage of basic food crops. Wine was cheap and plentiful during this period, while corn was scarce and expensive. Domitian's decree was the first recorded attempt to reduce a European winelake.

It is difficult to gauge how effective the ban was, but the vineyards were certainly flourishing again by AD 285, a mere five years after Domitian's order was rescinded. Emperor Probus, perhaps appropriately a gardener's son, issued the directive in AD 280 to replant the vineyards of Gaul.

The third and fourth centuries, however, also saw the waning of the Roman Empire, when the protection it offered to the population of border provinces began to weaken, giving rise to waves of 'barbarian' invasions from the east. In the early years of the fifth century the Roman province of Belgica, west of the Rhine frontier, was invaded by the Germanic-speaking Franks, the people who were to give their name to the country in which they settled. In the heart of this early Frankish kingdom lay the region which, much later, was to be called Champagne.

The Franks were not savages, but they did not settle easily into the sophisticated urban life-style of the local Gallo-Roman population. In a near-chaotic situation the formerly tranquil province – lying at a strategic crossroads for invading armies – became subjected to bands of looting Franks, Vandals, Burgundians and Goths. The most ferocious of these invaders was the 500,000-strong army of Attila the Hun, which stormed into the Empire in the spring of 451.

Although repelled initially by the bishop of Troyes (a town destined to become the capital of Champagne) the eastern hordes were able to sweep on, virtually unchecked, until they reached Orleans. The real turning point occurred just north of Châlons, during September when, in one of the bloodiest battles of human history, over 200,000 men were killed in hand-to-hand combat in less than twenty-four hours. Victory fell to the Roman commander Aetius, but only after he had desperately allied his legions with the forces of the Empire's declared enemies, the invading Visigoths and Franks.

The Roman Empire was already split into eastern and western halves, but its growing impotence was now demonstrated by the inability of its imperial armies to deal with Attila independently – it was a warning that the Roman Empire in the west was almost dead. Within twenty-five years it was.

In the 480s, the Franks, who were now established throughout Gaul, found a decisive ruler in their chieftain Clovis (465–511). He united their clans and established an expanding kingdom around the former Gallo-Roman city of Durocortorum: once the capital of the Gaulish tribe of Remi, the city is still commemorated today by its name Reims. Christianity came to the Franks when, in 496, Clovis was baptised by Bishop Remigius (better known to us as Saint-Rémy) whose name surely is a reminder of the ancient Remi. There had, of course, been Christians here, as elsewhere in the Empire, since the middle of the third century, but it was by Clovis's example – in fulfilment of a vow made in battle – that the heathen Frankish warriors accepted baptism from Remigius.

The glory of the Franks reached its apogee towards the end of the ninth century when their chieftain Charlemagne was crowned emperor of a revived Roman Empire in the West by the pope on Christmas day 800. The event to a large extent heralded the return of order and culture.

Charlemagne was succeeded in 814 by his son Louis the Pious (Louis I of France), the first in a long line of French kings to be crowned at Reims. From this traditional privilege of Reims, the fame and popularity of Champagne wines first began to spread. According to Alexander Henderson, in *The History of Ancient Wines* (1824), the ninth century saw the beginning of a distinction between the various wines of Champagne; references henceforth distinguish between the wines of the Vallée de la Marne and those of the Montagne de Reims. After the death of Louis I in 840 the Empire – which stretched from the Pyrenees in the south-east to the Elbe and the Danube in the west – was carved up into three kingdoms, shared between Charlemagne's three grandsons.

In the tenth century, the peace of Champagne was shattered in ten violent years of political battle by the house of Vermandois in its bid to secure the bishopdom of Reims. Bloodier, longer and also fought over Champagne soil was the struggle between Hugh Capet and Charles of Lorraine for the French throne. Reims suffered four sieges in sixty years, Épernay was pillaged half a dozen times and burnt twice. Hugh Capet executed the most proficient sacking of Épernay during the harvest of 947, when he set alight the entire region and carried off all of its wine. Heribert of Vermandois eventually guaranteed the bishopdom of Reims for his son Robert and the house of Vermandois assumed the title of Counts of Champagne. Hugh Capet paved the way for his son and namesake to be crowned king of France at Reims in 987.

Champagne became established as a political unit in the early eleventh century when the house of Vermandois united the counties of Troyes and Meaux. For a brief period in the province's history, its affairs became entwined in the broader struggles for the monarchy. Between 1019 and 1023, Champagne fell into the hands of Eudes II, the count of Blois and Chartres, who had a few years earlier annexed Sancerre. The power of Blois-Champagne now threatened the Capetian rule whose royal domain around Paris was encircled. But with the death of Eudes in 1037, the properties of Champagne were divided amongst his descendants while the strength of Blois naturally declined.

Champagne was reunited with Blois, however, under Thibaut IV who, upon the reunification of the two powerful provinces in 1125, became Thibaut II ('the Great') of Champagne. Thibaut was considered the second most powerful man in France after the king. A powerful rivalry developed between them, and the conflicts, first with Louis VI

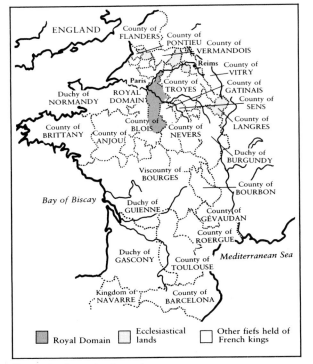

France in the early eleventh century

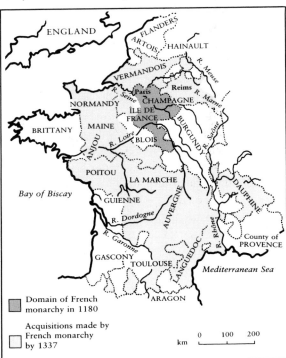

Growth of the French monarchy, 1180–1350

The House of the Musicians in the rue de Tambour, Reims, haunt of the *trouvères*

and then with Louis VII, ended only when Joan of Navarre and Champagne, the heir to the countship of Blois-Champagne, married the future king of France, Philip Augustus.

But Philip still did not trust the loyalty of Champagne and allowed the office of *sénéchal* (steward of the royal household), which was customarily awarded to a member of the count of Champagne's family, to lapse.

Thibaut IV of Champagne, the son of Thibaut III and Blanche of Navarre, was born after his father's death at Troyes in 1201. For four years of his early life he lived at the court of King Philip II, to whom he did feudal homage in 1214. After the king's death in 1223, he pledged his support for Philip's son Louis VII, but deserted him at the siege of Avignon in 1226. When Louis died a few months later, Thibaut aligned with a league of dissident barons who opposed the regent of France, Louis's widow Blanche of Castile, but he soon abandoned the barons and reconciled himself with Blanche.

The court of Champagne had meanwhile become a place of development for the ideal of courtly love and the medieval romantic poem.   Thibaut IV was a musician and probably the most famous of the aristocratic *trouvères,* the epic poets of Northern France. It was rumoured that he and Blanche were lovers and that many of his poems were addressed to her.

Champagne was also prospering during this time from the great trade fairs. While in times of war its uneasy location between the Frankish and German kingdoms rendered it prone to the ravages of invading armies, in times of peace, it was ideally situated at the crossroads to the great trade centres of Europe. Fairs were held annually and throughout the seasons of the year: there was the 'Warm' June Fair and the 'Cold' October Fair of Troyes, the May Fair and the September Fair of Saint Ayoul in Provins, the Lent Fair of Bar-sur-Aube and the January Fair of Lagny.

The fairs could last for up to forty-nine days and became a meeting place for merchants from Spain, Italy, England, the Low Countries and other parts of France. The counts of Champagne were quick to realise the lucrative sources of income that could be made from these fairs and dropped any inhibiting feudal dues, guaranteed the safety of the merchants and generally policed the fairs. Copious quantities of Champagne wine were consumed by such a large influx of visitors, enabling the vineyards to flourish and the *vignerons* to prosper, and leading to the export of both the wine and its reputation throughout the growing markets of Europe.

The importance of wine for Reims as a form of commerce in the early 1300s was demonstrated by the emergence of the *courtiers de vin*. In 1323 the appointment of these professional wine-brokers by the city's municipal authorities was opposed by the archbishop, who had traditionally held a vested interest in the local winemaking from which they derived an income. But his resistance was doomed to failure as the *courtiers'* position was confirmed by several royal decrees. A century later a royal charter of July 1412 gave the municipal authorities of Reims the sole right to appoint *courtiers* and expressly mentioned that Champagne wines formed the city's prime source of trade. The charter also attempted to curb the sharp practices of those *courtiers* who took commission from both seller and buyer.

In 1337, Edward III of England launched his assault on the French crown and so began the Hundred Years War, in which Champagne became one of the principal battlegrounds. Charles IV of France had died leaving no male heir, and the contest opened between two rival claimants, Philip VI of Valois, Charles's cousin, and Edward, whose mother Isabella of France was the daughter of Philip III. Ostensibly to recover lost English possessions, Edward's invasion of France followed almost immediately in the wake of Philip's unopposed seizure of the French throne. King John II succeeded Philip in 1350 and, after a series of English victories during which John was captured and sent back to England, Edward led his army on to Champagne. In 1359 he attempted to storm Reims in a bid to be crowned king of France in its cathedral. His attempt failed, but the Treaty of Bretigny was concluded which gave Edward sovereignty over Calais and the whole of Aquitaine, almost a quarter of France. Content with his achievement, Edward renounced his claim to the French crown.

But the plague returned to France in 1361, and the devastation it imposed, coupled with the laxity and incompetence of the English administration, weakened the English grip on its French territories. War was resumed, and the French now succeeded in reclaiming most of Aquitaine, leaving only Calais and a thin coastal strip under firm English control.

Ten years earlier, on 19 May 1364, the coronation of Charles V had taken place at Reims cathedral. The ceremonies and festivities attending the coronation of French kings at Reims did much to enhance the popularity and reputation of the wines of Champagne – though they cannot entirely have pleased the populace of Reims, who had to meet the expense of such occasions. Charles v's coronation, and the feast which followed it, cost the city over 7,712 *livres*, according to Varin's *Archives Administratives de Reims*. The spectacle, however, must have been a splendid one: Froissart records that the king and his queen (Jeanne de Bourbon) were accompanied by King Peter of Cyprus, King Wenceslas of Bohemia and the duke of Brabant, the dukes of Burgundy and Anjou and the counts of Eu, Dampmartin, Tancarville and Vaudemont.

Ever-increasing demand stimulated a great viticultural expansion in the last half of the fourteenth century. A list drawn up *c.* 1375 by Richard Pique, who as archbishop was due annual payments in the form of wine, reveals that virtually all the villages within a twenty mile radius of Reims were planted with vines.

Further anecdotes on the fame of Champagne wines in the fourteenth century are told by Max Sutaine in his *Essai sur l'histoire des vins de la Champagne* (1845); in particular he relates how, when the German king Wenceslas arrived in Reims in 1397 to discuss with Charles VI the division within the church over the popes of Avignon (a subject Henry Vizetelly describes in *A History of Champagne* (1882) as 'very fit for a drunkard and a madman to put their heads together about') he became so intoxicated on the local wines that he signed all the documents before him, departing without knowing what he had signed.

The further expansion of Champagne's vineyards suffered a temporary set-back in the early part of the fifteenth century when the old war with the English was resumed. King Henry V of England was recognised by a mad King Charles VI as heir to the throne of France, with the signing of the Treaty of Troyes in 1420, and Reims passed once again into English control. Charles VII, excluded from the succession by the treaty, was, however, recognised as king in the south of France and the bitter struggles for sovereignty continued. The tide turned for the French when, under the inspired leadership of Joan of Arc, Charles was taken to Reims to be crowned king in the cathedral in 1429. The triumphant coronation and surge of patriotic fervour which followed in its wake led a worried duke of Bedford, the English regent in France and uncle of Henry VI of England, to call for his nephew's own coronation on French soil.

French successes faltered, however, when the maid of Orleans, failing in her attempt to wrest Paris from the English in 1430, was captured and burned at the stake in Rouen on 30 May 1431. On 2 December Henry VI was crowned king of France in Saint Denis, Paris. But this did little to consolidate control over a country claimed but not subdued and when Duke Philip of Burgundy broke from his alliance with the English to pledge support for Charles VII at Arras in 1435, the days of English rule in France were numbered. Inspired by the martyrdom of Joan of Arc and backed by the forces of Burgundy, the French expelled the English from all their former possessions except Calais, bringing the so-called Hundred Years War to a successful conclusion in 1453.

Relative peace ensued in Champagne in the years which followed, although it was not until the coronation of Louis XI in 1461 that the French nobility were able to express their new solidarity. The coronation at Reims was a truly grand occasion, with all the major peers and bishops throughout the realm in attendance at one of the most expensive banquets ever lavished on a French king. Barely one month later, the city's generosity was rewarded by a special royal tax levied on its wines to fill the king's empty coffers!

In Reims during the early sixteenth century, visiting heads of state were often given wines of various growths from the Montagne de Reims and the Vallée de la Marne to compare with wines from the king's own vineyards at Aÿ. The fame of Aÿ was at its peak, and its wines were set apart from other growths; as beautifully understated by Paulmier in his treatise *De Vino et Pomaceo* (Paris, 1588), Aÿ was 'the ordinary drink of kings and princes'. According to Henry Vizetelly in his *History of Champagne*, many nobles went to the expense of having their own special buying commissioners stationed in the village to secure the finest vintages of this royal wine.

It is also from Aÿ and from this date that the oldest surviving Champagne house can be traced. In 1531 Jean Gosset was *seigneur d'Aÿ* and his son Claude Gosset was a *vigneron*. No documentary evidence exists to establish whether Claude actually traded his wines, and since a Champagne house deals essentially in the commerce of wines, the house of Gosset is deemed to have commenced with a Pierre Gosset from a later generation in 1584, who both made and sold his wines.

The reputation of Champagne was growing fast, as can be assessed from the record of rapidly rising prices. At the coronation of Francis II in 1559 a *queue*, a cask of ninety-six gallons, cost between 11s. 8d. and 15s. 10d., whilst at the coronation of Charles IX in 1561, just two years later, a *queue* had risen to between 23s. 4d. and 28s 4d. Fourteen years later, at the coronation of Henry III in 1575, it was between 45s. and 62s.

Towards the close of the sixteenth century, however, Champagne harvests suffered greatly from extraordinarily bad climatic conditions. According to Jehan Pussot's *Mémorial du temps* the price of wine varied enormously: it could be sold as cheaply as

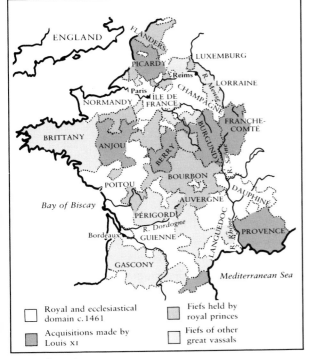

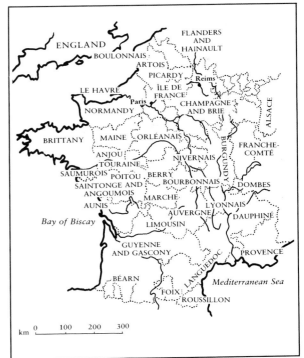

France in 1483

The *gouvernements* of France in 1789

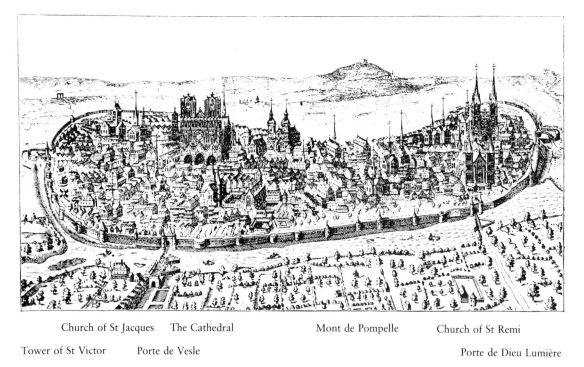

Church of St Jacques   The Cathedral   Mont de Pompelle   Church of St Remi

Tower of St Victor   Porte de Vesle   Porte de Dieu Lumière

THE CITY OF REIMS IN 1635 (from an engraving of the period)   Porte de Flèchambault

5s. 6d. a *queue* (as in 1579) if it was almost undrinkable, while on other occasions, the price would reach as high as 126s. 8d (1587) due to its scarcity. The vicissitudes of climate and harvest continued into the seventeenth century and Pussot goes on to record the contrast between the abundant vintage of 1604, when the *vignerons* were 'at their wits' end for vessels to contain their wine', and the devastating harvest three years later when the vintage was considered so poor that it 'had not been known within the memory of man'. Such vacillating fortunes of harvest were to become the norm for Champagne and, perversely, prove to be one of the reasons why this region is able to produce a sparkling wine superior to any other.

The development of Champagne as a sparkling wine

Up to the seventeenth century the wines produced in Champagne were not the sparkling, brilliant white wines we know today: they were still wines, or *vins tranquils*.

It is difficult for us to imagine the characteristics of wines described by critics writing a mere generation ago, let alone those of wines described centuries ago. Nevertheless, it is useful to know that numerous contemporary sources described the various hues of the wines of this period as 'pale coloured and tawny', 'with a rosy tinge' or even like a 'partridge's eye'. Since earliest times it seems that attempts were made to make wine as red as possible: in those places where vines producing white grapes thrived, it is likely that any black grapes available would have been thrown into the brew to give the wine a little colour, but in Champagne's naturally crisp climate, the skins of black grapes rarely give much colour to a wine, hence the weak and insipid impressions of early descriptions. However, as early as the sixteenth century, we know from the fame already achieved by the wines of Aÿ that a few winemakers had begun to experiment with wines made from white grape only. Of course the cruder methods of pressing grapes in those days would often have resulted in rather murky-looking wines which failed to clear properly. Later, in a treatise written in the eighteenth century, *Mémoire sur la manière de cultiver la vigne et de faire le vin en Champagne* (written, it is believed, by Jean Godinot *c.* 1718), it is stated that the Champenois had begun to study how to produce a 'grey ... almost white wine' some fifty years before, that is to say approximately 1668.

If one takes wines such as these together with the inevitably ill-fated attempts to make a red wine from black grapes grown in a climate barely hospitable enough to ripen a grape, let alone colour it, a wealth of curiously coloured, clouded wines must have constituted the norm, despite a half-hidden glint of pink or red in a few instances.

We know that Champagne was not the first sparkling wine: references in the Bible like 'wine ... when it moveth itself' (Proverbs 23:31) and 'Neither do men put new wine into old bottles; else the bottles break' (Matthew 9:17) confirm the existence of sparkling wine long before viticulture was even introduced to the Champagne region. But because of the obvious difficulties encountered in the fermentation process, the wines of antiquity would have been drunk, more often than not, before the first fermentation had finished or whilst undergoing the second fermentation the following spring. The earliest sparkling wines were undoubtedly discovered by accident, probably by the trial and error methods employed by anguished winemakers ironically trying to avoid the nuisance of fizzy wines.

Nobody can say for sure when the earliest purpose-made sparkling wine was produced, but documentary evidence exists to prove that the monks of the abbey of St Hilaire in southern France had intentionally produced sparkling wines as early as 1531, well over one hundred years before anyone attempted to do so in Champagne. These sparkling wines of St Hilaire, known as vin de blanquette, were and still are produced, just east of Limoux, south of the old walled city of Narbonne, by the so-called 'rural method'. The 'rural method' entails no separate second fermentation; it is merely a continuation of the first process, the wines being bottled before it terminates and thus allowing the first fermentation to continue in the bottle. The sediment deposited in the bottle during the final stages of the 'rural method' is not removed and the wine will thus be a little cloudy unless expertly handled.

Dom Pérignon

Nobody knows exactly when the first sparkling Champagne was made but the famous Benedictine monk from the abbey of Hautvillers certainly was a crucial figure in its early development. The legend enshrines a popular belief that it was Dom Pérignon who created sparkling wine and invented Champagne as we know it today. But he did not: the man's life has become a fable of great imagination and his prowess as a winemaker has assumed almost mythical proportions. It is therefore important that the precise nature of his achievements should be clarified.

Pierre Pérignon was born at Sainte-Ménehould near the Champagne-Lorraine border in 1638. Little is known of his early life, except that he was the son of a judge's clerk, of upper-middle class background, and that the male members of the family were engaged in either the legal or ecclesiastical professions.

On 3 July 1658 Pierre Pérignon entered the Benedictine abbey of Saint-Vanne at Verdun, a congregation founded by Dom Didier de la Cour (1550–1623), a strict monk who insisted on a high degree of learning and intellectual activity.

Didier's example was built upon by his successors and the esteem of the abbey grew. The strict selection of monks applying to Saint-Vanne and the high standards of learning it demanded of them provide an early insight into Pérignon's own capabilities. Moreover, within just eleven years he had been elevated to the honorific status of 'Dom' and sent to the abbey of Hautvillers to take up the post of cellarmaster, a position second only to that of abbot.

During his forty-seven years at Hautvillers, Dom Pérignon earned the reputation of being a generous, intelligent and meticulously minded man. As a winemaker, his skills were greatly revered by other cellarmasters, who attributed, in part, the outstanding quality of his wine to the fastidiousness of his studies. Even in his own day his wines were called, not after Hautvillers, but after the man himself, *vins de Pérignon*. His fame spread far and wide and the price of his wines soared.

Hautvillers Abbey

Madame Veuve Clicquot *née* Ponsardin (1777–1866):
painting by Léon Cogniet

The classic grapes of Champagne: Pinot Noir
(ABOVE), Pinot Meunier (LEFT) and
Chardonnay (BOTTOM LEFT)

Dom Pérignon grew blind in his final years but this did not prevent – it rather enhanced – his passion for the art of winemaking. He died at Hautvillers in 1715 at the age of seventy-seven.

What did he specifically invent, create or achieve? Patrick Forbes gets right to the heart of the matter when, in his scholarly work *Champagne* (1967), he refers to a treatise, *Traité de la culture des vignes de Champagne*, written by a certain Frère Pierre, a member of the community at the abbey of Hautvillers during and after the time of his mentor Dom Pérignon. Written by Dom Pérignon's pupil and immediate successor at Hautvillers, the treatise must be regarded as the most authoritative contemporary account, not only of the state of viticulture and viniculture in Champagne in the late seventeenth and early eighteenth centuries, but also of Dom Pérignon's particular contribution to the art of winemaking. From this treatise and other evidence, it can be deduced that Dom Pérignon achieved the following innovations: he was the first person in Champagne to produce a truly red wine; the first person to produce a perfectly limpid white wine from black grapes; he invented the traditional Champagne press; perfected the art of blending wines from many different vineyards to produce one consistent and superior *cuvée*, or blend; reintroduced the cork-stopper to France; and pioneered the use of stronger English glass to withstand the internal pressure generated by sparkling wine.

Because of Champagne's northerly latitude and the cold, wet influence of the Atlantic, all grapes must struggle to ripen in this region and black grapes rarely possess sufficient pigment in the skins to properly colour a wine. The problem of how to produce a red wine was as acute in Dom Pérignon's time as it is today, but according to Frère Pierre he found a solution to the problem by using old vines and selecting only the ripest grapes; he was thus able to achieve three or four successful vintages of decently coloured wines for about every ten, when the vines might enjoy exceptional warmth during the summer.

In a letter dated 25 October 1821, Dom Grossard, the last cellarmaster of Hautvillers, informed Monsieur d'Herbes, the deputy mayor of Aÿ, that it was Dom Pérignon who had discovered the secret of making starbright white wines. 'Before him,' he said, 'people only knew how to make a grey wine or one that was the colour of straw.' Dom Grossard need not be correct; certainly Pérignon perfected the art of producing starbright white wines, but it is possible that others succeeded before him – the fame of the white wines of Aÿ, for example, suggests this. But what Dom Pérignon did accomplish, which was unique at the time, was the production of a clear, untainted, white wine from black grapes.

The discovery is doubly important. Since Pérignon's time it has become evident that although the climate of Champagne barely manages to colour black grapes one particular variety, the Pinot Meunier, is the region's most prolific producer and the vine least prone to the severe frosts experienced in the Marne valley. Today nearly half of all the vines grown in the white wine vineyards of Champagne are of the Pinot Meunier variety – a practicality only possible because of Pérignon.

To obtain a clear white wine from black grapes Dom Pérignon would have had to employ sophisticated pressing techniques; it is most likely, therefore, that it was Pérignon who invented the traditional Champagne press, designed exactly for this purpose. The juice of all wine-producing black grapes is clear, but in order to extract it it has to be pressed through the grape's skin which, even in chilly Champagne, contains enough pigment to discolour the liquid. Traditional Champagne presses can be either round or square, but both compress a wide and thin cross-section of grapes which, unlike those in other areas, are not de-stalked. The press is uniquely designed to ensure that the pressure exerted is swift – to reduce the skin-contact time – and yet gentle enough to avoid the escape of unfavourable tannins and oils residing naturally in the pips and stalks. It was Dom Pérignon who conceived of the idea that the stalks would act as channels through the relatively thin cake of grapes, allowing the flow of juice to be speeded up.

A further innovation, one of the most significant accomplishments of Dom Pérignon, was his creation of the *cuvée* concept, or the blending together of different wines, some of them inferior, to achieve one superior and consistent *cuvée*. Both Frère Pierre and Dom Grossard record at length how Pérignon constructed his *cuvées*. Grossard declared that it was the 'marriage of our wines to which they owe their goodness'. The blending of wines was not an uncommon practice prior to Pérignon's time, either in Champagne or elsewhere, but it was Dom Pérignon's innate ability to construct a final *cuvée*, far exceeding in quality any previous blends, which led to his esteemed reputation in his own lifetime, creating a unique demand for the *vins de Pérignon*. Frère Pierre recorded:

He composed his blends not only according to the flavour of the juice, but also according to what the weather had been like that year – an early or late development, depending on the amount of cold or rain there had been – and according to whether the vines had grown a rich or mediocre foliage. All these factors served him as rules for the composition of the blends.

Dom Grossard further informs us that 'He could tell at once which grapes were from which vineyards and would say, "The wine of that vineyard must be married with the wine of that one", and never once did he make a mistake.' Grapes for pressing would be brought in from many different vineyards, following Dom Pérignon's explicit instructions. According to Patrick Forbes, in *Champagne*, the abbey of Hautvillers owned one hundred *arpents* (an *arpent* is an old French measure which varied in size between thirty-five and fifty ares) of vineyards some thirty years before Dom Pérignon's time and this estate would have certainly increased in his lifetime. In addition, the abbey received wines in the form of tithes. The demand for *vins de Pérignon* far exceeded supply and, as a consequence, grapes had to be purchased from outside the abbey's holdings to meet increased production levels. This meant seeking out even more diverse wines from hitherto unknown sources, which further taxed the new-found art of blending.

Dom Pérignon cared little for the wooden plugs wrapped in oil-soaked hemp which were in use during his time. Not only did he find this crude form of seal unsuitable for his normal still wines, but when he began to produce sparkling wines the total inadequacy of wooden pegs for imprisoning the carbonic gas was such that he set out to discover a more efficient seal. Cork-stoppers had been used by the Romans as long ago as 500 BC, but were 'lost' to the French when the Romans left Gaul some twelve hundred years before Dom Pérignon's day, though they were available elsewhere in Europe. How exactly corks came to be adopted at Hautvillers remains a mystery, but one story relates that when Spanish monks stopped at Hautvillers on their way north from Santiago de Compostela, Dom Pérignon noticed that their water-bottles were sealed with corks and requested supplies of this spongy material to be sent to him. Another suggests that Dom Pérignon spent several years in the Benedictine monastery at Alcántara in Spain and that it was he, not the monks of Santiago de Compostela, who brought the cork to Hautvillers. It hardly matters whether either of these stories is true, we know that cork was available, although not in France, and that Dom Pérignon did eventually use cork-stoppers for his wines, as corked bottles were dug up at Hautvillers when Moët & Chandon renovated the abbey in the late 1970s during its operations to turn it into a museum.

Once Dom Pérignon had learned how to produce a constant sparkling wine, and how to prevent any gas escaping from the bottle, through the use of a cork-stopper, the problem of breakages, a frequent occurrence, must have been acute. It was almost predictable that a perfectionist like Pérignon would not rest until he found a bottle strong enough to withstand the internal pressure exerted by a sparkling wine.

The use of the bottle to store and contain wine was an English custom; the French at this time generally preferred the use of casks to store, serve and transport their wines. *Verre anglais*, named thus because of its English origin, was the result of Admiral Sir Robert Mansell's concern for the future of British shipbuilding. He was worried by the decimation of forests by charcoal burners and persuaded King James I to forbid glass furnaces to be fired with wood in 1615. Turning to coal instead, the higher temperatures it achieved enabled English glass makers to develop an intrinsically stronger product.

How he heard of *verre anglais* is unclear, but it is not beyond belief that it stemmed from rumours that effervescing Champagne had become a popular drink in England. Before Dom Pérignon had made his name as a great winemaker, the effects of sparkling Champagne had achieved sufficient significance in England to merit the occasional mention, as the following verse from *The Man and the Mode*, written by Sir George Etherege in 1676, indicates:

> To the Mall and the Park
> Where we love till 'tis dark,
> Then sparkling Champaign
> Puts an end to their reign;
>   It quickly recovers
>   Poor languishing lovers,
> Makes us frolick and gay, and drowns all sorrow;
> But, Alas, we relapse again on the morrow.

The idea of 'accidentally sparkling' Champagne is far more plausible than it may at first seem. In Champagne's chilly climate the fermentation process would stop when winter took its grip, probably before all the grape sugars had been converted to alcohol, but certainly before any malo-lactic fermentation could naturally occur. The wine, transported in cask and bottled in London in the superior *verre anglais*, would remain dormant until the warmth of the following spring or, maybe, the warmth of a local tavern. Alcoholic or malo-lactic fermentation would commence, possibly a combination of both, and the result would be a sparkling wine along the lines of Limoux's Vin de Blanquette. If indeed this was how he happened upon *verre anglais*, it could well be that it was in England, not Spain, that Dom Pérignon rediscovered the cork.

I doubt whether the legend of Dom Pérignon would necessarily have survived to this day but for the fact that the Abbey of Hautvillers, where he devoted his life to the perfection of wine, happened to be in Champagne. One wonders whether he would still be so well remembered had he lived his monastic life in the Abbey of Saint-Hilaire in Roussillon. Moreover, it should not be forgotten that in 1823 Moët & Chandon purchased the Abbey of Hautvillers, along with its vineyards, and they certainly (to their credit) cannot be accused of allowing the legend of Dom Pérignon to die.

Frère Jean Oudart

According to Henry Vizetelly in his *A History of Champagne*, another monk whose reputation in the art of winemaking rivalled that of Dom Pérignon's was Brother Jean Oudart, the cellarer at the abbey of Saint Pierre-aux-Monts in Châlons, and just sixteen years younger than Dom Pérignon. The abbey of Saint Pierre-aux-Monts had considerable vineyard holdings at Pierry, Chouilly and Cramant which collectively boasted an average annual production of around 400 hectolitres. As cellarer to the abbey it was Brother Oudart's responsibility to manage these estates together with a staff of some 130 women and 20 men. Like Dom Pérignon, Brother Oudart was interested in perfecting the art of winemaking and we know, from a record of a transaction which took place at Pierry on 9 September 1713, that he was visited at least once by the older cellarmaster from Hautvillers.

It is uncertain exactly what contributions Brother Oudart made to the development of the Champagne method but we know that he also used corks from Spain and it has been suggested that he was the first to use a *liqueur de tirage*. But it should be remembered that if there are doubts about the precise nature of Brother Oudart's accomplishments, there is also uncertainty about Dom Pérignon's.

It was not until the eighteenth century that the word Champagne became synonymous with the sparkling wine of the region. Even with the fame of Dom Pérignon in the seventeenth century the name Champagne was strictly reserved for the still wines, although the slightly *pétillant* wines were also included. Before the turn of the century fully *mousseux* wines were referred to simply as *vins mousseux*, *sauté bouchant*, *flaçon mousseux* or *vins de Pérignon*.

Champagne wines became immensely popular in the eighteenth century amongst the English aristocracy. Princess Charlotte-Elizabeth declared the regent's passion for it in a letter dated 13 August 1716 exclaiming, 'When my son gets tipsy, it is not on strong drinks or spiritous liquors, but on the pure wines of Champagne.' In *Champagne*, Patrick Forbes indicates the indispensability of popping champagne corks for the success of a ball, stating that no less than 1,800 bottles of *mousseux* were consumed during a party held on 30 August 1739 at which Louix XV apparently attended *incognito*. But its boom in popularity was still a selective one – probably due to the fact that it was not until 1830 that the transport of Champagne in bottles became legally permitted. Prior to this time it had to travel in cask and the resultant 'sparkling' wine must have been a sorry product, hardly an advertisement for its quality and reputation. Only the very rich could afford to get hold of the real product, bottled and matured in the region itself.

The eighteenth century, however, saw the founding of ten Champagne firms, the first traceable houses since Gosset was established in 1584 and eight of which are still thriving today. They were: Ruinart (1729), Chanoine Frère (1730), Forest Fourneaux (present-day

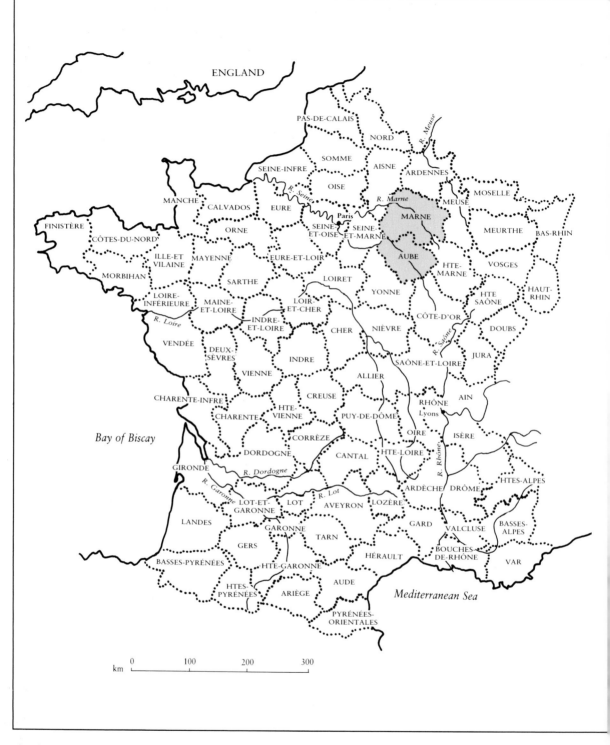

ENGLAND

PAS-DE-CALAIS

NORD

R. Meuse

SOMME

SEINE-INFRE

AISNE

ARDENNES

OISE

MOSELLE

MANCHE

R. Seine

R. Marne

MEUSE

CALVADOS

EURE

Paris

MARNE

MEURTHE

FINISTÈRE

ORNE

SEINE-
ET-OISE

SEINE-
ET-MARNE

BAS-RHIN

CÔTES-DU-NORD

ILLE-ET-
VILAINE

MAYENNE

EURE-ET-LOIR

AUBE

HTE-
MARNE

VOSGES

MORBIHAN

SARTHE

LOIRET

YONNE

HTE
SAÔNE

HAUT-
RHIN

LOIRE-
INFÉRIEURE

MAINE-
ET-LOIRE

LOIR-
ET-CHER

CÔTE-D'OR

R. Loire

INDRE-
ET-LOIRE

CHER

NIÈVRE

R. Saône

DOUBS

VENDÉE

DEUX-
SÈVRES

INDRE

SAÔNE-ET-LOIRE

JURA

VIENNE

ALLIER

CHARENTE-INFRE

CREUSE

AIN

Bay of Biscay

CHARENTE

HTE-
VIENNE

PUY-DE-DÔME

RHÔNE
Lyons

CORRÈZE

OIRE

ISÈRE

DORDOGNE

CANTAL

HTE-LOIRE

R. Rhône

GIRONDE

R. Dordogne

ARDÈCHE

DRÔME

HTES-ALPES

R. Garonne

R. Lot

LOT-ET-
GARONNE

LOT

AVEYRON

LOZÈRE

LANDES

GARONNE

TARN

GARD

VALCLUSE

BASSES-
ALPES

GERS

BOUCHES-
DE-RHÔNE

VAR

BASSES-PYRÉNÉES

HTE-GARONNE

HÉRAULT

HTES-
PYRÉNÉES

ARIÈGE

AUDE

Mediterranean Sea

PYRÉNÉES-
ORIENTALES

km   0   100   200   300

The *départements* of France in 1815

Taittinger, founded in 1734), Moët (present-day Moët & Chandon, founded in 1743), Vander-Veken (present-day Henri Abelé, founded in 1757), Delemotte (present-day Lanson, founded in 1760), Dubois Père & Fils (present-day Louis Roederer, founded in 1770), Clicquot (present-day Veuve Clicquot-Ponsardin, founded in 1772), Heidsieck (present-day Charles Heidsieck, Heidsieck & Co. Monopole and Piper Heidsieck, founded from one firm in 1785) and Ernest Jacquesson (1798).

Many of the Champagne houses established at this time were born as a direct result of the Reims textile trade. This city once possessed possibly the most important woollen manufacturing industry in France and the great textile barons took advantage of the rising reputation of Champagne by giving bottles away to customers. In some cases customers would demand more Champagne than woollens which led the sharpest businessmen to quickly diversify into this lucrative new commerce.

The nineteenth century saw the emergence of two specific practices which separated the so-called *méthode champenoise* from the 'rural method' of Limoux. These were: *dégorgement* (the act of removing sediment from the bottle after the second fermentation) and *liqueur de tirage* (the addition of sugar and yeast at the time of bottling to promote and guarantee a second fermentation). Without these two crucial procedures Champagne would not be the sophisticated product it is today, yet we cannot trace the precise date when they first occurred, nor identify any particular person responsible for their innovation.

Dégorgement

The first documented mention of *dégorgement* occurs in André Jullien's *Manuel du sommelier*, published in 1813. But *dégorgement* dates back at least as far as Dom Pérignon, who we know kept bottles stored, neck downward, in a bed of sand in order to encourage the sediment to drift down to the base of the cork. Keeping the bottle in an inverted position Dom Pérignon would have carried the Champagne to the table, before removing the cork and releasing the sediment. In a very fast and expert manner the bottle would then be brought to an upright position, thus preventing very little more than the sediment from escaping.

Such operations, although unquestionably *dégorgement à la volée*, would have been privately practised prior to any commercial application. But even the ingenious Dom

Early *dégorgement à la volée* performed by a *caviste* into a *guérite* to capture the cork and sediment

Pérignon failed to grasp how close he was to radically improving sparkling wine production. If only he had thought of recorking his wine after *dégorgement*, then the perfectly limpid sparkling wine he had managed to achieve for himself and, no doubt, passed on as a 'tip' to others, would have been available to everybody.

The commercial procedure of *dégorgement* crept in in gradual steps sometime in the latter part of the eighteenth century, or soon after, and might have been the producers' response to an increasing number of complaints about their clouded wines. In 1821 J. MacCulloch published *Remarks on the Art of Wine-Making* stating:

Another process is sometimes adopted for getting rid of the sediment without the trouble of decanting in this mode; the bottles are reserved in a frame proper for the purpose, for a certain number of days, so as to permit the foulness to fall into the neck; while in this position, the cork is dexterously withdrawn and that portion of the wine that is foul, allowed to escape, after which the bottle is filled with clear wine, permanently corked and secured with wire.

Liqueur de tirage

Initially, sugar was added after fermentation (*liqueur d'expédition*) purely to improve the flavour of wines which could sometimes be green and tart in a northerly region like Champagne. In 1718 Jean Godinot claimed that Dom Pérignon added one pound of sugar per *pièce* of wine, a charge which was hotly contested much later by Dom Grossard. Whether or not Dom Pérignon added sugar is of little importance here, but it is likely that *someone* somewhere had engaged in the practice and, in all probability, the sugaring of wine may have been quite commonplace.

But the addition of sugar to promote or assist fermentation, as distinct from its use after fermentation to improve flavour, can be firmly fixed in the history of winemaking. Adding sugar to the grape must to raise the wine's potential alcoholic content was first outlined in Chaptal's *Traité théorique sur la culture de la vigne, avec l'art de faire le vin* in 1801. Jean-Antoine Chaptal (1756–1832) from whom the operation of assisting the grape must, *chaptalisation*, derives its name, was a brilliant chemist and technocrat who served Napoleon as minister of the interior from 1800 to 1805. As minister, he issued instructions to vignerons on the advantages of adding sugar at the time of pressing and it was the vignerons of the more northerly winemaking regions, like Champagne, who benefited the most.

Shortly after Chaptal's publication a few Champagne manufacturers began to add the sugar, not at the time of pressing, but immediately prior to bottling in order to promote the second fermentation or, as the French call it, the *prise de mousse*. The difficulty was in gauging just how much sugar should be added to yield the desired degree of *mousse*: too little would merely result in a *vin pétillant*; too much would burst the bottle.

It was not until 1836 that it became possible to measure the amount of sugar left in a wine after the first fermentation, when Professor François of Châlons-sur-Marne published his *Nouvelles observations sur la fermentation de vin en bouteilles, suivies d'un procédé pour reconnaître la quantité de sucre contenu dans le vin immédiatement avant tirage*. François invented a simple device called the *sucre-oenomètre* which provided a scale of measured dosages to add to the wine to obtain given pressures of *mousse*. The

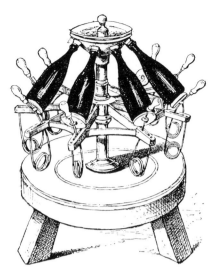

Nineteenth-century apparatus for delivering equal measures of *liqueur de tirage* to each bottle

system, known at the time as *réduction François*, was not accepted immediately in the Champagne community, despite being held in great esteem elsewhere and, ironically – which was most damaging of all to the Champagne industry – used to further the production of German sparkling *sekt*. Most nineteenth-century Champagnes continued to be made by methods akin to the old 'rural method', but with the additional advantage of *dégorgement*. It was not until the 1880s that the calculated use of a *liqueur de tirage* (a mixture of wine, sugar and yeast) became widespread in Champagne, elevating it finally, rather late in the day, to its present revered status.

Remuage

The simple method of inverting the bottles, as Dom Pérignon had done in his sand-pit, although adequate for the small amounts required by individuals, soon proved to be less than perfect for large commercial quantities. Certain particles in the sediment would not descend to the base of the cork, often remaining firmly stuck to the inner surface of the bottle. The sediment created during second fermentation is composed of various waste-products, several types of which possess a sticky character; to encourage these more cohesive particles to descend to the base of the cork requires a certain amount of physical persuasion and, as a result, a method of supplying this encouragement, *remuage*, was developed.

Remuage was pioneered by the house of Clicquot when, upon the death of her husband in 1805, the twenty-seven-year-old widow, Nicole Barbe (née Ponsardin), found herself in control of a major Champagne firm. She took personal charge of the cellars and, well aware of the problem posed by the obstinate particles of sediment which refused to fall easily, spent night and day trying to rid herself of this nuisance. It was her kitchen table that finally provided the ingenious solution. Taking it down to her cellars she cut holes in its surface to accommodate the inverted bottles of Champagne. Then, by periodically removing the inverted bottles from their positions, she would shake them, then replace them in the holes. By 1806 the Widow, or *Veuve* as she was known, and her kitchen table were the talk of Reims.

Remuage in fact required a modification of the original shaking process developed by the widow, involving a fractional tilt of each bottle (from horizontal to perpendicular) following every short, sharp twist to loosen the sediment. After several twists and tilts, the sediment is not only disturbed and encouraged to leave the sides of the bottle, but the bottle finally achieves a fully inverted position ready for *dégorgement*.

Sometime between 1806 and 1813 the twisting action we know today as *remuage* evolved, but it was the angled cut of the holes as much as the twisting motion which provided the key to the solution sought by the widow. This enabled each bottle to start in an almost horizontal position, but finish perpendicular having gone through a full 90° of movement without leaving the hole.

According to a letter from Alfred Werlé, the son of one of the widow's associates, it was an employee of Veuve Clicquot, Antoine Müller, who, in 1818, hit upon the supreme importance of cutting the bottle holes at an angle of 45°. Antoine Müller became the widow's *chef de caves*, or chief cellarer between 1810 and 1822, although in March of 1822 he resigned from his position and was able to set up his own Champagne establishment, calling it Müller-Ruinart. He employed the future founder of the house of Bollinger, Jacques Bollinger, then aged nineteen, to sell his wines in Germany, but it was Müller's experience at Veuve Clicquot which made him realise that the Russian market possessed the greatest potential for sales. Consequently he placed advertisements in Russian newspapers, stating that he had been in charge of the production and clarification

The original planks with holes cut by Antoine Müller at an angle of 45° upon which the Veuve Clicquot carried out her *remuage* experiments

of Veuve Clicquot wines for a number of years where he succeeded in achieving perfect limpidity.

Sometime between 1823 and 1824 the guarded secret of *remuage*, including Müller's angled holes, leaked out and, between 1830 and 1850, became common practice throughout the Champagne industry.

It was thus the house of Clicquot which placed the production of Champagne on a more sophisticated level than that of other sparkling wines. Without *dégorgement* and Clicquot's *remuage*, the Champagne process would have been no different from the medieval 'rural method' utilised elsewhere.

Today, manual *remuage* is still widely used, but it is carried out on specially designed wooden boards, hinged together to stand like an inverted 'V' and known as *pupitres* (the French for reading desks). Throughout the nineteenth century, following Madame Clicquot's inspired use of her kitchen table, wooden planks drilled with holes and supported on trestles were used for *remuage*, while some firms used similar planks but affixed to the walls of their cellars or *caves*. *Pupitres* were adapted from these structures, although it is still uncertain who first employed them commercially for *remuage*.

Dégorgement à la glace

The *à la volée* method of *dégorgement*, as practised by Dom Pérignon and others, was totally inadequate for the enormous quantities of Champagne being produced in the last quarter of the nineteenth century. Output had been steadily growing by about five million bottles every fifteen years, and was destined to reach a total of no less than thirty million bottles a year by the turn of the century.

With no trouble in selling their products, Champagne houses should have been heartened by such healthy expansion, but theirs was a labour-intensive business, where every bottle produced was taken through each stage of a complex operation by hand. What was needed was a new system of *dégorgement*, able to cope with far greater capacity levels at a significantly higher speed than the traditional *à la volée* process.

The *à la glace* or freezing method was invented by Armand Walfart in 1884 and is still the method of *dégorgement* most commonly used today. The necks of the inverted bottles are dipped in a freezing brine which freezes the wine and sediment at the base of the cork sufficiently to make it adhere to the bottle's inner-surface; the *dégorgeur* can then bring the bottle back to its upright position without disturbing the sediment. The frozen wine is not a block of ice, however, but a small amount of frozen wine with a consistency closer to slush. When the cork is extracted the slush-like sediment shoots out of the bottle and, because the rest of the wine remaining in the bottle is at a much lower temperature than normal, the gas is reluctant to escape, hence there is no spray of foam and the bottle may be topped up and recorked with a minimal loss of pressure.

Anybody seeing this operation in the modern bottling halls of Champagne houses today will find it difficult to imagine that it was in regular use a hundred years ago, yet the two pioneers of the *à la glace* system, Moët & Chandon and Perrier Jouët, both introduced the process in 1891, independently of each other, and five years before it was patented by Walfart on 14 November 1896. By 1908 the *à la glace* method was well enough established to be described by Ernest and Arthur Vizetelly in their book *Wines of France*.

By the late nineteenth century Champagne had become big business, as the very industrialised impression of this drawing of Moët & Chandon's bottling hall depicts

These developments were the minutiae by which an intrinsically superior sparkling wine came to be refined, but without a raw product of unique potential there would have been nothing to refine. Without the specific grape varieties that go to make Champagne; without the viticulturally begrudging climate – a combination of the region's northern latitude and its proximity to the Atlantic; and without the precise elevation found in the Montagne de Reims, the Vallée de la Marne and the Côte des Blancs, there would be no great sparkling wine called Champagne.

Phylloxera

Phylloxera first appeared in the Champagne vineyards at Treloup, in the Aisne *département*, in 1890. The dreaded disease had taken almost thirty years to reach Champagne since it was first identified in the Côtes-du-Rhône region, where it had arrived on experimental vine stocks shipped from America via London.

Initially, the vignerons in the south and south-west of France had tried to ignore the louse, but as its crippling devastation spread throughout the vineyards of the major wine regions various methods of eradication were attempted. These were usually chemically based, many of which contained a high proportion of potassium, but perhaps the most imaginative scheme was the deliberate introduction of *Tyroglyphus phylloxera*. *Tyroglyphus*, harmless to the vine but a deadly enemy of *Phylloxera vastatrix*, was imported in 1873 in an attempt to kill off the pest; unfortunately, however, unlike phylloxera, *Tyroglyphus* did not care for the European climate and failed to settle. Eventually it became apparent that every vine in every vineyard would have to be grafted on to phylloxera-resistant American rootstock. Costly and time-consuming (the operation was unfinished at the outbreak of the First World War), it was none the less essential.

Phylloxera is generally considered to be the greatest disaster in French viticultural history, but in some respects it has also been a blessing. Prior to its arrival in France, the greatest vineyards had undergone gradual devaluation as a result of the increasing demand for wine, which had led to the planting of inferior varieties and the extension of vineyards into unsuitable areas of land. Grafting on to American rootstock led to a much needed rationalisation, whereby only the best sites in the classic regions were replanted and only noble vines were cultivated.

The Champagne trade: its evolution and expansion

Formation of *syndicats*

A further setback, which directly affected the Champagne industry towards the end of the nineteenth century, was the publication of incorrect export figures by the French ministry of agriculture. This led to American charges that inferior quality Champagne had caused the drop in shipments outlined by the ministry which, in turn, created increased domestic interest in Californian sparkling wine. The ministry's figures had erred by no less than 8,243 dozen bottles of Champagne: shipments were not down – they were up. Thus, but for their own agricultural ministry, there would have been no American criticism, nor would there have been such a well-publicised fillip for the Californian sparkling wine industry.

The Champagne houses were naturally outraged at the government's ineptitude and drew up a vociferous protest, signed by eighty participants, condemning the publicity given to the ministerial communiqué. On 19 September 1882, at a special session of the Société Industrielle de Reims, three Champagne houses – Heidsieck & Co., G. H. Mumm & Co. and Giesler & Co. – tabled a motion to form a *syndicat* to defend the name and honour of Champagne. The motion was unanimously adopted and the first meeting of the *syndicat* took place on 4 November 1882 when twenty-two houses were represented. Aims were defined, certain statutory regulations laid down and five officers elected for the first three-year term. Although only twenty-two houses were represented the *syndicat* recognised that it stood for the rights of some sixty Champagne houses, virtually the entire trade at the time.

The *syndicat* was soon put to the test. In November 1883 a quantity of bottles purporting to be Champagne made by Deutz & Geldermann attracted attention in Munich. They were of abominable quality and obviously not genuine Champagne. The wine belonged to Herr A. Einhorn and the bottles had been dressed with forged Jockey Club labels. After exhaustive investigations the supplier was identified as Herr Ignatz of Wurzburg and a solicitor by the name of Medicus was recommended by Deutz & Geldermann to settle the matter. Another case in 1883 revealed that a *marque* of Veuve Clicquot-Ponsardine was being sold, but with the insertion of an extra 'o' in the label, reading 'Veuve Cliocquot-Ponsardin' and going for a ridiculously low price. The *syndicat* obtained some of the wine from an agent named Herr A. Centawer and its members were amazed by the almost identical labels; the spelling variation was virtually unnoticeable. Again, the quality was strikingly poor, provoking the *syndicat*'s action, not simply to combat unfair trading, but to defend the image of Champagne.

The *syndicat* very quickly established a reputation for acting firmly, swiftly and in any country, in defence of Champagne.

On 21 March 1884 a law was passed establishing the legal existence of the Syndicat du Commerce des Vins de Champagne, comprising the following 61 houses: Henri Abelé; Ch. Arnould & Heidelberger (later de Saint Marceaux); Barnett & Fils; F. Bernard & Co.; Veuve Binet Fils & Co.; Boll & Co.; Burchard-Delbeck & Co.; Carré & Barrau; Eugène Clicquot; F. Duchâtel-Ohaus; Ch. Farre; Gustave Gilbert; Gondelle & Co.; George Goulet & Co.; Henri Goulet; Heidsieck & Co.; Charles Heidsieck; Henriot & Co.; Ernest Irroy; Krug; Kunkelmann & Co. (Piper Heidsieck); Lanson Père & Fils; Veuve Ch. Loche; Manuel & Co.; A. Morizet; G. H. Mumm & Co.; Jules Mumm & Co.; Veuve Pommery & Fils; Louis Roederer; Ruinart Père & Fils; Werlé & Co. (Veuve Clicquot-Ponsardin); Chandon & Co.; Gallice & Co. (Perrier-Jouët); E. Mercier; Pol Roger & Co.; de Venoge & Co.; Wachter & Co.; J. Bollinger; C. Braeunlich; E. de Ayala; Deutz & Geldermann; Duminy & Co.; Auger Eysert & Hatton; A. Bissinger & Co.; Ch. de Cazanove; Desbordes & Fils; Dinet Peuvrel & Fils, G. Loche succr.; Giesler & Co.; Koch Fils; Lecureux & Co.; G. Planckaert-Grandjean; Billecart Père & Fils; Bouché Fils & Co.; Bruch Foucher & Co.; A. de Montebello; Dagonet & Fils; Freminet & Fils; I. Goerg & Co.; Joseph Perrier Fils & Co.; Baron de Launay, Berry & Eugène Perrier succr.

Throughout the *syndicat*'s first two or three decades of existence, however, its membership declined and in 1912 a second, alternative organisation was formed, the Syndicat des Négociants en Vins de Champagne. Those remaining in the original *syndicat* took the view that they comprised the élite of the trade and, by protecting the élite, the *syndicat* would achieve the best possible image for Champagne. The houses which established the break-away *syndicat* were less illustrious in name and thus believed little could be gained from an organisation run by the élite for the élite and they therefore grouped together.

On 11 May 1945 a merger of convenience took place between the associations of Champagne houses, the Syndicat du Commerce des Vins de Champagne and the Syndicat des Négociants en Vin de Champagne under the auspices of the Union des Syndicats du Commerce des Vins de Champagne. Both *syndicats* retained their separate titles, policies and regulations and continued to control their own destinies, the Union merely providing a co-operating and co-ordinating service which enabled all *négociants* in the trade to be represented should the need arise.

The Champagne Riots

It had been decided that the Champagne-producing area must be legally delimited in order to protect the quality of grapes being included in the *cuvées* and to safeguard the traditional areas able to grow them. Everyone agreed that this was a sensible decision, with the exception of growers from the more outlying districts, in particular the Midi, who had a vested interest in selling to Champagne and who would certainly be excluded.

In the absence of any positive action from the government to stop the trade with the Midi, the Fédération des Syndicats de la Champagne (which changed its name in 1919 to the Syndicat Général des Vignerons de la Champagne) was founded by Marne vignerons in 1904 to protect the quality of grapes being used for Champagne. Many of the rules laid down by this *syndicat* in 1904 were later taken as the basic framework around which the AOC regulations for Champagne were formulated in 1927.

Because of the continuing antagonism between the Marne (which includes the Montagne de Reims, the Vallée de la Marne and the Côte des Blancs), the Aube (the region south of Troyes) and, to a lesser extent, the Aisne (all the vineyards around Château-Thierry and to the east of Soissons), the government avoided all questions concerning boundaries. Initially this satisfied the Marne growers, since they were pleased that the government had not ratified the Aube's claim that it too was part of Champagne. But the arguments soon broke out again, because the Aube wines, although not officially included as Champagne wines, were not officially excluded either. Aube wines had long been used by several Champagne houses, albeit on the quiet, and with no delimited region fixed the practice began to increase. Fears soon began to be expressed that wines from the Midi too would again find their way back into Champagne cellars.

The rivalry grew acute, with the houses splitting into two camps. Those which used Aube wines put forward the argument that the Aube was not only part of the historic province of Champagne, but its chief town, Troyes, was the ancient provincial capital and once the seat of the counts of Champagne. The Marne camp pointed out that it would be ridiculous to include every hectare of the ancient province for purely historical reasons with no consideration for soil, aspect or other factors contributing to the quality of wine. Furthermore, they argued, such an area would cover one-twentieth of all France, stretching into Chablis and part of the Loire.

The government finally gave way and, on 17 December 1908, passed a bill which restricted the term 'Champagne' to certain named communes in the Marne and Aisne *départements* only. There was some dissent in the Aube, but not a great deal, for there was little chance of enforcing the law and the Aubois were content with continuing their business of supplying those houses in the Marne which covertly required their wines.

Marne growers (as opposed to Marne houses) however, felt much aggrieved by the continued blending of Aube wines, a situation aggravated by the financial hardship they faced after three bad harvests in 1907, 1908 and 1909 and culminating in the disastrous vintage of 1910. Disquiet grew and, on 11 February 1911, the ever-appeasing government brought in tougher laws restricting the use of Aube grapes.

While a sigh of relief could be felt in the Marne, the Aube population nigh on fermented with anger. In the face of government determination to enforce the February 1911 laws more than eight thousand Aube growers marched through the streets of Bar-sur-Aube carrying on their backs *paniers de mannequin* (grape harvesting baskets) full of tax-forms which they ceremoniously set fire to. Everyone joined in the protest, town bands, mayors and priests. An effigy of the prime minister, Monsieur Monis, was burned and thirty-six mayors resigned.

Such was the dismay of the Monis government that it hastily announced its intention to annul the laws of 1908 and 1911, weakly declaring that it was 'abandoning the territorial

delimitations which may provoke divisions among Frenchmen'. But such reconciliatory
action only made matters worse, reawakening hostilities in the Marne. On the afternoon
of 11 April, when the news of the impending annulment was announced, word went out
to all growers in the Marne and their supporters. Men could be seen grouping together,
bugles and horns were sounded. The storm broke over the little townships north of
Épernay: before dusk, the cellars and premises of producers in Dizy had been sacked,
those in Damery soon followed and by noon the next day some ten thousand
demonstrators descended upon Aÿ. The protestors had intended to enter Épernay, but
were prevented from doing so by a squadron of cavalry which had barricaded the road.

The squadron of cavalry was but a small contingent of a much larger military force
despatched to Champagne by the Monis government: Épernay was to be protected at all
costs and between twenty and forty thousand cavalry, dragoons and infantry poured into
the town.

Civil war was averted, but while the 120-strong squadron of cavalry were able to hold
back the rioters in Aÿ, they were unwilling to engage their fellow citizens in open conflict
and failed to prevent the mob from sacking and burning the premises of Ayala, Bissinger
and Deutz & Geldermann in Aÿ. According to Cyril Ray in his penetrating profile
Bollinger (1971), one house was spared and he records that fifteen years after the riots
Madame Bollinger overheard a passer-by outside one of her windows say, 'That's the
Bollinger house, you know: we didn't touch it during the riots here – as a matter of fact,
we lowered our flag to it when we passed!' 'Probably the red flag,' Madame is supposed to
have commented with pleased irony.

In the immediate aftermath of the rioting the vignerons tried to excuse their actions by
claiming that only houses which practised the blending of wines from the Midi had been
molested, but there was no evidence to bear this out and even houses which had kept
strictly to the noble blends had been attacked.

The Monis government had been guilty of foolish panic, the Marne growers of mob
violence. One of the last acts of the short-lived vacillating Monis government was to draft
a new bill recognising both the Marne and the Aube, but as two distinct districts. The
classic area of the Marne would be called 'Champagne', while the Aube and those districts
of the Marne excluded by the 1908 decree would be known as the 'Champagne Deuxième
Zone'. Both sides seemed satisfied and although it is unlikely that a two-tier Champagne
classification would have been workable in the long term, it sufficed for the present
although it was still being debated in the Senate when war broke out three years later.

The First World War

In European warfare invading armies normally choose harvest to launch their attacks, and
the year 1914 was no exception. On 3 September Reims fell to the German forces at the
end of their month-long advance; three days later Épernay too succumbed. But the power
of the German sweep faltered and French forces were able to regroup and mount a
counter-attack from the Paris region. There then followed, between 7 and 9 September, a
most bitter clash of armies in the normally tranquil vineyards of Champagne, the Battle of
the Marne.

Strategically, the Marne is important for the last line of defence it presents before the

Seine. Once the Seine is crossed, Paris lies open to the invader. It was therefore vital for the French to retake the north bank and this they acheived amidst vines heavily laden with fruit, reoccupying both Épernay and Reims by 13 September. Waged on the high ground in the Montagne de Reims, between Épernay and the Marne to the south and Reims to the north, there followed one of the most gruelling and protracted battles in human history, the line of trenches moving barely a hundred yards throughout four long and bloody years.

Nobody who has ever taken the trouble to visit General Gouraud's observation post on a cold, dank winter's day, could ever escape the hell-hole ambiance of such a deathly place which seems to reach out over the decades of time to shame and sicken the human race. My own memory is vivid: it was a bitterly cold morning, below $-14°C$, and the ground I trod, in which only days before I would have been up to my knees in mud, was as solid as rock. As I picked my way through the frozen woods towards the observation post which commands a unique view over the former battle-ground of the Marne, I wondered what it must have been like to be a soldier. It is a strenuous physical effort to scale on a good spring day, but in the pouring rain, amidst hailing bullets, laden with uniform and the tools of war ...

The north-facing slopes of the Montagne de Reims bore the brunt of the hostilities, yet the damage done to the vineyards during the Battle of the Marne was negligible compared with the inhuman slaughter and tragic loss of lives in the trenches. Work in the vineyards continued, with women and children dying while servicing the vineyards that the soldiers on both sides manipulated for their own strategic purposes. More than twenty children were killed bringing in that first wartime crop of 1914.

The collapse of world markets

In October 1917, while the attention of all France, particularly that of the people of Champagne, focused on the progress of the battles on the Western Front, Russia rose in revolution. This had considerable impact on the Champagne trade for, at a single stroke, 10 per cent of its annual production, normally consumed in royal and aristocratic Russian circles, suddenly had no market. Quite predictably, the revolutionary government refused to pay any outstanding bills for their former masters' frivolous luxuries, a state of affairs which had disastrous consequences for champagne houses, like Roederer, whose main market was Russian. Furthermore, after the Allied victory in 1918, Germany and the former Austro-Hungarian Empire were bankrupt and unable to make any significant purchases for a long time.

The bitterness and confusion over delimitation, which had led to the drafting of a bill in 1911 outlining the two distinct districts, 'Champagne' and 'Champagne Deuxième Zone', was still unsolved and an amended law was passed through the new government in 1919. This instigated for the first time the right of appellation in the form of the *Appellation d'Origine Contrôlée* (AOC) and regulations were imposed including a cunning proviso which dumped the entire issue of the Aube wines and the controversial 'Champagne Deuxième Zone' firmly in the lap of the judiciary. After six years of litigation, the courts decided in favour of the Aube growers and, in 1927, a new law quashed the *deuxième* designation once and for all, outlining a detailed list of communes eligible for the appellation Champagne (see Appendix IV), the broad outlines of which are still in existence today.

Meanwhile, on 20 January 1920, the dwindling sales of Champagne suffered yet another downward spiral, when the American Prohibition Bill was passed (although 'bootleggers' still managed to smuggle in substantial consignments). Prohibition was also imposed in various degrees in Scandinavian countries, another formerly prosperous market.

Traditionally the British had been Champagne's most lucrative customers – after the drink had been popularised in society by the Marlboroughs and the Prince of Wales in the last half of the nineteenth century. Soldiers had since picked up the habit of wine-drinking in France during the war and upon returning to England had educated the middle classes, further increasing the popularity of Champagne in the immediate post-war years. But when Britain went off the Gold Standard in 1931, the Champagne houses found themselves receiving just two-thirds of the price they had come to expect.

The disruption of world markets in the aftermath of the war, the waves of protectionism and concurrent fall in export sales inevitably affected the Champagne trade as it razed other industries; 1932 proved disastrous with virtually no buyers for Champagne. Despite a run of small harvests, the cellars in Reims and Épernay were brimming, and it was estimated that had sales maintained their 1932 level, the Champagne houses possessed sufficient stock in hand to tide over sales for the next thirty-three years. The last thing Champagne required was a plentiful harvest, but that was precisely what it got with the bumper crop of 1934.

Most houses simply refused to buy any grapes, even though the growers were practically giving them away. But little could be done to redress the situation since the houses were in just as bad a position as the growers. Some of the larger growers, however, who could afford the investment, began to make their own Champagne instead of relying purely on the sale of grapes. It was a costly investment requiring several years to come to fruition and the vast majority of growers could not afford the necessary equipment. It was at this time that many growers began to group together to form the earliest co-opératives in Champagne.

Unresponsive export markets led many houses to turn their attention inwards and focus on long-neglected domestic sales. This they achieved with stunning success, building up a trade several times the size of their previous home market. In 1927 Champagne sales on the French market accounted for eight million bottles, by 1935 it had passed twenty-four million. The French domestic market remains to this day far and away the largest consumer of Champagne.

Prior to the setting up of the CIVC, the single most effective body responsible for guarding the quality of Champagne today, a decree was passed on 28 September 1935 creating an inter-professional organisation called the Commission Spéciale de la Champagne, which soon became known as the Commission de Châlons because its meetings were held in the Prefecture (the administrative centre) at Châlons-sur-Marne. The Commission was composed of representatives from Champagne houses, growers, local officials, the ministry of agriculture and the treasury and its aims were 'to ensure the respect of local custom and tradition, the observation of which is necessary in order to preserve the quality of Champagne'. But apart from establishing an annual committee empowered to fix the price of grapes each year, the Commission was an unimaginative and ineffective institution.

The Second World War

From May 1940 until August 1944 the Champagne region was occupied by German troops. But the Champenois were not unprepared: many houses were able to seal up their cellars; those wishing to escape German occupation left for southern France, while others remained organising themselves into an effective network of resistance, the extent of which was unknown even to most Champenois.

The various houses hid as much Champagne as they dared by sealing up some of their cellars, but they had to be very careful not to attract attention. A famous Champagne house sporting blatantly low stocks, or declaring cellars which could easily be judged too small for the firm's recorded production, would have invited the Nazis to make an intensive search.

Throughout its period of occupation, the region's wine industry was under the control of a Rhineland wine-maker, Herr Klaebisch, who assumed the title of Führer of Champagne. As Patrick Forbes put it in *Champagne*, 'The news of his appointment was received with a certain relief by most people, for, if you were going to be shoved around, it was better to be shoved around by a wine-maker than by some beer-drinking Nazi lout.'

The German occupation proved useful in one respect, however: it spurred the formation of the Comité Interprofessionnel du Vin de Champagne (CIVC), an organisation which has since established itself as the most successful of its type in France. In November 1940 the Vichy government abolished the ineffective Commission de Châlons, intending to replace it with an organisation called Le Bureau de Repartition du Vinicole de Champagne, but in April the following year the Germans set up the CIVC.

Robert-Jean de Vogüé and Maurice Doyard, both members of the Commission de Châlons, convinced the German authorities that the Commission was powerless and unable to influence the trade on any matters raised, or to issue orders on the Führer's behalf or from other agencies of the occupation forces. Together de Vogüé and Doyard indicated that the Bureau intended by the Vichy government to replace the Commission would be no better and what was required, if the Germans wanted their orders carried out quickly and efficiently, was a body with real powers. Thus, playing to the Germans' appeal for order, these two brave Frenchmen secured for the trade a buffer in the form of the CIVC which took on the day-to-day unpleasantries of dealing with an alien administration. The Germans naturally played the major role in shaping the CIVC and its undoubted success, both immediate and since, must to some extent be credited to the Germans' reputation for organisation, efficiency and detail.

The Germans had intended blowing up the cellars of Champagne before retreating, but on 28 August 1944 they were caught napping as General Patton and his 3rd Army swept into Épernay.

2

Terroir

Was it really a fact that a significant section of the public really did not know
– not that Champagne came from a Province in France historically called
Champagne – but from France at all?
André Simon debating the Costa Brava Spanish Champagne case, *The History of
Champagne,* 1962

NO WORD IN THE ENGLISH LANGUAGE accurately captures the meaning of 'le terroir'
when used in a viticultural sense. Effectively, it refers to all environmental factors which
can affect the production of grapes in a given area and thus the potential of the wines that
area may produce. It is, without doubt, a contentious subject, but there is no doubt in the
mind of this author that it is only in Champagne that all these elements combine, albeit
precariously, with a special method of production, to produce a sparkling wine of such
incomparable finesse.

Location

Champagne is the most northerly of the AOC (Appellation d'Origine Contrôlée) wine
regions of France, lying approximately 150 kilometres north-east of Paris, and separated
from Belgium to the north by the hills and dense forests of the Ardennes. The VDQS (Vins
Délimités de Qualité Supérieure) production area Vins de Moselle is slightly further north
but it is negligible in terms of quantity and quality.

The area legally delimited between 1908 and 1919 as the Champagne-producing region
covers 34,500 hectares. Of these, 31,050 hectares may be planted, about 26,400 hectares
are planted and approximately 25,000 hectares are actually in production. As can be seen
from the table below, the area of Champagne under vine which is in production has
increased by 40% since 1970. There are two basic reasons for the apparent anomalies in
what generally appears to be a steady expansion of the vineyard area: first, the uprooting
of old, commercially non-productive vines; and second, the decimation of large patches of
vines due to natural causes like frost, hail, disease, pests, etc. In 1985, for example, one in
ten vines was killed by winter conditions when the temperature dropped as low as −23°C.

Before grapes are allowed the full AOC status of Champagne, the vines from which they
come, whether situated in a virgin vineyard or an old one just replanted, must attain their
'third leaf', by which is meant that the plants, having produced foliage for the third time,

will be three years old. Vineyards under 'first leaf' and 'second leaf' cannot, therefore, be considered as part of the area in production.

From 1970 to 1975, the planting of new vineyards was particularly hectic and the figures for 1982–5 are but an indication of yet another intensive period of viticultivating new land within the delimited region. After a dismal harvest in 1978, exacerbated by increased pressure on stocks from the record sales of 1978–9, the situation worsened the following year with a poor flowering in the spring of 1980, and some 1,600 hectares were

Champagne Viticole (expressed in hectares)

Year	Area of vines in production				Area of vines under '1st leaf'				Area of vines under '2nd leaf'				Total area under vine
	Marne	Aube and H. Marne*	Aisne and S. et M.†	Total	Marne	Aube and H. Marne*	Aisne and S. et M.†	Total	Marne	Aube and H. Marne*	Aisne and S. et M.†	Total	
1970	15,048	2,000	782	17,830	1,664	306	128	2,098	–	–	–	–	19,928
1971	15,735	2,183	845	18,763	812	196	69	1,077	719	155	62	936	20,766
1972	16,115	2,309	903	19,327	738	218	74	1,030	821	214	70	1,105	21,462
1973	16,524	2,510	968	20,002	783	226	91	1,100	762	229	77	1,068	22,170
1974	17,009	2,730	1,031	20,770	849	275	106	1,230	794	247	93	1,134	23,134
1975	17,600	2,983	1,124	21,707	661	268	100	1,029	889	298	113	1,300	24,036
1976	18,445	3,306	1,237	22,988	303	97	24	424	664	287	104	1,055	24,467
1977	19,045	3,599	1,336	23,980	142	51	15	208	308	98	25	431	24,619
1978	19,228	3,675	1,353	24,256	128	34	11	173	148	50	14	212	24,161
1979	19,183	3,689	1,362	24,234	145	55	12	212	129	36	11	176	24,622
1980	18,951	3,735	1,371	24,057	250	81	13	344	155	60	11	226	24,627
1981	18,734	3,728	1,361	23,823	517	161	52	730	255	83	12	350	24,903
1982	18,131	3,748	1,709	23,588	612	280	117	1,009	506	164	70	740	25,337
1983	18,255	3,869	1,779	23,903	728	356	133	1,217	623	285	126	1,034	26,154
1984	18,626	4,114	1,899	24,639	568	322	116	1,006	739	375	139	1,253	26,898
1985	19,596	3,960	1,473	25,029	n.a.	n.a.	n.a.	n.a.	n.a.	n.a.	n.a.	n.a.	26,398?

* Haut Marne.   † Seine et Marne.

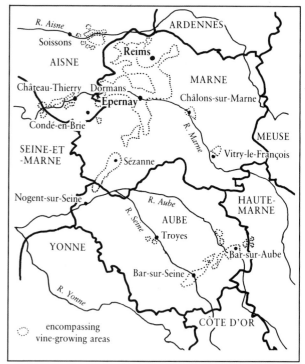

Location of the Champagne region relative to other major wine areas of France

The principal wine-growing areas of the Champagne region

released for planting between 1980 and 1983. While many people frowned at such a huge expansion programme, it soon became apparent that it was insufficient to guarantee the avoidance of another crisis, and official approval was immediately secured for the planting of a further 5,000 hectares by the year 1990.

It is likely that in the next few years there will be pressure to bring into production the remaining hectares of delimited land, although economics and the overall strategy of the Champagne market will also play their part.

Climate

The northern climate of Champagne is barely adequate to support the cultivation of the vine, let alone guarantee a crop of ripe grapes. Yet it is precisely this unfriendly climate which is the most crucial factor in determining the inimitable quality and character of Champagne. This viticultural twilight zone stretches the duration of the vine's growth cycle to the limit, resulting in a longer ripening period, providing grapes with a high degree of acidity. But a fine sparkling wine must also possess a certain richness of flavour of ripe grapes. Champagne's harvest must therefore reach a reasonable level of ripeness and as the ripening process, or *véraison* as the French call it, increases the sugar content, the high degree of acidity necessary for these wines is important only in ratio to the sugar content. In even a marginally warmer climate than Champagne's, the sugar-acid ratio would be unsuitable for a fine sparkling wine. Champagne's high sugar-acid ratio – a quality which would seem horrendously out of balance for a still wine – is essential in order to carry the flavour of the wine on to the palate through the sensation of thousands of bubbles bursting in the mouth.

In Champagne itself, in exceptionally hot vintages like 1947, 1959 and 1976, the sugar-acid ratios were inappropriate for the fine balance of Champagne. The wines from these years attained great ripeness, but the *véraison* was far too quick and the Champagnes produced were very high in alcohol and extract and low in acidity, resulting in big, overtly rich, fat wines. Great wines they may be, but it is hard to define these wines as good *sparkling* wines and classic Champagnes they most certainly are not.

It is not merely the northerly situation of Champagne which is responsible for its unique climate, the region is also influenced by the Atlantic. Some German vineyards can be found in more northerly locations, but they are subjected to the greater continental influence of colder winters and hotter summers. The Atlantic has a cooling effect on Champagne's summers and makes the seasons generally more variable.

The mean temperature in Champagne is 10.53°C sheltered at 2 metres above the ground and 11.21°C at 0.2 metres above the ground. It can fall below −5°C but rarely rises above 25°C. Because of the humidity, below freezing temperatures feel colder than they are and can have the harmful effect of biting deep into the vine and this can be fatal if the sap has started to rise. Any frost of −4°C or less at 0.3 metres above the ground will affect the vine. In the spring young shoots will be damaged by such frosts and, if the frosts are severe or prolonged, they may be killed. Second or tertiary shoots will grow but the crop will be reduced and the fruit may not ripen in time. Flat ground and the slopes of the Marne valley are particularly prone to frost. There are, on average, between sixty and eighty days of frost a year throughout the region.

The average amount of sunshine the vines receive annually is only 1,537 hours (Bordeaux: 2,071 hours) spread over 289 days. Some hold the view that there is an extra intensity to the sunlight due to its reflection from the chalky-white soil. Whether this has any significant effect upon the vine's growth has yet to be determined but it is true that the light in Champagne is exceptional for so northern a latitude.

A vineyard needs at least 400–500 millimetres of water per year: in Champagne the vines receive an annual average of 662 millimetres of rain over 176 days. Compared with

Month	Average temperature at 0.2 metres above ground in Celsius	Hours of sunshine	Millimetres of rainfall
January	2.15	42.5	59.8
February	3.70	70.1	50.5
March	7.30	123.8	44.6
April	11.00	157.8	43.2
May	15.20	193.2	54.0
June	18.30	198.3	54.0
July	19.85	203.7	56.9
August	19.60	192.3	61.5
September	16.65	163.7	56.2
October	11.55	107.0	54.9
November	6.20	50.8	63.1
December	3.00	34.0	63.4

other regions, such as Bordeaux (750–950 millimetres), Burgundy (630 millimetres in the Côte d'Or; 700 millimetres in Beaujolais) and the Loire valley (620–700 millimetres), however, this does not appear to be so high. However, a combination of the limestone subsoil and the profusion of rivers, canals, lakes and reservoirs reduces Champagne's water requirement (due to low evaporation), making its 622 millimetres of rainfall relatively heavier than it at first appears.

Hydrography

One of the most striking features of the hilly terrain of viticultural Champagne is its network of rivers and canals. The contribution of Champagne's waterways to the prosperity of its vineyards is often neglected, but these waters together provide excellent drainage to the slopes on which the vineyards are planted, whilst also sustaining a reliable water table.

The most important river in the region is the Marne which starts life in dramatic surroundings a few kilometres south of Langres, not far from the magnificent Château le Pailly. Langres, a fortress town enclosed by four kilometres of ancient ramparts and perched on top of a 100-metre-high plateau, some seventy-five kilometres north of Dijon

Overlooking the Marne valley from Hautvillers

Aspersion is a method of frost-protection involving a water-sprinkling system (BELOW) which automatically switches on whenever the temperature drops below freezing. The frost expends its energy in freezing the water, not the vine, as the delicate bud (RIGHT) safely cocooned in its igloo of ice so vividly demonstrates

and the Côte de Beaune, dominates the Marne valley. From here the Marne flows north, maintaining a parallel course with the N19 highway to Chaumont and the N67 to Dizier, before bending a little to the west, gathering strength, and flowing through Châlons-sur-Marne and Épernay. Keeping adjacent to the N3 from Châlons, it rushes through Château-Thierry and out of the delimited region towards Paris, where it feeds the Seine at Charenton.

Barely fifty kilometres from its source, the Seine flows through some of the southern Champagne vineyards in the Aube at Bar-sur-Seine. Keeping parallel to the N71 until Troyes, it follows the N19 to Nogent-sur-Seine – just south of the often forgotten delimited districts between Sézanne and Villenauxe-la-Grande – before heading north-west towards Paris.

The Aube, the Vesle and the Ardre are the three other important rivers in the region. With its source barely twenty kilometres south-west of le Pailly and Langres, the Aube flows through Bar-sur-Aube – whose vineyards, together with those of Bar-sur-Seine, provide about fourteen per cent of the total production of Champagne – before joining the Seine fifteen kilometres from Nogent-sur-Seine.

The Vesle and the Ardre play significant roles in the drainage of the vineyards of the Petite Montagne, the hilly extension of the Montagne de Reims just west of the city. The Vesle rises just east of Châlons-sur-Marne and flows north-westwards, fed by a small tributary, the Noblette, and accompanied by the Aisne–Marne Canal, before flowing through Reims and part of the northern section of the Petite Montagne into the Aisne *département*, east of Soissons. The Ardre starts life in the Montagne de Reims, just west of the N51, at a point roughly half-way between Reims and Épernay. Gradually picking up strength, it flows north-westwards following the N386 through the vineyards until it joins the Vesle at Fismes.

Other more minor rivers, streams and tributaries of local importance are: the Cubry and Sourdon, in the area south and west of Épernay; the Semoigne, Belval and Flagot, all of which feed the Marne; the Berle and Gubersault, south of the Côte des Blancs; the Surmelin, Petit Morin, Verdonelle and Moulin, which skirt the southern parts of the region; and the Aisne river which, while not a minor waterway, dips into the northern Champagne vineyards in the area east of Soissons.

Topography

The name Champagne comes from the Latin *campagna*, signifying open, unforested land: an ambiguous origin for those who have seen only the hilly vineyards of Champagne surmounted by forest. But the classic viticultural region occupies only a small proportion of the old historical province which was, by and large, open and flat.

The viticultural zone occupies that part of Champagne known as the *falaises* or Champagne cliffs. The chalk hills of the *falaises* are situated in the Reims and Épernay districts and comprise the Montagne de Reims, the Vallée de la Marne and the Côte des Blancs, the entire area of which, before human interference, was totally covered in forest.

It is difficult to offer a succinct description of the countryside of Champagne *viticole*. On the one hand, the Montagne de Reims suggests a much higher, tougher topography

All classic vineyards in Champagne possess a very thin layer of drift (ABOVE LEFT), under which exists a seam of brilliant-white chalk up to 300 metres thick. The infamous *boues de ville* (BOTTOM LEFT) contains anything from cigarette packets to Lego (INSET) but always, mysteriously, ends up dominated by blue plastic

than it actually represents; yet, on the other, to talk of rolling hills would give too tame an impression of the region.

On the Reims side of the Montagne de Reims, from Chamery just north of the Ardre, through Rilly-la-Montagne in the Grande Montagne proper, to Verzenay at its edge, the vineyards mostly have north-facing aspects. This is very unusual for a European wine region (in most cases, vineyards generally face south to some degree) and especially for one as northerly in latitude as Champagne. From Verzy to Trépail, however, the vines face eastwards, after which they take more southerly aspects.

The vineyards of the Vallée de la Marne face both north and south, depending on which bank they are situated. Going west, the vineyards on the right bank, from Mareuil towards Dormans, have an excellent south-facing aspect and far outmatch in terms of quality the north-facing, left bank vineyards of Mardeuil, Boursault, etc. Going south out of Épernay into the so-called Cubry valley, the vineyards of Pierry, Moussy and Vinay have south and south-east facing aspects, while across the valley towards Vaudancourt and Chavot they again face north, yet like those in the Montagne, seem to thrive.

Further south, where the vineyards of Monthelon and Morangis face Mancy across a small valley, the vines are nicely trapped in east and west-facing aspects. The south-west-facing vines of Grauves mix with those of Cuis before bending around the northern extremity of the Côte des Blancs to meet the superbly situated , east and south-east-facing vineyards of Cramant, Avize, le Mesnil and Vertus.

The vineyards in the Côte de Sézanne in the south-western Champagne district are noticeably less concentrated. They are planted in east and south-east-facing aspects along a ridge which stretches from Allemant, seven kilometres north-east of Sézanne, to Villenauxe-la-Grande, twenty kilometres south-west.

In the Aube *département* between Bar-sur-Aube and Bar-sur-Seine, the patches of vines are even more scattered and, although the best sites face south-east, most seem to have no general trend of aspect. Yet despite the generally low-lying and frost-prone valleys of this region, there are some good Champagnes produced from a handful of vineyards well situated on the steeper slopes of hillsides ranging between 200 and 300 metres in height.

Soil

Topsoil, which eventually becomes man-made when constantly cultivated, is of primary importance: some eighty per cent of the vine's root system, including most of the feeding network, remains in the upper sector of soil. On the other hand, subsoil will always remain geologically true, however cultivated the vineyard may be. Main roots penetrate several different layers of subsoil, the structure of which influences the root system's depth, its drainage and its ability to collect essential minerals.

In general, the ideal medium in which to grow vines for wine production is one that has a thin drift topsoil for good drainage and an easily penetrable, thus well drained subsoil of good water retention characteristics. Thus the metabolism of the vine is well known, and the interaction between it and the soil generally understood. But the finer details concerning the interaction between specific varieties of vine and particular types of soil are an area of knowledge which is still in need of serious research. Dr P.H.T. Beckett, head of the Soil Science Laboratory of the Department of Agricultural Science, University of Oxford, told me:

I did once try to collect information to that purpose ... Although I asked various qualified people if soil altered the flavour of wine from the same grape variety and district I got no clear answer ... I visited a one-man research station of the Cyprus Department of Agriculture who invited me to taste the products of many combinations of variety and soil. It was my impression that slightly casual management may have turned them all to vinegar. At least the wines tasted very curious to my inexpert palate.

Perhaps the greatest quality characteristic possessed by vines grown in Champagne is the ability to produce ripe grapes with a relatively high degree of acidity. Certainly climate is essentially responsible for this but soil plays a part too. A soil with free lime present (i.e. high pH) such as Champagne's Belemnite and Micraster chalk soil, provides grapes with a high cation, or acid, content. There are other soil factors which influence plant growth and the most pertinent of these in the case of Champagne is lime-induced chlorosis. High free lime content in soil restricts access to iron and, to a slightly lesser extent, manganese. This interferes with the synthesis of chlorophyl, an essential green colouring matter in the leaves which uses sunlight to convert simple elements into plant food, causing chlorosis, which is the yellowing of a plant's leaves. In Champagne this is normally countered by the selection of highly resident rootstock varieties and through the choice of sites where the chalk is thinly covered by drift or where man has added rich sandy or clayey lignite soils to the surface.

Most arguments supporting the importance of certain soil types for the production of quality wines hinge on the availability of minerals and other nutrients. These life-sustaining ingredients can be applied directly to the vine by man, indeed are so applied by man in commercial viticulture, yet according to Mike Woodhead, the owner of 'Le Bonheur' in South Africa, it is possible to effect a permanently natural and desirable nutrient cycle in those soils considered inferior by some. Mike Woodhead studied science in Holland and put it to good use when he purchased his wine estate. Composed of four basic soil-types, pot-clay, drained red loam, deep sand and quite deep sand over pot-clay, his estate had insufficient phosphorus, calcium and magnesium, with an unsuitably low pH. But by an expensive, slow and very laborious liming, composting and cover-cropping, he has established a natural cycle which no longer requires topping up with nutrients. The chemical analysis of his soil 'before and after' reveals an astonishing change.

	1972	1982
pH	4.1	6.5
Phosphorus	9 ppm	150 ppm
Potassium	165 ppm	145 ppm
Calcium	100 ppm	1,400 ppm
Magnesium	16 ppm	300 ppm

Glossary of rocks and soils

Alluvium Material which has been transported by river and deposited. Often sand and gravel, but in Champagne alluvial deposits may also include chalky pebbles and concentraions of chalk debris cemented into convex banks several metres thick, and younger alluvial soils may contain chalk clay.

Belemnite chalk See *Chalk* first. In *Champagne*, Patrick Forbes categorically states the gospel as held in Champagne: 'Now, it so happened that most of the top layer of chalk found on the Falaises is of a type known as *Belemnita quadrata*, which is markedly different from the Micraster chalk found on the plain below. Had the top layer of chalk found on the surface soil of the Falaises been mostly of the Micraster type, it is extremely improbable that there would ever have been champagne. For only where there are seams of *Belemnita quadrata* chalk, covered by a layer of Tertiary debris, will the vines produce radiant crops on the Falaises, and grapes that can be turned into champagne which has champagne's unique, inimitable flavour.' This implies something special about Belemnite chalk which is falacious.

As Dr Geoffrey Tresise, Keeper of Geology, Merseyside County Museum, has pointed out in a series of articles for the trade magazine *Wine & Spirit*, there is no physical or chemical property of Belemnite chalk which makes it either superior or inferior to Micraster for viticultural purposes and the grand cru towns of the northerly Montagne adequately demonstrate this. About the number of authors who write that 'the Champagne vineyards are confined to the belemnite-rich chalk and that the lower beds, where belemnites are lacking, produce inferior grapes which are never used for Champagne', he comments: 'They infer that the Campanian has some special but undefined property which makes it superior for vine-growing. Geologically this seems unlikely, if only because the Campanian chalk is widely distributed in the Paris Basin and is certainly not confined to the Montagne de Reims.' Indeed, belemnites, the small, dart-shaped molluscs whose strong rod-like fossilised calcareous shells encouraged geologists to name this particular Campanian chalk *Belemnita quadrata*, are only common in *relative* terms. All chalks, including Belemnite chalk, are fundamentally composed of coccoliths; the belemnites are but a tiny percentage and are also to be found in some seams of Micraster chalk to a greater or lesser degree. Geologists are notorious for latching on to the name of a particular life-form present in rock formations when thinking up names and equally notorious for changing their minds and the rock's name afterwards, hence *Belemnita quadrata* no longer exists because they have renamed it *Gonio teuthis quadrata*.

Chalk Chalk is commonly used as a synonym for limestone but, whereas all chalk is limestone, not all limestone is chalk. Limestone applies to any sedimentary rock consisting essentially of carbonates, but chalk is geologically unique, the white, very fine-grained limestone of the Upper Cretaceous period. Ninety-five million years ago, sea covered most of what is now Europe and, for thirty million years, while the earth experienced great calm, the microscopic calcareous material secreted by unicellular planktonic algae built up a lime-mud on the sea-floor. During this monumental length of time, numerous forms of sea-life evolved, flourished, and became extinct, their calcareous bodies forming thin layers in the ever-thickening lime-mud. Some sixty-five million years ago this seemingly endless sedate marine activity was abruptly halted when earth movements lifted up part of the sea-bed to form the continental land mass. The lime-mud dried up to form chalk up to three hundred metres thick, creating, for example, the South Downs of England, parts of the Loire and, of course, Champagne. The geological conditions under which the chalk formed are unique, and, as a result, so is the chalk.

Clay An argillaceous compound with plastic characteristics when wet.

Colluvium Recent weathered material or hill wash transported by gravity.

Lignite The 'brown coal' of Germany, a brown carbonaceous material intermediate in character between peat and coal.

Limestone Any sedimentary rock consisting essentially of carbonates.

Loam A soil with roughly equal proportions of clay, sand and silt. Depending on the proportions, clayey loams and sandy loams can be identified.

Loess An accumulation of wind-borne material, mainly silty in nature. Sometimes calcareous, but usually weathered and decalcified.

Marl A calcareous clay.

Marlstone Clayey limestones.

Micraster chalk (See *Chalk* first, then *Belemnite chalk*.) There are two main types, Santonian and Coniacian. This is the chalk of the plains, although it encroaches upon the slopes, most notably in the northern Montagne. If this was the chalk of the Falaises and Belemnite chalk the chalk of the plains, I wonder whether the Champagne gospel might not be extolling the virtues of the wonderful heart-shaped Micraster sea urchin?

Sand Particle-shaped quartz, often mixed with fine grains of calcareous origin in Champagne.

Local soil conditions

Montagne de Reims

Topsoil Soils developed in loess drift derived from sandy and clayey-lignite, chalk rubble and clayey colluvium.

Subsoil Principally Belemnite chalk on the upper slopes, with Micraster chalk on the lower slopes. Also, but to a much lesser degree, lignite (the Montagne is dotted with lignite quarries), sand and sandstone. Marlstone high up on some north-facing slopes, with an isolated stratum of fine calcareous sand up to fifteen metres thick in places.

Local conditions AMBONNAY: The south-eastern half of this commune is Micraster plain, but all vines are planted on the Belemnite continuation of Bouzy's vineyards. BOUZY: An isolated patch of loess and granular decalcified chalk immediately west of the village, much of which has never been viticultivated, otherwise completely Belemnite chalk. CHIGNEY-LES-ROSES: Fairly complex structure of interbedded subsoils: Belemnite and Micraster chalks, calcareous-silty deposits, colluvial clay and ferrous-brown calcareous clay. Higher slopes reveal widening seams of calcareous marl, sand and thin seams of marl, sandy-lignites and clayey-lignites. MAILLY: Complex structure of interbedded subsoils: Belemnite and two forms of Micraster chalks, calcareous-silty deposits, fine gravelly beds, colluvial clay and ferrous-brown calcareous clay. Higher slopes reveal widening seams of calcareous marl, sand and thin seams of marl, sandy-lignites and clayey-lignites. PUISIEULX: Fine gravelly bed. RILLY-LA-MONTAGNE: Fairly complex structure of interbedded subsoils and ferrous-brown calcareous clay. Higher slopes reveal widening seams of marl, sand and thin seams of marl, sandy-lignites and clayey-lignites. SILLERY: Fine gravelly beds and Micraster chalk. TRÉPAIL: A white chalky-marl is exposed at the very top of the slopes. VAUDEMANGES: The village itself and most of the commune is on Micraster but its vines are shared with Billy-le-Grand on Belemnite. VERZENAY: Complex structure of interbedded subsoils: Belemnite and two forms of Micraster chalks, calcareous-silty deposits, fine gravelly beds, various layers of ferrous siliceous pebbles and colluvial deposits of ferrous-brown flint-bearing clay. Higher slopes reveal calcareous marl, sand and thin seams of marl, sandy-lignites and clayey-lignites. VERZY: Complex structure of interbedded subsoils: Belemnite and two forms of Micraster chalks, calcareous-silty deposits, fine gravelly beds, various layers of ferrous-brown flinty pebbles east of the village and colluvial deposits of ferrous flint-bearing clay to the north. Higher slopes reveal calcareous marl, sand and thin seams of marl, sandy-lignites and clayey-lignites.

Vallée de la Marne

Topsoil Marl, lignite, sandy-loam and clay.
Subsoil No vines are planted on the alluvial soils close to the river, but on nearby higher ground Belemnite chalk can be seen as the major subsoil. However, west of Vauciennes on the south bank and Damery on the north bank, the chalk outcrop narrows to an ever thinner strip, eventually petering out just before Troissy and Châtillon-sur-Marne. The marl, lignite, sand, sandstone, clay and flinty-clay are in evidence above the narrow chalk slopes, taking over completely with an increasing emphasis on sandstone and clay.
Local conditions AVENAY: Brown coloured loess and granular decalcified chalk. AŸ: Loess and gravel behind village, both planted. BOURSAULT: Belemnite chalk on a few of the very lowest slopes, mainly sand, sandstone, clay and lignites mixed with various calcareous deposits. CUMIÈRES: Belemnite chalk, with seams rich in sand, sandstone, clay and lignites exposed on the highest slopes. HAUTVILLERS: Sand, sandstone, lignites and clay west of the village, and Belemnite chalk to the north-east, south and south-east. The famous hollow beneath Hautvillers, the Côtes-à-Bras, has filled with an accumulation of loess, or colluvial weathered clacareous deposisits, clayey-silts and iron-rich flint pebbles. MARDEUIL: Belemnite chalk on the middle slopes, running down into alluvial soil, with sand, clay and lignites higher up. MAREUIL-SUR-AŸ: Belemnite chalk on the slopes beneath Mutigny, alluvial soil approaching Mareuil-sur-Aÿ itself. TOURS-SUR-MARNE: A continuation of Bouzy's Belemnite chalk slopes. VAUCIENNES: Thin strip of Belemnite chalk, mainly sand, sandstone, clay and lignites.

Côte des Blancs

Topsoil Lignite, sand and clay.
Subsoil Principally Belemnite chalk, with some Micraster chalk at the edge of the lower slopes and lignite, sand, sandstone, clay and flinty-clay exposed in a thin strip on the

highest slopes. The Belemnite chalk is less dense than the Montagne de Reims and turns sandy towards the bottom of its twenty-metre depth.

Local conditions AVIZE: Mainly Belemnite chalk, but with Micraster extending from the plains into lower vineyards east of the railway line on the south-side of the village and west, beyond the line, to the north of the commune. An accumulation of weathered loess and colluvial deposits forms a band from the Cramant boundary, through the hollow between the two villages, beyond Avize and Oger, eventually petering out on the communal border of le Mesnil-sur-Oger. In a bowl-like depression at the Cramant end of this band, rich deposits of clay, sand, sandstone and lignites are to be found. BERGÈRES-LES-VERTUS: The accumulation of loess and colluvial weathered deposits of calcareous, clayey-silt and iron-bearing flinty soils radiating out from Vertus is found on the lower slopes of Bergères-les-Vertus, but the bulk of this village's vineyards are to be found on Belemnite chalk, with sand on some of the higher slopes. CHOUILLY: Vines closest to the village are on Micraster chalk, but the Butte de Saran is pure Belemnite, becoming heavily influenced by sand, sandstone, clay and lignites. CRAMANT: Those vines on the south face of the Butte de Saran belonging to the commune of Chouilly are planted on rich sand, sandstone, clay and lignite soil, while those which belong to Cramant, being physically beneath those of Chouilly, are of Belemnite chalk. This Belemnite chalk extends to the border of Avize, but Micraster bites into the vineyards on the lower slopes, reaching as far up as the D9–D10 cut which runs around the southern edge of the Butte de Saran. The vineyards on the Cuis side of the village are on rich clay, sand, sandstone and lignite soil, covered in places by an accumulation of loess and colluvium. CUIS: Apart from Belemnite chalk on the west-facing slopes overlooking Mancy and on the slopes closest to the D10 between Cuis and Cramant, most vines are to be found on soils derived from clay, sand, sandstone and lignite. LE MESNIL-SUR-OGER: The track skirting the highest slopes southwest of the village winds its way through a thin strip of clay, sand, sandstone and lignites. Apart from this, the entire vineyard belonging to this commune is situated on Belemnite chalk. OGER: Very little Micraster encroaching upon the Belemnite chalk hills of this village, just a small patch overlapping the D9 north of St Michel farm. A central core along the côte of accumulated loess and colluvial weathered deposits of calcareous, clayey-silt and iron-bearing flinty pebbles. Complex geological folds where the vines are planted either side of the village road leading west into the forest reveal various layers of yellowish-grey calcareous flint-bearing marl, sand, hard white limestone, clay, sand, sandstone and lignites. OIRY: Entirely Micraster. VERTUS: An accumulation of weathered deposits of loess and colluvial calcareous clayey-silt and iron-bearing flinty pebbles radiates outwards from the village, two particularly large legs of which follow the Côte north and south. Beyond this accumulation Belemnite chalk predominates, encroached upon by Micraster in one small patch between the railway line and the D9 north-east of the village and by sand noticed on the highest strip of vines south-west of Vertus.

Côte de Sézanne

Topsoil Marl, clay, sandstone and sand.
Subsoil East and north-east of Sézanne the subsoil is substantially chalk, both Belemnite and Micraster. South and south-west of Sézanne, the chalk subsoil exists in fairly large

pockets, broken up by marl, clay, sandstone, sandy-clay and sand. Yellow and red sand north of Sézanne, giving away sandstone with high iron levels further south. Lignite seams also exist as this Sparnacian deposit is quarried at Sans-Souci, just two kilometres north of Sézanne.

Aube Département

Topsoil Gravelly limestone, either weathered or oolitic, and granular limestone, Portlandian in origin.

Subsoil Kimmeridgian, mostly Upper Kimmeridgian, except for the Upper Oxfordian slopes of Trannes, Mussy-sur-Seine and on the Valanginien.

Local conditions BAR-SUR-AUBE: A cohesion of marl beds, calcareous marl (Upper and Middle Kimmeridgian) and much harder Portlandian calcareous rocks. BAR-SUR-SEINE: Beds of marl and calcareous marl (Upper and Middle Kimmeridgian) covered by Portlandian calcareous rocks broken down by frosts in the glacial period, providing excellent surface drainage, yet reserves of water for deep penetrating roots. BUXIÈRES-SUR-ARCE: A light-beige calcareous rock of Upper Portlandian origin called Barrois. COLOMBÉ-LE-FOSSE: This village is huddled between Portlandian hills of Barrois limestone. COURTERON: Local gravelly-textured limestone called la Bellerée. ESSOYES: A local limestone called d'Oisellemont of early Kimmeridgian age. MONTGUEUX: Heavily fissured Coniacian and Upper Turonian chalk, older than Belemnite and Micraster, both of which are Campanian. PLAINE-SAINT-LANGE: Grey limestone and marl just north of the village. VILLE-SUR-ARCE: Fine slopes for viticulture consisting of Kimmeridgian marls covered by Portlandian calcareous rocks broken up by frost in the glacial period, providing excellent surface drainage while deep roots can penetrate the marls for reserves of water. VOIGNY: Gravelly and oolitic limestone of Kimmeridgian age approaching the village, nestling between the steep slopes of a pure Portlandian mount, topped by the Bois de Voigny.

3

Vineyard Classification

*Very good in its way
Is the Verzenay,
Or the Sillery, soft and creamy.*
Henry Wadsworth Longfellow (1807–82)

The échelle des crus

ALL GROWTHS within the legally delimited Champagne zone are classified on a percentage basis known as the *échelle des crus* (see Appendix v). This was originally set at a minimum of 50% and a maximum of 100%, although recent reclassifications have increased the minimum *échelle* to 80%. Villages with vineyards rated between 90 and 99% inclusive are considered to be *premiers crus* while those classed at 100% are *grands crus*. Both terms are allowed to be used on the label by all Champagne manufacturers, although in general only growers who make and sell their own Champagne take advantage of this.

The échelle des crus is the basis upon which the price of grapes destined to become Champagne is fixed. Every year at harvest time the CIVC announces the price per kilo of grapes after consultation with the growers and *négociants* or houses. This is the price applied to grapes coming from 100%-rated grand cru vineyards, the produce of lesser rated vineyards commanding proportionately lower prices.

Thus, if one takes a hypothetical case where the price was fixed at 10 francs per kilo, all grapes coming from the 100% crus – like Avize, Cramant, Bouzy, for example – would cost 10 francs per kilo, while grapes coming from the 94%-rated Rilly-la-Montagne would cost 9.40 francs and so forth. Added to this, a premium is usually paid for so-called 'noble' grapes, such as Chardonnay or Pinot Noir, which encourages the cultivation of these better, but less prolific, varieties.

The advantage of the échelle des crus system is that it recognises a distinction in quality between two undeniably fine and relatively similar growths. This allows a premier cru to stand out and get appropriate recognition even if it should be considered a grand cru. But it must also be remembered, too, that while a 95%-rated vineyard may be superior to a 94%-rated one, healthy, ripe 80% grapes are vastly superior to 100% grapes which have been affected by disease, rot, or damaging weather conditions like hail or frost.

Grand cru villages There are seventeen villages in Champagne officially rated at 100% and thus designated grand cru status. These are: Ambonnay, Avize, Aÿ, Beaumont-sur-Vesle, Bouzy, Chouilly, Cramant, Louvois, Mailly-Champagne, le Mesnil-sur-Oger, Oger, Oiry, Puisieulx, Sillery, Tours-sur Marne, Verzenay and Verzy.

It is only recently that Champagne has been able to boast as many as seventeen grands crus. Until the 1985 harvest-time declaration of the échelle des crus, Chouilly, le Mesnil-sur-Oger, Oger, Oiry and Verzy merely held premier cru status. The event was an unprecedented one: Champagne's grand cru villages remained at twelve for almost forty years. Yet, despite increasing their number by almost half and achieving this reclassification in one speedy stroke, the CIVC was curiously quiet about it. No press release was made and I experienced extraordinary difficulties in trying to obtain the 1985 échelle des crus, Quite why this historic event was clothed in such secrecy is a mystery. Le Mesnil-sur-Oger, Oger and Verzy were long overdue this honour and Chouilly and Oiry, both very fine premiers crus, are far superior to quite a few traditionally established grand cru villages.

Interestingly, only part of Chouilly and Tours-sur-Marne can claim the grand cru classification. The black grapes of Chouilly and the white grapes of Tours-sur-Marne have an échelle of 95% and 90% respectively, and as such may claim only premier cru status. This therefore means that of the 4,339 hectares cultivated in Champagne's top villages, only 4,309 hold the rank of grand cru. Should Chouilly and Tours-sur-Marne replant these vineyards with the appropriate varieties, they would of course assume full grand status.

Of the 4,309 hectares of grand cru vineyards in Champagne, 2,251 hectares (52.2%) are planted with Chardonnay, 1,960 hectares (45.5%) with Pinot Noir and 98 hectares (2.3%) with Pinot Meunier.

Premier cru villages   There are thirty-eight premier cru villages in Champagne, plus those vineyards growing black grapes in the grand cru of Chouilly and those growing white grapes in the grand cru of Tours-sur-Marne, making a total of forty villages entitled to the status of premier cru. These are, in descending order of échelle:

99%	Mareuil-sur-Aÿ	93%	Avenay
	Tauxières		Champillon
			Cumières
95%	Bergères-les-Vertus (white grapes only)		Hautvillers
	Billy-le-Grand		Mutigny
	Bissueil		
	Chouilly (black grapes only)	90%	Bergères-les-Vertus (black grapes only)
	Cuis (white grapes only)		Bezannes
	Dizy		Chamery
	Grauves (white grapes only)		Coligny (white grapes only)
	Trépail		Cuis (black grapes only)
	Vaudemanges		Écueil
	Vertus		Étréchy (white grapes only)
	Villeneuve-Renneville		Grauves (black grapes only)
	Villers-Marmery		Jouy-les-Reims
	Voipreux		les Mesneux
			Pargny-les-Reims
94%	Chigny-les-Roses		Pierry
	Ludes		Sacy
	Montbré		Tours-sur-Marne (white grapes only)
	Rilly-la-Montagne		Villedommange
	Taissy		Villers-Allerand
	Trois Puits		Villers-aux-Noeuds

Of the 4,928* hectares of premier cru vineyards, 1,892 hectares (38.4%) are planted with Chardonnay, 1,412 hectares (28.7%) with Pinot Noir and 1,624 hectares (32.9%) with Pinot Meunier.

The reclassifications of 1985

The recent upgrading of grands and premiers crus has radically altered the proportions of grape varieties grown within these groups of villages. Most importantly the Chardonnay in the grand cru sector has risen from nearly a third to over a half of the vines cultivated, while in the premiers crus it has dropped from just under a half to less than 40%. The Pinot Noir in the grands crus has dropped from almost 65 to 45%, while the difference in the premiers crus is less than 3%. Not much of a change for the grand cru Pinot Meunier, but a significant increase for the premiers crus, jumping from a less than 25% coverage to almost one-third.

Champagne's échelle des crus is essentially a fairer system than other classifications in France where, as in Burgundy or Bordeaux for example, villages or properties are either steeped in glory or barely known, as the case may be. Yet this exceedingly sensible system has not always been applied in an even-handed manner. While some grand and premier cru villages do not justify such illustrious titles, certain superior premiers crus are, even after the reclassification of 1985, still denied the grand cru status they truly deserve. However, the issue is not quite as simple as that – many individual sites within premier cru villages can, and do, consistently produce wines as good as the best grands crus and infinitely better than the worst. This also applies, to a degree, to some lower-ranking villages. It seems a pity that the rationale of a percentage rating system is not extended a little further by incorporating a *lieux dits* scale classifying named sites within each village.

In the following village by village assessment of the famous grands and premiers crus of Champagne, I express my opinion on the merits and demerits of the major vineyards within each commune. Some vineyards may not be mentioned because they have only recently been cultivated and, therefore, have not been in production long enough to establish any sort of reputation.

The reader should note that the term Grower Champagne used throughout this chapter refers to a *récoltant-manipulant*, that is to say a grower who sells Champagne under his own name. More particulars about these growers can be located in the Village Directory of Champagne Growers. As the definition of a true *récoltant-manipulant* is a contentious subject, the author strongly advises that the section in Chapter 12 headed 'The Growers or *Récoltants*' is fully digested before consulting entries in the Directory.

*This figure does not include the villages of Bezannes, Chamery, Coligny, Jouy-les-Reims, Pargny-les-Reims, Villers-aux-Noeuds and Voipreux, all of which were elevated to premier cru status in 1985.

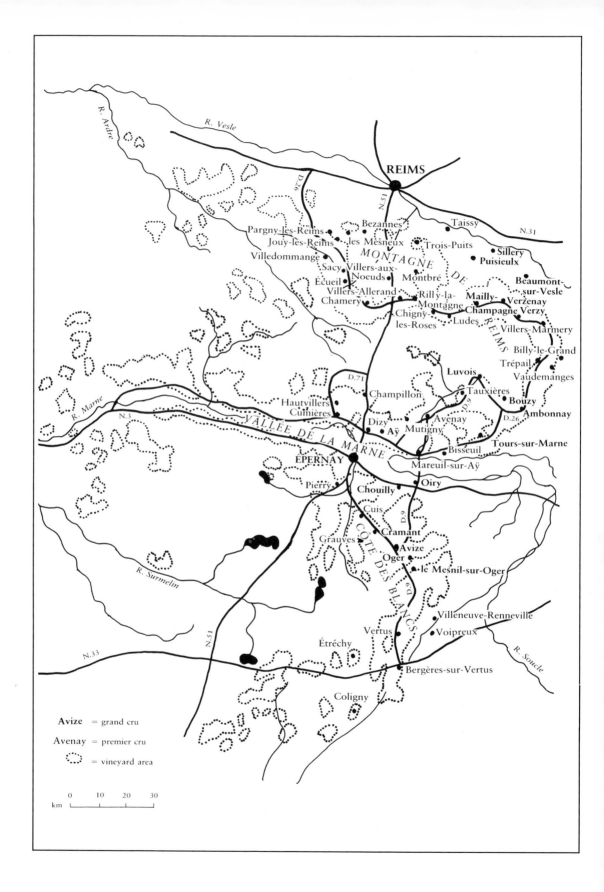

Avize = grand cru

Avenay = premier cru

⬭ = vineyard area

0   10   20   30
km

The grand cru villages

Ambonnay

Population 980   **Situation** 15 kilometres north-east of Épernay along the D1 and D19, on the southern slopes of the Montagne de Reims.
Surface area planted 364 hectares
Grape varieties Chardonnay: 54 hectares (14.84% of surface area); Pinot Noir: 310 hectares (85.16% of surface area)

The village is thought to have been named after a Roman officer, Amboniacus, at the time when the Emperor Probus ordered the replanting of vineyards throughout Gaul.

A sleepy hamlet which has miraculously escaped the scars of many battles, with quaint narrow streets and a Gallo-Roman church, Ambonnay is one of the prettiest villages in the region.

After Verzenay, the vineyard of Ambonnay is the second largest of all the grands crus. The majority of the vineyards are located to the north and north-west of the village, commencing half a kilometre north-west of Ambonnay itself, where the land rises to about 20 metres. Most of the vines are planted at a height of between 120 and 180 metres, although a few plots can be found at 200 to 220 metres in the northern part of the vineyard, bordering the vines of Bouzy.

The vines of Ambonnay are, in fact, a physical extension of those of Bouzy, but there is a subtle distinction in the aspect of these vineyards and, consequently, a difference in the character of the wines they produce. Unlike the south-facing vines of Bouzy, the vineyards of Ambonnay are essentially south-east and east-facing.

The wines of Ambonnay have a certain edge and show fine definition. Like those of neighbouring Bouzy, they possess qualities somewhere between the solid, full-bodied and strongly perfumed Verzenay and the smooth, exceptionally aromatic Aÿ but their great strength and vinosity edges them closer to the former than the latter.

Considerably lesser wines, however, are made from an isolated plot of vines around the south-western edge of Ambonnay – obviously these vines cannot be compared to those situated north of the village.

Ambonnay has long been famous for its production of still red wines. Since the early eighteenth century the red wines of Ambonnay have ranked alongside those of the now more famous Bouzy.
Houses owning vineyards Chauvet; Veuve Clicquot-Ponsardin; Heidsieck & Co. Monopole; R. et L. Legras; Moët & Chandon; G. H. Mumm & Co.; A. Secondé Prevoteau; Taittinger
Grower Champagnes André Beaufort; Claude Beaufort; Lucien Beaufort; H. Billot Fils; Bernard Bremont; R. and H. Coutier; Roger Croizy; Paul Déthune; Michel Egly; Robert Foureur; Roger Gauthier; Michel Ledru; Marguet-Bonnerave; A. Michel-Huguet; C. Millot; Jean B. Rodez; Michel Rodez; Georges Simon; Jean Varlot; Gaston Warin

Avize

Population 2,200   **Situation** 9 kilometres south-east of Épernay along the D9, in the Côte des Blancs.
Surface area planted 258 hectares
Grape varieties Chardonnay: 258 hectares (100% of surface area)

'Belles cottes, pas de chemise' sums up Avize in *parler Champenois*, perhaps because, according to local tradition, the young women of this village would lie naked upon the slopes of Mont-Arme (now, Mont-Aimé) on the early morning of 1 March every year, to catch the first rays of sun upon their glistening bodies. Sadly, this pagan custom, called 'Salut au Soleil du 1er Mars', is now no more than legend.

The east-facing slopes of Avize, at a height of between 110 and 210 metres, are planted entirely with Chardonnay grapes. The vines surround the village on all sides, but those grown on the highest slopes, on either side of the D10 to the west of Ambonnay, are by far the most successful; on the plain, either side of the D9, the vineyards are noticeably inferior.

At their very best the vineyards of Avize yield classic Chardonnay wines which have no superiors. Opinions vary, however, when comparing the qualities of Avize wines with those of its neighbouring grand cru Cramant. Some say that the Avize Chardonnay has more

OPPOSITE
Distribution of the grands and premiers crus

finesse, but I find that while Avize may have more clarity of flavour, Cramant and, for that matter, le Mesnil-sur-Oger have finer qualities of bouquet.

Houses owning vineyards Albert le Brun; Veuve Clicquot-Ponsardin; Duval-Leroy; Heidsieck & Co. Monopole; Jacquesson; Lanson; Larmandier; Laurent Perrier; Moët & Chandon; G. H. Mumm & Co.; Oudinot; Perrier-Jouët; Pol Roger; Pommery & Greno; Louis Roederer; Taitinger

Grower Champagnes Agrapart & Fils; F. Bonville; Pierre Callot; Michel Ghys; Michel Gonet; Jacques Selosse

Aÿ or Aÿ-Champagne

Population 4,900 **Situation** 3 kilometres east of Épernay along the D201, at the foot of the south-facing slopes of the Montagne de Reims on the right bank of the Marne valley.
Surface area planted 352 hectares
Grape varieties Chardonnay: 32 hectares (9.09% of surface area); Pinot Noir: 281 hectares (79.83% of surface area); Pinot Meunier: 39 hectares (11.08% of surface area)

The vineyards of Aÿ stretch out behind the village, up fairly steep slopes to a height of about 200 metres on the Mutigny side. These vines overlook a small north–south running valley, on the other side of which a 170-metre-high spur of vines drops down to the north-western edge of the village. Beyond this spur the vineyards continue for another 2 kilometres towards Dizy. But it is in the complex configuration of slopes, dips and valleys immediately behind the village that the greatest vines of Aÿ are found. In this miniature valley extending up towards the Bois de Charlefontaine, the slopes provide a unique micro-climate which, together with the protection of the village itself, shields the vines from the major winds and traps the sun. In the centre of the south-west facing slopes of this favoured valley lies the famous 'Côte aux Enfants', a single-site vineyard possessing exceptional qualities. Although it is possible to sample a pure Côte aux Enfants red wine made by Bollinger and matured in small oak casks, the production is tiny and availability correspondingly restricted.

Half-way along the 2 kilometres of vineyards towards Dizy, a crumpling of the contours twists the ground into a full, frontal, southern exposure. One of the most reputed single-site vineyards of this area is 'Le Léon', named after Pope Leo the Magnificent, who drew supplies from here in the first half of the nineteenth century.

Henry Vizetelly remarks (*A History of Champagne*, 1882) that the soil of Aÿ 'lends a flavour of peaches', but as he also records that an anonymous document, entitled 'Mémoire sur la Manière de cultiver la Vigne et de fair le Vin en Champagne', dated 1718, reveals that the secret of Dom Pérignon was to add four or five stoned peaches to a pièce of wine, the source of such an exotic flavour must be questioned. While it is unlikely that Dom Pérignon himself employed such methods, it is more than probable that others did. Monsieur Boudin of Perrier Jouet told me that in 'the old days' the Pinot Noir of Aÿ once had a *goût de terroir* which, I am glad to say, has since been 'lost'.

Aÿ Champagnes have great finesse and style, a good alcoholic potential and a strength which is belied by a delicacy of bouquet and a smoothness of flavour.
Houses owning vineyards Ayala & Co.; J. Bollinger; Veuve Clicquot-Ponsardin; Collery; Deutz & Geldermann; Roland Fliniaux; Emile Hamm et Fils; Henriot; Bernard Ivernel; Jacquesson; Krug; Mercier; Moët & Chandon; G. H. Mumm & Co.; Perrier Jouët; Pommery & Greno; Louis Roederer; de Venoge
Grower Champagnes Gosset-Brabant; Henri Goutorbe

Beaumont-sur-Vesle

Population 400 **Situation** 13 kilometres south-east of Reims along the N44, on the plain north of the Montagne de Reims.
Surface area planted 25 hectares
Grape varieties Chardonnay: 2 hectares (8% of surface area); Pinot Noir: 22 hectares (88% of surface area); Pinot Meunier: 1 hectare (4% of surface area)

The two parcels of vines belonging to Beaumont-sur-Vesle are located on a small patch of flat ground, west of the road leading out of the village towards Verzenay and, a kilometre further on, adjoining the edge of some of the poorest vineyards of Verzenay. Although it holds *grand cru* status Beaumont-sur-Vesle can in no way be described as a great growth. Even in 1824, André Jullien rated the

'light and agreeable but weak wines' of Beaumont-sur-Vesle no more than a fifth growth in his five-tier ranking of Champagne. Its wines were once upon a time combined in the vat with those of Verzenay and it is from the reputation of that great village that Beaumont-sur-Vesle has wrested its misplaced status.
Grower Champagnes Camille Bernard; Virgille Portier; Maurice Vautier; Pierre Vautier

Bouzy

Population 900 **Situation** 14 kilometres north-east of Épernay along the D1 and D19 on the south-facing slopes of the Montagne de Reims.
Surface area planted 357 hectares
Grape varieties Chardonnay: 43 hectares (12.04% of surface area); Pinot Noir: 314 hectares (87.96% of surface area)

The great amphitheatre of vines which rises up from the village of Bouzy represents one of the most famous vineyards in the world. Yet not all of the vines which sweep north – from Mont Écouve in the west up to the edge of the Bois des Dames, and trailing south down the ridge towards the village – produce top grade Bouzy wines. Roughly speaking, the quality is determined by location in the vineyard, which can be divided into bands: the most northerly band, elevated at a height of between 180 and 220 metres, comprises some of the finest grand cru slopes in all Champagne and represents about a third of Bouzy's hectarage; below this is a wide strip situated at a height of between 160 and 180 metres which, in my estimation, should hold the rank of a top premier cru; the lowest band, at about 170 metres, runs around the flat northern edge of the village and produces vines of a markedly inferior quality.

The characteristics afforded to Champagne by the inclusion of Bouzy wines in a *cuvée* are those of great weight and extract, richness of flavour, powerful Pinot bouquet and a high alcoholic content. Pure Bouzy Champagnes, though profuse in number, are consistently high in quality and often improve over a period of eight to ten years in bottle. Its red wines have all the qualities of colour and body found in the northern Montagne around Mailly, Verzenay and Verzy, but with an added degree of delicacy.
Houses owning vineyards Barancourt; J.

Bollinger; Chauvet; Veuve Clicquot-Ponsardin; Heidsieck & Co. Monopole; Lanson; Laurent Perrier; Moët & Chandon; G. H. Mumm & Co.; Pommery & Greno; A. Secondé Prevoteau; Taittinger
Grower Champagnes Paul Bara; H. Beaufort & Fils; R. le Clapart; André Clouet; Jérôme Collard, Dauvergne-Baron et Fils; René Dauvergne; Delavenne; Pierre Hulin et Fils; René Lallement; Gabriel Ledru; Bernard Mangin; Paul-Louis Martin; Pierre Paillard; Jean Plener Fils; Émilien Rémy; Camille Saves; Bernard Tornay; Alfred Tritant; Alain Vesselle; Georges Vesselle; Jean Vesselle; Maurice Vesselle; Michel Waroquier

Chouilly

Population 1,000 **Situation** 4 kilometres east of Épernay along the RD3 towards Châlons-sur-Marne.
Surface area planted 497 hectares
Grape varieties Chardonnay: 487 hectares (97.99% of surface area); Pinot Noir: 9 hectares (1.81% of surface area); Pinot Meunier: 1 hectare (0.2% of surface area)

Since 1985 the white grapes of this village have been elevated to grand cru status, but, while its black grapes have increased from 90% to 95% échelle, they maintain the rank of premier cru. While there are a few vines on the flat ground just south of the village, the vast majority are found on the slopes of the Butte de Saran, the northern extremity of the Côte des Blancs, and on the eastern slopes of Mont Bernon, edging the suburbs of Épernay. Those on the Butte de Saran are on north-east and south-east-facing slopes, the best of which are between 100 and 120 metres in height. Some particularly fine plots can be found around the southern side of the butt on south-east-facing slopes, which rise to a height of 220 metres. But this strip of superior vines is very thin, just a hundred metres in parts, as the communal boundary of Cramant hives off most of the vineyards. The lower vines around the village of Chouilly and those on the eastern slopes of Mont Bernon, towards Épernay, are relatively inferior.
Houses owning vineyards Henriot; Larmandier; R. et L. Legras; Mercier; Moët & Chandon; Oudinot; Pol Roger; Louis Roederer
Grower Champagnes Vazart-Comte; Vazart-Coquart & Fils; Lucien Vazart; Voirin

Cramant

Population 1,000 **Situation** 7 kilometres south-east of Épernay along the D40 and D10, lying in a valley on the northern edge of the Côte des Blancs between the Montagne d'Avize and the Butte de Saran.
Surface area planted 323 hectares
Grape varieties Chardonnay: 323 hectares

The vineyards of Cramant lie close to Moët & Chandon's splendid Château de Saran. Indeed, the thin strip of steep-sloping east to south-east-facing vines, situated on the north side of the D9 to D10 cut, are some of the best in Cramant. The communal borderline between Chouilly and Cramant slices through the middle of these slopes, the higher vines belonging to Chouilly. The south side of the cut dips down into a beautiful hollow of vines, all but the lowest locations being ideally situated. To the north-east of the dip, the eastern ridge of the Butte de Saran provides a few slopes of almost full southern exposure. On the east side of the village, however, only those slopes leading up to the Bois d'Avize are comparable.

Cramant, Avize, le Mesnil-sur-Oger and Oger are close rivals for the production of the best Chardonnay. Avize and Oger have great distinction, but there is something spectacular about the Chardonnay perfume from grapes grown in Cramant and le Mesnil-sur-Oger – it is a pure essence of the Chardonnay aroma, and apparently restricted to these two villages.
Houses owning vineyards Barancourt; Veuve Clicquot-Ponsardin; Duval-Leroy; Heidsieck & Co. Monopole; Larmandier; Laurent Perrier; Mercier; Moët & Chandon; G. H. Mumm & Co.; Oudinot; Perrier Jouët; Pol Roger; Pommery & Greno; Taittinger
Grower Champagnes Bonnaire-Bouquemont; Caroff-Gimonet; P. Guiborat; René Jumel; Krier-Busson; Collective Lebrun-Vignier; Pierre Lesage; Lilbert-Fils; Melat; G. Morizet; Pertois-Lebrun; Sugot-Feneuil

Louvois

Population 300 **Situation** 13 kilometres north-east of Épernay along the D201 and D9, on the southern slopes of the Montagne de Reims, nestling between the Bois du Mt St Hulin and the Bois des Dames.
Surface area planted 38 hectares
Grape varieties Chardonnay: 4 hectares (10.53% of surface area); Pinot Noir: 34 hectares (89.47% of surface area)

Strictly speaking, Louvois should not be considered a grand cru village. With only 38 hectares, its few vineyards are merely an extension of Bouzy's, growing over the ridge of the Bois des Dames and down the slopes of forested valley in which Louvois is situated.
Houses owning vineyards J. Bollinger; Veuve Clicquot-Ponsardin; Laurent Perrier; Louis Roederer; A. Secondé Prevoteau
Grower Champagnes Yves Beautrait; Guy Mea

Mailly-Champagne

Population 800 **Situation** 12 kilometres south-east of Reims along the N51 and D26, on the north-facing slopes of the Montagne de Reims, under the Moulin de Verzenay.
Surface area planted 272 hectares
Grape varieties Chardonnay: 22 hectares (8.09% of surface area); Pinot Noir: 228 hectares (83.82% of surface area); Pinot Meunier: 22 hectares (8.09% of surface area)

The vineyards of Mailly-Champagne are situated at the northern end of the village on fairly flat ground where they fare exceptionally well. A thermal blanket of warm air protects the vines in the winter months and hastens maturity through the summer. Exceptional vines are also found east of the village and south of the D26 huddled around sharply contoured ground which gives north, north-west and south-west-facing aspects. A small patch of vines also exists right at the top of the village where the ground rises steeply to more than 220 metres.

The red wines of Mailly have a long-standing reputation, and are often ranked, for their qualities of finesse and bouquet, alongside the famous, well-coloured wines of Verzenay and Verzy. Pure Mailly wines can be purchased from the local *co-opérative* (on the left as you enter the village on the D26 from Rilly) which is one of the best co-ops in Champagne.

Mailly is principally known for its Pinot Noir vines, but there are also now 22 hectares of Chardonnay, which since 1972, have been accorded grand cru status.
Houses owning vineyards Veuve Clicquot-Ponsardin; Moët & Chandon; G. H. Mumm & Co.; Perrier Jouët; Pommery & Greno; Louis Roederer; Taittinger
Grower Champagnes Barbier-Gosset; Jacques

Chance; M. Cheyallier; Paul Decotte; Gilbert Devarenne; Jean-Pierre Floquet; Michel Garitan; Michel Henroux; Lucien Roguet; Lucien Richez; M. Vanzella

le Mesnil-sur-Oger

Population 1,400 **Situation** 20 kilometres south-east of Épernay along the D40 and D10, on the eastern slopes of the Côte des Blancs.
Surface area planted 412 hectares
Grape varieties Chardonnay (100% of surface area)

Situated halfway between Avize and Vertus, le Mesnil-sur-Oger regularly produces some of the finest Chardonnay Champagnes. For forty years this village suffered the injustice of a 99% échelle de cru. While lesser villages grabbed a few per cent here and there, le Mesnil-sur-Oger was denied that one vital per cent required for full grand cru status. The slopes which produce these prized vines are generally east-facing, but in a few specific cases they are exposed in northern and southern directions. The vines grow at an altitude of between 140 and 240 metres, although those growing between 160 and 220 metres are the most successful. The lower slopes, which descend at a lesser incline to a height of 110 metres, also produce fine wines, although not quite the same exalted standard as the rest of this village.

It has long been acknowledged that the Chardonnay in le Mesnil-sur-Oger is a special clone of exceptional quality and character. It produces wine of great finesse and penetrating perfume which can dominate an entire *cuvée* even when its presence might only be a small proportion of the whole. The uniqueness of these localised vines was first recognised at the beginning of the century by Eugène-Aimé Salon, the founder of Champagne Salon; more recently, in the early 1970s, the house of Krug purchased the entire single-site, wall-enclosed vineyard of 'Clos du Mesnil', which is situated inside the village itself.
Houses owning vineyards Veuve Clicquot-Ponsardin; Henriot; Krug; Moët & Chandon; Salon
Grower Champagnes François Billion; Claude Cazals; Guy Charlemagne-Peters; François Gonet; André Jacquart; Léon Launois; Launois Père & Fils; Pertois-Morizet; Pierre Peters; Alain Robert

Oger

Population 700 **Situation** 11 kilometres south-east of Épernay along the D10 in the Côte des Blancs.
Surface area planted 383 hectares
Grape varieties Chardonnay: 100% of surface area

Oger is a small hamlet, its few houses set well back from the D10 towards the Forêt d'Oger, and barely noticeable from the road. Since the reclassification in the échelle des crus this village has risen to 100%, giving it full grand cru status. Its vineyards are situated on the same east-facing slopes as those of the superb grands crus of Avize and le Mesnil-sur-Oger, and its wines are comparable in quality. Pure Chardonnay Champagnes from the best vineyards of Oger have great finesse and all the true aromatic characteristics of the Chardonnay grape.
Houses owning vineyards Veuve Clicquot-Ponsardin; Henriot; Pommery & Greno
Grower Champagnes René Henry; Thomas Hussenet

Oiry

Population 400 **Situation** 7 kilometres east of Épernay along the D3 towards Châlons-sur-Marne, east of Chouilly.
Surface area planted 83 hectares
Grape varieties Chardonnay: 82 hectares (98.8% of surface area); Pinot Meunier: 1 hectare (1.2% of surface area)

The vineyards of Oiry are located well away from the village on the lower slopes of the Butte de Saran at a level of between 100 and 120 metres. In the main, they are an extension of the vineyards of Cramant, with a few hectares encroaching into the communal borders of Chouilly and Avize on either side. Of the various aspects here, there are some with excellent south and south-east exposures and the vines here produce unquestionably fine wines. Since 1985 the échelle de cru of this village has risen to 100%. Although there are some good sites, they are limited and, without doubt, the vineyards of Oiry are generally less favourably positioned than those of Chouilly which, unjustifiably, had a lower échelle until they both qualified for grand cru status.
Houses owning vineyards Larmandier; Pol Roger

Puisieulx

Population 300 **Situation** 9 kilometres south-east of Reims along the N44, D8 and D33, on the plain north of the Montagne de Reims and south-west of Sillery.
Surface area planted 18 hectares
Grape varieties Chardonnay: 5 hectares (27.78% of surface area); Pinot Noir: 11 hectares (61.11% of surface area); Pinot Meunier: 2 hectares (11.11% of surface area)

Puisieulx is the smallest of the grand cru villages and certainly does not merit its exalted status. It owes its position to the fame of Sillery which, equally overrated, owes its reputation to the vines of Verzeray.

On my first visit to the village I was unable to find any of its vines and when I asked several people from the larger Champagne houses, few had even heard of its vineyards, let alone of their elevated status. The vines are in fact situated on a hint of a mound just west of the town, growing at an altitude of between 100 and 105 metres which must be a classic example of frost-prone cultivation.
Houses owning vineyards Moët & Chandon

Sillery

Population 900 **Situation** 10 kilometres south-east of Reims along the N44 and D8 on the plain north of the Montagne de Reims.
Surface area planted 92 hectares
Grape varieties Chardonnay: 38 hectares (41.3% of surface area); Pinot Noir: 51 hectares (55.44% of surface area); Pinot Meunier: 3 hectares (3.26% of surface area)

Hardly a true grand cru, Sillery gained its prominence from the slopes of Verzenay which were part of the estate of the famous Brularts. The Brularts, who held the rank of Marquis of Sillery and Marquis of Puisieulx, were a winemaking family whose reputation goes back to the sixteenth century. Roger Brulart, the fourth Marquis of Sillery, was a member of the Ordre des Coteaux, a group of aristocrats intent on glamorising the wines and food of Champagne. He succeeded in glamorising his own wines extraordinarily well, but the reputation of Sillery did not attain its zenith until the eighteenth century when, under the Maréchale d'Éstrées, the only child of Louis-Philogène, the sixth Marquis, the estate had accumulated a vast holding of vineyards. It was from these vines, which stretched into Verzenay, Mailly and Verzy, that the wines of Sillery were made.

The vineyards of Sillery are indeed an extension of the lower slopes of Verzenay, where they stretch out along the flatter, frost-prone ground on the plain beneath the Montagne de Reims, taking a good kilometre and a half to rise a mere twenty metres or so. Within days of the first autumn frosts a large brown patch of vines can be seen growing out from this area. In spring the effect is less noticeable, but potentially more dangerous.

At the little crossroads two kilometres north of Mailly, if you look to your extreme left you will see the lower edge of some vineyards one-and-a-half kilometres away. These are the lowest-quality vines of Verzenay, a relatively small percentage of the grand cru's 403 hectares. But the long and very flat strip of vines immediately to your left, which extend back to the A4 motorway, are inferior to Verzenay's poorest vines; these are the vineyards of Sillery.
Houses owning vineyards Lanson; Laurent Perrier; Moët & Chandon; Pommery & Greno; Ruinart Père et Fils

Tours-sur-Marne

Population 1,300 **Situation** 12 kilometres east of Épernay along the D201 and D1, on the plain south of the Montagne de Reims, backing on to the Marne canal and the Bois Marteau.
Surface area planted 54 hectares
Grape varieties Chardonnay: 20 hectares (37.04% of surface area)*; Pinot Noir: 33 hectares (61.11% of surface area); Pinot Meunier: 1 hectare (1.85% of surface area)

The vineyards of Tours-sur-Marne are an extension of the lower and middle slopes of Bouzy and lie some distance north of the village. The best of the west and south-facing slopes are far superior to either Puisieulx or Sillery, but they nevertheless merit a modest premier and not grand cru status.
Houses owning vineyards Mercier
Grower Champagnes Clos Babot (resident in Bisseuil); Yves Delaporte; Lamiable Frères

Verzenay

Population 1,400 **Situation** 15 kilometres south-east of Reims along the N44 and D7, on the northern tip of the Montagne de Reims.

* Chardonnay can only claim an échelle of 90% and its wines are thus considered to be premier cru, not grand cru.

The Moulin à Verzenay

Surface area planted 403 hectares
Grape varieties Chardonnay: 40 hectares
(9.93% of surface area); Pinot Noir: 351
hectares (87.1% of surface area); Pinot
Meunier: 12 hectares (2.97% of surface area)

Verzenay is the largest of the grands crus and is
the best growth on the northern slopes of the
Montagne de Reims.

Situated on the turn of the Montagne –
before it bends around its eastern extremity
into Verzy, Villers-Marmery and Trépail – the
vineyards of Verzenay have either north or
west-facing aspects and are planted up to a
height of 220 and, in a few places, 240 metres.

Verzenay is reputed to produce the blackest
grapes in the region and its red wines are famed
for their richness of flavour and strongly
scented aromas. The Chardonnay grape grows
less well on these north-facing slopes and,
though less in evidence, has recently, perhaps
over-generously, been accorded full grand cru
status (1972).
Houses owning vineyards J. Bollinger;
Canard-Duchêne; Chauvet; Veuve Clicquot-
Ponsardin; Heidsieck & Co. Monopole; Moët
& Chandon; Laurent Perrier; G. H. Mumm &
Co.; Perrier Jouët; Pommery & Greno; Louis
Roederer; Ruinart Père et Fils; Taittinger
Grower Champagnes Michel Arnould; Pierre
Arnould; Jean Bovière; Christian Busin; Alain
Collas; Floquet-Gelot; J. C. Foureur; Joseph
Godme; Bertrand Godme; Marc Henriet;
Bernard Hatte; Rémi Hatte; Hervy-Quenardel;
Longueville; Michel Pithois; Quenardel-
Esquerre; Quenardel & Fils

Verzy

Population 1,100 **Situation** 2 kilometres
east of Verzenay along the D7.
Surface area planted 400 hectares
Grape varieties Chardonnay: 68 hectares
(17% of surface area); Pinot Noir: 316 hectares
(79% of surface area); Pinot Meunier: 16
hectares (4% of surface area)

The vineyards of Verzy lie adjacent to those of
Verzenay on the eastern edge of the northern
slopes of the Montagne de Reims. Most of the
vines are east-facing and located to the north of
the village, with the best sites found at heights
between 140 and 220 metres.

Verzy has an unusual viticultural history for
a growth of the Montagne; in the late
eighteenth century its vineyards were almost
entirely planted with white grapes. Exactly why
is unclear as the origins of these vineyards go
back to the days of the Knights Templars. It
was once thought that the Chardonnay vine
was brought to Champagne from Cyprus by
knights returning from the Crusades, which
might have provided some sort of answer, but
this theory has since been discredited. Perhaps
it is sufficient to say that prior to cutting back
parts of the Forêt de la Montagne, the slopes of
Verzy were not dissimilar topographically to
those of the Côte des Blancs.

When Verzy was practically a white grape
village (now almost eighty per cent Pinot Noir),
the exception was the vineyards near St Basle,
which is above the village bordering the famous
Faux de Verzy*. Today Verzy produces
excellent, full-bodied wines, rich in fruit and of
distinct style which more than deserve their
recent elevation to grand cru status.
Houses owning vineyards Chauvet; Veuve
Clicquot-Ponsardin; Heidsieck & Co
Monopole; Henriot; Moët & Chandon; Louis
Roederer
Grower Champagnes Cuperly; Jean-Paul
Deville; R. Juillet-P. & A. Lallement

* The Faux de Verzy is an eerie section of the Forêt de
la Montagne much stranger than the fictitious witch-
infested forests of Hollywood films. These trees, some
of which are over a thousand years old, are a type of
mutated beech, originally thought to have been freaks
of a mineral imbalance in the soil, although the
current theory is that a virus infection was
responsible. It is possible that one led to the other,
but whatever the cause, the result is a spooky copse of
stunted trees with disproportionately long and
spindly branches which must be seen to be believed.

The premier cru villages

Avenay

Population 1,100 **Situation** 8 kilometres north-east of Épernay along the D201 and D9, on the southern slopes of the Montagne de Reims in the Val d'Or.
Échelle de cru 93%
Surface area planted 211 hectares
Grape varieties Chardonnay: 19 hectares (9.01% of surface area); Pinot Noir: 143 hectares (67.77% of surface area); Pinot Meunier: 49 hectares (23.22% of surface area)

The complexly contoured east and south-facing vineyards in the Val d'Or produce excellent wines, far superior to the 93% grading of Avenay, and significantly better than the wines of its grand cru neighbours, Tours-sur-Marne and Louvois. Some of the north-facing slopes are less favoured and, while most of the vines are found at a height of between 140 and 180 metres, a few to the east and north of the village grow above 200 metres.
Houses owning vineyards Charbaut; Heidsieck & Co. Monopole; Henriot; Mercier; G. H. Mumm & Co.; Philipponnat; Pommery & Greno
Grower Champagnes Roger-Gabriel Pagin; Ricciuti-Revolté

Bergères-les-Vertus

Population 500 **Situation** 21 kilometres south of Épernay along the D40 and D9, at the southern tip of the Côte des Blancs, south of Vertus.
Échelle de cru 95% white grapes; 90% black grapes
Surface area planted 205 hectares
Grape varieties Chardonnay: 191 hectares (93.17% of surface area); Pinot Noir: 12 hectares (5.85% of surface area); Pinot Meunier: 2 hectares (0.98% of surface area)

The vineyards of Bergères-les-Vertus are largely an extension of the lower slopes of Vertus reaching down to the southern tip of the Côte des Blancs. Growing usually at a height of between 120 to 160 metres the vineyards curve round from an eastern to south-eastern aspect, and climb on to higher ground towards the edge of the Bois de Cormont. A smaller patch of lesser quality vines extends southwards on to the north-east-facing slopes of Mont Aimé. The wines of Bergères-les-Vertus are firm and fruity, with good extract and fine balance and well deserving of greater recognition.
Grower Champagnes Roger Gabriel-Pagin

Bezannes*

Population 600 **Situation** 2 kilometres south-west of Reims along the D6 between les Mesneux and Murigny.
Echelle de Cru 90%
From no specific mention in the échelle this growth acquired premier cru status in 1985.

Billy-le-Grand

Population 60 **Situation** 27 kilometres north-east of Épernay along the D201, D1, D37 and D19, on the lower eastern extremity of the Montagne de Reims, north of Vaudemanges.
Échelle de cru 95%
Surface area planted 59 hectares
Grape varieties Chardonnay: 39 hectares (66.1% of surface area); Pinot Noir: 20 hectares (33.9% of surface area)

The vineyards of this village are physically, though not communally, a continuation of the higher slopes of Vaudemanges; they are separated from the main belt of the Montagne on a lower eastern extremity. Some of the vines are planted up to 180 metres, but most are grown at an altitude of between 140 and 160 metres on full south-facing slopes. The vines from these slopes produce wine of an extremely dependable quality.
Grower Champagnes Roger Lapie

Bisseuil

Population 400 **Situation** Almost 10 kilometres east of Épernay along the D201 and D1, on the plain south of the Montagne de Reims, east of Tours-sur-Marne.
Échelle de cru 95%
Surface area planted 120 hectares

---

* This and the other villages newly accorded premier cru status in 1985 – Chamery, Coligny, Jouy-les-Reims, Pargny-les-Reims, Villers-aux-Noeuds and Voipreux – can here be only summarily noted, as full data were unavailable to the author at the time of writing.

Grape varieties Chardonnay: 66 hectares (55% of surface area); Pinot Noir: 40 hectares (33.33% of surface area); Pinot Meunier: 14 hectares (11.67% of surface area)

The vineyards of Bisseuil are set some distance back from the village and grow at a height of about 160 metres on the south-east-facing slopes of Mont Aigu, which forms the eastern side of the Val d'Or in which Avenay is located.
Houses owning vineyards Charbaut
Grower Champagnes Clos Babot

Chamery

Population 400　**Situation** 10 kilometres south-west of Reims along the D22 and D26.
Echelle de cru 90%
The village achieved its premier cru status in 1985 when it was upgraded from 88% to 90%.

Champillon

Population 400　**Situation** Between 5 and 6 kilometres north of Épernay along the N51 towards Reims, on the southern slopes of the Montagne de Reims.
Échelle de cru 93%
Surface area planted 69 hectares
Grape varieties Chardonnay: 7 hectares (10.14% of surface area); Pinot Noir: 16 hectares (23.19% of surface area); Pinot Meunier: 46 hectares (66.67% of surface area)

The panoramic view over Épernay and the Marne valley from the top of Champillon's 250-metre-high vineyards is one of the most impressive in Champagne. At the top of the shell-shaped vineyard is a full, frontal, south-facing aspect which descends on to south-east and south-west-facing slopes, to a level of 120 metres on the lowest slopes. The vineyards comprise less than 70 hectares, but nearly all produce wine of a superb quality which would seem to justify an upgrading of their 93% status. The best wines of Champillon have good extract and lend a certain edge to the *cuvée*.
Houses owning vineyards Mercier: Oudinot; Louis Roederer
Grower Champagnes G. E. Autreau Père et Fils

Chigny-les-Roses

Population 500　**Situation** 14 kilometres south of Reims along the N51 and D26, on the northern slopes of the Montagne de Reims.

Échelle de cru 94%
Surface area planted 118 hectares
Grape varieties Chardonnay: 13 hectares (11.02% of surface area); Pinot Noir: 26 hectares (22.03% of surface area); Pinot Meunier: 79 hectares (66.95% of surface area)

The delightfully named village of Chigny-les-Roses is situated south of Reims, on the northern slopes of the Montagne, a few kilometres west of the grand cru villages of Mailly-Champagne and Verzenay. Its vines are planted on north and north-east-facing slopes at an altitude of between 130 and 180 metres.
　Anyone who has drunk one of the bottles of Fred Leroux 1920 at Le Vigneron in Reims (in the days when it was an unpretentious little bistro, not the big, brash restaurant it is now) will know that some wines of Chigny are capable of maturing for great periods of time. Tasted in 1980, the Fred Leroux 1920 still had a vigorous *mousse*, even if the palate was well into the 'cheesy' stage of old age. The wines of this village often show great varietal character, good vinosity and fine balance.
Grower Champagnes Cattier; J. Lassalle; Patrice Leroux; Gilbert Menu; Michel Tixier

Coligny

Population 300　**Situation** 22 kilometres south of Épernay along the D40, D10, D9, and D39.
Échelle de cru 90% white grapes, 87% black grapes
Although this village is situated on the plains south-west of Bergères-les-Vertus, its vineyards can be found on the lower slopes of the southern tip of the Côte des Blancs and Mount Aimé. Classification of Coligny's white grapes jumped from 85% to 90% in 1985, assuming premier cru status.

Cuis

Population 400　**Situation** 4 kilometres south-east of Épernay along the D40, on the northern edge of the Côte des Blancs.
Échelle de cru 95% white grapes; 90% black grapes
Surface area planted 159 hectares
Grape varieties Chardonnay: 140 hectares (88.05% of surface area); Pinot Meunier: 19 hectares (11.95% of surface area)

If one considers the Butte de Saran as separate

from the headland of the Côte des Blancs, then the vineyards of Cuis can be seen as the northernmost edge of the Côte. Its vineyards, which have grown both black and white grapes for well over a hundred years, form a horseshoe around the Montagne d'Avize, starting with south-west-facing slopes south-west of the village, bending into a bank of north-facing vines at the back of the village and curving round into north-east-facing slopes close to the village of Cramant. Most of the vines are planted at a height of between 160 and 200 metres and provide wines of excellent, if differing, character. A small patch of vines on flat ground to the north of the village are less well exposed.

Houses owning vineyards Larmandier; Moët & Chandon; Pol Roger

Grower Champagnes Pierre Gimmonet & Fils; Paul Michel; Guy Vallois

Cumières

Population 1,000 **Situation** 3 kilometres north-west of Épernay along the D301, on the southern slopes of the Montagne de Reims.

Échelle de cru 93%

Surface area planted 163 hectares

Grape varieties Chardonnay: 18 hectares (11% of surface area); Pinot Noir: 58 hectares (35.6% of surface area); Pinot Meunier: 87 hectares (53.4% of surface area)

Overlooked by the Bois de St-Marc and the upper slopes of Hautvillers to the north, the vineyards of Cumières stretch out along south and south-east-facing slopes immediately above the village. Planted at an altitude of between 100 and 200 metres, the higher situated vines are less prone to the dangers of frost and provide well-structured, fruity wines.

Houses owning vineyards Moët & Chandon; Joseph Perrier; Louis Roederer

Grower Champagnes Denois Père & Fils; Pierre Bertrand; Blosseville-Marniquet; Gabriel Boutet; Jacques Delabaye; Deny-Dany; E. Duchenne; Jean-Marie Ettienne; René Geoffroy; Roger Geoffroy; Raymond Godart; José Gruget; B. le Guedard; Fernand Hutasse; Laval-Louis; Roger Locret; Veuve Maitre Geoffroy; Michel Malabré; Paul Martin; Michel Mignon; Yves Mignon; Charles Millet; Henri Plateau; Roger Plateau; Alphonse Poittevin; Claude Poittevin; Ludolph Poittevin; Reineville Père & Fils; Marcel Stinlet; Sinice Suisse; Vadin Plateau

Dizy

Population 1,000 **Situation** 2 kilometres north of Épernay along the N51 towards Reims, on the southern slopes of the Montagne de Reims.

Échelle de cru 95%

Surface area planted 166 hectares **Grape varieties** Chardonnay: 36 hectares (21.69% of surface area); Pinot Noir: 37 hectares (22.29% of surface area); Pinot Meunier: 93 hectares (56.02% of surface area)

As you leave Épernay for Reims, the vineyards of Dizy are those marvellous south-west-facing slopes which you wind your way through while climbing the steep ascent on to the Montagne plateau. The vines grow at a height of between 100 and 200 metres and produce dependable wines of a style somewhere between the well structured, fruity Hautvillers and Cumières and the classic but cavalier Aÿ.

Houses owning vineyards Jacquesson; Mercier; Moët & Chandon; Oudinot; Perrier Jouët; Pommery & Greno

Grower Champagnes J. L. Bernard; Gaston Chiquet; Paul Letuvée; Francis Tarillon; Jean Tarillon; Marcel Vautrain

Écueil

Population 300 **Situation** 7 kilometres south-west of Reims along the N51 and D26, on the Petite Montagne.

Échelle de cru 90%

Surface area planted 129 hectares **Grape varieties** Chardonnay: 4 hectares (3.1% of surface area); Pinot Noir: 121 hectares (93.8% of surface area); Pinot Meunier: 4 hectares (3.1% of surface area)

Écueil's vineyards are largely east-facing, growing at an altitude of between 180 and 220 metres, and overlooked by the Pâtis d'Écueil on the Petite Montagne. Écueil provides strong wines which can be useful in blending a *cuvée*. Some interesting pink Champagnes are made in this village which was once known for its long lived red wines.

Grower Champagnes Brochet-Hervieux & Fils; Marc Brugnon

Étréchy

Population 100 **Situation** 30 kilometres south of Épernay along the RD51, D36 and D40, on the southern edge of the Côte des

View of Hautvillers and the forest

Blancs, west of Bergères-les-Vertus.
Échelle de cru 90% white grapes; 87% black grapes
Surface area planted 9.6 hectares
Grape varieties Chardonnay: 9.12 hectares (95% of surface area); Pinot Noir: 0.1 hectares (1% of surface area); Pinot Meunier: 0.38 hectares (4% of surface area)

Étréchy is the smallest of the premiers crus, its two tiny patches of vines situated north-west of the village, on gentle south and south-west-facing slopes, at an elevation of between 170 and 180 metres. As far as I am aware, no pure Étréchy Champagnes are made and it is of little importance in terms of blending.

Grauves

Population 500   **Situation** 8 kilometres south of Épernay along the D40 in the Côte des Blancs on the south-western slopes of the Montagne d'Avize.
Échelle de cru 95% white grapes; 90% black grapes
Surface area planted 175 hectares
Grape varieties Chardonnay: 136 hectares (77.72% of surface area); Pinot Noir: 2 hectares (1.14% of surface area); Pinot Meunier: 37 hectares (21.14% of surface area)

Grauves has some well-sheltered vineyards which face each other on opposite slopes of a small valley beneath the Bois d'Avize at the northern end of the Côte des Blancs. The best wines are made from the highest vines north-west of Grauves, which grow up to a height of 220 metres, and from those in an east-facing gulley, south-west of the village.

These wines are exceptionally big and fleshy for the Côte des Blancs, an area more noted for style than strength. Individual sites like les Roualles, a vineyard belonging to Bollinger, have reputations for producing full-bodied, fruity wines comparable to those from the Montagne de Reims.
Houses owning vineyards Moët & Chandon; Pol Roger
Grower Champagnes Roland Marchand

Hautvillers

Population 800   **Situation** 4 kilometres north of Épernay along the N51 and D386, on the steep, southern slopes of the Montagne de Reims.
Échelle de cru 93%

Surface area planted 256 hectares
Grape varieties Chardonnay: 23 hectares (8.98% of surface area); Pinot Noir: 66 hectares (25.78% of surface area); Pinot Meunier: 167 hectares (65.24% of surface area)

The vineyards of Hautvillers lie in four distinct zones: one below the village, one above l'Écluse, one between Hautvillers and Champillon, and one above Cumières. The differing quality aspects of these zones make it impossible to specify a particular style of wine for Hautvillers.

The vines immediately below the village, facing Dizy, have an elevation of between 100 and 180 metres, and lie on east and south-facing slopes which become increasingly steep as the village approaches. Below these, immediately above the village of l'Écluse, in the hollow either side of the D386, the vines are mostly grown at below 100 metres, and the wines from here had a considerable reputation in the past. Above this group is a third zone situated in a cleavage between the vineyards of Champillon and the village of Hautvillers. Here the vines are mostly grown at a height of between 140 and 180 metres on south-east and south-west-facing slopes although some climb steeply from the outskirts of Hautvillers and rise to a height of around 250 metres. The fourth zone of Hautvillers vineyards are really an extension of those of Cumière but they rise higher, to an elevation of between 180 and 220 metres, and their aspect changes slightly, affording more south-facing slopes.

The reputation of Hautvillers has, understandably, grown from the legend of Dom Pérignon; at that time, although very few hectares of the abbey's vineyards were actually located within the commune of Hautvillers, some of its finest wines were made from the group of lower-lying vineyards above l'Écluse. Today, it is difficult to define a particular Hautvillers style: all have a good fruit content, and although some are perhaps lacking in definition, the finest attain great distinction, belancing high extract with a delicacy of flavour.
Houses owning vineyards Jacquesson; Mercier; Moët & Chandon; Joseph Perrier
Grower Champagnes J. Desruets; J. M. Gobillard; Jean Hugues; Fernand Lemaire; Serge Landragin; Locret-Lachaud; G. Sauvignier; G. Tribaut

Jouy-les-Reims

Population 200   **Situation** 8 kilometres south-west of Reims along the RD380 D26.
Échelle de cru 90%
Superbly sited south-facing slopes adjacent to Villedommange which deservedly earned a vital extra per cent in 1985, climbing from 89% to 90% and thus premier cru status.

Ludes

Population 700   **Situation** 7 kilometres south of Reims along the D9 and D233, on the northern slopes of the Montagne de Reims.
Échelle de cru 94%
Surface area planted 313 hectares
Grape varieties Chardonnay: 28 hectares (8.95% of surface area); Pinot Noir: 78 hectares (24.92% of surface area); Pinot Meunier: 207 hectares (66.13% of surface area)

The vineyards of Ludes are sandwiched between those of Chigny-les-Roses and the grand cru of Mailly-Champagne on the northern slopes of the Montagne de Reims. On either side of the village the vines are exposed on north-facing slopes, ranging between 140 and 200 metres in height. If you approach the village from the north, however, along the D9 or D33, you see that at the northern edge of the village, the vineyards bank up on both sides to form a hollow where the vines dip down to 120 metres, giving east and west-facing exposures on either side.

Ludes wines are welcomed for their use in blending of *cuvées*, they have the body and vinosity of a true Montagne wine, but I have yet to be convinced that a single growth Ludes can be a complete wine on its own.
Houses owning vineyards Canard-Duchêne
Grower Champagnes Brixon-Coquillard; Lamarche; Forget-Bereche; Forget-Brimont; Forget-Chemin; Gaidoz-Forget; Forget-Menu; Collective Monmarthe & Fils; Quatresols-Gauthier; Quatresols-Jamein; Serge Rafflin

Mareuil-sur-Aÿ

Population 1,200   **Situation** 5 kilometres east of Épernay along the D201, on the southernmost edge of the Montagne de Reims.
Échelle de cru 99%
Surface area planted 264 hectares
Grape varieties Chardonnay: 18 hectares (6.82% of surface area); Pinot Noir: 201 hectares (76.14% of surface area); Pinot Meunier: 45 hectares (17.04% of surface area)

The village of Mareuil-sur-Aÿ is situated beside the Marne canal, just east of Aÿ-Champagne and south of Avenay: few of its vines are located near the village itself, except for its best vineyard, a remarkable spur called the Clos des Goisses. Its very steep, fully south-facing slope can hardly be missed as one aproaches the village from Tours-sur-Marne. Behind this superb spur the vines of Clos des Goisses extend for a further 8 hectares on north-east-facing slopes and rise at a lesser incline from 100 to 138 metres, after which the land flattens out towards Avenay.

Most of Mareuil's vineyards are set a little distance from the village on south-east-facing slopes immediately beneath Mutigny. Almost adjacent to the vineyards of Aÿ, these vines have long had a reputation for producing wines of similar quality and character to the famous grand cru. They are planted at a height of between 100 and 190 metres. Below these slopes, between the D201 and the D9, there are more vineyards planted on flatter ground which provide wines of a much inferior quality to the rest of Mareuil.

In the nineteenth century, according to André Jullien in his *Topography of all known vineyards* (1824), Mareuil wines were no different from those of Aÿ 'and pass, in commerce, as *Vins d'Ay*', hence the village's name Mareuil-sur-Aÿ, the wines being sold on the back of the wines of Aÿ. Today, the wines produced from the slopes below Mutigny and on the spur of the Clos des Goisses are of the highest grand cru quality. The former have all the dash and flair of the neighbouring wines of Aÿ, while those of the Clos des Goisses, which belong exclusively to the house of Philipponnat, are high in alcohol, somewhat richer and possess great longevity.
Houses owning vineyards Charbaut; Robert Driant; Henriot; Mercier; Moët & Chandon; Philipponnat; Montebello
Grower Champagnes Roland Benard

les Mesneux

Population 300   **Situation** 2 kilometres north-east of Villedommange in the Petite Montagne south-west of Reims.
Échelle de cru 90%
Surface area planted 47 hectares

Grape varieties Chardonnay: 3 hectares (6.38% of surface area); Pinot Noir: 11 hectares (23.41% of surface area); Pinot Meunier: 33 hectares (70.21% of surface area)

The vineyards of les Mesneux are relatively unimportant and hardly merit premier cru status. They are situated on a slight south-east incline amidst surrounding flat lands.
Houses owning vineyards Mercier

Montbré

Population 100 **Situation** 4 kilometres south of Reims along the D9, on the plain north of the Montagne de Reims.
Échelle de cru 94%
Surface area planted 38 hectares
Grape varieties Chardonnay: 3 hectares (7.69% of surface area); Pinot Noir: 17 hectares (43.59% of surface area); Pinot Meunier: 19 hectares (48.72% of surface area)

Situated on a plain beneath Rilly-la-Montagne the vineyards of Montbré are not of true premier cru quality.

Mutigny

Population 100 **Situation** 7 kilometres north-east of Épernay along the D201, on the southern slopes of the Montagne de Reims.
Échelle de cru: 93%
Surface area planted 75 hectares
Grape varieties Chardonnay: 3 hectares (4% of surface area); Pinot Noir: 50 hectares (66.67% of surface area); Pinot Meunier: 22 hectares (29.33% of surface area)

Unfortunately, the best vines grown on the south-facing slopes beneath Mutigny come within the communal borders of Mareuil-sur-Aÿ. Mutigny's considerably smaller hectarage is located largely on the upper slopes of Avenay, while a few of its vineyards grow on slopes high above Mareuil. The relatively small production of Mutigny is, however, of good premier cru quality.
Houses owning vineyards Philipponnat; Henriot; Pommery & Greno
Grower Champagnes Sergé Humbert; Robert Husson; Jean Lefevre; Raymond Thibaut

Pargny-les-Reims

Population 300 **Situation** 8 kilometres south-west of Reims along the RD380.
Echelle de cru 90%
Elevated from 89⅔ to 90% in 1985.

Pierry

Population 1,300 **Situation** One kilometre south of Épernay along the RD51, at the opening of the Cubry valley.
Échelle de cru 90%
Surface area planted 102 hectares
Grape varieties Chardonnay: 12 hectares (11.77% of surface area); Pinot Noir: 10 hectares (9.8% of surface area); Pinot Meunier: 80 hectares (78.43% of surface area)

Pierry, once a separate village, is now a continuation of the southern suburbs of Épernay. Its vineyards, all south-east and east-facing, are located behind Pierry on a steep slope leading up to the Forêt d'Épernay. This slope climbs as abruptly as the southern slopes of the Montagne de Reims, starting at 100 metres and rising quickly to 200 metres.

Pierry derives its name from a stratum of flint in the subsoil which reputedly gives its wine a marked flinty taste. In the nineteenth century the wines of Pierry were considered on a par with the best wines of Aÿ. Today it is definitely a premier cru, and if one of the more classic varieties of Pinot Noir or Chardonnay could be exploited to the full on this favourable slope, its 90% classification would certainly be upgraded.
Houses owning vineyards G. Billard; Paul Gobillard; Pol Roger
Grower Champagnes Michel Mandois-Bernier

Rilly-la-Montagne

Population 1,100 **Situation** 11 kilometres south of Reims along the N51 and D26, on the northern slopes of the Montagne de Reims.
Échelle de cru 94%
Surface area planted 304 hectares
Grape varieties Chardonnay: 55 hectares (18.09% of surface area); Pinot Noir: 79 hectares (25.99% of surface area); Pinot Meunier: 170 hectares (55.92% of surface area)

Rilly-la-Montagne is the first significant growth, in terms of quality and quantity, to be encountered on the D26, as one winds one's way eastwards from the N51 through the northern slopes of the Montagne de Reims. Most of the vines have a slightly east to north-facing aspect, although those near Montbré are found on a gentle east-facing ridge. The best vines are those closest to the village growing at a height of between 140 and 200 metres. Rilly

produces wines which are appreciably lighter in style than those of neighbouring villages and has an unusually high proportion of Chardonnay for the Montagne de Reims.
Houses owning vineyards H. Germain & Fils
Grower Champagnes Adam Garnotel; Michel Fagot; Vilmart

Sacy

Population 400　**Situation** 7 kilometres south-west of Reims, between Villedommange and Écueil, in the Petite Montagne.
Échelle de cru 90%
Surface area planted 139 hectares
Grape varieties Chardonnay: 11 hectares (7.91% of surface area); Pinot Noir: 20 hectares (14.39% of surface area); Pinot Meunier: 108 hectares (77.7% of surface area)

The village is surrounded by vines, but it is those behind Sacy on steeply climbing, north-east-facing slopes leading up to the Bois de la Fosse which are the most favourably located. Lacking somewhat in definition, the wines of Sacy are, however, solid and dependable and, with those of neighbouring Villedommange, rank as the best wines of the Petite Montagne.
Houses owning vineyards Mercier
Grower Champagnes Raymond Bailly; André Chemin; Jean Luc Chemin; Bernard Damien; Gilbert Damien; Jacques Degennes; Philippe Degesne; René Dezautez; Roger Dumez; Jacques Goulin; Jean-Claude Grill; Gerrard Guillemart; Lucien Guillemart; André Hervieux; Jean Léger; Henri Leroy; Jean-Michel Leroy; Robert Leroy; Sergé Leroy; Roger Macquart; Lucien Martinet; Jean-Marie Mimin; Philippe Mobillion; François Perseval; Jean-Louis Perseval; Jacques Poncelet; Patrick Ponsart; Jany Poret; Gaetan Prévost; Jean Ravary; Sergé Rigaut; Denis Menu Robert; René Roualet; Jean-Louis Valentin; Bernard Wafflart; Michel Wafflart

Taissy

Population 700　**Situation** 3 kilometres south-east of Reims along the D8 from Cormontreuil, north of the Montagne.
Échelle de cru 94%
Surface area planted 148 hectares
Grape varieties Chardonnay: 46 hectares (31.29% of surface area); Pinot Noir: 34 hectares (23.13% of surface area); Pinot Meunier: 67 hectares (45.58% of surface area)

Like the overrated grand cru growths of Puisieulx and Sillery close by, the vineyards of Taissy are located on the plain north of the Montagne de Reims. Its best vines are located some distance from the village on the gentle southern slopes of Mont Ferré, on the eastern edge of a small hamlet called Varsovie. These are mainly south-east-facing and are at an elevation of between 130 and 155 metres. At one time, Taissy had a reputation for red wines comparable to that of Hautvillers. Its best wines today are probably as good as Puisieulx and Sillery – possibly better.

Tauxières

Population 1,000　**Situation** 12 kilometres north-east of Épernay along the D201 and D9, on the southern slopes of the Montagne de Reims.
Échelle de cru 99%
Surface area planted 229 hectares
Grape varieties Chardonnay: 39 hectares (17.03% of surface area); Pinot Noir: 172 hectares (75.11% of surface area); Pinot Meunier: 18 hectares (7.86% of surface area)

The vines found on the south and south-east-facing slopes above Tauxières and Mutry are at an altitude of between 140 and 180 metres. Across the little Livre valley the vines grown on the east and south-east-facing slopes of Mont Écouvé, at a height of between 150 and 170 metres, are an extension to those of Bouzy just over the hill. The wines produced by these vines are lighter than those of Bouzy, but are of good quality and can be very attractive in a blend.
Houses owning vineyards Mercier; Möet & Chandon; Oudinot
Grower Champagnes Marcel Banette; Pierre Banette; Sergé Banette; Louis Bernard; Robert Clément; Ste. Cochut; Max Cochut; Jean de Medts; Roger Fournier; Gille Gianocelli; Hubert Leblanc; Émile l'Hôpital; Henri Louvet; Yves Louvet; François Mahe; Frédérick Mauvignant; Yvon Mauvignant

Trépail

Population 500　**Situation** 20 kilometres north-east of Épernay along the D1, D19 and D26, on the south-eastern edge of the Montagne de Reims, north of Ambonnay.
Échelle de cru 95%
Surface area planted 242 hectares
Grape varieties Chardonnay: 211 hectares

In the nineteenth century black and white grape varieties were cultivated in adjacent square plots at the aptly named Château Marqueterie in Pierry. This picture shows two young girls collecting mixed bunches of black and white grapes with the château in the background

(87.19% of surface area); Pinot Noir: 31 hectares (12.81% of surface area)

Tréhail is just 3 kilometres north of the grand cru villages, Bouzy and Ambonnay, on the south-eastern extremity of the Montagne de Reims. The best vines are located south of the village, growing high up at between 160 and 220 metres on south and south-east-facing slopes. Below these slopes, north of the village and on various plots scattered throughout the commune, the vines are not as well sited, but they provide wines outshining other premiers crus.

Houses owning vineyards Henriot
Grower Champagnes Claude Beaufort; Jean Darreye; Carre Guebels; J. C. Dupont; Pierre Gabriel & Fils; Guebels-Bernadin; Kleber Jacqueminet; Machet-Griffon; Petiau & Fils; Redon-Lapoulle

Trois-Puits

Population 200 **Situation** 2 kilometres south of Reims along the D9, branching off at Cormontreuil, north of Montagne de Reims.
Échelle de cru 94%
Surface area planted 39 hectares
Grape varieties Pinot Noir: 10 hectares (25.64% of surface area); Pinot Meunier: 29 hectares (74.36% of surface area)

Low-grade vines, situated on flat ground – probably the most boring village in Champagne.
Grower Champagnes Jean Baillette; Maurice Baillette; Pierre Baillette; Sergé Cousin; Michel Larnaudie; René Trichet

Vaudemanges

Population 200 **Situation** 20 kilometres
north-east of Épernay along the D1 and D19,
on the lower eastern slopes of the Montagne de
Reims.
Échelle de cru 95%
Surface area planted 34 hectares
Grape varieties Chardonnay: 25 hectares
(73.53% of surface area); Pinot Noir: 9
hectares (26.47% of surface area)

Vaudemanges is just 2 kilometres south of
Billy-le-Grand. Its vineyards, bordered by the
Marne à l'Aisne canal to the east, are grown on
fully south-facing slopes on the lower, eastern
extremity of the Montagne de Reims. The
elevation of these vineyards is between 120 and
140 metres, those higher up merging with the
vineyards of Billy-le-Grand. The wines
produced here have good structure, balance
and fruit and are of dependable quality.
Houses owning vineyards G. H. Mumm & Co.
Grower Champagnes Chaudron & Fils

Vertus

Population 2,700 **Situation** 18 kilometres
south of Épernay along the D40, D10 and D9,
at the southern end of the Côte des Blancs.
Échelle de cru 95%
Surface area planted 498 hectares
Grape varieties Chardonnay: 408 hectares
(81.93% of surface area); Pinot Noir: 85

Carrying the blessed new wine from the church at Vertus during the St Vincent day celebrations on
23 January

hectares (17.07% of surface area); Pinot Meunier: 5 hectares (1% of surface area)

Vertus, at the southern end of the Côte des Blancs, is the largest of the grands and premiers crus. Most of its vines face east, although some of the slopes north of the village have south-east, south and even south-west exposures; virtually all are superbly positioned. The prime locations are found at a height of between 140 and 220 metres, below which, and north of the village, the vines are grown on flatter ground. Most of Vertus's hectarage is taken up with Chardonnay vines, but, interestingly, the 85 hectares of Pinot Noir are descended from pre-phylloxera vines brought from the famous Burgundy village of Beaune.

The reputation of Vertus's richly perfumed still red wines goes back to the fourteenth century; in the seventeenth century these wines were favoured by William of Orange. Vertus produces fruitier Champagnes than those of its northern neighbours on the Côte and, although the Chardonnay does not achieve the remarkable perfume and definition of les Mesnil or Cramant, the wines are of very high quality and well deserve upgrading.

Houses owning vineyards Veuve Clicquot-Ponsardin; Duval-Leroy; Henriot; Larmandier; Moët & Chandon; Louis Roederer

Grower Champagnes Bonnet Launois; René Bouche; Jean-Paul Boulonnais; Doquet-Jeanmarie; Bernard Doublet; Doublet-Hadot Père & Fils; Veuve A. Fourny & Fils; Larmandier-Bernier; J. C. Launois; Charles Pougeoise; Michel Rogue; Eraldo Schirru; Severin-Doublet.

Villedommange

Population 400 **Situation** 7 kilometres south-west of Reims along the D380 and D6 in the Petite Montagne.

Échelle de cru 90%

Surface area planted 178 hectares

Grape varieties Chardonnay: 10 hectares (5.62% of surface area); Pinot Noir: 29 hectares (16.29% of surface area); Pinot Meunier: 139 hectares (78.09% of surface area)

The village of Villedommange is surrounded on all sides by vineyards which are a continuation northwards of the slopes of Écueil and Sacy. The elevation of these vines ranges between 115 and 240 metres, those over 160 metres being steeper and more favourably positioned. Although Villedommange is of the same échelle as its neighbouring premiers crus, its highest vineyards, which do not adjoin a dense mass of forest and are thus free from the ill-effects of transpiration, produce grapes of a superior quality. These are full-bodied, richly flavoured wines which, with the wines of Sacy, are the best of the Petite Montagne.

Houses owning vineyards Veuve Clicquot-Ponsardin; Oudinot

Grower Champagnes Bardoux Père & Fils; François Bergeronneau; Raymond Devilliers; Fresne Ducret & Fils

Villeneuve-Renneville

Population (Villeneuve-Renneville-Chevigny) 300 **Situation** 25 kilometres south-east of Épernay along the D40, D10 and D12, on the plains east of the southern end of the Côte des Blancs.

Échelle de cru 95%

Surface area planted 95 hectares

Grape varieties Chardonnay: 94 hectares (98.95% of surface area); Pinot Noir: 1 hectare (1.05% of surface area)

Although the village of Villeneuve-Renneville is located on the plains beneath the Côte des Blancs, its vineyards are set back, and occupy the lower slopes of le Mesnil-sur-Oger. They are south-east-facing and are at a height of 110 metres. The wines from this village are modestly good but do not merit top premier cru status – despite the elevation of the échelle of this village in 1985 from 93% to 95%.

Houses owning vineyards Henriot

Grower Champagnes Yannick Castel; Robert Fery

Villers-Allerand

Population 700 **Situation** 7 kilometres south of Reims along the N51, on the northern edge of the Montagne de Reims.

Échelle de cru 90%

Surface area planted 125 hectares

Grape varieties Chardonnay: 17 hectares (13.6% of surface area); Pinot Noir: 25 hectares (20% of surface area); Pinot Meunier: 83 hectares (66.4% of surface area)

The vineyards of Villers-Allerand lie on either side of the main Épernay to Reims road as it descends from the Montagne on to the plain.

They are grown on north, north-east and north-west-facing slopes at an altitude of 150 to 200 metres. The best-situated vines are found east of the village on a slope which is a continuation of the vineyards of Rilly-la-Montagne, but are not of exceptional quality.

Grower Champagnes Michel Jobart; Claude Prevot; Jean-Claude Prevot; René Prevot; Stroebel Frères; Marcel Stroebel

Villers-Marmery

Population 600 **Situation** 20 kilometres south-east of Reims along the N44 and D326, on the eastern edge of the Montagne de Reims.
Échelle de cru 95%
Surface area planted 228 acres
Grape varieties Chardonnay: 217 hectares (95.18% of surface area); Pinot Noir: 9 hectares (3.95% of surface area); Pinot Meunier: 2 hectares (0.87% of surface area)

The vineyards of Villers-Marmery are well placed on the eastern slopes of the Montagne de Reims, between those of Verzy to the north and Trépail to the south. They are planted at a height of between 120 and 190 metres on east and south-east-facing slopes. This village produces strong wines of good varietal character well deserving premier cru status.
Grower Champagnes B. de Berland; G. Boutillez-Vignon; A. Brassart; Gaston Dayer; Henri Rémy

Villers-aux-Noeuds

Population 100 **Situation** 8 kilometres south of Reims along the N51 and turn right just after Champfleury.
Échelle de cru 90%

Not specifically mentioned in the échelle des crus prior to 1985.

Voipreux

Population 90 **Situation** 16 kilometres south-east of Épernay along the D3, D9, D12 and D37.
Échelle de cru 95%

Although Voipreux seems to have jumped from nowhere to a 95% premier cru, it does possess some choice sites nestled between Vertus and Villeneuve-Renneville on the lower east-facing slopes of the Côte des Blancs.

4

The Varieties of Vine and their Cultivation

Come, thou monarch of the vine,
Plumpy Bacchus with pink eyne!
In thy fats our cares be drown'd,
With thy grapes our hairs be crown'd.
Cup us till the world go round,
Cup us till the world go round!
William Shakespeare, *Antony and Cleopatra*, II, 7

THERE ARE THREE CLASSIC GRAPE VARIETIES which give Champagne its superlative flavour: Chardonnay, Pinot Noir and Pinot Meunier. Approximately 45% of all grand and premier cru vineyards are planted with Chardonnay, 36% with Pinot Noir and 19% with Pinot Meunier. Taking the Champagne region as a whole, it can be seen that Pinot Meunier assumes the greatest general importance, covering 36.5% (47% in 1982) of the total viticultural hectarage, followed by Pinot Noir with 35.8% (28% in 1982) and Chardonnay with 27.7% (24% in 1982). If the relative proportions of these grape varieties are compared on a *département* basis, an indication of the quality and character of these large areas can be discerned. Chardonnay: Marne 37.2%, Aube and Haut Marne 7.7%, Aisne and Seine-et-Marne 5.3%; Pinot Noir: Marne 25.2%, Aube and Haut Marne 80%, Aisne and Seine-et-Marne 11.2%; Pinot Meunier: Marne 37.6%, Aube and Haut Marne 12.3%, Aisne and Seine-et-Marne 83.5%. Other varieties are grown too: Pinot Blanc Vrai, Arbanne, Petit Meslier and even Gamay. These lesser varieties are not widely planted, nor do they contribute significantly to the quality and reputation of Champagne as we know it today, but they exist and do possess a certain curiosity value and are therefore dealt with in this chapter.

Note Although most Champagnes are a blend of all three classic grapes, their individual varietal characters are described to give readers an idea of how each may affect the style of a *cuvée*.

Chardonnay

Chardonnay is the noble grape from which some of the world's finest dry white wines are produced, notably those from Burgundy. Famous names of grands crus like Corton-Charlemagne or le Montrachet conjure up mouth-watering images of bright golden wines, lusciously rich and complex in flavour. The colder climate of the Marne, however, and the *prise de mousse* combine to create a much leaner animal in the sparkling wine of Champagne.

In Champagne, the Chardonnay is a strong growing variety which buds early, making it

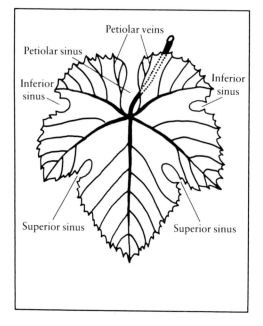

LEFT
Fig. 1 Basic shape of a vine leaf

BELOW
Fig. 2 Champagne's three classic grape varieties

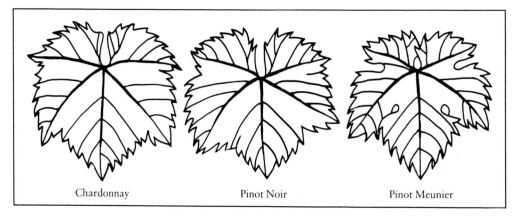

Chardonnay   Pinot Noir   Pinot Meunier

susceptible to spring frosts, but which also ripens in good time for so northerly a wine. It is particularly resistant to low winter temperatures and has some immunity against downy mildew, although it is somewhat sensitive to botrytis (rot) and to powdery mildew.

Chardonnay vines can be recognised by the dull, yellow-brown colour of the canes which have a noticeable bloom and darker nodes (the point where buds will emerge); their slightly bullate (bubbly) leaves, the edges of which have a tendency to curl upwards (some varieties curl downwards or not at all); and the compact clusters of small, round, yellow-amber grapes.

Chardonnay wines are notably lighter in body than those made from Pinot Noir, with a naturally higher acidity and a finer bouquet. In the early stages of maturity the fruit of a pure Chardonnay Champagne (ie, a blanc de blancs) can appear to be understated and cut by a certain 'steely' character, the deceiving taste of undeveloped and unharmonious extract. Chardonnay is, however, potentially the longest lived of all Champagne's grape varieties and a good blanc de blancs left to mature will achieve an incomparable intensity of flavour. From a hard and virtually tasteless youth, the fruit of a Chardonnay Champagne develops a zippy, zingy, almost citrusy tang of concentration, yet retains the delicacy and finesse for which the highest quality blancs de blancs are renowned. Opinions differ as to when this wine should be drunk. Many drinkers enjoy the freshness and vitality of a young Chardonnay Champagne, while others prefer some maturity. If the reader has been disappointed by one, then he should try the other.

Ancient and contemporary synonyms*

Arnaison Blanc; Arnaison; Arvosier; Aubaine; Auvernat Blanc; Auscerois; Auscerois Blanc; Auxois Blanc; Beaunois; Blanc de Cramant; Chardennet; Chaudenay; Chaudenet; Chasselas; Épinette Blanche; Feiner Weisser Burgunder; Gamay Blanc; Luisant; Maconnais; Melon Blanc; Melon d'Arbois; Morillon Blanc; Moulon; Muscadet; Noiren Blanc; Petit Chatey; Petite Sainte-Marie; Pinot Blanc; Pinot Blanc Chardonnay; Pinot Chardonnay; Plant de Tonnerre; Rousseau; Roussot; Weisser Clevner; White Pinot.

Pinot Noir

The Pinot Noir is another Burgundian grape, famous for that region's delicious, velvety red wines. Still red wines in Champagne are rare, however, and hardly ever exciting. The principal use of this variety is to provide the backbone essential to Champagne blends.

A delicate plant, the Pinot Noir is difficult to nurture through the freezing cold winters of Champagne. It is susceptible to botrytis and, with an earlier bud-break than Chardonnay, is prone to spring frosts. Nevertheless, it is an early maturing variety well suited to the long ripening period of a northern wine region. Field trials have for many years been concerned with finding a clone less susceptible to frost and this was initially seen as a way of upgrading some of the frost-prone vineyards of the Marne Valley which are traditionally planted with the hardier Pinot Meunier. Clonal selection now concerns

---

*This and the following lists include erroneous synonyms originating from mistaken identity in less well-informed times. Many are the names for what we would now call localised clones (see Glossary).

all three of Champagne's major varieties and the current emphasis is to ensure that each village has the clones best suited to its own *terroir*.

Pinot Noir can be recognised by the pale pink colour and greyish bloom of the young canes, the nodes of which are revealed by their contrasting dark-brown colour: the thick, extremely bullate, dark green leaves; and compact clusters of tough-skinned, heavily bloomed, blue-black, ovoid (egg-shaped) grapes.

Fermented from the clear, uncoloured juice of the black grape, Pinot Noir Champagnes have a deeper hue of gold than blanc de blancs Champagnes (which can sometimes be almost water-white). Compared to the Chardonnay it has a more obvious fruit character and in its youth possesses a greater depth of flavour and bouquet. The most important role of the Pinot Noir is to provide much of the body, flesh and grip of a Champagne *cuvée*, especially in the middle term of maturity. There should be a certain lusciousness about the style imparted to a blend by top quality Pinot Noir grapes, although this can be marred by an earthy taste if the vines are grown in a less than favourable site.

Ancient and contemporary synonyms

Auvernat; Blauburgunder; Blauer Spätburgunder; Franc Pinot; Golden Plant; Gros Plant Dore d'Aÿ; Klevner; Morillon; Nagi-Burgundi; Noiren; Petit Plant Dore; Pineau; Pinet; Pinoz; Plant d'Aÿ; Plant Dore; Plant Jeanson; Pinot Verot; Savagnin; Savagnin Noir; Cortaillod; Schwartz Klevner; Spätburgunder; Vert Dore (refers to its vivid green leaves).

Pinot Meunier

The Pinot Meunier is a variant of the Pinot Noir, dating back to the sixteenth century. There has been a radical reappraisal of the Pinot Meunier in the last ten years and growers and houses alike are nowadays more willing to admit the commercial worth of this grape, a variety which was once conspicuous by its absence from various famous firms' promotional pamphlets. It is similar in many ways to its more aristocratic relative, but the characteristics of its wines are less well defined.

Only in Champagne has this grape proved so successful. It is more prolific and easier to grow than the Pinot Noir and, with a later bud-break, is less prone to frost, hence its extensive cultivation in the Marne Valley. Like all Champagne varieties, it too has the advantage of ripening early, although this is often accompanied by a sensitivity to powdery mildew and to botrytis.

Pinot Meunier vines are easily recognised in the vineyard by their leaves which have deep sinuses, accentuated lobes and white undersides, hence Meunier or 'Miller' suggesting a brushing over with white miller's flour. Its new growth canes are a well defined brownish-red with a natural bloom and indistinct nodes and the grapes are small, round, thick-skinned, blue-black in colour and loosely clustered.

The Pinot Meunier produces honest, fruity wines which are attractive and easy to drink. These wines do lack, however, the depth, elegance and persistence of the Pinot Noir and its characteristics tend to peak early and fall away quickly. Champagnes made with a high proportion of Pinot Meunier sometimes have an earthy tone of fruit and when the grapes have come from less favourable sites, there can be a distinctly sweet aroma which reminds

Avize (above), one of the most famous crus of the Côte des Blancs, shrouded in autumn mist. Virtually all vines, not just in Champagne but across the world, have to be grafted on to American rootstocks (below) to avoid phylloxera. A few phylloxera-free areas, like this small patch outside Bouzy (right) which belongs to Bollinger, do exist, however. The vines beyond Bollinger's signboard have to be grafted and are, those before it do not and are not

Villedommange, a premier cru
responsible for some of the best wines
of the Petite Montagne

one of a confectioner's shop. But for relatively inexpensive, early drinking, Champagnes, the judicious addition of good quality Pinot Meunier to a *cuvée* is indispensible and provides an immediate appeal to both nose and palate.

Ancient and contemporary synonyms

Auvernat Gris; Blanche Feuille; Gris Meunier; Meunier; Morillon Tacone; Müller Rebe.

Other varieties

There are three other varieties authorised for the production of Champagne – the Pinot Blanc Vrai, the Arbanne and the Petit Meslier – but their hectarage is scattered and found in minute quantities only. The presence of the Pinot Blanc Vrai is almost negligible, while the Arbanne and Petit Meslier are found almost exclusively in the less favoured regions in the Aube. Production is declining for all three grapes and the vineyards are gradually being replanted with one of the three classic varieties.

Pinot Blanc Vrai

At one time the Pinot Blanc and the Chardonnay, which used to be erroneously called the Pinot Chardonnay, were considered to be one and the same, which is why there is usually evidence of its existence wherever the Chardonnay is traditionally cultivated.

Many growers, not only in Champagne but throughout France, still innocently cultivate Pinot Blanc Vrai believing it to be Chardonnay, although anyone with doubts need only look at the leaves on the vine. Both varieties bear leaves of the same basic shape, but whereas the leaves on the Chardonnay are concave, turning upwards at the edges allowing the underside to obscure the upper surface, the leaves on the Pinot Blanc are not. Furthermore, the leaves on the Pinot Blanc are far less bullate, that is to say not so bubbly between the leaf's veins.

When using leaves to help identify a vine, the grower must take care to select samples from the mature foliage occurring beyond the sixth node from the base of a shoot coming from the previous year's wood. The vines must not be suffering from any disease, nor should the leaves be those which have been distorted by herbicides.

Pinot Blanc wines in Champagne have more body than the Chardonnay and a greater alcoholic potential, but they lack finesse and usually remain neutral or possess a slightly earthy taste.

Arbanne

This variety gained considerable local repute in the nineteenth century, when 100% Arbanne Champagne was produced in Bar-sur-Aube. Very few Arbanne vines exist today, maybe one for every nine or ten Petit Meslier.

A white variety, this grape ripens early and its wines mature well. It has a very pleasant, extremely distinctive aroma which experienced vignerons in the Aube claim can be detected in a *cuvée*, despite the fact that its presence can only be, at the very most, a few percent of the overall blend.

The very aromatic nature of the Arbanne suggests it might well be an ancient variant of

Reterrage or *épandage*, the laying of new earth or manure (TOP LEFT), takes place between December and February every year. A vigneron pruning vines (BOTTOM LEFT); the off-cuts are burned as he goes

the Chardonnay Blanc Musque or, possibly, the Muscadelle of Bordeaux, both of which ripen early enough to survive in the southern extremities of Champagne. Other aromatic varieties are either too delicate to cultivate in Champagne or too late ripening to bear fruit.

Petit Meslier

Some sources suggest that as much as 4.5% of the Aube was planted with this variety as recently as ten or 15 years ago. Now greatly reduced, but still common compared to the Arbanne, the Petit Meslier is confined, for the most part, to the Aube *département*, except for a very small amount cultivated in Fleury-la-Rivière, west of Épernay.

It is a white variety which is difficult to ripen, hence the yield is small and its contribution to a *cuvée* is to increase the acidity and reduce the alcohol content. This provides the reason why it was once extensively cultivated in the Aube, where its more southerly location and lack of limestone subsoil sometimes renders wines lacking the desirably high degree of acidity required for classic Champagnes.

In big years, Aube wines may also possess too much alcohol to allow for a second fermentation and effect the correct balance. The function of the Petit Meslier has thus been similar to that of the Petit Verdot in Bordeaux.

The grapes produced are very small, round and dark yellow in colour. If vinified separately the Petit Meslier would make a thin wine, with an agreeably fruity nose, but an unpalatable extremely tart flavour.

Gamay

The Gamay is not one of the authorised varieties for Champagne, but it has been cultivated in the region for centuries and, at the last count in 1976, there were 38 hectares. It is estimated that there are still about 20 hectares in production, mostly in the Aube and in Vertus on the Côte des Blancs.

The vine is unimportant, but how and why its cultivation still persists in Champagne must be fascinating to anyone who has ever been intrigued by the curiously eclectic attitude to rules and regulations often displayed by the French.

The Gamay was rightly considered inferior for the production of Champagne when AOC laws were introduced in 1927 and its cultivation was restricted, but a generous transitory period of 18 years was allowed for growers heavily dependent on the vine, because the authorities recognised the financial burden of replanting with the authorised varieties.

At the time, the year of expiry would hardly have seemed significant, but when it arrived, Champagne was still recovering from four years of German occupation. It was 1949 before the authorities got around to this trivial matter and their solution was to slap another seven years on the original 18.

Fair enough in the circumstances, but since the extended expiry date in 1952, several growers have received individual concessions and, although the overall aim has been to gradually reduce the Gamay, the fact that at least 20 hectares exist, some 60 years after the law intent on banning the grape was first introduced, surely indicates that a certain laisser-faire attitude has been taken by successive administrations.

Who are these people still growing Gamay in Champagne and why do they want to continue? According to the regulations currently in force a grower would have to satisfy the following conditions in order to cultivate the Gamay today:

i) Only Aube growers qualify.
ii) The Gamay vines must have been planted prior to 1948.
iii) The proprietor of the vines in 1948 had to be at least 60 years of age in 1952.
iv) If the proprietor was between the ages of 50 and 60 in 1952, at least 50% of his vineyard must be planted with authorised varieties.
v) These conditions are only transferable to the grower's wife.

Why some growers, who must be at least 93 years of age by now (or 83 provided half their vineyard contains authorised varieties), wish to continue with very old, low-yielding and inferior-quality Gamay vines, God only knows. If the regulations are being enforced, and there is no reason to believe they are not, then bearing in mind that most growers own less than one hectare of vines, there still must be quite a few of these stubborn old vignerons around.

Cloning

Experiments to find vine clones best suited to the solumological and climatical conditions of Champagne have been continuing for more than twenty years. The first objective was to develop a Pinot Noir clone which could resist the frosts in the Marne valley and thus enable vineyards in this predominantly Pinot Meunier area to be replanted with a more noble variety. Over the last two decades, however, the commercial demands of the Champagne trade have tended to favour the more prolific yields and early maturing advantages of the Pinot Meunier which is increasingly being recognised as a classic variety. Hence, the emphasis on selection today is more to identify specific clones of Pinot Noir, Pinot Meunier and Chardonnay which are best suited to each individual village.

Rootstock varieties

Since the advent of phylloxera, when it became necessary to graft all European vines on to American rootstock, literally hundreds of rootstock varieties have been developed for virtually every permutation of vinestock and growing conditions. The major factors to be taken into consideration when selecting a rootstock variety are: its suitability to the vinestock on which it is to be grafted; its suitability to the geographical location and to climate; solumological effects; and the effect upon the quality and character of the fruit produced. Selection of suitable rootstocks in Champagne are greatly influenced by the solumological factor. A soil with a high active lime content can induce chlorosis or 'green sickness'. In the Marne valley the active lime content, which is not directly proportional to the total lime content, is high – up to 43% in the calcareous topsoil and as much as 53% in the pure chalk subsoil stratas – but the average active lime content is considerably lower.

Since the three most effective phylloxera-resistant species are the *Vitis Berlandieri*, the *Vitis Rupestris* and the *Vitis Riparia*, most rootstock crosses and hybrids (crosses between different species) are derived from these. Of the twenty-eight varieties of rootstock permitted in the cultivation of Champagne's vineyards, the most significant ones are: the *41 B Millardet et Grasset*, which has a fair resistance to phylloxera and an excellent active lime resistance (up to 40%); the *Selection Oppenheim No. 4* or *So 4*, which has very good phylloxera resistance and reasonable active lime resistance (up to 18%); and the *3309 Couderc*, which has excellent resistance to phylloxera and fair resistance to active lime (up to 11%). Of these, the *41 B Millardet* and the *So 4* both promote an early ripening of grapes, while the *So 4* must be seen as the most effective in terms of drought resistance, suitability to the humid conditions of Champagne and increased yields. Three further rootstock varieties cultivated in Champagne are: the *1103 Paulsen* which has an 18% active lime resistance; the *333 École de Montpellier*, with more than 40% active lime resistance and satisfactory resistance to phylloxera; and the *161–49 Couderc*, which has 25% active lime resistance and excellent resistance to phylloxera. Field trials in Champagne have also involved the *99 Richter*, the *110 Richter*, and the *5BB Selection Kober*, but as yet, these are not seen as major competitors to the established rootstock varieties.

Grafting

The difference in technique between all styles of grafting is simply the shape in which both the rootstocks and the vinestocks are cut, the prime purpose being to present the largest possible growing surface between the two canes. It is crucial that the growth of the rootstock should be in advance of the vinestock, or the scion will begin leaf before the union is complete and all such grafts will die from lack of water and nourishment. For the union to be successful the grafted vine forms a protective callus around the wound while the two plants seek compatibility.

No vines may be brought into production for Champagne until they have attained their 'third leaf', that is to say, when they are three years old. So vignerons purchasing bench grafted vinestock will save one year of productivity from their vineyard, a substantial proportion of their income. Many vignerons, however, will wait until the fourth or fifth year to avoid over-straining the young vines, which in turn will ensure a longer and more productive life. As with so many economies, the choice is between the short and the long term.

There are two basic methods of grafting the rootstock on to the desired scion (vinestock): bench grafting and field grafting.

Bench grafting

Cuttings of both rootstocks and scion are taken in autumn and stored until mid or late winter. They are then cut by one of the several methods to effect a good join. At this stage the rootstock will be about ten inches in length and the scion somewhere between one and three inches depending on the specific method employed. After being grafted, the joints are dipped into paraffin wax for protection. In modern viticultural establishments the grafts will spend some time in hot-room callusing boxes* to develop a protective skin or callous over the grafting wound before thay are planted into the nursery beds, and finally into the vineyard the following season. Examples of bench grafting styles are: Jupiter; Omega; Bench Cleft; Saw-type or Hengl; Log-whip; and Short-whip.

Field grafting

This is when the rootstock is simply planted into the vineyard in the autumn and, in the following March, the scion is grafted on to those vines which have taken. Cleft grafting on the spot is the primary example of field grafting and is widely used in California where varieties of vines cultivated change rapidly with fashion: a grower simply cuts off the *whole* of his existing variety at rootstock level and clefts on the new desired variety. Other styles employed, which are modifications of cleft grafting, are: Aerial; Cadillac, Mayorquine, and field budding. These can all be applied to existing vines but without removing any of the top foliage, the advantage being that if the new scion fails to take, the vine still lives and further attempts can be made.

The life of the vine

It is believed that some vines can live as long as five hundred years although such a plant would yield a negligible crop of grapes. Before the advent of phylloxera classic wine producing vines lived an average productive life of around fifty years, although a hundred years was not uncommon. Since the introduction of American rootstocks, however, the impaired circulatory effect upon the sap inflicted by the grafting wound reduces a vine's potential age to about thirty-five years, the most productive of which are those between ten and twenty-five years.

The reason why it is more productive in these middle years is simple. A vine has one aim in life: to reproduce itself. Growth by suckering is merely an extension of its own life; it achieves reproduction by producing seeds which are encased in the edible fruit so fondly admired by birds. To shorten the odds on reproducing itself it must produce a significant crop of attractive fruit, but it cannot do this without the framework on which to hang and parade its wares. To evolve this framework it requires energy from its roots. Thus while it is young, the vine's efforts are directed towards extending its root system, after which it concentrates on forming the structure of branches which will bear its flowers and fruit. As the vine matures, so more and more energy is used in the production of its fruit. With age the strain to produce fruit gradually erodes the vine's life-force with the result that fewer and fewer grapes are produced.

---

*Boxes in which the grafts are packed, up to 500 at a time, in sawdust, charcoal or moss, or a combination thereof, to facilitate the growth of callus tissue over the grafting wound. The callus cells require warmth, a constant temperature between 26–28°C, and a free flow of air in order to grow.

Vine control

Left to itself, however, a vine (grafted or ungrafted) would concentrate all its energies into sending out suckers, which would in turn push down roots to start the cycle all over again. Within two or three years, the majority of a grafted vine's network would be dependent not upon the grafted roots, but upon the regenerated root system of the producing vine and as such would be at the mercy of phylloxera. Ironically, that part of the vine still receiving its principal nourishment from the grafted rootstock would send out its own shoots and, unchecked by any sort of pruning, these would produce hybrid fruit of an unplanned nature. Before phylloxera, it had not been necessary to prune and train, although vine training systems were widely practised – after phylloxera it became essential. Thus the first reason for pruning and training vines is to avoid phylloxera and prevent reversion.

In addition to this, pruning and training are vital functions in the cultivation of the vine to help maintain the purity of its fruiting stock. As well as sustaining the health and vigour of the plant, they can control the quantity and quality of its fruit and direct its size, shape and height to positive effect.

Pruning cuts out damaged and diseased branches, thus averting the spread of decay, while at the same time rechannelling the vital sap back into the productive parts of the plant. It can also control both the quantity and quality of fruit by preventing the over-production of new, sappy growth at the expense of the fruit, and by halting the production of too many fruit buds at the expense of new, healthy growth which will result in poorer fruit and gradually weaken the vine.

In order to understand why certain pruning practices are adopted by various vine-training systems, it helps to know what happens when the shoots are cut. Except when the vine is dormant, sap rises to the top of every shoot and the uppermost bud of a shortened stem is the one that will burst into growth first. Removal of wood above a growth bud or shoot diverts energy into that bud or shoot. The harder the pruning the stronger the response, therefore the more growth required in one direction the more severe the pruning of that part of the vine should be. It should be remembered, however, that pruning deprives the vine of some of its food manufactured through the leaves: this should be replaced by feeding the roots or the plant will weaken. Pruning will also delay the flowering while new shoots grow – a very important point in northern wine regions like Champagne. Precocious growth of the vine in late winter or early spring could well render the vital flowering vulnerable to the severest of spring frosts.

Reducing the amount of fruiting buds lowers the quantity, but raises the quality of the grapes produced. Horizontal or diagonal branches produce more flowering shoots, and therefore more fruit, than vertical ones.

The manner in which a vine is trained will guide the size, shape and height of the plant towards reaping maximum benefits from the local conditions of aspect and climate. Vines can be lifted high off the ground to avoid frost; dropped as low as possible to benefit from heat reflected by stony ground at night; generously spaced along the rows to attract the sun and avoid humidity; or intensively cultivated into a canopy of foliage to avoid too much sun and encourage humidity in dry areas.

Systems of vine training

Four systems of vine training are allowed in Champagne: Chablis, Cordon, Guyot and Vallée de la Marne. The Guyot is a 'cane pruning' system, the other three being 'spur pruning'. Cane pruning is where no permanent branch exists, all canes being cut back each year to provide a vine consisting of entirely new growth. This gives a good spread of fruit over a large area and the annual production is easier to control because the number of fruiting buds can be increased or decreased. Spur pruning is where there is no annual replacement of the main branch, thus good thick wood is formed providing a solid framework and a stable yield.

The use of the four authorised systems is regulated by both grape variety and échelle de cru:

Vine variety	Échelle de Cru	Authorised methods
Chardonnay and ⎱ Pinot Noir ⎰	90%–100%	Chablis, Cordon
	80%–89%	Chablis, Cordon, Guyot
Pinot Meunier	90%–100%	Chablis, Cordon
	80%–100%	Chablis, Cordon, Guyot, Vallée de la Marne

Generally speaking, the Chablis system is used for Chardonnay vines planted in the Côte des Blancs, the Cordon system for Pinot Noir vines in the Montagne de Reims and the Vallée de la Marne method for Pinot Meunier vines grown in the Marne valley.

Chablis

The Chablis system was developed in the Chablis district in the nineteenth century. At least 90% of all Chardonnay vines in Champagne are trained by this method.

A maximum of four shoots per branch is allowed. For the Chardonnay, however, to which it is best suited, four shoots require five buds, as the first bud on this vine is always

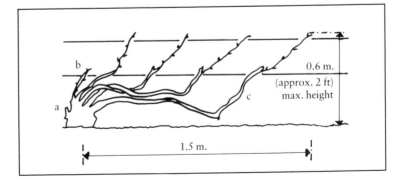

Fig. 3
Chablis system of
vine training

infertile. Either three, four or five permanent branches may be cultivated, each being grown at yearly intervals. Effectively this means that a three-year-old vine (the minimum age for AOC Champagne) will have three branches, a four-year-old four branches and so forth, unless the vigneron for some reason decides not to cultivate as many as he is entitled to.

The distance between each vine in the same row determines the eventual life of the main branches: every time one reaches the neighbouring plant it will be removed and a new one cultivated. In Fig. 3 the oldest branch (c) will soon have to be cut right back to the vine stump and it can be seen that the vigneron tending this vine has already decided to cultivate another branch (b) in preparation. At the same time a third branch (a) is allowed to develop but cut back until required. Should a main banch be broken off for some reason (by vineyard machinery, for example), it is permissible to bring out a shoot half-way along the next branch to fill the gap.

Cordon

Sometimes referred to as the *Cordon de Royat* system, this is primarily recommended for the Pinot Noir. Only one main branch is permitted, along which shoots above branch level are spaced at a minimum of 15 centimetre intervals. Each shoot may have two buds (three for Chardonnay, the first being infertile). An end shoot is also allowed which is itself an extension of the main branch; along this shoot may be four buds (five for Chardonnay or Pinot Noir).

In Fig. 4 (a) has been brought out in readiness but cut back until required. In Fig. 5 shoot (a) has been allowed to grow and is being trained to eventually replace the main branch (b), while another replacement shoot (c) has again been encouraged but cut back. Fig. 6 illustrates how the system may be adapted to replace a missing vine.

The most graphic impression of Cordon-trained vines can be seen in the late winter months, as one travels from Louvois on the D34. Take the first turning left for Bouzy and look at the formation of vines on your right as you approach the village. The vines look like columns of gnarled old men in perfect formation; they are all face on, bent almost double, as if with one arm dug into the pit of the back and the other seeking the support of a stick.

Guyot

This system is not allowed in vineyards of superior classification but is recommended for all authorised vine varieties in lesser growths. In contrast with the other three systems, the Guyot is a cane pruning system. Its main branch (or branches if the Guyot *double* is used) is not permanent. The quickest comparison is to liken it to the replacement branches mentioned above, shoot (a) in Fig. 5, for example.

In Guyot *simple* a single, annually renewable branch is allowed with ten productive buds, whereas for Guyot *double* two annually renewable branches are permitted with eight buds each. Fig. 7 shows how in both versions of the system shoots (a) will replace the main branches (b) in the following year.

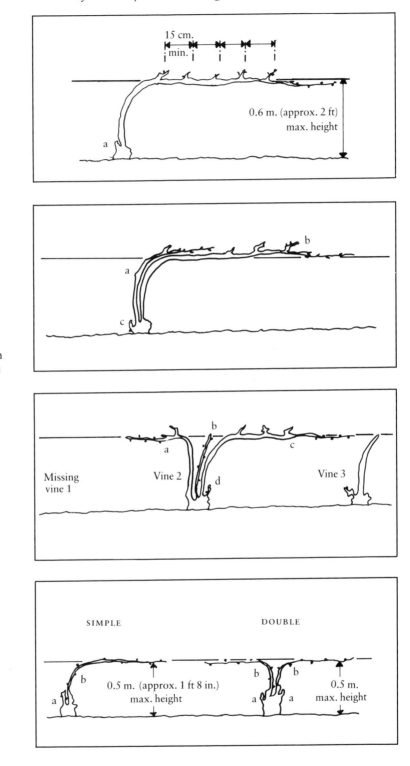

Fig. 4
Cordon system

Fig. 5
Cordon system with
replacement branch

Fig. 6
Cordon system
adapted to replace
missing vine

Fig. 7
Guyot system

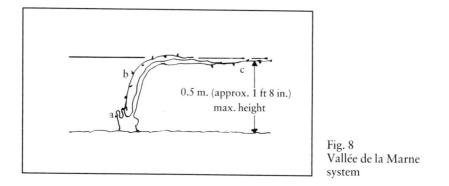

Fig. 8
Vallée de la Marne
system

Vallée de la Marne

The Vallée de la Marne system is restricted to the Pinot Meunier vine only or to vineyards of 89% échelle or lower. There are four variants of this system, all of which have different shoot requirements. In Fig. 8 I have illustrated the basic version which permits six buds on the main permanent branch and nine on the secondary branch. When the main branch (c) reaches the next plant it is replaced by the secondary branch (b) and the reserve shoot (a) will become the next secondary branch.

Density of growth

The space between vines in the same row and the distance between individual rows is strictly controlled: between vines the space ranges from 0.9 metres (minimum) to 1.5 metres (maximum); between rows it is 1.5 metres (maximum). The important factor for the vigneron in deciding the spread of his vines is that the 'sum of spread', that is, the distance between each vine added to the distance between each row, does not exceed 2.5 metres, thus the minimum number of vines planted per hectare is 6,666. A few examples should explain the meaning of 'sum of spread':

Distance in Metres				
Between Rows (Maximum 1.5)	+	Between Vines (0.9–1.5)	=	Sum of Spread (Maximum 2.5)
1.5	+	1.0	=	2.5
1.5	+	0.9	=	2.4
1.5	+	1.5	=	3.0*
1.0	+	1.5	=	2.5
1.25	+	1.25	=	2.5

In the above table all except the asterisked example would be legitimate planting spreads. Here although both distances, 1.5 metres between the rows and 1.5 metres between the vines, are within the maximum lengths allowed, the 'sum of spread' is 0.5 metres over.

Pre-phylloxera vines

Phylloxera infests all wine-producing regions of France, and most of those throughout Europe. A few areas in the world are phylloxera-free and the vines there are sometimes ungrafted. Extraordinarily, there are also some phylloxera-free patches existing in infested regions. This is usually explained by the presence of sand, a soil type not liked by phylloxera, but, curiously, there are also some wall-enclosed vineyards which shelter phylloxera-free, ungrafted vines.

Bollinger own just such a patch of phylloxera-free vines in Aÿ; whereas its high walls might well repel a small army, it remains a mystery why the little bug has not simply walked in under the gate. But if Bollinger's phylloxera-free vines in Aÿ are a puzzle, then their patch on the edge of Bouzy is even more astounding. Driving from Louvois to Bouzy, and taking the left turn into the village itself, one cannot miss the corner section of vines proudly signposted as 'Bollinger's Vieilles Vignes'. This small site is simply a three-sided plot which extends down to the road, its largest border merging into a vast hectarage of vines which have to be grafted in order to survive the threat of phylloxera.

Where the vines are ungrafted they are normally cultivated *en foule*, following the system of vine training which was universal in Champagne during the nineteenth century. As the name suggests, *en foule* is a rather crowded method of training the vine. Left to itself a vine would carpet the land in every direction, albeit making haphazard progress. Initially the vineyard is planted in one corner or at one end, in a very compact fashion, with about six vines per square metre. Within two or three years these vines are ready for *provignage* or layering. In the late autumn or early winter one or two two-year-old shoots from each 'mother' vine are buried six to eight inches deep, leaving the one-year-old shoots for production the following year. Suckers from the buried two-year-old shoots develop roots and within two years a 'new' vine is bearing fruit. There are two variations of this system: *Provignage à l'avance* where progress forward is by one shoot per vine: and *Provignage à l'écart*, a form of deflected layering where two or more canes progress forward. When a vine is five years old it is rested for a while before the practice of

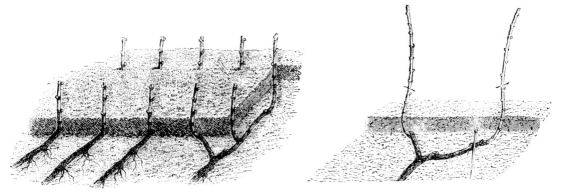

Provignage à l'avance   *Provignage à l'écart*

provignage is resumed, after which the layering process may continue for upwards of fifty years. Although a vineyard thus cultivated always appears to contain vines of no more than three years of age, they do of course all issue from their parent plants, thus a 'pre-phylloxera' vine nowadays will be either three or eighty years old, depending upon how it is viewed. From time to time the 'mothers' need renewing and the simple answer is to turn the nearest two-year-old shoot in full circle and bury it next to the tiring parent.

In April each of the canes seen protruding starkly from the ground in February is cut back to the second bud and stakes are planted for their support. In May or June they are secured to the top of the stakes in a bush-like fashion similar to the Goblet system practised in Beaujolais. By the time of harvest there may be as many as four or five fruiting branches. Excessive foliage may be cut back when the stakes are removed in late autumn. This leaves the vine curled in a heap, a condition in which it will remain until the January or February pruning when all but the one-year-old growth is either cut away or buried for advancing into new vines. And so the cycle begins again.

When *en foule* vineyards are uprooted, this is done in reverse order, starting with the oldest, the mother vine, and working down to the youngest. If the vineyard is still fertile a new mother vine will be created by bending back one or two of its two-year-old vines before grubbing up commences. Should the soil be in need of replenishment all the vines are grubbed up and the land left to fallow for a few years before new vinestock are planted and the entire cycle begins again.

A vineyard planted *en foule* will have something like 25,000 vines per hectare, compared with between 7,000 and 8,000 under post-phylloxera systems such as Cordon. Of course each individual vine yields much less, but the overall production per hectare is significantly higher and it lives up to three times as long, in productive terms, as a grafted vine.

Production levels

In 1935 the maximum production for Champagne was set at 50 hectolitres per hectare which could be annually modified by a special commission up or down to suit the specific conditions of the harvest. As the maximum extraction of grape juice or must was also set

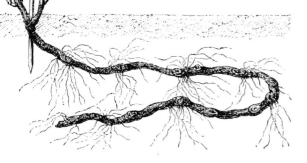

Vine prior to the January–February pruning, showing the extent of root

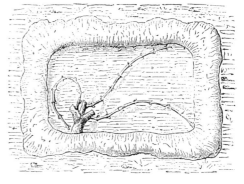

Triple *provignage* to replace the parent stock

at one litre of juice per one and a half kilograms of grapes, this production limit could also be expressed as 7,500 kilograms per hectare.

Initially the reasoning behind this law seemed sensible for a region like Champagne, which is set in a viticultural twilight zone where the size of harvest fluctuates from year to year. But it very soon became clear that any mention of a maximum was unnecessary and, with hindsight, it can be seen as a future source of embarrassment. If the commission, which since its inception has been the CIVC's ComCon (Commission Consultative), required a yardstick on which to base their annual increase or decrease of production limits, then it would have been more rational at the time to term the figure, whether or not it was actually 50 hectolitres per hectare, an average for the region. It was thus inevitable that whenever the official limit was declared higher than the 50 hectolitre/7,500 kilogram mark, Champagne's critics would declare that it was over-producing and its reputation would be tarnished.

With the advance of viticultural techniques the volume of grapes produced in Champagne naturally tended to rise and, always provided that they did not over-produce – a responsibility of ComCon which must be ratified by the non-partisan decree of the minister of agriculture – the quality of the fruit yielded also rose.

Since 1940 the average yield, which should in theory have been lower than the official limit but in practice was not always so, has steadily increased:

Period	Average Yield
1940–49	3,670 kgs per ha.
1950–59	5,000 kgs per ha.
1960–69	7,634 kgs per ha.

By 1970 the official limit, not for the first time, was set at no less than 12,000 kilograms, a fair bit up on the 1935 maximum of 7,500 kilograms, while the average yield topped 13,800 kilograms per hectare and, after setting the official limit at 13,000 kilograms in 1973, a law was passed the following year placing an absolute ceiling of 13,000 kilograms per hectare on all AOC Champagne vineyards, beyond which the so-called maximum could not be stretched.

The average for the 1970s was 9,200 kilograms per hectare, but in 1982 it rose to as much as 13,870 kilograms and in 1984 an even higher figure of 14,190. Looking coldly at the figures and at the *Plafond Limité de Classement* (PLC) of 13,000 kilograms per hectare, it would seem that most of Champagne's production in those two years should have been sent off to the distillery. This did not happen however.

It has to be understood that the enormous 1982 crop was a welcome relief after the miserly vintages of 1978, 1980 and 1981. Champagne's prayers had been answered, the only problem was how to legally recognise what was, technically, an illegally oversized crop. What happened first was that the CIVC told the growers to harvest an extra 10% over the official 13,000 kilograms limit for that year, but to store it separately until the situation clarified. Later it transpired that the INAO (Institut National des Appellations d'Origine des vins et eux-de-vie) would accept this 10% as a *stock régulateur*, a reserve without appellation to be kept for possible classification should any future shortfall require it. This was not without precedent in France; Bordeaux, for example, operates a similar system.

This reserve may be replaced annually, keeping the *stock régulateur* as fresh as possible, but it cannot be increased unless and until the INAO grant another *blocage* of excess production.

In 1983 another massive crop occurred – this was again met with joy, although the Champenois would certainly have been dismayed had 1984 turned out to be the third consecutive bumper year. This time a yield of 15,200 kilograms per hectare was authorised, but instead of the regulation 100 litres of juice per 150 kilograms of grapes, a unique declaration of 100 litres per 160 kilograms was enforced. It was pointed out that this ensured the highest quality from such a large harvest and that the overall permitted yield of 95 hectolitres per hectare was in fact lower than the 95.3 hectolitres per hectare granted in 1982. Of course this ignores the fact that 8.6 hectolitres of the 1982 crop was *not* Champagne, but an unclassified reserve. It also ignores the fact that the PLC of 13,000 kilograms represents just 86.66 hectolitres per hectare.

These were the right decisions, I believe, but had they adopted an average yardstick in 1935, rather than a maximum, and kept the yardstick in line with actual average production figures, the necessary steps taken would have appeared less dramatic. In 1935 the French were free to arrange their own wine laws, but they are now subject to EEC regulations and I doubt that Champagne, despite its unique viticultural situation, would be allowed to dispense with a maximum yield in favour of an average production yardstick.

I would be far happier seeing 15,000 kilograms of grapes in a fine, ripe and healthy year yielding 86.66 hectolitres of juice, than 13,000 kilograms stretched to supply the same volume of juice, leaving 2,000 kilograms of grapes of the same quality to rot on the vine. In the final analysis, however, *if* the AOC laws are applied effectively, all Champagnes must be passed by laboratory analysis and an organoleptic test (blind tasting) which should assure its future quality and reputation, whatever figures are found in the regulation books.

Enemies and disorders of the vine

With the advent of numerous chemical sprays to combat various disorders and pests, the greatest hazard facing the vine in Champagne today is frost. Many other dangers exist and the disorders which result can be just as harmful to the vine, but the risk of their occurrence is less and the vigneron's ability to contain the damage they cause is much greater. The full range of vine disorders fall within six categories: viral, parasitic, cryptogamic, pests, mineral imbalance (discussed in the following chapter) and climatic.

Viral

Virus infections seldom kill, but they do tend to affect vigour, reduce the crop, delay ripening and generally impair the plant's efficiency, although not all virus infections are necessarily harmful to the vine. The two most common virus infections display very obvious visual symptoms known as 'fan-leaf' and 'leaf-roll'; other virus infections may be less conspicuous and difficult to detect, yet may still have undesirable effects. The Chardonnay is particularly prone to 'fan-leaf' or *court-noué*, as it is also known.

Some viruses, including *court-noué*, are spread by microscopic worm-shaped organisms called nematodes, of which there are two basic types – root-knot and root-lesion – and many different species, all of which, in addition to infecting the vine, can inflict damage to the roots which can be confused with phylloxera. *SO 4* and *99 Richter* rootstock varieties are recommended for nematode-infested soils.

Fumigation of vineyards with Telone has improved conditions, but no control measure has yet eradicated nematodes on a field scale. Thermosensitive processes (the sensitivity of *court-noué* to heat treatment has been known since 1921) together with clonal selection are the primary methods of producing so-called 'virus-free' vinestocks. However, as new viruses are being discovered all the time, no vine can be regarded as truly virus-free.

Parasites

Without question the most feared of all vine parasites is *Phylloxera vastatrix*. Derived from the Greek words *phyllon* (leaf) and *xeros* (dry), the phylloxera lives only on the vine and cannot survive on any other host. Phylloxera occurs on the leaves and on the roots: the leaf form termed *Phylloxera vastatrix gallicola*, and the root form *Phylloxera vastatrix radicicola*. There are, however, four distinct stages in the development of phylloxera, all of which belong to the same *Phylloxera vastatrix* life-cycle: the sexual, the leaf, the root and the winged form.

The sexual form originates from eggs laid by the winged form on the under surface of young leaves. The sexual form has no digestive system and, after the male and female sexual forms have mated, the female lays just one winter egg in the dead bark of the vine's trunk. Both male and female of the sexual form die after mating.

From the winter egg an insect called the leaf form hatches out and begins to suck the lower surface of its birthplace, a young leaf, causing the formation of a hollow gall. In this gall the leaf form lays a number of eggs by parthenogenesis (self-propagation) which, usually in the autumn, hatch as root forms. Like the leaf form (only smaller), the root form is a wingless insect. It crawls down the vine and enters the soil, whereupon it reaches and punctures the roots for nourishment. In sucking out its nourishment the root form infects its lacerations of the root with a poisonous secretion which prevents the vine from healing itself.

The root form has the ability to reproduce itself by parthenogenesis several times throughout the year for a few years without passing into another form. Eggs laid by the root form which hatch in the late autumn, turn into larvae which hibernate in the roots, not emerging until the spring temperatures rise above 10°C the following year, when they attain maturity. Many of these mature offspring of the root form work their way to the surface and those which are winged fly off in search of new vines. These are the winged forms which lay the eggs which hatch into the sexual form, and the cycle is complete.

The more complex the life-cycle, the easier it should be to interrupt it and thus eradicate the parasite, but each link in the phylloxera chain appears to be capable of regenerating a modified cycle. In the mid-west United States, for example, where phylloxera originated, none of the above-ground forms occur, yet the cycle still thrives.

There are only three ways of controlling phylloxera: by grafting on to phylloxera-resistant rootstocks, the accepted method; by planting into 'phylloxera-proof' soil of at least 85% sand content; or by submersion (flooding the vines) for a period of sixty days in slightly permeable soils and ninety days in very permeable soils, sufficient to kill phylloxera but hardly practical for a working vineyard, especially when there is every likelihood that the parasite will return.

The sight of silken threads woven over the vine's flowers or fruit will indicate the presence of certain types of grape moths, possibly *cochylis* or *eudemis*. These moths lay their eggs, usually on the buds, in spring and summer. Depending when the eggs hatch, the larvae will feed on the tender vine shoots, the flowers or the fruit.

Other parasitic insects which may attack the vine are *pyralis* (the larvae of the meal-moth which feeds on young shoots and leaves); *altise* (a beetle which feeds on the leaves); *phyptus vitis* (a microscopic mite which attacks leaves, flowers and grapes, rendering a condition known as *erinosis*, first recognised by red leaf blisters which gradually turn yellow) and *cochenilles* (various bugs which feed on the sap, weakening the vine).

All the parasitic insects which may attack the vine in Champagne, with the exception of phylloxera, can be kept under control with numerous proprietary brands of insecticide, if treated early enough.

Cryptogamic

Cryptogamic or fungoid diseases are encouraged by a combination of humidity and heat and the vigneron has a choice of proprietary brands of spray which can prevent or cure these conditions.

Downy mildew, also known as 'false mildew', *Plasmopara viticola* or *peronospora*, is the most dangerous of all, mostly attacking the green parts of a vine, but also the flowers or clusters of grapes. In the autumn this fungus develops its winter spores, which are dark brown in colour, round, and 25–30 microns in diameter. Via infected leaves these winter spores enter the soil where they can remain alive for several years. The control of downy mildew is preventative, not curative, therefore the vigneron must commence spraying as early as possible prior to the flowering if the first infection is to be prevented. If the primary infection is not prevented, as many as three or four further outbreaks may occur throughout the growing season and the disease may assume epidemic proportions.

Powdery mildew, also known as 'true mildew', *Uncinula necator* or *oidium*, is first recognised by a white powdery deposit on the shoots, upper surfaces of the leaves and on young berries (it seldom attacks ripe grapes). Vines under stress from drought are vulnerable and, unlike most forms of cryptogamic disease, powdery mildew can be rife in dry conditions. It is best controlled by dusting the green parts of the vine, especially when it is hot, with finely powdered sulphur. In Champagne the Pinot Noir is the variety least affected by powdery mildew.

Grey rot, also known as *pourriture grise*, is a common danger in Champagne's humid climate; *brown rot*, or *pourriture brune*, also occurs but less frequently. At the first sign of rot the vigneron removes some of the outer foliage, exposing the vine to the drying effect of direct sunlight and improved aeration, and sprays with copper sulphate.

Pests

Birds can be a considerable problem in Champagne as the grapes begin to ripen. Great swarms of starlings and thrushes raid the vineyards by day, pecking at large numbers of grapes but eating few and causing more damage indirectly by rot than by anything else. Anyone who has made the mistake of parking at harvest-time under the trees which line the Place Drouet d'Erlon in Reims, will realise that most of Champagne's bird life return each night to this one street to rest and make room for the following day's gorging of grapes.

Climatic

Frost is the biggest killer as far as the size of crops harvested in Champagne is concerned. A spring frost at the time of flowering can cause imperfect fertilisation resulting in *millerandage*, the formation of tiny hard berries which will not swell or ripen. An autumn frost kills off the leaves, preventing any chance of further ripening. It may also swell the juice within the grapes to bursting point, ruining the fruit for winemaking unless harvested and transported to the press while still frozen, which would hardly be practicable for any significant area of vines affected by frost.

The traditional method of reducing frost damage is to use paraffin burners called *chaufferettes*. These can be seen dotted about the vineyards, either lit manually by the vigneron when the temperature drops to freezing setting off noisy alarms in the middle of the night, or fed by an automatic system which fires the burners by thermostatic control. More use today is being made of the aspersion method, a system of dissipating the freezing effect of frost by spraying the vines with water. As a vine will generally withstand a temperature as low as $-5°C$ water-spraying systems are set up to come into operation as soon as the temperature drops to $1°C$. The frost freezes the water, not the vine, and a protective cocoon is formed, within which even the tenderest shoots remain safe. But the spraying must continue for as long as the temperature remains at freezing point or below, as the energy of the frost must be spent on forming more and more ice outwards. If the spraying should stop, as can happen with blockages or burst pipes, the freezing effect travels inwards and the damage may be greater than if no precautions had been taken.

Whereas if the weather is bad (frosts) the vine might be affected by *millerandage*, if it is too good it can suffer from *coulure*. The symptoms of *millerandage* and *coulure* are often confused with each other, but they are not related. Good flowering is dependent on temperature, the ideal being between 20 and 25°C, but if growing conditions are *too* favourable when the flowering takes place, essential nutrients rush up to the tips, not to the clusters, wood growth takes precedence and the barely formed seeds dry up and fall to the ground.

Hail storms frequently ravage localised areas of vines in Champagne, as do, occasionally, tornadoes. Although it is not beyond the ingenuity of the vigneron to protect his vineyards from such isolated hazards, in fact little can be done which would be economically viable.

5

Work in the Vineyard

Once I was in a graveyard beside a vineyard when, on the other side of a high wall, I heard a succession of grunts interrupted by endless repetitions of 'Bad horse, Poulette, ready for the sausage machine'. On peering through a hole in the wall I saw that Poulette was a strapping Ardennaise, performing her duties admirably, but that her poor master was having to press so hard to keep the plough in the soil that the entire weight of his body was being taken by his arms and he was advancing across the vineyards behind Poulette with his feet off the ground.

Patrick Forbes, *Champagne*, 1967

November

The viticultural new year starts in November when the longer shoots of the vine are cut away, conserving the plant's energy for the cold winter months ahead. It also allows the vigneron easier access to the vineyard and to the vine, enabling him to carry out his next operation, the scattering of fertiliser pellets. Without cutting back the vines, too many of these pellets would be wasted, wedged in the vines' dead or dying foliage. By now the autumnal coloured leaves will begin to drop from the vine to reveal a skeleton of canes. Inside the vine the sap begins to withdraw to the roots.

The effort of yielding a good crop of grapes expends a great amount of the vine's energy and its roots will be active over the winter months searching out fresh supplies for the next year's growth. By scattering the fertiliser pellets over his vineyard the vigneron is helping to restore the vine's balance of resources. The foundation of each pellet is the so-called 'golden tripod', which includes the three basic requirements of all plant life: potassium, phosphorus and nitrogen.

Potassium, usually in the form of sulphate of potash, improves the vine's metabolism, assisting the movement of food within the plant and enriching the sap. This should lead to a better quality of grape in the following season. Phosphorus, usually in the form of superphosphate of lime, directly encourages root development and, because it is essential for respiration and photosynthesis, indirectly promotes an earlier *véraison* or ripening of the grapes. Nitrogen, usually in the form of nitrates, encourages leaf growth and will be stored by the plant until the following spring.

A late-autumn, early-winter fertiliser pellet will have a higher phosphorus content, those applied in the spring will contain more nitrogen, while those in the summer, more potassium. In addition to the basic 'golden tripod', the pellets also contain certain essential trace elements. Most trace elements are found in the numerous soils exploited for commercial cultivation, but the amounts which are availabe to the plant vary for several reasons. The minerals may simply be absent or present in negligible amounts, either naturally, through exhaustion by previous crops, or leeched out by climatic conditions. The pH level of a soil – the extremes of acidity or alkalinity – can actually prevent access to minerals which may be there in significant quantities: a high lime content, for example, denies or restricts a plant's access to iron and manganese. The proportion of these trace elements in the fertiliser pellets will vary significantly from one wine region to another, but they normally include one or more of the following: iron, indispensable for photosynthesis (plants lacking sufficient iron salts suffer from chlorosis); magnesium, the only mineral constituent of the chlorophyll molecule (lack of magnesium also causes chlorosis); and copper, zinc and boron, which are important for the overall metabolism of the vine.

Immediately after fertilising operations have ceased, banking-up is performed by ploughing an angled blade between each row of vines. This buries the pellets near to the roots and forms a protective mound of earth over the grafting wound which, although fully taken, will always be sensitive. It also allows frost to permeate the soil, aiding the infiltration of rain and essential for breaking up the clods into manageable sizes.

December to February

Between the months of December and January a solitary woman can often be seen progressing through the vineyards removing the twists of wire which had been used the previous spring to attach the vines to the guide wires. At the same time she will cut away any straggly shoots or twigs, generally tidying up the vines as she goes along.

By this stage the sap in the vine will have withdrawn into the roots. Above the ground the vine looks dormant, but below the roots are going through their most active period of the year. They dig deep in search of mineral deposits to replenish those expended in the last year of growth. The deeper they go, the more secure the vine will be in times of flood and the more able it will be to obtain moisture in times of drought.

At this time of the year the *vigneron* bolsters the fertility of the topsoil by the application of manure, utilising the trench created by the banking-up operation. The use of either *cendres-noires* or organic manure is generally preferred today, but in the past the most popular fertiliser has been the *boues de ville*, quite literally, town refuse.

Cendres-noires, the 'black gold' of the Montagne de Reims, is a Sparnacian deposit comprised almost entirely of rich black lignite, a friable carbonaceous substance which is half-way between peat and coal. The Montagne is dotted with small lignite mines, many deserted, which have traditionally supplied the Champagne grower. It is especially prized because carbon, its major component, is by far the most important of all plant nutrients. These deposits also contain various other mineral trace elements.

Organic manure might be animal or vegetable derived although both are difficult to obtain in quantity in a modern society. The most common organic manure these days is the spent *marc*, the residue of skins, pips and stalks amassed after the pressing process, which can be seen in purple-black piles by the roadside from November onwards.

Fig. 9
The Champagne
vineyard calendar

Boues de ville was described by Patrick Forbes in 1967 as:

neither more nor less than the contents of Parisian dustbins. Each Autumn consignments arrive in the winefield by rail in sealed tanks, transport during the summer being forbidden on account of the stink. In theory, each consignment has been finely ground to remove danger from broken glass . . . (*Champagne*, p. 255)

By the end of the 1970s, however, Champagne had no need to transport the *boues de ville* from Paris since the city of Reims was able to provide its own. Whether Parisian or Reims produced the great mounds of town refuse which one can see piled up on the roadside are a dusty grey colour interspersed with flecks of pale blue; the stench they give out, far outweighing that of the spent piles of *marc*, cannot be missed. There is a marked difference in colour between the dusty grey-brown of these mounds and the bright, light blue colour they spread over the vineyards. This is because the 'goodness' of the *boues* rots away into the soil leaving the bulk of non-bio-degradable material remaining which is largely blue plastic.

According to Alain Collery of Champagne Collery in Aÿ, there has been concern about the cadmium content in the soil from batteries which are also minced up along with other refuse in the *boues de ville*. In fact the Champenois are now moving away from the use of *boues* in favour of *cendres-noires*, but apparently this is not due to concern over the cadmium problem, it is because the *boues* is now more expensive than mining lignite deposits, due to the high price being paid by refuse-fuelled energy plants.

March to April

As the sap begins to climb into the vine, dormant buds start shooting: this is the signal to prune. But this poses a dilemma for the vigneron because the vine, once pruned, is at its most vulnerable to frost, while to wait for the danger of frost to subside would be to waste the vine's limited and precious energy: the decision of when to prune can prove an expensive one. The first indication of how large or small the yield might be is when the first leaves and tendrils begin to appear, followed by embryo bunches of grapes. But it should be remembered that this is merely an early indication growth.

Pruning begins in earnest in mid-March, cutting back to the number of shoots and fruiting buds stipulated by the various systems of vine cultivation. General vineyard maintenance of wires, stakes and machinery also takes place and, at the same time, the vines are secured to their training frames. In April the protective mound of soil safeguarding the grafting wound is ploughed back, burying the manure applied in the winter and levelling off the ground between the rows of vines.

May to July

Spraying commences in May and continues right up until the harvest, although the number of times the vines are sprayed and the types of spray used will depend on the local conditions of pests and disease. The spraying operations are carried out by hand, tractor and helicopter.

Spraying the vines by tractor

Beginning in June, the old sterile growth is picked off and hoeing starts in earnest. It is customary for workers to go collectively through the vines eradicating excess foliage, which improves the circulation of air around the vine and also reduces the risk of fungi developing. Care has to be taken not to remove too many leaves as it is the effect of sunlight upon the leaves immediately above the fruit which will ripen the grapes and not the sun directly on the fruit itself.

The grapes begin to form, after natural pollination, during the months of June and July. Ripening, or the *véraison*, commences in August and continues throughout September.

August to October

Spraying, hoeing and thinning continue throughout the ripening months between August and October. Harvest usually takes place in mid-October, although in extreme cases it has commenced as early as August and as late as November. After the vintage, when the leaves begin to turn, the operation to cut away any long shoots begins again and the cycle is complete.

6

The Presshouse

... usually powerful presses of modern invention, worked by a large fly-
wheel requiring four sturdy men to turn it, are employed.

Henry Vizetelly, *A History of Champagne*, 1882

The pressing operation

MOST LARGE PRODUCERS have their own presshouses conveniently situated in the
vineyards, otherwise growers take their grapes to co-operative presshouses or perhaps
make private arrangements with other producers. The presshouse is only utilised one
month in twelve, but when it is in operation, it is manned twenty-four hours a day. The
staff, dressed in the French labourer's ubiquitous blue overalls, work in non-stop shifts to
process the harvest as it comes in.

During the pressing operation, the first juice to emerge from a grape is called the *cuvée*
and it comes from the central zone of pulp. This part of the grape's flesh produces the
richest juice in terms of sugar, acids and trace elements, and goes to make the highest
quality Champagnes.

After the central portion from the grape is exhausted, the flesh nearest to the pips and to
the skin is pressed, that is, the pulp which is both inside and outside the richer central
zone. These outer and inner zones yield the *taille*, a juice which becomes increasingly
weaker in acidity and sugar, although some minerals may be in greater abundance. As
more and more juice flows through the pith of skins, pips and stalks it gradually becomes
discoloured; even white grapes at this stage yield a relatively dark and murky juice.

According to the *Code du Vin* (a publication codifying the regulations of the INAO), one
*marc** of 4,000 kilograms will yield 2,266 litres of juice, or must, as it is sometimes
called†. Still adhering to the old fashioned measurement by *pièce* (a cask which in
Champagne contains 205 litres), the 2,666 litres of must, as it comes through the pressing
operation, is separated into three portions in order of quality: the *cuvée*, which amounts
to the first ten *pièces* (2,050 litres); the *première taille*, which includes the next two *pièces*
(410 litres); and the *deuxième taille*, or the last *pièce* (205 litres). The traditional thirteen

---

* This term usually refers to the residue of grape
skins, pips and stalks left after pressing, but can, as in
this case, also refer to the grapes (must or vine) of an
individual pressing. If one refers to a *marc* of grapes
in Champagne, one is talking about 4,000 kg of

grapes because that is the traditional capacity of one
pressing.

† 100 litres of juice from 150 kg of grapes being the
maximum extraction allowed.

pièces in fact add up to one litre short of the mathematically equated 2,666 litres but this appears to have been overlooked. If pressing continues beyond the 2,666 litres limit the final dregs of the juice obtained, known as the *rebêche*, may not be used for the production of Champagne, Coteaux Champenois (the still wines of Champagne) or, indeed, any other officially classified wine.

Tannin increases as the pressing continues, particularly during the *rebêche* stage when the constituents of the stalks and pips progressively dominate the flow of juice. Unlike still red wines, sparkling Champagne does not benefit from a detectable tannin content, although a little tannin will be added prior to the last racking to activate the fining agent. It is therefore interesting to compare the increase of undesirable tannin with the decrease in desirable active acidity:

	pH	Tannin (in grams) per litre
Cuvée	2.60–2.96	0.017
Première taille	3.00–3.20	0.028
Deuxième taille	3.25–3.40	0.040
Rebêche	3.40–4.00	0.045

It is a long-established fallacy that both the *cuvée* and the *taille* are officially divided into three: the first, second and third *cuvées* and the first, second and third *tailles*. When Patrick Forbes proffered such divisions in his excellent work *Champagne* it had no bearing on the regulations. He was merely quoting his old textbook from the École de Viticulture et d'Oenologie at Avize which examines the practices of Champagne in the 1940s; no doubt, the breakdown of *cuvée* and *taille* merely indicated the number of press operations it took, in less sophisticated times, to squeeze out these two parts of extraction. Subsequent writers, however, have copied Patrick Forbes's work without checking for themselves, and the misleading myth has evolved in which the first thousand litres of the *cuvée* is believed to be officially designated the *première cuvée*. From this false premiss, it is easy to see how the public might wrongly think that Moët & Chandon's Première Cuvée Champagne is made entirely from the first thousand litres of the *cuvée*. Patrick Forbes is the first to point out that this is not so and that the title is just a brand name, but the confusion still persists.

In the years when no rain occurs between the last spraying of the vine and the harvest, the first sixty-five litres of the *cuvée* will often be tapped off and added to the *taille*. The reasoning behind this is that the first 65 litres will contain any contaminates which might be present on the grape skins, but readers should not be alarmed because the wines must pass an analytical examination before being sold. In typical Gallic fashion, the Champenois are just being extra careful.

Presses

Two types of presses are used, the horizontal press and the traditional Champagne press. At present, horizontal presses of between 2,000 and 8,000 kilograms are allowed, but trials with larger machines have been in progress for several years. Moët & Chandon, for example, is operating a 12,000-kilogram press on an experimental basis in conjunction with the CIVC. There are two principal kinds of horizontal press: the hydraulic press (the simplest of all), usually a Vaselin model, which has two flat metal plates at either end that push together, squashing the grapes in between and issuing the juice from a duct in the inner cylindrical sleeve; and the pneumatic press, of which the Willmes is the most common. The lateral membrane and the central membrane are two variations of the pneumatic press, the principle being the same for both: the membrane is a long and large taste-free rubber balloon which inflates when the press is full, gently crushing the grapes against the inside of the horizontal cylinder which has channels and ducts. The lateral membrane takes up the entire length of one side of the chamber, pushing the grapes against the other side. The central membrane is threaded lengthways through the centre of the cylinder and also blows up like a balloon when the chamber is filled with grapes, only the pressure outwards is even, gently crushing the fruit in all directions. The CIVC particularly recommends pneumatic presses for their speed and careful method of extraction.

The traditional, vertical Champagne press, based on the concepts employed by Dom Pérignon, is still considered by many to be the best means of pressing grapes for the sparkling wine of Champagne. Known as the *pressoir coquart*, it is by far the most common machine in Champagne presshouses; in other areas the hydraulic and pneumatic horizontal presses are more commonly used. However, since power sources have changed significantly since Dom Pérignon's day, there are no longer many of the giant, hand-operated, wheel-type presses.

Each press, which may be round or square, takes a *marc* of 4,000 kilograms. The bottom half, known as the *maie*, is made from oak and has a series of ducts around the inside rim at the base, through which the juice runs out. Its lid, or *mouton*, is also made of oak and consists of two semi-circular or rectangular flaps which fold down to make a horizontal plate that presses the grapes inside the *maie*.

Obtaining the *cuvée*

The *cuvée* is the highest quality juice and many Champagnes are made entirely from this first pressing.

In between each pressing required to extract the *cuvée* (or the first 2,050 litres) an operation called *retroussage*, meaning 'to turn up' or 'to tuck up', is carried out. During *retroussage* the *mouton* is raised, exposing the squashed mass of grapes which are then scooped into a pile in the centre of the *maie* using blunt wooden shovels called *pelles*.

Obtaining the *taille*

The term *taille* means 'cut' and that is precisely what is done to the *marc* in the *maie* after the *cuvée* has been extracted. At this stage the *marc* is like a solid cake which needs an instrument called a *bêche plate* to sever the mass into chunks which can then be forked into the centre of the *maie*. This enables greater pressure to be applied to the already compressed cake of grapes, skins, pips etc. The juice from this residue, called the *taille*, is the poorest in terms of quality which may be used for Champagne. Even so, the *taille* can sometimes be surprisingly good, especially in favourable years, and would in those Champagnes which utilise it, represent but a small proportion of the overall blend of a wine.

Because the *taille* does not reflect the same quality appeal as the *cuvée*, it is common practice for many houses to declare they never use *vins de taille* in their Champagnes, preferring to sell on any they may have. Some might admit that they use the best *vins de taille* in their *demi-sec* Champagnes where the extra sugar content is likely to mask any defects which may appear, but every house naturally declares that all inferior *vins de taille* are sold. This leads to the inevitable question 'Where does it all go to?' and the simple answer is that most of it goes to several firms specialising in BOB (Buyer's Own Brand: ie, supermarket brands etc.) Champagnes. These BOB specialists are, however, quite often the principal firms involved in an internal trade route rarely discussed in polite company in Champagne. Some of the Champagne houses which make a point of declaring they never use *vins de taille* in their own products have purchased ready-made Champagnes from the very houses to which they sold their *vins de taille* in the first place. Much of this secretive internal trading is conducted at *sur lattes* stage, when the wines have undergone secondary fermentation, thus Champagnes which have been blended and rendered sparkling by one firm end up being sold under the label of another. These Champagnes probably contain a significant proportion of *vins de taille* despite declarations to the opposite by the purchasing houses which end up selling them. But what is more dishonest is the simple fact that the wines are not what they purport to be. Champagne houses owe their success to brand image, they play on their reputation and they earn this from the quality, consistency and style of the Champagne they produce. It might make sense to the financial director faced with a demand which far outweighs supply; after all, this recycling of other houses' wines is perfectly legal, but it is at the same time deliberately hoodwinking the public. There is tremendous customer loyalty involved in the fortunes of Champagne, but this loyalty can only survive if it has a two-way traffic. This loophole should be closed.

Obtaining the *rebêche*

The *rebêche* is the unclassified juice pressed after the first and second *taille* have been extracted. It is so-called because the *bêche plate* must be reused to cut up the even denser *marc*. The chunks of *marc* are often transferred at this stage to a *séchoir* – a smaller, deeper, vertical press – or to a horizontal press to be squeezed out.

Producing the juice to make *vin de rebêche* is optional if pressing grapes for Champagne, but for some reason not even the CIVC could answer, obligatory by law if pressing grapes for Coteaux Champenois. It is neither a desirable nor a necessary product. Traditionally it was used for *ptisannes*, a very bitter, still wine recommended by physicians as a laxative and diuretic. Today the *rebêche* is only used for distillation (into either *prestation vinique* – alcohol for oath-taking, or *eaux-de-vie* – grape brandies) and table wine (if the natural alcoholic content is 6% or more, unlikely for *vin de rebêche*) or 'wine not fit for human consumption' (but presumably fit for distillation into industrial spirits) if less than 6% natural alcoholic content.

Since the Common Market annually produces such vast quantities of wine fit for nothing better than compulsory distillation, it is puzzling why the authorities still require producers of Coteaux Champenois to churn out as much as one or two *pièces* of this liquid for every *marc* pressed.

Débourbage

Débourbage, or cleansing, of the must can take place at either the presshouse or the winery and is, in its simplest form, merely a resting of the must to enable the particles of skin and other impurities to settle on the bottom of the vat. If a Champagne house buys its requirements in the form of must (as opposed to grapes), *débourbage* might well take place at both the presshouse and the winery. Lowering the must in temperature to 5°C encourages *débourbage* and the result is superior and quicker. In nearly all cases the must will be dosed with sulphur dioxide, which will encourage this settling process as well as act as an aseptic agent and as an antioxidant. If bentonite, a fining agent, is added at this stage, it improves protein stability and reduces the risk of spoilage from the sedimented waste.

7

Principles of Vinification

Authoritative books on wine before World War II make no mention of vinification, but since then the art of wine-making has made great strides...
Steven Spurrier and Michel Dovaz, *Académie du Vin Wine Course*, 1983

The components of grape juice

WINE IS AN ALCOHOLIC BEVERAGE obtained by the process of fermenting the juice of freshly gathered grapes where the biochemical action of yeast enzymes converts the sugars into ethyl alcohol and carbon dioxide. Before examining the process of fermentation in detail, its basic requirements and its products, it is necessary first to look at the components of the grape itself.

Depending on the variety of grape, the situation of the vineyard and the conditions under which it ripens, a grape is composed of approximately 90% pulp, 7% skin and 3% pips. The fresh grape juice, or must as it is often called, is made up of:

Components	% by volume	Comment
Water	70–85	
Carbohydrates	15–27	Mostly sugars: produced as sucrose in the leaves and converted in the grapes to approximately 50/50 glucose and fructose, although more fructose (the sweeter sugar) than glucose is made as the grape ripens. Small amounts of pentoses, pectin and inositol.
Acids	0.3–1.5	Tartaric and malic are the major grape acids, with a little citric and traces of succinic and lactic. Grapes contain twice as much tartaric as malic.
Minerals	0.3–0.6	Essentially potassium, phosphate, sodium, magnesium, calcium, iron, chloride, sulphate and traces of aluminium, silicic acid, iron, copper, zinc, boron, manganese, phosphorus, molybdenum, rubidium.
Tannins	0.01–0.1	Tannins are either hydrolysable or condensed; most grape tannins are condensed, up to 73% are catechin tannins.
Vitamins	T–0.001	Thiamine, riboflavin, pyridoxine, pantothenic acid, nicotinic acid and ascorbic acid.
Nitrogenous matter	0.03–0.2	Amino acids, protein etc.
Other matter	0–T	Various alcohols, esters, acids, aldehydes, anthocyanins (colouring pigments), enzymes, ammonia, iodine and unknown substances.

Note T = traces only.

Definition of fermentation

In 1810 a French chemist, Joseph-Louis Gay-Lussac, expressed the chemical process of fermentation as:

$$C_6H_{12}O_6 \longrightarrow 2\,C_2H_5OH + 2\,CO_2$$

(hexose sugar)   (ethyl alcohol)   (carbon dioxide)

Interestingly, the role of yeast, the agent which is responsible for converting the natural sugars of the grape into ethyl alcohol and carbon dioxide was not indicated by Gay-Lussac. The relevance of a living catalyst in the form of yeast cells had not been accepted and fermentation was thus believed to be a purely chemical process. Even ignoring the absence of any biological factor, Gay-Lussac's formula is merely a simplified expression for a series of complex chemical reactions, the full extent of which has not yet been identified by oenologists, or wine scientists.

The components of fermentation

The basic requirements of fermentation are thus yeasts, nutrients and sugars.

Yeasts

Yeasts can be put into two categories in winemaking, natural and cultured.

'Natural yeasts' are to be found adhering to the pruina, a waxy substance which covers the skin of ripe grapes and other fruits. By the time the grape has fully ripened, the coating of yeasts and other micro-organisms, commonly referred to as the bloom, contains an average of ten million yeast cells. These yeasts are of numerous varieties but can be divided into two groups: 'wine yeasts' and 'wild yeasts' – arbitrary categories for anyone but an oenologist. Of the ten million yeast cells found on a ripe grape, only 1 per cent or just 100,000 cells are so-called 'wine yeasts'.

The primary species of wine yeast is *Saccharomyces cerevisiae*: *cerevisiae* being a species of the genus *Saccharomyces*. A variety of *cerevisiae* widely used in winemaking is *Saccharomyces ellipsoideus* (also called *S. cerevisiae var. ellipsoideus*, *S. allypsoideus* or *S. oviformis*). There are numerous strains of *cerevisiae* and *ellipsoideus*, many taking their name from the various regions, districts or villages where they are found. A single village could well have hundreds of strains and a local winegrower might well possess a preference for one of these, developing it as a cultured yeast.

'Wild yeasts' are so named because if they are allowed to take control of the fermentation, they produce wild and unwanted characteristics, resulting in wines which can often become cloudy and have off-flavours and off-tastes. Yeasts of the following genera are amongst those considered to be wild yeasts: *Kloeckera* and *Hanseniaspora*, both of which form an excessive amount of acid (about double that produced by ordinary wine yeasts) and which give a sharp cidery off-flavour; *Pichia*, which contributes to an increased ethyl acetate content, creates various esters and oxidises available alcohol into acetaldehyde, giving vinegary or rancid off-flavours and sherry-like aromas; and

Hansenula, which, like *Pichia*, creates various unwanted esters and sherry-like characteristics. Added to these are the so-called 'pseudo-yeasts' of the genera: *Candida*, which is responsible for rancid off-flavours and converts alcohol into carbonic gas and water; and *Torulopsis*, which imparts a sliminess to the texture of wine. Several species within the *Saccharomyces* genus are also considered to be wild, unwanted yeasts.

'Cultured yeasts' are nothing more than thoroughbred strains of natural wine yeasts raised in a laboratory for specific purposes. They may be used because a winemaker prefers their greater reliability, because of the subtle nuances of bouquet and flavour which they produce, or because the particular strain of yeast has been cultured for specific conditions of fermentation: higher concentrations of alcohol or sulphur dioxide (SO_2), or higher osmotic pressure (as experienced in bottle-fermented wines such as Champagne).

A yeast cell is only 1/5,000th of an inch, yet under favourable conditions it has the ability to split ten thousand sugar molecules every second during fermentation. The wine yeasts on just one grape have, therefore, the capacity of splitting one billion sugar molecules every second, which is why the initial stage of fermentation is called the *bouillage,* due to the boisterous bubbling effect of such frenzied activity.

Yeast nutrients

Just as we need various nutrients to function properly, so do yeasts. For winemaking purposes yeast nutrients are required in minute amounts only, larger quantities would inhibit fermentation. These nutrients are: amino acids, vitamins (thiamine) and minerals (potassium, sulphate, phosphate and magnesium). Trace elements of iron, copper, zinc, boron and manganese are also responsible for stimulating yeast growth, but calcium, although it activates enzymes, is not essential.

Sugars

Yeasts need carbohydrates (sugar) to grow. Between 15 and 25% of a grape is sugar, the proportion varying according to the variety of grape, how ripe it is and the conditions under which it has ripened. The two main sugars present are both mono-saccharides: glucose (which comprises approximately 8–13% of the total grape) and fructose (which is between 7 and 12%). These sugars contain six carbons and are therefore known as hexose. Pentose, a mono-saccharide with only five carbons may also be found in fresh grapes, but it is unfermentable and always remains in the finished wine, however dry it may be to taste. If the grape must has insufficient sugar it can be chaptalised by the addition of sucrose (common white sugar), a di-saccharide.

The fermentation process

Unless it has been *thoroughly* cleansed of all micro-organisms, freshly pressed grape juice contains sufficient yeasts to commence a good fermentation. There is, however, a great danger that an unwanted wild fermentation might occur in the initial phase when the 'wild yeasts' greatly outnumber the true wine yeasts. It is, therefore, a normal practice to lightly cleanse the must with a little sulphur dioxide which will subdue the larger quantity of wild yeasts.

As the true wine yeasts are able to withstand heavier concentrations of sulphur dioxide they take control of the fermentation from the start. Most wild yeasts cannot operate in the presence of between 6 and 7% alcohol, therefore the true wine yeasts, whether *S. cerevisiae* or *S. ellipsoideus*, dominate naturally in the latter stages of fermentation. Of course, if the must *has* been thoroughly cleansed of all micro-organisms and a cultured yeast added, the dangers presented by wild yeasts are obviated.

It is not the yeast cell itself which is directly responsible for converting sugar into alcohol, but various enzymes, complex protein catalysts, secreted by the cell. This was discovered accidentally in 1897 when two German scientists, the brothers Eduard and Hans Buchner, were trying to provide an extract of medicinal value by squeezing yeast with sand and kieselguhr (a silicaceous earth often used for fining) under a hydraulic press. In order to preserve their extract they added sugar and, to their astonishment, they found that the mixture of juice and sugar fermented, forming alcohol and carbon dioxide. The juice had been obtained from the yeast but contained no yeast cells whatsoever.

Of the great number of enzymes which may be secreted by a yeast cell, some twenty-two are required to complete the chain reaction known as fermentation. Each acts as a catalyst for one activity and is specific for that purpose and no other. Sucrase, for example, splits the di-saccharide sucrose into the mono-saccharides fructose and glucose and is therefore essential for the fermentation of any must which has been chaptalised. Enzymes of the zymase complex produce the long chain of reactions which result in the reduction of fructose and glucose into alcohol and carbon dioxide.

The sugar content of a normal healthy and unchaptalised must is roughly 50/50 fructose and glucose. As mono-saccharides, these simple sugars are converted directly into alchohol by yeast enzymes. If chaptalised the enzymes ignore sucrose, a di-saccharide, until all the mono-saccharides are exhausted. Only when this has been achieved is the sucrose converted, by the enzyme sucrase, to fructose and glucose, readily fermentable mono-saccharides.

Pentose is an unfermentable mono-saccharide normally found in minute quantities in all healthy musts, chaptalised or unchaptalised. Thus even the driest of wines has an infinitesimal amount of sugar present.

The conversion of sugar to alcohol by Gay-Lussac's classic formula can be equated in proportional terms:

$$C_6 H_{12} O_6 \rightarrow 2C_2 H_5 OH + 2 CO_2$$

$C_6 H_{12} O_6$	$\rightarrow$	$2C_2 H_5 OH$	$+$	$2 CO_2$
100 parts		47–48 parts		48.9 parts
(hexose sugar)		(ethyl alcohol)		(carbon dioxide)

The balance of 3.1 to 4.1 parts is accounted for by glycerol, various aldehydes, volatile acids, esters and higher alcohols.

Alcoholic fermentation ceases when the supply of simple sugars is exhausted (the result being a bone-dry wine); when the alcoholic content reaches a point beyond which the yeast enzymes cannot operate (depending upon the initial sugar content of the must, the wine might be anything from dry to sweet); or when fermentation has been artificially stopped.

Fermentation may be terminated in a number of ways: by applying extreme heat (above

36°C yeast cells die, above 65°C the enzymes die – in extreme cold the yeasts are not harmed, but just become dormant and cause fermentation when the temperature rises sufficiently); by dosing with permitted additives (sulphur dioxide can actually encourage some yeasts to become active, therefore its use alone is insufficient, sorbic acid is very efficient in stabilising wine, especially sweet wine, but too much can cause an unpleasant geranium-like smell and is best used in conjunction with sulphur dioxide); by centrifuging the fermented wine or by extremely fine filtration (physically removing the micro-organisms); or by the addition of pure alcohol (thus artificially raising the alcoholic content to the point beyond which yeast enzymes cannot operate).

Depending on the style of wine made and the various traditional practices of vinification employed, after fermentation ceases the wine undergoes a certain ageing, a few weeks or a few years, in vat or cask before being bottled. During this time a deposit collects at the bottom of the vessel in which the wine is stored. This deposit is called the lees and contains dead yeast cells, bacteria, tartrates and numerous undesirable by-products of the fermentation process, the precise contents and proportions being dependent on the mode of vinification. If the wine is left in contact with the lees for an extended period of time there is a danger of bacterial spoilage due to yeast decomposition or autolysis (autolysis is, however, vital to the character of Champagne when it occurs inside the bottle after the secondary fermentation, but before *dégorgement*). The wine is, therefore, usually subjected to regular 'racking', where it is simply tapped-off free of its lees from one container to another.

Before the last racking the wine is either fined, or filtered, or both. Fining is the addition of an agent which attracts unwanted matter (gums, pectins, proteins, etc.) suspended in the wine, forming heavier combinations and thus dropping to the bottom with the rest of the lees.

Malo-lactic 'fermentation'

Not an alcoholic fermentation, this biochemical process converts the malic acid, a grape acid, into two parts lactic acid, an acid found in wine but not normally in grapes, and one part carbon dioxide. In this conversion small amounts of ethyl alcohol and acetic acid are also produced. Malo-lactic fermentation occurs naturally in some wines after the true alcoholic fermentation has finished.

The malic acid of the grape is reduced by cellular respiration during the ripening process, thus the further north a grape is grown, or the less ripe it is, the more malic acid it contains. Malic acid is a strong acid and is responsible for that sharp, refreshing crispness found in apples (hence the Latin appellation *malum* for apple).

Lactic acid, a weaker acid, is sometime called milk acid because it is the acid produced in sour milk by *Lactobacilli*. In low-acid wines lactic acid is undesirable because it may cause spoilage, but it can be useful in high-acid wine where it replaces the stronger malic acid.

Stronger acids like malic acid obviously have a sharper taste than the equivalent amount of a weaker acid and are less welcome in red wines than in white: in some white wines, such as *vinhos verdes* (the 'green wines' of Portugal), an obviously high malic acid content is considered desirable. Certain houses in Alsace deliberately avoid malo-lactic fermentation, the wines they produce are often hard and reserved in their youth, but last longer and soften with age, developing a greater depth of flavour than other Alsace wines which have undergone malo-lactic conversion. But as with so many aspects of wine, the preference of one style or another is simply one of personal taste.

In simple chemical terms malo-lactic fermentation is expressed as:

$$
\begin{array}{ccccc}
CH_2COOH & & CH_3 & & CO_2 \\
| & \rightarrow & | & + & \\
CHOHCOOH & & CHOHCOOH & & \text{(32.8 parts} \\
\text{(100 parts} & & \text{(67.2 parts} & & \text{carbon} \\
\text{malic acid)} & & \text{lactic acid)} & & \text{dioxide)}
\end{array}
$$

Before the days of temperature controlled wineries this malo-lactic conversion normally happened during the spring following the harvest, stimulated by the increasing warmth. In some cases the conditions required to activate this biochemical process took one, two or more years to develop, or never occurred. The conditions essential for malo-lactic fermentation are:

1 Temperature must be above 15°C.
2 Bacteria of the correct type must be present, the chief one being *Bacterium leuconostoc* (which used to be known as *Bacterium gracile*), although many other genera can convert malic acid to lactic acid.
3 Low sulphur dioxide is important if the lactic acid bacteria are not to be inhibited.
4 Nutrients are required by the bacteria. These particular nutrients are often to be found in the lees and racking is, therefore, often delayed until after the malo-lactic fermentation is complete.
5 pH levels outside the ideal range of between 3.2 and 3.4 can inhibit bacterial activity.

Without a favourable combination of the above conditions, malo-lactic fermentation does not occur. But just as yeast cultures may be used to start an alcoholic fermentation, so can cultures of suitable bacteria be utilised to ensure a malo-lactic fermentation. Modern wineries are, therefore, quite capable of inducing the conversion process at will.

The products of fermentation

The process of fermentation alters the constitution of grape juice, adding new compounds and changing the proportions of certain original ingredients.

Alcohol (C_2H_5OH)

There are many alcohols in wine but when considering the alcoholic content it is ethyl alcohol (also known as ethanol), and only ethyl alcohol, which is measured. Most wines contain between 8 and 14% alcohol.

Carbon dioxide (CO_2)

As one of the two major products of an alcoholic fermentation carbon dioxide is normally allowed to escape, unless deliberately restrained to produce a sparkling wine. However, in all good healthy wines a small amount remains dissolved as carbonic gas (H_2CO_3), enhancing the fruity flavour and giving a fresh taste in the mouth. In most countries white wines are considered to benefit more than red wines from a higher H_2CO_3 content (except for sparkling and semi-sparkling red wines), although all red wines need a very tiny amount in order not to seem dull, flat and lifeless.

Carbon dioxide is most noticeable at the *bouillage* stage of fermentation when large quantities of this gas are produced so rapidly that the wine appears to be boiling fiercely.

Glycerol ($C_3H_5[OH]_3$)

Glycerol is a viscous, colourless and odourless alcohol with a sweet taste. In most wines a glycerol content of between 0.5 and 1.5% by weight is found, although it can be, in the exceptional cases like the very sweet wines made from grapes affected by noble rot, as high as 3%.

Glycerol's sweetness is not usually detected below 1.5% and, as higher contents of glycerol are normally associated with sweet wines, its intrinsic sweetness is often swamped by the sugar. The effect of glycerol upon a wine's viscosity is minimal in the presence of ten times its amount of ethyl alcohol. At one time the so-called 'tears' or 'legs' in a wine (when swirled, some wines leave vertical threads of liquid clinging to the inside of the glass) were attributed to its glycerol content, but this has now been disproved (M. A. Amerine & E. B. Roessler, *Wines: Their Sensory Evaluation*, W. H. Freeman & Co., San Francisco, 1976) and it is in fact ethyl alcohol which is responsible. Ethyl alcohol, if suspended in water, produces long sinewy threads on the inside of the glass.

Aldehydes

Aldehydes are an intermediary stage between alcohols and acids, formed by the oxidation of alcohols. They are formed in small quantities during the normal fermentation process or in larger quantities by way of spoilage.

Acetaldehyde, the intermediary stage between ethyl alcohol and acetic acid, is the most important aldehyde in wine terms. In most low strength wines between 25 and 40 mg/l of acetaldehyde contributes essential wine flavours and aromas but larger amounts are undesirable, unstable, halfway to complete oxidation, evoke a sherry-like character and can turn very quickly into acetic acid. In a high strength wine like sherry the acetaldehyde content is nearer 200–300 mg/l, but it is stable and essential to the flavour and character of the wine.

Other aldehydes which are found in wines, but in very minute quantities, are: formaldehyde, propionaldehyde, cinnamaldehyde, cenanthaldehyde, capraldehyde, benzaldehyde, methyl-ethylketone and vanillin.

Volatile acids

Apart from carbon dioxide, the most common of volatile acids (sometimes called fatty acids) found in wine is acetic acid (CH_3COOH). Small amounts of acetic acid contribute positively to the attractive flavour of a wine and are produced by normal healthy alcoholic fermentations: 300–600 mg/l for white wines, 500–800 mg/l for red wines. Large amounts, in excess of 800–1,200 mg/l, are stable in high alcohol, deliberately oxidised wines like sherry, but too much acetaldehyde in low strength wines can, however, result in the production of excessive quantities of acetic acid by direct Cannizaric chemical reaction.

    Further volatile acids which may be found in wines include: butyric acid, propionic acid and formic acid.

Esters

While aldehydes are a half-way stage between alcohols and acids, esters are a combination of the two. Thus, whereas acetaldehyde is the mid-way product between the oxidation of ethyl alcohol and the formation of acetic acid, ethyl acetate ($CH_3COO.C_2H_5$) is the result of a combination of ethyl alcohol and acetic acid. In very low concentration ethyl acetate and other esters contribute to the fruity flavours of wine. Excess quantities can be less desirable, however: if ethyl acetate is allowed to dominate, it will give a wine the 'pear drop' smell of nail varnish (amyl acetate) or bubble-gum.

Higher alcohols

Higher alcohols, or fusel oils as they are sometimes called, are found in the minutest quantities in wine. Highly toxic in their pure form fusel oils are never produced in wine in even mildly harmful quantities. Amyl is by far the most predominant of these higher alcohols, followed by isoamyl, butyl, isobutyl, hexyl, propyl, etc.

Packing grapes into a traditional Champagne press
which works twenty-four hours a day during the harvest

Contrasting styles of vinification: cask-fermentation (LEFT) yields a complex Champagne which can be rich and biscuity with malic strength, while the hallmark of Champagne initially vinified in stainless steel under temperature-controlled conditions (BOTTOM) is one of freshness and uncomplicated fruit

8

The Champagne Method

Champagne is a wine in which adulteration is most obvious to such as are
well acquainted with it in the genuine state, and it is adulterated in England
with more boldness than any other.

Cyrus Redding, *A History and Description of Modern Wines*, 1833

THE CHAMPAGNE PROCESS, OR *Méthode Champenoise*, is merely a sophistication of the
commonly held art of winemaking, with the addition that the wine is allowed to ferment a
second time in the bottle to attain its sparkling character. At the start of the winemaking
process two crucial factors will affect quality: time and temperature. *Débourbage* takes
about ten to twelve hours, although there are various techniques which can shorten its
duration. If fermentation does not commence soon after this cleansing operation, an
undue amount of oxidation will result, turning the must into a noticeably ruddy-brown
colour.

Oxidation inevitably commences from the moment a grape is pressed. In itself it is not
harmful, but it is the *rate* at which it happens which can be damaging to wine. Some
degree of oxidation is essential to wine – the chemical and biochemical reactions which
occur as a result of the slow pace of oxidation form the myriad of complexities we call
maturation – but it must be tightly controlled by the winemaker from the start if its
progress when bottled is to be good and slow.

Excessive oxidation and bacterial spoilage can result from pressing grapes which are too
warm, or from vinifying hot musts. Even in Champagne the grapes harvested on a sunny
autumn day can be detrimentally hot, especially if left for hours outside a busy presshouse.
Cooling the must between pressing and *débourbage* is therefore recommended: it both
reduces the rate of oxidation and speeds up the cleansing process, and most modern
installations in Champagne are now equipped for this.

The first fermentation

From the cleansing vats and *débourbage* the wine is transported by pump, gravity or road
tanker to the fermentation vat. Many Champagne houses today employ the carefully
regulated, temperature-controlled, stainless steel vats for the fermentation process. Vats of
concrete, glass, enamel, epoxy resin and fibreglass can also be found, but they are on the
decline. Oak casks, once traditional in Champagne, are rarely used. Except for Krug and
Alfred Gratien which still ferment entirely in oak, and Bollinger which ferments one third

of its wines in oak, it is generally only the small growers who perpetuate its use in Champagne today, employing either the 205-litre *pièces* or the 1,000-litre-plus *foudres*; occasionally intermediary vessels like the 600-litre-*demi-muid* are also used.

The essential difference between Champagnes fermented in stainless steel vats and those fermented in oak is their relative rates of oxidation. The fresh oak characteristics deliberately sought by other winemakers – whether in Bordeaux, Burgundy, Rioja or California – are obviously not sought in Champagne. Oak casks average thirty years of life in Champagne, compared to maybe three years elsewhere. The slightest hint of an 'oaky' character would bring despair, even to oak enthusiasts like Krug, who would consider it ungainly, unbalanced and lacking in the finesse for which Champagne is so well known. Oak casks in Champagne mean permeability. They must be be watertight but they are obviously not airtight: when filled, the staves swell to prevent seepage, restricting the penetration of air (which is 21% oxygen) but not preventing it. As the Krugs say, 'the results are better for the type of Champagne we want to produce', giving characteristics of bouquet and flavour which are achieved through the 'breathing' facility of their oak barrels.

It must be emphasised that the increased rate of oxidation during a fermentation carried out in wood is not detrimentally fast, but merely 'faster' than that which takes place in less permeable vessels. Cask-fermented Champagnes and, for that matter, Champagnes which are initially fermented in non-porous containers like stainless steel, but subsequently matured in wood, acquire an increased acetaldehyde content and possess additional aldehydes and esters. The difference can be detected on the nose by an experienced taster and gives rise to descriptions such as biscuity (wholemeal, digestive or crumbly), nutty (hazelnuts or walnuts, but not almonds) and toasty (although this may well be a varietal characteristic of the Chardonnay grape). Good Champagne should, however, never reveal a sherry-like aroma which is the result of too high a level of acetaldehyde due to a precociously advanced state of oxidation induced, probably, by poor handling techniques in cask.

Cask-fermented Champagnes can be stunning examples of their kind, but in general only small growers and houses with a limited production can afford the time, space and labour necessary to nurse each barrel of wine to perfection. As the vast bulk of Champagne is produced by a relatively small number of very big houses, the larger, cleaner, stainless steel vats are obviously better suited to their needs, guaranteeing fresher and fruitier wines than those fermented in wood.

The temperature at which fermentation takes place varies according to the vessel used and control techniques applied, but between 18 and 20° would be normal for an establishment employing modern stainless steel vats. It should be realised that the temperature of fermentation is only initially influenced by the temperature of the must: some 60% of the energy released by the process of fermentation is given off in heat and it is this heat generated during the process which has to be countered by temperature control techniques. The three principal techniques employed in Champagne to cool stainless steel vats are: *ruissellement*, or the trickling of cold water down the side of a vat; *glycol*, the use of two or three hollow bands wrapped around the circumference of a vat carrying a super-cold liquid called glycol; and *environmental control*, where the temperature of the winery itself is controlled, a facility which might be used in conjunction with direct means of cooling vats.

Fermentation usually lasts for about ten days, although at Billecart-Salmon, a small *grande marque* in Mareuil-sur-Aÿ, it lasts for one month, the reason being that they carefully maintain a temperature of just 8°C throughout the entire fermentation process.[*] During fermentation the must might be enriched with sugar, an operation called chaptalisation. This is quite common in Champagne's lean climate and is best carried out in a series of small doses which are applied while the fermentation process is well underway. At the time of writing the EEC proposes to outlaw chaptalisation in 1989 in favour of grape concentrate (which affects the flavour) or rectified grape concentrate (which is supposed not to affect the flavour) manufactured from Europe's excess grape production in an attempt to reduce the EEC's wine lake, but there is much opposition to this.

Evaporation inevitably occurs during the *bouillage* stage of fermentation, the quantities extracted during pressing being reduced as follows:

	After pressing	*After bouillage*
Cuvée	2,050 litres	2,000 litres
Première taille	410 litres	400 litres
Deuxième taille	205 litres	200 litres

In a perfect situation, until *assemblage*, the wines are kept separate during the fermentation and maturation processes according to grape variety, village of origin, and whether the wines are *vin de cuvée* or *vin de taille*. But the degree of separation possible will depend on the ratio of vats (and their respective sizes) to the total volume of production. Obviously, with his larger number of small casks the traditionalist has the ideal facilities for the job.

During the winter months, up until the time of *assemblage*, the wine is racked twice and malo-lactic fermentation may be encouraged. Racking is simply the practice of running the wine off its sediment from one container to another and derives its name from the day when this operation would be conducted by gravity from one rack of casks to another, lower, rack.

Assemblage

Champagne's critical operation of *assemblage* is a highly skilled and painstaking performance. To consistently blend together one wine which accurately reflects the house style, a non-vintage Champagne, out of the annually endless variety of elements, is a vinicultural feat admired by oenologists the world over.

The *chef de caves*, or cellarmaster, does the important groundwork, making recommendations based not only on his years of experience, but on the behaviour of the wines

[*] The pros and cons of a longer, cooler fermentation are:
Pros: Less susceptible to bacterial spoilage; requires less SO$_2$; wines contain less volatile acidity and more aromatics and possess greater tartrate stability.
Cons: Lower glycerine and extract content; reduced effervescence and relatively expensive.

currently maturing in his cellar. He sets up tasting after tasting, some wines of which eventually go into the final blend in various proportions. In some cases it is the *chef de caves* who is responsible for the final decision, but it is often the head of the firm, one of the directors, and sometimes a consensus of a panel.

When constructing the blend most houses start from a rough formula: a certain *cépage* or proportion of grape varieties coming from specific villages it has been traditional to use. This may be controlled by the firm's vineyard holding, or by a commitment by contract to purchase grapes from numerous growers. But even the most thoroughly planned blends may need to be adapted after the arbitrary hazards of frost, rot, hail or insects have taken their toll.

In addition to natural disasters, even favourable harvests can pose problems. A great harvest requires that a certain proportion has to be put aside for use as vintage Champagne. The choice and quality of wines has to be carefully worked out. Even vintage Champagnes have to be blended, albeit from one year's wines. The final blend must convey both the quality and character of the year and also the house identity. In deciding how much vintage wine to put to one side, every house is restricted by law to no more than 80% of its total produce. This ensures that reserves of wines for blending future non-vintage Champagnes always benefit from at least 20% of the very best the region can produce.

The task for the *chef de caves* is a difficult one: most houses offer a range of Champagnes which could include a Cuvée de Prestige, a Blanc de Blancs, a Blanc de Noirs, and a Rosé, and each can be either vintage or non-vintage.

After the final blend has been effected on a model basis in the laboratory and checked for stability by chemical and biological analysis, the job of *assemblage* is carried out in massive vats (even in the case of traditional houses practising cask-fermenting or cask-maturing), each of which has a large internal propeller that drowsily rotates, thoroughly marrying the different wines.

The blending together of numerous wines with different chemical properties encourages a further fall of waste matter and the wine must undergo a third and final racking. But before this is accomplished, the wine is fined. Fining encourages the fall of various suspended particles which have not dropped out in the natural course of events.

The most common fining agent used in Champagne is gelatine; it is purchased commercially and may be of fish or animal origin. Gelatine uses primarily electrolytic reaction to remove unwanted matter suspended in wine: the positively charged gelatine attracts the negatively charged waste matter, and the greater density of the coagulated particles then falls to the bottom of the vat. Negatively charged tannin combines with the gelatine to propel the electrolytic process into motion, but as Champagne has a very low tannin content naturally, it has to be added.

An increasing number of Champagne producers are using a clay called bentonite for fining. Its active ingredient for the precipitation of wine sediments is a volcanic ash derivitive called montmorillonite. The reaction of montmorillonite in wine is also an electrolytic one but, as its charge is of the opposite polarity to gelatine, the prime use of bentonite is to fine out a positively charged protein haze. Depending on the wine to be fined, its use may be in conjunction with gelatine and tannin, or completely separate.

Another fining agent, isinglass, is preferred by some houses, including Bollinger and Krug. As it reacts well in low tannin wines, it is ideal for Champagne. Other fining agents are also employed in Champagne, but are less commonly used.

Many houses subject their wines to a cold stabilisation treatment where the temperature is dropped to −4°C for 8–10 days to precipitate the formation of tartrate crystals. Without such precautions calcium tartrate and potassium bi-tartrate crystals, soluble at normal temperatures, could form in Champagnes stored in very cold conditions. Tartrates are harmless and the *cognoscente* would not be bothered one way or the other by the presence of crystals. Most drinkers are, however, unenlightened in these matters and liable to object, thus manufacturers attempt to preclude such possibilities. A relatively recent technique has evolved which cuts down the duration to just a few days. This involves seeding the wine with a solution of 3–5% ground tartrate crystals which quickly generates the crystal forming process.

At this stage in the Champagne-making process we have a rather dry, but unremarkable white wine called a *vin clair*, fully fermented in the traditional, but universally practised winemaking method. The style and quality of this base wine is generally disappointing – over-acidic, clumsy and unbalanced – but it is exactly those qualities which, when lifted by the *prise de mousse*, will provide all the excitement, panache and perfect balance of a fine sparkling wine. From now on, the methods used will be those of the *Méthode Champenoise*, or Champagne method.

Addition of the *liqueur de tirage*

After the final racking the wine is transferred to the bottling line, but before bottling takes place the *liqueur de tirage*, or bottling liquor – a mixture of wine, sugar and selected yeast culture – is added to the base wine. The purpose of the *liqueur de tirage*, which may also include various yeast nutrients, is to stimulate a second alcoholic fermentation. This fermentation takes place, not in vats, nor in casks, but in bottles. Since there are some sparkling wines made by the so-called 'transfer method', which entails a second alcoholic fermentation in the bottle after which the wine is then decanted, filtered and re-bottled under pressure, it should be emphasised that the bottle in which Champagne and for that matter any *Méthode Champenoise* wine undergoes its second fermentation is precisely the same bottle in which it is later sold.

The traditional type of sugar still preferred by some for the *liqueur* is cane sugar although for the biochemical process of fermentation there is no difference between the sucrose of cane sugar and the sucrose of beet sugar. Beet sugar is, however, the type used today because it is cheaper to buy and easier to obtain, with a ready supply cultivated on the plains around Champagne.

Sugar (or sucrose) is a necessary ingredient in the *liqueur de tirage* because all base wines for champagne are dry and completely devoid of fermentable sugars. In a few exceptional cases, however, some producers may opt for a base wine with some residual sugar, therefore the amount added at the time of the *liqueur de tirage* will be adjusted accordingly.

Abnormally hot years can provide base wines with an alcoholic strength of over 10–

11.5%. Champagnes which are too high in alcohol are considered to lack balance and elegance, but there is a more fundamental reason why base wines should not be so strong: even the highly developed yeast cultures of Champagne have difficulty functioning under great osmotic pressure in the presence of more than 13.5% alcohol. Some strains are more able than others, but most find it impossible to secrete the necessary enzymes in bottle-fermented wines approaching 14% alcohol.

Although in many years the base wines produced in Champagne require assistance by chaptalisation, in a very few – just three since the last war: 1947, 1959 and 1976 – base wines of 13–14% were common. In such instances a producer might decide to stop the first alcoholic fermentation before all the sugar is converted to alcohol and reduce the *liqueur* accordingly, or to blend in weaker wines from less favourable years, or effect a combination of both. As is not the case in other wine-producing regions of France, a vintage wine in Champagne must be entirely of the year stated. Although technically illegal, the addition of a little wine from other years is occasionally practised by some houses for vintage Champagne, whether exceptionally hot ones or otherwise. I also know of at least one producer genuinely unaware of the full extent of the regulations concerning vintage Champagne.

The *liqueur de tirage* is usually added in a ratio of 50 kilograms of sugar to 100 litres of *liqueur*, that is 33.33 litres of sugar to 66.66 litres of wine. A *liqueur* of this ratio is said to have a 50% saturation. In general, the *liqueur* will give the *cuvée* 22–24 grams of sugar to every litre of wine to be fermented. This will result in a 1.2–1.3% increase in alcohol and sufficient carbonic gas to effect a pressure of between 4.9 and 5.3 atmospheres. (An atmosphere is a unit of pressure, 1 atmosphere being the equivalent to the atmospheric pressure experienced at sea-level, ie, 15 pounds per square inch. Measurements of pressure vary according to temperature – all measurements given in this text are as at 20°C.) As the sugar content permitted at the *liqueur de tirage* stage (including any natural residual grape sugar in the base wine) is restricted to a maximum of 27 g/l, the amount of alcohol and carbonic gas produced during the secondary fermentation is also restricted. Through this indirect control, the alcohol achieved by the *liqueur de tirage* cannot be more than 1.5% by volume and the greatest pressure of *mousse* possible is 6 atmospheres.

Dosed with a suitable amount of *liqueur*, the wines are bottled and capped with a temporary closure. The *liège et agrafe*, or cork and metal clasp, was once the only method of seal used for Champagne while undergoing fermentation in bottle, but crown-caps with plastic inserts are now virtually universal. The *liège et agrafe* might still be used by a few firms for a special *cuvée*, particularly a limited production of a *cuvée de prestige* (special upmarket brands like Taittinger's Comtes de Champagne for example), but these distinctive seals are mostly reserved for the various Coteaux Champenois today.

The crown-cap was initially treated with suspicion by many famous Champagne houses, but after lengthy experimentation, even great traditionalists like Bollinger began to adopt the use of these beer-bottle tops.

A plastic insert is fitted into the neck of the bottle and secured by the crown-cap. This insert is shaped like a flanged pot, its purpose to catch the sediment produced by the second fermentation. Inside the cap there is a thin wafer of cork which acts as a cushion and prevents any rust forming on the glass lip.

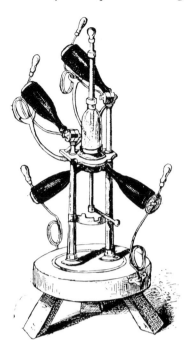

A nineteenth-century
dosing machine

Despite the claim of some writers to the contrary, there is no contact between the wine and the cap's slither of cork. In the first place this is because the cap's sole job is to hold the plastic pot tightly in place, effectively sealing the neck, thus allowing no wine to seep out around the insert's flange. In the second place, the cork itself is covered by plastic-coated paper, the diameter of which is wider than the hole in the bottle's neck.

There are various grades of crown-cap which have been tested, but those currently in use fall into two major categories and their effectiveness differs. The cheapest are usually made of aluminium and maintain a reasonable seal for three years, after which time the aluminium gradually oxidises, loosening the cap's grip on the bottle. This grade is suitable for non-vintage Champagnes. The more expensive are normally stainless steel and these perform well for between five and seven years and are therefore recommended for vintage or prestige Champagnes. After seven years it is not the stainless steel cap which deteriorates but the plastic insert. No doubt advances will be made and superior plastics created, enabling the use of less degradable inserts, but in the meantime Champagne houses wanting to keep wines *sur pointes* (after *remuage*, before *dégorgement*, the bottles are stacked in an inverted vertical position with necks lodged in the punts of the bottles beneath) for a considerable length of time will have to rely on the tried and trusted *liège et agrafe*.

It is possible to tell at a glance whether a Champagne being served has been capped or corked. A crown-cap requires a lipped bottle-neck, whereas the metal clasp which secures a cork requires an exaggerated ring moulded into the bottle-neck around which it can grip.

Creating the 'sparkle' or the *prise de mousse*

Once bottled and capped, the wines pass along the automatic line to a mechanical device which shakes each bottle, ensuring an even dispersal of the *liqueur de tirage*. At this point, many of the lines make a 90° downward turn carrying the bottles, perpendicularly attached to the vertical track, through a hole in the ground to the next floor.

The wines are then stacked *sur lattes* in the deepest *caves* (many of which, in Champagne, were constructed by tunnelling between *crayères* – chalk pits dug in the Gallo-Roman period to provide building materials) while the second fermentation takes place. In many firms, stacking the wines *sur lattes* merely entails packing the wines horizontally in pallets. In others it refers to the traditional horizontal stacking of bottles into massive piles, each row of bottles separated from the one above and the one below by thin strips of wood called laths or *lattes*.

Whether in pallets of a few hundred bottles or in piles of a hundred thousand, it is important that Champagne undergoing the *prise de mousse* should be stored in the deepest *caves* available. The deeper a firm's cellars are cut into the chalk subsoil, the cooler and less variable the temperature. Cooler temperatures cause slower fermentations and slower second fermentations result in better sparkling wines with greater aromatic

Nineteenth-century illustration of the excavation of Deutz and Geldermann's new cellars at Aÿ

Bottles stacked *sur lattes*

properties, more complex flavours and smaller bubbles. The ideal temperature for the second fermentation of any sparkling wine is a constant one between 10 and 12°C.

Most of the second fermentation process is over within two weeks, but the final stages, hampered by the high osmotic pressure, can draw out much longer. It is possible to encourage completion of the process in less than ten days, but when a top *cuvée* is placed in a deep cellar, it may be left there for as long as three months.

During the *prise de mousse* the *sur lattes* piles are dismantled and restacked several times, at which juncture each bottle is briefly but briskly shaken, an operation called *poignetage*. This shaking is because the deposit during the second fermentation tends to fall in layers. These layers consist of various waste products that may range from harmless granular matter to extremely sticky sediments. The sticky sediments can prove difficult to remove at the *remuage* stage, and shaking the bottles disturbs the layered sediment into a less sticky whole. If the wines are stored on pallets the dismantling and restacking operation may be achieved by fork-lift truck. Seeing these pallet-burdened fork-lift trucks whizz about the cellars, it is easy to understand why it is unneccessary to undertake the labour-intensive task of shaking each bottle.

Occasionally one comes across a shattered bottle in the *sur lattes* piles, but the occurrence is much less frequent than when Patrick Forbes was writing about Champagne in 1967: 'the modern Champagne-maker considers himself lucky if loss through breakage is less than half of one per cent' (Patrick Forbes, *Champagne*, p. 320); the figure today would be nearer to one in two thousand. Since the force exerted inside a *grand mousseux* or fully sparkling Champagne is equivalent to the pressure inside a tyre of a double-decker bus, it is small wonder that breakages of up to 50% were commonplace in the eighteenth century.

Remuage

From the *sur lattes* piles, the bottles are transferred to *pupitres*, two hinged heavy rectangular boards containing sixty holes, each of which has been bored at an angle of 45°. The cut of these holes will allow a bottle to be held by the neck in any position from horizontal, through 90°, to vertical. Traditionally *pupitres* were made of wood, but concrete casted boards are now quite common.

To begin with, the bottles in the *pupitres* are barely sloping, but each day a *remueur* gives each bottle a sharp twist back and forth (to loosen the sediment's adhesion to the bottle), a slight turn to the left or right of maybe an eighth of a revolution (to ensure that the sediment settles on a different section of the bottle's inner surface) and a gentle nudge upwards (to encourage the sediment to move down the bottle towards the plastic pot held by the crown-cap).

Some *remueurs* perform each operation separately, others effect a combination, but they all glide over the contents of a *pupitre* with astounding accuracy in just a few seconds, appearing to barely touch each one of the sixty bottles. After numerous nudges upwards over a period of several weeks, or a few months, the bottle will eventually reach an upright, inverted position. The sediment will be neatly deposited in the plastic pot and the wine will be ready for *dégorgement*.

Mechanical methods of *remuage* are also becoming increasingly widely used. Whether computer-controlled or manually operated, all forms of mechanical *remuage* follow the basic principle of the Catalan 'Girasol', called a *gyropalette* in Champagne. After the *prise de mousse* a pallet, which contains 504 bottles, is placed on an octangular base, the bottle-necks facing downwards. Every eight hours the pallet is moved across the axis of the base, each movement causing the sediment to spiral down the inner surface of the bottles. In this way *remuage* can be reduced from two to three months duration to just one week.

Despite the obvious success of mechanical *remuage* some houses still feel that the manual, labour-intensive system is more effective and retain their highly-skilled *remueurs* for their top *cuvées*, marketing them, of course, as wines made by purely traditional methods. Other smaller establishments have opted for hand-operated systems to lessen the redundancy problem. Both methods, if applied correctly, are effective.

Stacking *sur pointes*

After *remuage* the bottles are ready for disgorging to facilitate the removal of their sediments, but many will undergo an ageing period *sur pointes*. In the case of cheaper Champagnes disgorging the sediment happens soon after the minimum sixty-day *prise de mousse* period. The more expensive Champagnes are stacked vertically, though still inverted, in large piles with the neck (*pointe*) of each bottle lodged in the punt of the bottle beneath.

Better-quality Champagnes undergo the *prise de mousse* and *remuage* in the deepest cellars

The benefit of ageing *sur pointes* is two-fold: first, the wine's flavour and bouquet benefit from an extended contact with the yeasty sediments; second, its longevity is improved by avoiding an early *dégorgement*. During the disgorging operation the wine is exposed to the air when the temporary closure is removed; this obviously results in an increased rate of oxidation. The exposure to the air is very short and the increase in the rate of oxidation very slight, but it is sufficient to affect the potential ageing capability of the wine. No Champagne, therefore, whether cheap or expensive, is ever disgorged until absolutely necessary ie, until it is required for shipping.

Most ordinary non-vintage Champagnes remain *sur pointes* for just a few months, perhaps a year, although some houses like to allow two or three years. Vintage Champagnes may be left four or five years, while for some prestige *cuvées*, whether non-vintage like Laurent Perrier's Grand Siècle or vintage like Bollinger's Tradition RD, the duration can be much longer. The period of ageing before *dégorgement* gives Champagne the qualities of autolysis by which its greatness can be measured. This autolytic character can be recognised in a fine Champagne of relatively youthful age by a clean yeasty aroma which, with a little more maturity, will evolve into a slightly fuller, often sweeter, bouquet reminiscent of fresh baked *brioche* paste, but the potential of a great Champagne finally emerges as a deep, mature character which is rich and has a biscuity or nutty complexity. Any youthful sparkling wine can be rendered more drinkable by giving it a year or two in bottle after *dégorgement*, but it is only through an extended ageing period before *dégorgement* that its basic quality may be improved.

Disgorging or *dégorgement*

There are two basic methods of disgorging: *à la volée* and *à la glace*. The first, *à la volée*, is the oldest, involving the use of a curved blade to remove the *agrafe* and a pair of pincers to extract the cork. The *dégorgeur*, who wears a leather apron and a face mask for protection against the possibility of an exploding bottle, works in front of a *guerite*, half a barrel on a stand used for catching the cork and sediment. He carefully holds each bottle upside down to avoid disturbing the sediment. With a quick flick of the wrist, the *agrafe* is removed and, after a little wriggle, the cork is propelled into the *guérite*, immediately followed by the sediment.

The art is in timing when to bring the bottle upright – too early and some of the sediment remains in the bottle, too late and valuable Champagne gushes out. Another difficulty (as I discovered when trying to perform *à la volée* on a thirty-year-old Champagne at the house of Philipponnat) is that the heads of very old corks can disintegrate while the *agrafe* is being removed.

The second method, *à la glace*, although not as ancient as *à la volée* has, nevertheless, been in use since 1891. The necks of the bottles are dipped two or three inches into a tank of freezing brine (calcium chloride prevents the water from solidifying). There seems to be no uniformity of temperature and duration for this process: the temperature of the brine can vary between $-15°$ and $-30°C$, and the length of time the bottles remain dipped in this freezing mixture ranges from three to twenty-five minutes. There appears to be no oenological reason to influence producers in their choice between colder temperatures for shorter durations and less severe temperatures for longer durations. Most temperature/duration combinations are arrived at in order to match the capacity of the bottling line in question.

As the bottles emerge from the brine they are turned the right way up, with no ill-effect, as the freezing sediment adheres to the crown-cap's plastic pot. They then pass along the automatic line to a bottle-opening robot. With a sharp popping noise the caps are speedily removed and each plastic pot containing the sediment is propelled out of its bottle by the internal pressure within.

The sediment is not in fact a frozen pellet but a semi-frozen slush, the colour and texture of fine wet sand. As one looks at the bottles after they have been dipped in the freezing brine, they appear to contain solid blocks of frozen wine. But this is an illusion created by a thin film of soft ice coating the inner surface of the bottle's neck. Although not made of solid ice it is sufficiently robust for the slush to adhere to the top of the bottle for the few minutes that it takes to reach the bottle-opening plant.

À la glace is obviously the most universally practised method in Champagne today, *à la volée* being reserved for wines that have undergone a second fermentation using the traditional *liège et agrafe* seal. But even then, most houses will modify this form of disgorging by using freezing brine.

Addition of the *liqueur d'expédition*

At this stage the bottles of Champagne are on the production line, but with no cork. They need to be both topped up and finally sealed. The opportunity is also taken to dose the wine with sugar in the form of the *liqueur d'expédition*, or shipping liquor.

Most Champagnes are non-vintage Brut wines and, even after two or three years ageing *sur pointes*, they are green and raw, due to the relatively high acidity essential for fine sparkling wines. So-called Ultra Brut, Brut Non Dosage, Brut Sauvage and Brut Zero wines are not dosed, but all regular Brut Champagnes are. In general the older the product, the less dosage required: vintage Champagnes have smaller doses than non-vintage and when old vintages are disgorged they rarely have any dosage at all, merely being topped up with the same wine from other bottles.

The *liqueur d'expédition* contains wine (usually the same or similar *cuvée* as the Champagne being dosed), sugar (cane sugar is preferred) and grape spirit (rarely used, its function being to bolster the alcoholic strength of very sweet Champagnes).

It is usual to talk in percentage terms when discussing relative doses of the *liqueur d'expédition*, comparing the 0.75% dosed Brut of one house with the 1% dosed Brut of another, but the sugar content of the *liqueur* may vary between 50 and 75 kilograms per 100 litres. The only sensible comparisons are those which use residual sugar (grams per litre) of the finished Champagne.

The various terminologies in use to describe the relative sweetness of a Champagne can be confusing. The table below, however, sets out the approved sugar levels and their official appellations which are legally binding for Champagne:

French term	Residual sugar (grams per litre)	Translation	Realistic description
Brut	Less than 15	Raw or bone dry	Can vary between dry and very dry
Extra Sec	12–20	Extra dry	Can vary between dry and medium dry
Sec	17–35	Dry	Can vary between medium and medium sweet
Demi Sec	35–50	Semi dry	Sweet
Doux	More than 50	Sweet	Intensely sweet, virtually non-existent

Such flexible limits are crucial when dealing with sparkling wines, in order to achieve the balance between acidity and sugar which is so vital to the relative sweetness perceived by the palate.

Each firm obviously makes full use of this flexibility for reasons of house style and, in some instances, when bottling for specific world markets. The flexibility is particularly apparent for the Brut category of non-vintage wines. It is the house style that puts, for example, Bollinger and Krug at the driest end of the Brut scale and Veuve Clicquot at the sweeter end. I generally prefer my Bruts to be very dry, but Veuve Clicquot Brut, in particular, has the weight, acidity and richness of flavour to balance the extra sugar content, not always apparent in other sweeter Champagnes.

Most firms put larger doses of sugar in Champagnes being shipped to hot or third world countries where the conditions the wines will have to endure before being consumed are either unfavourable or uncertain. Some countries prefer Champagne sweeter or drier than others. In 1882 Henry Vizetelly noted in his *A History of Champagne*: 'The saccharine addition varies according to the market for which the wine is destined: thus the high-class English buyer demands a dry Champagne, the Russian a wine sweet and strong as a "ladies' grog", and the Frenchman and German a sweet light wine.' He later adds: 'Instances have been known of additions of 25 and even 30 per cent of liqueur, though the average may be taken to be for Germany and France, 15 to 18 per cent; America, 10 to 15 per cent; England, 2 to 6 per cent.'

Finally, the standards of dosage held by each firm change with fashion. The trends may barely be recognised at the time, yet while nobody would argue that a traditional Champagne today is Brut, connoisseurs of the past would have been adamant that traditionally it was sweet in the nineteenth century, dry in the eighteenth century and 'still'

A *doseur* in the late nineteenth century

in the seventeenth century. The current trend is for ever lighter, ever drier wines; yet surveys show that while most people look for dry on the label, some sweetness is generally desired in the bottle.

Corking and labelling

After being topped up with the *liqueur d'expédition* the bottles quickly move along the production line to be corked. Many people are surprised at the cylindrical shape of an unused Champagne cork expecting to see the mushroom-like form of a used Champagne cork. But it is not until a cork is put into a Champagne bottle that it assumes its familiar shape. The first thrust of the corking machine drives the cork half-way in and the bottle emerges with a peculiar cone-shaped section jutting from the neck. Further along the line it receives another pulverising blow and a metal cap is placed onto the cork: – it is the combination of the two acts which gives the Champagne cork its mushroom-like head. Both cork and bottle-neck are then clasped together with a wire muzzle (the function of the metal cap is to prevent the muzzle from severing the cork).

At one time Champagne corks were made from a single piece of cork, but today they consist of an upper part of agglomerated cork and one, two or three discs of natural cork

Further operations as carried out in the nineteenth century:

LEFT Corking
BELOW LEFT Putting the wire muzzle on cork and bottle-neck

BELOW Evolution of the Champagne cork: 1) unused cylinder shape; 2) the mushroom shape (*juponne*) indicates recently bottled Champagne, maybe two to three years old in this case; and 3) the straight-sided (*cheville*) cork which suggests a well matured bottle

which are in contact with the wine. The more discs there are, the better the grade of cork. Entirely agglomerated corks are sometimes attached to BOB (Buyer's Own brand) Champagnes.

After being corked each bottle is automatically shaken (to ensure complete diffusion of the *liqueur d'expédition*) and, unless sent back down to the cellars for further ageing, labelled in full glory. Champagne is well known for its attractive *habillage* of foil and label; very few can be described as gaudy, and even the humblest grower in Champagne has an innate sense of style.

Except for the best *cuvées* which are often kept a while before shipping, the Champagne is now ready for sale. Some countries like Britain have a tradition of giving Champagne a year's ageing on landing, but few firms are able to maintain the practice. It is always advisable to give Champagne, especially non-vintage Champagne, a year or two of extra ageing before drinking it. During the final resting period the alcohol combines with various acids to create esters which are important to the change in bouquet and flavour.

9

Styles of Champagne and Other Wines and Spirits of the Region

Lily on liquid roses floating!
So floats yon foam o'er pink Champagne!
Fain would I join such pleasant boating,
And prove that ruby main,
And float away on wine!

John Kenyon, 1837

AFTER EACH CATEGORY IN THIS CHAPTER I will offer a personal choice of houses that I believe make leading examples of the different styles of wine. Sometimes a producer might make more than one *cuvée* of a certain category and in these cases it is advisable to check under the house in question. Regarding the vintage years, the Champagnes will naturally vary in character according to the year but while there are bound to be discrepancies, the houses I select have all shown consistent form. Entries marked ^{V}, however, offer particularly good value, while those marked ^{Q} are outstanding in quality.

Non-Vintage or *Sans Année*

Non-vintage (NV) Champagne must have a minimum 'total' alcoholic content (which includes the actual alcohol plus the potential alcohol – the residual sugar which could still be fermented out) of at least 10% in volume, including any *liqueur d'expédition*, and cannot be sold until it is at least one year of age – although this period could be extended to fifteen months in the not too distant future. As this applies to the youngest wine in a blend, most are much older and many non-vintage Champagnes have an average age which ranges from between two and three years.

There are several houses making non-vintage Champagne of a disappointing or variable quality (their numbers swelled in the early 1980s after the short harvests of 1978, 1980 and 1981) yet possess individual de luxe or vintage *cuvées* of an exceptional character and style. This is unfortunate since the reputation of a house generally depends on the quality and the consistency of its non-vintage Champagne.

It is difficult to gauge the precise percentage that non-vintage represents of all Champagne produced as this varies enormously depending upon the number of vintage years. Some say 80%, others estimate the figure to be nearer 90%.

In most regions blending is frowned upon and the best wines are made on one estate and from a single vintage. In Champagne the traditional view could not be more contrasting –

the most classic Champagnes are a blend of different grape varieties from different areas and from different harvests. Vintage Champagnes fetch an extra premium because the public demand it, but because of Champagne's variable harvests, the harmonious blend of different years permits the producers to provide far better non-vintage wines. While non-vintage Champagnes are not necessarily the finest wines in a particular house's selection, they are capable of being so, and in specific vintages where the character of the wines might not suit an individual's taste (for example, lovers of light elegant Champagnes could find the 1976 too heavy) it is sensible to pay less and to buy the non-vintage.

As non-vintage Champagnes are produced every year, it is quite obvious that the bulk of the blend will be from the current vintage, thus non-vintage blends are often described in this book as being 1980-based, or 1981-based, etc., depending upon the year in question.

Leading NV Brut producers　Barancourt^Q, Boizel, Bollinger^Q, de Castellane^V, Veuve Clicquot, Collery, Deutz, Charles Heidsieck, Heidsieck & Co. Monopole, Piper Heidsieck, Henriot, Krug^Q, Laurent-Perrier^V, Joseph Perrier, Philipponnat^V, Pommery, Louis Roederer, Ruinart and de Venoge^V

Leading NV demi-sec producers　Ayala^{VQ}, Veuve Clicquot, Mumm

Leading NV doux producer　Louis Roederer (this is the only house I know of which still makes a Doux Champagne, although there may be other less well-known producers)

Vintage or *Millésimé*

Opinions differ as to when the first vintage or, in French, *millésimé* Champagne was declared. André Simon, in *The History of the Champagne Trade in England* (1905), names Perrier-Jouët as one of the first houses to indicate a vintage on the label and mentions that George Goulet sold a vintaged 1870; yet he goes on to mention that the Ayala Very Dry 1865 received much acclaim, being favoured by the Prince of Wales at the Bullingdon Club, which suggests that the superiority of certain years above others was widely acknowledged by the second part of the nineteenth century. The first vintage Champagne mentioned in a Christie's catalogue was Moët's Sillery 1815; I have also seen a Claude Moët 1743 Vin Mousseux – there are no doubt many such examples.

André Simon explained the succession of vintages being declared at the turn of the century, 1892/3/5/8/9 and 1900, as being due to 'the public [which has] now been educated to ask for a vintage in preference to a non-vintage Champagne ... so that some shippers have decided to ship nothing but vintage wines.'

Branding the vintage on Champagne corks also became a common occurrence in the late nineteenth century, the British publication *Wine Trade Review* having urged the practice in its issue of 15 December 1880.

The actual alcoholic content of vintage Champagne must be at least 11% by volume at the time of sale, the potential alcohol derived from any residual sugar present being in addition. It cannot be released for sale until at least three years old, but as a brief survey of the current vintages on offer should reveal, the minimum age is usually nearer five years.

Not more than 80% of the harvest in question may be sold as vintage Champagne; this conserves at least 20% of the best years for future blending of non-vintage wines, thus perpetuating high standards for basic Champagnes too. Vintage Champagnes should always reflect the characteristics of the year in question and yet maintain a definite house style, but on occasion the conflict betwen these two stipulations is too great to be resolved. All vintage Champagnes must by law contain only wine of the declared vintage; however, a number of producers have blended in tiny amounts of wines from other years (much smaller proportions than for the non-vintages), an illegal but, I would say, commendable practice. A perfect vintage year in Champagne simply does not exist and a tiny admixture of other wines is often a wise step to redress the balance of a particular vintage without altering its overall style.

Bollinger has labelled its vintage Champagne *Grande Année* since marketing its 1979 *cuvées*, thus emphasising that Bollinger at least declares in only the finest years. This is a welcome move, especially after other houses had offered vintage Champagnes from the poor harvest of 1977 and the unexceptional one of 1978. It is reprehensible to maintain that some 'passable' vintages can be made in even the poorest of years since a vintage should, by definition, be of a year in which exceptional quality was the rule rather than the exception.

Leading vintage Champagne producers Ayala[V], Barancourt[Q], Billecart-Salmon[Q], Bollinger[Q], de Castellane[V], Veuve Clicquot, Collery, Deutz[Q], Gosset, George Goulet, Alfred Gratien[VQ], Heidsieck & Co. Monopole, Henriot, Jacquesson[Q], Krug, Lanson[V], Mercier[Q], Moët & Chandon, Joseph Perrier[VQ], Perrier-Jouët[Q], Philipponnat[Q], Pol Roger[Q], Pommery[Q], Napoleon[Q], Louis Roederer[Q], Salon[Q], Taittinger[Q].

Blanc de Blancs

Literally 'white of whites', Blanc de Blancs defines a white wine made from white grapes. It is not a term specifically reserved for Champagne but can be used for any wine, still or sparkling, vinified from white grapes.

Until recently a blanc de blancs in Champagne could be made from one or more of four varieties: Chardonnay, Pinot Blanc, Arbanne and Petit Meslier, although it has virtually always been pure Chardonnay and since 1980 the regulations have restricted production to just this one grape variety. Although a great many blancs de blancs are produced in the area of the Côte des Blancs, there is no requirement that they should be. Examples of blanc de blancs Champagnes can be found from the Montagne de Reims, the Vallée de la Marne, the Côte de Sézanne and the Aube.

A typical blanc de blanc is the lightest of Champagnes, yet it can take the longest time to mature and possess the greatest potential longevity. Even the simplest blancs de blancs require several years to develop their true Chardonnay flavour. Initially they can appear severe in acidity, light in fruit, with an austere flavour and a short finish. But all blancs de blancs should gain in fruit and length with time, and the very best will develop in bouquet: the Chardonnay grown in Mesnil, le Mesnil-sur-Oger, Cramant and Avize all possess a unique, highly perfumed aroma.

Blanc de blancs Champagnes have been made at least since the thirteenth century, when Aÿ achieved its earliest reputation. Eugène-Aimé Salon was, however, the first to coin the term 'blanc de blancs' for commercial purposes in the second decade of this century, although a *blanc de blancs des Arbanne* was produced in Bar-sur-Aube in the early nineteenth century.

Leading blanc de blancs producers   Ayala[V], Barancourt, Billecart-Salmon, Bruno Paillard[VQ], Deutz[V], Jacquesson[Q], Mumm[Q], Joseph Perrier[VQ], Pol Roger[Q], Ruinart[Q], Salon[Q], Taittinger[Q] and de Venoge[V]

Blanc de Noirs

Literally 'white of blacks', this wine is made from either the Pinot Noir, the Pinot Meunier or from a blend of the two. It too may be used to describe wines other than Champagne and is in fact enjoying a new vogue as a synonym for very pale rosé wines in various countries but, unlike blanc de blancs, blanc de noirs Champagnes are rare. Bollinger is one of the few houses to produce a blanc de noirs and their Vieilles Vignes Françaises is one of the even fewer number to indicate the term on the label. Most blancs de noirs are, however, grower Champagnes and are made by circumstance rather than by choice.

In contrast to blanc de blancs, blanc de noirs Champagnes possess a heavy, ponderous, fruity flavour and are often slightly earthy in taste; they are, moreover, golden-yellow in colour where blancs de blancs are water-white. While a blanc de blancs can attain immaculate equilibrium, the weight of a blanc de noirs is intrinsically out of balance for the finesse expected of a classic Champagne. Curiously, however, their imbalance can prove useful when partnering wine with food. When a fine sparkling wine is needed to cut the texture of a particular dish which also has a powerful flavour, a Roquefort soufflé for example, only a blanc de noirs Champagne will be able to survive in such very rich company.

Leading blanc de noirs producers Bollinger[Q] and Bruno Paillard[VQ]

Pink Champagne or Champagne Rosé

Earlier references to pink Champagne have not always been entirely complimentary.

Cyrus Redding, in *The History and Description of Modern Wines* (1833) claims that 'No one who knows what the wines are at all would drink rose-coloured Champagne, if he could obtain the other kind.' Similarly, Alexander Henderson, in *The History of Ancient and Modern Wines* (1824) reveals that 'At present the pink Champagne is less requested than the colourless.' Pink wines had been produced for several centuries before these writers spoke of pink Champagne and, no doubt, much would have been sparkling, whether by design or accident; the first record of a commercially produced pink sparkling Champagne is that of Clicquot's in 1777.

Pink Champagne has, however, enjoyed ephemeral bursts of popularity; its most widespread success coincided with the early-Victorian fashion for saucer-shaped glasses.

The spectacle provoked by these crystal glasses filled with pink liquid and contrasting snow-white foam was apparently so irresistible that it became *de rigueur* in certain circles. Its popularity peaked in the 1850s, declined, and then peaked again at the end of Victoria's reign, the vogue continuing into the frivolous years of the Edwardian era before finally fading. Subsequent interest has been relatively small.

But for a minority of instances, black grapes have clear juice and it is through maceration of grape skins and juice that coloration is achieved. The longer the skin contact, the greater the colour, especially when the juice contains alcohol which is more efficient in the extraction of anthocyanins or pigments from the skins than non-alcoholic must. The production of all European pink wines must by law utilise a form of this skin contact as the only method of coloration. Whether this skin contact is achieved by pressing, maceration, or bleeding (*saignée*), the duration of this process will be much shorter than for red wine. Generally the blending of red and white wine to make pink wine is strictly forbidden, but not in the case of Champagne which may be produced by both methods, although most of it is produced by blending. This has always been the traditional method and, as the AOC regulations were initially based on the general consensus of local practice and tradition, French and Common Market laws recognise the fact.

Between 10 and 20% (of the whole *cuvée*) of red AOC Champagne, not Coteaux Champenois, may be used as the base wine for the *liqueur de tirage*. As the amount of colour which can drain out during the *prise de mousse* varies, the base wine of the *liqueur d'expédition* may also be red Champagne. Fierce arguments have arisen, however, over the use of this method, with revered oenologists pontificating over the rights and wrongs of what is called 'cutting' (the cutting of white wine with red to produce pink). But whatever their criticisms, it is impossible to distinguish between the two methods under stringent blind-tasting conditions.

Leading pink Champagne producers Besserat de Bellefon[VQ], Billecart-Salmon[Q], Bollinger[Q], de Castellane[VQ], Gosset[Q], George Goulet, Charles Heidsieck, Lanson[V], Laurent-Perrier, Moët & Chandon, Mumm, Perrier-Jouët[V], Philipponnat, Pol Roger[Q], Pommery[Q], Ruinart, Taittinger[Q] and Veuve Clicquot[Q]

Crémant

In Champagne the term *crémant* is used in its most traditional sense. This is in contrast to other regions, particularly with the recent appellations of the early 1970s such as Crémant d'Alsace, Crémant de Bourgogne and Crémant de Loire, where the term is merely synonymous with fully *mousseux*.

Most Champagnes are fully *mousseux*, although the house style of some firms may produce slightly softer sparkling wines (as in the case of Philipponnat, for example), but a *crémant*, if properly made, should be noticeably less fizzy. Fully *mousseux* Champagnes will have an internal pressure of five to six atmospheres (as pressure is affected by temperature, all measurements in atmospheres are given at 20°C). A *crémant* is traditionally 3.6 atmospheres, but all Champagnes, including *crémants*, cannot be less than 3.5 atmospheres, unless in half-bottle, in which case the minimum is three atmospheres.

In the eighteenth century a *crémant* (or *sablant* as it was often called), was regarded as superior to the 'green' fully *mousseux* products. Bertin du Rocheret, the Abbot of Bignon, in a letter dated 1736, extolled the virtues of *sablant* wines, but condemned those wines with 'the strongest foam' as 'furiously green' and possessing 'not much vinosity'. Even in the nineteenth century, long after fully *mousseux* Champagnes had received acceptance and praise, certain gourmets persisted in drinking only the still wines of the region, or the slightly *pétillant*. On no account would they lower themselves to touch a fully *mousseux* Champagne. The premiss being that such strongly effervescent wines must be intrinsically harsh and tart and smelling of fermentation.

A good *crémant* is hard to come by as few possess the required lower pressure and an even fewer number portray the correct 'creaming' character of minuscule bubbles which slowly and constantly unfold like the frothing of boiling butter.

Leading *crémant* producers Besserat de Bellefon^{VQ}, Alfred Gratien^Q, Abel Lepitre and Mumm^Q

Non-Dosage

Synonyms in current commercial use: Brut Zéro, Brut Sauvage, Brut Non-Dosage, Sans Sucre, Ultra Brut.

As long ago as 1889, Laurent Perrier sold a 'Grand Vin Sans Sucre' and, in an announcement published on 6 May 1895, the same firm described its 'Sans Sucre 1893' Champagne as:

The natural highest class Champagne of remarkably fine flavour, taste and bouquet, without any added sugar or alcohol, shipped by Laurent-Perrier & Co. A wine of marvellously clean taste, invigorating and exhilarating properties, superior to all Champagnes containing sugar.

Although these Champagnes are sold as ready to drink, they can be very austere in their youth. The best non-dosage Champagnes attain a greater depth and complexity with keeping and as such should be cellared as for vintage Champagnes.

Leading non-dosage producers Besserat de Bellefon^{VQ}, Laurent Perrier and Piper Heidsieck^Q

De luxe Champagnes or *Cuvées de Prestige*

The *cuvées de prestige* – the flagships of the Champagne houses – offer the absolute in great Champagnes. Or they are intended to: some can be over refined and mellow, lacking the dash and flare that should make Champagne so exciting.

A typical *cuvée de prestige* might well be made entirely of grand cru wines, often confined to vineyards belonging to the house and, if not reserved for the best vintages, then blended 'from only the finest years'. Many such wines are marketed on a 'purely

'Now, George, my boy, there's a glass of Champagne for you. Don't get such stuff at school, eh?' 'H'm! Awfully sweet. Very good sort for ladies. But I've arrived at a time of life when I confess I like my wine dry.' (From a late nineteenth-century drawing by John Leech in *Punch*)

traditional process' concept and the house may still employ oak casks for fermentation or ageing, *liège et agrafe* for the *prise de mousse* and disgorge each bottle *à la volée* by hand. Many are bottled and labelled in eighteenth-century form and all such *cuvées* are naturally highly priced.

Moët & Chandon's Dom Pérignon vintage 1921, first marketed in 1937, was the commercial pioneer of prestige *cuvées*, although Louis Roederer's equally well-known Cristal was in existence at least sixty years earlier. We know that intricate details of the composition and design of Roederer's Cristal were registered as early as 8 November 1877, but the wine was originally produced specifically for the Russian Imperial Court and, as it was not generally available to ordinary customers, it cannot at that time be considered as a commercial product. The Russian Court was a lucrative market for Louis Roederer until the firm's existence was jeopardised by the Revolution. This left Roederer with an enormous, unpaid bill and a considerable stock of unsold Cristal. Unlike today, Cristal was very sweet and ideally suited to the palate of its sole purchasers, the Tsars of

Russia; although Champagnes were generally sweeter in the nineteenth century, Louis Roederer nevertheless had to search hard to find an appropriate market. Eventually this was found in South America and the entire surplus stock was off-loaded in 1919.

Between the two world wars Cristal was not sold on the open market, but the brand was kept alive by small *cuvées* for the firm's own use and as gifts. From 1923 to 1939 a total of 90,000 bottles was produced, but the first commercial production was the vintage of 1945, a good twenty-four years after the first *cuvée* of Dom Pérignon.

Leading *cuvée de prestige* producers   Bollinger (RD)^Q, Deutz (Cuvée William Deutz)^Q, Heidsieck & Co. Monopole (Cuvée Diamant Bleu)^Q, Henriot (Réserve de Baron Philippe de Rothschild), Laurent-Perrier (Cuvée Grand Siècle), Moët & Chandon (Dom Pérignon)^Q, Perrier-Jouët (Belle Epoque)^Q, Philipponnat (Clos des Goisses)^{VQ}, Pol Roger (Réserve Spéciale PR and Cuvée Sir Winston Churchill)^Q, Louis Roederer (Cristal)^Q, Ruinart (Dom Ruinart)^Q and Taittinger (Comtes de Champagne)^Q. NB Krug claim not to have a specific *cuvée de prestige*.

Coteaux Champenois

In 1927, during the formative years of the AOC regulations, the still wine of Champagne was given the awkward title *Vin Originaire de la Champagne Viticole*, a rather pedantic way of saying Champagne, without indicating the wine's still or *tranquil* state. In 1953 it became known as *Vin Nature de la Champagne*, which did at least qualify the wine. It only became known as *Coteaux Champenois* as recently as 1974.

Still wines produced in the Champagne region have a much longer history than the now famous sparkling varieties, but it must be said that, by modern standards, the appellation of Coteaux Champenois is generally a very poor one. The region of Champagne is, in a viticultural sense, so critically situated that it produces intrinsically superior sparkling products, yet inherently inferior still ones.

Few Coteaux Champenois produced by the famous Champagne houses are of a reasonable quality and an even fewer number display any signs of consistency. There is a wealth of much better still wine – red, white and rosé – produced in other areas of France under the more humble VDQS and *vin de pays* appellations, which are sold at a fraction of the price of Coteaux Champenois. The general quality of still wines of Champagne could be raised, but their potential will always be limited by the region's unfavourable climate.

Throughout its chequered official existence, most producers have rarely attempted to market Coteaux Champenois wines, tending to treat the appellation as a form of reserve which could, in times of shortage, be proffered to the authorities for upgrading to full Champagne status. Upon acceptance, such wines would be bottled and subjected to the normal second fermentation process for the *prise de mousse*.

Whereas the price of grapes for Champagne is fixed, no such control exists for Coteaux Champenois grapes, which are, inevitably, cheaper. Yet if the Coteaux Champenois wines are later reclassified, as happened to the crops of 1975, 1976 and particularly 1977, the price of Champagne does not come down.

The area of production, the permitted varieties of vine and the methods of cultivation

A rare example of pink Champagne produced from naturally macerated pink or rosé wine, blending red and white wine being the most widespread practice. Even more rarely, the wine here is cask-fermented

Remuage is a labour-intensive job; every day the *remueur* must gradually riddle the bottle to encourage the yeast sediment to descend to the base of the cork, gradually tilting the bottle a fraction after each operation until it is fully perpendicular and ready for *dégorgement*

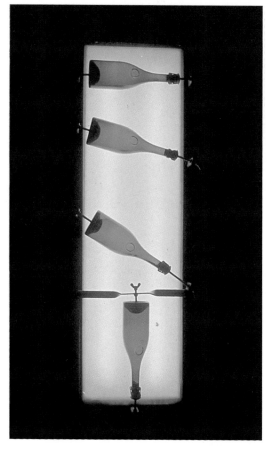

are all identical to those used for Champagne. Coteaux Champenois has a maximum yield set at 13,000 kilograms per hectare or 86.66 hectolitres per hectare, but can be decreased by annual declaration (as opposed to Champagne, which is usually modified upwards).

Red

Perhaps in two or three years in every ten, it is possible for many growers and producers in Ambonnay, Aÿ, Bouzy, Cumières and Mareuil-sur-Aÿ to produce a reasonable Coteaux Champenois Rouge. In maybe one year in ten a few growers in scattered locations, not necessarily in the famous growths, will make a truly fine red wine.

Most of the few houses specialising in the production of Coteaux Champenois make red wines which are very pedestrian; the vast numbers of small grower-producers (*récoltants-manipulants*) possess the greatest potential in this sector. One notable exception is Bollinger's La Côte aux Enfants, but this is produced in very much the same way as a grower's red wine: the production is limited, coming from one small vineyard belonging to the house. The wine is made only in exceptional years (like 1976) and matured in small casks of new oak. The wine is variable in quality, as are even the best years of Champagne. Some is very good and the style and character is improving, but Bollinger readily admit that they are only in the experimental stage and welcome discussion on the merits and demerits of the wine. Tiny quantities of La Côte aux Enfants were released for export in 1985. The Bouzy-based house of Barancourt (effectively three growers merged into one company) is in a similar position. I have tasted some really fine vintages of Barancourt's Bouzy Rouge.

Leading red wine producers Bollinger and Barancourt. The best buys are usually found by tasting around the villages after unusually hot vintages.

White

Most of these wines are thin in fruit and high in acid. Growers and houses alike seem to lack the capacity to produce successful still white wines in Champagne. The two exceptions are Ruinart's Chardonnay (not a fine wine, but very enjoyable) and Moët & Chandon's Saran (vastly superior to the Ruinart though still not quite a fine wine). I doubt many could emulate Saran, but serious Coteaux Champenois producers would benefit if they strove to obtain the simple but pleasant style of Ruinart's Chardonnay. In Champagne's crisp climate, the French would do well to take a tip from German winemakers, as a restrained practice of *süssreserve* (the addition of sterilised unfermented grape must) could give these wines the fresh fruitiness that they generally lack. It would require amending the regulations, but the effort would be beneficial and parallels could be drawn with the addition of Champagne's *liqueur d'expédition*.

Leading white wine producers Moët & Chandon[Q] and Ruinart

Rosé

Relatively few Coteaux Champenois are pink, but of all such wines that I have tasted, none has been inspiring and most of them were simply dry and dull. There seems less inclination in Champagne to produce a decent still rosé than there is to make a good red and white wine.

Rosé des Riceys

This is not a Coteaux Champenois, but a completely separate appellation for a pure Pinot Noir still, pink wine made in the commune of les Riceys in the Aube *département*. Locally the wine is something of a legend, its fame dating back to Louis XIV, who apparently served Rosé des Riceys on frequent occasions.

Production, averaging about 10,000 bottles annually, is erratic, as an honest producer knows that the special character of Rosé des Riceys only emerges in the very best years. The wine should be dark for a rosé, almost, but not quite, the colour of a light red wine. When successful, Rosé des Riceys has an aromatic bouquet often reminiscent of chocolate, herbs and mint and with a deep penetrating flavour which is fruity and very smooth. It is not what one expects from Pinot Noir, but the surprise can be extremely pleasant.

Currently there are only three producers of Rosé des Riceys, all *récoltants-manipulants*; they are Alexander Bonnet, Horiot Père & Fils and Morel Père & Fils.

Ratafia

Various flavoured cordials and alcoholic beverages have been proffered under the name of Ratafia since the sixteenth century. The definition of Ratafia has thus differed according to time and place, but there is only one origin of the word; parties to an agreement would share a glass of some form of alcohol to ratify their contract and, according to the *Dictionnaire éthymologique de la langue française* (PUF, 1950), the word stemmed from a West Indian misspelling of the Latin phrase used by lawyers: 'rata fiat conventio'.

Today Ratafia is similar to Pineau de Charente – a sweet, alcoholic and grapy tasting apéritif, which should be served chilled. Some people like to accompany the dessert with a glass of Ratafia and others even drink it as an *apéritif* or as a *digestif*.

Ratafia may be red, white or pink. It is an alcoholic beverage which has not undergone fermentation, this being prevented by the addition of grape spirit (an operation called *mutage*) of at least 90% alcohol by volume. The must used for Ratafia has to conform to the same specifications of production area, vine varieties and methods of cultivation as Champagne or Coteaux Champenois. After the *mutage*, the raw Ratafia may be stored in cask or vat for twelve to fifteen months. The minimum alcoholic strength of Ratafia is 18% by volume in France and 23% by volume for exportation. Exported Ratafia is often sweetened up.

There is much argument as to whether the *cuvée* or the *taille* is best. Certainly there is less confusion as to which grape varieties are best, Pinot Noir-based Ratafias definitely show more elegance and have less chance of developing a *rancio* character. The following list of producers, by no means a complete list, gives an indication of the principal ingredients involved. A number of these are made by Goyard, the largest distillery in the region, but only one which I know for sure to be Goyard products has been indicated. The *mutage* is usually accomplished with a neutral spirit, although mention is made where cognac is known to be used.

Producer	Notes on Ratafia	Producer	Notes on Ratafia
Billiard	Produced by Goyard	Abel Lepitre	Pure Pinot Noir
Binet	Pinot Noir from Ludes and Rilly-la-Montagne	Moët & Chandon	Pure Pinot Noir from Aÿ
		Montaudon	Pure Chardonnay from Cramant
de Castellane	Marne Valley Pinot Meunier	Oudinot	Pure Pinot Noir, including some *cuvée*
A. Charbaut	Black grapes only		
A. Chauvet	Fifty/fifty black and white grapes	Joseph Perrier	Pure Pinot Noir from Cumières
H. Germain	Pinot Noir from Ludes and Rilly-la-Montagne	Philipponnat	A single-site vineyard Ratafia. Pure Pinot Noir from the Clos des goisses which includes no *taille*
Gosset	Taille de Pinot		
Paul Golillard	Black grapes from Pierry, muted with *esprit de cognac* and aged for 3–4 years in wood	Roederer	Matured five years in wood
		A. Secondé Prevoteau	Purely *première taille de Pinot Noir*
Lanson	Pure Chardonnay	de Venoge	Black grapes from Dizy and Hautvillers
Laurent-Perrier	Black grapes only		

Those who like the oxidised *rancio* character, which is quite a popular taste in France, will not, of course, agree with my choice of leading producers.

Leading Ratafia producers Joseph Perrier[Q]

Eaux-de-Vie

Eau-de-vie is the French term for brandy, in the loose sense that a distillation of wine provides a drinkable spirit. The literal translation is 'water of life' and is the equivalent of *aqua vitae* and the Gaelic *uisge beatha*. In Champagne there are four Appellation d'Origine Réglementée eaux-de-vie under two basic categories – Marc and Fine Marne.

Marc (pronounced 'mar') is distilled from the presshouse waste, the residue of skins, pips and stalks which remain after the very last drop of grape juice has been squeezed out. This *marc* can be so solid that it can sometimes be seen being wheeled down the presshouse yard. At the distillery the gentle art of brandy-making often starts with bulldozers which are used to pack the broken-up *marc* into massive silos where the whole mess is turned into a dirty-brown slurry by the addition of water. It is then fermented and distilled to a high strength, after which the spirit may be aged for between three to ten years.

For the appellation of *Eau-de-vie de marc de Champagne*, the brandy must be made from *marc* which was destined to become Champagne or Coteaux Champenois and should have a minimum alcoholic strength of 40%. If made from non-AOC grape varieties, the appellation of *Eau-de-vie du Centre-est* will be used.

Personally, I find all *marc* brandies rough and fiery, having no subtlety whatsoever.

Fine Marne (pronounced 'feen marn') is distilled from wine made from grapes which were destined to be Champagne or Coteaux Champenois but which failed to qualify for its appellation. Such wine may be thought to be healthy, but below standard at the time of

The gentle art of making Eaux-de-Vie de Marc de Champagne

OPPOSITE A spent *marc* destined to become *Eaux-de-Vie de Marc de Champagne* or vineyard fertiliser

disgorgement, or it may be the residue liquid from rackings, *vin de rebêche*, the result of over-production, or Champagne or Coteaux Champenois found to contain insufficient alcohol to qualify for its appellation. If produced from non-AOC grape varieties it will have the appellation of *Eau-de-vie de vin du Centre-est*.

Although marketed as 'Fine Marne' or 'Fine de la Marne' (but never 'Fine Champagne' or 'Grande Fine Champagne', terms reserved exclusively for cognac), these are not the actual appellation. A bottle of Fine Marne will read: *Appellation Eau-de-vie de vin de la Marne Réglementée*.

A good Fine Marne can be compared with the very best Spanish brandies or modest cognacs, although a Fine Marne is much lighter. Unlike Marc, the Fines Marnes can be quality products.

Buying, Storing and Appreciating Champagne

Bishops' boots Mr Radcliffe also condemned, and spoke highly in favour of tops cleaned with champagne and apricot jam.

Robert Smith Surtees, *Handley Cross*, Chapter 27

Buying

The single most important consideration when buying wine is its storage, and thus the best place to buy Champagne is from the house in question. While the product may be more expensive than the special offers in a local supermarket, a Champagne bought from its producer has a guaranteed record of perfect storage. Obviously not everyone can purchase from source, but the question of storage must be uppermost in the mind of a buyer. How does the supplier store his wines? How often does he turn over his stocks? Do you know where he gets his supplies from and how they are stored? Often the response to these questions will be negative or unsure, and therefore the only sensible method of buying will be to taste the wine first. A bottle opened up over dinner is a minor expense in comparison to the financial loss that can be experienced after buying several bottles, let alone cases of dud, untested Champagne.

An auction room is an excellent place to pick up a relatively rare Champagne at a reasonable price, but it can also be a minefield of disasters. Frequently the full provenance of a wine is unknown and, unlike a local wine-merchant, the auction house will be unwilling to grant refunds to disappointed customers. Buy at auctions by all means, but never without a prior tasting of the wine.

Ready for sale

When offered for sale to the general public Champagne should, by all rights, be ready to drink, but there are different standards of 'readiness', the French conception often diverging from the British, not to mention the myriad of views in between. Many decades have passed since British shippers were able to afford to give Champagne the landed-age* it deserves and the British are now, like most other nationalities, rapidly adopting the early-drinking vinicidal habits of the French.

---

*The French used to ship Champagne at a far more mature age than they do now, in addition to which the British used to give the wines what is called 'landed-age', that is to say they kept the wines an extra year or two after landing before they considered them fit for selling.

The ageing laws of Champagne are far stricter than those applied to other sparkling wines, yet they are so woefully inadequate – these wines need only be aged for twelve months – that even the humblest producers mature their wines far in excess of the regulatory minimum. In the early 1980s, when the average age given to non-vintage Champagnes fell below the oft-quoted three years, the reputation of the entire trade suffered. Most Champagne houses would ideally like to give their Champagnes, especially their non-vintages, longer ageing. It is therefore advisable to keep most Champagnes at least one or two years before drinking and some, like Krug and Piper Heidsieck, for a much longer period.

There is one exception, however: recently disgorged venerable vintages. As soon as disgorgement takes place, the exposure to air speeds up oxidation, the rate of oxidation being directly proportionate to the duration that the wine has been matured before its first closure: the longer it has been kept, therefore, the faster the rate of oxidation on disgorgement. Classic vintages from the 1920s or 1930s, for example, can be almost unbelievably fresh and lively when disgorged, yet dull and cheesy within a few weeks of being recorked.

Storing

The prime storage conditions for Champagne are the same as for other wines: a relatively cool temperature and darkness. Although the ideal storage temperature of Champagne is the same as that at which it was subjected to the *prise de mousse*, between 10 and 12°C, the consistency of temperature is far more important. Thus wine stored in conditions where the temperature varied between 6 and 14°C, would not be as well off as wine stored at a constant 20°C. Of all the sizes of bottle available for storing or serving Champagne the single bottle is the handiest, but the magnum has the greatest potential for longevity. Quarter-sized and half-sized bottles should be avoided and caution taken when buying sizes larger than magnum, most of which are filled under pressure (*transvasage*) and are therefore liable to age far more rapidly and be under-fizzed. With such a variety of bottle types on the market, it can be difficult to remember the sizes:

Bottles		Metric contents	Imperial measure of contents
Quarter		20 centilitres	6½ fluid ounces
Half		40 centilitres	13 fluid ounces
Imperial pint		60 centilitres	19½ fluid ounces
Bottle		80 centilitres	1 pint 6 fluid ounces
Magnum	(2 bottles)	1.6 litres	2 pints 12 fluid ounces
Jeroboam (or			
Double Magnum)	(4 bottles)	3.2 litres	5 pints 4 fluid ounces
Rehoboam (or			
Triple Magnum)	(6 bottles)	4.8 litres	7 pints 16 fluid ounces
Methuselah	(8 bottles)	6.4 litres (1.3 gals)	10 pints 8 fluid ounces
Salmanazar	(12 bottles)	9.6 litres (1.95 gals)	15 pints 12 fluid ounces
Balthazar	(16 bottles)	12.8 litres (2.51 gals)	20 pints 16 fluid ounces
Nebuchadnezzar	(20 bottles)	16.0 litres (2.625 gals)	21 pints

Serving

Temperature is of paramount importance when serving Champagne, especially if the effects of the *prise de mousse* are not to be wasted: chilled not iced is the best advice. Traditionally, white wines have been served chilled and red wines at so-called room temperature. The aromatic compounds found within all wines are more volatile at higher temperatures, hence the practice of serving full-bodied red wines at room temperature.

One of the major effects of chilling wine is that more carbonic gas is retained at lower temperatures. This adds a quality of crispness and freshness and tends to liven the impression of fruit on the palate. But with modern refrigerators and central heating, white wines, especially sparkling wines, are frequently served too cold and red wines often far too warm.

Champagne is best served at between 6 and 8°C; the only time I would advise a colder temperature would be when serving Champagne at a crowded reception, when the number of visitors and bustle of party activity will obviously warm the room up very quickly.

If the day is cold enough, the best way to chill Champagne is by leaving it outside for a couple of hours, although there is a lot of humbug surrounding the use of refrigerators for cooling wine, especially Champagne. Provided that it is not used as a means of storage, a refrigerator is a good place to chill down any wine. A couple of hours is all that is necessary, but a few more would do no great harm to the product provided it is allowed to warm to the appropriate service temperature before drinking. What should be avoided at all costs is the habit of leaving unopened bottles upright in a refrigerator for extended periods: this will adhere the cork to the bottle-neck and the refrigeration process will eventually dry out the cork from the outside.

If one is pressed for time, a bucket filled with ice and water will accomplish in twenty minutes what the refrigerator does in two hours. Ice on its own is useless, as it needs the medium of water to exchange temperature with the wine inside the bottle. But care must be taken when opening a Champagne cooled in an ice-bucket, as the top couple of inches containing the first gas to escape will be warmer than the rest of the bottle. If ice is not available, a few minutes in the deep freeze would not unduly impair the flavour. But such a step should be taken only as a last resort.

Opening a Champagne bottle and pouring the wine is not a complicated operation, although many think it is. Do not be flustered by the task, it is really very simple to look expert. First discard sufficient foil to remove the wire muzzle and extract the cork. This can be accomplished, either by pulling a rip-cord which may be present in the foil, or by fingering out the looped-end of the twist of wire holding the cork. In either case, the next step is to untwist the wire. Some people at this stage think they should break the wire, but this only hinders matters. All that is required is to observe which way the wire twists and to untwist it, which enables the grip of the muzzle on the bottle-neck to be loosened. Lift the wire cage up and over the cork, taking with it part of the foil if not removed by possible existence of a rip-cord. Thus freed, temperature permitting, the cork is gently eased out, holding the bottle firmly and twisting the cork. It might be necessary to lever the cork, first to the right, then to left, in between twisting it. In any case, the cork should be eased out, not with a theatrical bang but with a barely audible 'phut'.

When serving Champagne, the trick is to pour a very little amount into each glass first, then return to the first glass, by which time its frothing should be over. It is always the first drop of Champagne in a glass which is the liveliest and it is surprising how easy it is to pour on top of existing wine. To avoid spilling, try giving the bottle a little twist combined with a tilt upwards, before removing the bottle from the glass. It is just a tiny action which, in time, becomes part of the style of pouring.

The one-handed method of pouring Champagne which is practised by professional *sommeliers* is the easiest manner to adopt. Simply place your thumb in the deep punt in the bottom of the bottle and spread your fingers out to support the body. It is not only easy, it is the only way to serve Champagne from magnums if dropped bottles and smashed glasses are to be avoided.

Glasses

Two glasses have been synonymous with Champagne throughout history: the *coupe* and the *flûte*. The *coupe* was created *c.* 1663 by Venetian glass-makers at the Duke of Buckingham's glass factory in Greenwich. In deference to its Italian inventors, the glass was originally known as a *tazza* (cup), but this name faded during its two-hundred-year-growth in popularity. It had been designed specifically for Champagne, which was not guaranteed to be fully *mousseux* at that time, but it was not until Victorian commerce marketed the Champagne *coupe* that it became widely known in fashionable English society and shortly afterwards in America. The most famous production of this sort of vessel was the eighteenth-century Sèvres porcelain *coupes* which once adorned the Queen's Diary Temple at the Château de Rambouillet, and which were modelled on the breasts of Marie-Antoinette.

The *flûte* is of a much earlier origin, dating back to Gallo-Roman times. Fine examples made at Murano near Venice became immensely popular during the sixteenth century, stimulating exports and generating the production of copies in the Netherlands and in England. At the court of Charles II the exiled St Évremond constantly tried to promote the *flûte* as 'the glass of fashion' and, indeed, it became universally accepted for Champagne in France and England throughout the eighteenth century.

No connoisseur would use a *coupe* for any sparkling wine, let alone Champagne. Not only does such a wide-brimmed glass provide a greater surface area in which the bubbles can escape, but its shape is completely incapable of retaining the bouquet. The taller, narrower and more elegant form of the *flûte* is obviously superior. But even the *flûte* is not ideal. The perfect vessel for drinking any wine, still or sparkling, fortified or unfortified, is the tulip-shaped glass. Its bulbous base and inwardly sloping sides concentrate the aromas in the top of the glass, allowing the drinker the full benefit of the wine's bouquet. The size of the glass is important: it must be sufficiently large to ensure that a 'good glassful' barely takes up more than half of the glass, thus leaving room above for the aromas to circulate. The tulip-shaped glass of specific dimensions has been accepted internationally as the standard tasting glass.

Tasting

All serious tastings require deep, intensive concentration, cutting out all distractions and, most especially, comments on the wines made by others. It is all too easy to be led when dealing with something as subjective as opinions of taste. Tasting a wine can be broken down into three basic operations which in the trade is known as the 'eye', the 'nose' and the 'palate'. The first object when evaluating the eye of a wine is to assess its limpidity. All wines should be clear; any samples which are cloudy, hazy or (for Champagne) contain sediment, should be rejected, thus rendering further tasting unnecessary. Some wines which are clear appear far sharper than others and such starbright wines should be marked up. Next one can observe the colour: most Champagnes are of a straw-coloured hue, although a blanc de blancs will be almost water-white while a blanc de noirs nearer to yellow-gold. Because white wines deepen in colour with age, old Champagne can attain the golden hue of a blanc de noirs, before full oxidation renders it amber-brown. Thus the lightest of Champagnes may be young blanc de blancs and the darkest, a very old blanc de noirs, with the varying shades in between giving clues to the proportion of grape varieties in the *cuvée* and an idea of age.

It is often claimed that the quality of a *mousse* can be assessed simply by looking at the bubbles in a glass and that a constant stream of fine, tiny bubbles is an indication of a fine, persistent *mousse*. But it should be borne in mind that the surface of every glass is microscopically different and that the generation of bubbles is influenced by friction between the Champagne and the glass itself. Thus the presence of large, uneven or infrequent bubbles is not necessarily the mark of a poor *mousse*. The most effective way of gauging the effervescing character of any sparkling wine is through the palate.

But before a wine is tasted it must be 'nosed'. The eye alone will leave open many options: is the gloriously golden Champagne a young blanc de noirs, an old blanc de blancs or a middle-aged blend? 'Nosing' the wine will provide several further clues. Before the first sniff is taken, however, the wine should be left to stand a few minutes in the glass and then given several good swirls. This releases the initial burst of carbonic gas, opening the way for the aromatics and the more longer lasting bouquet.

Two qualities are discernible at this stage: the freshness and grapyness of youth or the fuller, riper odours of maturity. Without being unnecessarily specific, it should be possible to place the Champagne in some category of age and grape variety – by playing off the colour clue against the nose – and also to formulate some idea of the wine's quality: top quality Champagnes almost invariably show some positive signs, whether the powerful varietal character of a youthful wine, or the biscuity complexities of a mature Champagne.

Only when the 'nosing' has finished should the Champagne be tasted. The taster must ask him/herself if all the facets of bouquet or aroma have been examined. Has the nose answered questions raised by the eye, or have yet more questions been proffered? Then, on to the palate. One can begin by taking a good mouthful of Champagne and, drawing air into the mouth and through the wine, making a gurgling noise. This will magnify the qualities and characteristics of the wine by volatilising some of the esters and ethers in the back passages of the throat and nose.

The self-questioning which should be conducted during tasting the wine is similar to that which takes place when 'nosing' it. One of the most important questions to be answered is whether the palate accurately reflects the nose. Perhaps the first consideration, in the case of Champagne, should be that of the *mousse*. A fine and persistent *mousse* is always sought, but it is sometimes difficult to discern in the mouth. Only through practice and experience, by comparing one Champagne with another, will anyone come to terms with the tactile impressions of the *mousse*.

There are four basic sensations experienced by the tongue – sweetness, acidity, saltiness and bitterness. The two immediate reactions to a wine when it enters the mouth are sweetness and acidity. Sweetness is primarily detected on the tip of the tongue and acidity on the sides, but the human mind is easily fooled and an excess of one can mask the true quantity of the other. It is essential, therefore, to ask the following questions: does it taste dry, is there plenty of acidity lengthening the flavour and, if so, might there not be more residual sugar than initially suspected?

Bitterness is mainly detected at the back of the tongue and this might be unpleasant. It may be the result of a concentration of the, as yet, undeveloped extract or it could simply be due to something unpleasant or unnatural in the wine. Distinguishing between the two is often difficult and, again, an ability acquired only through experience. But there are clues to be found in the characteristics of the wine surrounding such bitterness, and the question should always be asked as to whether there is any room for development. The answer will often classify the type of bitterness: if there exists a potential for development, then the bitterness is probably one of unharmonious extract, if the wine seems not to proffer any future development, then it is obviously a negative factor.

Next one can move on to the fruit: is there much of it, is it fresh and is it distinctive? Does it suggest a Pinot or a Chardonnay flavour? Is the fruitiness deep and penetrating or is it wide and complex? Is it pure fruit or more aromatic? Is it flowery and young, or round, biscuity and fully developed?

The Champagne should now be spat out (if tasting several wines) or swallowed. The taster can then discover whether the flavour on the palate remains and if it does, for how long and whether an aftertaste lingers. The balance of sweetness and acidity is the prime factor here, while there may be an aftertaste which persists long after the wine has gone. This may be a component part of the overall palate, or appear to be so, or it may introduce a completely new flavour. Length is an essential characteristic of quality, while an aftertaste, if a pleasant one, can be an added bonus.

It is the correlation of all these experiences, received from the eye, the nose and the palate, which forms the basis of an opinion on tasting. That opinion should indicate whether or not the Champagne is liked. It should enable one to classify the quality of the Champagne or, at the very least, one's perception of the quality which is, after all, all that matters.

II

The Provincial Cuisine of Champagne

The north is also Cabbage country, as soldiers who train on the lower lying areas of Champagne, the 'Champagne humide', know all too well: for many years the local cabbages have been a staple in their diet.

Anne Willan, *French Regional Cooking*, 1981

WAVERLEY ROOT, IN HIS PIONEERING BOOK ON FRENCH FOOD, *The Food of France* (1958) stated that Champagne presents 'the anomaly of being the only important wine region in the country which has not produced on its own soil an appropriate cuisine to accompany its wine.' On the same theme, although somewhat more generous in its expression, the meticulously researched *Larousse Gastronomique* enthuses about the excellence of cooking in Champagne but adds the deflating qualification that its 'repertoire is rather limited'.

What is often forgotten is that when the Italian culinary renaissance revitalised French cuisine in the mid-sixteenth century, the local wines of Champagne bore no resemblance to those of today. Throughout the famous provinces of France, culinary traditions evolved from a cohesion of regional foods and local wines. The success story of Champagne's rise as a great sparkling wine threw this culinary evolution off course and in the eighteenth century, while other provinces carried on along their well trodden paths to gastronomic glory, the cuisine of Champagne found itself up a blind alley. Thus, in this context, the views expressed in *The Food of France*, *Larousse Gastronomique* et al have the appearance of being correct if harsh.

While the aromatic, tomato and garlic laced dishes of Provence are as well known as the rich sauces of Burgundy, there is no equivalent image of the cuisine of Champagne. Yet it does exist and its repertoire, not so much limited as eclipsed by the more colourful reputations of other provinces, is as rich and varied as one might expect for a province which once extended north to include the Ardennes, west to encompass what is now part of the built-up outskirts of Paris, south to claim Chablis and eastwards into Touraine, reaching almost as far as the Loire valley. This enormous province covered almost one-twentieth of France, representing an area more than seven hundred times the size of Champagne *viticole* today. In establishing its cuisine, Champagne could thus draw on a wide range of culinary traditions and local produce, from the famous orchards and vegetable gardens of the Île de France, grown to feed the ever-expanding population of Paris, to the game and wild mushrooms of the forest of the Ardennes and the freshwater fish from the numerous rivers.

In one respect, the true cuisine of Champagne is no different from that of any other gastronmic region: the best cooking is, of course, found in the home. While some country *auberges* and city *bistros* do specialise in the local cuisine, any visitor to Champagne should be wary of the ubiquitous *au Champagne* dishes, nearly all of which are bland and fabricated for the tourist trade. The following examples of traditional foods and genuine country dishes should enable the reader to gauge the true depth and variety of Champagne's cuisine.

Soups

Country soups are really the classic preserve of Périgord and Provence, but the cabbage and potato cultivations of the Champagne plains yield some very honest and tasty versions. More than 40 per cent of France's potatoes are grown in Champagne and the north.

Soupe au lait ardennaise A leek, potato, *escarole* (Batavian endive) and milk soup.

Soupe à la bière de Mezières A brown onion soup garnished with grilled bread and Gruyère cheese.

Soupe au beurre White haricot beans, potatoes, cabbage and butter form the basis of this soup; it can also be flavoured with carrot, leek, celery and turnip.

Soupe aux choux et aux lardons A chunky potato, cabbage and onion soup garnished with crisply fried lardons of bacon.

Salads and vegetable dishes

Champagne is famous for its salads, which often include dandelion leaves, and which can be garnished with various hot ingredients such as poached eggs, crispy bacon lardons, chicken livers, fried croûtons and the widely cultivated potato. The old province was rich in salad and vegetable products: leeks and artichokes from the Ardennes; fat white chicory heads (called endives in France and America) from Flanders; potatoes and white, green and red cabbage from the plains; carrots from Crécy-en-Brie; succulent, white asparagus from Argenteuil; and mushrooms which used to be cultivated in some of the Gallo-roman *crayères* of Reims.

Bailline Halved new potatoes covered with sliced onions and slowly casseroled in white wine.

Champignons à la Sainte-Ménehould Mushrooms on egg-dipped toast.

Chou à l'ardennaise Cabbage braised with sliced apple and juniper berries.

Chou potagère Sliced cabbage casseroled in white wine, with onions, carrots and bacon.

Endives à l'ardennaise Chicory cooked in cream, draped in Gruyère cheese and grilled.

Fricassée de pommes de terre à l'ardennaise Sliced potato casseroled in white wine with onions, shallots and bacon.

Purée d'oignons Onions, butter, stock and Marc de Champagne cooked *en cocotte* at a low heat for three hours.

Salade des betteraves aux noix Beetroot, various green salad leaves and chopped walnuts tossed in vinaigrette.

Salade champenoise Curly endive (called chicory in France and America), chopped tomatoes, chicken livers, crispy bacon lardons, tiny croûtons garnished with poached eggs.
Salade au lard Various green leaves, potatoes, crispy bacon lardons and tiny croûtons.
Salade de pissenlit au lard Dandelion leaves, crispy bacon lardons and tiny croûtons.

Fish and crustacea

The cuisine of Champagne is richly endowed with dishes of eel, freshwater crayfish, trout, carp, barbel, pike, and salmon, all of which provide delicate partners to the wines of the region.
Anguille en matelote Eel and wine stew.
Anguille au vert Eel in green herb sauce.
Anguille Sainte-Ménehould Sliced-eel, poached in white wine, soaked in butter, coated in breadcrumbs and chopped mushrooms, and grilled.
Brochet farci à la rémoise Stuffed pike braised in white wine.
Carpe (or *truite*) *au bleu* In this dish the fish, which is kept alive until a few minutes before cooking, is gutted but never washed, and then plunged into a boiling *court-bouillon* containing a high proportion of wine vinegar and simmered for between five and seven minutes, the effect of which is to achieve a vivid blue coloration of the flesh.
Écrevisses à la mode de Monsieur le Prieur The famous gourmand Brillat-Savarin (1755–1826) mentions this extraordinary dish in *La Physiologie du goût* (Paris, 1825). It entails the reduction of a cooking liquor comprised of white wine, Champagne, bacon, carrots, onions, shallots, garlic, thyme, parsley, chervil, bayleaf, grated orange rind, uncrushed salt, white pepper and cayenne pepper. Having been reduced by half, this *court-bouillon* is used to cook the crayfish for between ten and twelve minutes before being passed through a sieve and poured over the crayfish as a sauce when serving.
Écrevisses en matelote A simple crayfish and wine stew.
Filets de brochet au vin des Riceys Fillets of pike cooked in the pink wine of les Riceys, with mushrooms, thyme and laurel.
Filets de truites au vin de Champagne Fillets of trout cooked in white wine, chives, cloves and truffles. One of the few true *au Champagne* dishes, the earliest recorded reference of this recipe is dated 1778.
Matelote à la canotière A sophisticated stew of carp and eel, cooked in white wine, and garnished with fried gudgeon in breadcrumbs and boiled crayfish.
Matelote champenoise A rich wine stew of eel, pike, and carp, bream or tench.
Pôchouse à matelote A freshwater fish stew of several types of fish, including eel, pike, carp and barbel, garnished with diced belly of pork, mushrooms and glazed button onions.
Quenelles de brochet There are various fish dumplings ingrained in the country cooking of Champagne, but only *Quenelles* of pike can claim true classic status. *Quenelles* come in many sizes and shapes; the most common type I have encountered is about the size and shape of a very small hen's egg. This is an exquisitely delicate dish based on a lightly poached dough containing finely pounded pike flesh. It looks and tastes deceptively simple.
Truite à l'ardennaise Trout sautéed with lardons of bacon and served in a cream sauce.

Meats, poultry and game

As much of Champagne's early wealth was centred on the wool trade, it is not surprising to discover that this region's cuisine sports a wealth of local mutton dishes. Sheep adapt well to the Champagne *pouilleuse*, a strip of land which stretches from the Ardennes to the Loire, sweeping east of Reims in an arc along the edge of the Franco-British Basin. The *pouilleuse* is unsuited for vegetable crops, but provides ideal land for sheep to graze on, much of it being carpeted in wild thyme and it is this which is said to give Champenois mutton its special flavour. These lamb dishes are many, varied and well worth the try, but it is not the province's only meat of gastronomic repute. The Fôret de la Montagne de Reims once teemed with game and the Ardennes, further north, is still considered to be one of the richest game areas in Europe. It is in such places that wild boar still roam, while rabbit, hare, duck and game birds are plentiful throughout the region.

Andouillettes The two basic forms of cured sausage in French *charcuterie* are the large, fat *andouille* and, most popular in Champagne, the thin *andouillettes* or chitterlings which are stuffed into the small rather than the large intestines. Most *andouillettes* are pork-based, but the greatest *andouillettes* in Champagne are mutton-based.

Andouillettes de mouton These *andouillettes* of Troyes are the most famous mutton-based *andouilletes* in all France.

Boudin blanc This is a white pudding made from white pork meat, chicken and onions, although some inferior ones contain veal and may be filled out with breadcrumbs. The *boudin blanc* of Rethel in the Ardennes is especially moist and delicious and is considered by some to be the best of this type of sausage.

Boudin noir This is the French equivalent of black pudding or blood sausage, made of pig's blood and pork fat and forced into an intestine. At harvest time they are usually sliced and grilled and served with mashed potato.

Boudin de Sainte-Ménehould A rabbit-based version which has a fine, rich flavour, but tends to dry out very quickly and should therefore be as fresh as possible.

Boeuf en éventail à la troyenne Rare steak covered with onions, white breadcrumbs, chopped parsley, sautéed mushrooms and grated Gruyère cheese.

Carbonnade de boeuf à la flamande This famous dish comes from that part of Belgium which was once part of Champagne. Scallops of beef and sliced onion are cooked in beer, mustard and a small amount of brown sugar.

Choucroute This pickled cabbage dish is the French version of *sauerkraut*. Found throughout most of north-east France, it is especially popular in Champagne. Vast tracts of Champagne's plains are cultivated with cabbages – this, plus the historic Germanic connection which persists to this day in the names of famous houses such as Krug, Heidsieck et al, obviously explains the local appeal of this dish. It is usually served with *andouillettes* and various cuts of meat, particularly pork. During a lunch with Jean-Marc Charles Heidsieck, I saw him pour more Champagne into his *choucroute* than his glass!

Civet de lièvre A rich red wine stew of leverets between three and six months of age.

Civet de marcassin A young wild boar no older than six months, stewed in red wine.

Coq au vin de Bouzy A local version of the famous Burgundian dish, the chicken cooked in the red wine of Bouzy, with onions, mushrooms, lardons of bacon and garlic and served with croûtons.

Côtes de porc à l'ardennaise   This is a dish in which a slice of Ardennes ham, spread with mushrooms cooked in white wine, cream and butter, is sandwiched between two boneless pork chops (or one very thick one slit horizontally) and cooked *en papillote* (formerly in hermetically-sealed baking paper, now in aluminium foil).

Crêpes au jambon   Thin pancakes filled with minced ham, shallots and mushrooms, sometimes browned in a coat of white wine, cream and Gruyère cheese sauce, spiced with nutmeg.

Dindonneau braisé au Champagne   Young turkey braised in white wine with onions, shallots, carrots, mushrooms, bacon and nutmeg. Young turkeys were traditionally reared south of Nevers.

Escalopes de veau à la rémoise   Veal cooked in locally made mustard, cream, white wine and butter, sprinkled with breadcrumbs and browned under the grill.

Faisan aux raisins   Pheasant cooked in butter, bacon, grapes and Marc de Champagne.

Faisan en daube à la sparnacienne   Pheasant casseroled in red wine, Marc de Champagne, mushrooms, onions, celery and carrots.

Galette à la flamme   This is a dish half-way between a *quiche* and a *pizza* which consists of a bread dough base topped with a mixture of beaten egg and lardons of bacon and cooked quickly in a hot oven.

Grives à l'ardennaise   Partly boned thrushes stuffed with *foie gras*, chopped thrush livers, and truffles. Braised and served in a *croustade* (a 'pot' hollowed out of loaf and deep fried) filled with bacon and mushrooms – often accompanied by a *demi-glace* sauce.

Grives en cocotte à l'ardennaise   Thrushes cooked *en cocotte* (individual casserole dishes) with juniper berries.

Grives sous la cendré   Thrushes stuffed with calf's liver, lightly smoked bacon and Marc de Champagne.

Hure de sanglier   Stuffed boar's head, with the ears and tongue cooked separately.

Jambon   Reims is justly famous for its hams, some of which are encased in pastry.

Jambon de bête rousse   Wild boar ham, cured in the same way as domesticated pig's ham, the animal being between six months and a year old.

Jambonneau   Specifically forelegs of ham.

Langues   Stuffed tongue and smoked tongue are specialities of Troyes.

Lapin en gelée   Rabbit cooked in white wine, bacon and onion and accompanied, separately, with its own liver. It can be served hot or set in its own juices and served cold.

Marcassin ardennais   Young boar marinaded in red wine and juniper berries and casseroled with celeriac and lardons of bacon.

Oie à la marnaise   Goose cooked in stock with whole peeled potatoes.

Pains   These 'loaves' were the forerunner to mousses and mousselines; once bound with a *panada* (a mixture of flour, salt, butter and water), they are now mixed with a *béchamel* (white sauce) and set with gelatine if served cold, or cooked in a *bain-marie* (a tray of water in the oven) if served hot.

Pain des Ardennes   A cold *pain* of smoked Ardennes ham.

Pain de poulet   A hot chicken *pain*, sometimes served with two sauces – tomato and chicken. It may also be eaten cold the next day.

Pâté en croûte à la champenoise An *en croûte* coarse pâté of rabbit, pork and veal, the meat having first been marinaded in Marc de Champagne for two days.

Pâté froid de grives A smooth thrush pâté originating from the Ardennes.

Pâté de lapin à la champenoise A coarse pâté of white-wine-marinaded rabbit, seasoned with nutmeg and thyme, baked *en croûte* and served hot or cold.

Pâté rémois or *Pâté de la Petite Maman* A coarse pâté cooked *en croûte* (in pastry) made from pigeon or partridge, veal, pork fillet, calf-liver and sausage meat, flavoured with nutmeg and marinaded in white wine and Marc de Champagne.

Pieds de cochon à la Sainte-Ménehould Pig's trotters cooked for up to 48 hours in a *court-bouillon* of white wine, stock, onions and carrots, they are then drained, coated in fresh breadcrumbs, masked with *beurre fondu* and grilled to a golden colour. Traditionally this dish is served with creamed potatoes or puréed peas.

Pieds de mouton farcis à la rémoise Sheep's feet stuffed with sausage meat, chopped pork crackling and breadcrumbs – a speciality of Reims.

Pieds de veau Saint-Ménehould Calf's feet prepared and served in a similar way to *Pieds de cochon à la Sainte-Ménehould*, but with an initial cooking time of between 2 and 3 hours.

Potée champenoise This dish is traditionally eaten by the *vendangeurs* during the harvest. It is a hearty 'meal-in-one' comprising slowly stewed meats, *andouillettes,* carrots, onions, potato, cabbage, turnips, green beans, and peas. The well-flavoured stock is prepared like soup in a bowl with floating grilled croûtons, while the drained vegetables are served separately, neatly arranged by type. The meats, which may contain various cuts of mutton, beef and pork, are offered on one communal plate.

Poularde au Champagne en gelée Chicken stuffed with foie gras, brandy and truffles, and baked in butter in the oven. The juices are drained-off, mixed with an equal amount of Champagne and used to 'baste' the bird while it cools.

Quenelles champenoises de lapin These are not really *quenelles* in the true sense, but more like *quenelle*-shaped, rabbit-based sausage cakes which are sometimes called *boudins de lapin*.

Queue de boeuf grillée Saint-Ménehould Braised ox-tail spread with mustard slightly flavoured with cayenne pepper, rolled in breadcrumbs, and grilled.

Rôties de pigeon à la rémoise Roasted pigeons garnished with their own livers and strips of Ardennes ham which have been sautéed in butter.

Sanglier à l'ardennaise Fillets of wild boar marinaded for three days in red wine and vinegar, flambéed in Marc de Champagne and cooked with a small amount of the marinade – should be served garnished with bilberries.

Saucisses de Champagne A sausage made from pork meat, the fat from around the pig's kidneys, Champagne and spices.

Pastries and other sweets

Champagne has an attractive array of original pastries, traditionally calling upon pears, apples, cherries and plums of the Île-de-France, wild-thyme-influenced honey of Châlons-sur-Marne and Saint-Ménehould and pure fruit *confitures* and *gelées* from the Aube.

Anglois Plum tart named after the red-clad English soldier.

Beignets aux pommes Flat pan-fried apple fritters.

Biscuits roses de Reims It is sociably acceptable to dunk the famous pink coloured biscuits of Reims in Champagne, but they may also be eaten on their own, served with light, creamy desserts like *sabayon* or used as an ingredient in other recipes.

Crème champenoise Every region has a variant of this dish which is similar to a *sabayon*, but with the added zest of lemon peel, and may be served either warm or cold.

Flan Champenois A dough-based flan in which the *crème de pâtissier* is flavoured with Marc de Champagne. Cherry flans and pear flans are particularly popular in Champagne.

Galette au sucre The special character of this cake is its texture which looks like that of an over-aerated madeira cake, but tears like bread. It is made from eggs, butter, flour and yeast, and baked with a crispy sugar topping.

Gâteau Tante Edmée A cake made from Reims biscuits, butter, eggs, and sometimes Marc de Champagne; it is served with *crème anglaise* (fresh custard made from eggs, cream and vanilla).

Macaron The origin of macaroons is uncertain, but those of Nancy, east of Champagne, were famous as early as the seventeenth century and they are now a speciality of the Aube.

Nonnettes de Reims Small rectangular cakes made with local honey and topped with royal icing.

Petit fours rémois Small biscuits made by chilling a mixture of crushed *biscuits de Reims*, sugar, eggs, butter and Marc de Champagne in the fridge for two hours.

Rabottes Apple stuffed with red fruit jam and baked in *en croûte*.

Sabayon au Champagne (or *Marc de Champagne*) This is a French version of the classic Italian zabaglione in which a mixture of eggs, beaten with wine or brandy, and sugar is cooked in *a bain-marie* while continuously whisking. It is best served warm.

Sorbet à la champenoise A presentation of three sorbets: Champagne flavoured, Marc de Champagne flavoured and ratafia flavoured which together present a white, grey and pink coloured dish.

Tarte au quemeu or *tarte au queneu* or *galette à la farce* This is a type of flan, with an egg custard filling baked on a pastry base which is traditionally served at fêtes in Chaumont in Haute-Marne.

Tarte aux raisins This grape tart is usually made with Pinot Noir or Chardonnay grapes, sometimes a pattern of both and is traditionally served following the *Potée champenoise* at harvest time.

Local cheeses

Champagne is well known for its soft, creamy cheeses, in particular *brie* which is made in the eastern reaches of the old province of Champagne. Although the best cheeses usually come from small farmhouses (indicated by the word *fermier* on the label) or from monasteries (look for *Abbaye*), factory-produced cheeses are not necessarily inferior, if they have been made using traditional methods and unpasteurised milk, but most are produced with pasteurised milk and as a consequence lack the flavour of *fermier* and *Abbaye* cheeses.

When cheeses are offered without wrappers (as is usually the case) look at their shape and finish: a factory-made cheese will be symmetrical and pristine looking, while a traditional cheese is often hand-shaped and the texture of the crust is much less even. But one should not spurn factory-produced cheeses on principle, any more than one should automatically reject the commercial production of famous Champagnes in preference to the rustic products of *récoltants-manipulants*. The quality of a factory-made cheese will be dependent on the character of the raw material and on the care taken over its production. The following cheeses are all made from the region which once formed the historical province of Champagne and are all produced from cow's milk.

Arrigny A small, square-shaped cheese, which is mild, soft and creamy.

Baguette laonnaise A cylindrical-shaped soft cheese, creamy-yellow in colour, with a smooth brown rind. It is high smelling and has an assertive flavour.

Bouquet de Thiérache A local farm-produced cheese from the Meuse river near the Franco-Belgian border.

Boursault A small, delicately textured triple-cream cheese, apricot or peach coloured inside with a skin which can develop a rosy bloom if carefully aged. Boursault is usually made from pasteurised milk, although the gold-labelled variety produced at Saint-Cyr-sur-Morin is unpasteurised.

Brie This soft, creamy-yellow cheese has been written about since the time of Charlemagne and no doubt has a history much longer. The *Pays de Brie* or classic *brie* country overlaps the Île-de-France and the old province of Champagne, the largest proportion being in Champagne. *Brie de Melun* is generally thought to be the first of the legendary *bries* but *Brie de Meaux* is currently considered the more classic product. Typically, *brie* is made as a flat disc, about fourteen inches in diameter and one to one and a half inches deep. The crust of a commercial *brie* is smooth and white, while a farm-made *brie* can be recognised by the ruddy-brown patches on its somewhat uneven surface.

Brie de Coulommiers Not a true *brie* although related, this cheese is mild and delicate in flavour and sometimes simply called *Coulommiers* or *Petit Coulommiers* when young.

Brie Laitier A factory-made *brie* using pasteurised milk and added stabilisers. This is supermarket *brie* – it is the lightest in colour and the mildest in flavour.

Brie de Meaux The largest of the genuine farm-made *bries*, it can weigh as much as six pounds and should be labelled *fermier*. It has a ripe, tangy flavour which is always rich, sometimes farmyardy, but should never be so high as to be ammoniac.

Caprice des Dieux Originating from the Bongrain creamery at Illoud in Haute-Marne, this double-cream cheese has white crust and a fine, mild flavour. It is small, oval-shaped and weighs about six ounces.

Carré de l'Est A small, square-shaped cheese with a soft white crust, usually factory-made and often regarded as a rectangular *Camembert*. Those with a washed rind (where the outer surface has been regularly wiped over with brine in order to sustain a high internal moisture level) can be quite pungent, but exported varieties are generally milder.

Cendré This is a generic term for the small soft cheeses ripened in ashes provided by discarded vine branches from local vineyards.

Cendré de la brie A farm-made cheese of low fat-content, rarely seen outside the locality. Traditionally *Cendré de la brie* was made from the left-over, low-fat curds of *brie*-making which were kept for the farmer's family. These were then rolled in ashes and matured to obtain a richer, stronger cheese from the relatively feeble ingredients.

Cendré des Riceys A small, wheel-shaped, soft cheese, about three-quarters of a pound in weight. Rolled in Pinot Noir ashes, it is high smelling and pungent in flavour, and sometimes known simply as *les Riceys*, *Champenois* or *Cendré champenois*.

Chaource A drum-shaped, soft cheese of varying size, usually well over a pound in weight. Named after the town of Chaource, near Troyes, it is widely produced by small creameries from unpasteurised milk. It has a white crust, a mild smell and a rich, tangy flavour.

Chaumont A small, spicy, Marne valley cheese, with a ripe, creamy flavour, produced in the locality of Chaumont. It can be either conical or fat-wheel-shaped and has a ruddy-brown 'washed' crust. Soft, ripe, creamy-tangy cheese, similar to *Époisses* of Burgundy.

Coulommiers (See also *Brie de Coulommiers*) Usually a factory-made cheese, although some smaller and richer farm-made versions from cream-enriched unpasteurised milk can be found. It is called *Brie de Coulommiers* if aged.

Coulommiers frais A very small, soft, double-cream cheese similar to the widely available *Petit Suisse*. It is unripened and unsalted and improves greatly if broken up and seasoned with a little salt and coarsely ground black pepper.

Ducs Ducs is the brand name for a factory-made, soft-ripened curd cheese made at Chapelle-la-Vieille-Forêt, near Chablis. It is round and flat with a soft, powdery skin and is ripened prior to sale.

Ervy-le-Châtel A truncated-cone-shaped soft cheese with a bloomy crust and a spicy, almost fruity, flavour. Produced around *Ervy-le-Châtel*, south of Troyes, it is often compared to *Chaource* fifteen kilometres to the east.

Explorateur A supremely rich, triple-cream, wheel-shaped cheese made in the Petit-Morin valley of Seine-et-Marne. It has a light white skin, a rather neutral aroma, but a luxurious, delicate, creamy flavour.

Fougeru This is a *Coulommiers*-type cheese made at Tournan-en-Brie with *fougères*, or fern leaves, which has a mild yet distinctive flavour.

Igny Also called *Abbaye d'Igny* this is a smooth, semi-soft, wheel-shaped cheese weighing about two pounds and produced by the Trappist monks of Igny, near Fismes.

Langres This is a high smelling, strong tasting soft to semi-soft cheese, truncated-cone or sunken-drum-shaped, with a smooth browny 'washed' crust.

Maroilles Originally Flemish, *Maroilles* has long been established in Champagne as a farm-made, brick-shaped cheese weighing anything between 8 oz and two pounds. It is soft in texture with a reddish 'washed' crust, a pungent smell and a piquant flavour.

Montreal A smooth, pungent, soft creamy cheese, farm-made in the Serein valley.

Rocroi A rectangular or wheel-shaped soft creamy cheese rolled in vine ashes and also called *Cendré des Ardennes*.

Saint-Florentin Similar to *Soumaintrain*.

Sorbais A smaller version of *Maroilles*, often called *Maroilles-sorbais*.

Soumaintrain This cheese is more commonly associated with Burgundy, although it is also made in Champagne. About 12 oz in weight, wheel-shaped, with a shiny-brown 'washed' rind, it has a high smell and pungent flavour.

Cheese dishes

Gougères de l'Aube Small baked choux pastry buns filled with Gruyère cheese-flavoured *béchamel*, sprinkled with grated cheese and crisped in the oven. *Gougères*, often considered a Burgundian speciality, were in fact originally cooked in Sens in the Aube département.

Beignets de fromage blanc Deep-fried choux pastry buns, lightly flavoured with *fromage blanc* and tossed in finely ground sugar.

Fondus au fromage A *béchamel*-based Gruyère and parmesan *pâté* cut into small rectangular slabs when cold, dipped in egg and breadcrumbs, and deep-fried.

Drinking Champagne with food

One school of thought is of the belief that Champagne partners most dishes adequately, yet none ideally, while another is of the opinion that Champagne does not go with food at all and therefore should only be drunk by itself. Such views are nonsense however. Of course, those who believe such things have the right to their own opinion, but most readers are unlikely to feel so restricted in their enjoyment of Champagne. Champagne does have the ability to accompany most foods, but it certainly rises above adequate in these partnerships and some combinations come close to perfection.

This does not mean that Champagne should be enjoyed with every course; although occasional showpiece menus make a feature of this, such meals are by definition unbalanced. An honoured guest at a Champagne house, for instance, will probably be offered a good red wine, usually a claret, with the main course, after drinking Champagne as an apéritif and with the first course. Some might feel it more natural, rational even, to follow Champagne with a red Burgundy, there being a direct relationship between the grape varieties involved. However, many houses feel Burgundy to be too heavy and believe the weight of a Bordeaux wine makes it the perfect choice. This is not a hard and fast rule – the food, the wine or the guest may encourage a normally pro-Bordeaux house to serve Burgundy on occasions.

Food and wine combinations

There are, in fact, no rules about which wines should be drunk with certain foods, merely broad guidelines which have evolved over the centuries. The concept of drinking white wine with seafood and white meats, for example, or red wine with dark meats, is merely a reflection of the fact that these combinations have suited the taste of most people most of the time. Nobody has to slavishly adhere to this sort of advice, but being the tried and tested wisdom of generations, it naturally makes sense to make use of it.

When analysed, whether a general guideline like white wine with seafood, or a specific recommendation such as Champagne with oysters, the common factor is always one of achieving a balance. If a gastronomic law does exist, then it has to be that the more delicate the food, the more delicate the wine, the richer the food, the fuller the wine. Thus, if one decides to experiment with, say, a red wine with chicken, it would be sensible to start off with a *light* red or seek a well flavoured chicken dish. How far from the main framework of generations of advice an individual's taste extends is of course a matter of personal interpretation.

Some partnerships of Champagne and food are classic; Champagne with oysters, as mentioned above, and with caviar, or with foie gras. But trends come and go and some classics tend to lapse: in former times, there was a general preference for Champagne *doux* (sweet Champagne) with unfermented cheese, but Champagne *doux* is virtually extinct today, thus we are unable to preserve the status of this old classic. Conditioning affects what is perceived to be classic, thus countries can develop combinations which may be classic on a national basis only. The French preference for a dry Champagne to accompany a sweet dessert is, for example, hard to appreciate in Britain and the United States.

Obviously the most important factor to consider when balancing Champagne with food is its effervescence. This is usually a positive quality in Champagne, although there are some foods with which an effervescence is less appropriate. The effervescence of Champagne can provide the perfect edge to cut across certain textures such as butter, eggs, cream and purées, while its relatively high acidity can act both to clean the mouth after bland flavours or to match the tartness of some tomato-based dishes.

Champagne is ideal to drink with fried food, from the humble pork sausage to the trout or salmon dishes of *haute cuisine*. Its sparkling property brings out the true earthy taste of most river fish (which should not be confused with the muddy character of fish from soft-bottom waters) and cuts through the myriad of cream and butter sauces in which so many fish and fowl are cooked. Champagne is also the perfect accompaniment to various vegetarian dishes, lifts the texture of pasta and rice dishes and delights all combinations of egg, from *en cocotte* to coddled, stuffed to scrambled or *souffléed*.

Champagne with a traditional English breakfast provides a superlative start to the day. It is absolutely indispensable with cold mousses, hot or cold mousselines and all cold dishes glazed *en gelée*, *en aspic* or with *chaud-froid*. Take the yawn out of soup and serve it with Champagne, a positive must with all cold soups and nothing less than revolutionary with hot *purée*, *velouté*, *bisque* and cream soups.

Some recommended combinations of Champagne and local cuisine:

WINES	DISHES AND CHEESES

Vintage and Non-vintage Brut Champagnes

Light styles
(Eg, Ayala, Billecart-Salmon, Jacquesson, Mumm, Perrier-Jouët)

Soupe au lait ardennaise, Endives à l'ardenaise, Salade au lard, Carpe au bleu, Boudin blanc, Pieds de cochon à la Sainte-Ménehould, Pieds de veau Sainte-Ménehould, Potée champenoise, Saucisses de Champagne, Fondus au fromage
CHEESES Arrigny, Boursault, Caprice des Dieux, Coulommiers Frais, Ducs, Explorateur

Medium styles
(Eg, Deutz, Henriot, Moët, Joseph Perrier, Piper Heidsieck, Philipponnat, Pommery, Ruinart)

Soupe au beurre, Chou potagère, Fricassé de pommes de terre à l'ardennaise, Salade champenoise, Brochet farci à la rémoise, Ecrevisses en matelote, Andouillettes de mouton, Boudin blanc, Choucroute, Galette à la flamme, Lapin en gelée, Potée champenoise, Saucisses de Champagne, Fondus au fromage
CHEESES Arrigny, Bouquet de Thiérache, Boursault, Brie de Colommiers, Caprice des Dieux, Chaource, Chaumont, Ducs, Explorateur

Rich, full styles
(Eg, Barancourt, Napoleon, Veuve Clicquot)

Soupe à la bière de Mezières, Chou à l'ardennaise, Salade champenoise, Aiguille Sainte-Ménehould, Matelote champenoise, Boudin de Sainte-Ménehould, Carbonnade de boeuf, Faisan aux raisins, Pâté rémois, Pâté en croûte à la champenoise, Potée champenoise
CHEESES Bouquet de Thiérache, Brie de Meaux, Chaource, Chaumont, Ervy-le-Châtel, Igny, Maroilles

Assertive, full styles
(Eg, Bollinger, Alfred Gratien, Krug)

Soupe aux choux et aux lardons, Bailline, Salade de pissenlit au lard, Aiguille au vert, Écrevisses en matelote, Matelote à la Canontière, Andouillettes de mouton, Boudin noir, Boeuf en éventail à la troyenne, Faisan en daube à la sparnacienne, Grives sous la cendré, Oie à la marnaise, Potée champenoise
CHEESES Baguette laonnaise, Brie de Meaux, Carré de l'Est, Cendré de la brie, Cendré de Riceys, Langres, Maroilles, Rocroi, Saint-Florentin, Sorbais, Soumaintrain

Blanc de Blancs Brut Champagnes

Young or light styles
(Eg, Ayala, Besserat de Bellefon, Jacquesson, Mumm, Bruno Paillard)

Salade au lard, Soupe au lait ardennaise, Truite au bleu, Quenelles de brochet, Boudin blanc, Crêpes au jambon, Grives à l'ardennaise, Pieds de cochon à la Sainte-Ménehould, Pieds de veau, Sainte-Ménehould, Potée champenoise, Saucisses de Champagne, Fondus au fromage
CHEESES Arrigny, Boursault, Caprice des Dieux, Coulommiers frais, Ducs, Explorateur

WINES	DISHES AND CHEESES
Medium styles (Eg, Billecart-Salmon, Deutz, Joseph Perrier, Pol Roger, de Venoge)	Soupe au lait ardennaise, Endives à l'ardennaise, Brochet farci à la rémoise, Écrevisses en matelote, Andouillettes de mouton, Boudin blanc, Choucroute, Galette à la flamme, Potée champenoise, Saucisses de Champagne CHEESES Arringy, Bouquet de Thiérache, Caprice des Dieux, Chaource, Chaumont
Mature or full styles (Eg, Barancourt, Comte de Champagne, Ruinart, Salon)	Aiguille Sainte-Ménehould, Chou à l'ardennaise, Matelote champenoise, Andouillettes de mouton, Boudin blanc, Faisan aux raisins, Escalopes de veau à la rémoise CHEESES Baguette Laonnaise, Brie de Meaux, Carré de l'Est, Cendré de la brie, Cendré de Riceys, Langres, Maroilles, Rocroi, Saint-Florentin, Sorbais, Soumaintrain

Blanc de Noirs Brut Champagnes

Mature or full styles (Eg, Bollinger, Bruno Paillard)	Pochouse à matelote, Boudin de Sainte-Ménehould, Carbonnade de boeuf, Civet de livre, Pâté en croûte à la champenoise, Pâté rémois CHEESES Baguette laonnaise, Brie de Meaux, Carré de l'Est, Cendré de la brie, Cendré de Riceys, Langres, Maroilles, Rocroi, Saint-Florentin, Sorbais, Soumaintrain

Pink Brut Champagnes

Light styles (Eg, Besserat de Bellefon, Billecart-Salmon, Mumm)	Champignons à la Sainte-Ménehould, Chou à l'ardennaise, Salade au lard, Truite au bleu, Quenelles de brochet CHEESES Arrigny, Boursault, Caprice des Explorateurs
Soft, medium styles (Eg, Belle Epoque, de Castellane, Gosset, Lanson, Philipponnat)	Filets de truites au vin de Champagne, Quenelles de brochet, Grives en cocotte à l'ardennaise, Langues, Lapin en gelée CHEESES Arrigny, Bouquet de Thiérache, Brie de Melun, Caprice des Dieux, Carré de l'Est, Chaource, Chaumont, Igny, Montreal
Crisp, medium styles (Eg, Bollinger, Krug, Pol Roger, Pommery, Veuve Clicquot)	Écrevisses en matelote, Filets de brochet au vin des Riceys, Coq au vin de Bouzy, Escalopes de veau à la rémoise, Faisan aux raisins CHEESES Baguette laonnaise, Brie de Meaux, Carré de l'Est, Cendré de la brie, Cendré de Riceys, Langres, Maroilles, Rocroi, Saint-Florentin, Sorbais, Soumaintrain
Rich, full styles (Eg, Barancourt, Comte de Champagne, George Goulet, Dom Pérignon, Veuve Clicquot's Wedding Cuvée)	Truite à l'ardennaise, Carbonnade de boeuf, Civet de marcassin, Côtes de porc à l'ardennaise, Dindonneau braisé au Champagne CHEESES Baguette laonnaise, Brie de Meaux, Carré de l'Est, Cendré de la brie, Cendré de Riceys, Langres, Maroilles, Rocroi, Saint-Florentin, Sorbais, Soumaintrain

WINES	DISHES AND CHEESES

Crémant Brut Champagnes

Authentic styles
(Eg, Besserat de Bellefon, Alfred Gratien, Abel Lepitre, Mumm)

Soupe au lait ardennaise, Endives à l'ardennaise, Champignons à la Sainte-Ménehould, Truite au bleu, Quenelles de brochet, Boudin blanc, Grives à l'ardennaise, Fondus au fromage, Gougères
CHEESES Arrigny, Bouquet de Thiérache, Boursault, Caprice des Dieux, Coulommiers frais, Ducs, Explorateur

Coteaux Champenois

Red
(Eg, Barancourt, Bollinger)

Coq au vin de Bouzy, Carbonnade de boeuf flammande, Boeuf en éventail à la troyenne, Civet de marcassin, Crêpes au jambon, Dindonneau braisé au Champagne, Pâté en croûte à la champenoise, Pâté rémois
CHEESES Bouquet de Thiérache, Carré de l'Est, Cendré de Brie, Cendré des Riceys, Fougeru, Igny Montreal, Rocroi

White

Salade au lard, Boudin blanc, Pieds de cochon à la Sainte-Ménehould, Saucisses de Champagne, Fondus au fromage
CHEESES Caprice des Dieux, Coulommiers frais, Ducs

Rosé des Riceys

Recommended wines
(Eg, Horiot, Bonnet)

Filets de brochet au vin des Riceys, Filets de truites au vin de Champagne, Champignons à la Sainte-Ménehould, Langues, Lapin en gelée, Chou à l'ardennaise, Salade au lard, Truite au bleu
CHEESES Boursault, Brie de Melun, Carré de l'Est, Cendré des Riceys, Chaource, Chaumont, Igny, Montreal

Ratafia

Recommended wines
(Eg, Joseph Perrier, Veuve Clicquot)

Anglois, Galette au sucre, Gâteau Tante Edmée, Nonnettes de Reims, Rabottes, Tarte aux raisins
CHEESES Sweet wines are best suited to rich, piquant, blue-veined cheeses, unhappily absent in Champagne.

12

Champagne Houses, Growers and Co-operatives

When John Finley complained there was water in the cellar of the house rented from Grover Cleveland, Cleveland replied, 'Well, my dear fellow, what did you expect – Champagne?'
Cleveland Finley, *Scribner's Magazine*, April 1927

HISTORICALLY, THERE HAS ALWAYS BEEN A DIVISION between viticulture and viniculture in Champagne. Before the great Champagne houses of today emerged it was the local Champenois who tended the vine while various monastic orders made and sold the wine. From the eighteenth century onwards the role of the monks was gradually superseded by entrepreneurs – often of foreign origin as names such as Bollinger, Heidsieck, Krug, Roederer, Schreider, and Vander-Veken imply. Today, while the Champagne houses produce most of the wine, they own very little of the land. Of the 23,618 hectares of vineyards which were productive in 1982, the houses owned 3,388 hectares (or 14.3%) and the growers 20,230 hectares (or 85.7%).

The Houses or *Négociants-Manipulants*

Initially the houses negotiated with the growers to purchase their grapes, which they then processed into Champagne, thus becoming known as *négociants-manipulants*. Today, an increasing number of houses also have vineyard holdings, although the amount they own varies between 5% and 95% of their total production needs. Obviously any firm with a large viticultural estate can rest assured that in times of shortage its production will be bolstered by supplies from its own vineyards. Not only will its own grapes cost considerably less than the statutory fixed price per kilo, but the continuity of style can be more confidently maintained and its quality more easily guaranteed.

There are 120 *négociants-manipulants* of varying size. At the lower end of the scale, between twenty-five and thirty are barely more than growers; they have applied to become *négociants-manipulants* and have a combined production which represents about 2% of the *négociants-manipulants'* total trade. At the top end of the scale ten houses represent 50% of the trade.

In the popular image of Champagne great and particular weight is given to the term *grande marque*, but the term is ambiguous, especially in English speaking countries where it has evolved into some sort of 'official' classification akin to the concept of a grand cru. Literally, *grande marque* means a 'great brand' or famous make and refers to a reputation gained either through great quality or sheer volume: thus Harrods and Woolworth, Parker and Biro, Rolls Royce and Ford are all *grandes marques*. In Champagne a *grande marque* should simply refer to a well-known brand, but its use has been complicated since the mid-sixties due to its adoption by a Syndicat of *négociants*.

In 1964 the Syndicat des Grandes Marques de Champagne came into being, emerging out of the former Syndicat du Commerce des Vins de Champagne. At that time membership included Ayala, Billecart-Salmon, J. Bollinger, Veuve Clicquot-Ponsardin, Delbeck (which has since been taken over by Piper Heidsieck), Deutz & Geldermann, Heidsieck & Co. Monopole, Charles Heidsieck, Irroy, Krug, Lanson Père & Fils, Massé Père & Fils, Moët & Chandon, Montebello, G. H. Mumm & Co., Perrier-Jouët, Joseph Perrier, Piper Heidsieck, Pol Roger, Pommery & Greno, Ch. & A. Prieur, Louis Roederer, Ruinart Père & Fils, A. Salon & Co. and Taittinger.

Since 1964 Canard-Duchêne, Henriot, Laurent-Perrier, and Mercier have all been elected. Although the Syndicat includes houses which the majority of Champagne afficionados would regard, through quality or volume, as 'great brands', there are several which certainly do not qualify. Irroy had a fine reputation over a hundred years ago, but it is currently no more than a second label of Taittinger. I would place Massé, belonging to Lanson, and Montebello, belonging to Ayala, in the same category. Despite its high quality, Champagne Napoleon of Ch. & A. Prieur plainly is not a *grande marque*, while Salon, although produced in tiny quantities, seems still to have enough of the reputation it established in the twenties and thirties to merit 'great brand' status.

Those who maintain that a Champagne *grande marque* can only be called such if it is a member of the Syndicat de Grandes Marques de Champagne must, by their own definition, agree that prior to 11 March 1964 there were no *grandes marques* at all! But there is nothing to stop any Champagne proclaiming itself a *grande marque* as, for example, Henri Abelé's 'Grande Marque Impériale' does and has done since the beginning of the century, long before the Syndicat's change of name in 1964.

All *négociant-manipulant* Champagnes, whether *grandes marques* or not, can be recognised by the matriculation number, usually located at the base of a label, commencing with the initials 'NM'.

The Growers or *Récoltants*

There are approximately 14,000 owners of productive vineyards in Champagne, between 7,000 and 8,000 of whom are resident growers, *or récoltants*; the remainder are absentee landlords or part-time growers. All except 300 of the 14,000 owners belong to the Syndicat Général des Vignerons de la Champagne, the remaining 300 being the *négociants* and a few rebel *récoltants* who apparently have no desire to belong to any organisation.

Of the 7,000 to 8,000 *récoltants*, only 4,860 are grower-producers or *récoltants-manipulants*, selling all or part of their harvest under their own label; the rest sell their entire crop either to the *négociants-manipulants* or to the *co-opératives-manipulants*. The production of a *récoltant* can vary from between 50 bottles a year (for entirely private use), to 300,000 bottles (which is larger in volume than some of the smaller houses). The average *récoltant-manipulant* produces 10,000 bottles from a 1.5 hectarage vineyard.

A survey of owners in 1981, when their numbers totalled 14,305 and the area of productive vineyards they owned covered almost 20,930 hectares, shows the breakdown of vineyards owned:

Size of Vineyard	Number of Growers	Proportion of Growers	Total Area under Vine	Proportion of Total
Less than 1 ha.	7,881	55.10%	3,092 ha.	15%
1–2 ha.	2,769	19.35%	4,020 ha.	19%
2–3 ha.	1,753	12.25%	4,322 ha.	21%
3–5 ha.	1,324	9.25%	4,971 ha.	23%
over 5 ha.	578	4.05%	4,524 ha.	22%
TOTAL	14,305	100.00%	20,929 ha.	100%

Sales by the *récoltants-manipulants* are no longer insignificant. Once a bare two to three million bottles, production rose in the mid-1950s when *récoltants* became disenchanted with supplying the houses. The *négociants-manipulants* were to many growers disproportionately wealthy and increasing numbers of *récoltants* took the financial risk of manufacturing their own Champagnes. Not only was the monetary investment in equipment a substantial one (much more so that in other regions where the *méthode champenoise* is not required) but the growers often had to wait for two to three years before a significant return could be realised. For most it paid off and sales rose steadily, although it was not until they broke through on to the domestic French market in the mid-1970s that sales rose steeply, peaking at over fifty-one million bottles in 1979 (or sixty-three million if *co-opératives-manipulants* are included).

Some *récoltants-manipulants* Champagnes are produced utilising a *co-opérative* for all or part of the process, although many undertake the entire operation themselves. Wines are generally sold on the premises and naturally new customers are welcomed. Many people prefer the more personalised product of the *récoltant-manipulant*, returning year after year to the same grower for perhaps just one case of Champagne and a reception which is always warm and sincere.

It cannot be denied that grower Champagnes show less consistency than house Champagnes, but it is understandable when 4,860 different grower *marques* exist, each having anything from one to half a dozen styles of wine on offer, yielding a possibility of 17,000 different labels. Seeking out quality can be a daunting task.

In a year of favourable climatic conditions, and when the growers' situation is not exacerbated by acute or abnormal economic conditions, *récoltants'* own-label production can expect to average some 45 million bottles of which 6.5 million could be classified as 'co-oped clones'. A co-oped clone refers to a Champagne produced by a *co-opérative*, but sold under numerous different *récoltant* labels by members of the *co-opérative*. The wine may be of very good quality, but it is not the individual product of a specific grower.

Where the wine is an individual product, it is usually a single growth or mono-cru and, like Krug's Clos du Mesnil and Philipponnat's Clos des Goises, does not therefore conform to the classic concept of a blended Champagne. It is the uniqueness of these Champagnes which should be enjoyed.

Some growers do own several plots of vines in different villages and grow more than one variety of grape, but their ability to effect the complicated permutations of blend practised by the houses is naturally restricted by the quantity of each variety they are able to obtain to achieve a particular *cuvée*. *Récoltants-manipulants* are prevented from buying more than 5% as a proportion of their preserved stock of grapes. Whereas growers can apply to become *négociants-manipulants* and thus deal freely in the purchases of grapes, musts and wines, few would be willing to sacrifice the obvious tax benefits of being a grower.

There are future possibilities for growers to band together, not as *co-opératives*, but as small groups of three or four *récoltants*, or one 'family' of growers. The firm of Barancourt evolved in this way: three *récoltants* Brice, Tritant and Martin, merged their holdings into one sizeable estate of forty-six hectares. With prime Chardonnay sites in Avize balancing top Pinot Noir vineyards in Bouzy, the newly named firm of Barancourt has managed to establish a reputation for quality, balance and consistency. But not all combinations need result in a change of status, smaller unions can be, and are, just as effective.

A *récoltant-manipulant* Champagne can be recognised by the initials 'RM' appearing before the matriculation number on the label.

The *Co-opératives* and *Co-opératives-Manipulants*

Prior to 1939 there were just thirty *co-opératives* in Champagne, but the CIVC has since encouraged their development, resulting in the current total of 146. These fall into four basic categories:

1 *Presshouse co-opérative* which merely presses grapes.
2 *Vin clair co-opérative* which presses grapes and vinifies still wines.
3 *Sur lattes co-opérative* which presses grapes, vinifies still wines and takes the Champagne process to the *sur lattes* stage.
4 *Commercial co-opérative* which presses grapes, vinifies still wines and makes and sells Champagne under one or more of its own labels recognised by the initials 'CM' (*co-opérative-manipulant*) appearing before the matriculation number.

The above indicates the capacity of a *co-opérative* within each category, but it does not necessarily follow that all the grapes a *co-opérative* receives are processed to the full extent of its functions. A commercial *co-opérative* may, for example, merely press some of its grapes if it so wishes – it does not have to commercialise its entire turnover.

The *Négociants-non-Manipulants* and BOBS

The *négociants-non-manipulants* and BOBS (Buyer's Own Brand) are a further marketing outlet for Champagne. They are the wholesale buyers who buy their Champagne from the producers and market it independently, either as true wholesalers (or *négociants-non-manipulants*) – such as de Courcy, which buys its Champagne from A. Charbaut & Fils and wholesales it direct to hotels, restaurants and various retailers in France and abroad –

or as retailers – such as Maxims or Marks & Spencer, which retail it under their own-label restaurant or supermarket brands. The brands are obviously owned by the wholesalers and retailers who are free to change the firms producing their Champagnes at will, although this right would be more likely to be exercised in the case of retailers, such as Marks & Spencer, than by a *négociant-non-manipulant* like de Courcy.

The two initials appearing before the matriculation number on a bottle of Champagne which refer to this group are 'MA', standing for *marque auxiliaire*. The regulations concerning *marques auxiliaires* are far from satisfactory as 'MA' does in fact represent two very different sorts of wine: the *marque d'acheteur* and the *sous marque*. The *marque d'acheteur* or 'Buyer's Own Brand' (BOB) applies to a wine belonging to a wholesaler or retailer; the *sous marque* is a true *marque auxiliaire*, an auxiliary or secondary *marque* or brand belonging to its producer, some examples of which are Giesler, Gauthier, Eugène Clicquot, Pol Gessner and Giesmann, all of which are made by and belong to Marne & Champagne.

To further confuse the 'MA' issue, a Champagne house may have up to three different *marques* with 'NM' matriculation numbers, thus a *sous marque* might bear either 'MA' or 'NM' according to circumstance. At the time of writing, changes in the regulations were being considered which would oblige producers to clearly indicate their name on the label. This would be a welcome step, especially if the same rationale could be applied to famous brands of Champagne which have been purchased *sur lattes* from BOB houses.

13

Champagne's Future

A cause may be inconvenient, but it's magnificent. It's like champagne or highshoes and one must be prepared to suffer for it.
Arnold Bennett, *The Title*

WHAT LIES AHEAD for the future of Champagne? Is its expanding viticultural Champagne area, commonly predicted to reach 29,000 hectares by 1991, compared to 25,500 hectares today, going to enhance the luxury image of this product? Will the expected annual production of 200 million bottles spread the gospel far and wide, or will it damage the 'limited supply' theme that Champagne's viticulturally meagre climate has solidly built up over the centuries? We can look back to the sixties, when the area under vine was around 12,000 hectares and a harvest of 75 million bottles was considered large. In the past the quality of Champagne could not be disputed. But what can we look forward to?

Vineyards outside Champagne *viticole*

Some of Champagne *viticole* delimited in 1927 can now be found under roads and buildings, supporting bridges and in other locations which have become impossible to cultivate. As some of the land once deemed suitable for viticulture is now unavailable, due to progress, does this mean, maybe, that there could be a reverse hypothesis? Is it possible, due to progress in viticultural techniques, that some areas hitherto inappropriate for cultivation might now be considered suitable?

Certainly some people think so and there are already two schools of opinion on this subject in Champagne. I expect one of these, the pro-expansionists, to become more vociferous towards the end of the eighties. It is hard not to be at least cautiously in support of a controlled expansion into new areas within the general Champagne region, if the exploitation of those areas can be viticulturally justified.

Land suitable for the growing of Champagne vines

In *Champagne*, Patrick Forbes points out that the law of 1927 made provision for the setting up of local government-sponsored commissions 'to determine the eligibility of individual vineyards ... empowered to strike off the list all vineyards situated on flat, clayey ground and on ground overlying micraster chalk, neither of which is suitable for the growing of Champagne vines.' If this had been carried out with any efficiency, the surface area now under vine would be much smaller and programmes involving the plantation of new vineyards would be severely hampered.

The fact is, right or wrong, Champagne today is made, in part, from vines grown on flat ground, on clayey ground and on ground overlying Micraster chalk, but in the melting pot which is Champagne, the overall effect on most of the wines that we drink is not perceptible.

I say that the effect is not perceptible on 'most wines that we drink' because, of course, it is true that a relatively small quantity of specific and unblended wine from flat and clayey vineyards is made which, denied the benefit of the melting pot, provides a distinct contrast to our classic concept of Champagne.

Many, though certainly not all, of these flat and clayey vineyards, can be located in the more southerly Bar-sur-Aube and Bar-sur-Seine area, where an even greater influence than soil or aspect on the character of the wines produced is the different climatic conditions experienced.

As the different character of wines produced on flat, clayey, Micraster or other miscellaneous soils is lost in the overall blend of most Champagne *cuvées*, the inclusion of what might be called non-classic sites in the overall collection of Champagne vineyards is not, in itself, detrimental. What is vital however is that the current balance of classic to non-classic sites should at least be maintained.

Champagne region or Champagne *viticole*?

Before the rights or wrongs of the expansion proposals can be assessed, and the potential ways of putting into effect such proposals might be pondered, we must first realise the essential difference between the Champagne region (I am not referring to the historical province) and Champagne *viticole*.

The Champagne region is bounded by the communal borders referred to in the delimitation law of 1927 and is perhaps fifty times the size of Champagne *viticole*, a term which only covers land under vine designated AOC Champagne. Champagne *viticole* is, therefore, currently 25,500 hectares and by the law of 1927 may only be extended to, in total, the 31,050 hectares delimited by that law.

It is because the expansion of Champagne *viticole* will be closely approaching its potential of 31,050 hectares by 1990 that some, mostly producers, have expressed the need to re-evaluate the future extent of Champagne *viticole* to cope with the projected increased demand for Champagne. To be fair, it must be added that even the most extreme fringes of the pro-expansionists realise that the appeal of a luxury product like Champagne comes, in part, from its limited production – nobody, as far as I know, has suggested an expansion the size of which might endanger the quality image of Champagne.

Expansion of Champagne *viticole* over and above 31,050 hectares, but within the communal boundaries of the general Champagne region, would require a fundamental change of law. If that could be achieved, and it is a distinct possibility that it could, how then could the vineyards be expanded and what would be the justification?

The infrastructure and superstructure of Champagne

Expansion of Champagne viticole could be undertaken in two basic areas, the infrastructure and the superstructure.

Consolidation of the infrastructure   As already mentioned, there are sites within the Champagne region, in villages right across the board, from the lowly to Premiers and Grands Crus, that are not classed AOC Champagne, yet are every bit as suitable (or unsuitable) as some that are. In addition to these, there are those sites that might genuinely have been ill-positioned for cultivation in 1927, but which, with modern clonal selection, new rootstock varieties and other viticultural developments, may now be adaptable.

Developing the superstructure   There are great tracts of land within the communal boundaries of the Champagne region which have never been cultivated. In some cases, whole islands of Champagne have been delimited well away from the mainstream, yet few or no vines have been planted there. At the time of writing some of these areas relatively devoid of vines were:

East of Soissons	South and east of Arrigny
North-east of Vitry-le-François	South and east of Marcilly-le-Hayer
North of Chagny	West of Troyes

There are also many substantial districts devoid of vines in between intensively cultivated classic areas. Many of these areas, whether islands of delimitation or districts between the classic growths, might be suitable for viticultural development. Much of the land would prove totally inappropriate, but the vast expanses of land involved (and by that I do not mean that it is open flat ground, it is not) do contain areas ripe for controlled expansion.

Guarantee of quality

I think that the best opportunities for expansion will be found in consolidating the infrastructure, particularly in and around the growths of the Montagne de Reims, but the future quality of Champagne could, in any case, be safeguarded by surveys of potential sites and test cultivations prior to expansion. When production has commenced, of course, the analytical and tasting examination which all Champagne wines must undergo would be applicable.

Dog-fighting in the pro-expansionist camp

If and when such expansions take place, should the land be divided equally between the Champagne houses and the growers or shared out on a scale proportionate to their present ratio? Because the latter would mean that the houses would receive only one hectare in eight, such talk has led some pro-expansionist houses to moot the possibility of reversing the current ratio to redress the situation.

Money has a lot to do with all this heated talk: a plot of arable land suddenly receiving full AOC Champagne status would be worth between twenty-five and fifty times its original value. A moderately wealthy grower would literally become a (sterling) millionaire overnight and Champagne houses facing financial difficulties, including several big names, could instantly become some of the strongest business in the trade.

Many growers have ownership of plots favourable to re-classification and several houses, notably the larger ones, are not far behind. As promising sites have come onto the market certain firms have been quietly buying them up. It has been virtually impossible to buy AOC Champagne land for a long time, therefore houses have either purchased ailing firms with vineyard holdings or, believing in the inevitability of expansion, purchased arable land they consider to be potentially AOC plots.

The question of dividing out newly classified vineyards should not even arise. All decisions should be based upon the suitability of the land to grow Champagne vines and the suitability only. It is not as if there are tens of thousands of hectares, all with equally appropriate aspect, elevation, soil and location. The land which is appropriate for viti-cultivation should be listed in order of its intrinsic quality and released in that order.

Growers – a way forward?

In 1983 the French domestic market for Champagne showed a welcome upturn, recovering to its 1981 level. Strangely, the growers and *co-opératives*, who have so successfully penetrated the home market in the late seventies, had their poorest performance for five years. It must be a bitter disappointment for them and as they have little impact on the export market, the options open seem few indeed.

But perhaps they should look to the export market, not individually, or even as a collective group of individual growers, but as an entity with one product. In this day and age of super-*co-opératives*, the growers should seriously consider pooling their wines to produce a range of Champagnes under one label which could be effectively marketed and promoted, not by a super-*co-opérative*, but by their *syndicat*. It would certainly give them openings, contacts and experience, all of which could be followed up by some of the more dynamic individual growers at a later date.

Certainly they will have to do something if they wish to remain a force in the market place.

Invention of the 'yeast capsule'

Research started about ten years ago into a second fermentation yeast capsule, the use of which should dispense with the need to perform *remuage* of any kind. The CIVC and the Institut National de la Recherche Agronomique (INRA), in conjunction with Moët & Chandon, have now perfected such a capsule, but the wines produced still have to undergo several years of trials.

To create this capsule, a new technology was developed enabling the imprisonment of yeast cells in alginate* beads, the walls of which permit the flow of sugar, alcohol and

* Alginate is a natural polymer extracted from marine algae.

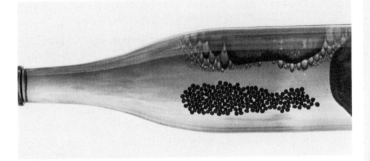

The miraculous 'yeast capsule' may one day obviate the need for *remuage*. Each capsule imprisons yeast cells within alginate walls which allow sugar, alcohol and carbonic gas molecules to pass through while being impervious to the sediment created by the second fermentation. Within seconds the 'yeast capsules' in a bottle lying *sur lattes* 1 (ABOVE) descend to the neck of the bottle and 2 (RIGHT) are ready for disgorging

carbon dioxide molecules, yet prove impervious to the waste material generated by the enzymatic activity. Thus fermentation takes place normally, but with no sediment other than that residing inside the alginate beads. As these capsules are a few millimetres in diameter and of a higher density than the wine, they easily drop into the crown-cap's plastic pot as soon as the bottle is inverted.

The idea was simple, but the advances in microbiological techniques necessary to develop it were not. Yeast capsules were used to produce a Blanquette de Limoux in 1975, but the first successful Champagnes utilising the alginate beads were made in 1982 and, so far, they appear to be indistinguishable from traditionally elaborated Champagnes constructed from the same raw materials. But the CIVC will require a much longer trial period before any stamp of approval may be considered. In the meantime, the commercial manufacture of these yeast capsules has yet to be evaluated and, if viable, there is still the problem of inserting the beads into each bottle prior to the *prise de mousse*. It will be necessary to develop some sort of automatic dispensing system readily adaptable to most modern bottling lines. The new yeast capsule process, although showing very encouraging results, will not be available for several years at the most, but towards the end of the 1990s, it could well make the expensive computerised gyropalette system as redundant as the *remueurs* they have replaced.

Taittinger's computerised *gyropalettes* of the 1980s – will they be redundant in the 1990s?

The *sur lattes* scandal – a blot on Champagne's copybook

The amount of *sur lattes* business which is known to go on is alarming enough, but most houses are reluctant to admit such dealings and that which is known is but the tip of a very dirty iceberg.

It goes something like this ...

A house (big or small, famous or not) proudly declares that it uses no *vin de taille* or very little. The *vin de taille*, mostly the *deuxième taille* is sold to 'a firm specialising in BOBS'. In a lot of instances this firm is Marne & Champagne (it produces 10 million bottles, but in many other cases, the *taille* is sold to other 'specialist' *négociants*. It should be said at this point that Marne, and the others, can and do make some very decent Champagnes.

In periods of shortage and by this I do not only mean great gulfs of time when the entire trade faces a crisis like that of a few years ago, I mean when individual firms find their stocks cannot meet orders, these 'no *taille* for us' houses turn desperately to other firms with stocks to spare. These are usually wines which are at the *sur lattes* stage and may therefore be dosed according to the purchasing firm's recipe. Such *sur lattes* stocks are often purchased from the very same firms to which they sold their *taille* (if they actually did sell it in the first place) and consequently it is not beyond the bounds of possibility that they end up selling pure *vin de taille* Champagnes.

Some firms will buy better *sur lattes* than others and a few manage to get hold of some very good Champagnes indeed. It can turn out that the house buying *sur lattes* ends up with a better product than it normally makes for itself, whether this is because the 'specialist' is really very good at its job, or because the firm buying up the stock is just a downright poor Champagne house, it matters not.

I have heard houses claim that it is in the *dosage* that they turn a simple *sur lattes* product into one worthy of the reputation of that house. Poppycock! I have heard others say that they are just as meticulous in seeking out wines *sur lattes* to match their house style as they are at buying in grapes, must or *vin clair* and try to pretend there is no difference. Rubbish! Grapes, grape must and *vin clair* are all raw products a long way short of the all important *assemblage* stage and it is at the *assemblage* that such products may be rejected. A few have even told me that they purchase *sur lattes*, open every bottle and pour the sparkling, cloudy wine into the blending vat. I have seen 'over the hill' or sub-standard wine going back into the melting pot, but I have yet to see a house buying significant stocks *sur lattes* to help it out of a tight spot, then opening up all the bottles and waiting a year for the finished product.

These houses are no different from *négociants-non-manipulants* when they rely on such underhand practices. At least *négociants-non-manipulants* are honest about it, but the houses, especially the more famous houses, selling *sur lattes* Champagne under their own label deceive their customers. It might be legal, but what moral right have they to hoodwink a loyal customer who buys a brand because he trusts the label? I will probably upset, not only some houses, but the Syndicat Professionnel des Courtiers en Vins de Champagne, for trying to deny them a living, but I think the customer comes first and I would hope that most of the Champagne trade does too.

It might be possible to argue one exception, a particular *cuvée*, exclusively *sur lattes* wines purchased from the same source year after year, but as a general rule, I would prefer to see legislation forcing producers to use a completely separate *marque*, one which would give a customer no false impression that the wine is made by his favourite Champagne house.

Champagne has created a huge world market for bubbles, but it must constantly guarantee the highest quality of its luxury product if the bubbles are not to burst.

14

Champagne House Profiles

Farewell, then, Pommery Seventy-Four!
With reverential sips
We part and grieve that never more
Such wine may pass our lips.
'Ode to Pommery 1874' by Richard John Lloyd Price,
Vanity Fair, 27 December 1894

Key to common abbreviations

CH = Chardonnay; PN = Pinot Noir;
PM = Pinot Meunier; NV = non-vintage;
blended = pink Champagne made by blending
a little red wine into a white Champagne; skin-
contact = pink Champagne where the colour is
achieved through a limited contact with the
skins of Pinot grapes.

Explanatory notes
The échelle of purchases indicates the average
rating for all the grapes or musts bought in.
Where a breakdown of grape varieties in a
cuvée is given (known in France as the *cépage*),
the percentages given may alter slightly
according to the nature of the vintage. The
figures stated are, however, as valid as the
proportions of grape varieties included in a
Bordeaux château which are equally susceptible
to the vagaries of vintage.

The following notes on individual wines are
based largely on a series of tastings conducted
at each house between January 1980 and
November 1983, often supplemented by
separate encounters of the wine in France or in
Britain during the 1970s and 1980s up to 1985.
Indication is given where experience of the wine
is very slight, while no notes are given for
products not tasted. The years appearing after
the notes on vintage wines are not an indication
of vintages recently declared, but specific
vintages the author recommends. In most cases,
the last year commented on will be 1979
(rightly so, bearing in mind how much bottle
age a vintage wine should have), but the reader
may look forward to a string of fine future
vintages: 1981, 1982, 1983, 1985.

Prise de mousse in half-size bottles and
bottles larger than magnums is uncommon and
I have therefore recorded instances where I
have seen bottles of this size either *sur lattes*,
sur pointes or in *pupitres* for *remuage*.

Other *marques* mentioned are NMS or MAS
and, if MAS, may be owned by either vendor or
purchaser.

Visits to the larger houses usually include
commentaries in various major languages,
including English, and traditionally end with a
glass of Champagne, but do not expect it in
some of the smaller establishments. Those
houses which advertise visits for the purpose of
purchasing Champagne may be willing to show
visitors around, whether or not a purchase is
made, but prior contact should be established.
Not all firms sell their products direct, but
where they do it is advisable to take advantage
of the service, even if the same Champagne may
be on offer at a lower price in a local
supermarket: knowledge that the wine has been
stored under perfect conditions is of much
greater value to the knowing customer, and its
storage history will assume even greater
importance if the Champagne is to be laid
down for further maturation.

Henri Abelé

52 rue de Sillery, Reims
Telephone (26) 85.23.86
Origin Established in 1757 by Théodore
Vander Veken, this house is one of the oldest in
Champagne. In the archives of Reims townhall
a copy of a letter dated 1765 reveals that the
firm of Vander Veken had a 'flourishing
sparkling champagne trade'. When Théodore's
son Rémi took over, he extended the family
vineyards in Rilly-la-Montagne and developed
sales, exporting to Belgium, Holland and Italy.

Leaving no immediate heirs, Rémi left the
firm to his nephew Auguste Ruinart de Brimont
in 1828. In 1834 Auguste formed an
association with Antoine Müller, the former
chef de caves of Veuve Clicquot who had
helped the Widow discover the intricacies of
remuage. From this partnership the house
passed to François Abelé de Müller who, in
1842, transferred the business to new premises
in Ludes.

When François died in 1876 his son Henri
took over and in 1903 changed the name of the
house to Abelé-Vander Veken. In 1942 control
passed to the Compagnie Française des Grands
Vins, a house founded in 1908 by Eugène
Charmat (inventor of the bulk method of
sparkling wine production *cuve close* in 1910),
and today the firm which makes and markets
the *marque* of Henri Abelé.
Production 1 million bottles
Exports 5–10%
Vinification notes Mechanical *remuage*
utilising *gyropalettes*
Special interest Turnover is mostly by direct
sales from the house or by mail-order.

WINES
House style: Very dry wines heavily influenced
by high Chardonnay content averaging 60% in
most of the *cuvées*.
N V Brut Sourire de Reims A consistently fine
wine. NV sec and demi-sec also produced
N V Grande Marque Impériale Brut Wine not
tasted
N V Rosé Brut Skin-contact
Vintage Impérial Club Brut Only the 1976
tasted, but highly recommended.

Jean Arnoult

Celles-sur-Ource, Bar-sur-Seine
Origin This small house was the first to be
established in the Aube *département*. It was
founded in 1919 by Jean Arnoult (1860–1943)
who became involved in the Champagne trade
late in life.

WINES
N V Carte Blanche Royale Brut NV sec and
demi-sec also produced
Fleur de Raisin *Cuvée de prestige*

Ayala & Co.

Château d'Aÿ
2 boulevard du Nord, Aÿ-Champagne
Telephone (26) 50.13.40
Visits By appointment
Origin The idea that Ayala is an anagram of 'à
la Aÿ' is attractive but etymologically unsound.
It is purely coincidence which brought Raphael
Edmond Louis Gonzague de Ayala, the son of a
Columbian diplomat, to the little town of Aÿ.
With his marriage to Berthe Gabrielle
d'Albrecht, the daughter of the Vicomtesse
Marie-Caroline Durand de Mareuil, he
acquired certain important vineyards, and to
sell the Champagne they produced he founded
the house of Ayala in 1860.

In 1937 the house was bought by Monsieur
René Chayoux (1891–1969) who, the previous
year, had taken control of the Champagne firms
of Duminy and Montebello. In 1961 he also
acquired Château La Lagune, a troisième cru
classé in the Médoc, Bordeaux. Since the death
of René Chayoux the house of Ayala has been
run by Monsieur Jean-Michel Ducellier.
Vineyards Some 25 hectares as part of the
Montebello estate.
Purchases Only grapes from the Côte des
Blancs and Montagne de Reims are used for
Ayala Champagnes.
Production 900,000 bottles
Exports 30–35%
Vinification notes *Prise de mousse* occurs in
halves and jeroboams.
Average bottle-age of N V *cuvées* 2½ years
Other *marques* Montebello

WINES
House style: Honest, fruity and generous wines
of *grand mousseux*; exceptionally good value.
N V Carte Blanche Demi-sec (50–60% PN,
15–25% CH, 25% PM; 95% échelle) Fine
mousse, delightfully clean bouquet, very
perfumed flavour; sweet, luscious and well
balanced.

N V Brut (50% PN, 25% CH, 25% PM; 95% échelle) Vigorous *mousse*, small bubbles and yeasty nose. The 1980-based N V in 1983 was quite exceptional: beautiful nose – light and elegant; ultra-fine *mousse*; good acid balance and a pleasant yeasty after-taste.

Rosé N V Brut (100% PN; blended) Only a very small quantity of this wine is produced, made entirely from grapes grown on the Montagne de Reims and marketed in a special clear bottle. It is a soft, peach-coloured, fruity wine with a clean, stylish finish.

Vintage Brut (75% PN, 25% CH; 97% échelle) Usually a much richer wine than the NV with a riper nose and a mellow but elegant fruit flavour. Recommended years: 1973, 1975, 1979.

Vintage Blanc de Blancs Brut (100% CH) Light, stylish wine made from blends of up to five growths including those of Cramant, Vertus and le Mesnil-sur-Oger; it has a fragrant nose and a very creamy *mousse*. The 1975 is superb, while the 1979 had a pâté-like nose, but should develop. Recommended year: 1975.

Barancourt

Brice-Martin-Tritant
Place Tritant, Bouzy
Telephone (26) 59.00.67
Visits April to October, seven days a week, 8 a.m.–7 p.m., no appointment necessary
Origin The line of Barancourt ceased to exist when Philogone Barancourt died in 1941. It was one of the oldest and most respected names in the history of Bouzy and for this reason it was adopted by three young growers when they merged their vineyards to form the Champagne house of Barancourt in 1969.

Two sons of Bouzy *récoltants* Jean-Paul Brice and Pierre Martin, who had studied viticulture together at Avize, joined in partnership with Raynald Tritant, also a grower's son, but born in Reims and a graduate of accountancy and management. In 1966, prior to setting up the company, Monsieurs Brice, Martin and Tritant purchased a considerable amount of land in the Barsequanais country which had been abandoned at the time of phylloxera, and set about planting new vineyards – a serious undertaking for three young men, the oldest of whom was barely twenty years old. In 1969 the three families backed their enterprising sons by pooling their vineyard holdings to form the Domaine de Barancourt and in 1975 the house

of Brice-Martin-Tritant was officially set up. In its brief existence, Barancourt has already established a reputation for producing Champagnes of the highest quality.
Vineyards Bouzy (13 hectares), Cramant (3.3 hectares), Ambonnay (2 hectares), Tauxières (0.3 hectares), Bar-sur-Seine (3 hectares), Loches-sur-Ource (13 hectares) and Merrey-sur-Arce (10 hectares). The total holding comprises 44.6 hectares which supplies 90% of the company's needs.
Production Average 350,000 bottles
Sales 230,000 bottles
Exports Approximately 20%
Stocks 1 million bottles (1983)
Vinification notes Oenologist Michel Joly is responsible for constructing the blends of the wines.
Average bottle-age of N V *cuvées* 2–4 years depending on the cuvée.
Other *marques* Michel Olivier, Stafford Hotel

WINES
House style: Barancourt Champagnes can definitely be classed as *vins de garde*, that is to say wines capable of improving greatly with age. They may be tight in their youth, requiring several years longer in bottle than most, but given the sort of ageing any great Champagne deserves, the wines of Barancourt will show their true class and style.
Réserve N V Brut (67% PN, 33% CH) This is a good commercial standard of N V brut with a high alcohol content and firm grip which many famous houses would be happy to sell. It is not as brut as the other Barancourt Champagnes and still relatively young.
Bouzy N V Brut (80% PN, 20% CH; 100% échelle; mono-cru). This wine has a very strong *mousse* of small bubbles and a powerful nose; normally about four years old, it is a well-structured, top quality Champagne with a high extract which will take time to mature.
Cramant N V Brut (100% CH; 100% échelle; mono-cru) This wine has a very fine *mousse* with perfumed nose; it is packed tightly with fruit which will need a good amount of time in bottle.
Bouzy Rosé N V Brut (35% PN, 65% CH; 100% échelle; blended) This is a dark-coloured pink Champagne which is almost red. I normally prefer more delicate renditions, but this is a great wine with strong red wine nuances of Pinot Noir on the nose and palate.
Coteaux Champenois Vintage Bouzy

Rouge (100% PN; 100% échelle) Average years of this wine can be soft and lacking, but great years are spectacular, if one is clever enough to prise a few of the older vintages out of Barancourt.

Beaumet Chaurey

3 rue Malakoff, Épernay
Telephone (26) 54.53.34
Visits By appointment
Origin The house of Chaurey, founded in 1840, was taken over by the house of Beaumet (founded 1878) in the 1950s. Beaumet Chaurey then passed through the hands of Charbaut and Leclerc-Briant before it was finally acquired by Jean Trouillard in 1974.
Vineyards 62 hectares owned, supplying 90% of the firm's annual needs
Purchases 10%   **Production** 800,000 bottles
Average bottle-age of N V *cuvées* 3 years

WINES
N V Brut (67% PN, 33% CH; 92% échelle)
Vintage Brut (67% PN, 33% CH; 94% échelle)
Vintage Brut Cuvée Malakoff (100% CH; 99% échelle; *cuvée de prestige*)
Vintage Brut Rosé (100% PN; skin-contact)

Besserat de Bellefon

Allée du Vignoble, Route Nationale 51, Murigny, Reims
Telephone (26) 06.09.18
Visits Appointment preferred but not essential.
Origin This firm was founded in 1843 when Edmond Besserat established a small Champagne house bearing his name in Aÿ. But it was not until the period between the two wars, when the business was in the hands of his two sons, Victor and Edmond (who had married Mlle Yvonne de Méric de Bellefon), that the business took off. When in the 1920s they launched their Crémant Brut, the Besserat brothers became the first to specialise in this style of Champagne on a truly commercial scale. In 1959, Victor and Edmond sold out to Cinzano. Under new ownership Besserat de Bellefon began to increase production and in 1963 purchased the famous *grande marque* house of Salon. In 1970 the firm moved into the luxurious surrounding of a purpose-built complex at Murigny, a suburb on the southern edge of Reims. The powerful Pernod-Ricard group acquired control of Besserat de Bellefon in 1976.

Vineyards 10 hectares at Aÿ and the use of Salon's 1 hectare at le Mesnil-sur-Oger when not declared a vintage.
Purchases Average échelle of 94%
Production 2 million bottles
Sales 1½–2 million bottles
Exports 250,000 bottles
Stocks 8 million bottles (1983)
Vinification notes The modern winery has temperature- and humidity-controlled cellars and a computerised *cuverie* of stainless steel vats, where the precise location of every litre of wine is illuminated on an electronic control panel.
Average bottle-age of N V *cuvées* 2–3 years depending on the *cuvée*
Other *marques* Morlant de la Marne (19% of sales)
Special interest In contrast to all its 'high-tech' production Besserat de Bellefon also owns the more traditional house of Salon, a member of the Syndicat des Grandes Marques de Champagne.

WINES
House style: Besserat de Bellefon wines are light, fresh and always technically correct. The house specialises in producing fine, top quality *crémant* Champagnes of true character, which are appreciated on the home market, but little known and undervalued abroad.
N V Réserve Brut (50% PN, 17% PM, 33% CH; 90% échelle) This wine has a strong and persistent *mousse* with a big Pinot nose, allowing the Chardonnay to come through on the palate giving good fruit and acidity.
N V Crémant Blanc Brut (33.3% PN, 33.3% PM, 33.3% CH; 90% échelle) This wine has excellent creaming *mousse* with a full nose and lots of fruit. It is light, long and elegant, and is best drunk young. Has been ranked first in many of the 'blind' tastings I have organised.
N V Crémant des Moines Rosé Brut (50% PN, 10% PM, 40% CH; 90% échelle; blended) This is a wonderful rosé and quite simply the very best early drinking *crémant* I have ever tasted.
N V B de B Brut (60% PN, 40% CH; 100% échelle) A *cuvée de prestige* launched in October 1984 and assembled from old reserve wines of between six and seven years of age. Very rich, fine bubbles, gently moussing, a wine for lovers of old-style Champagne.
Vintage Réserve Brut (50% PN, 50% CH; 95% échelle) This is a richer wine than others in the range with a lively *mousse*, some complexity and a very long Pinot after-taste.

Recommended years: 1973, 1975.

Vintage Brut Intégral　(50% PN, 50% CH; 95% échelle) This is an excellent *non-dosage* wine with a fine *mousse* and great depth and finesse, although the 1977 was a mistake.

Recommended year: 1975.

Vintage Rosé Brut　(50% PN, 50% CH; 95% échelle; blended) This rosé has always been disappointing in the years I have tasted it.

Billecart-Salmon

40 rue Carnot, Mareuil-sur-Aÿ
Telephone (26) 50.60.22
Visits　By appointment
Origin　The Billecart-Salmon family have resided in Mareuil-sur-Aÿ since the sixteenth century, but it was not until 1818 that one of them, Nicolas-François, entered the Champagne trade by establishing this firm. He soon gained a reputation for his wines, opening up markets throughout the world, but an inept American agent lost Billecart-Salmon a staggering '100,000 golden francs' in 1830, which led to a gradual decline of the business in the second and third generations.

When Charles Roland-Billecart took control in 1917 he inherited a poor state of affairs. Yet despite the low turnover, the ill-effect of the First World War and the collapse of world markets soon after, he steadily built up the business and in 1926 took the decision to sell the family's vineyard holdings to finance further growth. It was a prudent decision and today his successor Jean Roland-Billecart continues to maintain a steady annual growth of 3½–4%, determined that an increase in sales should not mean a decrease in quality.

Vineyards　None

Purchases　Traditionally from twenty-five different growths, 40% of the musts purchased coming from the Côte des Blancs, 30% from the Montagne de Reims and 30% from the Vallée de la Marne, close to Épernay.

Production　500,000 bottles

Sales　400,000 bottles　**Exports**　25%

Stocks　1.3 million bottles (December 1983)

Vinification notes　All grape must purchased is subjected to an extra *débourbage* at 5°C. Since this removes almost all of the natural grape yeast Billecart-Salmon uses a cultured yeast for both the first and second fermentations, formulated out of the growths from Avize, Cramant and Verzenay. The first fermentation is deliberately slow, as the temperature in the

vats is strictly maintained at just 8°C. Billecart-Salmon has a very modern approach to vinification, avoiding oxidation at all costs. The use of between sixty and seventy small 4,000-litre vats permits complex blending of the *cuvée* from between twenty-three and twenty-five separate growths. Since 1962 all wines have undergone malo-lactic conversion. The *assemblage* is performed by Jean Roland-Billecart and his able winemaker James Coffinet. *Prise de mousse* is conducted in jeroboams.

Average bottle-age of N V *cuvées*　3 years

Special interest　The firm is a member of the Syndicat des Grandes Marques de Champagne.

WINES

House style: The lightness and fragrance of these wines belie their Pinot content and indeed their potential longevity. In 1983 I asked Jean Roland-Billecart if I could taste a few of his older vintages to see how they age under perfect conditions. Enthusiastically, he dispatched James Coffinet to the cellars. The tasting of 1978, 1976, 1975, 1974, 1973, 1971, 1969, 1959 and 1955 was a rare privilege. Obviously the vintages varied in quality, but the oldest of all, the 1955, was awarded maximum marks for its superb depth and complexity, brilliantly balanced by the freshness of its almost thirty-year-old *mousse*. These wines have a tremendous capacity for ageing and, if one might be tempted to drink them young, they certainly do repay keeping.

N V Brut　(50% PM, 25% PN, 25% CH; 93% échelle) This wine is not quite as dry as some brut Champagnes, but it is an attractive, well-made wine of fine character. It is light in body, elegant in style and possesses good balance.

N V Sec　(50% PM, 25% PN, 25% CH; 93% échelle) Similar to the brut, but the sec has a slightly higher *dosage*.

N V Demi-sec　(50% PM, 25% PN, 25% CH; 93% échelle) This is one of the very few Champagnes to include *eau-de-vie* in the *dosage*. None is used in any other Billecart-Salmon wine.

Vintage Blanc de Blancs Brut　(100% CH; 99–100% échelle) A strong *mousse* of very fine bubbles, with a soft bouquet, medium body and delicate finish.

Vintage Brut Cuvée N. F. Billecart　(60% PN, 40% CH; 100% échelle) Light-golden in colour, this Champagne has a firm *mousse* of small bubbles with good depth and muscle, yet is also elegant with a superb Chardonnay finish. Recommended year: 1973.

Rosé N V Brut (60% PN, 40% CH; 93% échelle; blended) Just with the barest hint of colour, this rosé has a vigorous, crisp white *mousse* with a delicate nose and palate and delightful balance. It is the one Billecart-Salmon Champagne I would recommend drinking early. The house produced its first sparkling pink Champagne called 'Silley Rosé' in 1830, and since 1970 their Rosé N V Brut has represented no less than 10% of sales, an abnormally high proportion for this type of wine.

G. Billiard

78 rue de Général de Gaulle, Pierry
Telephone (26) 54.02.96
Visits Yes, but check opening days and hours by telephone.
Origin The house was founded in 1935 by Graetan Billiard (1894–1967), a former cellarer for Pol Chauvet.
Vineyards 2 hectares at Pierry and in the Vallée de la Marne, representing 15% of total production.
Purchases Grape musts averaging 90% échelle from *co-opératives*.
Production 80,000 bottles **Exports** 15%
Vinification notes There are no reserve wines; the firm's non-vintage Champagnes, almost 88% of Billiard's total production, are the product of one year only.

WINES
NV Cachet Rouge Brut (80% PN/PM, 20% CH; 90% échelle) Sec and demi-sec also produced.
NV Blanc de Blancs Brut (100% CH; 90% échelle)
NV Brut Rosé (blended) Red wine from Cumières used
Vintage Brut (80% PN/PM, 20% CH; 90% échelle)
Vintage Blanc de Blancs Brut (100% CH)

Boizel

16 rue de Bernon, Épernay
Telephone (26) 55.21.51
Visits By appointment
Origin Established in 1834 by Auguste Boizel, a native of Étoges, this house has had a strong association with Hedges & Butler, its British agent, since 1887. The firm, still an independent family business, is now run by Erica Boizel-Hotte of Dutch nationality.

With no vineyards, Boizel must buy in all of its requirements. Most purchases of Pinot Noir are from Aÿ and Bouzy, while its Chardonnay grapes come from Chouilly, Vertus, Cumières and Hautvillers.
Vineyards None
Purchases Average 92% échelle
Production 500,000 bottles (300,000 as Boizel)
Exports 55%
Vinification notes Mechanical methods of *remuage* are employed, utilising *gyropalettes* for part of the production.
Average bottle-age of NV *cuvées* 3 years
Other *marques* Louis Kremmer, Camuset

WINES
House style: Boizel Champagnes are fruity, well made and good value for money.
NV Brut (55% PN, 30% CH, 15% PM; 92% échelle) This wine has a good *mousse* with a pleasant, mellow nose and a ripe, fruity palate.
Vintage Brut (65% PN, 30% CH, 5% PM; 92% échelle) The vintage brut is big, firm and rich, but still possessing its typical easy-going fruity style. Recommended years: 1971, 1973, 1975, 1979.
Vintage Joyau de France (65% PN, 35% CH; 95–100% échelle; *cuvée de prestige*) Wine not tasted.
NV Brut Rosé (70% PN, 30% PM; 92% échelle; blended) Wine not tasted.

J. Bollinger

Rue Jules Lobet, Aÿ-Champagne
Telephone (26) 50.12.34
Visits By appointment
Origin In 1803 Joseph-Jacob-Placide Bollinger, later simply known as Jacques Bollinger, was born in the Germanic kingdom of Württemburg. He joined the Champagne trade in 1822 at the age of nineteen, selling wines in Germany for Müller-Ruinart, a small house set up that year by a fellow German Antoine Müller, who combined his name with his wife's to trade under. Müller was the *chef de caves* at Veuve Clicquot who had assisted the Widow in her invention of *remuage*.

After seven years with Müller Jacques Bollinger was asked by Athanase-Louise-Emmanuel de Villermont, later Comte de Villermont, to form a company to sell the wines produced from his vineyards. De Villermont had already traded with customers in Jersey and Guernsey, but needed to restore his fortunes and sought to exploit the rapidly expanding Champagne trade. However, he did not want his family name connected with anything so lowly as commerce and thus it was that Jacques Bollinger and Paul Renaudin were set up in business in 1829 to trade under the name of Renaudin, Bollinger & Co.

Jacques Bollinger, who in 1837 married Louise-Charlotte de Villermont, the comte's daughter by a second marriage, extended his father-in-law's initial eleven-hectare holding by planting a new vineyard in Verzenay. After Jacques's death in 1888 his two sons Georges and Joseph expanded the vineyards further, acquiring further sites in Louvois, Bouzy and Tauxières. Jacques Bollinger's grandson and namesake took over the firm in 1918. He improved the firm's properties and replanted one vineyard of particular repute, la Côte-aux-Enfants in Aÿ. He was too ill to fight for his country during the Second World War; the strain of being mayor of Aÿ under German occupation proved all too much and he died in 1941, aged forty-seven.

Madame Bollinger, or as the workers knew her, Madame Jacques, took over on her husband's death. There have been many great women in the history of Champagne, but only the legendary Madame 'Lily' Bollinger can challenge the reputation of the Widow. She went everywhere by bicycle, personally supervised every operation – whether in the vineyard or in the cellar – and was well known for her insistence on perfection. Cyril Ray in his thorough and affectionate profile *Bollinger* (1971), states that it was her severity over *épluchage*, a grape sorting procedure, which was most often quoted by workers when discussing her strictness. If performed at all, *épluchage* sifts out the bad grapes bunch by bunch – Madame Bollinger, however, insisted that *épluchage* should be carried out grape by grape!

Bollinger was one of the few houses spared in the uprising of 1911. Cyril Ray records that fifteen years after the riots Madame Bollinger overheard a passer-by outside one of her windows say, 'That's the Bollinger house, you know: we didn't touch it during the riots here – as a matter of fact, we lowered our flag to it when we passed!' 'Probably the red flag', Madame added, with pleased irony.

Although 'Lily' Bollinger travelled the world, opening up new markets with her personal charm and appeal, she was happiest at home with the simplicities of life in Aÿ where she could peddle her way around the Bollinger estate. She increased the firm's viticultural holdings, securing a vineyard called Beauregard at Aÿ-Mutigny, and through her nephews was responsible for adding sites at Grauves, Bisseuil and Champvoisy to the Bollinger estate. This extraordinary lady succeeded in doubling the firm's production whilst sacrificing none of its reputation.

The line of Bollinger is now extinct; when Madame 'Lily' died in 1977 her nephew Christian Bizot took over. He joined the firm in 1952 and is now helped by his two nephews and fellow-directors Michael Villedey and Arnould d'Hautefeuille.

In June 1984 Bollinger launched its range of updated label designs. This was an important step for such a traditional house, seeking to come to terms with modern marketing conditions and yet to maintain a classical design which would emphasise the tradition and quality of Bollinger. The results are certainly chic, but they are presented in a restrained style which firmly anchors the products to their esteemed past.

Vineyards 141.75 hectares of which 120.65 are planted. The vineyards meet, on average, about 70% of total production needs. The principal villages in which vineyards are owned are listed below, individually named sites following in brackets.

AVENAY 15 hectares of 93% échelle (Monthurlet, Champ Bernard)

AŸ 22 hectares of 100% échelle (Cheuzelle, Cognet Robert, Côte-aux-Enfants, Chaudes Terres, Valnon Froid Cul, Charmont, Beauregard)

BISSEUIL 5.4 hectares of 93% échelle (les Tuillières)

CHAMPVOISY 17 hectares of 84% échelle (les Millots)

CUIS 21.15 hectares of 95% échelle (les Roualles, les Fétés, les Saints Julien, les Gouaisses, les Blancs Chiens)

GRAUVES 6.6 hectares of 95% échelle (les Roualles, le Mont des Charmes, les Terres des Hurlaux)

LOUVOIS 15.7 hectares of 100% échelle (les Navandières, les Barsaulx)

MUTIGNY 3.95 hectares of 93% échelle

TAUXIÈRES 17.95 hectares of 99% échelle (les Jolis, les Vigneules, les Putiers)

VERZENAY 17 hectares of 100% échelle (le Champ du Clerc, les Aumonières, les Coutures, le Poirier Saint-Pierre, les Chardonnières, la Barbarie)

Purchases Averaging 97% échelle

Production 1.3 million bottles

Sales 1.3 million bottles **Exports** 70%

Stocks 7 million bottles (1983)

Vinification notes The first fermentation takes place one-third in cask and two-thirds in stainless steel vats. The cask-fermented wines are not filtered and it is uncertain how much of it actually undergoes malo-lactic conversion, probably very little. The more acid wines are deliberately vinified in the vats where the malo-lactic process can be controlled. In the case of individual *cuvées* the amount of cask-fermented wine can be as high as 80–85%. Most producers keep their reserve wines (required for future blending of NV Champagnes) in vats, a very few use casks, but even fewer go to the trouble and expense of storing their wines in magnums as Bollinger do. The *prise de mousse* takes place in jeroboams and all vintage wines are sealed with *liège et agrafe*.

Average bottle-age of NV *cuvées* 3–4 years

Special interest The house is a member of the Syndicat des Grandes Marques de Champagne. Since Bollinger's RD Champagnes are so well known, it is worth giving an indication of the extra ageing involved in the production of these wines. The following vintages were being shipped in 1985: 1979 (Grande Année), 1975 (RD) and 1970 (Année Rare). Ten years may seem a long time in bottle, even for a vintage Champagne, therefore, by the use of RD on the label, Bollinger is saying this is not old stock, it has been recently disgorged and is ready to drink. While most aficionados may be aware that RD stands for *récemment dégorgé* or recently disgorged, few realise that 'RD' is actually registered as a trademark.

WINES

House style: All Bollinger Champagnes are classics of their kind and all vintages are recommended, those indicated being absolute favourites. Occasionally the Pinot Meunier is used, and in the non-vintage it may be as high as 10%.

NV Special Cuvée Brut (65–70% PN, 5% PM, 20–25% CH; 97% échelle) This has a fine, long-lasting *mousse*, always with a good mature flavour, yet fresh and crisp. It is a firm-flavoured wine, not as austere as Krug, but equally a *vin de garde*.

Vintage Grande Année Brut (65–70% PN, 5% PM, 20–25% CH; 97% échelle) A richer wine of higher quality than the non-vintage but with more individual character. Recommended years: 1970, 1975, 1979.

Vintage RD (65–70% PN, 5% PM, 20–25% CH; 97% échelle) This Champagne is exactly the same wine as Bollinger's normal vintage, but the bottles are left *sur pointes* when the Grande Année is disgorged, allowing longer contact with its lees and thus resulting in a richer wine of great complexity. Recommended years: 1964, 1966, 1970, 1975.

Vintage Année Rare (65–70% PN, 5% PM, 20–25% CH; 97% échelle) The same wine again, but left for a longer period *sur pointe* to achieve even greater richness and complexity. A relatively new addition to the range, Année Rare is a sort of RD RD.

Vintage Vieilles Vignes Françaises Blanc de Noirs Produced from Bollinger's ungrafted pre-phylloxera vines growing *en foule* in Bouzy and Aÿ. The first vintage produced, the 1969, coincided with Madame Bollinger's seventieth birthday. The 1970, of deep old-gold colour, had a soft *mousse* of exceptionally fine bubbles for Pinot Noir, with a big, rooty vegetal nose, great strength and depth, although rather heavy and cumbersome in balance without food. The 1975 was equally rooty but it had a stronger *mousse* and a better fruit–acidity ratio, although it was still a little ungainly. The depth of these wines can be unbelievable, but they are curiosities rather than classics.

Vintage Grande Année Rosé (Vintage brut plus red wine; 97% échelle; blended) This is a classic, refined wine which delightfully counter-balances Madame Bollinger's declaration that 'Champagne is a white wine' – quoted by Cyril Ray in *Bollinger* (1971) to emphasise that this house would never make a pink wine.

Coteaux Champenois La Côte aux Enfants (100% échelle) A vintaged dry red (still) wine produced in limited quantities (between 15 and 20 *pièces* a year) entirely from one named site, the south-facing slope of la Côte-aux-Enfants in Aÿ. Although potentially good, the 1976 was short-lived, according to Arnould d'Hautefeuille, because old rather than new casks were used in its fermentation.

Château de Boursault, once the property
of Mme Veuve Clicquot

The 1981 I tasted had an excellent colour, an
oaky nose – unfortunately spoiled by too much
acetaldehyde – but with a good round and
fruity flavour, some varietal character and a
peppery, tannic finish. The 1979 was much
lighter, thinner in fruit and higher in acidity,
but with an elegance to its oaky nose that was
missing in the 1981.

F. Bonnet & Fils

Rue de Mesnil, Oger
Telephone (26) 50.52.43
Visits By appointment
Origin The house was founded in 1922 by the
récoltant Ferdinand Bonnet and is now owned
by three sisters of the Bonnet family.
Vineyards 22 hectares on the Côte des Blancs,
averaging 95% échelle and above, and
two-thirds of the firm's total production.
Production 140,000 bottles
Vinification notes Mechanical *remuage* is
employed using *gyropalettes* for half the
production.
Average bottle-age of NV *cuvées* 4 years

WINES
House style: The range is generally influenced
by a high proportion of Chardonnay in the

blends. I have rarely tasted the wines, but
Bonnet's vintage Blanc de Blancs is good and
the 1976 came top in a *Decanter* tasting
(reported in the July 1983 issue).

Château de Boursault

Boursault, Épernay
Telephone (26) 50.42.21
Origin A twentieth-century house based on a
seventeenth-century château of truly Loire
proportions once owned by the famous Widow
of Veuve Clicquot.
    The house of Château de Boursault is set in
beautiful surroundings a few kilometres west of
Épernay on the left bank of the Marne, access
being gained from the N3 via a couple of
narrow, winding lanes. Unfortunately there
was no one there to keep my appointment, and
I was unable to taste any of the wines, but the
setting is enchanting, and no doubt any
château-bottled Champagne would market
extremely well, especially from a property of
great historic links such as Boursault.
Vineyards 15.5 hectares comprising 50%
Pinot Meunier, 40% Pinot Noir and 10%
Chardonnay, some 80% of which is sold off as
grapes.
Production 20,000 bottles   **Exports** 35%
Vinification notes The *dosage* of the brut is 1%
at 50% saturation. Reserve wines added to NV
cuvées amount to 15%.
Average bottle-age of NV *cuvées* 2½–3 years
Other *marques* N. Fringhian

Bricout & Koch

7 route de Cramant, Avize
Telephone (26) 57.53.93
Visits For purchases
Origin This house can be traced back to 1820,
when Charles Koch set up business in Avize.
His three sons, Charles, Eugène and Gustave,
joined up with Arthur Bricout, the technical
director of the house de Venoge. In 1869
Bricout married the daughter of Christian
Adalbert Kupferberg, the famous *sekt* producer
in Mainz, and seven years later he established
the house of Bricout in Épernay.
Vineyards 4 hectares at Bethon, representing
little more than 10% of total production.
Purchases Averaging 87% échelle
Production 1½ million bottles   **Exports** 20%
Vinification notes Various fermentation vessels
are used, including wooden *foudres* and vats of

glass-lined cement, enamel-lined steel and stainless steel. The *remuage* employs a combination of traditional and mechanical methods, the latter utilising *gyropalettes*. *Dosage* for the brut Champagnes is given as 1% at 70% saturation.

Average bottle-age of NV *cuvées* 1½–4 years depending on the *cuvée*

WINES

NV Carte Blanche (mainly PN *cuvée* and some CH *taille*; 87% échelle) One and a half years ageing.

NV Carte Noire Brut (70% PN/PM, 30% CH; 87% échelle) Also in demi-sec. Two to two and a half years ageing.

NV d'Or Brut (70% PN/PM, 30% CH; 87% échelle) Also in demi-sec. Four years ageing.

NV Blanc de Blancs Brut (100% CH; 87% échelle) Two and a half years ageing.

NV Rosé Brut A blend of Carte Blanche and Carte Noire, to which red wine from les Riceys, Bouzy or Cumières is added. Three years ageing.

Vintage Charles Koch Brut (50% PN, 50% CH; 100% échelle; *cuvée de prestige*). A 1919 tasted very well, a fine wine by any standards.

Albert le Brun

93 avenue de Paris, Châlons-sur-Marne
Telephone (26) 68.18.68
Visits By appointment
Origin The house of Albert le Brun was established in 1860 at Avize in the heart of the Côte des Blancs. Still run by the le Brun family, the firm moved its headquarters away from Avize some years ago, and now occupies modern premises in Châlons-sur-Marne which include three kilometres of cellars originally owned by the firm, Jacquesson & Fils.
Purchases Averaging 86% échelle
Production 300,000 bottles **Exports** 50%
Average bottle-age of NV *cuvées* 2 years
Other *marques* Arlit & Cie

WINES
House style: Traditionally vinified, well matured and good value.
NV Cuvée Réservée Brut (65% PN, 35% CH; 90–95% échelle) This wine is a blend of Pinot Noir from Hautvillers, Vertus, Troissy and Vinay, with Chardonnay from Avize and Bethon. It has a well-formed *mousse*, a developed nose, with a biscuity, fruity character

on the palate and a lingering aftertaste of some complexity.

NV Blanc de Blancs Brut (100% CH; 100% échelle) Pure Avize Chardonnay – rich, ripe and mature.

Vintage Cuvée Réservée Brut (Blends vary, the 1976 contains 41% PN, 59% CH; 96% échelle) A blend of Pinot Noir from Hautvillers, Ludes and Chigny-les-Roses, with Chardonnay from Avize.

Vintage Vieille France Brut (Blends vary, the 1979 contains 54% PN, 46% CH; 96% échelle) A blend of Pinot Noir from Hautvillers, Vertus, Vinay and Chigny-les-Roses, with Chardonnay from Avize.

Édouard Brun & Cie

14 rue Marcel Mailly, Aÿ-Champagne
Telephone (26) 50.10.55
Origin Édouard Brun was born in 1875 into a family of coopers based in Aÿ. He set up his wine business in Aÿ in 1898, but his *marque* was not established until as recently as 1960.
Production 250,000 bottles

WINES
NV (brut, sec and demi-sec), Vintage, Crémant and Rosé Brut.

René Brun

4 place de la Libération, Aÿ-Champagne
Telephone (26) 50.11.98
Origin For five generations the Brun family had been *récoltants*, but René Brun trained as a cooper before deciding to make Champagne under his own name in 1941. Madame Brun took over in 1976 and the firm is now run by her two sons André and Roger.
Production 200,000 bottles

WINES
NV (brut, sec and demi-sec), NV Cuvée de Réserve Brut, Rosé Brut, Vintage Brut and Cuvée Spéciale (the *cuvée de prestige*).

Canard-Duchêne

1 rue Edmond Canard, Ludes, Rilly-la-Montagne
Telephone (26) 61.10.96
Visits Open seven days a week between 1 May and 30 September
Origin The firm was founded in 1868 by Victor-François Canard, who was married to

Françoise-Léonie Duchêne. Very little is known about the early history of this house as most of its records were destroyed during the First World War.

Between the two world wars, however, sales rose to 300,000 bottles, but the real growth in business came in the 1950s when François and Jean-Pierre Canard joined the firm: sales increased from 0.6 million bottles in 1950 to 2.3 million bottles in 1980. Piper-Heidsieck acquired a 33.6% share of the company in 1973 but sold this to Canard-Duchêne's current owner Veuve Clicquot in 1978.

Vineyards .16 hectares at Ludes, Taissy and Verzenay representing just 3½% of total production.

Purchases 40% of Canard-Duchêne's purchases are from the Aube *département* and 60% from the Vallée de la Marne and the Côte des Blancs.

Production 2.5 million bottles

Sales 2.3 million bottles   **Exports** 20%

Stocks 8½ million bottles (December 1983)

Vinification notes Part of the *remuage* is achieved by mechanically operated pupimatics, a form of jumping *pupitres*.

Other *marques* Chanoine Frères

Special interest The house is a member of the Syndicat des Grandes Marques de Champagne.

WINES

House style: Despite the modern, technically well-equipped premises, and an extremely friendly management, the wines of this house are disappointing and rather dull.

NV Brut (67.5% PN, 7.5% PM, 25% CH; 87% échelle) A good *mousse*, although rather coarse in style, with a sweet and gamey nose and an earthy, somewhat rooty flavour.

Charles VII Brut (33% PN, 67% CH; 95–100% échelle) This wine is certainly the best in the selection: a *cuvée de prestige*, it has a good persistent *mousse*, a clean nose and a well-balanced structure. The wine is sold in some markets as a vintage and in others as a non-vintage.

Vintage Brut (67% PN/PM, 33% CH) No Aube wines are included in this blend. The 1975 was quite good, but the 1976 had an almost pork-pâté character on the nose.

Vintage Blanc de Blancs Brut (100% CH) The 1973 had a particularly active *mousse* of fine bubbles.

Vintage Imperial Star Brut Wine not tasted.

Coteaux Champenois Rouge Wine not tasted.

De Castellane

57 rue Verdun, Épernay

Telephone (26) 55.15.33

Visits by appointment

Origin The cupola-topped tower of de Castellane is such an oddity on Épernay's skyline that a visitor should have no excuse for not finding the place. The vineyard was established in 1890 by Vicomte Florens de Castellane, of Provençal origins; the first manager was Fernand Merand, the descendants of whom still operate the company. Laurent-Perrier took a 20% share in the business early in 1984.

Vineyards None   **Purchases** 90% échelle

Production 1.5 million bottles

Sales 1 million bottles   **Exports** 30%

Stocks 3.9 million bottles (December 1983)

Vinification notes A large percentage of the wines are cask-fermented in 600-litre *demi-muids*, but stainless steel vats are being introduced. Until 1972, de Castellane used *eau-de-vie* in its *liqueur d'expédition*.

Average bottle-age of NV *cuvées* 3 years

WINES

House style: There has been a change in de Castellane's non-vintage house style in recent years. In 1980 it was definitely one of ripeness of fruit and maturity of bottle-age; in 1984 the wine was fresher and much lighter. Part of this change has come about as a result of cooler fermentation in stainless steel, but the four intervening years also saw de Castellane's stock dwindle by 1.1 million bottles as a consequence of the short vintages. However, production is now averaging one-and-a-half times the amount of wine actually sold, thus replenishing its stocks.

NV Brut (30% PN, 55% PM, 15% CH; 87% échelle) Sometimes a full and penetrating Pinot flavour with no earthy-Meunier undertones; at other times livelier, younger and with more than a hint of fragrant Chardonnay (see above), but always a well-made wine with a super-fine *mousse* and excellent value.

NV Blanc de Blancs Brut (100% CH; 88% échelle) Pale lemon colour, firm and fine *mousse*, ripe perfumed Chardonnay on nose and palate, usually more mellow than expected for a non-vintage Blanc de Blancs.

Vintage Brut (50% PN, 25% PM, 25% CH; 93% échelle) Rich, honeyed and long, always a

Resting *sur lattes*, Champagne undergoes a second fermentation
to create the carbonic gas which gives the wine its natural sparkle.
This process, known as the *prise de mousse*, takes place in
the deepest, coolest cellars of Champagne

good-quality wine. Recommended years: 1973, 1975, 1976, 1979.

Vintage Blanc de Blancs Brut (100% CH; 96% échelle) The 1973 and 1975 were superb, the 1976 excellent but just lacked the finesse of the earlier vintages.

Vintage Rosé Brut The 1974, exceptional for any year, was extraordinary for this year with its enchanting strawberry character on nose and palate. The 1979 was much firmer, yet not quite the class of the 1974, although attractively ripe and full.

Vintage Commodore (75% PN, 25% CH; 97% échelle) The vinification is traditional, with the use of *liège et agrafe*. The *mousse* is very fine – the most delicate of the de Castellane range. The 1974 was another success for such an unmemorable year, with a delicious honeyed nose and almost exotic fruit on the palate.

Other wines include the occasional production of Coteaux Champenois Rouge and Blanc.

De Cazanove

26 rue Pasteur, Avize
Telephone (26) 57.54.98
Origin The house was established at Avize in 1811 by Charles-Gabriel de Cazanove. Charles-Gabriel was one of a family of ten children and the father of five himself. By the last quarter of the nineteenth century, this house had built up a big enough reputation for Henry Vizetelly to deem a visit necessary. In his *A History of Champagne*, 1882, he records,

More important than all, however, is the quality of wine with which these cellars are stocked; and, following the rule observed by Champagne firms of the highest repute, it has been a leading principle with M. de Cazanove always to rely on the choicer growths – those light, delicate, and fragrant wines of the Marne which throw out the true aroma of the flower of the vine. M. de Cazanove, who is distinguished for his knowledge of viticulture, occupies an influential position at Avize, being Vice-President of the Horticultural Society of the Marne, and a member of the committee charged with guarding Champagne vineyards against the invasion of phylloxera. His own vines include only those fine varieties to which the crus of the Marne owe their great renown. He possesses an excellent vineyard at Grauves, near Avize; and his mother-in-law, Madame Poultier of Pierry, is one of the principal vine-growers of the district.

The house of de Cazanove was purchased by the Moët-Hennessy group in 1979 and sold to SAME in 1985.

NV Brut, NV Extra Dry, NV Demi-sec, Ruban Azur, Vintage Brut, Vintage Cuvée Spéciale Magnum Blanc de Blancs

A. Charbaut & Fils

17 avenue de Champagne, Épernay
Telephone (26) 54.37.55
Visits By appointment
Origin Established in 1948 by André Charbaut, the firm were essentially *récoltants* until about 1955, from which time this company has advanced from success to success. André Charbaut is still in charge and it is warming to see the sparkle in his eye when he is tasting his own product. He is assisted by his two sons, René and Guy.
Vineyards 56 hectares between 90% and 100% échelle; the most important of the vineyards is at Mareuil-sur-Aÿ, but they also extend to Bisseuil, Avenay and, in the Aube, Viviers-sur-Artaut. These vineyards supply 17% of the company's needs.
Purchases Between 88% and 90% échelle
Production 2 million bottles **Exports** 40%
Average bottle-age of NV *cuvées* 1½–2 years
Other *marques* The *marque* of de Courcy (owned by a *négociant-non-manipulant*) has been spectacularly active on export markets. There are various house labels for top French restaurants.

WINES
House style: Once of a decent quality, the wine has fallen off considerably. I only hope this has been due to a stock shortage situation which can be rectified in the light of recent large harvests.
NV Selection Brut (60% PN, 20% CH; 80–85% échelle) Also sec and demi-sec. Reasonable *mousse*, medium-sized bubbles, clean, fresh commercial blend.
NV Cuvée de Réserve (66% PN, 34% CH; 80–85% échelle) Also sec and demi-sec
NV Brut Extra (60% PN, 20% PM, 20% CH; 90% échelle).
NV Blanc de Blancs Brut (100% CH; 96% échelle) Very pale colour, reticent nose, light flinty character coming out after about ten to twenty minutes.
NV Crémant Blanc de Blancs Brut (100% CH; 96% échelle) Lighter in weight than the straight Blanc de Blancs, yet more mature in flavour.
NV Rosé Brut (100% PN; 98% échelle; skin-contact) A mono-cru from Mareuil-sur-Aÿ. It

used to be tangerine-pink in colour, very fruity and with plenty of acidity to match, but recent examples have been too pink, mild and characterless.

Vintage Brut (50% PN, 50% CH; 95–100% échelle) The 1973 and 1975 were good solid blends with a persistent *mousse* and deserving decent ageing.

Vintage Certificate Blanc de Blancs Brut (100% CH; 95–100% échelle) The Crémant Blanc de Blancs is better value, but the 1973 was a good, lively wine showing classic Chardonnay traits and a big, long *mousse*.

A. Chauvet

11 avenue de Champagne, Tours-sur-Marne
Telephone (26) 59.92.37
Visits Week-ends by appointment
Origin The house was founded in 1848
Vineyards 4 hectares on the Montagne de Reims at Bouzy, Ambonnay, Verzenay and Verzy; 5 hectares in the Vallée de la Marne at Bisseuil, representing 80% of total production.
Production 50,000 bottles **Exports** 10%
Average bottle-age of NV *cuvées* 2.5 years

WINES

House style: Wines not tasted. Chauvet is situated opposite Laurent Perrier in Tours-sur-Marne and, despite the numerous occasions I have been there, including a two-week stay at the local auberge, I am ashamed to say that I never visited this small house. This is more the pity as Chauvet are the only house, apart from Besserat de Bellefon and de Venoge, to produce a *crémant* rosé, they produce two, in fact.

NV Carte Blanche Brut (60% PN/PM, 40% CH; 98% échelle)
NV Cachet Vert Blanc de Blancs Brut (100% CH)
NV Grand Crémant Rosé Brut (blended)
Vintage Brut (50% PN, 50% CH; 98% échelle)
Vintage Crémant Rosé Brut (blended)
Coteaux Champenois Bouzy Rouge

Collery

4 rue Anatole France, Aÿ-Champagne
Telephone (26) 50.01.20
Visits Every day, no appointment necessary. Visiting is a speciality at Collery; they have welcomed callers from no less than eighty-three countries and, in 1983, some 10,000 individuals toured this small house and its accompanying museum. Their target is 50,000.
Origin The Collery family of Aÿ supplied grapes to the Abbey of Hautvillers before Dom Pérignon's day. In 1893 they decided to keep part of their harvest to produce and sell their own Champagne. Known variously as 'Collery-Merlin', 'Collery-Herbillon' and 'Jean Collery', this small house, now simply called Champagne Collery, is currently directed by Alain Collery, a lecturer at a Paris business school.
Vineyards 7 hectares at Aÿ and 2 at Mareuil-sur-Aÿ
Production Annually averaging 120,000 bottles prior to 1977, 90,000 between 1978 and 1981, and just 60,000 in 1982 and 1983. They are reverting more and more to their own production and are buying in less and less.
Exports 20–30%
Vinification notes They stopped using *eau-de-vie* in 1970.
Average bottle-age of NV *cuvées* 3 years
Special interest Officially the house is a *négociant-manipulant*, yet it qualifies as a member of the Club de Viticulteurs Champenois, producing a Special Club Champagne.

WINES

House style: Collery's skilful use of the Pinot Noir belies the influence of this grape, which might be as high as 100% in some of the *cuvées*. These are elegantly fruity wines which have a touch of flamboyance, characteristic of Aÿ but they are let down by the poor standard of labelling. It is puzzling that Alain Collery, whose wines are extremely stylish, should use labels which would look vulgar on a bottle of cheap vin mousseux!

NV Cuvée Réserve Brut (70% PN, 20% PM, 10% CH; 95% échelle) Also in extra dry. Full-flavoured, well-balanced wine.

NV Rosé Brut (100% PN, 100% échelle) Made exclusively from Collery's own vineyards in Aÿ. Sometimes sold as a vintage, the 1973 had a delightful strawberry liqueur nose, an extremely fine *mousse*, deliciously perfumed Pinot fruit, fine balance, great length and an elegant after-taste. The 1971 was less successful.

Vintage Cuvée Herbillon Brut (100% PN; 100% échelle in earlier vintages, currently 90% PN, 10% CH; 99–100% échelle) Made exclusively from Collery's own vineyards in Aÿ. Persistent *mouse*, very rich and long flavour. Recommended years: 1966, 1969, 1973.

Vintage Cuvée Special Club Brut (100% PN; 100% échelle in earlier vintages, currently 90% PN, 10% CH; 99–100% échelle) Made exclusively from Collery's own vineyards in Aÿ. Exceptional elegance for a Blanc de Noirs. Recommended years: 1971, 1973.

Delamotte Père & Fils

5 rue de la Brêche d'Oger, le Mesnil-sur-Oger
Telephone (26) 57.51.65
Origin François Delamotte began making and selling Champagne in 1760, adopting the name Delamotte Père & Fils in 1786, when he brought his two sons Alexandre and Nicholas-Louis into the business. The founding of this firm led to the emergence of another: Lanson Père & Fils. In 1828, after the death of his brother, Nicholas-Louis Delamotte changed the house's name to Louis Delamotte Père & Fils and went into partnership with a certain Jean-Baptiste Lanson. At the end of 1837 Lanson's two nephews, Victor-Marie and Henri, joined the firm, whose name was now changed to Veuve Delamotte-Barrachin. In 1856 Delamotte's widow died and, shortly afterwards, the Lansons gained full control of the firm and changed its title to Lanson Père & Fils, although the *marque* of Delamotte was often exploited over the years which followed. After the First World War, the Delamotte *marque* was acquired by Marie-Louise de Nonancourt, the sister of Victor and Henri Lanson; the Nonancourts were destined to purchase the *marque* of Laurent Perrier, which prospered under their direction. In 1927 Delamotte Père & Fils set up business in le Mesnil-sur-Oger under the direction of Charles de Nonancourt.
Production 160,000 bottles
Sales 160,000 bottles **Exports** 40%

WINES
NV Brut, NV Sec, NV Demi-sec, Vintage Brut, Blanc de Blancs, Crémant and Rosé Brut

A. Desmoulins & Cie

44 avenue Foch, Épernay
Telephone (26) 54.24.24
Visits By appointment
Origin The house was established in 1908 by Albert Desmoulins.
Production 180,000 bottles
Sales 180,000 bottles
Average bottle-age of NV *cuvées* 2.5 years

WINES
The Cuvée Prestige (tasted once, 1983) has a soft, creamy, lightly-matured-yeasty nose, good depth of fruit and a fine balance.
NV Cuvée Reserve Brut (90% échelle) NV Sec, NV Demi-Sec, NV Cuvée Brut Royal, NV Cuvée Prestige (50% PN/PM, 50% CH), Cuvée Brut Idéal

Deutz & Geldermann

16 rue Jeanson, Aÿ-Champagne
Telephone (26) 55.15.11
Visits By appointment
Origin The house was established in 1838 by William Deutz and Pierre Geldermann, two young men in their twenties. Both came from Aachen, then part of France under the First Empire, when it was known as Aix-la-Chapelle. It was a partnership of Deutz's six years of experience gained at J. Bollinger, another Aÿ house, and Geldermann's capital – a joint venture which was strengthened by the marriage of William Deutz's son to Pierre Geldermann's daughter.

In November 1883 a quantity of bottles purporting to be Champagne Deutz &

Poster based on a painting *La Belle Époque* by Marie Félix Hippolyte Lucax (1854–1925)

Geldermann attracted attention in Munich. They were of atrocious quality and obviously not genuine Champagne. The Syndicat du Commerce des Vins de Champagne, technically not established until May 1884, was nevertheless already enquiring into such frauds and it was soon discovered that the wine belonged to one Herr A. Einhorn. After exhaustive investigations it was established that the bogus Champagne had forged Jockey Club labels. The Syndicat tracked down the source of supply to a certain Herr Ignatz of Würzburg, and a solicitor by the name of Medicus acted for Deutz & Geldermnn to settle the matter.

Deutz & Geldermann's cellars suffered badly during the riots of 1911, but recovered sufficiently to acquire considerable assets in other wine regions. These currently include a Sekt factory in Germany, Château de l'Aulée in the Loire, the Rhône shippers Delas Frères and some land in California which has recently been planted and will eventually produce a sparkling Californian *Méthode Champenoise* wine.

Vineyards 11.46 hectares at Aÿ (PN); 4.46 hectares at Bisseuil (PM); 5.94 hectares at Mareuil-sur-Aÿ (PN); 11.46 hectares at le Mesnil-sur-Oger (CH); 1.52 hectares at Moussy (PM); 5.76 hectares at Pierry (PM): a total of 40.60 hectares, averaging 97% échelle and representing 40% of total production.
Purchases From sixteen growths averaging 96% échelle
Production 750,000 bottles   **Exports** 50%
Vinification notes There is no fining or filtering of these wines, which receive an extra six months ageing in their cellars after the final corking. *Prise de mousse* is carried out in half-bottles and jeroboams.
Average bottle-age of NV *cuvées* 3–4 years
Special interest The house is a member of the Syndicat de Grandes Marques de Champagne.

WINES
House style: Delicacy, grace and breeding, with exceptional quality in the vintage sector. Some 40% of the production is vintage Champagne. Sometimes the brut dosage tends to rise, in which case the wines benefit from extra ageing.
NV Brut (60% PN, 15% PM, 25% CH; 96% échelle) Also in extra dry and demi-sec. Lively *mousse* of tiny bubbles, fragrant nose, well balanced palate of gentle fruit and elegant finish. Can improve with age.
NV Crémant Brut (67% PN/PM, 33% CH; 96% échelle) Fully *mousseux*, not *crémant*,

some fruit, but not true brut dryness. Mainly Pinot Meunier; tasted in 1980 but not seen since.
Vintage Brut (60% PN, 15% PM, 25% CH; 96% échelle) Wines of great style and finesse, rich in extract and finishing very attractively. Recommended years: 1973, 1975, 1979.
Vintage Blanc de Blancs Brut (100% CH; 99–100% échelle) Crisp white-lemon colour, always star-bright, with an incessant stream of pin-head bubbles – a classic Chardonnay *mousse*. A complete wine. Now marketed in a clear bottle protected from harmful ultra-violet rays by a silver wrapping. Recommended years: 1973, 1975, 1979.
Vintage Rosé Brut (80% PN, 20% PM; 96% échelle; blended) Attractive apricot colour with gold reflections; a solid, fleshy wine, but not one of the best pink Champagnes and, for that matter, not one of the best Deutz wines. The 1973 was disappointing, the 1978 attractive, but too heavily dosed. Recommended years: 1975.
Vintage Cuvée William Deutz (60% PN, 10% PM, 30% CH; 99–100% échelle) Pale lemon-straw colour, good *mousse* of fine bubbles, true brut dryness; usually a fuller wine, but well balanced with acidity to effect the Deutz style. Recommended years: 1971, 1973.
Vintage Cuvée Georges Mathieu (60% PN, 15% PM, 25% CH; 96% échelle) Deutz & Geldermann's answer to Bollinger's RD (that is to say, exactly the same as the ordinary vintage, only left longer *sur pointes*), but rather flashy, with its white and red labelling designed by Georges Mathieu. Only the 1971 and 1978 tasted: the 1971 was everything it should be, but the 1978, though not a bad wine for its year, seems to defeat its late disgorged objective.

André Drappier

Urville, Bar-sur-Aube
Telephone (25) 26.40.13
Visits By appointment
Vineyards 24 hectares; 80% échelle and representing 100% of total production
Production 150,000–200,000 bottles
Vinification notes Cool-fermentation is carried out in stainless steel, with very low levels of SO_2; also automatic *remuage*, with *gyropalettes* being used for part of the production.
Average bottle-age of NV *cuvées* 2 years

WINES

House style: Well made wines of great strength and intensity of fruit. A modern style preferring fruit flavour to the autolytic character of traditional Champagne.

NV Brut (75% PN, 25% PM; 80% échelle) A good *mousse*, penetrated by rich Pinot Noir fruit. Also in extra dry and demi-sec.

Vintage Grande Sendrée Brut (40% PN, 5% PM, 55% CH; 80% échelle) Same overtly fruity style as above, but with more Chardonnay character and finesse.

Vintage Brut (40% PN, 5% PM, 55% CH; 80% échelle)

Vintage Val des Desmoiselles Rosé Brut (100% PN; 80% échelle; skin-contact) Also Coteaux Champenois

Émile Driant

12 rue Marie-Coquebert, Aÿ-Champagne
Telephone (26) 50.13.43
Visits Welcome, but check opening days and times by telephone
Origin Established in 1920 by Émile Driant
Vineyards 20 hectares at Mareuil-sur-Aÿ
Production 50,000 bottles

WINES

Extra Brut Special (60% PN, 40% CH) An assemblage of Aÿ, Avize and Grauves originally prepared for a restaurant in Vauciennes
NV Brut, NV Sec, and NV Demi-Sec

Duval-Leroy

Rue du Mont Chenil, Vertus
Telephone (26) 52.10.75
Visits By appointment
Origin The house was established in 1859 by the merging of Jules Duval & Fils with Édouard Leroy; since then it has been run by the Duval family. Some 70% of Duval-Leroy's total production is sold under various BOB labels, but the quality of these BOBs is, for the most part, superior for these types of wine.
Vineyards 80 hectares: some 30 hectares at Le Mesnil-sur-Oger, Cramant and Avize, the balance at Vertus, Bergères, Villeneuve and Loisy and the Côte de Sézanne, averaging 90% échelle, 25% of total production.
Purchases Grape must is purchased only from traditional *pressois coquarts*, as this house believes that Vaslin and Mabile presses cannot distinguish between the *cuvée* and the *taille*.
Production 2–2.5 million bottles
Exports 10%

Vinification notes Mechanical *remuage* is employed, utilising *gyropalettes* for part of the production.
Average bottle-age of NV *cuvées* 3 years
Other *marques* Paul Vertay (*sous marque*), Veuve Morlant (BOB) and Paul Reisder (BOB)

WINES

House style: Full flavoured wines, well made, well aged and relatively inexpensive.

NV Fleur de Champagne Brut (30% PN, 70% CH; 95%+ échelle) Well formed *mousse* of small and persistent bubbles, full open-knit nose; rich, fruity and lengthy on the palate. A higher standard than at some famous houses.

NV Crémant Blanc de Blancs Brut (100% CH) The first time I tasted this was at a St Vincent day reception in Vertus. It had been mixed with a lot of grower Champagnes, many of which were very poor, but this stood out for its very fine, clinging *mousse*, penetrating flavour and lovely balance.

NV Rosé Brut (20% PN, 80% CH; 95% échelle, blended) Not tasted.

NV Cuvée du Roys Brut (5% PN, 95% CH; 95% échelle) Six to seven years' average bottle-age give this wine extra depth.

Vintage Fleur de Champagne Brut (20% PN, 80% CH; 95% échelle) A vintage which I have rarely tasted; the 1978 was strange, with an egg custard and pineapple nose and very rich, fruity palate – enjoyable in an unusual sort of way.

Coteaux Champenois Vertus Rouge (100% PN; 95%+ échelle) Tasted young and fresh (as Duval-Leroy recommend) it is light and fruity – an expensive alternative to Beaujolais; tasted with an extra year's bottle-age, it begins to tire.

Coteaux Champenois Blanc de Blancs de Chardonnay (100% CH; 95%+ échelle) Very typical of its appellation!

Roland Fliniaux

1 rue Léon Bourgeois, Aÿ-Champagne
Telephone (26) 55.17.17
Visits By appointment
Origin Established in 1905 by Joseph Fliniaux, a *récoltant* who owned a highly regarded site called Les Rocherets near Épernay.
Vineyards 4 hectares at Aÿ, representing 25% of total production
Purchases Averaging 98% échelle
Production 80,000–100,000 bottles
Vinification notes *Prise de mousse* in half-bottles

Average bottle-age of NV *cuvées* Minimum of 3 years

WINES

NV Cuvée de Réserve, Carte Bleue Brut (80% PN, 20% CH; 95%+ échelle) Also in demi-sec

NV Cuvée Supérieure, Carte Rouge Brut (80% PN, 20% CH; 95%+ échelle) Also in demi-sec

NV Cuvée Spéciale, Carte Noire Brut (80% PN, 20% CH; 95%+ échelle) Also in demi-sec. Five years bottle-age.

NV Sélection Rosé Brut (100% PN; 95%+ échelle; skin-contact) Marketed in a clear bottle

Vintage Carte Noire Brut (100% PN; 100% échelle) Exclusively vin d'Aÿ. The 1979 had a fine *mousse*, good body and length; it seemed a little unreliable in 1983, requiring more bottle-age, but had a nice biscuity finish.

Gardet & Cie

13 rue Georges Legros, Chigny-les-Roses, Rilly-la-Montagne
Telephone (26) 03.42.03
Visits By appointment
Origin Established in 1895
Production 600,000 bottles
Vinification notes A small percentage of the wine is treated by mechanical *remuage*, *gyropalettes* being used.
Average bottle-age of NV *cuvées* 3 years

WINES

NV Extra Quality Brut (70% PN, 30% CH; 92% échelle) Also in sec and demi-sec.

NV Selected Réserve Brut (70% PN, 30% CH; 95% échelle) Blend of vintages with an average bottle-age of 5 years.

NV Rosé Brut (100% PN; skin-contact)

Vintage Brut (50% PN, 50% CH; 95% échelle) Also Crémant, Vintage Cuvée Royal England and Coteaux Champenois.

H. Germain & Fils

36 rue de Reims, Rilly-la-Montagne
Telephone (26) 03.42.03
Visits Weekdays – no appointment necessary
Origin This house was established by Henri-Antoine Germain in 1898. Champagne exploding into the middle of a football match, even with the cathedral of Reims in the background, is not everyone's idea of how to market a product renowned for its elegance and sophistication; but then not everybody is the football enthusiast that the recent incumbent of

the business, Henri-Edmond Germain, obviously was. This house has now been sold to Frey, a local furniture firm, and marketing methods may now change.
Vineyards 24.45 hectares at Rilly-la-Montagne, representing 20–25% of total production.
Purchases Averaging 90% échelle
Production 1 million bottles **Exports** 12%
Average bottle-age of NV *cuvées* 2 years
Vinification notes *Liège et agrafe* for magnums and all bottles of Cuvée Venus.
Other *marques* An average of 180,000 bottles of Binet are produced under NV Brut, NV Sélection (*cuvée de prestige*), Vintage Brut, Vintage Blanc de Blancs, Vintage Rosé and Coteaux Champenois Rilly Rouge labels. This *marque*, established at Reims in 1849, was purchased from Piper Heidsieck in 1943. At the time of writing, Germain & Fils were proud that Roger Verge takes a thousand cases per year of this *marque* for his four-star restaurant Le Moulin de Mougins, just outside Cannes.

WINES

House style: Competent *cuvées*, rarely exciting, but usually enjoyable drinking and good value for money.

NV Carte Blanche Brut (50% PN, 50% PM; 90%+ échelle) Good commercial blend, very fruity, good rooty Pinot flavour, soft and well made.

NV Réserve Brut The same wine, with the same dosage.

NV Carte d'Or Rosé Brut (100% PN/PM; 90%+ échelle) Decent standard, but unremarkable.

Vintage Brut (60% PN, 40% CH; 90%+ échelle) Normally a persistent *mousse*, and good depth of well matured flavour. Recommended years: 1973, 1975.

Vintage Blanc de Blancs Brut (100% CH; 90%+ échelle) Only the 1979 tasted: a very full and mellow nose, and extremely round on the palate for a blanc de blancs; a richly flavoured wine, long and clean on the finish. Some Chardonnay from Rilly-la-Montagne apparently gives this *cuvée* its generous style.

Vintage Grande Cuvée Venus Brut (30–40% PN, 60–70% CH; 90%+ échelle) This really is a very enjoyable Champagne, with good fruit, smooth and mellow, and balanced by the freshness of a fine and lively *mousse*; despite its class, however, its marketing must be hampered by a rather cheap-looking label.

Grande Cuvée Venus Blanc de Blanc Not tasted.

Coteaux Champenois Rilly Rouge Light, well made, Beaujolais-style wine – its quality average for the appellation.

Paul Gobillard

43 rue Léon Bourgeois, Pierry, Épernay
Telephone (26) 54.05.11
Origin Paul Gobillard, born in 1836, was a vigneron in Pierry, but it was the success of his grandson and namesake before the last war which established this house in 1941.
Visits By appointment
Production 150,000–180,000 bottles
Exports Negligible
Average bottle-age of NV *cuvée* 2–3 years

WINES
House style: Wines not tasted.
NV Carte Blanche Sec (also demi-sec), NV Brut Réserve, Vintage Brut (high proportion of Chardonnay), NV Rosé Brut, NV Régence Brut (prestige *cuvée* launched in 1968, predominantly Pinot character), Ratafia and Marc.

Gosset

69 rue Blondeau, Aÿ-Champagne
Telephone (26) 50.12.51
Visits By appointment
Origin Four years before Paulmier described the wines of Aÿ in *De vino et pomaceo* (Paris, 1588) as 'the ordinary drink of kings and princes' Pierre Gosset established the oldest house in Champagne. Those who maintain that Ruinart is the most ancient of Champagne houses are always referred to the Bibliothèque Nationale in Paris, where the Dossiers Bleus are housed: No. 29867 [322] contains a manuscript clearly showing that Pierre Gosset was not only a *récoltant*, but also a *négociant* of wines at Aÿ in 1584.

The Gossets can trace their family back sixteen generations to Jean Gosset, who was Seigneur d'Aÿ in 1531. It is recorded that Jean's son Claude was a vigneron in 1555, but as there is no documentary proof that he marketed the wine which he made, the honour of founding the house of Gosset must go to Pierre. Another honour which accrues to Pierre Gosset is that, as mayor of Aÿ (1584–92), he had the privilege of receiving Henri IV. There is no evidence to indicate whether the king was given any of Gosset's wines, but it would seem more than likely that he was.
Vineyards 10 hectares, representing 25% of total production
Production 200,000 bottles **Exports** 34%
Vinification notes Two-thirds cask-fermented, one-third (the biggest, fullest wines) fermented in small vats. Malo-lactic conversion is avoided to provide 'fresher wines' of 'greater longevity'. Mechanical *remuage* utilising *gyropalettes* is

Part of a document held by the Bibliothèque Nationale establishing the sixteenth-century origins of the house of Gosset

adopted for a small proportion of the wines.

Average bottle-age of NV *cuvée*   2–3 years

Special interest   At the end of the 1970s Gosset took over the house of Philipponnat. Gosset celebrated its four hundredth anniversary in 1984 with the launch of Cuvée 4me Centenaire.

WINES

House style: Rich, soft wines of luxurious style in all but their standard NV Brut

NV Réserve Brut   (60% PN/PM (maximum 10% PM), 40% CH; 93% échelle) I often find this wine malic and disjointed.

NV Spécial Réserve Brut   (65% PN, 35% CH; 95% échelle) The luxurious style of *mousse* and delightfully delicate, soft-fruit palate of the Spécial Réserve is everything one expects of a fine Gosset wine.

NV Rosé Brut   (15% PN, 85% CH; 93% échelle; blended) Elegant peach colour, strong *mousse* of minuscule bubbles, fragrant Chardonnay on the nose, but good, big, rooty Pinot flavour on the palate. A very distinguished pink Champagne, sold in a transparent bottle.

Vintage Brut   (60% PN, 40% CH; 93% échelle) Wines of increased depth, character and body. Recommended years: 1971, 1975, 1976.

Grand Millésime   (60% PN, 40% CH; 93% échelle) As for the ordinary vintage, but the Chardonnay appears to dominate, giving greater complexity, finesse and depth. Recommended years: 1971, 1973.

Vintage Cuvée 4me Centenaire   (36% PN, 63% CH; 93% échelle) Fewer than 2,500 cases were produced of this cuvée, which contains various years, including the 1971, which was very successful for Gosset. The bottles are numbered 1–200 (for use by the Gosset family), 201–1,500 (en magnum) and 1,501–28,500 (in 'other bottles'). A very smooth Champagne, ripe, round and lightly rich on a palate which is delicately balanced by a luxuriant *mousse* so typical of Gosset. The wine must contain top class Pinot Noir from superb sites because the character of this grape sings through, despite its minority presence.

Vintage Brut Intégral 1961   (35% PN, 65% CH; 95% échelle) This wine, released in September 1979, I found to be showing its age and generally disappointing, despite the enthusiastic reviews devoted to it in *Paris Match* and *Figaro*.

Other products include Coteaux Champenois Blanc de Blancs and Coteaux Champenois Bouzy Rouge.

George Goulet

Les Grands Champagnes de Reims
2 and 4 avenue du Général-Giraud, Reims
Telephone (26) 85.05.77
Visits   By appointment
Origin   Established in 1834 as Goulet Frères by François André Goulet, the business was abandoned in 1849 before being re-established in 1867 as George Goulet, for the founder's third son George. Because this house supplied Champagne to both King George IV and King George V, it has been suggested that the 's' in George(s) Goulet was dropped as a mark of respect for those monarchs. This, however, is not the case: the third son's name was, in fact, spelt George, not Georges.

In 1960 George Goulet was acquired by Abel Lepitre. Shortly afterwards the current umbrella company, Le Société des Grandes Champagnes de Reims, was formed, embracing Abel Lepitre, George Goulet and de Saint Marceaux.

An interesting story concerning George Goulet concerns a young English gentleman, hard up on his luck in New York in 1933, about to embark upon an ephemeral career selling, amongst other products, George Goulet Champagne. In April 1933, he heard that two acquaintances, Jack Kreindlar and his friend 'Charlie', were going into the wine business. They introduced him to one of the backers, Frank Hunter (of Tilden and Hunter, the world champion tennis doubles). The Englishman was duly enlisted and his first sale, which happened to be George Goulet Champagne, was to one Woolly Donahue. The deal was struck just before midnight 4 December which, as Prohibition was not repealed until 5 December, was a crime. Who was he? None other than the late David Niven! How do we know? Niven confessed to this little escapade in his autobiography *The Moon's a Balloon*. Niven was an awful salesman (hired on a wage of $40 a week based on sales of $400 at 10% commission, he rarely achieved this and hardly ever exceeded it), but his colleague Harry Rantzman was not – his selling acumen was so sharp, he ended up owning several apartment blocks in the Bronx. Niven was one of the founding sons of '21's and to this day his photograph (an FBI mug-shot in which he had to hold a board around his neck with a registration number on it) adorns the offices bearing the caption 'First and worst salesman'.

Purchases 90–95% échelle
Production 350,000 bottles **Exports** 25%
Other *marques* Henry Goulet

WINES
House style: Full, rich and smooth wines
greatly influenced by Pinot Noir.
NV Extra Quality Brut (50% PN, 10% PM,
40% CH; 92% échelle) Also in sec and demi-
sec. A finely based wine, with plenty of fruit
and balancing acidity, but sometimes let down
by a vigorous but coarse *mousse*.
NV Goulet G Blanc de Blancs Brut (100% CH;
92% échelle) Not tasted.
Vintage Extra Quality Brut (60% PN, 40%
CH; 95% échelle) Strong *mousse* of small
bubbles, generous nose, full and fruity on the
palate, with a smooth rich finish.
Recommended years: 1975, 1976, 1979.
Vintage Crémant Blanc de Blancs Brut (100%
CH; 95% échelle) Not tasted.
Vintage Extra Quality Rosé Brut (100% PN;
95% échelle; blended) Always big in body and
full in fruit, often herbal in character,
eventually gaining much elegance.
Recommended years: 1975, 1976, 1979.
Vintage Cuvée du Centenaire (55% PN, 45%
CH; 92–99% échelle) Launched in 1967 to
celebrate one hundred years of the *marque*
George Goulet, this *cuvée* undergoes its *prise de
mousse* sealed by *liège et agrafe* and is
disgorged *à la volée*, without the use of freezing
brine. The *mousse* tends to be softer than in the
other blends, the nose having a certain flowery
character derived from the Chardonnay; the
wine is always very ripe and well matured, with
a long, delicate finish. The 1974 was
surprisingly successful. Recommended years:
1970, 1974, 1975.

Alfred Gratien

Gratien, Meyer, Sedoux & Cie
30 rue Maurice-Cerveaux, Épernay
Telephone (26) 54.38.20
Visits Welcome, but an appointment is
appreciated.
Origin In 1864 the firm of Gratien & Meyer
set up business in Épernay and in Saumur
(Loire). The correct company name today is
Gratien, Meyer, Seydoux et Cie. In the Loire
this firm markets its range of *méthode
champenoise* wines under the Gratien & Meyer
marque, while in Épernay the Champagnes are
sold under the Alfred Gratien label.

Vineyards None
Production 200,000 bottles
Exports In excess of 50%
Vinification notes The wines are entirely cask-
fermented, reserves being kept in wood. All
Champagnes sold under the Alfred Gratien
marque undergo *prise de mousse* in bottles
sealed by *liège et agrafe*, although crown-caps
are used for supermarket brands and for a
certain percentage of the NV. The wines are,
therefore, more traditionally produced than
either Krug or Bollinger.
Average bottle-age of NV *cuvées* 3–4 years
Special interest The firm supplies the IEC Wine
Society and the House of Commons in London.

WINES
House style: Very mature and biscuity; the
vintage wines are always first class, but the non-
vintage *cuvées* can be too oxidised on the nose
for my liking. The company specialise in
supplying a range of older vintages.
NV Cuvée de Réserve Brut (67% PN/PM, 33%
CH; 80–90% échelle) Good *mousse* of fine
bubbles, fully developed bouquet (though too
strong for my taste), plenty of extract, well
balanced and long.
NV Rosé Brut Mainly based on Chardonnay,
this wine has sometimes been very malic, which
is understandable considering its cask-
fermentation. When this occurs it repays to
keep the wine several years; this may result in
the alteration of its colour to an orange hue,
and although this might be less attractive to
look at, the wine is certainly better to drink.
Vintage Crémant Brut (60–70% PN/PM, 30–
40% CH; 92% échelle) Some really great
vintages have been produced by this house over
the years. The impression on the nose is one
that is absolutely clean and ripe in fruit for at
least ten years, after which the wines age
gracefully, developing a vastly more refined
nose than the NV and a truly rich and complex
biscuit flavour on the palate. Recommended
years: 1970, 1971, 1973.

Hamm

Émile Hamm & Fils
16 rue Nicolas Philipponnat, Aÿ-Champagne
Telephone (26) 50.12.87
Visits For purchases.
Origin Established in 1930 by Émile Hamm,
who, although born locally, was of an Alsace
family.

Vineyards 3.5 hectares in Aÿ, representing 10% of the total production.
Purchases Averaging 90% échelle.
Production 200,000 bottles **Exports** 4%
Vinification notes *Prise de mousse* in half-bottles.

WINES

NV Sélection Brut An *assemblage* of minor growths and 33% of *vins de taille* from Chardonnay grapes.
NV Réserve 1er Cru Brut (60% PN/PM, 40% CH; 97% échelle)
NV Rosé Brut Made by adding vin d'Aÿ rouge to the above wine. Production of this *cuvée* began as recently as 1973.
Vintage Brut (50% PN, 50% CH; 97% échelle)

The Heidsieck Houses

Many people are confused by the existence of three Champagne houses each bearing the name Heidsieck. Some are surprised that there *are* three, having believed there to be but one house marketing several brands. In the light of this widespread misunderstanding, it seemed sensible to depart from alphabetical order and discuss all three Heidsieck houses in turn at this point in the book, even though they are completely independent, with no connection other than a common name. Opposite is a chronological table which serves to separate and identify the origin of each house and explain the differences between them which obtain today.

Charles Heidsieck

3 Place des Droits-de-l'Homme, Reims
Telephone (26) 40.16.13
Visits By appointment
Origin The firm of Heidsieck was founded in 1785 by Florenz-Louis Heidsieck, but the first use of Charles Heidsieck as a *marque* did not occur until 1851. In 1845 Charles-Camille Heidsieck (the son of Charles-Henri, one of Florenz-Louis' three nephews, partners in the original Heidsieck firm) joined the company of H. Piper & Co., a firm run by his aunt and her second husband, Henri Piper. In 1851, after marrying Amélie Henriot (his father had also married an Henriot), he left Piper to join his brother-in-law Ernest Henriot at the house of Henriot. The two worked together to market a new Champagne, using the Heidsieck name,

and so the house of Charles Heidsieck was formed in 1851.

In 1857 Charles-Camille made the first of many trips to America, in which he combined selling Champagne with the sport of shooting; through his flamboyant life-style he soon became known as 'Champagne Charlie'. The often quoted verse from George Leybourne's famous music-hall song rarely mentioned Heidsieck, as, for a shilling, he would fit in any Champagne name:

Champagne Charlie was my name,
  Champagne drinking gained my fame,
So as of old when on a spree,
  Moet and Shandon's [sic] the wine for me.

On one trip to America, in 1861, Charles-Camille was imprisoned in a 'Yankee' fort on the Mississippi delta. This was during the Civil War, and his jailers had not taken kindly to the contracts Heidsieck was carrying in a diplomatic bag; they were from certain French companies committed to supplying the Confederate armies.

In 1976, just over one hundred years after Ernest Henriot left the company to concentrate on his own *marque* (which he had established in 1808) the house of Henriot returned to take over Charles Heidsieck. On the surface, it looked like an equal association, Henriot's considerable vineyard and Charles Heidsieck's much larger sales, but in effect Henriot held the controlling shares. It proved to be a successful merger. But the ramification was an ephemeral one and, in 1985, Charles Heidsieck was sold to Rémy Martin the Cognac house which also controls Krug.

While Charles Heidsieck is technically the youngest of the three Heidsieck houses, it is also the only one run by directly descended members of the Heidsieck family. All Heidsiecks who work for Charles Heidsieck append 'Charles' to their Heidsieck surname.
Vineyards None.
Purchases Averaging 93% échelle
Production 3.5 million bottles **Exports** 60%
Average bottle-age of NV *cuvées* 3 years
Special interest The house is a member of the Syndicat de Grandes Marques de Champagne. In 1982 Jean-Marc Charles-Heidsieck mounted an enlightening tasting of the *vins clairs* used to construct the NV Brut. As a *cuvée* may contain as many as sixty different villages, the normal construction of the Charles Heidsieck NV was

Evolution of the Heidsieck Houses

1785 The firm of Heidsieck founded by Florenz-Louis Heidsieck.

1794 The firm's title changed to Heidsieck & Co.

1795 Henri-Louis Walbaum, nephew of Florenz-Louis, entered the firm.

1805 Charles-Henri Heidsieck, nephew of Florenz-Louis, entered the firm.

1808 Christian Heidsieck, nephew of Florenz-Louis and younger brother of Charles-Henri, entered the firm.

1818 Charles-Henri Heidsieck married Émilie Henriot.

1824 Charles-Henri Heidsieck died.

1828 Florenz-Louis Heidsieck died. The firm ceased trading for a short while before the two surviving nephews regrouped and continued trading as Heidsieck & Co., but without the direction of Florenz-Louis, Henri-Louis Walbaum and Christian Heidsieck soon split up, each to go his own way.

Heidsieck & Co. Monopole

1834 Henri-Louis Walbaum founded the firm of Walbaum Heidsieck & Co.

1846 Henri-Louis' son-in-law Auguste Heidsieck took over the firm and changed its title back to Heidsieck & Co.

1858 August Luling, nephew of August Heidsieck, entered the firm.

1860 The brand name of 'Monopole' was first registered by the firm.

1870 Auguste Heidsieck died.

1870–1910 As a result of various changes in the firm's personnel its name was altered successively to Veuve Heidsieck; Walbaum, Luling, Goulden & Co.; Walbaum, Goulden & Co.

1923 Acquired by Édouard Mignot of Comptoirs Français, the firm's name was changed to Heidsieck & Co. Monopole

1972 Acquired by the Mumm Group.

Piper Heidsieck

1834 Christian Heidsieck formed a company to sell Champagne, using the *marque* Heidsieck.

1835 Christian Heidsieck died. The firm's name was changed to Veuve Heidsieck.

1837 Heidsieck's widow married her brother-in-law Henri Piper. The firm's name was changed to H. Piper & Co., but sold under the Heidsieck *marque*.

1845 The firm's label was changed to Piper-Heidsieck, but the rights to the Heidsieck *marque* were kept. Charles-Camille Heidsieck, the son of Charles-Henri (d. 1824), entered the firm.

1850 J. C. Kunkelmann was made a partner of H. Piper & Co.

1851 Charles-Camille Heidsieck married Amélie Henriot and left the firm to work with his brother-in-law and found the firm of Charles Heidsieck.

1870 Henri-Piper died. Kunkelmann took over the firm whose title was changed to Kunkelmann et Cie. After Kunkelmann's son died, the firm was left to the Marquise de Saurez d'Aulan.

Charles Heidsieck

1851 Charles-Camille Heidsieck left H. Piper & Co. to join Henriot Frères, Soeur & Co. (established 1808). Charles-Camille and hs brother-in-law Ernest Henriot founded the house of Charles Heidsieck.

1871 Charles-Eugène Heidsieck took over control of Charles Heidsieck.

1875 Ernest Henriot left Charles Heidsieck to concentrate on the house of Henriot.

1976 The firms of Charles Heidsieck and Henriot were merged, with Henriot in control.

1985 History repeated itself as Henriot and Charles Heidsieck split. Charles Heidsieck was acquired by Rémy Martin.

broken down into seven basic categories, and wines which are always used in the *cuvée* of this house were offered under each of these as indicative of their type. The following descriptions and my comments are intended to help the reader to understand how the final blend can be greater than the sum of its component parts. Since the date of the tasting was 30 November, the wines had not completed their fermentation and some were not quite *vins clairs*.

Grand Blanc (20% of final blend)
Description: Chardonnay from Avize.
Author's tasting notes: Straw-yellow, bright, youthful Chardonnay aroma, fine acidity, balance and length.

Petit Blanc (5% of final blend)
Description: Chardonnay from the Côte de Sézanne.
Author's tasting notes: Pale-straw, murky, reticent on the nose, aromatic on the palate, fatter than the Grand Blanc and with less acidity.

Grand Noir (30% of final blend)
Description: Pinot Noir from Bouzy.
Author's tasting notes: Dirty pink-grey, attractive full and fruity nose, rich concentrated flavour, malic acidity still very active.

Petit Noir (10% of final blend)
Description: Pinot Meunier from Damery.
Author's tasting notes: Slightly deeper colour than the Grand Noir, but a bit less murky; simple fruity nose, round, overtly fruity and forward on the palate, earthy undertone, short.

Montagne de Reims (20% of final blend)
Description: Pinot Noir from Ludes.
Author's tasting notes: Deepest colour, ruddy reflections, bright; reticent nose, richness and elegance on the palate.

First Pressing Noir (5% of final blend)
Description: Pinot Noir from various villages of the Montagne de Reims and Vallée de la Marne.
Author's tasting notes: Peach-coloured (will fade during the second fermentation), fresh and fragrant fruit on nose, lightweight palate.

Reserve wine (10% of final blend)
Description: An *assemblage* of 80% Pinot Noir and Pinot Meunier and 20% Chardonnay from the 1981 vintage.
Author's tasting notes: Pale straw colour, perfectly limpid, precociously perfumed nose, Pinot richness on the palate.

WINES

House style: Champagnes which offer very good value: fine *mousse*, generous bouquet, well structured, with good fruit and length.

NV Brut (40% PN, 40% PM, 20% CH; 95% échelle) Well made Champagne, showing more Chardonnay elegance than these proportions might suggest.

NV Blanc de Blancs Brut (100% CH; 96% échelle) Not tasted.

Vintage Brut (75% PN/PM, 25% CH; 95% échelle) Always well made, with a contrast between fulness of flavour and elegance of style. The 1976 has a fine balance for that big year. Recommended years: 1975, 1976.

Vintage Cuvée Royale Brut (60% PN, 40% CH; 95–100% échelle) Well bred wine with Pinot Noir, which comes mainly from Aÿ, Ambonnay, Bouzy, Mailly and Verzenay, dominating the initial palate, with Chardonnay adding elegance to the finish. Recommended years: 1973, 1975.

Vintage Blanc de Blancs Brut (100% CH; 99–100% échelle) From Avize, Cramant Chouilly and elsewhere; throughout Henriot's nine-year ownership, this *cuvée* was precisely the same as Henriot's Vintage Blanc de Blancs Brut.

Vintage Rosé Brut (74% PN, 18% PM, 18% CH; 96% échelle; blended) Vintage Brut with as much as 25–30% red wine from Bouzy. Elegant peach-pink colour, smooth *mousse*, refined nose; very fruity indeed, with an underlying 'big' fruit flavour waiting to burst out, and a stylish finish. Recommended years: 1973, 1975.

Vintage Cuvée 'Champagne Charlie' Brut Only the 1979 tasted. Gentle *mousse*. Light lemon-gold colour, enchanting hint of honey on the nose; big, fleshy Pinot character on the palate, Chardonnay showing on the finish. The wine needed another four years at least in 1983.

Heidsieck & Co. Monopole

83 rue Coquebert, Reims
Telephone (26) 07.39.34
Visits By appointment
Origin The history of this house, like that of Charles Heidsieck, also stretches back to the founding by Florenz-Louis of Heidsieck & Co., in 1785; but this particular Heidsieck firm established its own identity in 1834, when

Henri-Louis Walbaum, the first of the three nephews whom Florenz-Louis brought into the original firm, started his own house, Walbaum, Heidsieck & Co. Although his son-in-law August Heidsieck took over the firm in 1846, and various partners by the name of Luling and Goulden came and went, this branch of the Heidsieck legacy remained under the control and direction of the Walbaums until 1923. In that year Édouard Mignot, of Comtoirs Français, purchased the firm and changed its title to Heidsieck & Co. Monopole, after the great brand which it had first registered in 1860.

In 1972 Heidsieck & Co. Monopole was acquired by the Mumm Group, which also owns Perrier-Jouët and is itself part of the huge multi-national company of Seagram.

Vineyards 23 hectares of Pinot Noir at Bouzy and Ambonnay, 43 hectares of Pinot Noir at Verzenay and Verzy, and 44 hectares of Pinot Meunier at Savigny-sur-Ardre and Faverolles, averaging 94% échelle and representing 30–33% of total production.

Purchases Averaging 97% échelle

Production 1.6–1.9 million bottles

Sales 1.6–1.85 million bottles **Exports** 50%

Stocks 6.5 million bottles (December 1983)

Vinification notes *Prise de mousse* in half-bottles using crown-caps; in jeroboams and methuselahs, using *liège et agrafe*. The last time this firm produced a Champagne Doux (in excess of 50 grams per litre of residual sugar) was in 1970, but the use of *eau-de-vie* in the *liqueur d'expedition* was discontinued in the 1940s.

Average bottle-age of NV *cuvées* 3 years

Special interest Heidsieck & Co. Monopole is in the process of replanting its entire estate with selected clones. The house is a member of the Syndicat de Grandes Marques de Champagne.

WINES

House style: Always a Champagne of good depth, it can pursue richness while forsaking flare, yet its excellent base wine and sound *mousse* raise its quality above that of many other wines.

NV Dry Monopole Brut (67% PN/PM, 33% CH; 95% échelle) Maximum of 5% Pinot Meunier. Carefully developed *mousse*, well developed nose, indicative of the richness revealed on the palate; very good fruit. The wine is an extremely well made commercial brut.

NV Red Top Sec and Green Top Demi-Sec (As above, but PN might be 15–20%) Not tasted.

Vintage Dry Monopole Brut (67% PN, 33% CH; 97–98% échelle) Firm, lasting and mature; Pinot is dominant, with plenty of fruit and acidity. Recommended years: 1971, 1973, 1975, 1979.

Vintage Rosé Brut (70–72% PN, 28–30% CH; 97–98% échelle) Only the 1973 tasted (1980) – very orangy, the colour of Tavel Rosé; plenty of ripe fruit, well matured, very soft.

Vintage Cuvée Diamant Bleu (50% PN, 50% CH; 100% échelle) Many Champagnes are fifty-fifty blends, but few have such an immaculate balance of Pinot Noir and Chardonnay; an exquisitely fine wine in all respects: *mousse*, nose, palate and finish. Recommended years: 1973, 1975, 1976.

Piper Heidsieck

Kunkelmann & Cie
51 boulevard Henri Vasnier, Reims
Telephone (26) 85.01.94

Visits Monday to Friday throughout the year; weekends, April to November. An electric train takes visitors around some of the twelve kilometres of cellars.

Origin Like the other two Heidsieck houses, the firm owes its earliest origins to Florenz-Louis, but, as with Heidsieck & Co. Monopole, its real history began in 1834, when one of the original three nephews brought into the business by Florenz-Louis established his own house. For Piper Heidsieck, the nephew in question was Christian Heidsieck, but he spent barely one year selling Champagne under the simple *marque* of Heidsieck before he died. In the hands of his widow the house became known as Veuve Heidsieck, but her mourning lasted just two years, for, in 1837, she married Henri-Guillaume Piper, her brother-in-law. Henri Piper, who was a great-nephew of Florenz-Louis, had been an associate in the firm since its inception. Under his control, the business changed names to H. Piper & Co., but continued selling its Champagne under the *marque* of Heidsieck until 1845. In that year, although the firm held on to the rights of the Heidsieck *marque*, it began selling its Champagne as 'Piper-Heidsieck' in deference to its American customers, who had insisted on calling the wine 'Piper's Heidsieck'.

Jean-Claude Kunkelmann, who had been representing H. Piper & Co. in America, returned to Reims in 1850 with a veritable fortune (possibly earned by commissions) and was duly made a partner, as was Christian Walbaum, who had been representing the firm in Russia. When Henri Piper died in 1870, he left H. Piper & Co. to Kunkelmann, who changed its title to Kunkelmann et Cie, which has remained the firm's legal title to this day.

When Kunkelmann died in 1881, he left the business to his son Ferdinand Kunkelmann. In 1930, Ferdinand's daughter, the Marquise de Saurez d'Aulan, inherited Kunkelmann et Cie. Her husband, the Marquis, helped administer the company's affairs (in 1936 he was, incidentally, a member of the French Olympic bobsleigh team). He was decorated posthumously with the Croix de Guerre and the Légion d'Honneur for his daring exploits in the Second World War.

The Marquise later remarried, her second husband being Général d'Alès. Her son François d'Aulan is now chairman of the firm, which, although publicly quoted, is still firmly controlled by the d'Aulan family's majority share-holding.

Vineyards None

Production 4–6.5 million bottles

Sales 4–4.5 million bottles   **Exports** 60%

Stocks 15.5 million bottles (December 1983)

Vinification notes After its first fermentation the wine is centrifuged, and is not submitted to malo-lactic conversion. This firm has one of the largest and fastest *transvasage* lines in Champagne, where bottles are decanted under pressure and half- and quarter-bottles are similarly filled. It is a system much in demand by other firms – I have seen many famous labels moving down this line, most of them having nothing to do with Piper! The house was also one of the first to use computer-controlled mechanical *remuage*, utilising *gyropalettes*, an operation which is now virtually 100% automatic at this house.

Average bottle-age of NV *Cuvées* 2.5–4 years.

Other *marques* Becker (second quality) and Heidsieck.

Special interest The house is a member of the Syndicat de Grandes Marques de Champagne.

WINES

House style: The Piper Heidsieck Champagne is underrated because it is all too often drunk too young. While these wines cannot possibly be compared with those of Krug for longevity, Piper Champagne, like Krug, does not go through the malo-lactic process and thus requires more time in bottle. Krug is made to be aged, which is why it might appear austere in its youth; Piper is not made to be aged, which is why it can be tightly closed in its youth. Given a decent period of maturity, Piper wines achieve depth and finesse.

NV Brut Extra (40% PN, 30% PM, 30% CH; 90–100% échelle) Also in demi-sec. Strong *mousse*, fresh nose, true fragrant brut flavour, lengthening and deepening with time in bottle.

NV Brut Sauvage (25% PN, 25% PM, 50% CH, 90–100% échelle) Piper's experiments with this non-dosage Champagne began in 1965. Prior to its general release in 1980, it was test-marketed in Germany under the Brut Dosage Zero label. At that time it was a very tight wine, but with a deep rasping quality which seemed to be trying to break free. Precisely the same *cuvée*, tasted in 1982, had rounded out, but still required three or four years' extra ageing in bottle. It has a strong *mousse*, a full nose and fine quality; like any sound non-dosage Champagne, it should be given as long as a vintage wine to mature.

Vintage Extra Brut (25% PN, 25% PM, 50% CH; 90–100% échelle) Full mature nose, often nutty or biscuity; a fine *mousse* of tiny bubbles and, with ten years of bottle-age, when the Chardonnay catches up with the Pinot, a complete flavour, long and complex. The 1961 still had a lively *mousse* with a honey and macaroon flavour, when drunk in 1980, despite the fact that the sample tasted had been normally disgorged and left unattended in the chef de caves' locker for several years. Recommended years: 1973, 1975, 1976.

Vintage Florenz-Louis Brut (20% PN/PM, 80% CH; 99% échelle) A delicate wine shedding gentle nuances of bouquet and flavour. Well made, with a good *mousse* and an appropriate amount of fruit, but not quite enough character to attract customers as a *cuvée de prestige* should be expected to do. Recommended years: 1973, 1975.

Vintage Rosé Brut The Vintage Extra Brut is the base wine for this *cuvée*, to which 15–20% of red wine from Bouzy is added. I did not taste enough to proffer a sensible opinion; the 1975 was darkish in colour, with a soft fruit nose and very rich palate, while the 1976 had far too much acetaldehyde on the nose.

Vintage Rare (40% PN, 60% CH; 100% échelle; 93g/l residual sugar) Launched on 1 September 1984, this wine is a blend of wines from all twelve then grand cru villages. The vintage of 1976 was selected for Champagne Rare, a special *cuvée* introduced to celebrate Piper's bicentenial year in 1985. The label is a reproduction of that designed by Peter Carl Fabergé for Piper's centenary in 1885. Not tasted.

Also Heidsieck NV Brut, NV Demi-Sec Vintage Brut, Vintage Brut Rosé and Vintage Jubilé Brut, Becker NV Brut, NV Demi-Sec, Vintage Brut, Vintage Brut Rosé and Vintage Amorial.

Henriot

3 Place des Droits-de-l'Homme, Reims
Telephone (26) 85.03.27
Visits By appointment
Origin In 1808, Appoline Henriot, née Godinot, the widow of Nicolas-Simon Henriot, established the house of Veuve Henriot Aîné to make and sell Champagne produced from her father's vineyards. After twenty-four years of establishing the house of Charles Heidsieck with his brother-in-law Charles-Camille Heidsieck, Appoline's grandson Ernest Henriot took control of Veuve Henriot. In 1875 the firm's name was changed to Henriot & Cie, and in the years which followed Ernest was responsible for greatly enlarging the business, most notably by the acquisition of some seventy-five hectares of prime vineyards on the Côte des Blancs.

In 1976 Henriot resumed its close association with Charles Heidsieck by a merger which, in fact, gave Henriot controlling shares in both businesses. However, Charles Heidsieck was sold to Rémy Martin in 1985 and by what has been termed a 'reverse takeover' of Veuve Clicquot, M. Joseph Henriot received an 11% holding of that great house in return for stock, premises and vineyards.
Vineyards 125 hectares, comprising 70% Chardonnay and 30% Pinot Noir, averaging 95% échelle and representing 20% of the combined production of Charles Heidsieck-Henriot.
Purchases Averaging 90% échelle
Production 1.5 million bottles **Exports** 30%
Vinification notes There is a 6,000 kilogram Mabile central-membrane press at le Mesnil-sur-Oger, also an 8,000-kilogram Blucher horizontal press. There is a brand-new *cuverie* of temperature-controlled, nitrogen-blanketed, stainless steel vats, which was built during the Charles Heidsieck-Henriot days, which utilises the most modern of techniques.

Average bottle-age of NV *cuvées* 3 years.
Special interest The house has been a member of the Syndicat de Grandes Marques de Champagne since its acquisition of Charles Heidsieck.

WINES
House style: Mild, gently rich Champagnes of good *mousse* and quality, which deserve to be well known.
NV Souverain Brut (40–50% PN/PM, 50–60% CH; 90%+ échelle) Pale straw colour, good strength of *mousse*, often a pleasant yeasty-mushroomy nose; an old-style wine, showing good fruit and length.
NV Crémant Blanc de Blancs Brut (100% CH; 99–100% échelle) A large proportion of grapes from le Mesnil-sur-Oger and Oger are used. Not tasted.
Vintage Souverain Brut (67% PN, 33% CH; 90%+ échelle) Very ripe and fruity, firm *mousse* and character. Recommended years 1975, 1976.
Vintage Blanc de Blancs Brut (100% CH; 99–100% échelle) From Avize, Cramant Chouilly and elsewhere; precisely the same as Charles Heidsieck's Vintage Blanc de Blancs Brut when Henriot controlled that company.
Vintage Rosé Brut This is NV Souverain blended with some red wine from Ambonnay, Bouzy and Verzenay. Not tasted.
Vintage Le Premier Brut (50% PN, 50% CH; 99% échelle) Not tasted.
Réserve Baron Philippe de Rothschild (50% PN, 50% CH; 99% échelle) Fine *mousse*, full and generous nose, rich fruit on the palate, definitely brut. The 1975 had a pleasant but strange taste of tea leaves! Recommended years: 1973, 1975.

Herard & Fluteau

Route Nationale: Gye-sur-Seine, Mussy-sur Seine
Origin Established in 1935 by Émile Herard and his brother-in-law Georges Fluteau.
Production 100,000 bottles

WINES
NV Brut, NV Sec, NV Demi-Sec, Vintage Brut.

Irroy

44 boulevard Lundy, Reims
Telephone (26) 88.37.27
Origin The name of Irroy can be traced back as far as the fifteenth century in Mareuil-sur-Aÿ

M. Ernest Irroy's establishment at Reims in 1882

and Avenay, but the house of Irroy was not established until 1820. In the second half of the nineteenth century Ernest Irroy, then head of the firm, expanded the business to include vineyards at Bouzy and a presshouse at Ambonnay. He was known for the consideration he gave his employees, greatly improving their conditions of work. Although this little house has now slipped into relative obscurity, Ernest Irroy built up a considerable reputation for his wines. Henry Vizetelly, in *A History of Champagne* (1882), declares that Irroy's wines were 'prepared with scrupulous care and rare intelligence ... They are emphatically connoisseurs' wines'. Today Irroy is treated as a *sous marque* by its parent company, Taittinger.

Special interest The house is a member of the Syndicat de Grandes Marques de Champagne.

WINES

NV Brut, Vintage Cuvée Marie Antoinette So named because Mary Antoinette stayed at Château d'Irroy in 1786.

Ivernal

4 rue Jules Lobet, Aÿ-Champagne
Telephone (26) 50.11.00
Visits By appointment
Origin The house was established in 1955 by Bernard Ivernal, whose family has lived in Aÿ since at least the fifteenth century.
Vineyards 2 hectares at Aÿ
Purchases 6–7%
Production 190,000 bottles   **Exports** 30%
Vinification notes *Prise de mousse* in halves, jeroboams and methuselahs. Ivernal has always disgorged *à la volée*, but only recently has Bernard decided to give up dipping the wines into freezing brine (as in *à la glace*) prior to this manual operation. The reason is that while freezing gives his *dégorgeurs* more flexibility, thus rendering their task easier to perform, they complain that it makes their hands too cold! Ivernal must be the only house to disgorge its entire production *à la volée* without the aid of freezing brine.
Average bottle-age of NV *cuvées* 3 years

Other *marques* Jacques Mathier, Marignan, Delande Frères, Raoul Gauthier.

WINES

House style: The following notes relate to one tasting at Bernard Ivernal's home in November 1983. I certainly preferred his vintage wines, but it was not possible to make a valid assessment of Ivernal's house style. His wines are to be found in some of the finest restaurants in France.

NV Réserve Brut 60% PN/PM, 40% CH; 94% échelle) Sweet and simple, young and broad; not a true *brut*, and the *mousse* was also not satisfactory.

NV Rosé Brut The base wine is similar in construction to the NV Réserve Brut, to which is added red wine from Bouzy and Aÿ. I tasted two Rosé NVs: one based on the 1981 vintage was dark and sweet, the red wine was not well married and it was much too young; the one based on the 1980 vintage was lighter in colour, fuller on the nose and richer on the palate, with a good strong *mousse*.

Vintage Brut (50% PN/PM, 50% CH; 94% échelle) The 1973 was a pale straw colour, mature and full on the nose, fresh and vigorous on the palate; a well balanced, well made wine.

Vintage Cuvée du Roi François 1er Brut (formerly 40% PN/PM, 60% Chardonnay; now 50% PN/PM, 50% CH) The 1978 tasted was of the earlier construction. A good *mousse* of small bubbles, delightful balance of fruit and acidity, very round and drinking well; a better than average 1978 for early drinking.

Jacquesson & Fils

Société Léon de Tassigny
68 rue du Colonel Fabien, Dizy
Telephone (26)53.00.66
Visits By appointment
Origin Claude Jacquesson and his son Memmie established this house in 1798; in 1802 they opened their magnificent offices, and ten kilometres of cellars, built at great expense, in Châlons-sur-Marne. When Napoleon visited this lavish organisation in 1810 he was so impressed that he presented the firm with a special gold medal, awarded for the 'richness and beauty' of its *caves*.

Adolphe Jacquesson succeeded his father Memmie in 1837; four years later his English sister-in-law, Emma Anne Jaunay, married (at

the British Embassy in Paris) a German who had been employed by Jacquesson since 1834. The man's name was Joseph Krug, who, eighteen months after his marriage to Emma Anne, surprised everybody by leaving to set up his own Champagne house (see Krug & Co.)

By 1867 the house of Jacquesson boasted annual sales in excess of one million bottles – big business for any Champagne firm at that time and about three times Jacquesson's turnover today. Adolphe Jacquesson died in 1875, his descendants chose other careers and in 1920, after a transitional period, the house of Jacquesson became the property of a broker called Léon de Tassigny. Tassigny moved the firm to Reims, the centre of the Champagne trade. In 1974 the house was purchased by Jean Chiquet, who took it to its present location in Dizy.

The good ship *Niantic* . . .

Built at Chatham in 1835, the *Niantic* was a three-masted sailing ship which began her life trading in tea and silk in the China Seas around the time of the Opium Wars. In 1849 it was transporting gold miners to San Francisco and, on July 4, the *Niantic* was anchored in San Francisco Bay with her passengers disembarked. When the captain awoke the following morning, he found his entire crew had deserted to join the gold rush. This was

The Niantic Hotel, Clay Street,
San Francisco, *circa* 1860

but one of hundreds of similar occurrences which, by early 1850, resulted in no less than seven hundred such ships abandoned in the waters of Yerba Buena Cove. Some were later sailed away, others were deliberately sunk and quite a number – including the *Niantic* – were beached and used for all sorts of purposes, from churches to jails, whorehouses to hotels.

Beached at the end of Clay Street, the *Niantic* was first a warehouse but, in 1851, one of the numerous fires which swept the city razed her to the keel. Almost before the ashes had cooled, a wooden three-storey building was constructed over them; the upper two floors comprised the Niantic Hotel. When this building was demolished in the 1870s some thirty-five baskets of Champagne bearing the Jacquesson brand were found. The wine, which had originally been in the ship's hold, had been submerged in mud and water and had thus survived the fire nineteen years earlier. Newspaper clippings on file in the San Francisco Museum reported this wine had been 'so completely covered as to be almost excluded from the air, and some of the wine effervesced slightly on uncorking, and was of a very fair flavour.'

But the story does not end here, for the site provided the foundation of a four-storey brick-built structure, which remained in use until the earthquake and fire of 1906. This razed the building to the ground once more and again the *Niantic* rose phoenix-like from the ashes to give forth yet more Champagne Jacquesson! Quoted in *The Story of the Niantic*, 1949, an old-time San Francisco resident recalled that 'The cork of the bottle was drawn with much ceremony, but on the first sip there was a great sputtering by the anticipating partakers – the bottle had been submerged so long that the salt water had forced through the cork. I will leave it to you to imagine the flavour.'

Vineyards 11 hectares at Aÿ, Dizy and Hautvillers and 11 hectares at Avize, averaging 98% échelle and representing 35% of the total production.
Purchases Averaging 90–95% échelle
Production 350,000 bottles   **Exports** 20%
Average bottle-age of NV *Cuvées* 2–2.5 years.

WINES
House style: Light, delicately balanced wines.
NV Perfection Brut (80–90% PN/PM, 10–20% CH; 94% échelle) I have not been much impressed by this *cuvée*, although recent bottles tasted in the United Kingdom seemed appreciably better. The wine needs more bottle-age.
NV Blanc de Blancs Brut (100% CH; 100% échelle) In contrast to my criticisms of the Perfection, I have only the highest praise for this, certainly one of the most elegant Blanc de Blancs Champagnes available. Water-white, ultra-fine, with a silky-smooth *mousse* and gentle Chardonnay on both nose and palate revealing deliciously delicate fruit, this is a great wine.
NV Rosé Brut (55% PN, 35% PM, 10% CH; 94% échelle; blended) Pale apricot colour, good *mousse*, open knit nose, full, fruity and earthy; an honest, fleshy wine, showing a true brut dryness, but unremarkable.
Vintage Perfection Brut (60–70% PN/PM, 30–40% CH; 95% échelle) I have tasted too few vintages to form a valid impression, but those I tried have all had a smooth, yet persistent *mousse*, a rich nose and a good point of acidity on the palate.
Vintage Signature Brut 50% PN, 50% CH; 95% échelle) Made entirely from the house's own grapes, fermented in 75-hectolitre wooden vats. Not tasted.
Vintage Brut Zero Blanc de Blancs 1969 (100% CH) A relatively new launch of a recently disgorged *cuvée de prestige* without dosage. A superb rendition of pure Chardonnay unhindered by any sign of dosage.
Coteaux Champenois Avize Blanc de Blancs and Dizy Rouge.

Jamart & Cie

Saint-Martin d'Ablois, Épernay
Telephone (26) 54.34.20
Origin The house was established in 1936 by Émilien Jamart.

WINES
Carte Blanche, Cuvée de Réserve, Blanc de Blancs, Rosé Brut.

Krug & Co.

5 rue Coquebert, Reims
Telephone (26) 88.24.24
Visits By appointment
Origin Born Johann-Josef Krug at Mainz in 1800, Krug later gallicised his Christian names as Jean-Joseph. He entered the Champagne trade with the firm of Jacquesson & Fils in 1834. On 8 March 1841 he married Adolphe

Early days at the house of Krug, rue Coquebert

Jacquesson's English sister-in-law, Emma Anne
Jaunay, at the British Embassy in Paris. Barely
eighteen months later Joseph Krug left
Jacquesson, much to everyone's surprise. In
1843, assisted by a friend and partner,
Hippolyte de Vives, Joseph Krug established
the house of Krug & Co. in a rented cellar at 8
rue Saint-Hilaire, in Reims.

When Joseph Krug died in 1866, the
company was reorganised; the outcome was
that Krug's widow and de Vives each possessed
a 25% interest in the firm and Joseph's son Paul
(born in 1842) held 50%, also drawing a salary
for running the business. When de Vives retired
two years later, Paul Krug was given control
and, married to Caroline Herle, set about
establishing the dynasty of Champagne Krug by
fathering a family of ten children – none of
whom, however, showed any desire to join the
family business. The eldest son, Joseph Krug II
(born in 1869), had always dreamed of being a
sailor, but, now that the dynasty of Champagne

Krug seemed to be under threat, he was cajoled,
or possibly bullied, by his father into working
for the firm.

By 1893 the house of Krug was established in
its current premises in rue Coquebert and the
business was jointly run by father and son. In
1910, upon his father's death, Joseph Krug II
assumed control, but relinquished his business
career at the outbreak of the First World War
to join the French army. In 1915 he was
wounded and captured while serving in the
Ardennes. During his absence, Joseph's wife
managed the firm and it was she who made the
famous Krug vintage of 1915. Joseph returned
in 1918, but his health was so bad that it was
feared he would be unable to continue control.
In 1924, when his son, Paul Krug II, was only
six years of age, Joseph decided to enlist the
help of his nephew, Jean Seydoux. Joseph
eventually proved the doctor's estimate of his
expected life-span to be nearly fifty years out,
since it was not until 1959, when Joseph was

celebrating his ninetieth birthday, that Paul Krug II eventually took over the company. Jean Seydoux, greatly respected by the Krugs for his contribution to the reputation of their house, died in 1962, and Joseph outlived his would-be successor by five years.

Between 1970 and 1972, Paul Krug invested in 15.5 hectares of vineyards at Aÿ and le Mesnil-sur-Oger (a growth favoured by successive generations of the family). These were to form the basis of a new *marque* called Grand Cuvée, launched in 1979. The expense of such substantial land purchases was made possible by finance from the great cognac house of Rémy Martin. This firm had many social and commercial ties with the Krugs and had long distributed its Champagnes in France before acquiring a shareholding in the firm. Rémy Martin eventually acquired a controlling interest, but the day to day running of the house remained firmly in the hands of Henri and Rémi, the fifth generation of Krugs.

Paul Krug officially retired in 1977, but he still continued to give the benefit of his advice, based on forty years of experience, to his two sons. This is the secret of Krug: not merely the continuation of a dynasty, but the tradition of two generations always working together and respecting each other. In this way the house of Krug has maintained a smooth transition of style and quality from one generation to the next: today, Henri and Rémi adhere to the same thinking that Joseph Krug propagated in the nineteenth century.

Vineyards 9 hectares of Pinot Noir at Aÿ and 6.5 hectares of Chardonnay at le Mesnil-sur-Oger, representing 20–30% of the total production.
Purchases Averaging 95% échelle
Sales Between 400,000 and 500,000 bottles, limited by the amount of stock at the time of sale
Exports 70%
Stocks 3 million bottles (December 1983)
Vinification notes The single most important aspect of the house of Krug's thinking about Champagne lies in its strict adherence to the first fermentation in wood. All wines are vinified in 205-litre casks, made from well weathered Argonne oak, of which Krug have over three thousand. There is no filtration – just two rackings by gravity, from cask to cask. The wine does not go through malo-lactic conversion before the *prise de mousse*,

although Henri believes it might well develop in bottle in some cases; should this be so, the six years of cellarage before disgorgement should be more than enough to complete the process. The occurrence of malo-lactic fermentation in bottles of lesser age could lead to cloudy and unstable Champagne due to a mannitic fermentation but with the luxury of Krug's ageing, all biochemical activity is completed long before the wines are released for sale. Crown-caps are used for the second fermentation and stainless steel vats for the preservation of reserve wines.
Special interest The house is a member of the Syndicat de Grandes Marques de Champagne. Rémy Martin has a connection with Chateau Remy, an excellent sparkling wine, produced at great expense by the *Méthode Champenoise* in Australia.

WINES
The Krugs claim that they do not possess a house NV Brut, only producing 'what is now referred to as *Cuvées Spéciales* or *Prestiges Cuvées*'. This is merely playing with words. The reputation of the house, which always used to be based on the quality of Krug Private Cuvée, is now firmly based on Krug NV Grande Cuvée, and if this *cuvée*, which accounts for some 80% of all Krug sales, is not a house NV wine then one wonders what is. Certainly it would not be misleading to point out that Krug's house NV Brut is in the same price range as a *cuvée de prestige*.

House style: Krug produces great wines which can appear so austere in their youth (although they may have as many as six years' bottle-age) that many consumers have found them too tough to enjoy. Even experienced tasters, under blind conditions, have been known to make uncomplimentary remarks about Krug Champagne.

In the 1970s I found that Krug Private Cuvée, purchased in the United Kingdom (wine which must have been at least as mature as that sold in other markets), required at least a further four years in bottle, and, although it is impossible to be as sure about Krug Grande Cuvée which replaced it recently, I suspect that the same pattern is developing for this wine too. Given the appropriate amount of time, all Krug wines achieve an unsurpassable balance of great depth and complexity. A mature Krug is, in Champagne terms, the epitome of breeding.
NV Grande Cuvée Brut (50% PN, 15% PM,

35% CH; 95% + échelle) The first shipment of this wine, despite its five years' average bottle-age, tasted very green and hard, but successive shipments appear to be 'older' and have tended to be comparatively full and mellow. The wine is an assemblage of forty to fifty wines from twenty to twenty-five growths, from seven or eight different vintages. It has an extremely fine *mousse*, distinctive scent, very complex nose and palate, and a deep flavour, showing plenty of Pinot, supported by the grip and bite of top-class Chardonnay, carrying through to a long finish. The Private Cuvée was a bigger wine, much fatter, with only half the Chardonnay content of the Grande Cuvée.

NV Rosé Brut (First blend, 52% PN, 24% PM, 24% CH; 95% + echelle; blended) Very round and fruity for a Krug wine, with an impression of soft fruit (strawberries and raspberries) on the nose, a classic Pinot rooty-richness on the palate, and a very fine finish.

Vintage Brut (50% PN, 20% PM, 30% CH; 95% + échelle) A richer wine than the above, requiring a long time in bottle. Always true to both the character of the vintage and the style of its producer. All vintages recommended, but especially 1971, 1973, 1975, 1976. The 1928, which has often been called the greatest of all Krug vintages, contained a high proportion of Pinot Meunier, which contradicts the common belief that this particular variety does not age well. According to Rémi Krug, his grandfather Joseph said that he had never spent his time better than while constructing the complex 1928 *cuvée* from a 'mosaic' of growths.

Vintage Krug Collection A recent release of classic wines from the vintages of 1964 and 1969. Not tasted, but recollections of the standard Krug 1964 leave my mouth watering at the thought of perfectly preserved bottles of this vintage.

Vintage Clos du Mesnil, Blanc de Blancs (100% CH; 99% échelle) Produced entirely from a single site called Clos du Mesnil in the village of le Mesnil-sur-Oger on the Côte des Blancs. This vineyard of 1.87 hectares has been totally enclosed by walls since 1698 and is now actually situated inside the village itself. The first vintage produced was the 1979, of which less than thirteen hundred cases were made, all the bottles being individually numbered and the label even carrying the date of harvest. Although I tasted this wine only once, I was astonished by Krug's ability to capture the quintessential character of Mesnil-Chardonnay and, at the same time, create a wine which is unmistakably Krug. A great wine which deserves to be kept until the next century.

Lang Biémont

'Les Ormissets'. Oiry, Épernay
Telephone (26) 59.62.55
Visits Monday to Friday; appointment required for weekends.
Origin The house was founded in 1875 by Henri Paul Lang and his wife Phanelie Héloïse Biémont in their native village of Avize.
Vineyards 50 hectares, representing up to 95% of the total production.
Average bottle-age of NV *cuvées* 3 years

WINES
House style: Heavily influenced by Chardonnay, but wines seldom tasted.
NV Carte d'Or Demi-sec and Brut (10% PN, 10% PM, 80% CH)
NV Cuvée Réservée Brut (10% PN, 10% PM, 80% CH)
NV Rosé Brut (20% PN, 80% CH)
Blanc de Blancs and **Vintage Brut**

Lanson Père & Fils

12 boulevard Lundy, Reims
Telephone (26) 40.36.26
Visits By appointment
Origin The founding of this firm dates back to 1760, when François Delamotte began making and selling Champagne, adopting the name Delamotte Père & Fils. In 1786 he brought his two sons Alexandre and Nicholas-Louis into the business. In 1828, after the death of his brother, Nicholas-Louis Delamotte changed the house's name to Louis Delamotte Père et Fils and associated with a certain Jean-Baptiste Lanson. At the end of 1837, Nicholas-Louis Delamotte died, the firm's name was changed to Veuve Delamotte-Barrachin and Lanson's two nephews, Victor-Marie and Henri, entered the business. In 1856, Delamotte's widow died, and, shortly afterwards, the Lansons gained full control of the firm, changing its name to Lanson Père et fils. The Lansons have been in control ever since.

Victor and Henri began purchasing vineyards in the 1930s: a shrewd decision, in the light of the size of the vast Lanson estate now. Classified AOC land rarely changes hands these days and, when it does, it does so for enormous sums of money. In 1970, the pastis firm of Ricard purchased a 48% share in Lanson, and in 1976, Lanson bought the once famous house of Masse. In 1980, the Gardinier Group, which already had a significant holding in Lanson (the connection being that Pierre Lanson had married Hélène Gardinier in 1960), purchased Ricard's share for 65 million francs and took control.

In November 1983, without any warning, Gardinier (which had by then acquired Pommery & Greno) sold Lanson-Pommery to BSN, the giant French food group. There had not been even a whisper amongst the houses, the trade found out at breakfast-time on Friday 11 November, when the news hit the French headlines. Despite the initial shock that the take-over created ('What does a yoghurt firm know about Champagne?' was the remark on everyone's lips), it was soon widely realised that BSN had a considerable amount of marketing muscle and that this startling development could benefit the whole of Champagne.

Vineyards 47 hectares on the Montagne de Reims, 75 hectares on the Côte des Blancs, 72 hectares in the Vallée de la Marne and 16 hectares in the Aube *département*, averaging 96% échelle and representing 40% of the total production.
Purchases Averaging 96% échelle
Production 5 million bottles
Exports 50–55%
Vinification notes Cool fermentation in stainless steel vats; no malo-lactic conversion.
Average bottle-age of NV *Cuvées* 2.5 years.
Special interest The house is a member of the Syndicat de Grandes Marques de Champagne.

WINES
House style: Soft and flowery, contrary to what might be expected from Champagnes which have not undergone malo-lactic fermentation.
NV Black Label Brut (45% PN, 10% PM, 45% CH; 96% échelle) Excellent *mousse*, full and fragrant on the nose, round and soft on the palate, with a mild, fruity finish. The sec and demi-sec are not marketed with a black label and, although of similar construction to the brut, actually contain more *vins de taille*.
Vintage Noble Cuvée de Lanson Brut (20% PN, 80% CH; 100% échelle) Blended from eight grands and premiers crus, this is Lanson's relatively new prestige *cuvée*, produced in limited quantities and bottled in an exact replica of the bottle used for Lanson's first

Champagnes in 1760. It shows an ability to improve if given time in bottle.
NV Rosé Brut (45% PN, 10% PM, 45% CH; 96% échelle; blended) Delicate pale peach colour, beautiful *mousse* of super-fine bubbles, simple Pinot fruit on the nose and palate. An acceptable wine.
Vintage Brut (45% PN, 10% PM, 45% CH; 98% échelle) The wine always has a good, fine and persistent *mousse*, is richer in colour than the NV, and has a distinctive flowery nose which often appears almost Germanic in style. Recommended years: 1971, 1975, 1979.
Special Cuvée 225 (100% échelle) The 1980 vintage launched this new prestige *cuvée* created to celebrate Lanson's 225th anniversary. Containing slightly more Chardonnay than Pinot Noir, this wine is blended from wines of Avize, Cramant, Ambonnay, Bouzy and Verzenay. On the limited basis of one vintage only, it is hard to predict its potential. What can be reported is its paradoxical character – very forward on the nose, yet not developed, or together, on the palate. Bottled in the same eighteenth century replica used for Noble Cuvée de Lanson.
Coteaux Champenois Blanc (100% CH; 96% échelle) Technically sound, but best used on salads.
Coteaux Champenois Rouge (100% PN; 96% échelle) Again technically sound, but dull.

Larmandier Père & Fils

BP 4, Cramant
Telephone (26) 50.52.19
Visits For purchases
Origin The house was founded in 1978 by Dominique Larmandier, a member of a great family of wine-growers.
Vineyards 8 hectares on the Côte des Blancs, Chardonnay at Chouilly, Oiry, Avize, Cuis and, with a little Pinot Noir, Vertus, averaging 95% échelle and representing 85% of the total production.
Purchases Averaging 95% échelle
Production 100,000 bottles **Exports** None
Vinification notes *Prise de mousse* in half-bottles.
Average bottle-age of NV *cuvée* 3 years.

WINES
NV Brut (20% PN, 80% CH; 99% échelle) A blend of Chardonnay from Cramant and Pinot Noir from Vertus.

NV Brut Perlé A lightly *mousseux* Blanc de Blancs made from an *assemblage* of Chouilly, Avize, Cramant and Oiry. This wine represents more than half of Larmandier's total production.

NV Cramant Blanc de Blancs Brut (100% CH; 100% échelle) A wine with three years' bottle-age.

Vintage Special Club Brut A kind of de luxe Cramant Blanc de Blancs, but bearing a vintage.

Laurent Perrier

Veuve Laurent-Perrier & Co.
Avenue de Champagne, Tours-sur-Marne
Telephone (26) 59.91.22
Visits By appointment
Origin On 12 December 1812 the Laurent family moved from their native village of Chigny-les-Roses on the Montagne de Reims. As coopers, the Laurents were tired of seeing other people's wines in their own casks and decided therefore to set up in the business of making and selling Champagne in the remains of an eleventh century abbey at Tours-sur-Marne. When their son Eugène Laurent, who had married Mathilde Émile Perrier, died in 1887, the firm's name was changed to Veuve Laurent-Perrier.

Mathilde Laurent-Perrier died on 29 May 1925 without heirs; eventually Marie-Louise de Nonancourt, the sister of Victor and Henri Lanson, acquired the *marque* in 1938. The house only became really successful after the Second World War when Bernard de Nonancourt (the son of Marie-Louise) took over the firm. At that time it was ranked a mere ninety-eighth amongst the Champagne houses but its activities since have pushed it into the top half dozen with an increase in sales of 5000%.

Vineyards 80 hectares representing 10% of the total production.
Purchases Averaging 90% échelle
Production 6 million bottles **Exports** 55%
Stocks 27 million bottles (November 1983, including the 1983 production)
Average bottle-age of N V *cuvées* 3 years.
Special interest The house is a member of the Syndicat de Grandes Marques de Champagne. Early in 1984 Laurent Perrier took a 20% share in the house of de Castellane. A recent joint venture with the company of Almaden has resulted in the production of a sparkling Californian Blanc de Blancs under the Laurent Perrier label.

WINES
House style: The wines have a light richness, are fresh, long and elegant, and are excellent value for money.

NV LP Brut (50% PN, 15% PM, 35% ch; 90–95% échelle) Pale lemon colour, excellent *mousse* of extremely fine and persistent bubbles, fresh nose, crisp, lightly rich fruit; a wine long and elegant on the palate.

NV Crémant Brut (33% PN, 33% PM, 34% CH; 80–95% échelle) The wine contains *vins de taille* and wines from the Aube *département*. Lacking in *mousse*, which dies too quickly, the wine, although solid and clean, fails to achieve the true Laurent Perrier quality. The wine represents some 15% of the total production, it is not exported, and is often seen at very low prices in supermarkets.

NV Ultra Brut The first *cuvée*, launched in 1981, was a Pinot-dominated wine; it has a biscuity nose and very fleshy palate, with a great deal of extract.

Cuvée Grand Siècle (50% PN, 50% CH, 100% échelle) Blended from wines of vintage years only. Exquisite *mousse*, fragrant almost floral nose, fresh, crisp fruit; a beautiful wine of great length, style and consistency.

NV Rosé Brut (100% PN; 90–95% échelle; skin-contact) With a full, distinct and generous nose of some complexity and a rich, soft-fruit flavour this is an individual wine of some finesse.

Vintage LP Brut (75% PN, 25% CH; 95% échelle) Persistent *mousse*, fine depth, flesh and fruit; a distinguished medium-term vintage Champagne. Recommended years: 1973, 1975, 1976, 1979.

Vintage Millésimé Rare Brut (75% PN, 25% CH; 95% échelle) At the time of writing only the 1966 and the 1969 had been released. Small quantities of outstanding years are kept *sur pointes*. The 1966 was fresh and vital-looking, with an excellent *mousse*, a rich nose, beautifully mellow berry flavours on the palate and a most attractive finish.

Coteaux Champenois Bouzy Rouge (100% PN; 100% échelle) Not tasted.

Coteaux Champenois Pinot Franc (100% PN; 90–95% échelle). The name is confusing; 'Franc' merely indicates the ancient origins of red wines produced in the Champagne area. Very well made, this is a clean wine, with a certain fruitiness and a character not dissimilar to that of an inexpensive, early drinking *petit château* wine from Bordeaux, despite its pure Pinot content. The wine has obviously been aged in wood at some stage, but would benefit from being blended with a small amount of wine matured in new oak, which would add grip and character.

Coteaux Champenois Rosé A skin-contact wine produced mainly for the German market. Not tasted.

Coteaux Champenois Blanc de Blancs de Chardonnay A simple, well made wine produced entirely from growths on the Côte des Blancs. The samples I have tasted all lacked a real fruitiness. A one-off vintage version, dated 1973, would have died by the time I tasted it in 1980, had it not been for its extreme acidity.

R. & L. Legras

10 rue des Partelaines, Chouilly
Telephone (26) 54.50.79
Visits For purchases
Origin The Legras family have a long history as vignerons dating back to the eighteenth century. As recently as 1972, René and Lucien were registered as *récoltants-manipulants*, but began operating as a *négociant-manipulant* the following year.
Vineyards 21 hectares on the Côte des Blancs and 1 hectare on the Montagne de Reims, representing 40–50% of the total production.
Purchases 95% échelle
Production 250,000 bottles
Exports 18%

WINES
House style: All wines are pure Chouilly Blanc de Blancs. NV Grand Vintage, Vintage Présidence, Vintage Cuvée Saint-Vincent and Coteaux Champenois Blanc Réserve. One or two wines tried over the years and all of them interesting. A tasting note of one vintage of Cuvée Saint-Vincent reminded me of a classic Salon.

Lenoble

BP 6, Damery
Telephone (26) 58.42.60
Origin The house was founded in 1924 by Armand Raphael Graser.

WINES
NV Brut, NV Sec, NV Demi-Sec, Blanc de Blancs, Rosé Brut and Vintage Brut.

Abel Lepitre

Les Grands Champagnes de Reims
2 and 4 avenue du Général Giraud, Reims
Telephone (26) 85.05.77
Visits By appointment
Origin The humble grape-growing Lepitre family had been cultivating the slopes of the Montagne de Reims for many generations when Abel Lepitre was born in 1920. At barely twenty-four years of age, he established a Champagne house bearing his name in the village of Ludes.

Throughout the Second World War, with Abel Lepitre in a German prison camp, the house remained inoperative. He died in captivity and, in 1947, his son Jacques took over the business. The present premises were purchased in 1955. In 1960 substantial acquisitions of other Champagne *marques* were made, including those of George Goulet, Henry Goulet, Girard & Co and Gustave Gilbert & Gravet; and the current umbrella company of Les Grands Champagnes de Reims was set up. In 1970, the Ricard Group took control through Les Établissements Vinicoles Champenois. This company held a 48% share in Les Grands Vins de Champagne and thus Ricard, now Pernod-Ricard, became a sleeping partner. In 1974, during Abel Lepitre's fiftieth anniversary, Les Grands Vins de Champagne acquired the *marqe* of de St Marceaux. Pernod-Ricard sold its share of the business to Felix Chatellier, the owner of Château Dauzac, a 5ème Grand Cru Classé in Margaux. M. Chatellier now owns Les Grands Vins de Champagne.
Vineyards None
Purchases Averaging 92% échelle
Production 500,000 bottles   **Exports** 25%
Vinification notes *Prise de mousse* in half-bottles and jeroboams, also (I was told) in methuselahs, but I did not see any in *pupitres*.

WINES
NV Carte Blanche Brut (50% PN, 10% PM, 40% CH; 92% échelle) An impression of sweetness on the nose, reminiscent of confectionery, and a light *mousse* which quickly fades. It is a pity that the more mature NV Idéal Cuvée Brut, with its greater Pinot Noir content, was dropped in favour of this *cuvée*. The same wine, bottled in quarters under transvasage, is labelled NV Karal Brut.
NV Cuvée No. 134, Blanc de Blancs

Two vignerons take the autumn sun in
the grand cru vineyards of Avize

Brut (100% CH; 92% échelle) Not tasted.
Vintage Idéal Cuvée Brut (60% PN, 40% CH; 95% échelle) Too infrequently tasted.
Vintage Crémant Blanc de Blancs Brut (100% CH; 95% échelle) Flowery nose, good *mousse*, fragrant Chardonnay flavour.
Vintage Rosé Brut (100% PN; 95% échelle; blended) Strong *mousse*, rich and generous in fruit; a fine wine by any standards. Recommended year: 1975.
Vintage Prince A. de Bourbon-Parme Brut 40% PN, 60% CH; 97% échelle) Very soft and full for a Chardonnay dominated blend, fragrant and ripe on the palate, with a gentle finish. Recommended years: 1970, 1974, 1975. *Prise de mousse* is employed with the use of *liège et agrafe*, this wine being disgorged *à la volée*, without the use of freezing brine.
Coteaux Champenois Bouzy Rouge (100% PN; 100% échelle) Usually sold when one year to two years old. Not tasted.
Coteaux Champenois Saint-Rémi Blanc de Blancs Not tasted.

Marie Stuart

Comptoir Vinicole de Champagne
8 Place de la République, Reims
Telephone (26) 47.92.26
Visits For purchases
Origin Established in 1919, this *marque* was acquired by André Garitant in 1927, by Champagne Trouillard in 1954, by Prat-Fontaine & Longuet in 1962, and finally by the Société Anonyme Magenta-Épernay in 1972.
Vineyards None
Purchases Averaging 88% échelle
Production 800,000–900,000 bottles
Exports 30%
Average bottle-age of NV *cuvées* 3 years

WINES
House style: On little experience, the vintage Champagnes would seem to have an edge over the NVs, with the prestige *cuvées* superior.
NV Standard Brut (80% PN/PM, 20% CH; 90% échelle)
NV Blanc de Blancs Brut (100% CH)
NV Cuvée de la Reine (40% PN, 60% CH; 96% échelle)

(OPPOSITE) The home of Champagne Ivernal, with its walled courtyard and heavy ancient gates, is one of the oldest buildings in Aÿ-Champagne

NV Rosé Brut (80% PN/PM, 20% CH, 90% échelle; blended)
Vintage Brut (40% PN, 60% CH; 95% échelle)
Vintage Grande Réserve Brut (25% PN, 75% CH; 96% échelle)

G. H. Martel & Cie

23 rue Jean Moulin, Magenta, Épernay
Telephone (26) 51.06.33
Visits By appointment
Origin The house was established in 1869 by a vigneron at Avenay and developed as a *marque* by André Tabourin in the 1920s. When Tabourin died in 1979, the business was acquired by Rapeneau & Cie.

WINES
NV Sec, NV Extre-sec, NV Demi-Sec, NV Carte d'Or, Vintage Brut, Crémant Brut, Blanc de Blancs, Rosé Brut and Cuvée Henry Leopold.

Massé

48 rue de Courlancy, Reims
Telephone (26) 47.61.31
Visits By appointment
Origin Established at Rilly-la-Montagne in 1853, this house is now little more than a *sous marque* of Lanson.
Production Averaging about 200,000 bottles in 1976, when the firm was purchased by Lanson, the current annual output now stands at close on 700,000 bottles.
Exports 5–6%
Special Interest The house is a member of the Syndicat de Grandes Marques de Champagne.

WINES
House style: I was unable to discern a style at my one tasting of these wines conducted at Lanson in 1980.
NV Brut (45% PN, 20% PM, 35% CH) Good *mousse*; a simple fruity nose and a delicate flavour, which soon faded, however; the wine is hollow, short and off-balance, with excessive acidity and no fruit to back it up.
NV Cuvée Henry Massé Brut Again, a Champagne with a well formed *mousse*, but lacking the flavour and character to sustain it. This so-called *cuvée de prestige* lacked any outstanding qualities, except for a certain *goût de terroir* which stuck at the back of the throat.
Vintage Brut Only the 1971 tasted. Vegetal nose; thin, short and lacking acidity.

Medot & Cie

30 rue Werlé, Reims
Telephone (26)47.46.15
Origin The house was established in 1897 by
Jules Pascal (1848–1919), but the wines made
were mostly sold *sur lattes*. Pascal's daughter
Léonie, who married Jules Medot, was the first
to sell Champagnes under this *marque*.

WINES

NV Brut, NV Sec, NV Demi-Sec, Vintage Brut,
Blanc de Blancs Brut, and the *cuvée de prestige*
Clos des Chaulins.

Mercier

75 avenue de Champagne, Épernay
Telephone (26) 54.71.11
Visits Daily and some weekends; electric train,
as at Piper Heidsieck.
Origin The house was founded in 1858 by
Eugène Mercier, when he combined the five
Champagne houses of Berton, Philippe
Bourlon, Dufaut Père & Fils, René Lesecq and
Veuve Soyez into one called Maison Mercier
Union de Propriétaires, based at 20 du
Boulevard Poissonnière in Paris.

Eugène Mercier was an imposing figure of
ancient Champagne stock. He successfully
marketed his wines to the population as a
whole, rather than to a select group of
privileged customers, the established practice of
most other prosperous houses in the nineteenth
century. The legend of Eugène Mercier is still
strong: he never missed an opportunity to draw
attention to his wines and thus attract sales; his
style was solid but spectacular. He is perhaps
best remembered for his use of a team of
twenty-four white oxen to haul a huge and
fabulous carved cask through Paris on 7 May
1889 – this was during the Paris Exhibition and
the streets were crowded with sight-seers. The
cask was almost one-thousand times the size of
a traditional Champagne *pièce* and it had taken
no less than twenty years to construct.

In about 1930 the house of Mercier
established itself at its present premises in
Épernay. No. 75 Avenue de Champagne was
dubbed Château de Pékin by Mercier
employees, because they had to walk so far
from the city centre to reach it.

Much in the tradition of its owner, Mercier
has always concentrated first and foremost on a
wide appeal in France itself, exports always
coming second.

In 1970, Mercier was taken over by Moët &
Chandon, and its prestigious restaurant, the
Royal Champagne at Champillon, was
absorbed by a subsidiary of Moët-Hennessy
called Provital.

Vineyards 3.36 hectares at Chouilly (CH); 0.07
hectares at Cramant (CH); 9.96 hectares at
Épernay (33% CH, 49% PM, 18% PN); 3.04
hectares at Hautvillers (PM); 1.21 hectares at
Champillon (PM); 0.36 hectares at Dizy (PM);
1.92 hectares at Aÿ (PN); 8.89 hectares at
Mareuil-sur-Aÿ (PN); 1.90 hectares at Avenay
(PM); 28.04 hectares at Tauxières (38% PN,
62% PM); 6.61 hectares at Tours-sur-Marne
(CH); 6.38 hectares at Germaine (PM); 10.56
hectares at les Mesneux (85% PM, 15% PN);
11.95 hectares at Sarcy (PM); 22.18 hectares at
Poilly (80% PM, 20% CH); 13.91 hectares at
Nesles-la-Montagne (PM); 15.19 hectares at
Étampes-sur-Marne (PM); 1.66 hectares at
Chierry (PM); 4.07 hectares at Château Thierry
(PM); 9.03 hectares at Essômes (PM), and 52.25
hectares at Chézy-sur-Marne (90% PM, 10%
PN), making a total of some 212 hectares in
production (of 250 hectares owned),
representing 20% of the total production.
Production 6 million bottles   **Exports** 15%
Stocks 17 million bottles (1984)
Vinification notes A centrifuge is used after
alcoholic and malo-lactic fermentations, prior
to bottling. Wines are blended by Dominique
Foulon, *chef de caves* for both Mercier and
Moët & Chandon.
Average bottle-age of NV *Cuvées* 2–2.5 years.
Special interest The house is a member of the
Syndicat de Grandes Marques de Champagne.
Mercier is the best-selling brand on the
domestic French market, beating Moët &
Chandon.

WINES

House style: I invariably find the NV Brut
much better in the United Kingdom than in
France.
NV Brut Réserve (40–50% PN, 40–60% PM,
10–20% CH; 80–95% échelle) In France I find
this a sturdy little wine with a good *mousse*, but
with a stewed apple nose and generally lacking
any finesse. In the United Kingdom I rarely
notice the stewed apple nose and find the wine
fuller and fruitier.
NV Demi-Sec Réserve (60–70% PN, 30–40%
PM; 80–95% échelle) Only tasted in France:
straightforward, unexciting, stewed apple and
sugar flavour.

NV Crémant Brut (40–60% PN, 20–40% PM, 10–20% CH; 85–90% échelle) A small production of less than a thousand cases annually. Not tasted.

Vintage Réserve Brut (20–80% PN/PM, 20–50% CH; 90% + échelle) Not really a true brut, but usually a wine with a good base, rich in natural extract, full on the nose and fine in *mousse*. Recommended years: 1971, 1975.

Vintage Rosé Brut (90–100% PN/PM, 0–10% CH; 90% + échelle) Fairly deep-peach coloured wines that can be shy and lacking in character initially, but which may develop in the glass.

Vintage Réserve de l'Empereur Brut Only the 1975 tasted: pale straw colour, good strength of *mousse*, small bubbles, similar in style to the Brut Réserve 1975, but heavier and meatier. This is Mercier's *cuvée de prestige* sold on the French market.

Émile Michel

Verzenay
Telephone (26) 49.40.40
Origin The house was established in 1932 by Émile Michel, from the Ardennes.
Production 60,000 bottles

WINES
NV Brut, NV Sec, NV Demi-Sec, Vintage Brut, and Rosé Brut.

Moët & Chandon

Moët-Hennessy
20 avenue de Champagne, Épernay
Telephone (26) 54.71.71
Visits Monday to Friday throughout the year; weekends and public holidays April to October.
Origin It has been suggested that the first Moët was a fifteenth-century Dutchman named Le Clerc. No doubt the family was originally from Holland, but the name of Moët was already established when Le Clerc is said to have run at the head of a crowd of Rémois, shouting, 'Het moet zoo zijn' ('It must be so') at the English who were trying to prevent Charles VII from entering the city. A Jean Moët and a Nicholas Moët are documented as being magistrates of Reims in the early 1400s, and a Moet, in the capacity of municipal magistrate, stood next to Joan of Arc in Reims Cathedral when Charles VII was crowned in 1429.

The house of Moët was established in 1743 by Claude Moët, a *courtier en vin* since 1716 and the owner of some well known vineyards in the Marne Valley. It was, therefore, natural that he should become a producer.

It was Jean-Remy Moët (1758–1841), the grandson of Claude, who really created the reputation of the house of Moët, although the firm was already an important one when he took it over in 1792. Six years later he was faced with what must have been his most taxing challenge when the Monneron Bank, which held most of the company's capital, failed. Jean-Remy travelled to Paris and stationed himself outside the bank. Enquiring of every visitor to the bank whether or not he held a note signed by him, Jean-Remy paid the full value of the bill in cash for everyone who did hold such a note, and in due course, returned to Épernay – virtually penniless, in terms of cash, but with his credit intact. He then swiftly rebuilt his business and, within four years, his standing was such that he was elected mayor of Épernay.

But what undoubtedly set the house of Moët on the road, not just to success, but to an unassailable domination of the entire Champagne industry, was the comradeship struck up between Jean-Remy and the young Napoleon, at a time when Napoleon was a student at the military school of Brienne, to which Jean-Remy Moët (it is assumed) was sent by his father to collect orders from the mess. After Napoleon was proclaimed Emperor in 1804, Jean-Remy benefited from a decade of influential patronage that was to lay the foundations of Moët's 180 years of astonishing success. As mayor of Épernay, it was Jean-Remy's responsibility to welcome and entertain Napoleon on his frequent visits to the town, which lies on the route between Paris and Germany which the Emperor and his war-weary troops so often trod. On Napoleon's remark that it would be useful to have a country home nearby, Jean-Remy commissioned the miniaturist Jean-Baptiste Isabey to design the Trianon, twin houses which were built opposite his own home in the Avenue de Champagne.

Shortly before Napoleon was banished to Elba, he paid his last visit to Moët and decorated Jean-Remy with the Légion d'Honneur. In 1815 Jean-Remy resigned as mayor of Épernay, and the year after that brought his son-in-law into the firm, thinking it best to retire from the public view after his long association with Napoleon.

Jean-Remy need not have feared unpopularity, however, on the contrary, after the Battle of Waterloo the world-famous Champagne Moët chimed in with the post-war mood and the Trianon was even livelier and more crowded than before, with names like those of Wellington and Blücher replacing those of Napoleon and his entourage. In fact, Moët's order books of the period read like a Who-was-Who of post-Waterloo Europe.

The Bourbons, restored to the throne, were clearly unaffected by Jean-Remy's overt Bonapartist sympathies, since Charles X visited Moët's cellars in 1825, accompanied by his daughter-in-law, the Duchesse d'Angoulême, who thirty-four years earlier had been mauled and nearly killed by an Épernay mob.

When Jean-Remy retired in 1832, his son Victor and his son-in-law Pierre Gabriel Chandon took over the firm, whose name they changed next year to Moët & Chandon.

They built upon Jean-Remy's reputation, consolidating Moët & Chandon as brand leader on the French market and in England and other major export countries throughout the mid-nineteenth century. By the 1880s, the range of Moët & Chandon's famous 'Star' brand Champagnes, which then consisted of Brut Imperial, Creaming, Extra Superior, Extra Dry Sillery, White Dry Sillery and First, had established such a global reputation that this firm must be considered the first, truly international *grande marque*. The firm employed a total of 800 vineyard workers and 350 cellarmen, all of whom received free medical assistance and legal aid, were paid during illness and benefited from a non-contributory pension.

At this juncture Moët & Chandon was producing approximately 2.5 million bottles of Champagne each year, held stocks totalling 12 million bottles and owned the largest single vineyard holding in Champagne with an estate of 360 hectares. But it was not solely the size of this estate which was so impressive, the quality of its vineyards could not, for the most part, be faulted; 85 hectares at Aÿ; 75 hectares at Cramant and Chouilly; 50 hectares at Verzenay and Verzy; 40 hectares at Grauves and Pierry; 35 hectares at Hautvillers; 30 hectares at le Mesnil-sur-Oger; 25 hectares at Épernay; 20 hectares at Bouzy; and press-houses stretched across the Côte des Blancs, Montagne de Reims and Vallée de la Marne. It was from the

strength of this viticultural base that Moët & Chandon was destined to dominate the Champagne trade in the twentieth century.

Moët & Chandon suffered vast damage in its vineyards and building during the First World War. The reconstruction of its offices at 20 avenue de Champagne was completed in 1929. In 1930 Moët purchased the unused *marque* of Dom Pérignon from Mercier and commercialised this as the first *prestige cuvée* in 1937. During the Second World War, Comte Robert-Jean de Vogüé, a descendant of Jean-Remy Moët, was primarily responsible for establishing the CIVC, but his continual obstruction of the German authorities resulted in his arrest by the Gestapo. He was condemned to death, but, thankfully, the sentence was never carried out. After the war, Robert-Jean de Vogüé increased Moët & Chandon's production to 12 million bottles. In 1962 the company went public and became the first Champagne house to be quoted on the Bourse. Moet & Chandon took over Ruinart in 1963, bought into Christian Dior in 1968, merged with Mercier in 1970 and purchased de Cazanove from Martini in 1979 (then sold it to SAME in 1985). In 1971 the first in a series of complex financial transactions took place between Moët & Chandon and the Cognac house of Hennessy to form what is today the powerful Moët-Hennessy group.

Vineyards 48.67 hectares at Chouilly (CH); 0.64 hectares at Cuis (CH); 38.33 hectares at Cramant (CH); 5.11 hectares at Grauves (75% CH, 25% PM); 1.72 hectares at Avize (CH); 29.05 hectares at le Mesnil-sur-Oger (CH); 3.78 hectares at Vertus (CH); 12.42 hectares at Épernay (56% CH, 26% PM, 18% PN); 0.81 hectares at Moussy (PM); 1.59 hectares at Vinay (PM); 5.35 hectares at Mancy (60% CH, 40% PM); 5.22 hectares at Cumières (PN); 40.59 hectares at Hautvillers (50% PN, 50% PM); 5.81 hectares at Dizy (60% CH, 40% PN); 37.91 hectares at Aÿ (80% PN, 15% CH, 5% PM); 29.63 hectares at Mareuil-sur-Aÿ (PN); 7.79 hectares at Tauxières (72% PN, 28% PM); 9.41 hectares at Bouzy (PN); 5.58 hectares at

ABOVE Looking across the sunken garden at the twin pavilions of Trianon flanking Jean-Remy Moët's house, now used as Moët's offices
BELOW The view of the Orangery in all its Napoleonic splendour, sited at the bottom of Isabey's magnificent gardens of Trianon

Ambonnay (PN); 2.05 hectares at Verzy (PN); 25.74 hectares at Verzenay (70% PN, 30% CH); 2.98 hectares at Mailly (PN); 14.94 hectares at Sillery (CH); 3.25 hectares at Puisieulx (CH); 42.71 hectares at Taissy (65% PM, 35% CH; 20.30 hectares at Pontfaverger and Selles (70% CH, 30% PM); 10.08 hectares at Mardeuil (CH); 7.48 hectares at Mareuil-le-Port (PM); 17.93 hectares at Jaulgonne (PM); 1.36 hectares at Courtemont (PM); 13.95 hectares at Crezancy (PM); 6.58 hectares at Connigis (PM); 2.00 hectares at Monthurel (PM); 19.96 hectares at Mont-Saint-Père (PM); 8.27 hectares at Château-Thierry and Essômes (70% PN, 30% PM); and 6.32 hectares at Essoyes (PN), making a total of 485.48 hectares, representing 20–30% of the total production.
Production 18 million bottles. **Exports** 70%
Stocks 75 million bottles (1984)
Vinification notes In addition to the traditional *pressoirs coquarts* found in most of Moët's pressoirs, the house operates two horizontal presses, 8,000 and 12,000 kilograms. The latter press is under trial with the CIVC, as the limit for Champagne is 8,000 kilograms. A centrifuge is used after alcoholic and malo-lactic fermentations, prior to bottling. Wines are blended by Dominique Foulon, *chef de caves* for both Moët & Chandon and Mercier.
Average bottle-age of NV *Cuvées* 2–3 years
Special interest The house is a member of the Syndicat de Grandes Marques de Champagne. Although Moët is shipped to no less than 150 different countries and is the best-selling brand in many of them, including the seven largest export markets (the United Kingdom, the United States, Germany, Belgium, Italy, Switzerland and Holland), it is outstripped on the domestic French market by its own second-ranking brand, Mercier. Moët & Chandon has owned the abbey at Hautvillers (where Dom Pérignon perfected his wines) since 1823, when it was purchased from one Joseph Dubois, who had acquired the abbey when it was auctioned as a national property in 1791.

The Moët-Hennessy Group includes Ruinart Père et Fils, Mervier and de Cazanove in the Champagne sector, and Christian Dior Perfumes and Roc in perfumes and cosmetics.

Moët-Hennessy conducts many diverse operations outside France. The Munich-based company Chandon GmbH markets about 750,000 bottles of M. Chandon Sekt in West Germany and Austria. Rozès (Port and Madeira wines) were acquired and consolidated in 1977.

Some three million bottles of still and sparkling Argentian wines are produced annually by Proviar (49% of the company is owned by Moët-Hennessy under the labels M. Chandon and H. Mercier.) Another subsidiary company is Provifin, a Brazilian venture jointly run with Cinzano and the Montero Aranha Financial Group, which owns seventy hectares of vineyards in the Rio Grande do Sul and a winery complex capable of handling two and a half million bottles. The still and sparkling Brazilian wines produced here are sold under the M. Chandon label.

The most exciting excursion by the Moët-Hennessy Group in recent years must be its acquisition of 800 hectares in the Napa Valley, California: the first French-owned vineyards in America. In 1983 three million bottles of sparkling wine were produced under the Chandon Napa Valley Brut and the Chandon Blanc de Noirs labels. Moët-Hennessy also owns the Simi winery in the Sonoma valley.

WINES
House styles: This is hard to assess: the NV is a decent, straight, commercial wine; the vintage Champagnes are excellent and the Dom Pérignon is legendary. It is easy for writers to find fault with Moët, but as this house has done so much for Champagne, critics really ought to balance its few negative aspects with its wealth of positive points. I admit that I never choose Moët NV when offered a range to select from, but I must equally admit that, when given the wine without choice, I am usually surprised by just how good it is, considering the sheer volume which is produced. In some instances it might be downright poor, but this is sometimes true of other NVs and on not a few occasions I have been staggered by the occasional outstandingly fine bottle of basic Moët. Strangely, I seem to prefer Moët when in France and Mercier when in Britain.
NV Première Cuvée Brut (50% PN, 20% PM, 30% CH; 85% échelle) Good strong *mousse*, correct on nose and palate, medium in weight and fruit. This wine is called NV Brut Impérial in France, but the dosage may be in wine sold on the domestic market.
NV Crémant Demi-Sec (40% PN, 40% PM, 20% CH; 80–90% échelle) Light, rapidly fading *mousse*; fresh, but hollow and sugary at the finish.

Vintage Brut Impérial (30–40% PN, 40–50% PM, 20–30% CH; 90% + échelle) This wine shows particularly well in magnum; my only real criticism is that it seldom has a true *brut* dryness. In 1980, at a memorable tasting of Impérial (going back to 1959), the various vintages displayed a definite house style of rooty Pinot character, lifted by Chardonnay. The 1959 (disgorged in 1972) was remarkably fresh and elegant for such a strong year and the 1962 contiued to release a steady stream of minuscule bubbles one hour after opening. Recommended years: 1970, 1971, 1975. There is also a Vintage Dry Impérial, which I have not tasted.

Vintage Brut Impérial Rosé Made by blending a little red wine, usually from Bouzy. Most vintages have ranged from delicate peach to deep-red and invariably disappoint – the 1975 seemed out of balance when tasted two or three times in 1981. Only the 1970, in magnums, has appealed to me on a consistent basis, even though it looked like a sparkling red wine (and I prefer the more delicate pink Champagnes); it has an extremely persistent and fine *mousse*, clinging to the rim of the glass, and an aroma evocative of wild mountain strawberries; it is a clean wine with rich fruit and a good acid balance, the deep colour belying its elegance. Recommended year: 1970. There is also a Vintage Dry Impérial Rosé which I have not tasted.

Vintage Dom Pérignon Brut (50% PN, 50% CH; 100% échelle) This always has an impeccable *mousse* of ultra-fine bubbles, and an enticing nose of complex fruity fragrances – rich, stylish and succulent. The remarkable year of 1961 was good in Champagne, but nowhere near as exceptional as in Bordeaux. However, I chanced on a supply of Dom Pérignon 1961 in 1982 and, after selling on all but half a dozen botles for more than my original outlay, I set about drinking all six bottles in as many weeks and can testify that, for Dom Pérignon, 1961 was indeed an extraordinary year. Other recommended years: 1962, 1966.

Vintage Dom Pérignon Rosé (60% PN, 40% CH; 100% échelle; blended) I have only tasted the 1969: it has an extremely fine *mousse* and an enticing, ripe, soft-fruit aroma, delicious and rich on the palate and long and delicate on the finish. The first vintage was the 1959, produced in a very small quantity exclusively for the banquet held by the Shah of Iran in Persepolis to celebrate the two-thousand-year history of the Persian Empire. It was not until 1970 that the first Dom Pérignon Rosé was sold commercially, the vintage being 1962.

Coteaux Champenois Saran Blanc de Blancs (100% CH; 100% échelle) An aristocrat of a wine, despite the peasant character of its appellation. It is a non-vintage wine, but varies, according to the time of purchase, from soft and buttery (like a Côte Chalonnaise) to the firm, fruity acidity of a lesser Chablis. A tasting of samples collected over a five-year period revealed vintage-like differences in character, but at least demonstrated the wine's capacity to age in varying degrees, depending on the 'vintage' – a quality singularly deficient in any other Coteaux Champenois Blanc de Blancs. The grapes come exclusively from the vineyards of Château Saran. The majority of the estate is in Chouilly, but the vines used for this Coteaux Champenois are those located within the boundaries of neighbouring Cramant, to the side and rear of the house. As the Saran vineyards are also part of those reserved for Dom Pérignon (which consists of equal proportions of Chardonnay and Pinot Noir), each bottle of pure Chardonnay Saran produced prevents two of Dom Pérignon being produced.

Montaudon

6 rue Ponsardin, Reims
Telephone (26) 47.53.30
Visits Check opening days and time by telephone.
Origin Auguste-Louis Montaudon (1867–1932) was sent by his employers, Bouvet-Ladubay, the *Méthode Champenoise* firm at Saumur in the Loire (now owned by Taittinger), to l'Union Champenoise in Épernay. Here he studied the methods and practices used in the making of Champagne, and the knowledge and skills which he required he duly passed on to his son Auguste-Eugène. At barely nineteen years of age, Auguste-Eugène decided to set up as a *négociant* in rue Pasteur, Épernay. With his father's advice and guidance, Auguste-Eugène was able to steer his newly founded house to success and prosperity. In 1957 he transferred the business to the premises of Champagne Vander Gucht, a house in Reims which he had recently bought.

Vineyards 15 hectares at les Riceys, representing 20% of the total production.
Production 300,000–400,000 bottles
Exports 15%
Average bottle-age of NV *cuvées* 3 years
Vinification notes There is automatic *remuage* for part of the production.

WINES

NV Brut (50% PN, 25% PM, 25% CH; 90% échelle) Very mild, lacking acidity on the few occasions tasted. Also available in sec and demi-sec.
NV Blanc de Blancs Brut (100% CH) Not tasted.
NV Rosé Brut (75% PN, 25% CH; blended) Red wine from les Riceys is used for blending. Not tasted.
Vintage Brut (50% PN, 50% CH; 95% échelle) I drank a memorable bottle of the 1976, and a 1979 showed promise.
Coteaux Champenois Blanc An unusual blanc de noirs, made from Pinot Noir of Avirey, Lingey and Gye-sur-Seine in the Aube département.
Coteaux Champenois Rouge As above, but vinified red.

Montebello

Société Générale de Champagne
Château de Mareuil-sur-Aÿ, Mareuil
Telephone (26) 50.13.40
Origin The Champagne house of Montebello was established at the Château de Mareuil-sur-Aÿ in 1834 by the Duc de Montebello, eldest son of Maréchal Lannes (1769–1809), who was Napoleon's friend, was created Duc de Montebello by him, and died at the battle of Essling after a distinguished career. The Duc de Montebello was a successful ambassador, Minister of Foreign Affairs and Minister of the Navy. He was thus obliged to travel a great deal, and consequently, brought his two brothers, the Marquis Alfred and General Comte Gustave, into the business. It was they, rather than the Duc, who looked after the château, its estate and Champagne Montebello. The Duc's daughter married Édouard Werle, the Widow's principal partner in the house of Veuve Clicquot.

In 1936, Stanislas de Montbello sold the house to René Chayoux, who purchased Champagne Ayala the following year.
Vineyards 23 hectares at Mareil-sur-Aÿ

Production 250,000 bottles **Exports** 20%
Special interest The house is a member of the Syndicat de Grandes Marques de Champagne.

WINES

House style: Only tasted once, in a side-by-side comparison with Ayala, in the company of Jean Michel Ducellier, at Château d'Aÿ in November 1983. In view of the history of the *marque*, it is baffling that Montebello labels should be, with those of de Courcy (a *négociant-non-manipulant*), quite the ugliest in Champagne.
NV Brut (50% PN, 25% PM, 25% CH) Fuller than the Ayala Brut on the nose, rounder, less dash and flare; fine, light *mousse*, some fruit, rather mild – a much simpler wine, but very respectable. Also in sec and demi-sec, but these I have not tasted.
Vintage Brut (50% PN, 25% PM, 25% CH) I tasted only the 1976: an 'old' nose, showing excessive acetaldehyde; this wine also has a light, fine *mousse* and full Pinot flavour on the palate, but is lacking in acidity.

G. H. Mumm & Co.

29 and 34 rue du Champ-de-Mars, Reims
Telephone (26) 40.22.73
Visits Monday to Friday throughout the year; weekends and public holidays from March until October.
Origin The house was founded in 1827 by two Germans, Peter Arnold de Mumm and Frederick Giesler, who together formed P.A. Mumm, Giesler & Co. After ten years, Giesler left to start Giesler & Co. at Avize, which attained great fame, but is now simply a *marque* belonging to Marne et Champagne. In 1852, Peter Arnold's son Jules de Mumm left the firm to found his own house, leaving his brother Georges-Hermann (born Georg Hermann) to run the business on his own. In 1873, G. H. Mumm & Co launched its now famous Cordon Rouge brand and the company went from strength to strength. Jules de Mumm produced some of the most aesthetically appealing labels for his Champagnes, but as a business his house did not survive; G. H. Mumm & Co. acquired the right to the *marque* and still ship a few cases every now and then, to keep the name alive.

Despite nearly one hundred years of trading, the Mumms had not sought naturalisation, unlike so many other German founders of

Champagne houses. This turned out to be a most unwise decision because the firm was confiscated after the First World War and put up for sale. In 1920 G. H. Mumm & Co was purchased by several parties with varying shareholdings. One of the shareholders was Dubonnet, and René Lalou, whose wife was a Dubonnet, took control of the firm. As chairman, he guided Mumm from 1920 until 1973 with steady success, building it into one of the largest houses in Champagne. G. H. Mumm & Co acquired Perrier-Jouët in 1959, G. Chauvet Frères in 1969, and Heidsieck & Co. Monopole in 1972. In the same year that it purchased Chauvet, Mumm itself was taken over by one of its shareholders, the giant Canadian-based multi-national Seagram Group.

Vineyards 219 hectares, averaging 95% échelle and representing some 20% of the total production. The vineyards include 21 hectares at Mailly (PN); 12.5 hectares at Vaudemanges (PN); 12.5 hectares at Ambonnay (PN); 11 hectares at Bouzy (PN); 40 hectares at Avenay (PN); 16 hectares at Aÿ (PN); 5 hectares at Cramant (CH); 26 hectares at Avize (CH); and 35 hectares at Chambrécy (PM).

Purchases 95% échelle.

Production 8 million bottles **Exports** 67%

Average bottle-age of NV *Cuvées* 3 years

Special interest The house is a member of the Syndicat de Grandes Marques de Champagne.

WINES

House style: Like Veuve Clicquot, Mumm bruts tend to be relatively sweet, and thus the Champagnes from both houses appeal to a very wide public. The analogy cannot be pursued further, however, as the styles of Mumm and Clicquot could not be more different: Mumm Champagnes are light and fragrant.

NV Cordon Rouge Brut (75% PN/PM, 25% CH; 93% échelle) Pleasant, persistent *mousse*; attractive nose, open and quite full; lightly rich flavour, with a clean and fragrant finish – not a true brut dryness, but the wine is a distinguished NV for those with something of a sweet tooth.

NV Cordon Vert (75% PN/PM, 25% CH; 93% échelle) One of the better demi-sec Champagnes, but a touch mild and too soft on the finish for me. Whereas Cordon Brut Champagnes are composed entirely of *vins de cuvée*, Cordon Vert is a blend of *première* and *deuxième taille* of Chardonnay and *première taille* of Pinot Noir, with 38 grams per litre of residual sugar.

NV Crémant de Cramant, Blanc de Blancs Brut (100% CH; 100% échelle) Although the quality of this wine appeared to plunge a few years ago, it is once again at the peak of its perfection. It has an exquisite *mousse* of tiny bubbles, creaming and clinging to the glass, is slightly drier than the Cordon Rouge and fine and delicate in both flavour and style: a superbly balanced, early drinking delight.

Vintage Cordon Rouge Brut (70% PN, 30% CH; 93% échelle) It has more brut dryness than the above and is well made, but never seems to excite me. Nevertheless, the 1976 was one of the better wines of that great, but difficult, year.

Vintage René Lalou Brut (up to 50% PN, 50% CH or more; 98–100% échelle) I tasted only the 1973: top-quality *mousse*, very generous nose, true brut flavour, and a certain muscle balanced by graceful fruit and a gentle finish.

Vintage Rosé Brut (72% PN, 28% CH; 93% échelle; blended) The base wine of Vintage Cordon Rouge, to which is added 8–10% of red wine from Mumm's own vineyards in Bouzy. Obviously a little red wine is just what the Cordon Rouge needs because, although it rarely thrills me, Mumm's Rosé always does. It has a delightful pale colour, barely hinting at peach and topped with a wisp of white *mousse*; and a refined fruity flavour: a wine of style and finesse. The sensitively designed label, with its pastel pink rose, reproduced from Leonard Foujita's painting *La petite fille à la rose* is visually reminiscent of the nineteenth century labelling of Jules de Mumm's.

La petite fille à la rose
by Leonard Foujita

Napoleon

Ch. & A. Prieur
2 rue de Villiers-aux-Bois, Vertus
Telephone (26) 52.11.74
Visits By appointment
Origin Born at Mailly in 1799, Jean-Louis
Prieur moved to Vertus in 1820. Five years later
he married Marie-Reine Pageot and began
selling Champagne under the name Prieur-
Pageot. His sons Charles and Alfred gave their
initials to the firm's present titles, but it was
Charles' sons, the founder's grandsons, Louis-
Charles and Alfred M. Ernest, who thought of
using the *marque* of Napoleon after taking
control of the business in 1898. The first
Napoleon Champagne was a small shipment
sent to Volgograd in Russia at the turn of the
century, and the Prieurs have ever since had the
sole right to use the name of Napoleon on a
Champagne bottle.
Vineyards None **Purchases** Averaging 94%
Production 100,000–150,000 bottles
Exports 50%
Vinification notes Some 70% of the
production is fermented in stainless steel vats,
the balance in oak casks.
Average bottle-age of NV *Cuvées* 3 years.
Special interest The house is a member of the
Syndicat de Grandes Marques de Champagne.
WINES
House style: Honest, generous wines, with
some vintages that are as fine as can be found
anywhere in Champagne.
NV Napoleon Carte Verte Brut (75% PM,
25% CH; 80–90% échelle) Honest, mild and
earthy Champagne which improves for a
couple of years, but not for much longer.
NV Napoleon Carte Orange Brut (60% PN,
40% CH; 90–100% échelle) A wine in a
distinctly higher class: creamy-rich and fruity,
with a fine *mousse* and a relaxed character.
This unpretentious wine is better than many
more famous NV brands.
NV Napoleon Rosé Brut (60% PN, 40% CH;
90–100% échelle; blended) Not tasted.
Vintage Napoleon Brut (50–60% PN, 40–
50% CH; 90–100% échelle) Rich, distinctive
wines, with a persistent *mousse* of fine bubbles;
the elegance of Chardonnay often shows on the
nose, but the wine is always well fleshed with
Pinot flavour, dominating the palate and finish.
Napoleon Brut ages gracefully into the sort of
ultra-clean aroma and flavour of honey and

vanilla sought after by lovers of old
Champagne. Recommended years: 1971, 1973,
1975, 1976.

Oudinot

12 rue Roger Godart, Épernay
Telephone (26) 54.60.31
Visits Telephone for details
Origin This house, established at the end of the
last century by Jules Édouard Oudinot, was at
first run by his son Marcel. In 1979 the firm
acquired the *marque* of Jeanmaire, and at the
close of 1981 Oudinot was acquired by Michel
Trouillard, who had previously sold his
Trouillard-de-Venoge group to Charles-
Heidsieck-Henriot – keeping, however, the
family vineyards. The combination of
Trouillard's vineyards with the cellars, stock
and estate of Oudinot created a modest new
force in Champagne, which has yet to realise its
true potential.
Vineyards 65 hectares at Tauxières, Dizy,
Champillon, Villedommange, Bouzy, les
Mesneux, Chouilly, Cramant and Avize,
averaging 92% échelle and representing 90%
of the total production.
Purchases Only from the Côte des Blancs.
Production 600,000 bottles **Exports** 45%
Vinification notes The house uses Vaslin
horizontal presses and glycol-cooled stainless
steel vats.
Average bottle-age of NV *cuvées* 3 years
Other *marques* Jeanmaire, Royal Onzane, A.
& S. de Perrot.

WINES
House style: As I have only tasted Oudinot a
few times in London in the late 1970s, prior to
its acquisition by Michel Trouillard and its
subsequent reorganisation, I am unable to
express an opinion about its Champagnes
today.
NV Brut, NV Demi-Sec, NV Blanc de Blancs,
Vintage Brut, Vintage Rosé Brut, Vintage Blanc
de Blancs Brut, and the *cuvée de prestige*
Vintage Cuvée Particulière.

Bruno Paillard

Rue Jacques Maritain, Reims
Telephone (26) 36.20.22
Visits By appointment
Origin The fastest rising star on the
Champagne scene, Bruno Paillard first
appeared on the market as recently as 1981, but

at that time it was merely a *marque auxiliaire*; not until 1984 was this *marque* granted *négociant-manipulant* status by the CIVC. The story of the house starts, however, not in the 1980s, but in the economic decline of the 1950s.

Rémy Paillard, Bruno's father, had inherited four hectares of vines in Verzenay, but found it impossible to make a decent living from them. With the help of a couple of sleeping partners (the Feuillatte brothers, of Vernhes in Paris), he began planting twenty-two hectares in the Petite Montagne: eleven at Crugny and eleven at Buleuse. With supermarkets selling *grandes marques* to the public at lower prices than wholesalers like Vernhes could offer the hotel and restaurant trade, the Champagne market had become increasingly difficult for everyone. Henriot was at that time producing a BOB for Nicolas, and this gave Vernhes the inspiration to market their own brand – hence their investment in Rémy Paillard, whom they had entrusted with the selection of their wine.

Despite the massive devaluation of the franc in 1960. Paillard's BOB business was so successful that Rémy decided to limit his sales to the home market. Bruno joined the family firm in the mid-1970s and by the time I met him in 1980, had doubled his father's turnover. He was also export consultant for Marne & Champagne, the king of BOBs, and was acting privately as a *courtier en Champagne*. In this last capacity he was uniquely positioned: houses specialising in BOBs were restricted to their own stocks, whereas Bruno was the only BOB broker actually based in the region. On the one hand he had the best possible entrée to the largest stocks of BOB Champagne at Marne & Champagne while, on the other, he had an incomparable list of contacts at other houses made through both Marne & Champagne and his father. He soon gained a reputation with foreign buyers for being able to come up with the right wine at the right price.

Occasionally Bruno came across a parcel of wine of such outstanding quality that it would have been a crime to sell it as just another BOB. He therefore brought out his own *marque auxiliaire* and it was from tiny quantities of this extraordinary wine sold to the Sunday Times Wine Club that a wider demand grew for Champagne Bruno Paillard. Soon this *marque auxiliaire* could be purchased in six different styles, including such unusual *cuvées* as Brut Zero and Blanc de Noirs and it was not long

before Bruno was in a position to apply for full *négociant-manipulant* status. Knowing that, as a legitimate Champagne house, his reputation would depend upon the quality and consistency of wines made and blended by him, Bruno Paillard built a temperature-controlled *cuvérie* and cellars at Murigny, on the southern edge of Reims. Since it will be a few years before all his Champagnes are guided from grape to glass in this winery it is too early to know exactly what Champagnes this recently established house has in store, but it is safe to predict that they will be very good.

Production 240,000 bottles (1984)
Exports 100% (1984)
Average bottle-age of NV *cuvées*: 3 years

WINES
House style: Difficult to assess prior to 1984, impossible to predict after.
NV Brut (35% PN, 45% PM, 25% CH) A good strength of *mousse*; this is a fleshy, rooty-fruity wine, balancing freshness with a certain roundness; a good amount of old reserve wine is used.
NV Crémant Blanc de Blancs Brut (100% CH) One of the few true *crémants*: a delightfully perfumed Chardonnay.
NV Rosé Brut (90–95% PN, 5–10% CH; skin-contact) I have tasted this only once; it has a delightful peach colour and plenty of ripe fruit flavour, yet it seems to be lifted by more than a small percentage of Chardonnay. A distinguished wine.
Vintage Brut (40–50% PN, 50–60% CH) The 1973 (under Paillard's *marque auxiliaire* label) was extraordinarily good. The 1976 was a much bigger, richer wine, as would be expected, yet also one of the more elegant of that very hot year.

Wines under *marque-auxiliaire* labels which might still be available include NV Brut Zero (of the same construction as the NV Brut, but with nearly four years' ageing and no dosage) and Vintage Blanc de Noirs (an amazingly rich wine and one of the first *cuvées* to establish Bruno's reputation).

Joseph Perrier

69 avenue de Paris, Châlons-sur-Marne
Telephone (26) 68.29.51
Visits By appointment
Origin The house was established by Joseph Perrier in 1825 at Châlons-sur-Marne, where

Part of the correspondence dated 1865 between M. Pithois of Joseph Perrier and Pasteur on the subject of secondary fermentation

Perrier's father, François-Alexandre, had helped *his* father-in-law in a small wine business. Châlons-sur-Marne, now off the beaten track in terms of the Champagne trade, occupied a more central position in the nineteenth century. More firms had premises in the town then, and, just ten years before Joseph Perrier set up business, Napoleon had visited Châlons-sur-Marne to see for himself the cellars of Jacquesson, which were reputed to be the finest in all Champagne. In *The History of Champagne* (1962), André Simon names thirteen Champagne shippers who had offices at Châlons-sur-Marne one hundred years before he was writing.

On his death in 1870, Joseph Perrier left a successful business to his grandson Gabriel Perrier (1858–1916), who, however, had little inclination to run a Champagne house and eventually sold the firm to Paul Pithois (1850–1918) in 1888. The Pithois had been in the wine business for many generations, having vineyards at Cumières, Hautvillers and Damery. The house has been in the Pithois family ever since, the current chairman being Georges Pithois and the managing director his nephew Claude Fourmon.

Vineyards 5 hectares at Cumières (PN); 2 hectares at Damery (PN); 1 hectare at Hautvillers (PN), and 12 hectares at Verneuil (PM), forming an estate of 20 hectares, averaging 90% échelle and representing 35% of the total production

Purchases Averaging 90% échelle

Production 600,000 bottles

Sales 550,000 bottles **Exports** 40–50%

Stocks 2 million bottles (1983)

Vinification notes It was with great surprise that I read Hubrect Duijker's claim, in his otherwise excellent work, *The Loire, Alsace and Champagne* (1983), that 'At Joseph Perrier they freely admit that the dosage contains a dash of brandy: many houses refuse even to discuss this', as the firm told me that they have not used any *eau-de-vie* in the *liqueur d'expédition* for the past twenty years and confirmed this in writing to me in the very year in which Duijker's book was published in its English translation. The tradition of brandying the dosage evolved at a time when sweet Champagne was all the rage. In order to produce this, a large amount of cane sugar had to be added, and this displaced so much wine that the strength was significantly reduced; therefore spirit was added to raise the alcoholic level. Joseph Perrier have not produced a truly sweet Champagne since the war. *Prise de mousse* is carried out in half-bottles, jeroboams and methuselahs.

Average bottle-age of NV *cuvées* 3 years

Special interest The house is a member of the Syndicat de Grandes Marques de Champagne.

WINES

House style: The wines are mellow and fruity, influenced greatly by the Pinot; they are made in a relaxed style and are very easy to drink. There have been some quite outstanding late releases of fresh Champagne classics. Perrier is one of my favourite houses.

NV Cuvée Royale Brut (25% PN, 45% PM, 30% CH; 88–90% échelle) Well-constructed *mousse* of small bubbles, fresh yet mature nose, plenty of uncomplicated fruit, great depth; a full but elegant wine. Also in sec and demi-sec.

NV Cuvée Royale Blanc de Blancs Brut (100% CH; 90% échelle) Very smooth and persistent *mousse* and a highly perfumed, creamy nose; a delicate wine on the palate.

NV Cuvée Cent Cinquantenaire Brut (40%

PN, 60% CH; 92% échelle) With a vigorous *mousse* of tiny bubbles, this is a full and generous wine, with a good edge of acidity and a long finish. It is made from a blend of vintage years.
NV Cuvée Royale Rosé Brut (15% PN, 55% PM, 30% CH; 88–90% échelle) The few times I have tasted this *cuvée*, it has been dark in colour and very open on the nose, showing good Pinot character but spoilt by too much residual sugar.
Vintage Cuvée Royale Brut (60% PN, 40% CH; 90–100% échelle) Persistent *mousse* of tiny bubbles, ripe fruit; a wine with an elegant style and a long, rich finish. A bottle of recently disgorged 1955 was quite sensational in the late 1970s. Recommended years: 1973, 1975, 1979.
Coteaux Champenois Cumières Rouge (100% PN; 90% échelle) An above-average Coteaux Champenois, like a cross between Chianti and Burgundy; a light, fresh, agreeable wine which improves with breathing.
Coteaux Champenois Blanc de Blancs Chardonnay (100% CH; 90–100% échelle) A clean, crisp, dry wine with good acidity, comparable to an inexpensive Macon.

Perrier-Jouët

28 avenue de Champagne, Épernay
Telephone (26) 55.20.53
Visits Daily from April to September
Origin In 1811, Pierre Nicolas-Marie Perrier (1786–1854), the uncle of Joseph Perrier, combining his wife's maiden name with his own founded the house of Perrier-Jouët. Within twenty years the firm had established itself on many export markets and, under Charles Perrier, Pierre's son, the reputation of this *marque* was consolidated: the house supplied wine for various distinguished customers, including Napoleon III, King Leopold of the Belgians and Queen Victoria.

Charles Perrier was not only successful at making and selling Champagne; he was a clever politician, who became mayor of Épernay. In 1863, he built Château Perrier opposite Maison Perrier-Jouët in the Avenue de Champagne. The building today houses the local library and museum and is well worth a visit. Upon Perrier's death in 1897, since he left no son to inherit the business, Perrier-Jouët passed into the control of his nephew Henri Gallice, a man

with an exceptional reputation for honesty. In 1934, the firm passed to Louis Budin, who was married to a member of the Gallice family.

Louis Budin's son Michel became head of Perrier-Jouët in 1959, and in the same year the house was acquired by the Mumm Group. Under the umbrella of the Canadian-based Seagram Group, along with Mumm and Heidsieck & Co. Monopole, it is no longer an independent house in terms of ownership, but it is run as a separate concern and has managed to retain its own identity. With Michel Budin still responsible for the blending of Perrier-Jouët's *cuvées*, this house continues to make traditional Champagnes of the very highest standard. I have always had a special affection for it and for its romantic wines.
Vineyards 12 hectares at Mailly (PN); 12 hectares at Aÿ (PN); 10 hectares at Dizy (PN); 29 hectares at Cramant (CH); 10 hectares at Avize (CH); 13 hectares at Vinay (PM), and 22 hectares at Orbais l'Abbaye (PM), the total forming an estate of 108 hectares, averaging 96% échelle and representing 40% of the total production.
Purchases Averaging 94% échelle
Production Average for 1982–3, 2.9 million bottles
Sales Average for 1982–3, 1.9 million bottles (2.4 million in 1984)
Exports 60%
Stocks 8.5 million bottles (December 1983)
Vinification notes The last time *eau-de-vie* was used in the *liqueur d'expédition* was as recently as 1976, although the quantity used had gradually decreased in previous years.
Average bottle-age of NV *cuvées* 2–3 years
Special interest The house is a member of the Syndicat de Grandes Marques de Champagne.

House style: The wines have great elegance and breeding, being lighter and more fragrant than the proportional dominance of Pinot grapes would indicate.
NV Grand Brut (70% PN/PM, 30% CH; 94% échelle) Fine, persistent *mousse*; very fresh aroma, sometimes lively and appley when too young, but always able to develop if the wine is laid down for a couple of years; good acidity and fruit. Also in sec and demi-sec.
Vintage Extra Brut (70% PN/PM, 30% CH; 94% échelle) An impeccable wine year in and year out: ultra-fine *mousse*, delicate aroma,

with the small proportion of Chardonnay stabbing through, perfect fruit and acid balance. The 1966 was magnificent at the end of the 1970s. Recommended years: 1973, 1975, 1976, 1979.

Vintage Blason de France Brut (60% PN, 40% CH; 100% échelle) I have only tasted the 1975: pale lemon-straw colour, gentle but persistent *mousse* of pin-head bubbles, penetrating flavour of juicy-ripe Chardonnay, trailing off gracefully.

Vintage Rosé Brut (70% PN, 30% CH; 94% échelle; blended) Lovely peach colour, extraordinarily good *mousse* of creaming minuscule bubbles for such a high Pinot content, full and very fruity Pinot nose, rich-fruit palate with a touch of earthiness; not quite the usual Perrier-Jouët elegance. Recommended year: 1975.

Vintage Belle Époque Rosé Brut (60% PN, 40% 100% échelle) Critics who insinuate that more effort goes into producing the bottle than into effecting the *cuvée* should be ignored. This is consistently one of the best half-dozen de luxe Champagnes available, and it is precisely because Perrier-Jouët realise that Belle Époque's unique bottle attracts so much attention for its design that they are so fastidious about the quality of the wine. Recommended years: 1964, 1969, 1971, 1975, 1976. With flowers painted in pink, gold and green enamel, the bottle is indeed the most attractive of any used for presenting Champagne. It was created for Perrier-Jouët by the great Art Nouveau glassmaker and cabinet-maker of Nancy, Émile Gallé (1846–1904), just two years before his death, to evoke the Belle Époque of the 1890s. The enamel-painted design has to be fired at 500° Celsius, a mere 50 degrees below the melting point of glass. A number of 'Belle Époque' by-products exist, the most tasteful being glass ice-buckets and matching tulip-shaped glasses.

Vintage Belle Époque Rosé Brut (60% PN, 40% CH; 100% échelle; blended) The first *cuvée* was the 1976, but I have only tasted the 1978; lovely soft and gentle *mousse*, delicate Pinot nose, very ripe Pinot fruit on the palate, edged with a lace of Chardonnay, great finesse and finish. A particularly outstanding wine, considering the year.

In 1984 Perrier-Jouët launched two new *cuvées*: NV Blason de France and NV Blason de France Rosé.

Petitjean

12 bis rue Victor Hugo, Épernay
Telephone (26) 54.44.52
Origin The house was established in 1846 by Paul Cochet at Ambonnay under the *marque* of P. Cochet. The business was acquired at the turn of the century by his son-in-law Henri Petitjean (1874–1961), who altered the name to H. Petitjean & Cie. In 1959, control of the firm passed to Henri Petitjean's grandson Michel, who was head of the Institut Oenologique de Champagne.
Production 130,000 bottles

WINES
NV Brut, NV Sec, NV Demi-Sec, NV Réserve Brut, NV Réserve Sec, NV Réserve Demi-Sec, Brut Crémant Rosé, Vintage Brut, Cuvée Tradition

Philipponnat

13 rue du Pont, Mareuil-sur-Aÿ
Telephone (26) 50.60.43
Visits By appointment
Origin The Philipponnat family has been established in the Marne Valley since at least the sixteenth century, although it was not until the mid-nineteenth century that they began growing grapes and making wine. It was in Aÿ that the Philipponnats first became involved in the Champagne trade, moving to Mareuil-sur-Aÿ in 1912 to set up the house of Philipponnat as it now exists. In 1935 the firm purchased six hectares of vines on the steep, south-south-facing slopes of the highly reputed Clos des Goisses, the sight of which, reflected in the Marne au Rhin canal, is world-famous. In the spring of 1980, the house of Philipponnat was taken over by Gosset.
Vineyards 10 hectares at Mareuil-sur-Aÿ (70% PN, 30% CH) and 2 hectares at Avenay and Murigny (PN), representing 15–20% of the total production
Purchases Averaging 90% échelle
Production 500,000–600,000 bottles
Exports 25%
Stocks 1.5 million bottles (November 1983)
Average bottle-age of NV *cuvées* 2.5 years

WINES
House style: Much of the delicate charm and feel of these wines can be attributed to the firm's substantial stocks of old reserve wines: it is not so much the average bottle-age of a non-

vintage Champagne that matters; it is how that average is constructed. Certainly not *grand mousseux*, the soft Philopponnat style of *mousse* will not be admired by those who require quantity, rather than quality, in this respect. These are Champagnes to relax with, but they are also excellent wines to match with food, particularly *cuisine nouvelle*.

NV Royal Réserve Brut (35% PN, 40% PM, 25% CH; 92% échelle) Classic nose with just a pleasant hint of yeast; gentle *mousse*, with very small bubbles, rich fruit, balanced with fine acidity; good grip and length.

NV Royal Réserve Rose Brut (Same base wine as the above, with the addition of red wine from Philipponnat's Clos des Goisses vineyard, 92%+ échelle) Delicately coloured wine; most attractive nose, with elegant Pinot Noir; beautiful varietal character on the palate. It is hard to believe that the wine is not pure Pinot Noir, except for the finish, where the finesse of Chardonnay lifts and lightens the blend.

Vintage Royal Réserve Brut (70–75% PN, 25–30% CH; 95% échelle). Greater muscle than the NV, with higher extract, yet still maintaining the graceful *mousse* that is Philipponnat's trademark. The 1976 was a great success, combining the strength of that drought year with the finesse of Philipponnat's style. Recommended years: 1971, 1973, 1975, 1976, 1979.

Vintage Cuvée Première Blanc de Blancs Brut (100% CH; 100% échelle) I have only tasted the 1976: a tight wine with a great intensity of fruit, long but firm, requiring plenty of bottle-age to loosen up and open out. It should be excellent.

Vintage Clos des Goisses (70% PN, 30% CH; 30% échelle) The late Colin Fenton, Master of Wine, who was perhaps the world's greatest admirer of Champagne Salon, stated that anyone who could not understand or like Salon would not appreciate Clos des Goisses, and vice versa. Although they are two very different wines – one a Marne Valley Pinot Noir dominated blend, the other a Côte des Blancs Chardonnay – both have a singular intensity which sets them apart from all other Champagnes. Like Salon, Clos des Goisses Changes so radically between ten and fifteen years that it comes to assume a completely different, and vastly more complex, identity. With Philipponnat's typically quiet *mousse*, this wine is initially fresh and fragrant on the nose, and strong and ripe on the palate. At its peak, it attains great depth and a penetrating richness, continuously unfolding to reveal such nuances of bouquet and flavour as broken creamy

The famous Clos des Goisses in 1910, when the configuration of trees was such that its reflection in the Marne au Rhin canal had the uncanny appearance of a Champagne bottle with its mushroom-shaped cork in the process of lift-off!

biscuits, hazelnuts, toast, yoghurt, honey, vanilla and more besides.

The micro-climate of Clos des Goisses is such that it is possible to select wines from the south-south slope with enough fruit to balance the acidity of even the meanest years. Few years in Champagne have been quite as mean as the year of my birth, 1951, yet a magnum of Clos des Goisses 1951 (I doubt if the house marketed the vintage), kept *sur pointes* at Mareuil-sur-Aÿ, was nothing short of remarkable – a great wine. Yet only a small part of Clos des Goisses is located on this exceptional slope, most of the vineyards stretching back over the gently rolling land behind. So, in really major years, when the grapes can literally roast on the frontal slope, Philipponnat can blend in the less generous wines to effect a perfect balance. Recommended years: 1961, 1970, 1971, 1973, 1976.

Jules Pierlot

15 rue Henri-Martin, Épernay
Telephone (26) 54.45.52
Origin The house was established in 1889 by Jules Pierlot.
Production 100,000–120,000 bottles
Exports 20%
Average bottle-age of NV *cuvées* 3 years

WINES
NV Casque d'Or Brut, NV Casque Blanc (Blanc de Blancs), Cuvée Spéciale Blanc de Blancs Brut, Cuvée Spéciale 'Jules Pierlot' Rosé Brut (blended), NV Cuvée des Archers (*cuvée de prestige*)

Ployez Jacquemart

Ludes
Telephone (26) 61.11.87
Origin In 1930, Marcel Ployez, a native of the Aube *département* and married to a certain Yvonne Jacquemart, founded the small house of Ployez Jacquemart at Ludes, in the Montagne de Reims. When Marcel Ployez died in 1957, his widow took control of the business and ran it for ten years until her two sons, Gérard and Jacques, were able to enter the firm.
Vineyards 2 hectares, representing 15% of the total production
Production 100,000 bottles
Average bottle-age of NV *cuvées* 2.5 years

WINES
NV Extra Quality Brut (50%– PN/PM, 50%+ CH; 97% échelle) Only Chardonnay in good years.
NV Séléction Brut (50%– PN/PM, 50%+ CH; 97% échelle) Only Chardonnay in good years.
Vintage Brut (50%– PN, 50%+ CH; 97% échelle) Only Chardonnay in good years.
Vintage Cuvée Liesse d'Hardonville Brut (100% PN/PM; 98% échelle) *Cuvée de prestige*
Vintage Rosé Brut (50%– PN, 50%+ CH; 97% échelle; blended)

Pol Roger & Co.

1 rue Henri Lelarge, Épernay
Telephone (26) 55.41.95
Visits Monday to Friday throughout the year, except public holidays
Origin The house was founded in 1849 by Pol Roger (1831–99; son of Charles Jean-Baptiste Roger), who the year before had begun winemaking at the tender age of eighteen. He shipped his first wine to England in 1876 and, by the time his two sons, Maurice (1869–1959) and Georges (1873–1950), took control in 1899, the business was well established. On 15 March 1900, the Roger family was officially renamed Pol-Roger – a change which necessitated a decree signed by the president of the Republic.

Maurice Pol-Roger was mayor when the Germans occupied Épernay for seven days in September 1914. During this short but unhappy period he withstood German threats to shoot him and burn the town to the ground, a stand which earned him the eternal gratitude of his fellow townsmen. Between the two world wars, Pol Roger is reputed to have shipped more Champagne to England, then as now the principal market, than any other house. When, in 1935, more than twenty years later, he declined to stand yet again for election as mayor, the people of Épernay took the unprecedented step of making him honorary mayor of the town for life. Upon his death, the house of Pol Roger passed to his son Jacques and his nephew Guy. The present incumbents are Christian Pol-Roger and Christian de Billy, both great-grandsons of the founder, Pol Roger.

The most famous and most ardent admirer of Champagne Pol Roger was Winston Churchill,

who has proved to be the firm's greatest advertisement. He often said of Champagne, 'In victory we deserve it, in defeat we need it', and Pol Roger was the Champagne with which he preferred to celebrate or drown his sorrows. Winston Churchill always had his Pol Roger bottled in Imperial Pints: he did not buy full size bottles in case he was unable to manage the entire contents by himself and, as he was often chastised by his beloved Clementine for drinking on his own, he considered half-bottles not worth the bother of being ticked off! Commenting at the launching of the Cuvée Sir Winston Churchill in 1984, Lady Soames said of her father's passion for Pol Roger, 'I saw him many times the better for it, but never the worse'. His favourite vintages were 1928, 1934 and 1947 and he liked to drink his Champagne much older than is the fashion now.

Vineyards 70 hectares at Chavot-Courcourt, Chouilly, Cramant, Cuis, Épernay, Grauves, Mardreuil, Moussy and Pierry, averaging 95% échelle and representing 35% of the total production.

ABOVE Courtyard of Messrs Pol Roger & Co's establishment at Épernay, 1882

RIGHT Vintage year

Purchases Averaging 95% échelle
Production 1 million bottles (1978–81), 1.7 million bottles (1982–3)
Sales 1.3 million bottles (1978–81), 1.2 million bottles (1982–3)
Exports 55–60%
Stocks 5 million bottles (1983)
Average bottle-age of NV *cuvées* 3–4 years
Special interest The house is a member of the Syndicat de Grandes Marques de Champagne.

WINES

House style: There is much truth in the claim that the character of the winemaker can be seen in the wines which he makes. The charm and ease of Christian Pol Roger is balanced in the house wines by the bubbly character of the ever-smiling, yet quietly deep, Christian de Billy.
NV Sec (25% PN, 45% PM, 30% CH; 90% échelle) Very pale straw colour, fine *mousse*, a simple sweet nose, some character and elegance on the palate, not cloying on the finish. Also in demi-sec.
NV Brut (30–35% PN, 30–35% PM, 30–40% CH; 95% échelle) A persistent *mousse* of tiny bubbles, a classic Pinot dominated blend, showing power and depth, although not quite brut in the true sense.
Vintage Brut (40–50% PN, up to 20% PM, 40–50% CH; 95% échelle) Classic vintage Champagne. Only the 1976 has disappointed, yet that had the feel of an 'ugly duckling' and I would not be surprised to find it completely transformed in ten years or so. The 1952, kept *sur pointes* for the Queen's Silver Jubilee in 1977, was simply the finest Champagne I have ever tasted, although it was closely followed by the 1964. Recommended years: 1971, 1975, 1979.
Vintage Chardonnay Brut (100% CH; 100% échelle) Ultra-fine *mousse*, seductive Chardonnay perfume on the nose; a wine absolutely correct on the palate, with ripe fruit, excellent acidity and good brut dryness. Recommended years: 1971, 1975.
Vintage Réserve Spéciale PR Brut (50% PN, 50% CH; 95% échelle) Again, ultra-fine *mousse*; an extraordinary balance of fruit and acidity gives a long finish and the extra Chardonnay adds a touch of flintiness to the aftertaste. Recommended years: 1971, 1975.
Vintage Rosé Brut The 1975 was 100% Pinot Noir, the 1971 75% Pinot Noir and 25% Chardonnay; both were made by blending in a little red wine from Bouzy. There is an extraordinarily fine and creaming *mousse* for such a Pinot-dominated wine, also a delightful pale peach colour; the wine is very fresh on the nose, with nuances of various soft fruit, lightly rich on the palate and shows great finesse. Recommended years: 1971, 1975.
Vintage Cuvée Sir Winston Churchill Brut This is an expensive wine, but it is also quite superb. The 1975 vintage (available in magnums only) with which this de luxe *cuvée* was launched may one day replace the Pol Roger 1952 as the best Champagne I have ever tasted. The follow-up vintage, 1979, will be available in bottles as well as in magnums. It would be apt if some future vintage could be released in Sir Winston's favoured Imperial Pints, EEC regulations permitting that is.

Pommery & Greno

5 Place Général-Gouraud, Reims
Telephone (26) 05.05.01
Visits Monday to Friday throughout the year; weekends and public holidays by appointment.
Origin In the year 860, when Charles II was king of France, Armand I, Vicomte de Polignac, was known as 'King of the Mountains' in Velay and the Wizard Merlin wandered in the woods – or so the Pommery & Greno advertising literature would have you believe, for Prince Edmond de Polignac, direct descendant of Armand I, presided over the destiny of the house of Pommery until very recently.

In 1836, Narcisse Greno took over the house of Dubois-Gosset, changing its name first to Dubois & Greno, then to N. Greno & Cie. Louis Alexandre Pommery became an associate in 1856, evidently investing substantially, because when he died two years later, his widow Jeanne Alexandrine Louise Pommery became head of the firm, despite the fact that Greno continued his participation in the business for a further two years. Until Pommery died in 1858, Madame Pommery had confined her attentions to her two children: Louis, then seventeen, and Louise, who was still a baby. Yet what followed was to be an example of an inexperienced woman stepping into her late husband's shoes and doing his job better.

Between 1870 and 1871, the Prince of Hohenhoe occupied the Pommery house during the Franco-Prussian War, turning it into his headquarters as the governor of Reims. After the Germans had withdrawn, Madame

Pommery acquired sixty hectares of land on what was known as the Butte Saint Niçaise, for the purpose of expanding her cellars. This site contained 120 Gallo-Roman crayères, which she had converted into nineteen kilometres of cellars. Above these cellars builders set to work on an eight-year task to construct a grand house to Madame Pommery's own design. Whether she had the builders work in isolation and ignorance of one another's allotted function is not known, but the resulting strange conglomeration of towers, spires and domes in brick and stone might suggest this assumption; in fact, it is said to have been inspired by the stately homes of Madame Pommery's five most important customers in England and Scotland. Those who were invited to the opening in 1878 were reported to be dumbfounded by the sight of what looked like five separate buildings stuck together – a weird but a magnificent piece of architectural fun.

In 1879 Madame Pommery married her daughter Louise to Prince Guy de Polignac, whose family could be traced back over forty generations, through eleven centuries, to Armand I. It was Prince Jules de Polignac who, as prime minister, had pursued the ultra-royalist policy which provoked the revolution of 1830 and was consequently imprisoned until 1836.

In 1979, Xavier Gardiner, already the owner of Champagne Lanson, purchased Pommery & Greno, becoming president of the company in June the following year. Barely a year after opening a £2 million *cuverie* of glistening stainless steel at Pommery, he sold both houses to BSN, the giant French food and beverage group.

Vineyards 307 hectares at Avenay, Avize, Aÿ, Bouzy, Cramant, Dizy, Mailly, Mutigny, Oger, Sillery, and Verzenay, averaging 99% échelle and representing 45–50% of the total production.
Purchases Averaging 90–95% échelle
Production 4 million bottles
Exports 65–70%
Vinification notes *Prise de mousse* is carried out in half-bottles, jeroboams and methuselahs.
Average bottle-age of NV cuvées 3 years
Special interest The house is a member of the Syndicat de Grandes Marques de Champagne.

WINES
House style: 'Sleeping beauties waiting to be discovered' was how someone once described these wines to me. I concur. They are caringly constructed, full-flavoured wines of consistently fine *mousse*, typically very dry and very long. Pommery must be one of the most underrated Champagnes available.
NV Brut Royal (70–75% PN/PM, 25–30% CH; 90% échelle) Very light in colour, with a persistent *mousse* of tiny bubbles; delightfully dry and deep-flavoured; a meaty wine with a long finish.

Also NV Extra Dry, NV Extra Sec, NV Drapeau Sec, and NV Demi-Sec: not tasted.
NV Rosé Brut (70–75% PN/PM, 25–30% CH; 90% échelle; skin-contact) The wine used to be vintaged (I remember a very attractive 1973), but is now a blend of different years. My notes for both versions emphasise the wine's perfumed character. The NV has a fresh and fragrant nose, reminiscent of strawberries, a fine *mousse*, perfumed Pinot on the palate and perfect balance; it makes delightful drinking.
Vintage Brut (50% PN, 50% CH; 100% échelle) A very distinguished Champagne which retains its freshness for a considerably longer period than most. Recommended years: 1973, 1975, 1979.
Vintage Blanc de Blancs Brut (100% CH; 100% échelle) Sadly, this wine has been discontinued. This single cru from Avize is full for a pure Chardonnay wine; extremely fruity, very distinctive and stylish, with a very dry and very long flavour – typically Pommery.
Louise Pommery (100% échelle) This is Pommery's relatively recent prestige *cuvée*, produced entirely from the firm's own vineyards, a classic blend of Pinot Noir from Aÿ and Chardonnay from Avize.

Rapeneau & Cie

4 rue Paul Bert, Magenta, Épernay
Telephone (26) 51.06.33
Origin The house was established in 1925 by Ernest Rapeneau. Between 1978 and 1980, the firm acquired the *marques* of Morel, Mortas and the houses of Jeanmaire (Châlons-sur-Marne), and G. H. Martel & Cie. In 1981, the turnover (in FF) was nearly twice that of Krug.
Vineyards 15 hectares
Sales 1.3 million bottles

WINES
NV Carte Verte Brut, Grand Réserve Brut, Blanc de Blancs, Vintage Brut and Rosé Brut

Louis Roederer

21 boulevard Lundy, Reims
Telephone (26) 40.42.11
Visits August to June by appointment
Origin The house of Roederer stems from the founding in 1760 of a firm called Dubois Père & Fils, which soon passed into the hands of Nicolas-Henri Schreider. In 1827, Schreider sought the assistance of his nephew Louis Roederer (1798–1870) in the running of his business. Roederer took over the firm six years later upon the death of his uncle and changed the firm's name to Louis Roederer. A hard worker, he soon made shipments to various export markets, including the Americas and England, but his greatest achievement was in conquering the Russian market; in fact, the Tsar became his best customer.

When Louis Roederer II assumed control in 1870 on the death of his father, sales were averaging two-and-a-half million bottles. In 1876, at the request of Alexander II, Louis Roederer created their now famous Cristal (then a sweet Champagne), presented in a special bottle of clear crystal made exclusively for the Russian imperial house. Roederer registered the label, and hence the *marque*, on 13 May 1876, and the intricate details of the bottle's design on 8 November the following year.

Louis II died suddenly in 1880, leaving the thriving business to his sister Léonie Orly, but she died eight years later and the great house of Louis Roederer consequently passed into the hands of her two sons Louis-Victor and Léon Orly, who both obeyed their mother's dying wish and appended Roederer to their surname.

The Revolution of October 1917 was a serious blow to the house of Roederer, not only depriving the firm of its principal market, but leaving it with the Tsar's outstanding bills, which the new régime naturally had no intention of paying. It also left a considerable stock of very sweet Champagnes on their hands, and it took a while to find a purchaser with a suitably sweet tooth. Eventually the entire stock was sold to a buyer in South America.

In 1932 Léon Orly-Roederer died and the following year his widow, Madame Camille Orly-Roederer, took control. Another outstanding widow of Champagne, Madame Roederer directed the firm with great energy for a period of some forty-two years, establishing a reputation for Louis Roederer Champagnes which became world-wide and is second to none. After Madame Roederer's death, the firm passed to her daughter, whose son Jean-Claude Rouzaud is in charge today.

Vineyards 28.46 hectares at Avize; 30.47 hectares at Aÿ; 11.14 hectares at Boleuse; 27.39 hectares at Chouilly; 2.46 hectares at Champillon; 16.30 hectares at Cumières; 1.41 hectares at Louvois; 21.28 hectares at Vertus; 23.98 hectares at Verzenay, and 21.76 hectares at Verzy, totalling an estate of 184.55 hectares, averaging 97.5% échelle and representing 80% of the total production.

Purchases Mostly Pinot Noir, always from the same vineyards and averaging 95% échelle.

Production 1.5 million bottles (1978–81); 1.7 million bottles (1982–3)

Sales 1.6 million bottles (1978–81); 1.5 million bottles (1982–3)

Exports 60%

Stocks 9 million bottles (1983)

Vinification notes Malo-lactic fermentation at Roederer is dependent on the natural acidity level of the must – in some years it is prevented. They ceased using *eau-de-vie* in 1972. The *vins de taille* of black grapes are submitted to a centrifuge; this is a sound practice, it is worth noting that such a prestigious and traditional house as Roederer makes use of it. Reserve wines are kept in casks of varying size.

Average bottle-age of NV *cuvées* 3.5–4 years

Other *marques* On 27 December 1907, the *marque* established in 1864, known as Théophile Roederer, was acquired. The wines consist of NV Brut, NV Extra Dry, NV Demi-Sec, Vintage Brut and a Crémant Brut. Traditionally they consist of two-thirds black grapes and one-third white grapes; the non-vintage wines have an average age of approximately three years.

Special interest The house is a member of the Syndicat de Grandes Marques de Champagne. The Krugs, who reside just across the street, told me that Roederer is the only house they consider worthy of trading an occasional case with.

During the early 1980s, when the economic situation in France was hastening the flight of spare capital out of the country, Roederer embarked on a venture in California. The firm invested some $15 million in an operation, totally under their control, which involved 200 hectares of land in the Anderson Valley, where it is cooler than other viticultural areas of

California and the harvest takes place in September, rather than in August. Using only Pinot Noir and Chardonnay, the firm planted a third of the land for three successive years (from 1982 to 1984), and the first crop, which is expected to yield one million bottles, is due in 1986.

WINES

House style: Roederer produce wines which have twice the average bottle-age of many Champagnes, but which are sometimes spoilt by an unnecessary touch of too much sugar. Presumably this is how Roederer devotees like their Champagne; if so, then these are great wines, which could be better if the firm's customers were willing to forgo a little sweetness.

NV Brut (66% PN, 34% CH; 95–100% échelle) Usually a classic NV, if not quite brut enough for my liking. This wine is the same as NV Extra Quality Brut, sold on the United Kingdom market. A new cuvée, NV Brut Premier, test-marketed in Germany in 1984, is due to be launched in the UK in 1986.

NV Extra Dry (66% PN, 34% CH; 95–100% échelle) The same as the brut, but with a higher dosage.

NV Grand Vin Sec and Demi-Sec (66% PN, 34% CH; 95–100% échelle) A rather contradictory label; the Demi-Sec is sometimes more accurately labelled 'Rich'.

NV Carte Blanche (66% PN, 34% CH; 95–100% échelle) With sixty grams per litre of residual sugar, this is the only *doux* Champagne I have come across. Just a thousand cases a year are produced for a few sweet-toothed Roederer customers. I have tasted it only once, at Roederer in 1983, when it had far too much acetaldehyde on the nose and no elegance to the bouquet or palate. It has a simple sugary flavour, although it is not as sweet as I had expected.

NV Rosé Brut (80% PN, 20% CH; 95–100% échelle; skin-contact) Some complexity on the nose; youthful and firm on the palate; a good balance of young wines and reserve wines.

Vintage Brut (66% PN, 34% CH; 97.5% échelle) There have been some memorable bottles of vintages from the 1960s, which seemed to become slightly sweeter during the 1970s, although with enough body and acidity to balance them. Recommended years: 1971, 1973, 1975, 1976.

Vintage Blanc de Blancs Brut (100% CH; 95–100% échelle) I have not tasted this recently

introduced wine. From the producer's description it would appear to be a *crémant* of true brut dryness: 'The lightest and driest of LR wines. Contains only about 60% of the CO_2 content usually present in Champagne'.

Vintage Cristal Brut (55–60% PN, 40–45% CH; 97.5% échelle) Lighter than the vintage brut, this is an elegant and lengthy wine with plenty of fruit. Recommended years: 1966, 1971, 1973. Roederer was the first house to use a protective wrapping on their bottles. The yellow cellophane around the clear glass bottle in which Cristal is sold protects the wine inside from the harmful effects of ultra-violet rays.

Vintage Cristal Rosé Brut A skin-contact pink Champagne; I have only tasted the 1976 vintage. In 1983, when I did so, the wine was relatively closed and still developing, with a compact, intense youthful flavour. A very refined wine.

A. Rothschild

Marne & Champagne
22 rue Maurice-Cerveaux, Épernay
Telephone (26) 51.21.66

Origin Few people have heard of Marne & Champagne, a house established in 1933 by its current owner, Gaston Burtin, yet only one other house makes and sells more bottles of Champagne than Marne, and that, of course, is Moët & Chandon. The reason why this house has remained invisible to consumers for more than fifty years is that its Champagnes are marketed under no less than three hundred different labels and even its flagship range is not sold as Marne & Champagne, but A. Rothschild. The three hundred fantasy labels of Marne & Champagne does not take into account the numerous labels of famous houses which buy *sur lattes* from Marne & Champagne. This supply of wines *sur lattes* to the rest of the trade has often caused *La Revue Vinicole* to label Marne & Champagne 'Champagne's life support system'.

While other houses were struggling to establish their reputations, Marne & Champagne decided to monopolise the BOB-trade. Virtually unopposed in this wide-open sector of the market, Marne & Champagne had little difficulty in raising their sales from one million bottles in 1939 to five million in 1959 and ten million in 1979, while customers remained totally ignorant of the house's name.

Vineyards None
Production 10 million bottles

Purchases While many houses admit that they use some *vins de taille* in certain NV Champagnes, particularly sec or demi-sec blends, very few dare declare that they use as much as they can acquire. Marne & Champagne, however, could not avoid making such an admission, if challenged, because nine out of every ten firms which sell *vins de taille* claim that it is Marne & Champagne that buys them. After *bouillage*, 23% of the total production of Champagne is classified as *vin de taille*, but most houses use much less (perhaps 15%), and then only in the cheaper blends. Marne & Champagne's purchases of *vins de taille* amount to 40%. As 20% of the total production consists of A. Rothschild Champagne (see below), composed entirely of *vin de cuvée*, the average *vin de taille* content of Marne & Champagne's other wines is no less than 50%, I say 'no less', because some customers demand pure *vin de cuvée* under their own labels (and pay accordingly), thus increasing the average for the other buyers.

Exports 50% of the A. Rothschild range

Stocks 30 million bottles (1983)

Vinification notes To assist the acidity of Champagnes made from such a high *vin de taille* content, malo-lactic conversion is prevented.

Average bottle-age of NV *cuvées* 3 years (A. Rothschild range)

Other *marques* Pol Albert, Eugène Clicquot, Denis Père & Fils, Gauthier, Pol Gessner, Giesler, Giesmann, Georges Martel, Guy Morin and others. A. Rothschild is the flagship *marque* and accounts for some two million bottles a year.

Special interest In 1983 Marne & Champagne purchased Château Haut-Brignon in the Premières Côtes de Bordeaux and Château des Tours in Montagne St Émilion.

WINES

House style: At first, the good quality and consistency of wines from a BOB house like Marne & Champagne might seem surprising, but, with enough *vins de cuvée* to make six million bottles (three times the production of A. Rothschild), the house is well able to be selective in the wines used for this range.

NV Brut Réserve (80% PN, 20% CH; 90–95% échelle) Fine, persistent *mousse*; fresh and ripe on nose and palate; good depth and length. A very acceptable wine.

Vintage Brut Réserve (60% PN, 40% CH; 90–95% échelle) The 1975 had a good *mousse* and a very mature 'billowing', vegetal nose; yet it was absolutely clean and fresh on the palate, full of flavour and well-balanced. The 1970 was a Chardonnay-dominated wine, with a persistent *mousse*, still quite backward on the palate (when last tasted in 1980) and with a very characteristic steely finish.

Vintage Grand Trianon Brut (60% PN, 40% CH; 90–95% échelle) The 1973 had a strong *mousse* of extremely fine bubbles; a very fresh and delicately flavoured wine.

Vintage Brut Réserve Rosé (60% PN, 40% CH; 90–95% échelle; blended) The 1975 had a gentle shade of peach colour, and a delightfully fragrant nose, belying a big flavour with a touch of tannin and an earthy fruit character, but a gentle, rather elegant, finish. The 1976 suffered from excessive dosage and bore no relation to the earlier vintage.

Ruinart Père & Fils

Société Rémoise des Grand Vins de Champagne
4 rue de Crayère, Reims
Telephone (26) 85.40.29

Visits Monday to Friday throughout the year; weekends and public holidays by appointment for parties of over twenty-five people

Origin The house was founded on 1 September 1729 by Nicolas Ruinart (1697–1769), the nephew of Dom Thierry Ruinart (1657–1709), a Benedictine monk of the congregation of Saint-Maur and a friend and confidant of Dom Pérignon. Nicolas Ruinart started in the linen trade and it became his custom to present his customers with Champagne as a token of goodwill. The Champagne became so popular that the account book containing the entry for the first consignment, which marked the founding of this house, gradually accumulated more entries for wine than for linen, so that the trade in linen was eventually totally replaced by the trade in wine.

When in 1764 Nicolas was joined by his son Claude Ruinart (1731–98), the house of Ruinart became Ruinart Père & Fils.

Claude Ruinart's eldest son, Irénée, was particularly active in selling Ruinart Champagne to such famous customers as Napoleon, Joseph Bonaparte, king of Spain, Joachim Murat, king of Naples, and Talleyrand. He also sold wine to the Empress Josephine, but she refused to pay her bills after her divorce. Apart from being an astute businessman, he was successful in his political ambitions. On 6 June 1817 he was ennobled as Vicomte de Brimont by decree of Louis XVIII and, as deputy of the Marne and mayor of Épernay, he received the Empress Marie-Louise and, later, Charles X, the last king of France to be crowned at Reims Cathedral.

Irénée retired in 1830 to write *Traité sur la culture en terre calcaire* and was succeeded as head of the firm by his son Edmond. Edmond Ruinart was received by President Jackson at the White House in Washington; his son Edgar, who inherited his father's taste for travel, visited St Petersburg in 1860 and opened up the Russian market.

André Ruinart, who took over control from his father, Edgar's brother Charles, in 1888, was a pioneer of aviation who sponsored, with others, the first cross-Channel air race. The firm's buildings were completely destroyed by shelling during the Battle of the Marne. André literally went underground, conducting the firm's affairs from one of Ruinart's spectacular *crayères*. When further shelling damaged a water-main, flooding this temporary accommodation, he simply lashed the office furniture to a wooden platform and it was business as usual from a raft floating around a massive gallery eighty feet beneath the ground! André was succeeded in 1919 by his son Gerrard, but it was not until 1950, one year after Gerrard's nephew Bertrand Muré assumed control, that the house of Ruinart began to expand its business. In 1950, after an injection of capital from Baron Philippe de Rothschild, Ruinart actively promoted its Champagne in unison with advertisements for Château Mouton Rothschild. This association, which lasted until Moët & Chandon purchased Ruinart in 1963, was responsible for quadrupling sales. Under Moët & Chandon, Ruinart has doubled its production, yet has retained its independent, upmarket image. The Moët-Hennessy Group now has a 99.82% share in the house of Ruinart.

Vineyards 8 hectares at Sillery and 7 hectares at Brimont, representing 20% of the total production.
Purchases 95% échelle
Production 1.3 million bottles **Exports** 60%
Vinification notes *Prise de mousse* is carried out in half-bottles and jeroboams.
Average bottle-age of NV *cuvées* 3 years

Special interest The house is a member of the Syndicat de Grandes Marques de Champagne. It has perhaps the most dramatic-looking *crayères* in all Champagne.

WINES
House style: The wines are very refined and Chardonnay-based; always technically sound and often aesthetically brilliant.
NV Brut Tradition (30–40% PN, 30–40% PM, 25–30% CH; 94% échelle) A good, even *mousse*; elegant on the nose; crisp and fruity on the palate, but rather short on the finish.
Vintage Brut (70% PN/PM, 30% CH; 95% échelle) Very little tasted
Vintage Dom Ruinart Blanc de Blancs Brut (100% CH; 99% échelle) A very good Champagne, fuller than most blancs de blancs; sometimes a touch earthy, but usually very rich in fruit. Recommended years: 1973, 1975. The first vintage of this *cuvée de prestige* to be released was the 1959. It is a blend of Avize, Cramant and le Mesnil-sur-Oger on the Côte des Blancs and Sillery and Verzenay on the Montagne de Reims.
Vintage Dom Ruinart Rosé Brut (50% PN, 50% CH; 99% échelle; blended in light years, skin-contact in big years) In my opinion this wine has a touch more class than its far more popular *blanc de blancs* stable mate. This has an elegant colour; very fine and persistent *mousse*, rich and deep flavoured, long and well-balanced. Recommended years: 1973, 1975.
Coteaux Champenois Ruinart Chardonnay (100% CH) Fresh and quaffing, with a crunchy grape flavour. Not a great wine, and not even quite a fine wine, but without doubt the best white Coteaux Champenois regularly produced by the houses after that of Moët & Chandon's Saran.

Sacotte

13 rue de la Verrerie, Magenta, Épernay
Telephone (26) 55.31.90
Visits Not permitted
Origin The house was established at Magenta in 1887 by Léon Sacotte, a vigneron from Avenay, in the Val d'Or, who started making his own Champagne. By a daughter from his second marriage to one Marie-Pauline Dezy, he became father-in-law to Gaston Burtin. Burtin and Sacotte's son Henri very successfully ran the business until 1933, when Gaston Burtin left to form his own house, Marne &

Champagne. Today the small house of Sacotte is run by Michel Sacotte, grandson of the founder.
Production 250,000 bottles

WINES
NV Carte Rubis Brut, Vintage Brut (66% PN/PM, 33% CH), Vintage Blanc de Blancs, Rosé Brut

Sacy

6 rue de Verzenay, Verzy
Telephone (26) 49.42.25
Origin The house was established in 1969 by the current owner, André Sacy.
Production 220,000 bottles

WINES
House style: Only tasted once at Olympia in 1981; I was not impressed.
NV Carte d'Or Brut (2 years' bottle-age), NV Carte Verte Brut (4 years' bottle-age), NV Carte Verte Rosé Brut, Vintage Carte Verte Brut

De Saint-Marceaux

4 avenue du Général Giraud, Reims
Telephone (26) 40.20.05
Visits By appointment
Origin The house was founded in 1837 by Jean Alexandre de Saint Marceaux, a son of Augustin Marie Guillaume de Paul de Saint Marceaux. It quickly established a reputation, it supplied the King of the Belgians and became popular throughout Europe, particularly in Russia. In the latter part of the nineteenth century, de Saint Marceaux produced several different labels; the Dry Royal was greatly esteemed in the United States of America, while the much drier Carte d'Or was favoured in England. After the death of Jean Alexandre's youngest son, Charles René, in 1915, de Saint Marceaux passed through various hands before it was purchased in 1974 by Jacques Lepitre. Lepitre had been producing de Saint Marceaux Champagne for its owner, a Monsieur Édouard Miailhe, for almost twenty years, therefore his acquisition was in fact maintaining a continuity of style for the de Saint Marceaux brand. Along with the brands of George Goulet and Abel Lepitre, de Saint Marceaux is now under the umbrella company of the Société des Grandes Champagnes de Reims.
Vineyards None   **Production** 170,000 bottles

WINES
House style: I have only tasted the NV Brut, which has always been well-made and offers a good mouthful of clean fruit.
NV Brut, NV Sec, NV Demi-Sec, Vintage Brut, Vintage Blanc de Blancs Brut (the 1977 was the last vintage produced of this *cuvée*) and Rosé Brut

Salon

le Mesnil-sur-Oger, Avize
Telephone (26) 50.53.69
Visits Not permitted
Origin The house was established in 1914 by Eugène-Aimé Salon (1867–1943), who was born at Pocancy, a small agricultural village on the plains of Champagne, to the east of le Mesnil-sur-Oger. Eugène-Aimé spent much of his boyhood assisting his brother-in-law, Marcel Guillaume, in his work as *chef de caves* for a small firm producing a single vineyard Champagne called Clos Tarin. In due course Marcel was to establish the *co-opérative*, the Union des Producteurs de la Côte des Blancs.

Although his boyhood experience kindled in Salon an enthusiasm for wine-making, he did not enter the trade for some years. Trained as a teacher, he rejected this profession in favour of commerce and joined a Parisian firm of furriers called Chapel. After achieving success in this business, and after involving himself in politics, he purchased five hectares of vines at le Mesnil-sur-Oger where, in his spare time, he set about realising his youthful ambition: to create a perfectly balanced Champagne from a single growth and from just one grape variety, the Chardonnay.

Whenever Eugène-Aimé entertained his associates he naturally offered them his own unlabelled Champagne, and was soon besieged with requests for supplies, which at first he declined, since he was still principally a furrier. As the requests mounted, however, he released a few bottles, business rapidly accumulated and he found himself running a Champagne firm.

Eugène-Aimé now enlarged his vineyard and started buying grapes from other growers in le Mesnil-sur-Oger. He used only the best fruit and only the *vin de cuvée*; all else was sold off. Furthermore, he only produced vintage Champagne and wines of undeclared years were also disposed of. Salon appears to have been the first house to exploit commercially a Blanc de Blancs Champagne.

Salon was Maxim's house wine during the 1920s and, throughout that decade and the 1930s it achieved its pinnacle of fame. Since Eugène-Aimé Salon died in 1943, the reputation of this exceptional Champagne has never quite remained at the level achieved in its earlier years, although the quality of the wine has not deteriorated in the slightest. The house was acquired by Besserat de Bellefon in 1963 and is now controlled by the Pernod-Ricard Group via that house.

Vineyards 1 hectare at le Mesnil-sur-Oger, representing 15% of the total production.

Purchases Only from le Mesnil-sur-Oger and therefore 99% échelle.

Production 55,000 bottles **Exports** 40%
Stocks 270,000 bottles (1984)

Vinification notes The wines of Salon never undergo malo-lactic fermentation. The first fermentation is carried out in vats, but maturation of the wine in *demi-muids*. Since the house was acquired by Besserat de Bellefon, the antithesis of Salon, respect for tradition has nevertheless been maintained, and the determination to conform to the highest standards of quality has seen the *à la glace* method of disgorgement abandoned in favour of the *à la volée*, in order that each bottle can be individually sniffed (the *à la glace* method kills the nose) by skilled *dégorgeurs*.

Special interest The house is a member of the Syndicat de Grandes Marques de Champagne.

WINES
House style: I can do no better than reiterate the description by Colin Fenton MW, whom it was my privilege to know for a short while. The following is extracted from a profile of Salon which Colin was compiling prior to his untimely death.

'The hallmark of the Salon flavour is its alluring taste of walnuts which is found in those grapes from its chosen vineyards: it is present when the wine is young and becomes more obvious – yet still subtle – as it grows older.

The second most striking quality of Salon le Mesnil is its richness in fruit – and yet at the same time it retains an enticing level of acidity which makes it beautifully fresh and vibrant. Its distinction comes from this combination of elegance and concentration, for it possesses a delicate balance of apparently contrary qualities – a dual excellence of depth and lightness – in a word, finesse.'

In addition to my notes, I give those of Colin Fenton, who obviously managed to taste more vintages of this very special Champagne than I:

1976 Cuvée 'S' Pale-lemon-gold colour; very fine and typically smooth *mousse*; crushed digestive biscuit nose and rich Chardonnay flavour; complexities just beginning to accumulate (TS).

1973 Pale-gold colour; super-smooth *mousse*; delightful blend of spring flowers and fresh cream on the nose; richer than most 1973s; already a long, complex wine with a marvellous and seductive balance, yet with plenty of room for development (TS). Flowery and fine, combines the qualities of 1969 and 1971 (CF).

1971 Pale-gold colour; fresh and elegant nose, with a crumbly biscuit character in the background; a very rich flavour seeming to lie gracefully on the palate, before tailing off into an exquisite finish. The same wine, tasted with Colin Fenton at his home in London, seemed to be very different, with an ultra-fine, but softer *mousse*, and a complex palate, accentuated with a hint of lemon-peel (TS). Not quite so heavy with fruit as 1969 but more elegant (CF).

1971 Cuvée 'S' Pale-gold colour; very fine, persistent *mousse*; much fresher and 'younger' than the other 1971, yet still rich; an intense wine with a penetrating flavour and great length (TS).

1969 Very fine: still youthful and full of fruit. Hint of walnuts (CF).

1966 Most attractive nose, with completely absorbed mild walnut flavour. Balanced and round without the fullness of the 1969 (CF).

1964 Light, pale colour, incredible freshness and outstanding balance (CF).

1961 Light golden colour, marvellous equilibrium between *mousse* and fruit. Full of charm and strength: racy and delicate (CF).

1959 Pale gold colour; persistent *mousse* of ultra-fine bubbles; yoghurt nose, amazingly youthful for its age; a strong wine with great depth (TS). Haunting creamy nose, pale colour showing maturity without age; minuscule *mousse*, and lovely race (CF).

1955 Extremely fine. Age has given it lusciousness without loss of freshness. Beautiful combination of fruit and elegance (CF).

1953 Nose a little tired: palate more vigorous with mature Chardonnay flavour; probably now at its zenith (CF).

1949 A legendary wine of surpassing beauty: a complex flavour of walnuts and warmth, in which an almost roasted element of grapes is marvellously apparent. Outstanding (CF).

1948 Strong structure and concentration but not so balanced as 1947: still has a point of hardness with an otherwise remarkable softness and ripeness (CF).

1947 Light gold colour, *mousse* has obviously softened, but its tenacity has not abated; an ever-unfolding and extremely complex nose, very rich with many nuances (one, unforgettably, of crushed 'Nice' biscuits); a deep, creamy flavour, with an indelible finish of walnuts, hazelnuts and macaroons (TS). Pronounced rich nutty nose: great depth: perfection (CF).

When Paul Bergeot (now in control of de Venoge) introduced the new packaging, including a slightly fatter bottle shape, he wanted to use it for the 1971 vintage. The difficulty was that the 1971 was already bottled and bubbly. There was, however, no stopping Monsieur Bergeot: the remaining bottles of 1971 were decanted into a vat, mixed with a light *liqueur de tirage* and rebottled in the new vessel to obtain a second *prise de mousse*. This treatment was also applied to some of the 1973 vintage (which I did not taste), but since then, all Salon Cuvée 'S' Champagnes have been normally processed. If you should acquire both 'old' and 'new' 1971 or 1973, a comparative tasting of these Champagnes (twice-fermented and thrice-fermented respectively) could be very instructive.

A. Secondé Prevoteau

2 rue du Château, Ambonnay
Telephone (26) 59.01.59
Visits For purchases
Origin André Secondé's family have long had close viticultural ties with the great house of Roederer. His grandfather and his great-grandfather both supplied Rouge d'Ambonnay, destined to tint the pink Champagne with which Roederer supplied the Tsars of Russia. André initially sold his wines as a *récoltant-manipulant*, but he is now a *négociant-manipulant*. However, all Secondé Prevoteau wines are entirely the production of his family's vineyards.
Vineyards 12 hectares at Ambonnay, Bouzy and Louvois
Production 80,000 bottles
Exports Small shipments to West Germany

WINES
House style: I have tasted only the NV Princesses de France Brut, and only on one occasion; it was dry, correct and well-matured. NV Cuvée de Réserve, NV Princesses de France Brut, NV Princesses de France Blanc de Blancs (single-vineyard wine from la Butte des Aguzon), NV Princesses de France Rosé, NV Fleuron de France (pure Ambonnay Blanc de Noirs), Coteaux Champenois Ambonnay Rouge.

SAME

Société Anonyme de Magenta-Épernay
1 rue des Cotelles, Épernay
Telephone (26) 54.23.46
Origin The house was established in 1925 by Eugène Charmat, the inventor of the *cuve close* bulk production process for making cheap sparkling wine. In 1972, under the control of Philippe Lombard, SAME acquired the house of Marie Stuart and, in 1985, bought de Cazanove from Moët-Hennessy.
Sales 2 million bottles
Special interest The house is a major producer of private label, BOB Champagnes and non-Champagne *vins mousseux*.

WINES
NV Brut, NV Demi-Sec, Rosé Brut, Blanc de Blancs

SOREVI

Société rémoise des vins
61 rue de Verdun, Reims
Telephone (26) 07.34.10
SOREVI's principal *marque*, Champagne Paul Bur, was established in 1861. It was acquired in 1950 by Robert Charmat, the creator of Veuve de Vernay, an inexpensive *vin mousseux* made by *cuve close*, the bulk production process invented by his father, Eugène Charmat. In 1976 the distribution of the Veuve Paul Bur range was undertaken by the Berger Group and sales (which had stood at 120,000 bottles in 1974) rose to a million in 1979. But the tiny vintage of 1978 had caused great problems for the rapidly expanding house and, in 1979, it was taken over by SOREVI, a subsidiary of Berger. The Champagne is now produced for SOREVI by the Centre Vinicole de la Champagne, a co-operative in Chouilly.
Special interest Bur is the only Champagne whose makers are permitted to use an image of Reims Cathedral on its label.

NV Brut, NV Demi-Sec, NV Rosé Brut,
Vintage Brut

Taittinger

Compagnie Commerciale et Viticole
Champenoise
9 Place Saint-Niçaise, Reims
Telephone (26) 85.45.35
Visits Daily throughout the year, with the
exception of Christmas and New Year. French
and English are spoken, and there are excellent
audio-visual facilities in many languages.
Origin The house of Fourneaux was one of the
very first Champagne firms to be established. It
was founded in 1734 by Jacques Fourneaux,
the son of an important vineyard owner in
Rilly-la-Montagne. Under the control of
Jérome Alexandre Fourneaux and Antoine
Martial Forest-Fourneaux, the firm's title was
changed to Forest-Fourneaux & Cie. It was to
Jérome Fourneaux that the young widowed
Nicole-Barbe Clicquot turned for help and
advice, when her husband died, and it was
Fourneaux who blended all the Veuve Clicquot
wines between 1805 and 1810.

The formative years of Forest-Fourneaux &
Cie were, however, relatively uneventful,
compared to the last fifty years. The
phenomenal success of this firm started when it
was acquired by the Taittinger family after the
First World War. It was Pierre Taittinger who
changed the firm's name, first to Ets Taittinger
Mailly & Cie, then, simply, to Taittinger. He
set about building up the company's vineyards
and purchased a château and estate called la
Marquetterie as a centre for these vine-growing
activities. The name la Marquetterie accurately
reflects the extraordinary viticultural
characteristics of this estate, which has a
history of cultivating alternating plots of black
and white grapes (currently there are nine
hectares of Pinot and eight of Chardonnay). It
was at la Marquetterie that Brother Jean
Oudart experimented with the production of
sparkling Champagne at the same time as Dom
Pérignon and for twenty-seven years after his
death.

In 1933, the house of Taittinger was
transferred from Mailly to the ancient home of
the Counts of Champagne in Reims. This was
built in the thirteenth century for Thibault IV, a
descendant of Charlemagne and heir to the
Counts of Champagne and the kingdom of
Navarre. The Taittingers restored the property
shortly after the First World War, under the
supervision of the French Ministry of Fine Arts.
Later on the firm moved to Place Saint-Niçaise,
keeping the ancient home for special banquets
and ceremonies. The cellars at Place Saint-
Niçaise contain traces of the thirteenth century
Saint-Niçaise Abbey which, in 1717, was
visited by Tsar Peter the Great of Russia. These
are showpiece cellars for Taittinger which are
reserved for the *cuvée de prestige* Comtes de
Champagne, the 'working' cellars being located
in the Rue de la Justice.
Vineyards 250 hectares in thirty growths (half
planted with Chardonnay), representing 50%
of the total production.
Sales 3.4 million bottles (1983)
Exports 55%
Stocks 15.2 million bottles (November 1983)
Vinification notes About a quarter of the
production is cask-fermented; the rest is
fermented in stainless steel, using modern
vinification methods. *Liège et agrafe* is used for
all Comtes de Champagne and *prise de mousse*
in jereboams for Comtes de Champagne. With
Piper-Heidsieck, Taittinger were one of the first
houses to adopt automatic *remuage*, utilising
computer-controlled *gyropalettes*.
Average bottle-age of NV *cuvées* 3 years
Other *marques* Irroy
Special interest The house is a member of the
Syndicat de Grandes Marques de Champagne.
Taittinger also own the *Méthode Champenoise*
houses of Monmousseau and Bouvet in the
Loire, the Concorde group of hotels, and many
other diversified interests.

House style: Sheer length, great style and
elegance. The wines are heavily influenced by
Chardonnay.
NV Brut Réserve (60% PN/PM, 40% CH;
95% échelle) This is a problematical
Champagne: sometimes it has a poor, almost
'soapy' style; at other times it can be so rich and
elegant that one would mistake it for a fine
vintage Taittinger. Half-bottles are invariably
disappointing, but if you chance on a bottle
from one of the exceptionally fine shipments –
then stock up.
NV Brut Absolu (60% PN, 40% CH; 95%
échelle) Taittinger's contribution to the non-
dosage market; not tasted.
NV Vintage Brut (60% PN, 40% CH; 95%
échelle) The Chardonnay seems to charge
through the Pinot, giving the vintage a greater

length than the NV, and a more refined style. Recommended years: 1976, 1979.

Vintage Collection (60% PN, 40% CH; 95–100% échelle) A new *cuvée* which will be packaged in various bottle designs created by famous artists. Victor Vasarély, the Hungarian-born Op-artist, was chosen to design the presentation for the 1978 vintage, the wine selected to launch this collection. He has adorned the gold-coloured bottle with an interesting illusion which he calls 'Vega' – rectangular turquoise shapes creating a spherical effect which we are told, is intended to suggest the idea of eternal renewal. The bottle itself is disappointing – unpainted, and sheathed in a clumsy plastic cladding. Arman, the French contemporary sculptor and painter, is responsible for the 1981 Vintage Collection. The wines are as exceptional as the designs.

Vintage Comtes de Champagne Blanc de Blancs Brut (100% CH; 95–100% échelle) It is always a privilege to drink this remarkable Champagne: a pure Chardonay wine first produced in the vintage of 1952, but in no way typical of a Blanc de Blancs. I am amazed by those who characterise Comtes de Champagne as 'light and delicate' and can only imagine that the people responsible for such misleading descriptions have all drunk the wine far too early. It has nothing to do with whether you like your Champagne young or old, because Comtes de Champagne retains a refreshing crispness of youth well into its second decade. Most vintages of this wine need at least eight years, and many require ten or twelve. The 1973 had reached its peak in 1985, but would remain there until the early 1990s, whereas the 1975 was only just beginning to turn into the truly beautiful wine it is destined to be. The 1970 reached its peak at some time about 1980 and I cannot imagine when it will drop from its current state of perfection, but the 1971 is already in a slow decline.

Vintage Comtes de Champagne Rosé Brut (100% PN; 100% échelle) In its short career (the first vintage, the 1966, was put on the market in 1972) this has proved to be a consistently attractive wine. Great finesse on the nose belies the fact that it is packed with plenty of mouthwatering fruit flavour. The 1970 was superb in 1983, the 1971 seemed highly dosed and thus spoilt, the 1975 was delicious and drinking well, but the 1976 was a long way from being ready.

De Venoge

30 avenue de Champagne, Épernay
Telephone (26) 55.01.01
Visits By appointment
Origin The house was established in 1837 by Henri-Marc de Venoge at Mareuil-sur-Aÿ; it moved to Épernay in 1839 and takes its name from the river which flows into Lake Geneva. Henry Vizetelly, in *A History of Champagne* (1882), described the firm as 'De Venoge, the great Épernay manufacturer of common-class champagne'. It achieved its greatest success between 1845 and 1869 under the control of Joseph de Verage, Henri-Marc's son. De Venoge was never considered a classic Champagne house and it has never pretended to produce great wines, but since its acquisition in 1958 by the Trouillard family, it has steadily built up a reputation as a consistent producer of well-made, good-value Champagnes. In January 1981, the Trouillard-de-Venoge group was sold to Charles Heidsieck-Henriot, but in March 1983 Paul Bergeot, formerly of Besserat de Bellefon, took control. Anyone who knows Monsieur Bergeot will realise that something will now happen here, whether it be rapid expansion and modernisation or going back to the most traditional of methods.
Vineyards 6 hectares at Aÿ (PN), representing less than 5% of the total production.
Purchases Averaging 90% échelle
Production 1.2–1.5 million bottles
Exports 50%
Stocks 4 million bottles
Average bottle-age of NV *cuvées* 3 years

WINES
House style: These wines used to have a good landed age, but, probably because the wine merchants in question now sell more Champagne, de Venoge appears to be getting younger. As I remember them, they are full, round and mature, with a creamy richness – not great, but very drinkable. As Monsieur Bergeot is now in complete charge, even blending the wines, the following notes may prove to be of no more than historical interest.
NV Cordon Bleu Brut (60% PN/PM, 40% CH; 91% échelle) This Champagne was first launched in 1864. It has a soft yeasty nose, persistent but not over-strong *mousse*, good depth of creamy flavour and a sound balance. Occasionally some half-bottles can crop up which are really delicious.

NV Blanc de Blancs Crémant Brut (100% CH; 95% échelle) With but a few exceptions this represents both the best wine and the best value. The most memorable *cuvée* I remember was based on the 1979 vintage: it had an extraordinary perfume, the sort that can only be obtained from Cramant, Avize and le Mesnil-sur-Oger, a soft and gentle *mousse* and a very long flavour, hinting at honey. A rare delight, but few bottles will be available by the time this book is published.

Crémant Rosé (95% échelle) First produced in the 1860s, this wine has been resurrected by Paul Bergeot, who after 13 years at the helm of Besserat de Bellefon, should know something about *crémant rosé*.

Vintage Brut (40% PN, 60% CH; 95% échelle) The 1976 was attractively soft and easy to drink for that difficult year.

Vintage des Princes Brut (100% CH; 98–100% échelle) I have only tasted the 1975: a full, rich and long Chardonnay wine, with the perfume of Chardonnay, but far smoother than I expected. This wine would command more respect if it was sold in something more akin to a standard Champagne bottle, rather than in a cross between a ship's decanter and a dandy's perfume jar.

Vintage Rosé Brut (100% PN; 95% échelle; skin-contact) Also a wine which I have only tasted once, and again, the 1975. It has a bright-pink colour, and is a fleshy, flavoursome wine, which is easy to drink, but lacks elegance.

Veuve Clicquot-Ponsardin

12 rue du Temple, Reims
Telephone (26) 40.25.42
Visits Daily
Origin In 1772, Philippe Clicquot Muiron opened a trading house in Reims, dealing mainly in fabrics and banking, with very modest transactions concerning Champagne. But it was through the supply of wines to friends and good customers that so many of the most famous names in Champagne were established, and thus it was that the house of Clicquot was born.

The total Clicquot production, in those early years, amounted to some five thousand bottles, made from some six hectares of vines at Bouzy and Ambonnay. In 1799, Clicquot's son François married Nicole-Barbe Ponsardin.

Although she was a daughter of a famous baron, the ceremony had to be held in a wine cellar as, in the aftermath of the Revolution, the Church was a banned institution.

After François had taken over his father's various commercial activities in 1801, it soon became evident that his preference was for wines, not drapery or banking. He spent much time in the vineyards and villages, supervising the operations of a much expanded Champagne production, and frequently travelled abroad, soliciting famous and influential clients. During these absences, François and Nicole-Barbe exchanged a wealth of correspondence. The young couple were obviously very close and, in the pursuit of business, decidedly of a single mind. A daughter Clementine was born in 1800, and five years later François died, aged only thirty, after suffering malignant fever for two weeks. Philippe Clicquot, who had retired four years earlier, was heartbroken by his son's death and, in the wake of the disastrous harvest of 1805, wanted to sell the business. But François' widow, Nicole-Barbe, then only twenty-seven years of age, had the greater part of her life in front of her. She also had to think of Clementine, her only link with François, and she therefore opposed her father-in-law's plan. The pain of her loss became the driving force which compelled her to take over the house of Clicquot. She sought the assistance of her late husband's principal associate, a Monsieur Bohne, and, for the purpose of effecting the blends, that of Jérôme Fourneaux, who was at that time head of Forest-Fourneaux & Cie (later Taittinger), and launched herself into the male preserve of the Champagne industry, giving her firm the title of Veuve Clicquot-Ponsardin, Fourneaux & Cie.

In the first of several letters of complaint which Bohne wrote from Russia in 1806, he criticised the *mousse* of the firm's Champagne: 'This is a terrible thing that gets up and goes to bed with me: toad's eyes! I like large eyes everywhere, except in champagne'. In 1810, when the firm was on a good financial footing, Madame Clicquot relinquished the services of Fourneaux and engaged a skilful *chef de caves* called Antoine Müller.

In the wake of Napoleon's defeats, yet before peace was finally achieved, the house of Clicquot took the calculated risk of shipping the vintage of 1811 to Russia through the Allied blockade in 1814. At Bohne's first stop,

Koenigsberg in Prussia, he wrote in a letter dated July 1814,

'They worship my wine ... of all the wines that have turned Northern heads, the *cuvée* of Madame Clicquot's 1811 has no equal. Delicious to taste, it is a real assassin, and whoever wishes to know it should tie themselves to the chair, otherwise they may find themselves under the table with the crumbs!'

The departure of Fourneaux and the arrival of Müller thus marked a dramatic change in the quality, and thereby in increase in the reputation, of Champagne Clicquot. It was Müller who was instrumental in developing the system of *remuage*, which Madame Clicquot had been working on since at least 1806. According to a letter written much later in the century by Alfred Werlé, the son of Comte Édouard Werlé (an employee of Madame Clicquot's since 1821 and her partner from 1831 – of whom more later), it was Antoine Müller, who, in 1818, hit upon the supreme importance of cutting the holes in racks in which the bottles undergoing *remuage* are racked at an angle of 45 degrees. In March 1822, Müller resigned from Veuve Clicquot and set up his own Champagne establishment, called Müller-Ruinart, employing the future founder of the house of Bollinger, Jacques Bollinger, then aged nineteen.

Madame Clicquot had married her daughter Clementine to the penniless Comte Louis de Chevigné on 13 September 1817. This was not a wise choice, but no doubt Madame Clicquot was charmed by the Comte's personality and felt sorry for his circumstances (his father had been killed during the royalist rising in the Vendée and his mother thrown into prison with her six children, including the newborn Louis).

However, Louis de Chevigné, although denied the grandeur to which his birth would have entitled him before the Revolution, was well-trained in the practice of extravagant living, and in the art of ingratiating oneself into the company of those who could afford to pay for such luxuries, by his mentor Richard Castel. Married to Clementine and ensuring that he was adored by his mother-in-law, he found in her a bottomless cash-box from which to draw to meet his gambling debts and other expenses.

It was upon Chevigné's urging that Madame Clicquot purchased and lavishly renovated the Château de Boursault, a few miles west of Épernay. She would probably have been led into other reckless ventures had it not been for one of her employees, Édouard Werlé. In 1828 a famous bank in Paris (with whom the Clicquot capital was deposited) collapsed. Without disclosing his intention to Madame Clicquot, Werlé set off to the city to trade in his own private fortune to pay off the creditors, who had started demanding immediate settlement of their debts. This was, in effect, a repetition of the daring action taken by Jean-Remy Moët exactly thirty years earlier (see under Moët & Chandon), with an equally successful result. The only difference was that the money used was not Clicquot's, but that of one of its employees. When the widow heard of this gesture, she repaid Werlé by making him a partner and by putting him in charge of the day-to-day running of the house. Now it was the sombre-faced Werlé that Louis de Chevigné had to approach when he wanted money, not his adoring mother-in-law. The amount of money going into Chevigné's pocket was from now onwards drastically reduced, but although this enabled the house of Clicquot to prosper, it did not completely foil Louis. He set about writing a rather risqué book of poems entitled *Les Contes Rémois*, which he had reprinted every time he required some money, knowing that his mother-in-law would buy up each edition to keep such licentious work out of the bookstalls.

Madame Clicquot died peacefully at her luxurious Château Boursault in 1866, at the age of eighty-eight, leaving the business – very sensibly – to Édouard Werlé. In 1884 the house of Clicquot passed to Édouard's son Alfred, who had married the grand-daughter of the Duc de Montebello. For fifty years the firm was controlled by Alfred's son-in-law, Comte Bertrand de Mun, whose son-in-law, Comte Bernard de Vogüé, today runs Clicquot.

Vineyards 280 hectares at Ambonnay (PN), Avize (CH), Aÿ (PN), Bouzy (PN), Cramant (CH), Hautvillers, Louvois, Mailly (PN), Mareuil-sur-Aÿ, le Mesnil-sur-Oger (CH), Oger (CH), Pargny-les-Reims, Vertus (CH + PN), Verzenay (PN), Verzy (PN), Villedommange (PN) and Villers-Marmery, averaging 96% échelle (more than 160 hectares are 99–100% échelle) and representing 30% of the total production.

Purchases 97% échelle

Production 6.5 million bottles

Sales 6 million bottles (6.5 million in 1978–81)

Exports 75%
Stocks 26 million bottles (1983)
Vinification notes *Prise de mousse* is carried
out in half-bottles. Large-scale mechanical
remuage is used, with *gyropalettes*.
Average bottle-age of NV *cuvées* 3 years
Special interest The house is a member of the
Syndicat de Grandes Marques de Champagne.
In 1978 Veuve Clicquot purchased full control
of the house Canard-Duchêne, situated at
Ludes, in the Montagne de Reims. Following
the example of Moët & Chandon, Clicquot
entered the perfume business when it acquired
Givenchy at the end of 1981 and the beginning
of 1982.

WINES
House style: Supremely rich and well-aged,
Veuve Clicquot Champagnes are of consistently
high quality.
NV Brut (50% PN, 20% PM, 30% CH; 97% +
échelle) Luxurious *mousse*; full-flavoured and
rich in fruit; a long wine, not as brut as some,
but with good body and vinosity.
NV Demi-Sec (50% PN, 20% PM, 30% CH;
97% échelle) Good creamy *mousse*; very
generous nose; well-balanced, deep-flavoured
and long. This demi-sec is sold as 'Rich' in the
United Kingdom.

Through the
enterprise of Mme
Veuve Clicquot
and Antoine
Müller, *remuage*
became
widespread in the
nineteenth century

Vintage Brut (67% PN, 33% CH; 97% + échelle) Perhaps best described as a fuller, richer version of the NV, which retains the Clicquot style while portraying the vintage in question. Recommended years: 1973, 1975, 1979.

Vintage Grande Dame Brut (67% PN, 33% CH; 97% + échelle) A much mellower wine than the rest of the Clicquot range, this wine can develop ripe, nutty and complex nuances of maturity, yet retain a pale colour and a great vitality, with a strong and persistent stream of tiny bubbles. Recommended years: 1973, 1975. Produced entirely from those vineyards which originally belonged to Madame Clicquot, the first vintage of 1969 launched this *cuvée* in 1972 to celebrate the firm's bicentenary. The metal cap on top of the cork carries a reproduction of a portrait of the great lady, painted by the nineteenth century artist Léon Cogniet.

Vintage Rosé Brut (67% PN, 33% CH; 97% + échelle; blended) A delightfully peach-coloured wine, always delicious yet often contradictory in character – full but light, rich but elegant. The Vintage Brut Rosé 1976 and the Royal Wedding Cuvée Brut Rosé 1976 (marketed in 1981) are two different wines. The former, being a true 1976, is of course much fuller than normal, but it is no match for the latter, a very deep-coloured Champagne with a big red wine nose, powerful flavour and a positive tannic finish. Recommended years: 1973, 1975. Veuve Clicquot first produced a pink Champagne in 1777: this is the oldest recorded vintage of such a wine from any house.

Coteaux Champenois Occasionally produced; very attractive presentation, but only average quality.

Vollereaux

48 rue Léon Bourgeois, Pierry, Épernay
Telephone (26) 54.03.05
Visits Monday to Saturday, preferably by appointment
Origin The house was founded in 1933.
Vineyards 40 hectares
Production 350,000 bottles
Average bottle-age of NV *cuvées* 3 years

WINES
NV Brut, NV Extra Dry, NV Demi-Sec, NV Rosé Brut, Blanc de Blancs Brut, Vintage Brut, Coteaux Champenois

Waris & Chenayer

1 rue Pasteur, Avize
Origin The house was founded by Vincent Waris (1875–1927) and his father Armand Waris in 1898 at Avize, on the Côte des Blancs. While the firm was under the control of Jean-Marie Waris (1904–77), Marcel Chenayer joined it, and its title was changed to Waris & Chenayer in 1927.
Production 80,000 bottles

WINES
NV Super Imperator Brut, Rosé Brut, Grand Crémant Brut, Blanc de Blancs Brut, Vintage Brut, Cuvée Étrusque (the *cuvée de prestige* of the house)

Other Houses

de Castelnau

Société Sparnaciennes de Vins de Champagne
9 rue J. Chandon Moët, Épernay
Telephone (26) 54.04.06

Chamcomex

67 rue de l'Hôpital, Épernay
Telephone (26) 54.20.10

Chaudron Guérin

Route de Billy-le-Grand, Vaudemanges
Telephone (26) 69.57.84

Cote & Sandrin

Celles-sur-Ource, Bar-sur-Seine
Telephone (25) 38.50.06

François Diligent

Buxeuil, Bar-sur-Seine
Telephone (25) 38.50.76

Jacquinot & Cie

St Martin d'Ablois, Épernay
Telephone (26) 54.36.81

Eugène Ralle

B.P. 6
51360 Verzenay
Telephone (26) 49.40.12

Théophile Roederer

20 rue Andrieux
51058 Reims
Telephone (26) 47.59.81
This house has had commercial links with the great house of Louis Roederer since 1904.

J. de Telmont

Damery, 51200 Épernay
Visits By appointment
Run by the l'Hôpital family, which owns 24 hectares of primarily Pinot Noir vines. J. de Telmont has been experimenting with huge 4,000-bottle *gyropalettes* for *remuage*. Champagnes of this firm are remarkably good value. The Grande Réserve Brut NV is a joy to drink – never a bad bottle – and the Blanc de Blancs repays a little ageing. A good value house deserving more recognition.

Vranken sa

39 rue du Général Leclerc, Vertus
Telephone (26) 52.23.54
This is an important small house with annual sales of almost a million bottles in 1984. The *marques* include: Veuve Monnier, Charles Laffite, Comte d'Avlone and Doyard.

15

Champagne Co-operative Profiles

I have no shame about being a Champagne Socialist – I believe in
Champagne for everyone.

John Mortimer, 'Wogan' TV Show, BBC 1, 25 February 1984

Ch. de l'Auche

Also Nectar de St Remi
Co-opérative Vinicole de Germigny-Janvry-
Rosnay
Janvry, Gueux, Marne
Telephone (26) 03.63.40
Origin The *co-opérative* was established in 1961.
Membership 126 members
Vineyards Total collective holdings of 130
hectares: 18.80 of Pinot Noir, 79.00 of Pinot
Meunier and 7.20 of Chardonnay
Production 754,000 bottles, plus the
equivalent of 937,000 kilograms of grapes sold
to *négociants*
**Sold direct under the *Co-opérative*
label** 200,000 bottles
Sold by members 430,500 bottles
Stock 1 million bottles maximum
Vinification notes Horizontal Vaslin hydraulic
presses are used. The first fermentation is
carried out in stainless steel, *remuage* in hand-
operated *gyropalettes*.

WINES
Ch. de l'Auche Grande Réserve Brut (20% PN,
80% PM)
Vintage Nectar de St Remi (50% PN/PM,
50% CH)

Richard de Ayala

Union des Propriétaires Récoltants
le Mesnil sur Oger
Telephone (26) 57.53.23
Membership 450 members
Vineyards 280 hectares
Production 200,000 bottles
Sold direct 120,000 bottles

Beaumont des Crayères

Co-opérative Vinicole de Mardeuil
64 rue de la Liberté, Mardeuil
Telephone (26) 55.29.40
Membership 200 members
Vineyards 70 hectares
Production 200,000 bottles
Sold direct 150,000 bottles

De Blemond

Co-opérative Vinicole de Cuis
Cuis
Telephone (26) 55.12.12
Membership 85 members
Vineyards 35 hectares
Production 150,000 bottles
Sold direct 60,000 bottles

Centre Vinicole de la Champagne

'Plumecoq', Chouilly
Telephone (26) 54.50.60
Origin The *co-opérative* was established in
1972, since when investment has been
continuous, with a corresponding expansion
programme. This is now the largest, most up-
to-date production plant in Champagne.
Membership CVC is not a *co-opérative* of
vignerons but a *co-opérative* of *co-opératives*. It
has seventy participating *co-opératives*,
through which it has an indirect membership of
4,000 growers.
Vineyards Total collective holding of 1,200
hectares: 264 of Pinot Noir, 792 of Pinot
Meunier and 144 of Chardonnay
Production 12 million bottles

Sold direct under the *Co-opérative* label 1.8 million bottles under the Bur label plus varying quantities of St Maurice, Besroches, Deprayères and Nicolas Feuillate. BOBS account for 30% of sales.
Sold by members 4 million bottles
Sold to *négociants* 2.5 million bottles (*sur lattes*)
Stock 25 million bottles

WINES
Various BOBS tasted mostly good, but Champagne Bur sold by SOREVI not tasted.

Cercle d'Or

Also Lacroix-Demiel
Union des Récoltants
Colombé-le-Sec
Telephone (25) 27.02.08
Origin The *co-opérative* was established in 1956 by eighteen local vignerons.
Membership 85 members
Vineyards 150 hectares around the villages of Colombé-le-Sec, Colombé-la-Fosse, Saulcy, Rouvres-les-Vignes and Lignol-le-Château
Sold direct under the *Co-opérative* label 80,000 bottles

WINES
Cercle d'Or: NV Brut, NV Extra Dry, NV Sec NV Demi-Sec, Cuvée Réservée
Lacroix-Demiel: NV Brut and NV Demi-Sec.

Chassenay d'Arce

Also Decôtanne
Co-opérative Vinicole des Coteaux de l'Arce
Ville-sur-Arce, Bar-sur-Seine
Telephone (25) 38.74.07
Origin The *co-opérative* was established in 1956.
Membership 130 members
Vineyards Total collective holding of 220 hectares: 194 of Pinot Noir, 6 of Chardonnay
Production 2 million kilograms
Sold direct under the *Co-opérative* label 500,000–800,000 bottles
Stock 2 million bottles

WINES
Chassenay d'Arce: NV Cuvée Séléction Brut, NV Cuvée Séléction Sec, NV Cuvée Séléction Demi-Sec, Blanc de Blancs Brut, Vintage Brut
Decôtanne: NV Brut, NV Sec, NV Demi-Sec

Clérambault

Co-opérative Vinicole de Neuville-sur-Seine & Buxeuil
Route Nationale, Neuville-sur-Seine
Telephone (25) 38.20.10
Origin The *co-opérative* was established in January 1951 by a group of thirty-eight vignerons cultivating some forty-four hectares of Gamay vines.
Membership 54 members
Vineyards Total collective holding of 110 hectares: 82.5 of Pinot Noir, 22 of Pinot Meunier and 5.5 of Chardonnay

WINES
Clérambault: NV Carte Blanche Brut, NV Carte Blanche Demi-Sec, NV Carte Noire Brut, NV Carte Noire Sec, NV Carte Noire Demi-Sec, Vintage Blanc de Blancs Brut, Rosé Brut, Coteaux Champenois Blanc

Clos de la Chapelle

Co-opérative Vinicole de Villedommange
2 rue de l'Église, Villedommange, Gueux
Telephone (26) 49.25.33
Sold direct under the *Co-opérative* label 120,000 bottles

WINES
Clos de la Chapelle: NV Brut Réserve

Raoul Collet

Co-opérative Générale des Vignerons
34 rue Jeanson, Aÿ-Champagne
Telephone (26) 55.15.88
Origin Established at Dizy in 1921, this is the oldest *co-opérative* in Champagne. In 1932 the *marque* of Alphonse Perrin was created to honour its founder, the *marques* of Gaston Delière and the Duc de Breuzy were launched in 1941 and, when its director for almost thirty years, Raoul Collet, died in 1960, a brand in his honour was introduced. These and other *marques* are sometimes used in addition to Champagne Raoul Collet.
Membership 300 members, with a further 100 from five intermediary *co-opératives*
Vineyards Total collective holding of 600 hectares: 390 of Pinot Noir, 150 of Pinot Meunier and 60 of Chardonnay, with an average échelle of 90%
Production 2 million bottles

Sold direct under the *Co-opérative* label 1.5 million bottles
Sold by members 300,000 bottles
Sold to *négociants* 200,000 bottles
Stock 3.5 million bottles

WINES
NV Carte Noire Brut (40% PN, 60% PM, 87% échelle)
NV Carte Rouge (90% PN, 10% CH; 94% échelle)
Vintage Carte d'Or (60% PN, 40% CH; 98% échelle)
Rosé Brut A fine, fresh and elegantly fruity wine.
Coteaux Champenois Blanc (80% PN, 20% CH; 96% échelle). Unusual for a still white wine of this region to contain a proportion of blanc de noirs.

René Florancy

Also Saint Gall and Orpale
Union Champagne
7 rue Pasteur, Avize
Telephone (26) 57.94.22
Origin The *co-opérative* was established in 1966.
Membership Union Champagne consists of 10 *co-opératives*, most of them situated on the Côte des Blancs, with a total membership of 1,100 vignerons
Vineyards Total collective holding of 1,000 hectares: 260 of Pinot Noir and 740 of Chardonnay, averaging 97% échelle.
Production 7 million bottles
Sold direct under the *Co-opérative* label 1 million bottles under René Florancy, Saint Gall, Orpale and various BOBs
Sold by members 1.2 million bottles
Sold to *négociants* 16,500 hectolitres of vin clair and 700,000 bottles *sur lattes*
Stock 10 million bottles

WINES
On the few occasions when I have tasted wines under the René Florancy label, I have been impressed by their quality and style. Union Champagne's ability, combined with its selective choice of membership (vignerons growing only Pinot Noir or Chardonnay in very high échelle vineyards), is evident in the final product.
René Florancy: NV Brut, NV Brut Tradition, Crémant Blanc de Blancs Brut, Brut Rosé
Saint Gall: NV Carte Noire Brut, NV Brut

Tradition, Blanc de Blancs Brut, Crémant Blanc de Blancs Brut, Blanc de Blancs Brut Non-Dosage
Orpale: Blanc de Blancs Brut. Tasted once only, it nevertheless showed remarkably well – marvellously mature and ripe, and truly indicative of how fine top-class Chardonnay can be with proper ageing.

Gruet & Fils

Co-opérative des Coteaux de Bethon
Rue du Chemin Neuf, Bethon
Telephone (26) 80.26.19
An association of sixty growers, producing a blanc de blancs, under the Champagne Gruet & Fils label, which they sell direct to customers.

Jacquart

La Co-opérative Régionale des Vins de Champagne
5 rue Gosset, Reims
Telephone (26) 07.20.20
Origin The *co-opérative* was established in 1961.
Membership 680 direct members and 14 local *co-opératives*
Vineyards Total collective holding of 1,000 hectares
Production 8 million bottles
Sold direct under the *Co-opérative* label 2 million bottles
Sold by members 3.5 million bottles

WINES
NV Brut Tradition, NV Brut Sélection (98% échelle), NV Brut Rosé (98% + échelle; blended with red wine from Bouzy, Ambonnay and Ludes), Vintage Brut (60% PN/PM, 40% CH, an *assemblage* of Mailly, Verzenay, Verzy, Aÿ, Chouilly and le Mesnil-sur-Oger wines), Vintage Blanc de Blancs Brut; a *cuvée de prestige* is due to be released soon.

Champagne Lancelot
Co-opérative Vinicole de Mancy

Mancy, Épernay
Telephone (26) 59.71.52
Origin The *co-opérative* was established in 1948.
Membership 120 members
Vineyards Total collective holding of 105 hectares: 15 of Pinot Noir, 60 of Pinot Meunier and 30 of Chardonnay, averaging 90% échelle

Production 750,000–800,000 bottles
**Sold direct under the *Co-opérative*
label** 600,000 bottles sold under supermarket
labels; the balance sold direct to private
restaurants and clients

WINES
NV Sélection Brut, NV Grande Réserve (a
Blanc de Noirs, with five to six years' bottle-
age), NV Rosé Brut (a base wine of Blanc de
Blanc to which red wine is added), Vintage
Brut, Vintage Blanc de Blancs Brut

Léonze d'Albe

Union Auboise des Producteurs de Vins de
Champagne
Domaine de Villeneuve, Bar-sur-Aube
Telephone (25) 29.85.57
Origin The *co-opérative* was established in
1967, and the first wines were marketed in
1970.
Membership 11 member *co-opératives*
Vineyards Total collective holding of 1,200
hectares, 98% of which are planted with Pinot
Noir
Production 1.1 million bottles
**Sold direct under the *Co-opérative*
label** 600,000 sold under the Léonze d'Albe
label in the UK, this wine being sold under the
Abel Jeannin label; 400,000 under other
marques
Stock 2.5 million bottles

WINES
These wines have been tasted once only, at the
co-opérative in 1980. A rosé and a vintage
Champagne are due to be added to the Léonze
d'Albe range.
NV Extra Quality Brut Réserve (Based on the
1977 vintage: relatively deep straw-yellow
colour; lively *mousse* of medium-large-sized
bubbles; an open, full and vegetal nose, earthy-
fruit flavour, good balance. Based on the 1969
vintage, not commercially available: noticeably
finer *mousse*; broken biscuit nose, rich and
fruity on the palate; the earthiness coming
through on the finish.
NV Grande Cuvée Brut (the 1976 vintage) A
much lighter straw colour; good yeasty nose;
an earthy-appley taste; coarse in texture and
short in finish. The annual production of this
cuvée is limited to some 7,000 bottles. The
union send their must to CVC at Chouilly,
where it is blended with an equal amount of

wine from the Marne and made into
Champagne; the bottles are returned *sur lattes*
to the *union*. The wine is marketed with three
years' age, one more than the Extra Quality
Brut Réserve.

Mailly-Champagne

Société de Producteurs Mailly-Champagne
Mailly-Champagne, Rilly-la-Montagne
Telephone (26) 49.41.10
Origin The *co-opérative* was established on 9
April 1929 by 24 founder members.
Membership 70 members
Vineyards Total collective holding of 70
hectares entirely within the commune of
Mailly: 52.5 of Pinot Noir and 17.5 of
Chardonnay
Production 450,000 bottles
Sold direct under *Co-opérative* label 450,000
bottles
Stock 1.5 million bottles

WINES
NV Brut Réserve (80% PN, 20% CH; 100%
échelle) Fresh, yeasty nose; very fine, very
strong *mousse*; lovely balance and length.
NV Brut Intégral (80% PN, 20% CH; 100%
échelle) Sampled once only (a blend of 1978
and 1979 tasted at Mailly in 1983). Too much
acetaldehyde on the nose; a strong, well-
structured wine with a powerful *mousse*, but it
needed a dosage.
NV Cuvée des Échansons Brut (80% PN, 20%
CH; 100% échelle) Sampled only once (a blend
of 1973 and 1975 tasted at Mailly in 1983)
A 'sweet' acetaldehyde-dominated nose and
appley flavour – I was not impressed.
NV Rosé Brut (100% PN, skin-contact) Very
open, almost 'sweet' nose; an extremely fruity,
well-balanced wine, reminiscent of strawberries
on the after-taste.
Vintage Brut (80% PN, 20% CH; 100%
échelle) Usually a sturdy, well-made wine, with
a fine and lasting *mousse*. The 1977 was
successful, if atypical for Mailly and unusual
for any Champagne: a soft and mature nose
strangely evocative of egg-custard and a fine
mousse; the wine has the nervousness of the
1977, but combined with a contradictory
elegance.
Coteaux Champenois Rouge, Coteaux
Champenois Blanc

Du Mont Hauban

Co-opérative Vinicole de Monthelon
Monthelon
Telephone (26) 59.70.27
Membership 150 members
Vineyards 120 hectares
Production 450,000 bottles
Sold direct 150,000 bottles

Palmer

Société Co-opérative de Producteurs des
Grands Terroirs de Champagne
67 rue Jacquart, Reims
Telephone (26) 07.35.07
Origin The *co-opérative* was established in
1947 at Avize, and relocated in Reims in 1959.
Membership 80 members
Vineyards Total collective holding of 160
hectares: 64 of Pinot Noir, 80 of Pinot Meunier
and 16 of Chardonnay, averaging 95% échelle
Production 1 million bottles
Sold direct under the *Co-opérative*
label 60,000 bottles under the Palmer label
and various *sous marques*
Sold by members 350,000 bottles
Stock 2.5 million bottles *sur lattes*

WINES
NV Brut (solid, harmonious, well made wine),
NV Sec, NV Demi-Sec, NV Cuvée Amazone,
NV Rosé Rubis Brut (blended with red wine
from Verzenay), NV Blanc de Blancs Brut,
Vintage Brut, Vintage Blanc de Blancs Brut,
Vintage Blanc de Noirs Brut (essentially an
assemblage of Verzenay and Rilly-la-Montagne
wines)

G. Pannier

Co-opérative de Champagnisation des Coteaux
du Val de Marne
23 rue Roger-Catillon, Château-Thierry
Telephone (23) 69.13.10
Origin The Champagne house of G. Pannier
was founded in 1937, but in 1963 it was sold to
a group of local growers who had been its
traditional suppliers, thus creating CO.VA.MA.
This *co-operative* produces various BOBS,
including Pol du Breuil and de Brienne, but
efforts are being made to place a greater
emphasis on its Pannier label by the end of the
decade.
Membership 180 members

Vineyards Total collective holding of 250
hectares: 4 of Pinot Noir, 190 of Pinot Meunier
and 6 of Chardonnay
Production 2 million bottles
Sold direct under the *Co-opérative*
label 600,000 bottles
Sold by members 700,000 bottles
Stock 4 million bottles

WINES
NV Brut An honest wine, well-made, rich in
fruit, with a typically earthy finish.
NV Brut Rosé Tasted only once; I was not
impressed.
Vintage Brut I have only tasted the 1979: a
fresh, well-balanced wine, but a touch green on
the finish.

Le Royal Coteau

Co-opérative de Grauves
Rue de la Co-opérative, Grauves
Telephone (26) 59.71.12
Membership 150 members
Vineyards 100 hectares
Sold direct under the *Co-opérative*
label 150,000 **bottles**

WINES
Grande Réserve Brut, Blanc de Blancs Brut

Saint Reol ou Nectar de Noirs

Sélection des Producteurs Associés
Ambonnay
Telephone (26) 57.01.46
Membership 125 members
Vineyards 130 hectares
Production 350,000 bottles
Sold direct under the *Co-opérative*
label 50,000 bottles

WINES
NV Brut, Vintage Brut

Saint Simon

Co-opérative la Crayère
Bethon
Telephone (26) 80.26.43
Membership 120 members
Vineyards 140 hectares
Production 300,000 bottles
Sold direct under the *Co-opérative*
label 250,000 bottles

The wines of 'la Crayère', as it is known, from
the vineyards of the Côte de Sézanne, are noted
for a particular style called *goût Bethon*.
NV Brut, Vintage Brut

Sanger et Vaubecourt

Co-opérative des Anciens Élèves de la
Viticulture
Lycée viticole de la Champagne
Avize
Telephone (26) 57.50.42
A co-opérative of old students which employs
students during the vacation.

Production 100,000 bottles
**Sold direct under the *Co-opérative*
label** 100,000 bottles

A. Vatel

Association Co-opérative des Premiers Crus de
la Marne
Aÿ Champagne
Telephone (26) 50.11.95
Membership 75 members
Vineyards 20 hectares
Production 100,000 bottles
**Sold direct under the *Co-opérative*
label** 100,000 bottles

16

Village Directory
of Champagne Growers
and their products

I want to be buried with a bottle of champagne at my head and another
bottle at my feet.

From the last will and testament of James McMillan Gibson, who died at
Palm Beach, USA, in 1966

Growers are listed under the village where they reside. In virtually every case, the growers own vines in the villages in which they live, but many may have vineyards in other communes – where these are known, they are mentioned.

It is impossible, in many cases, to discover which grower Champagnes are 'Co-op clones' (see chapter 12). On the other hand, it is easier to ascertain which wines are probably the individually produced Champagnes of a named grower. While some genuine *récoltants-manipulants* make just one *cuvée*, usually a non-vintage brut, very few vignerons selling 'Co-op clones' can offer a large range of Champagnes. If a grower sells an unusual *cuvée*, such as a *crémant* rosé, this may be an indication that his Champagnes are individually produced. Of course, if you are touring the region, you can always ask to visit his cellar and make sure you see evidence of where the wine is first fermented as well as some sign of *remuage*.

Although I have listed all the *cuvées* which are known to exist, or to have existed, it is possible that some growers may stock some which are not included here.

I should make some mention of Special Club *cuvées*. In 1971 several vignerons formulated the concept of an exclusive club of leading growers who were resolved to maintain the highest standards of production. This loose association of growers, who have named

themselves the Club de Viticulteurs Champenois, have created what is, in effect, the *récoltant*'s answer to the *cuvée de prestige* sector of the *négociant*'s market. Members of the club are entitled to sell their Champagnes in Special Club bottles with Club labels. To earn the right to the Special Club label, a grower must, firstly, agree to restrict the proportion of his production that he sells as vintage to just 20%. As the Special Club *cuvée* can only be a vintage Champagne, this rule ensures a strict selection of the wines used. Secondly, all members must submit their Special Club Champagnes for tasting tests by fellow members. Thirdly (and this is perhaps the most interesting point), club membership can only be applied for, and held, if members maintain at least three years' bottle-age for their non-vintage Champagnes. There are currently some fifty members of the Club de Viticulteurs Champenois, each with a minimum annual production of 25,000 bottles. Although the majority of the members are *récoltants-manipulants*, some *négociants-manipulants* (such as Collery), where Champagnes are produced entirely from their own vineyards, are members and sell Special Club *cuvées*.

Some *récoltants-manipulants*, in villages which are rated 100% échelle de cru, prefer to use the term Premier Cru, rather than Grand Cru, on their labels.

AMBONNAY 100% échelle de cru

André Beaufort
1 rue de Vaudemanges
Telephone (26) 59.01.50
WINES NV Grand Cru 100% Brut, Grand Cru
100% Rosé, Coteaux Champenois Ambonnay
Blanc, Coteaux Champenois Rouge
COMMENT No artificial fertilisers, synthesised
insecticides or synthesised fungicides are used.

Claude Beaufort
16 boulevard des Bermonts
Telephone (26) 59.01.32
WINES NV Brut 1er Cru, Brut Rosé, Coteaux
Champenois Blanc, Coteaux Champenois
Ambonnay Rouge

Lucien Beaufort
3 rue de Crilly
Telephone (26) 59.01.30
WINES NV Brut Cru 100%, Rosé Cru 100%,
Coteaux Champenois Ambonnay Blanc,
Coteaux Champenois Rouge

H. Billot Fils
Place de la Fontaine
Telephone (26) 59.00.14
WINES NV Brut Grand Cru 100%, Coteaux
Champenois Ambonnay Rouge

Bernard Bremont
1 rue de Reims
Telephone (26) 59.01.65
WINES NV 1er Cru Brut, NV 1er Cru Sec, NV
1er Cru Demi-Sec, Rosé Brut, Coteaux
Champenois Blanc, Coteaux Champenois
Ambonnay Rouge

R. & H. Coutier
7 rue Henri III
Telephone (26) 59.01.74
WINES NV Brut Grand Réserve, Blanc de
Blancs Brut, Rosé Brut, Coteaux Champenois
Blanc, Coteaux Champenois Ambonnay Rouge

Roger Croizy
5 rue de Trépail
Telephone (26) 59.01.52
WINES NV Grand Cru 100%

Paul Déthune
Rue de l'Espérance, Rue de Moulin
Telephone (26) 59.01.88
WINES NV Grand Cru Brut, NV Grand Cru
Sec, NV Grand Cru Demi-Sec, Brut Rosé, Blanc
de Blancs Brut, Coteaux Champenois Blanc,
Coteaux Champenois Ambonnay Rouge,
Coteaux Champenois Rosé
COMMENT Tasted twice – extremely well
made, traditionally styled wines.

Michel Égly
Route de Trépail
Telephone (26) 59.00.70
WINES NV Grand Cru 100% Brut, Grand Cru
Rosé, Coteaux Champenois Blanc de Noirs,
Coteaux Champenois Bouzy Rouge

Robert Fourer
4 Impasse des Pinots
Telephone (26) 59.02.68
WINES NV Grand Cru Brut, Rosé Brut,
Coteaux Champenois Blanc, Coteaux
Champenois Ambonnay Rouge

Roger Gauthier
Rue Bacchus
Telephone (26) 59.01.94
WINES NV Grand Cru 100% Brut, Rosé Brut,
Coteaux Champenois Blanc, Coteaux
Champenois Ambonnay Rouge, Coteaux
Champenois Bouzy Rouge

Michel Ledru
5 place de la Croix
Telephone (26) 59.00.71
WINES NV Grand Cru 100% Brut, NV Grand
Cru 100% Sec, NV Grand Cru 100% Demi-
Sec, NV Grand Cru 100% Rosé, Coteaux
Champenois Vin de Coteaux Blanc, Coteaux
Champenois Bouzy Rouge

Marguet-Bonnerave
14 rue de Bouzy
Telephone (26) 59.01.08
WINES NV Grand Cru 100% Brut Réserve,
NV Demi-Sec, NV Rosé, Coteaux Champenois
Ambonnay Rouge, Coteaux Champenois
Bouzy Rouge, Coteaux Champenois Blanc Cru
100%, Coteaux Champenois Rouge Cru
100%, Coteaux Champenois Rosé Cru 100%

A. Michel-Huguet
1 place de la Marie
Telephone (26) 59.01.45
WINES NV Grand Cru 100% Brut, Coteaux
Champenois Blanc

C. Millot
La Feraudière, rue Saint-Vincent
Telephone (26) 59.07.25
WINES NV Grand Cru Brut, Coteaux
Champenois Blanc, Coteaux Champenois
Ambonnay Rouge

Jean B. Rodez
Rue de Châlons
Telephone (26) 59.00.52
WINES NV Grand Cru 100% Brut, Coteaux
Champenois Vin de Coteaux Blanc, Coteaux
Champenois Ambonnay Rouge

Michel Rodez
3 rue Colbert
Telephone (26) 59.00.27
WINES NV Grand Cru 100% Brut, Grand Cru
Rosé, Coteaux Champenois Blanc, Coteaux
Champenois Ambonnay Rouge

Georges Simon
14 route de Trépail
Telephone (26) 59.00.59
WINES NV Grand Cru 100% Brut, Coteaux
Champenois Blanc

Jean Varlot
8 rue de Trépail
Telephone (26) 59.00.65
WINES NV Cuvée de Réserve, Coteaux
Champenois Ambonnay Rouge

Gaston Warin
1 rue de Bouzy
Telephone (26) 59.01.29
WINES NV Grand Cru Brut, Coteaux
Champenois Blanc

ARRENTIÈRES   80% échelle de cru

Jacques Chaput
Route de Bar-sur-Aube
Telephone (25) 27.00.14
WINES NV Brut

Nongin Pierre
Rue Principale
WINES NV Brut

AVENAY   93% échelle de cru

R. Gabriel-Pagin
22 rue Charles-de-Gaulle
Telephone (26) 50.64.61
WINES NV Premier Cru Brut, NV Premier Cru
Sec, NV Premier Cru Demi-Sec, NV Grande
Réserve Premier Cru Brut (55% PN, 45% CH),
Vintage Special Club Brut (100% PN), Vintage
Special Club Rosé Brut (the same as the Special
Club Brut, but with the addition of red wine),
ratafia

COMMENT The grower owns 6.5 hectares at
Avenay: 6 hectares of Pinot Noir and 0.5
hectare of Chardonnay.

Ricciuti-Révolte
Telephone (26) 52.30.27
WINES NV Brut, NV Sec, NV Demi-Sec, NV
Brut Réserve, NV Brut Rosé, Coteaux
Champenois Blanc
COMMENT The grower owns 3.5 hectares
(50% PN, 50% PM) at Avenay and 1 hectare
(25% PN, 75% CH) at Mareuil-sur-Aÿ,
producing 15,000 bottles a year and selling a
quarter of his grapes to G. H. Mumm & Co.

The legend of General Patton lingers on in
Avenay, through the presence of Albert
Ricciuti, the only American *récoltant-
manipulant* in all Champagne. He met Paulette
Révolte, the daughter of a local grower, when
Patton's 3rd Army swept into the region in
August 1944. They fell in love, but were
separated when Albert had to return to the
United States. He eventually returned to France
to find Paulette, and in 1963 they married,
subsequently setting up as Champagne
growers.

AVIZE   100% échelle de cru

Agrapart & Fils
26 avenue Jean-Jaurès
Telephone (26) 50.51.38
WINES NV Premier Cru Blanc de Blancs Brut
COMMENT The growers own vineyards at
Avize and Cramant.

F. Bonville & Fils
9 rue Pasteur
Telephone (26) 50.52.30
WINES NV Brut Sélection, NV Demi-Sec, NV
Blanc de Blancs Brut Grand Cru 100%
COMMENT Established in 1947, Bonville owns
13 hectares, producing 130,000 bottles in a
good year.

Pierre Callot
31 avenue Jean-Jaurès
Telephone (26) 50.51.57
WINES NV Blanc de Blancs Brut Grand Cru

Michel Ghys
2 rue des Gris
Telephone (26) 50.51.05
WINES NV Brut

Michel Gonet
21 avenue Jean-Jaurès
Telephone (26) 50.50.56

WINES NV Brut (50% PN, 50% CH), NV Blanc de Blancs Brut, NV 1er Cru Blanc de Blancs Brut (an *assemblage* of Oger and le Mesnil-sur-Oger wines), Brut Rosé (100% PN; blended; an *assemblage* of Vertus and Vindey), Coteaux Champenois Blanc (Montgueux and Vindey), Coteaux Champenois Rouge (Vertus and Vindey)
COMMENT The grower owns 7.5 hectares at Avize, Oger and le Mesnil-sur-Oger, 12 hectares at Vindey, 8 hectares at Montgueux and 5 hectares at Fravaux, producing 300,000 bottles a year. Fine wines of lightly-yeasty character, lesser quality wines are sold under a *marque auxiliaire*.

Jacques Selosse
61 rue Ernest Vallé
Telephone (26) 50.53.56
WINES NV Blanc de Blancs Brut, NV Vieille Réserve Blanc de Blancs Brut (the same as the standard *cuvée*, but with more bottle-age and less dosage), Vintage Blanc de Blancs Brut, Vintage Special Club Brut, Coteaux Champenois Blanc
COMMENT The grower owns 4.5 hectares of Chardonnay at Avize and 1 hectare of Chardonnay on the Côte de Sézanne, producing 30,000 bottles a year of consistently classic Champagnes.

AŸ-CHAMPAGNE 100% échelle de cru

Gosset-Brabant
23 boulevard du Maréchal-de-Lattre-de-Tassigny
Telephone (26) 50.10.26
WINES NV 1er Cru Brut

Henri Goutorbe
11 rue Léon Bourgeois
Telephone (26) 50.11.59
WINES NV Cuvée Traditionelle Brut, NV Sec, NV Demi-Sec, Cuvée Prestige Brut, Cuvée Blanc de Blancs Brut, Cuvée Rosé Brut, Vintage Brut, Vintage Special Club, Coteaux Champenois

BAGNEUX-LA-FOSSE 80% échelle de cru

Paul-Marie Bertrand
Rue du Vieux Château
Telephone (25) 38.30.58
WINES NV Brut

Jean Huart
'La Mansardière'

Telephone (25) 38.31.18
WINES NV Brut

BARBONNE-FAYEL
85% (black grapes) – 87% (white grapes) échelle de cru

George Logeard
Rue Saint-Michel
Telephone (26) 80.20.30
WINES NV Brut

BETHON
85% (black grapes) – 87% (white grapes) échelle de cru

Guy Petit
Rue du Chemin Neuf
Telephone (26) 80.26.31
WINES NV Blanc de Blancs Brut

Marcel Triolet
Rue du Chemin Neuf
Telephone (26) 80.26.24
WINES NV Blanc de Blancs Brut

BILLY-LE-GRAND 95% échelle de cru

Roger Lapie
Route de Vaudemanges
Telephone (26) 65.57.83
WINES NV Brut

BLIGNY 80% échelle de cru

Château de Bligny
Telephone (25) 26.40.11
WINES NV Carte Noire Brut, Rosé Brut (skin-contact), NV Blanc de Blancs Brut, Vintage Blanc de Blancs Brut
COMMENT The château is one of only two which bottles Champagnes; it owns 17 hectares at Bligny, producing 100,000 bottles a year. Malo-lactic conversion is not used.

BOURSAULT 84% échelle de cru

Jacques Berat
8 rue St Roch
Telephone (26) 58.42.45
WINES NV Carte Blanche Brut, Special Cuvée Brut, Carte Perlée Brut, Vintage Brut (50% PN, 50% CH)
COMMENT The grower owns 10 hectares, producing 110,000 bottles a year.

BOUZY 100% échelle de cru

Paul Bara

4 rue Yvonnet
Telephone (26) 59.00.50
WINES NV Grand Cru 100% Demi-Sec, NV
Grand Cru 100% Brut; (75% PN, 25% CH),
NV Grand Rosé de Bouzy (blended), Vintage
Grand Cru 100% Brut (75% PN, 25% CH),
Vintage Comtesse Marie de France Bouzy
Grand Cru 100% Brut (60% PN, 40% CH),
Vintage Special Club, Vintage Coteaux
Champenois Grand Cru 100% Bouzy
COMMENT The Bara family, who have lived in
Bouzy since 1657, have been vignerons since
1833. They own 11 hectares of Pinot Noir and
Chardonnay at Bouzy, producing 100,000
bottles a year.

H. Beaufort & Fils

32 rue de Tours
Telephone (26) 57.01.34
WINES NV Bouzy Grand Cru Brut (Carte
Blanche: Chardonnay and Pinot Noir; Carte
d'Or: Blanc de Noirs), Rosé Brut (skin-
contact), Bouzy Blanc, Special Club, Coteaux
Champenois Bouzy Rouge, Coteaux
Champenois Rosé de Bouzy
COMMENT The grower owns 16.5 hectares,
producing 100,000 bottles a year. The Bouzy
Rouge is very good.

Bernard Tornay

Telephone (26) 59.00.86
WINES NV Brut, NV Demi-Sec, Brut Rosé,
Vintage Brut, Coteaux Champenois
COMMENT The grower owns 10.5 hectares,
producing 120,000 bottles a year.

Alain Vesselle

Telephone (26) 59.00.88
WINES NV Grand 1er Cru 100% Brut, NV
Demi-Sec, Perlé du Coteau Bouzy, Coteaux
Champenois Blanc, Coteaux Champenois
Bouzy Rouge.
COMMENT The grower owns 12.4 hectares,
producing 110,000 bottles a year.

Georges Vesselle

16 rue des Postes
Telephone (26) 59.00.15
WINES NV Brut (100%), NV Brut Oeil de
Perdrix Grand Cru 100%, NV Brut Rosé, NV
Brut Réserve, NV Brut Sec, NV Brut Demi-Sec,
Vintage Brut, Vintage Brut Alexandre, Coteaux
Champenois Bouzy Rouge, Coteaux
Champenois Bouzy Rosé

COMMENT The grower owns 13 hectares of
Pinot Noir and 2 hectares of Chardonnay at
Bouzy, producing 150,000 bottles a year. The
Bouzy Rouge is usually well-structured and
finely perfumed and the Champagne Brut 1975
is excellent.

Jean Vesselle

2 place J.-B. Barnut
Telephone (26) 59.01.55
WINES NV Brut Réserve, NV Brut 100%
(85% PN, 15% CH; non-dosage), NV Oeil-de-
Perdrix Brut (100% PN; a light-coloured pink
Champagne; skin-contact), NV Rosé Brut
(deeper colour, skin-contact), NV Cuvée de
Prestige Brut, Vintage Coteaux Champenois
Bouzy Rouge
COMMENT The grower owns 4.2 hectares of
Pinot Noir and 0.7 hectares of Chardonnay at
Bouzy and 3.2 hectares of Pinot Noir at Loches-
sur-Ource, producing 45,000 bottles a year. I
have tasted a fine bottle of NV Rosé Brut and a
couple of bottles of Bouzy Rouge, both soundly
made.

Other growers

R. Leclapart, 22 rue de Tours and 1 rue Paul
Doumer

André Clouet, 8 rue Gambetta (a fine Bouzy
Rouge)

Dauvergne-Baron & Fils, 31 rue de Tours

René Dauvergne, 12 rue Jeanne d'Arc

Delavenne, 6 rue de Tours and 5 rue de Louvois

Pierre Hulin & Fils, rue de Tours

Lahaye, 1 rue Jeanne d'Arc

Gabriel Ledru, 27 rue Jeanne d'Arc

Jean Plener Fils, 2 rue A-Briand

Camille Savès, 4 rue de Condé (one glorious
1978 tasted in 1980: full, rich and long, with
honey and almonds on the aftertaste)

Alfred Tritant, rue de Tours

Maurice Vesselle, 2 rue Yvonnet (an excellent,
light but finely flavoured 1977 Bouzy Rouge
tasted in 1983: elegant and long)

Michel Waroquier, 22 rue Jeanne d'Arc

BRUGNY-VAUDANCOURT
86% échelle de cru

Maurice Hugot

13 rue de la Co-opérative
Telephone (26) 51.34.20
WINES NV Grande Réserve Brut

Étienne Oudart
8 rue de la Cloterie
Telephone (26) 51.34.25
WINES NV Brut, NV Sec, NV Demi-Sec, NV
Brut Réserve, Coteaux Champenois Blanc,
Ratafia
COMMENT I once tasted the NV Brut; it was
very soft and round, with a perfumed middle
palate, finishing simply.

BUXEUIL 80% échelle de cru

Moutard Père & Fils
Route de Polisy
Telephone (25) 38.50.73
WINES NV Brut, NV Demi-Sec, NV Blanc de
Blancs Brut, Brut Rosé, Vintage Brut, Vintage
Blanc de Blancs Brut
COMMENT The growers own 10 hectares,
producing 100,000 bottles.

LA CELLE-SOUS-CHANTEMERLE
85% (black grapes) – 87% (white grapes)
échelle de cru

Jean Gaudichau
Grande Rue
Telephone (26) 80.21.58
WINES NV Blanc de Blancs Brut

CELLES-SUR-OURCE 80% échelle de cru

Cheurlin-Dangin
Rue Principale
Telephone (25) 38.50.26
WINES NV Brut
COMMENT The grower is a producer of
significant quantity, but I have not tasted his
wines.

Daniel Cheurlin
WINES NV Brut

Paul Dangin & Fils
Rue du Pont
WINES NV Brut
COMMENT The grower is a producer of
significant quantity, but I have not tasted his
wines.

Delot Père & Fils
WINES NV Brut, NV Montre-Cul Blanc de
Blancs Brut

Maurice Delot
Place de l'Église
Telephone (25) 38.50.12
WINES NV Brut

Gautherot
Grande Rue
Telephone (25) 38.50.03
WINES NV Cuvée Réserve Brut

Pierre Gerbais
Telephone (25) 38.50.29
WINES NV Brut

Laurent
Rue des Huguenots
Telephone (25) 38.50.10
WINES NV Brut

Marcel Vezien
4 rue de la Montée
Telephone (25) 38.50.22
WINES NV Brut

CERSEUIL 84% échelle de cru

Gilbert Debargue
5 rue de la Gravelle
Telephone (26) 50.71.65
WINES NV Brut, NV Sec, NV Demi-Sec

Dehours
1 and 2 rue de la Chapelle
Telephone (26) 50.71.75
WINES NV Brut, Crémant Brut, Coteaux
Champenois Blanc de Blancs
COMMENT The grower, who owns 28
hectares, can trace his family back to vignerons
working in 1610.

CHAMERY 90% échelle de cru

Gilbert Bertrand
WINES NV Brut, NV Rosé Brut
COMMENT The grower produces traditionally
made wines. The pink Champagne is clean and
delicate.

Michel Labbé
WINES NV Brut, NV Rosé Brut, ratafia
COMMENT Clean and correct, this grower's
wines are consistent, but not exciting.

CHAMPILLON 93% échelle de cru

G. E. Autreau Père & Fils
15 rue Renet Baudet
Telephone (26) 51.54.13
WINES NV 1er Cru Brut, NV Demi-Sec,
Vintage Brut Réserve, Vintage Blanc de Blancs
Brut, Brut Rosé 1er Cru, Roualet des Bordes
Brut
COMMENT The growers own 21 hectares at
Champillon, Aÿ and Chouilly, producing
150,000 bottles a year. I have tasted the 1979 a
few times; it has a very fine nose and is rich in
fruit and firm in body; quite an elegant wine.

CHAVOT-COURCOURT
88% échelle de cru

Jean-Paul Arvois
WINES NV Brut, Vintage Brut, Vintage Rosé
Brut
COMMENT The growers own vineyards at
Chavot-Courcourt and Cramant, producing
10,000 bottles in a good year. The wines are
deeply flavoured and well-structured, often
with a pleasing earthy character to the finish.

Bartaux & Fils
16 rue du Mont Félix
Telephone (26) 51.42.23
WINES NV Brut

André Desmarest
Rue de l'Église
WINES NV Brut
COMMENT The grower is a producer of
significant quantity, but I have not tasted his
wines.

René Jacquesson
12 rue du Maréchal Juin
Telephone (26) 51.46.63
WINES NV Brut

Michel Lagache
3 rue Jean Mermoz
Telephone (26) 51.92.91
WINES NV Brut
COMMENT The grower owns vineyards at
Chavot-Courcourt and Cerseuil.

Robert Lebeau
13 rue de Général Leclerc
Telephone (26) 51.41.26
WINES NV Cuvée Réserve Brut

Lucien Leblond
26 rue du Général Leclerc
Telephone (26) 51.50.43
WINES NV Cuvée Blancs et Noirs Brut

André Tissier
19 rue d'Église
Telephone (26) 51.51.13
WINES NV 1er Cru Brut

Roger Tissier
22 rue du Général Leclerc
Telephone (26) 51.49.71
WINES NV Brut

CHIGNY-LES-ROSES 94% échelle de cru

Cattier
6 and 11 rue Dom Pérignon
Telephone (26) 03.42.11
WINES NV Brut, NV Extra Dry, NV Demi-
Sec, Rosé Brut, Clos du Moulin Brut, Vintage
Brut, Coteaux Champenois, ratafia
COMMENT The grower owns 20 hectares,
producing 200,000 bottles a year. I have tasted
the NV Brut once; it was full-bodied, deep-
flavoured and very traditional. A superb bottle
of Clos du Moulin tasted; rich, yet delicate and
fine.

J. Lassalle
Rue des Châtaigniers
Telephone (26) 03.42.91
WINES NV Impérial Préférence Brut, NV
Réserve des Grandes Années Brut Rosé,
Vintage Blanc de Blancs Brut, Vintage Cuvée
Agéline Blanc de Noirs, Vintage Chigny Rouge
Coteaux Champenois
COMMENT The house is run by a widow and
her daughter. The pink Champagne is
delightful and a special 1973 cuvée of the Blanc
de Blancs is outstanding.

Patrice Leroux
12 rue Georges Legros
Telephone (26) 03.42.01
WINES NV Carte Bleue Brut, NV Carte Bleue
Sec, NV Carte Bleue Demi-Sec, Carte Rouge Brut
COMMENT The grower owns 7 hectares,
producing 60,000 bottles a year.

Gilbert Menu
1 and 3 rue Jobert
Telephone (26) 48.43.35
WINES NV Brut Premier Cru, NV Sec, NV
Demi-Sec, Coteaux Champenois

Michel Tixier
8 rue des Vignes
Telephone (26) 48.42.61/03.42.61
WINES NV Carte Noire Cuvée Réserve Brut,
Carte Blanche Cuvée Grande Année Brut

CHOUILLY
95% (black grapes) – 100% (white grapes)
échelle de cru

Vazart-Comte
26 rue des Partelaines
Telephone (26) 59.60.06
WINES NV Premier Cru Blanc de Blancs Brut,
NV Brut, NV Demi-Sec, Coteaux Champenois
Blanc

Vazart-Coquart & Fils
6 rue des Partelaines
Telephone (26) 59.60.08
WINES NV 1er Cru Blanc de Blancs Brut
Réserve
COMMENT A bottle of NV Grand Bouquet,
based on the 1957 vintage, which I tasted in
1983, was very honeyed, soft and stylish – quite
remarkable for such an old 'off vintage'.

Lucien Vazart
2 rue d'Avize
Telephone (26) 59.61.15
WINES NV Private Cuvée Blanc de Blancs Brut

Voirin
Rue Dom Pérignon
Telephone (26) 50.60.20
WINES NV Brut, Vintage Special Club

COLOMBÉ-LE-SEC 80% échelle de cru

Bernard Breuzon
Telephone (25) 27.02.06
WINES Cuvée Marie-Louise Brut

Chrétien-Esseint
Telephone (25) 27.02.15
WINES NV Cuvée Réservée Brut

René Dosne
Telephone (25) 27.02.14
WINES NV Brut

C. Paradis & Fils
Telephone (25) 27.02.12
WINES NV Brut Sélection

CONDÉ-SUR-MARNE
80% échelle de cru

Norbert Potié
6 rue de Reims
Telephone (26) 69.57.14
WINES NV Grand Cru Blanc de Blancs Brut,
NV Grand Cru Rosé, NV Premier Cru Brut,
Coteaux Champenois Blanc, Coteaux
Champenois Ambonnay Rouge
COMMENT The grower owns vineyards at
Ambonnay and Trépail.

CONGY 85% échelle de cru

Breton Fils
12 rue Courte-Pilate
Telephone (26) 59.31.03
WINES NV Brut, NV Sec, NV Demi-Sec, Brut
de Brut, Blanc de Blancs Brut, Brut Rosé,
Vintage Brut, Coteaux Champenois
COMMENT The grower owns 10 hectares,
producing 100,000 bottles a year.

Jean Collard
Telephone (26) 59.31.31
WINES NV Brut

René Collin
Telephone (26) 59.31.20
WINES NV Brut

Robert Desbrosse
Telephone (26) 59.31.08
WINES NV Brut

CORMOYEUX 85% échelle de cru

André Faniel
Grande Rue
Telephone (26) 59.41.80
WINES NV Carte Blanche Brut, NV Carte
Blanche Sec, NV Carte Blanche Demi-Sec

Lemoine Fils
Telephone (26) 59.41.66
WINES NV Cuvée Réservée, NV Brut, NV
Rosé Brut, Coteaux Champenois Rouge

Daniel Mondet
Grande Rue
Telephone (26) 59.41.71
WINES NV Brut, NV Sec, NV Demi-Sec, Brut
Grande Réserve, Blanc de Blancs Brut

Tellier Père & Fils
Grande Rue
Telephone (26) 59.41.72
WINES NV Carte d'Or, NV Brut, NV Sec, NV Demi-Sec

COULOMMES-LA-MONTAGNE
89% échelle de cru

Norbert Hoche
Rue Neuve
Telephone (26) 49.20.47
WINES NV Brut

Christian Lépitre
Telephone (26) 49.20.34
WINES NV Brut

Gérard Lépitre
Rue de l'Église
Telephone (26) 49.20.21
WINES NV Brut

Michel Massonot
Telephone (26) 49.20.19
WINES NV Brut

F. Meriguet-Augé
Rue de l'Église
Telephone (26) 49.20.43
WINES NV Brut

Ponson Père & Fils
Telephone (26) 49.20.17
WINES NV Brut

COURMAS 87% échelle de cru

Y. Alexandre
Telephone (26) 49.20.78
WINES NV Brut
COMMENT The grower owns vineyards in many villages.

COURTAGNON 82% échelle de cru

Lutun
WINES NV Brut, Coteaux Champenois

CRAMANT 100% échelle de cru

Bonnaire-Bouquemont
105 rue du Courage
Telephone (26) 50.50.85
WINES NV Carte Noire Brut (mostly Pinot Meunier from the Aisne *département*), NV Blanc de Blancs Demi-Sec, NV Blanc de Blancs Brut (from Cramant and adjacent communes), NV Crémant Blanc de Blancs (the same base wine as the standard NV Blanc de Blancs, but with a reduced *liqueur de tirage*), Vintage Blanc de Blancs Brut (pure Cramant), Vintage Special Club Blanc de Blancs Brut (pure Cramant), NV Brut Rosé (blended with red wine made from grapes purchased* from Bouzy and Verzenay), Coteaux Champenois Blanc, Coteaux Champenois Rouge, Coteaux Champenois Rosé, ratafia
COMMENT The growers own 13.5 hectares of Chardonnay at Cramant and in the surrounding communes and 9.5 hectares of all three grape varieties in the Aisne *département*, producing an average annual total of 200,000 bottles. I tasted a very good Blanc de Blancs 1975 in 1983.

Caroff-Gimonet
2 rue de la Libération
Telephone (26) 50.54.44
WINES NV Blanc de Blancs Brut

P. Guiborat
5 rue d'Épernay
Telephone (26) 50.54.08
WINES Cuvée André-Paul Blanc de Blancs ND Brut (non-dosage)
COMMENT Good tasty Chardonnay character, well made wines, finely bubbled *mousse*.

René Jumel
Telephone (26) 50.50.13
WINES NV Grand Cru 100% Blanc de Blancs Brut

Krier-Busson
3 rue de la Libération
Telephone (26) 50.52.24
WINES NV Grand Cru Brut

Collective Lebrun-Vignier
2 place Carnot
WINES NV Brut

*Although debarred from purchasing grapes and wine in quantity, growers do have the right to buy up to 5% of their total production from elsewhere.

COMMENT The collective is a producer of significant quantity, but I have not tasted its wines.

Pierre Lesage

338 rue du Moutier
Telephone (26) 50.50.21
WINES NV Blanc de Blancs Brut

Lilbert-Fils

Rue du Moutier
Telephone (26) 50.50.16
WINES NV Blanc de Blancs Brut, NV Blanc de Blancs Brut Réserve, Crémant de Cramant, Coteaux Champenois Cramant Blanc de Blancs
COMMENT The Lilberts have been *viticulteurs* at Cramant since 1746. They produce good, biscuity Chardonnay wines.

Mélat

Rue du 8 Mai
Telephone (26) 50.52.27
WINES NV Premier Cru 100% Blanc de Blancs Brut Réserve, Cuvée Marie Chantel 1er Cru 100% Blanc de Blancs Brut

G. Morizet

19 rue du Moutier
Telephone (26) 50.50.92
WINES NV Grand Cru Brut, Coteaux Champenois Blanc de Blancs, Coteaux Champenois Bouzy Rouge

Pertois-Lebrun

28 rue de la Libération
Telephone (26) 50.54.25
WINES NV Premier Cru Blanc de Blancs Brut, NV Extra Dry, NV Demi-Sec, Vintage Cramant, Coteaux Champenois
COMMENT The grower owns 6 hectares, producing 75,000 bottles.

Sugot-Feneuil Fils

40 impasse de la Mairie
Telephone (26) 50.53.54
WINES NV Carte Rouge (67% PM, 33% CH), NV Carte Perlée Grand Cru Blanc de Blancs Brut, Vintage Special Club Brut, Coteaux Champenois 'Le Cramant' Blanc
COMMENT The growers own 4 hectares at Bergères-les-Vertus, Chouilly, Cramant and Oiry, and 2.7 hectares at Trigny, producing 35,000 bottles a year. I have tasted one or two superb wines from this grower.

CUIS

90% (black grapes) – 95% (white grapes) échelle de cru

Pierre Gimonnet & Fils

1 rue de la République
Telephone (26) 51.47.29
WINES NV Blanc de Blancs Brut, Vintage Blanc de Blancs Brut, Vintage Special Club Blanc de Blancs Brut, Coteaux Champenois Blanc de Blancs
COMMENT The growers own 20 hectares at Cuis, Chouilly and Cramant, producing 150,000 bottles a year. Tasted just once, the Special Club had a delightful, light-yeast nose and a delicate balance of fruit on the palate.

Paul Michel

20 Grande Rue
Telephone (26) 51.41.12
WINES NV 1er Cru Blanc de Blancs Brut

Guy Vallois

2 rue de l'Égalité
Telephone (26) 51.72.92
WINES NV 1er Cru Blanc de Blancs Brut

CUMIÈRES 90% échelle de cru

Denois Père & Fils

103 rue L. Dupont
Telephone (26) 51.42.45
WINES NV Carte Blanche Brut, Cuvée de Réserve Brut, Crémant Rosé Brut, Carte d'Or, Cuvée des Côtes-à-Bras, Cuvée Marie Antoinette, Coteaux Champenois Blanc de Blancs de Chardonnay, Coteaux Champenois Cumières Rouge
COMMENT Some half-bottles of Denois Cumières Rouge, sold at the Hôtel Chapon Fin, Épernay, in January 1980, were amongst the best examples of this appellation that I have had the chance to taste. Yet, such is the inconsistency of this appellation, that a few bottles purchased direct from Denois, at the same juncture, turned out to be well-made but not outstanding. The Crémant Rosé has an immediately appealing nose and an initially attractive palate, but disappoints after this and does not improve with age. The Cuvée des Côtes-à-Bras is a fine, meaty wine from a single site below the abbey of Hautvillers which *does* improve with more time in bottle. The Cuvée Marie Antoinette attains a balance earlier than the Côtes-a-Bras, but also improves with age.

René Geoffroy

150 rue Bois-des-Jots
Telephone (26) 51.51.01
WINES NV Brut, Coteaux Champenois
Cumières Rouge
COMMENT This is a very good, fruity
Cumières Rouge; tasted once.

Other producers

Pierre Bertrand, Blosseville-Marniquet, Gabriel
Boutet, Jacques Delabaye, Deny-Dany, E.
Duchenne, Jean-Marie Étienne, Roger
Geoffroy, Raymond Godart, B. le Guedard,
José Gruget, Fernand Hutasse, Laval-Louis,
Roger Locret, Veuve Maitre Geoffroy, Michel
Malabre, Paul Martin, Michel Mignon, Yves
Mignon (a good, fruity Champagne), Charles
Millet, Henri Plateau, Roger Plateau, Alphonse
Poittevin, Claude Poittevin, Ludolf Poittevin,
Reineville Père & Fils, Marcel Stinlet, Sinice
Suisse, Vadin Plateau.

Most growers in Cumières produce the
following wines: NV Brut, NV Sec, NV Demi-
Sec, Rosé Brut, Blanc de Balncs Brut, Coteaux
Champenois (this normally includes a Cumières
Rouge).

DAMERY 89% échelle de cru

A. Dessaint-Dubois

23 place Victor Hugo
Telephone (26) 50.51.70
WINES NV Brut, NV Sec, NV Demi-Sec

André l'Hôpital-Haton

Avenue de Champagne
WINES NV Brut

Jeeper

8 rue Georges Clémenceau
WINES NV Cuvée Ducale Extra Brut, NV
Cuvée Ducale Brut, NV Cuvée Ducale Demi-
Sec, Grande Réserve Blanc de Blancs, Dom
Grossard, Coteaux Champenois Damery
Rouge, ratafia
COMMENT The grower owns 37 hectares: 15
at Damery and Boursault, 11 at Bethon and
Montgenost and 11 at Vitry-en-Partois. Jeeper
produces an average of 300,000 bottles a year,
one third of which is exported. These wines are
well made: the Cuvée Ducale Brut is well
structured: it has a good *mousse*, well balanced
fruit and acidity and has more Chardonnay
character than most styles of house brut.

Claude Lemaire

19 rue Pasteur
Telephone (26) 50.41.31
WINES NV Cuvée de Réserve Brut, Carte d'Or
Brut, Carte d'Or Extra Dry, Carte d'Or Sec,
Carte d'Or Demi-Sec, Coteaux Champenois

M. Masson & Fils

3 rue Général-Sarrail
Telephone (26) 50.41.74
WINES NV Brut, NV Sec, NV Demi-Sec,
Cuvée Carte d'Or

Patrice Prévoteau-Rouchausse

13–15 rue A. Maginot
Telephone (26) 50.41.56
WINES NV Brut, NV Sec, NV Demi-Sec, Rosé
Brut, Coteaux Champenois
COMMENT The grower owns 10 hectares,
producing 100,000 bottles a year.

DIZY 95% échelle de cru

J. L. Bernard

1065 avenue du Maréchal Leclerc
Telephone (26) 51.23.34
WINES NV Cuvée de Réserve 1er Cru
COMMENT The grower owns vineyards at
Hautvillers.

Gaston Chiquet

912 avenue du Général-Leclerc
Telephone (26) 51.46.19
WINES NV Carte Blanche Brut, NV Carte
Verte Brut, NV Carte Verte Sec, NV Carte
Verte Demi-Sec, NV Blanc de Blancs d'Aÿ Brut,
NV Rosé Brut, Nouveau Crémant Brut,
Vintage Carte d'Or Brut, Vintage Special Club
Brut, Coteaux Champenois Blanc de Blanc
d'Aÿ
COMMENT The grower owns 4 hectares of
Pinot Noir, 8 hectares of Pinot Meunier and 8
hectares of Chardonnay at Aÿ, Cumières, Dizy
and Hautvillers, producing 120,000 bottles a
year. Claude de Lagrange is a *sous marque*
belonging to this grower.

Paul Létuvée

624 avenue Général-Leclerc
Telephone (26) 51.46.82
WINES NV Brut
COMMENT The grower's wine is produced
without the use of chemical fertilisers,
insecticides, herbicides or synthetic fungicides.

Francis Tarillon
423 route de Reims
Telephone (26) 51.33.93
WINES NV Brut, NV Sec

Jean Tarillon
807 avenue du Maréchal Leclerc
Telephone (26) 51.33.68
WINES NV Brut, NV Sec, NV Extra Dry, NV
Demi-Sec, 1er Cru Blanc de Blancs Brut

Marcel Vautrain
157 route de Reims
Telephone (26) 51.22.03
WINES NV Brut, NV Blanc de Blancs Brut

ÉCUEIL 90% échelle de cru

Brochet-Hervieux et Fils
Telephone (26) 97.65.92
WINES NV Brut, NV Sec, NV Demi-Sec,
Vintage Brut, Vintage Special Club
COMMENT The growers own 9.4 hectares of
Pinot Noir and 1.6 hectares of Chardonnay at
Écueil, producing 60,000 bottles a year.

M. Brugnon
WINES NV Brut, NV Rosé Brut, Vintage Brut
COMMENT The wines are of good strength and
sturdy balance, the Pinot Noir-dominated pink
Champagne being particularly successful.

ÉPERNAY 88% échelle de cru

Bauget-Jouette
60 rue Chaud-Ruelle
Telephone (26) 51.30.34
WINES NV Carte Blanche Brut (10% PN, 60%
PM, 30% CH; an *assemblage* of Pinots from the
Côtes d'Épernay and Chardonnay from
Grauves), Vintage Brut, Rosé Brut (100% PN
and PM from the Marne Valley), Coteaux
Champenois Blanc, Coteaux Champenois
Damery Rouge.
COMMENT The growers were established in
1949. They own a total of 9.5 hectares at
Mancy, Monthelon, Grauves, Venteuil and
Damery. The average annual production
amounts to 140,000 bottles, 20% of which
contain cask-fermented wine.

Leclerc-Briant
67–71 rue Chaud-Ruelle
Telephone (26) 51.81.60
WINES NV Brut (100% PN and PM), NV
Demi-Sec (100% PN and PM), NV Cuvée de
Réserve Brut (100% PN and CH), NV Rosé
Brut (100% PN), Vintage Brut, Vintage Special
Club
COMMENT The growers were established in
1872. They own 25 hectares in Cumières,
Damery, Épernay, Hautvillers and Verneuil.
Their average annual production amounts to
250,000 bottles.

F. Miltat & Fils
134 bis avenue du Maréchal Foch
Telephone (26) 51.64.85
WINES NV Grande Réserve Blanc de Blancs
Brut

Collective Testulat
23 rue Léger Bertin
WINES NV Brut
COMMENT The collective is a producer of
significant quantity but I have not tasted his
wines.

ÉTOGES 85% échelle de cru

Mancier-Lasnier
Route Nationale
Telephone (26) 59.32.81
WINES NV Brut

Jean Ruffin & Fils
Grande Rue
Telephone (26) 59.30.14
WINES NV Grand Vin de Réserve Brut

FÈREBRIANGES 85% échelle de cru

Albert Bergère
Telephone (26) 59.30.23
WINES NV Réserve Brut, NV Sélection Brut,
NV Blanc de Blancs Brut, Rosé Brut, Vintage
Special Club, Coteaux Champenois Blanc de
Blancs, Coteaux Champenois Rouge (100%
PM), ratafia
COMMENT The grower owns 16.5 hectares of
Chardonnay and Pinot Meunier at Fèrebrianges
and 5 hectares of Pinot Noir at Essômes. The
average annual production amounts to 100,000
bottles.

Marcel Pernet
Telephone (26) 59.30.58
WINES NV Brut

FESTIGNY 84% échelle de cru

Henri Loriot
WINES NV Brut (100% PM)
COMMENT I have tasted this wine once; it is dry and well-balanced, with good fruit and an interesting perfume on the after-taste.

FONTAINE-DENIS
85% (black grapes) – 87% (white grapes) échelle de cru

René Collet
Grande Rue
Telephone (26) 80.21.08
WINES NV Brut

GRAUVES 90% (black grapes) – 95% (white grapes) échelle de cru

Roland Marchand
4 rue du Baut
Telephone (26) 59.71.26
WINES NV 1er Cru Brut

GYE-SUR-SEINE 80% échelle de cru

Cheurlin & Fils
Rue de la Gare
Telephone (25) 38.56.27
WINES NV Spécial Réserve Brut

HAUTVILLERS 93% échelle de cru

J. Desruets
85 rue de Bacchus
Telephone (26) 59.40.13
WINES NV 1er Cru Brut, Coteaux Champenois Blanc

J. M. Gobillard
126 rue de Bacchus
Telephone (26) 59.40.18
WINES NV Brut, NV Rosé Brut, NV Blanc de Blancs Brut, Vintage Blanc de Blancs Brut, Coteaux Champenois Blanc, Coteaux Champenois Rouge, Coteaux Champenois Rosé

Jean Hugues
162 route de Fismes
Telephone (26) 59.40.56
WINES NV Brut, NV Extra Sec, NV Sec, NV Demi-Sec
COMMENT The grower owns vineyards at Pierry.

Serge Landragin
88 rue de l'Église
Telephone (26) 59.40.30
WINES NV 1er Cru Brut

Fernand Lemaire
88 rue des Buttes
Telephone (26) 59.40.44
WINES NV 1er Cru Brut

Locret-Lachaud
40 rue Saint-Vincent
Telephone (26) 59.40.20
WINES NV Brut, Coteaux Champenois Blanc

G. Sauvignier
Telephone (26) 59.40.17
WINES NV Brut

G. Tribaut
Telephone (26) 59.40.57
WINES NV 1er Cru Brut, Coteaux Champenois

LANDREVILLE 80% échelle de cru

Chaussin-Vetraino
Telephone (25) 38.52.61
WINES NV Brut

Jacques Dufour
88 Grande Rue
Telephone (25) 38.52.23
WINES NV Brut

Robert Dufour & Fils
4 rue de la Croix Malot
Telephone (25) 38.52.25
WINES NV Blanc de Blancs Brut

Daniel Lardoux
Rue de la Poste
Telephone (25) 38.52.87
WINES NV Extra Quality Brut

Royer Père & Fils
62 Grande Rue
Telephone (25) 38.52.16
WINES NV Cuvée de Réserve Blanc de Blancs Brut

LOCHES-SUR-OURCE 80% échelle de cru

Dautel & Jacquenet
10 rue Saint-Vincent
Telephone (25) 38.61.12
WINES NV Blanc de Blancs Brut

LOUVOIS 100% échelle de cru

Yves Beautrait
Allées des Cavaliers
Telephone (26) 59.03.30
WINES NV Brut Premier Cru, Vintage Rosé
Brut (blended), Vintage Special Club, Coteaux
Champenois Bouzy Rouge.
COMMENT The grower owns 16.5 hectares (11
of Pinot Noir and 5.5 of Chardonnay) at
Louvois, Bouzy, Tauxières and Tours-sur-
Marne. I tasted a fine bottle of Special Club
1975 in 1982.

Guy Méa
1 rue de l'Église
Telephone (26) 59.03.42
WINES NV Brut 1er Cru

LUDES 94% échelle de cru

Brixon-Coquillard
5 rue de Mailly
Telephone (26) 61.11.37
WINES NV Premier Cru Brut, NV Premier Cru
Sec, NV Premier Extra Dry, NV Premier Cru
Demi-Sec, Coteaux Champenois Blanc

Forget-Bereche
Forget-Brimont
Forget-Chemin
16 rue Victor-Hugo
Telephone (26) 61.12.17
WINES under each label: NV Carte Blanche,
NV Carte Verte, NV Rosé Brut, Special Club,
Coteaux Champenois

Gaidoz-Forget
Forget-Menu
4 rue Gambetta
Telephone (26) 61.10.30
WINES under each label: NV Brut, NV Sec,
NV Extra Dry, NV Demi-Sec, Coteaux
Champenois

Lamarche
Rue des Flammées
Telephone (26) 61.12.25
WINES NV Premier Cru Brut, NV Premier Cru
Demi-Sec, Rosé Brut, Coteaux Champenois
Blanc, Coteaux Champenois Rouge, ratafia

Collective Monmartre & Fils
Rue Victor-Hugo
Telephone (26) 61.10.99
WINES NV 1er Cru Brut, NV 1er Cru Sec, NV
1er Cru Demi-Sec

Quatresols-Gauthier
4 rue de Reims
Telephone (26) 61.10.13
WINES NV 1er Cru Brut, NV 1er Cru Sec, NV
1er Cru Demi-Sec, Coteaux Champenois Blanc,
Coteaux Champenois Bouzy Rouge

Quatresols-Jamein
34 rue Victor-Hugo
Telephone (26) 61.10 22
WINES NV Carte d'Or Brut, NV Carte d'Or
Sec, NV Carte d'Or Extra Dry, NV Carte d'Or
Demi-Sec

Serge Rafflin
10 rue Nationale
Telephone (26) 61.12.84
WINES NV Premier Cru Brut, Coteaux
Champenois Ludes Rouge, ratafia

MAILLY-CHAMPAGNE
100% échelle de cru

Barbier-Gosset
6 place Marceau
Telephone (26) 49.41.34
WINES NV Réserve Brut, NV Réserve Sec,
NV Réserve Extra Dry, NV Réserve Demi-Sec,
Coteaux Champenois Blanc

Jacques Chance
WINES NV Grand Cru Brut

M. Chevallier
9 rue A, Briand
Telephone (26) 49.41.27
WINES NV Premier Cru Brut, NV Premier Cru
Sec, NV Premier Cru Demi-Sec

Paul Decotte
Rue de la Libération
Telephone (26) 49.41.04
WINES NV Grand Cru Brut

Gilbert Devarenne
4 rue Jules Ferry
Telephone (26) 49.44.23
WINES NV Brut, NV Demi-Sec, Coteaux
Champenois Blanc

Jean-Pierre Floquet
Telephone (26) 49.48.13
WINES NV Brut

Michel Garitan
36 rue Gambetta
Telephone (26) 49.43.61
WINES NV Brut, NV Demi-Sec, Coteaux
Champenois

Michel Henroux
Rue Hautes des Carrières
Telephone (26) 49.48.05
WINES NV Grand Cru Brut

Lucien Roguet
7 rue Gambetta
Telephone (26) 49.41.36
WINES NV Grand Cru 100% Brut
COMMENT The growers have been established
from 1870.

Lucien Richez
Telephone (26) 49.41.23
WINES NV Brut

N. Vanzella
5 rue Joliot-Curie
Telephone (26) 49.41.67
WINES NV Brut, NV Sec, NV Demi-Sec,
Coteaux Champenois Blanc

MANCY   88% échelle de cru

Bourboin Fils
3 Grande Rue
Telephone (26) 59.71.64
WINES NV Brut

B. Domi-Marceau
11 rue de Bas
Telephone (26) 59.71.67
WINES NV Brut

Jacques-Fleury
21 rue de Bas
Telephone (26) 59.71.56
WINES NV Brut

Pernet-Lebrun
Ancien Moulin
Telephone (26) 59.71.63
WINES NV Brut

MAREUIL-LE-PORT   84% échelle de cru

Duval Roger
Impasse de la Recette
Telephone (26) 50.31.54
WINES NV Brut, NV Demi-Sec

MAREUIL-SUR-AŸ   98% échelle de cru

Roland Benard
21 rue Corbier
Telephone (26) 50.60.36
WINES NV Brut Sélection Or, NV Brut Noir,

NV Sec, NV Demi-Sec, Cuvée de Réserve Brut,
Blanc de Blancs Brut, Brut Rosé, Coteaux
Champenois Blanc
COMMENT The grower owns 6.6 hectares.

LE-MESNIL-SUR-OGER
100% échelle de cru

François Billion
4 rue des Lombards
Telephone (26) 50.51.24
WINES NV Premier Cru Blanc de Blancs Brut

Claude Cazals
Telephone (26) 50.52.26
WINES NV Blanc de Blancs Brut

Guy Charlemagne-Peters
4 rue Brêche d'Oger
Telephone (26) 50.52.98
WINES NV Blanc de Blancs Brut
COMMENT The grower is a producer of
significant quantity, but I have not tasted the
wines.

François Gonet
Rue du Stade
Telephone (26) 50.53.71
WINES NV Brut (50% PN, 50% CH), NV
Demi-Sec, NV Cuvée de Réserve Blanc de
Blancs Brut, Vintage Brut, Vintage Special Club
COMMENT The grower owns 7 hectares,
producing 70,000 bottles a year

André Jacquart
WINES NV Blanc de Blancs Brut, Rosé Brut,
Cuvée Spéciale Brut, Vintage Brut, Vintage
Special Club Brut.
COMMENT The grower owns 12 hectares,
producing 90,000 bottles a year. He makes
light, fresh wines, with a fruity, clean and well-
balanced taste.

Léon Launois
3 ruelle de l'Arquebuse
Telephone (26) 50.50.28
WINES NV Premier Cru Cuvée Réservée Blanc
de Blancs Brut

Launois Père & Fils
3 avenue de la République
Telephone (26) 50.50.15
WINES NV Premier Cru Cuvée Réservée Blanc
de Blancs Brut, Crémant Blanc de Blancs Brut,
Vintage Special Club, Rosé Brut
COMMENT The firm was founded in 1872. The
growers own 21 hectares, producing 200,000

bottles a year. I have tasted NV Cuvée Réservée on many occasions in Britain; it is a well-made, old-style, biscuity Chardonnay, with a fine *mousse*. It is ready for drinking straight away and improves little with age.

Pertois-Moriset
5 route d'Oger
Telephone (26) 50.53.04
WINES NV Premier Cru Grande Réserve Blanc de Blancs Brut

Pierre Peters
26 rue des Lombards
Telephone (26) 50.50.32
WINES NV Cuvée Réserve Blanc de Blancs Brut, Crémant Blanc de Blancs Brut, Vintage Blanc de Blancs Brut, Vintage Special Club Blanc de Blancs Brut, ratafia
COMMENT The grower owns 12 hectares at le Mesnil-sur-Oger, 4 hectares at Sézanne and 1 hectare at Baye, producing 140,000 bottles a year. I have tasted the NV Cuvée Réserve Blanc de Blancs Brut on several occasions. It has a hint of Mesnil perfume on the nose and is very dry and correct on the palate, but is fatter and has not quite the varietal purity of a classic Mesnil blanc de blancs; nevertheless, it is a well-made wine of fine *mousse* and extremely enjoyable character. The Crémant I have tasted only once; finely perfumed and with a gentle *mousse*, it is an exceptional wine.

Alain Robert
25 avenue de la République
Telephone (26) 50.52.94
WINES NV Blanc de Blancs Brut

MEURVILLE 80% échelle de cru

Bernard Capprest
Telephone (25) 26.41.14
WINES NV Cuvée Speciale Blanc de Blancs Brut

MONTGENOST 85% (black grapes) – 87% (white grapes) échelle de cru

Jacques Copinet
WINES NV Blanc de Blancs Brut, NV Rosé Brut
COMMENT The pink Champagne is a delicate Chardonnay-style wine.

MONTHELON 88% échelle de cru

René le Brun
6 and 12 rue Gaston Poittevin
Telephone (26) 59.70.30
WINES NV Brut

Julien Chopin
1 rue Gaston Poittevin
Telephone (26) 59.70.46
WINES NV Cuvée Réserve Brut

Georges Colin
Telephone (26) 59.70.03
WINES NV Cuvée de Réserve Brut, Blanc de Blancs Brut

Denis Frézier
8 and 50 rue Gaston Poittevin
Telephone (26) 59.70.16
WINES NV Brut

Gaspard-Parmentier
58–60 rue Gaston Poittevin
Telephone (26) 59.70.37
WINES NV Grande Réserve Brut

Marchand & Fils
16–18 rue Henri Martin
Telephone (26) 59.70.08
WINES NV Cuvée Réserve Brut

Du Mont-Hauban
3 route de Mancy
Telephone (26) 59.70.27
WINES NV Brut

Jacques Robert
Telephone (26) 59.70.21
WINES NV Extra Quality Brut, Coteaux Champenois Monthelon Rouge

MONTIGNY-SOUS-CHÂTILLON
86% échelle de cru

Charlier & Fils
4 rue des Pervenches
Telephone (26) 50.35.18
WINES Carte Blanche Brut, Carte Blanche Sec, Carte Blanche Demi-Sec, Carte Noire Brut, Carte Noire Sec, Carte Noire Demi-Sec, NV Rosé Brut (blended), Vintage Special Club, Coteaux Champenois Blanc, Vintage Coteaux Champenois Rouge, Coteaux Champenois Rosé de Saignée, ratafia
COMMENT The growers own 8 hectares at Montigny (4.8 of Pinot Noir, 2.4 of Pinot Meunier and 0.8 of Chardonnay), producing 90,000 bottles a year.

Lacrois
Telephone (26) 50.35.17
WINES NV Brut, NV Demi-Sec, Brut Rosé,
Cuvée des Sapeurs-Pompiers, Coteaux
Champenois Blanc, Coteaux Champenois
Rouge

MOUSSY 88% échelle de cru

Daniel Charlot
5 rue Jules Ferry
Telephone (26) 51.48.21
WINES NV Brut

Roger Crété
1 rue des Plantes
Telephone (26) 51.40.78
WINES NV Brut

Veuve Godart & Fils
Avenue du Mont Félix
Telephone (26) 51.44.64
WINES NV Cuvée Réserve Brut

Michel & Fils
Telephone (26) 51.49.57
WINES NV Carte Blanche Brut (80% PM, 20%
CH), NV Carte Noire Extra Dry (80% PM,
20% CH), Blanc de Blancs Brut, Brut Rosé
(100% PM), Vintage Special Club (50% PM,
50% CH), Coteaux Champenois Moussy Blanc,
Coteaux Champenois Moussy Rouge

Jean Michel
15 rue Jean-Jaurès
Telephone (26) 51.26.10
WINES NV Brut, Vintage Brut, Coteaux
Champenois Moussy Rouge
COMMENT I tasted a bottle of light and grapy
Moussy Rouge in 1983.

José Michel-Tisserand
14 rue Prélot
WINES NV Carte Blanche Brut, NV Carte
Blanche Demi-Sec, Rosé Brut, Vintage Blanc de
Blancs Brut, Vintage Crémant Brut, Vintage
Special Club, Coteaux Champenois
COMMENT The grower owns 15.2 hectares,
producing 125,000 bottles a year. Tasted once
only – an obviously elegant wine underneath,
spoilt by an ungainly hint of oxidation.

R. Renaudin
Domaine des Conardins
Telephone (26) 51.28.04
WINES NV Brut, Domaine des Conardins Brut,
Vintage Special Club, Coteaux Champenois
Moussy Rouge

COMMENT The grower owns 22.5 hectares,
producing 240,000 bottles a year.

Collective Thiercelin
2 place Léon Bourgeois
WINES NV Brut
COMMENT The collective is a producer of
significant quantity, but I have not tasted the
wines.

NEUVILLE-SUR-SEINE
80% échelle de cru

E. Carré
Telephone (25) 38.57.15
WINES NV Brut

Paul Hérard
Telephone (25) 38.56.14
WINES NV Blanc de Noirs Brut, NV Sec, NV
Demi-Sec Brut Réserve
COMMENT The grower owns 10 hectares,
producing 90,000 bottles a year.

NOÉ-LES-MALLETS 80% échelle de cru

Veuve Doussot
Telephone (25) 38.60.18
WINES NV Brut

OEUILLY 84% échelle de cru

Tarlant Père & Fils
WINES NV Cuvée de Réserve Brut

OGER 100% échelle de cru

René Henry
1 rue d'Avize
Telephone (26) 50.50.89
WINES NV Carte d'Or Blanc de Blancs Brut

Thomas-Hussenet
17 rue de 7 Vents
Telephone (26) 50.51.49
WINES NV Cuvée Spéciale Brut
COMMENT No chemical fertilisers or pesticides
are used.

PASSY-SUR-MARNE 85% échelle de cru

Alain Mercier
Telephone (26) 71.93.76
WINES NV Brut

PIERRY 90% échelle de cru

Michel Mandois-Bernier
66 rue du Général de Gaulle
WINES NV Brut
COMMENT The grower is a producer of
significant quantity, but I have not tasted the
wines.

PORT-À-BINSON 84% échelle de cru

Lecart-Cabaret
Route Nationale 3
Telephone (26) 50.30.08
WINES NV Grande Réserve Brut, NV Grande
Réserve Sec, NV Grande Réserve Demi-Sec

Claude Cordoin
Route Nationale 3
Telephone (26) 50.31.66
WINES NV Sec, NV Demi-Sec, Cuvée de
Réserve Brut, Carte d'Or Brut

LES RICEYS 80% échelle de cru

Alexandre Bonnet
138 rue de Général de Gaulle, Ricey-Haut
Telephone (25) 38.30.93
WINES NV Brut Tradition, NV Blanc de
Blancs Brut, NV Brut Prestige, Brut Rosé, Rosé
des Riceys, Coteaux Champenois Blanc,
Coteaux Champenois Rouge, Coteaux
Champenois Rosé
COMMENT Distinctive still red wines which are
rich, smoky, complex and capable of ageing
ten years or more.

Gallimard Père & Fils
18 rue du Magny, Ricey-Haut
Telephone (25) 38.32.44
WINES NV Brut, NV Brut Rosé
COMMENT The NV Brut is a blanc de noirs
and the rosé (skin contact) shows good Pinot
Noir varietal characteristics.

Horiot Père & Fils
11 rue de la Cure, Ricey-Bas
Telephone (25) 38.32.21
WINES NV Brut (50% PN, 50% CH), NV
Brut Rosé, Rosé des Riceys
COMMENT Certainly the pink Champagne and
Rosé des Riceys are Horiot's best products. The
former is on the dark side: a big, full and fruity
wine, which can tend to be earthy, according to
the vintage on which the blend is based (the
1977 was earthy, the 1976 pure fruit). Of the

Rosé des Riceys, the 1979 was elegant; the
1978 was rich and distinctive, with a minty
aroma and an excellent depth of flavour; the
1976 was big and dark, but rather short; and
the 1971 was superbly balanced, deceptively
light, yet intensely flavoured and velvet smooth.

Serge Mathieu
Avirey-Lingey
Telephone (25) 38.32.58
WINES NV Tradition Brut, NV Sec, NV Demi-
Sec, Brut Prestige, Vintage Brut, Brut Rosé

Morel Père et Fils
1 grande rue de l'Ecole, Riceys
Telephone (25) 38.35.67
WINES Rosé des Riceys
COMMENT One of the three producers of Rosé
des Riceys, but the only one concentrating on it
alone. Tasted only a few times, it was nothing
special, but it is a wine which favours
exceptional vintages and maybe the NV blends
were not based on particularly special years.
Tiny production of about 2,000 bottles a year.

Morize Père & Fils
122 rue du Général de Gaulle, Ricey-Haut
Telephone (25) 38.30.02
WINES NV Brut

Joseph Walczak
'Le Cadran Solaire', Ricey-Haut
Telephone (25) 38.31.57
WINES NV Brut

RILLY-LA-MONTAGNE
94% échelle de cru

Adam-Garnotel
Telephone (26) 03.40.22
WINES NV Extra Quality Brut, NV Demi-Sec,
Blanc de Blancs Brut, Rosé Brut (blended),
Vintage Brut
COMMENT The growers own 9 hectares. Their
average annual production amounts to 100,000
bottles.

Michel Fagot
4 bis rue de Chigny
WINES NV Brut
COMMENT The grower is a producer of
significant quantity, but I have not tasted the
wines.

Vilmart
4 rue de la République
Telephone (26) 48.40.01
WINES NV Cuvée Sélectionée Brut, Coteaux
Champenois Rilly Rouge

ROMERY 85% échelle de cru

M. Pingret-Sachet
Rue des Grappes d'Or
Telephone (26) 59.41.75
WINES NV Brut, NV Sec, NV Demi-Sec

SAINT MARTIN D'ABLOIS
86% échelle de cru

Cez-Danjou
3 place du Général de Gaulle
Telephone (26) 59.51.32
WINES NV Brut

T. C. Desmoulins
22 rue des Lambourgs
Telephone (26) 59.50.51
WINES NV Brut, NV Sec, NV Demi-Sec, NV
Brut Réserve, Coteaux Champenois Blanc,
ratafia

Didier-Niceron
1 route d'Épernay
Telephone (26) 59.50.23
WINES NV Brut

Maurice Diot
5 rue Marcel Soyeux
Telephone (26) 59.51.04
WINES NV Brut

Michel Hatat
4 place du Général de Gaulle
Telephone (26) 59.50.01
WINES NV Brut, NV Sec, NV Demi-Sec,
Coteaux Champenois Blanc

SERMIERS 89% échelle de cru

René Fresne
Place de l'Église
Telephone (26) 97.62.31
WINES NV Réserve Brut, NV Réserve Sec, NV
Réserve Demi-Sec, Coteaux Champenois Blanc,
ratafia

Froment-Griffon
Route de Champagne
Telephone (26) 97.62.37
WINES NV Grande Réserve Brut, NV Sec, NV
Demi-Sec, Coteaux Champenois Blanc, ratafia

Hury-Manceaux
Telephone (26) 97.60.88
WINES NV Brut

Lacuisse Frères
134 route de Champagne, Nogent
Telephone (26) 97.62.53
WINES NV Réserve Brut, NV Réserve Sec, NV
Réserve Demi-Sec

Roland Lagrive
Route de Montchenot
Telephone (26) 97.62.64
WINES NV Brut, NV Sec, NV Demi-Sec

Manceaux-Lantenois
Nogent
Telephone (26) 97.60.08
WINES NV Brut, NV Sec, NV Demi-Sec

André Rat
Rue du Clos des Moines
Telephone (26) 97.61.95
WINES NV Brut Sélection, NV Sec Sélection,
NV Demi-Sec Sélection, Coteaux Champenois
Blanc, ratafia

Jean Rat
Nogent
Telephone (26) 97.62.94
WINES NV Brut, NV Sec, NV Demi-Sec,
Coteaux Champenois Blanc, ratafia

TALUS-SAINT-PRIX 85% échelle de cru

André Triolet
Grande Rue
Telephone (26) 59.12.42
WINES NV Brut

TOURS-SUR-MARNE 100% échelle de cru

Yves Delaporte
Rue de la Haie du Bois
Telephone (26) 59.91.26
WINES NV Brut

Lamiable Frères
8 rue de Condé-sur-Marne
Telephone (26) 59.92.69
WINES NV Brut, NV Extra Sec, NV Demi-Sec,
Brut Rosé, Vintage Special Club, Coteaux
Champenois
COMMENT The growers own 6 hectares,
producing 60,000 bottles a year.

TRÉLOU-SUR-MARNE 85% échelle de cru

Belouis Fils
'Chassins'
Telephone (26) 71.92.48
WINES NV Brut

Veuve Olivier & Fils
Telephone (26) 71.93.51
WINES NV Carte d'Or Brut

TRÉPAIL 95% échelle de cru

Claude Beaufort
5 rue des Neigettes
Telephone (26) 59.05.63
WINES NV Premier Cru Brut, NV Premier Cru
Extra Dry, NV Premier Cru Demi-Sec, Blanc de
Blancs Brut, Coteaux Champenois Blanc

Carré-Guebels
Rue de l'Égalité
Telephone (26) 59.05.02
WINES NV Premier Cru Brut

Jean Darreye
2 rue d'Ambonnay
Telephone (26) 59.05.18
WINES NV Cuvée de Réserve, Coteaux
Champenois Blanc
COMMENT The grower owns vineyards at
Villers-Marmery in addition to those at Trépail.

J. C. Dupont
7 rue d'Ambonnay
Telephone (26) 59.05.59
WINES NV Premier Cru Brut, NV Premier Cru
Sec, NV Premier Cru Demi-Sec, Rosé Brut,
Blanc de Blancs Brut

Pierre Gabrielle & Fils
2 rue du Calvaire
Telephone (26) 59.05.46
WINES NV Brut, NV Sec, NV Demi-Sec,
Coteaux Champenois Blanc, Coteaux
Champenois Bouzy Rouge

Guebels-Bernardin
2 impasse du Général Abbé
Telephone (26) 59.05.58
WINES NV Premier Cru Brut, NV Premier Cru
Sec, NV Premier Cru Demi-Sec, Coteaux
Champenois Blanc

Kléber Jacqueminet
33 rue de Vaudemanges
Telephone (26) 59.05.75
WINES NV Brut, NV Sec, NV Demi-Sec,
Coteaux Champenois Blanc

Machet-Griffon
1 rue de Vaudemanges
Telephone (26) 59.05.25
WINES NV Premier Cru Brut, Coteaux
Champenois Trépail Rouge

Pétiau & Fils
9 rue Saint-Martin
Telephone (26) 59.05.48
WINES NV Premier Cru Brut, NV Premier Cru
Sec, NV Premier Cru Demi-Sec, Blanc de Blancs
Brut

Redon-Lapoulle
22 rue de Vaudemanges
Telephone (26) 59.05.66
WINES NV 1er Cru Brut, NV 1er Cru Sec, NV
1er Cru Demi-Sec, Blanc de Blancs Brut,
Coteaux Champenois Blanc

TRIGNY 84% échelle de cru

Robert Bertrand
Rue du Point du Jour
Telephone (26) 49.31.47
WINES NV Brut

A. Forest & Fils
Petite rue de l'Église
WINES NV Brut

Marcel Forest & Fils
Telephone (26) 49.32.57
WINES NV Brut

J. C. Malot Fils
Grande rue
Telephone (26) 59.31.81
WINES NV Brut

TROISSY 84% échelle de cru

Charles Orban
44 route de Paris
Telephone (26) 50.70 05
WINES NV Carte Blanche Brut (100% PM),
NV Carte Noire Brut (100% PM; Vincelles),
NV Carte d'Or Blanc de Blancs Brut (an
assemblage of Troissy and Vincelles wines),
NV Rosé Brut (100% PM; blended), Vintage
Special Club, ratafia
COMMENT The grower owns 4 hectares at
Troissy and 2 hectares at Vincelles and Treslon,
producing 60,000 bottles a year.

URVILLE 80% échelle de cru

André Drappier-Collot
Telephone (25) 26.40.15
WINES NV Extra Dry

VAUCIENNES 84% échelle de cru

Michel Laroche
WINES NV Brut, NV Rosé Brut
COMMENT These wines, made from a three-hectare vineyard called La Chaussée, are full-bodied, crisp, dry and stylish.

VAUDEMANGES 95% échelle de cru

Chaudron & Fils
Rue d'Ambonnay
Telephone (26) 26.69.59
WINES NV Brut

VENTEUIL 89% échelle de cru

Collective Guerre
Les Hurelles
WINES NV Brut
COMMENT The collective has a significant sized production.

Jean-Pierre Marniquet
23 rue de Champagne
Telephone (26) 50.46.01
WINES NV Brut, NV Sec, NV Demi-Sec, Brut Rosé, Coteaux Champenois Blanc, Coteaux Champenois Rouge

Prévoteau-Tintier
6 Faubourg d'Arnotay
Telephone (26) 50.47.28
WINES NV Brut, NV Sec, NV Demi-Sec, NV Doux, Coteaux Champenois

VERNEUIL 86% échelle de cru

Jean Vatel
Rue de la Tour
Telephone (26) 50.76.34
WINES NV Brut

VERTUS 95% échelle de cru

Bonnet-Launois
Route du Mesnil-sur-Oger
Telephone (26) 50.82.46
WINES NV Premier Cru Brut, Coteaux Champenois Blanc, Coteau Champenois Vertus Rouge

René Bouché
44 route de Voipreux
Telephone (26) 50.84.12
WINES NV 1er Cru Cuvée de Réserve Blanc de Blancs Brut

Jean-Paul Boulonnais
7 boulevard Paul-Georg
Telephone (26) 59.81.16
WINES NV Brut, Blanc de Blancs Brut, Coteaux Champenois Vertus Rouge

Henri Bourgeois
WINES NV Blanc de Blancs Brut
COMMENT I have tasted this wine only once; it was light, steely and correct.

Lucien Carré
WINES NV Blanc de Blancs Brut
COMMENT I have tasted this wine only once; it had an elegant Chardonnay on the nose, was light-bodied, had a hint of honey and a good finish.

Doquet-Jeanmaire
Route de Voipreux
Telephone (26) 52.16.50
WINES NV Carte d'Or Blanc de Blancs Brut, NV Sélection Blanc de Blancs Brut, Réserve Blanc de Blancs Brut, Vintage Brut, Rosé Brut
COMMENT The growers own 13 hectares, producing 100,000 bottles a year.

Bernard Doublet
15 'les Falloises'
Telephone (26) 50.84.47
WINES NV 1er Cru Brut, Coteaux Champenois Blanc, Coteaux Champenois Vertus Rouge

Doublet-Hadot Père & Fils
6 place Mont-Chenil
Telephone (26) 50.81.55
WINES NV Premier Cru Brut

Veuve A. Fourny & Fils
Route du Mesnil
Telephone (26) 50.80.76
WINES NV Blanc de Blancs Brut

Larmandier-Bernier
43 rue du 28 Août
Telephone (26) 50.81.89
WINES NV Brut (25% PN, 75% CH), NV Crémant Blanc de Blancs Brut (an *assemblage* of Chouilly, Cramant and Vertus), NV Blanc de Blancs Brut (the same as the preceding wine, but fully *mousseux*), NV Brut Rosé (NV Brut blended with red wine from Vertus), Vintage Special Club, Coteaux Champenois Blanc (100% CH; Cramant and Vertus) Coteaux Champenois Vertus Rouge
COMMENT The growers own 9.5 hectares of Chardonnay and Pinot Noir at Bergères-les-Vertus, Chouilly, Cramant and Vertus,

producing 65,000 bottles a year. I tasted the
NV Blanc de Blancs once in 1980; it had a
closed nose and initially good depth of flavour,
but it fell short on the finish.

J. C. Launois
32 route de Voipreux
Telephone (26) 50.84.78
WINES NV Brut, NV Sec, NV Demi-Sec,
Grande Réserve Blanc de Blancs Brut, Crémant
Brut, Rosé Brut, Coteaux Champenois

Charles Pougeoise
21–23 Boulevard Paul-Goerg
WINES NV Carte Noire Brut, NV Sec, NV
Demi-Sec, Crémant Brut, Carte Rouge Grande
Réserve Brut, Rosé Brut
COMMENT The grower owns 13 hectares,
producing 100,000 bottles a year.

Michel Rogué
15 rue Général Leclerc
Telephone (26) 50.82.12
WINES NV Premier Cru Brut, Rosé Brut,
Coteaux Champenois Blanc, Coteaux
Champenois Vertus Rouge

Eraldo Schirru
78 route de Voipreux
Telephone (26) 50.84.48
WINES NV Premier Cru Brut

Séverin-Doublet
10 rue des Falloises
Telephone (26) 50.81.63
WINES NV Brut (15% PN, 85% CH), NV
Blanc de Blancs Brut (less than 0.5% of the
total production)
COMMENT The annual production amounts to
approximately 50,000 bottles. A tiny amount
of vintage Champagne is made in the finest
years, but is not available commercially. The
1966, served as a pick-me-up after a long day of
St Vincent celebrations and ceremonies in
1980, was probably the best grower
Champagne I have ever drunk; with a rich,
toasty Chardonnay nose and palate, lifted by
the liveliness of a fine and persistent *mousse*, it
was an exceptional wine indeed.

VERZENAY 100% échelle de cru

Michel Arnould
28 rue de Mailly
Telephone (26) 49.40.06
WINES NV Brut Grand Cru, NV Brut Réserve,
Coteaux Champenois Blanc, Coteaux
Champenois Verzenay Rouge, Coteaux
Champenois Rosé

Pierre Arnould
1 rue Gambetta
Telephone (26) 49.40.12
WINES NV Brut, Coteaux Champenois Blanc,
Coteaux Champenois Verzenay Rouge

Jean Bovière
24 rue André Charpentier
Telephone (26) 49.41.76
WINES NV 1er Cru Brut

Christian Busin
Rue d'Uzes and 33 rue Thiers
Telephone (26) 49.40.94
WINES NV Grand Cru Brut, Coteaux
Champenois Blanc

Alain Collas
1 rue Heidsieck
Telephone (26) 49.42.70
WINES NV Brut
COMMENT The grower owns vineyards at
Serzy and Verneuil.

Floquet-Gélot
6 rue Corbet
Telephone (26) 49.42.92
WINES NV Brut Sélection, Rosé Brut, Coteaux
Champenois Verzenay Rouge, Coteaux
Champenois Blanc

J. C. Foureur
9 rue Buirette-Petit
Telephone (26) 49.41.99
WINES NV Sélection Brut, NV Sélection Demi-
Sec, NV Réserve Brut, Réserve du Vigneron
Brut, Spécialité Rosé Brut, Coteaux
Champenois Verzenay Rouge, Coteaux
Champenois Blanc de Blancs, Coteaux
Champenois Rosé, ratafia

Bertrand Godmé
11 rue Werlé
Telephone (26) 49.41.88
WINES NV Cuvée de Réserve Brut, Coteaux
Champenois Blanc
COMMENT I tasted a good-quality,
uncomplicated and fruity NV in 1983.

Bernard Hatté
1 rue de la Petite Fontaine
Telephone (26) 49.40.90
WINES NV Brut, Rosé Brut, Cuvée Special
CLub, Coteaux Champenois Blanc
COMMENT The grower owns vineyards at
Chambrécy in addition to those at Verzenay.
Tasted twice, several years apart, but superb
wines on both occasions.

Rémi Hatté
8 rue Thiers
Telephone (26) 49.40.81
WINES NV Brut, Rosé Brut, Coteaux
Champenois Blanc, Coteaux Champenois
Rouge

Marc Henriet
33 rue de Mailly
Telephone (26) 49.41.79
WINES NV Grand Cru 100% Brut Sélection

Hervy-Quenardel
12 rue Werlé
Telephone (26) 49.44.52
WINES NV Brut, Rosé Brut, Coteaux
Champenois Blanc

Longueville
Place de Mairie
Telephone (26) 49.40.63
WINES NV Brut

Michel Pithois
16 rue Moët et Chandon
Telephone (26) 49.41.77
WINES NV Brut Réserve, Coteaux
Champenois Blanc

Quenardel-Esquerré
7 rue Werlé
Telephone (26) 49.41.81
WINES NV Grand Cru 100% Brut

Quenardel et Fils
Place de la Mairie
Telephone (26) 49.40.63
WINES NV Cuvée de Réserve Brut, NV Cuvée
de Réserve Sec, NV Cuvée de Réserve Demi-
Sec, Vintage Special Club Brut
COMMENT I have tasted the Special Club 1978
only once; it had a biscuity nose, heavy fruit
and a peppery finish.

VERZY 100% échelle de cru

Jean-Paul Deville
13 rue Carnot
Telephone (26) 49.42.80
WINES NV Brut, Vintage Brut, Coteaux
Champenois Blanc, ratafia

R. Juillet – P. & A. Lallement
30 rue Carnot
Telephone (26) 49.42.42
WINES NV Brut, NV Rosé Brut (base wine of
NV Brut, to which red wine of Sillery is added),

Vintage Special Club, Coteaux Champenois
Blanc, Coteaux Champenois Sillery Rouge
COMMENT The growers own 4 hectares at
Verzy and Sillery.

VILLEDOMMANGE 90% échelle de cru

Bardoux Père & Fils
6 rue de Reims
Telephone (26) 49.25.10
WINES NV Brut

François Bergeronneau
10 rue de Vignes
Telephone (26) 49.24.18
WINES NV 1er Cru Brut

Raymond Devilliers
WINES Coteaux Champenois Villedommange
Rouge
COMMENT A traditional vinification, with the
wine kept two years in wood and no filtration,
produces a full red with a pronounced smoky
character. The 1978 possessed a strange but
interesting Emmenthal cheese nose!

Fresne Ducret Fils
Rue Saint-Vincent
Telephone (26) 49.24.60
WINES NV Brut Réserve

VILLERS-MARMERY 95% échelle de cru

B. de Berland
WINES NV Brut Réserve

G. Boutillez-Vignon
26 rue Pasteur
Telephone (26) 49.46.60
WINES NV 1er Cru Brut

A. Brassart
11 rue Pasteur
Telephone (26) 49.45.03
WINES NV Brut Réserve 1er Cru, NV Sec, NV
Demi-Sec, Blanc de Blancs 1er Cru

Gaston Dayer
3 rue Pasteur
Telephone (26) 49.45.27
WINES NV Premier Cru Brut

Henri Remy
5 rue Pasteur
Telephone (26) 49.45.45
WINES NV Premier Cru Brut

VILLE-SUR-ARCE 80% échelle de cru

J. M. Fériès
Telephone (25) 38.74.13
WINES NV Brut

Roger Marquant & Fils
Grande Rue
Telephone (25) 38.75.65
WINES NV Brut Réserve

Remy Massin & Fils
Telephone (25) 38.74.09
WINES NV Cuvée de Réserve Brut

Yvon Massin
Telephone (25) 38.75.20
WINES NV Brut Réserve

Raymond Thévenin
Grande Rue
Telephone (25) 38.75.21
WINES NV Brut

VILLEVENARD 85% échelle de cru

Collective Nominé-Renard
Telephone (26) 59.12.57
WINES NV Cuvée Spéciale Brut, Cuvée
Réserve Brut, Cuvée Rosé Brut, Cuvée Blanc de
Blancs Brut, Vintage Special Club
COMMENT The collective owns 20 hectares,
producing 160,000 bottles a year.

Renard-Barnier
Telephone (26) 59.12.51
WINES NV Brut Réserve

VINAY 86% échelle de cru

Roger Closquinet
4 rue de la Liberté
Telephone (26) 51.47.20
WINES NV Brut, NV Sec, NV Demi-Sec, Brut
Rosé, Vintage Brut, Coteaux Champenois
Blanc, ratafia

Mignon Père & Fils
5 rue de Champagne
Telephone (26) 51.35.16
WINES NV Brut, NV Sec, NV Demi-Sec,
Cuvée de Réserve Brut, Coteaux Champenois
Blanc, Coteaux Champenois Rouge, ratafia

VOIGNY 80% échelle de cru

Jean Aubriot
Telephone (25) 27.00.72
WINES NV Brut

B. Robert
Telephone (25) 27.11.53
WINES Grande Réserve 'Le Treizot' Brut

Claude Sampers
Telephone (25) 27.11.57
WINES NV Brut

VRIGNY 89% échelle de cru

Marie-France de Latour
Telephone (26) 48.60.41
WINES NV Private Cuvée

Appendices

Appendix I The Vintages from 1900 to 1985

The following notes provide a summary of the principal factors – climatic and viticultural – affecting the quality and longevity of Champagnes vinified annually since 1900. Before proceeding to the annual entries, arranged in reverse chronological order, certain phrases of definition need to be clarified. The alcohol and acidity mentioned refer to the average strengths recorded, including the first and second *tailles*; since the finer Champagnes are vinified predominantly from the *cuvée*, their levels will be correspondingly higher. Details of permitted alcohol levels refer to the strength of the *vin clair* prior to the extra alcohol acquired during the *prise de mousse*. Critical terms like 'of average blending quality' or 'extremely useful for maintaining non-vintage blends', although referring to wines far removed from classic vintages, are not intended derogatorily: without these cardinal blends there would be no such thing as Champagne. Discrepancies arise, however, the further back in time one goes, when views drawn from contemporary critics tend to be both more polarised and more simplistic. Thus 'vintage' may range from good to great, while 'non-vintage' years are invariably described as poor. Since I do not share this view, I must therefore advise readers to beware of the semantic implications involved.

1985
Ouverture des vendanges Commenced 30 September all communes were picking by 4 October, harvest ceased 7 November.
Vineyard area in production 25,029 ha
Total production 1,139,185 hl
Average yield per hectare 6,827 kgs
Maximum permitted yield per hectare: 6,500 kgs, but this was extended up to a maximum of 13,000 kgs in exceptional, isolated cases.
Minimum permitted natural alcoholic content 8.5%
The vintage Winter frosts, with temperatures as low as −25°C, destroyed one in ten of every vine in Champagne. The greatest damage occurred in the northern Montagne de Reims, between Verzy and Pargny, and in the Aube, where nearly 25% of the vineyards were destroyed. Good weather in early July permitted a successful flowering for the surviving vines of all three varieties, but the development and

maturity of the grapes was irregular. A sunny September and October saved the day, although the quantities harvested varied between 1,000 kgs and 13,000 kgs per hectare. The indian summer created the opportunity in some areas for a rare second harvest.
The wine The quality was excellent, with wines averaging betwen 9% and 11% alcohol and 8 to 9.5 g/l of acidity. Certainly 1985 will be declared by most houses and it is likely to produce well balanced Champagnes of great elegance and finesse, possibly similar in style to 1975.

1984
Ouverture des vendanges 6 October for the communes of Bethon and la Celle-sous-Chantemerle and for young vines aged three years. 8 October for the communes of Bassu, Bassuet, Saint-Lumier-en-Champagne, Vitry-en-Perthois, Trépail, Villers-Marmery, Cumières, Damery, Venteuil, Barbonne-Fayel, Chantemerle, Fontaine-Denis, Montgenost, Saudoy, Sézanne, Vindey, all the communes of the Aube, Aisne, Seine-et-Marne and Haute-Marne *départements* and all Pinot Meunier vines situated north of the Vesle. 9 October for the communes of Épernay, Pierry, Moussy, Avize, Bergères-les-Vertus, Chouilly, Cramant, le Mesnil-sur-Oger, Oger, Oiry and Vertus. 10 October for all vines in other communes. Picking ceased on 5 November.
Vineyard area in production 24,638 ha
Total production 1,490,000 hl
Average yield per hectare 9,150 kgs
Maximum permitted yield per hectare 10,500 kgs
Minimum permitted natural alcoholic content 8%
The vintage A late but rapid *débourrement* created an expectation of yet another bumper-sized crop, but May was cold and wet and during the vital mid-June flowering period the temperature fluctuated considerably, resulting in *coulure* and *millerandage* and thus effectively reducing the potential size of the harvest. With a cooler and less sunny August than July, the grapes did not commence *véraison* until the end of the month. At the beginning of September there appeared to be a fairly sizeable crop of healthy grapes beginning the ripening process, but there were very few hours of sun – less than half the amount

normally expected for September and the lowest on record since 1958 – and north and north-west winds brought in persistent rain, interspersed with damaging hailstorms in parts of the Aube and the Aisne. Picking started and finished in poor weather, with a combination of fog and damp throughout the region encouraging the development of rot, making rigorous *épluchage* essential.

The wine With careful pressing and an extended *débourbage* a good sized harvest of average blending quality wine was produced, the Pinot Noir generally proving more successful than the Chardonnay.

1983

Ouverture des vendanges 26 September for the Chardonnay on the Côte des Blancs and the communes of Sézanne, Trépail, Vitry-le-François, Montgueux and Villenauxe. 29 September for the Chardonnay in all other communes and for the Pinot Noir and Pinot Meunier on the Côtes des Blancs, the communes around Sézanne, Trépail, Vitry-le-François, Montgueux, Villenauxe, Épernay, Cuis, Grauves, Mardeuil, Vauciennes, those communes with direct access to the rivers Marne and Aisne, all the vineyards north of the Vesle and in the Aube *département*. 3 October for all vines in the remaining communes. Picking ceased on 1 November.

Vineyard area in production 23,900 ha

Total production 2,245,667 hl, of which approximately 575,000 hl was placed on one side as a *stock régulateur*, a supply of non-classified *vin clair* to be held as a reserve against the possibility of short crops in the future.

Average yield per hectare 15,012 kgs (as high as 18,000 kgs in places).

Maximum permitted yield per hectare 15,200 kgs, of which only 11,200 kgs was classified at the time of the harvest as AOC Champagne, the balance of 4,000 kgs being regarded as a *stock régulateur* and, whereas 150 kgs of grapes normally provides 100 litres of must, the requirement for 1983 was raised to 160 kgs for the entire maximum yield of 15,200 kgs.

Minimum permitted natural alcoholic content 8.5%

The vintage After an excellent *sortie*, almost perfect weather provided Champagne with a record harvest of healthy, well-ripened grapes. There were no spring frosts, warm and dry conditions prevailed throughout the flowering period, and a fine summer and autumn followed, resulting in a second, successive, bumper crop. The last occasion when two successive years were of such outstanding quality was almost a century and a quarter ago, according to the CIVC, in the years 1857 and 1858. Just the odd patch of rain caused isolated patches of mildew.

The wine Both 1983 and 1982 wines are of fine quality and will no doubt always be compared to one another. In comparison to 1982, 1983 wines are equally as rich but have a higher malic acid content. The general consensus at the time of writing is that the 1983 vintage may not be quite as great as that of 1982, but the wines are assured an excellent potential and their higher acidity could mean that the best 1983s will outlive the best 1982s.

1982

Ouverture des vendanges 17 September for the Chardonnay from the communes of Chouilly, Cuis, Cramant, Avize, Oiry, Oger, le Mesnil-sur-Oger, Vertus, Voipreux, Villeneuve-Renneville, Bergères-les-Vertus, Coligny, Trépail, Villers-Marmery, Billy-le-Grand, Vaudemanges, Fontaine-Denis, la Celle-sous-Chantemerle, Bethon and Montgenost, and for all varieties of vine in the commune of Cumières and throughout the Aube *département*. 20 September for all varieties of vine in the remaining communes. Picking ceased on 26 October.

Vineyard area in production 23,618 ha

Total production 2,214,222 hl; Champagne: 2,212,880 hl; Coteaux Champenois: 1,342 hl

Average yield per hectare 14,080 kgs

Maximum permitted yield per hectare 13,000 kgs

Minimum permitted natural alcoholic content 8.5%

The vintage A fine *sortie* was followed by excellent climatic conditions right up until the harvest. This meant plenty of rain at the correct times (52.3 mm above normal), with more than sufficient sun (comparable to the drought year of 1976) and heat (a mean temperature of 11.35°C compared to 11.25°C for 1976). There were a few isolated outbreaks of mildew in June and July, but the bunches of grapes were healthy, ripe and rich in extract when picking began, possessing a better overall balance than the 1976 vintage. After one week of brilliant sunshine at the start of the *vendange* it poured, but, although picking conditions were far from perfect, the rain served the purpose of preventing over-ripeness, a condition which would have yielded fruit low in acidity and prone to oxidation.

The wine Classic, vintage quality *cuvées* resulted from blending the rich, early picked harvest with the somewhat diluted wines of later picked vines. The ideal climatic conditions prior to the rainfall highlighted the varietal characteristics, resulting in a fine fruity Pinot Meunier, an exceptionally strong and well-structured Pinot Noir and Chardonnay of outstanding perfume, balance and finesse. There could be some phenomenal grower Champagnes made entirely of early picked Chardonnay from the top growths of the Côte des Blancs.

1981

Ouverture des vendanges 28 September for all varieties of vines throughout the region. Picking ceased on 4 November.

Vineyard area in production 23,823 ha

Total production 695,673 hl

Average yield per hectare 4,390 kgs

Maximum permitted yield per hectare 9,000 kgs (13,000 kgs where some growers have applied for an increase in advance of the *ouverture des vendanges*).

Minimum permitted natural alcoholic content 9%
The vintage 1981 was a very wet year with an extra
200 mm of rain falling principally in the months of
March, June, October and December. An
exceptionally warm March gave rise to a precocious
bud-break, which allowed spring frosts to destroy
between 20 and 25% of the potential crop through
millerandage. Widespread *coulure* coupled with
virulent outbreaks of *oidium* further reduced the
crop.
The wine These wines are certainly of vintage
quality, although the crisis of low stocks was
exacerbated by such a small harvest. The question at
the time was not whether a vintage could be achieved,
but whether the houses could afford to bring out a
vintage Champagne when every drop of wine was
required for maintaining the volume and quality of
non-vintage blends. In retrospect the vintage was
obtained and produced wines of good alcohol and
acidity levels displaying an elegant balance. The
Chardonnay has an exceptionally aromatic bouquet
and the depth of flavour and richness of the Pinot
Noir is remarkable.

1980

Ouverture des vendanges 9 October for all varieties
of vine throughout the region. Picking ceased on 8
November.
Vineyard area in production 24,057 ha
Total production 851,716 hl
Average yield per hectare 5,311 kgs
Maximum permitted yield per hectare 7,500 kgs
(13,000 kgs where some growers have applied for an
increase in advance of the *ouverture des vendanges*).
Minimum permitted natural alcoholic content 7.5%
The vintage With the exception of February, August
and September the year was generally colder than
normal. The flowering was late and very poor and
coulure was widespread, with the Pinot Noir and
Pinot Meunier affected more than the Chardonnay.
Rain persisted throughout June and July, while
August and September were dry and reasonably
sunny.
The wine Although not of vintage quality, the wines
are fresh and aromatic, with excellent acidity levels
and most of them showing a satisfactory alcoholic
content. This vintage should prove extremely useful
in maintaining the quality and vigour of non-vintage
blends.

1979

Ouverture des vendanges 3 October for the
communes of Cumières, Bethon, Chantemerle, la
Celle-sous-Chantemerle, Fontaine-Denis,
Montgenost, Bassu, Bassuet, Saint-Lumier and Vitry-
en-Perthois. 5 October for the communes of Aÿ,
Dizy, Hautvillers, Louvois, Bouzy, Ambonnay,
Trépail, Barbonne-Fayel, Saudoy, Vindey, Sézanne
and, for Chardonnay only, the communes of
Épernay, Pierry, Cramant, Avize, Oger, le Mesnil-

sur-Oger, Vertus, Bergères-les-Vertus and the Aube
département. 8 October for all vine varieties in the
remaining communes. Picking ceased on 31 October.
Vineyard area in production 24,000 ha
Total production 1,731,598 hl; Champagne:
1,661,278 hl; Coteaux Champenois: 70,320 hl
Average yield per hectare 10,650 kgs
Maximum permitted yield per hectare 12,000 kgs
(Coteaux Champenois – 13,000 kgs)
Minimum permitted natural alcoholic content 8%
The vintage After a long, cold winter vine growth
was retarded by as much as one month; but as is
often the case in Champagne, the delay prevented
damage to the tender shoots durig the bitter weather
of March. Pruning was carried out at the normal time
and only minimal harm resulted from the severe
frosts of 7 May. The third week of May was warm
and sunny, encouraging rapid growth which was
maintained throughout a summer not dissimilar to
that of 1970. All varieties in most districts fared well,
with the slight exception of the Pinot Meunier in the
Aisne *département* which was less prolific than
normal. The harvest commenced under ideal
conditions, providing mature, healthy and
wholesome grapes. Although persistent rain
interposed, the grapes showed little or no signs of rot
and remained high in sugar content. All the grapes
were thin-skinned and pressed easily, giving a rich
and well-balanced juice.
The wine 1979 was one of the most outstanding of
declared vintages, averaging 9–10% in alcohol and
around 6 grams of acidity, on a par with the quality
of 1975, although firmer in character. The wines are
classic in construction, with an elegance and finesse
which contrasts favourably with the rather syrupy
1978 vintage. Although delicious to drink now, the
best of this vintage will reach their peak around 1990.

1978

Ouverture des vendanges 9 October for black grapes
and 11 October for white grapes. Picking ceased on 8
November.
Vineyard area in production 24,255 ha
Total production 594,732 hl; Champagne:
594,314 hl; Coteaux Champenois: 418 hl
Average yield per hectare 3,862 kgs
Maximum permitted yield per hectare 7,500 kgs
(Coteaux Champenois – 9,000 kgs)
Minimum permitted natural alcoholic content 7.5%
The vintage Budding, which normally takes place in
mid-March, was irregular and occurred between 8
and 25 April, but the prospects were encouraging and
the *sortie* (the appearance of embryo bunches of
grapes prior to the flowering) showed well. Hopes
were dashed, however, after a near-fatal flowering
which was also one month late. Heavy outbreaks of
rot occurred, *coulure* and *millerandage* were
widespread and erratic hail caused further, if
localised, damage, particularly at Pargny, Jouy,
Saulchery and Charly.

The wine The wines from this year are fresh and fruity, but far from complete and, in most cases, lacking the structure required for a good vintage Champagne. Some houses have declared 1978 a vintage, but, with few notable exceptions, the majority of these wines are flabby, over-dosed and conspicuously cumbersome in style.

1977

Ouverture des vendanges 6 October for black grapes and 10 October for white grapes. Picking ceased on 14 November.
Vineyard area in production 23,900 ha
Total production 1,399,954 hl; Champagne: 1,306,116 h; Coteaux Champenois: 93,838 hl. Most of the Coteaux Champenois was reclassified after the shortage resulting from the disastrous 1978 harvest.
Average yield per hectare 8,850 kgs
Maximum permitted yield per hectare 8,500 kgs (Coteaux Champenois – 9,500 kgs)
Minimum permitted natural alcoholic content 7.5%
The vintage The *sortie* was average but extremely irregular, particularly in the Aube, most of which was feeble. After a cold and wet start, the spring frosts took their toll, especially in the Côte des Blancs where it affected ten per cent of the surface. Brenner was virulent and early attacks of mildew caused significant damage, especially in the Aube. The Pinot Meunier had a good flowering, but both the Pinot Noir and the Chardonnay suffered. Rougeau was reported in some sectors, widespread outbreaks of grey rot occurred in late July and hail touched various communes in the Aube and the Marne *départements*. Generally poor climatic conditions persisted throughout the summer until the end of August, but September was dry and sunny and October warmer than average, eventually eradicating the well established grey rot and producing a surprisingly sizeable crop of good blending quality wines. Conditions at harvest particularly favoured the Pinot Noir and Pinot Meunier varieties, while the Chardonnay, although reduced in yield, was generally high in mineral content and rich in extract and acidity.
The wine Not of vintage quality generally: with few exceptions the grapes were low in sugar and the wines, consequently, light in body and weak in alcohol. But some fine blancs de blancs were made and, in all cases, the high acidity of the wines has tended to hold the *mousse* well.

1976

Ouverture des vendanges 1 September for the Chardonnay throughout the region, and for all vine varieties in the Aube *département*. 3 September for other vine varieties in the remaining communes.
Vineyard area in production 22,900 ha
Total production 1,587,560 hl; Champagne: 1,368,400 hl; Coteaux Champenois: 219,160 hl. Most of the Coteaux Champenois was reclassified

after the shortage imposed by the disastrous 1978 harvest.
Average yield per hectare 10,515 kgs
Maximum permitted yield per hectare 9,000 kgs (Coteaux Champenois – 11,000 kgs)
Minimum permitted natural alcoholic content Chardonnay of 95–100% échelle – 10%, of less than 95% échelle – 9.5%; Pinot Noir of 95–100% échelle – 9.5%, of less than 95% échelle – 9%; Pinot Meunier – 9%
The vintage After a dry winter the *débourrement* took place between 6 and 21 April, followed by a spring with no frosts or hail, giving rise to a generous *sortie* which raised hopes for a bumper crop. Favourable conditions continued throughout the summer, benefiting especially from a dry June and July. No parasites or disorders affected the vineyards, although some of the younger vines suffered from a lack of water. The *véraison* commenced on 1 August and the harvest on 1 September. The crop was so plentiful that in many cases the vignerons were encouraged to press out only the must from the *cuvée*, or first extraction of juice.
The wine The wines from this bumper crop were rich in extract, high in alcohol, big and fat in character and relatively low in acidity. Some of the musts had a tendency to oxidise prior to, or during, the first fermentation, leaving an ungainly sherry-like aroma – the unsuccessful products of a generally fine year. Critics of this vintage have highlighted its low acidity level, suggesting that these wines will not last long. Contrary to these opinions, however, are the heavy-weight, long-lasting vintages of 1959 and 1947, both of which were lower in acidity, but, like the 1976, high in alcohol and extract. The 1976 is too fat and rich to be considered a great Champagne in the classic sense, but the best of this vintage will mature into some of the longest-lived Champagne ever made.

1975

Ouverture des vendanges 29 September for the Aube and Haute-Marne *départements*. 30 September for the Aisne *département* and for all communes in the Marne *département* other than those commencing on 2 October. 2 October for all vineyards on and north of a line drawn from Chambercy through Germaine to Verzy, on the left bank of the Marne west of Boursault and in the Surmelin valley. Picking ceased on 29 October.
Vineyard area in production 21,800 ha
Total production 1,314,930 hl; Champagne: 1,066,388 hl; Coteaux Champenois: 248,542 hl. Most of the Coteaux Champenois was reclassified after shortages resulting from the disastrous 1978 harvest.
Average yield per hectare 9,250 kgs
Maximum permitted yield per hectare 7,500 kgs (Coteaux Champenois – 10,000 kgs)
Minimum permitted natural alcoholic content 8.5%

The vintage The bud-break was late, occurring in most cases during the last week of April, but both the *sortie* and the flowering were big and bountiful. This was despite widespread *millerandage*, which was off-set by the heavy number of berries on each bunch. July and August were exceptionally sunny, although the total amount of sunshine for the year was considerably below average. The harvest began in late September, when very healthy, nicely ripened grapes were collected. In October a considerable amount of grey rot spread through the vineyards, but this was the only limiting factor to an otherwise high quality, high yielding crop.

The wine The grapes from this harvest were thin-skinned, pressed easily and yielded a rich must, with an elegant balance of sugar and acidity. Virtually every producer declared the musts of vintage quality, which soon developed into long, delicately flavoured wines, characterised by a certain roundness, a soft finish and a particularly striking Chardonnay aroma. Stylish wines for early drinking.

1974

Ouverture des vendanges 28 September for all varieties of vine throughout the region. Picking ceased on 31 October.

Vineyard area in production 20,900 ha

Total production 1,273,136 hl; Champagne: 1,246,652 hl; Coteaux Champenois: 26,484 hl

Average yield per hectare 9,240 kgs

Maximum permitted yield per hectare 11,000 kgs (Coteaux Champenois – 13,000 kgs)

Maximum permitted yield per hectare 7.5%

The vintage A year of exceptional climatic conditions, with certain months not conforming to their natural pattern. Another large harvest was expected after an extremely generous *sortie*, but severe spring frosts damaged 1,600 hectares, of which 860 hectares were completely destroyed. The Pinot Noir and Chardonnay flowered well, but cold weather conditions affected the Pinot Meunier resulting in *coulure*, and on 10 June hail storms struck at Tauxières and Tours-sur-Marne, damaging many of the vines. Harvesting began under wet, unpleasant conditions, making the picking long and tedious, with grey rot setting in.

The wine Wines extracted from the early picked grapes were of good to medium quality, but the quality declined as the harvest progressed. The year provided a large volume of good blending quality wines, with a few spectacular exceptions like de Castellane's vintage pink Champagne.

1973

Ouverture des vendanges 28 September for all varieties of vine throughout the region. Picking ceased on 31 October.

Vineyard area in production 20,000 ha

Total production 1,576,418 hl

Average yield per hectare 11,780 kgs

Maximum permitted yield per hectare 13,000 kgs

Minimum permitted natural alcoholic content 9%

The vintage A good *sortie*, although inferior to 1970 and variable responses for the three varieties of vine. Cold weather in April retarded growth initially but, except for isolated incidents in Congy, Villevenard and le Mesnil-sur-Oger on 3 May, spring frosts were almost non-existent. Flowering took place under ideal circumstances, with hardly any *coulure* or *millerandage* and, apart from a few stormy outbreaks, the summer was warm, dry and sunny. On certain directly south-facing slopes, the grapes were literally roasted on the vines on 10 and 11 April and, again, on 4 September. September, which was generally much wetter than normal, saw the development of rot prior to the harvest, a virulent attack of red spider and, on 20 September, a tornado ripped through the vines of Fèrebrianges.

The wine Like the 1975, the wines are recognised by a characteristic degree of acidity, but they are balanced by a certain roundness and should provide classical Champagnes capable of retaining their freshness and fragrance for as long as twenty years.

1972

Ouverture des vendanges 12 October for black grapes and 14 October for white grapes. Picking ceased on 15 November.

Vineyard area in production 19,380 ha

Total production 1,161,722 hl

Average yield per hectare 9,000 kgs

Maximum permitted yield per hectare 12,000 kgs

Minimum permitted natural alcoholic content 8.5%

The vintage All three varieties had a very good *sortie*, comparable to that of 1970, although the older vines fared less favourably. But a rapid growth of foliage was impaired by hailstorms after 17 April, and further damage was inflicted by black frost in various sectors of the Marne and Aube *départements*, with the vines in the Côte des Blancs suffering most. In June the vines were subjected to frequent and heavy downpours of rain and further bursts of hail. Flowering went well, despite widespread rot and rampant *coulure*, which was finally cleared up during the ripening period, leaving just a few patches of brown rot in parts. Early autumn frosts further plagued the vines prior to a late harvest, the most acute cases of this damage being experienced in 200 hectares on the Côtes des Blancs, 100 hectares in the area west of Reims, at Verzenay and in 30 hectares in the Aube *département*.

The wine Certainly not of vintage quality – a vast amount of thin, acidic and mediocre wine which required all the skills of blending and generous amounts of rich reserve wines to assemble into acceptable products.

1971

Ouverture des vendanges 18 September for all varieties of vine throughout the region. Picking ceased on 4 November.

Vineyard area in production 18,400 ha

Total production 637,091 hl
Average yield per hectare 5,100 kgs
Maximum permitted yield per hectare 12,000 kgs
Minimum permitted natural alcoholic content 9%
The vintage Foliage growth was promisingly rapid, but this was badly affected by severe spring frosts between 27 and 29 April which damaged 1,000 hectares. The Chardonnay, however, had an excellent *sortie*, comparable to that of 1970, and the Pinot Noir and Pinot Meunier also fared well. On 27 May hail devastated 650 hectares. Flowering took place successfully between 6 and 24 June, despite conditions which were cold and twice as wet as normal. *Coulure* and *millerandage* occurred in some vineyards in July but the vines generally benefited from exceptionally good weather during this month, enjoying 304 hours of sunshine instead of the normal 206; violent storms and strong winds on 27 July were the only negative aspects. The storms in late July and the vicious torrent of hail on 18 August together decimated no less than 2,650 hectares, reducing their production to zero. Rampant mildew forced growers to treat the vines continuously throughout the summer and the vines further suffered from widespread chlorosis and rot, following that fateful day of 18 August. A dry and sunny September cleared up all traces of the rot and picking took place in good climatic conditions. The grapes were healthy, but a substantial proportion were unripe.
The wine Climatic and other conditions reduced the volume for this year, but the effect on quality was minimal and the wines were, on the whole, solid, well constructed, agreeably flavoured and well balanced in alcohol acidity. A few of the wines have suffered from the ups and downs of the viticultural year, but most seem good maturing Champagnes hallmarked by a high degree of finesse.

1970

Ouverture des vendanges 27 September for all varieties of vine throughout the region. Picking ceased on 31 October.
Vineyard area in production 17,815 ha
Total production 1,642,629 hl
Average yield per hectare 13,830 kgs
Maximum permitted yield per hectare 12,000 kgs
Minimum permitted natural alcoholic content 7.5%
The vintage Ideal climatic conditions resulted in an excellent *sortie* for all three varieties. A little *coulure* and *millerandage* was noticed in a few growths, but the amount was tiny and did not affect the volume of the harvest. The only limiting factor was some hail in Aube *département* which destroyed nearly 300 hectares. At the time 1970 was the largest Champagne crop on record.
The wine Widely declared a vintage, these wines are richer and racier than the size of harvest might first suggest; often complex in bouquet and penetrating in flavour. The best are characterised by a completeness of style and perfection of balance.

1969

Ouverture des vendanges 1 October for all varieties of vine throughout the region. Picking ceased on 8 November.
Vineyard area in production 17,134 ha
Total production 684,480 hl
Average yield per hectare 6,100 kgs
Maximum permitted yield per hectare 12,000 kgs
Minimum permitted natural alcoholic content 9.5%
The vintage No spring frosts, but severe variations in temperature coupled with rainy periods proved unfavourable during the initial period of development for the Pinot Meunier. The entire region was beset with *coulure* and *millerandage* at the time of flowering and a generally good summer was disrupted by violent thunder, rain and hail storms, completely destroying 900 hectares of vines. Early attacks of mildew on both leaves and grapes were the most serious experienced in Champagne since 1958. Grey and brown rot were active in some areas, but the growers managed to control most of it. Beginning on 1 October, the harvest period was dry and sunny, eradicating any remaining rot and allowing for a slightly undersized (for the 1960s) crop of healthy, ripe grapes.
The wine Without doubt it is the high acidity in some of these wines which has kept them alive. Generally declared a vintage, the successful examples are full bodied, possessing an excellent varietal character, a fine acidity and an adequate alcoholic content.

1968

Vineyard area in production 16,516 ha
Total production 777,238 hl
Average yield per hectare 7,200 kgs
Maximum permitted yield per hectare 12,000 kgs
Spring frosts destroyed over 2,000 hectares throughout the region, wreaking the worst havoc in the Côtes des Blancs. *Coulure* and *millerandage* reduced the crop by 10% and hailstorms followed by grey rot caused further damage. A normal sized crop of unhealthy, underripe grapes was vinified into honest but thin blending quality wines. Some exceptional blancs de blancs were produced in a limited quantity.

1967

Vineyard area in production 16,016 ha
Total production 871,009 hl
Average yield per hectare 8,190 kgs
Maximum permitted yield per hectare 12,000 kgs
Spring frosts destroyed 1,200 hectares of vines, with *millerandage* and grey rot taking their toll too. Average quality wines only, although one or two producers declared it a vintage.

1966

Vineyard area in production 15,564 ha
Total production 700,084 hl
Average yield per hectare 7,000 kgs
Maximum permitted yield per hectare 12,000 kgs
Winter frosts limited the potential production, hail partially destroyed some 200 hectares and chlorosis was a problem in some areas. Generally declared a vintage. Firm, elegant and stylish wines.

1965

Vineyard area in production 14,721 ha
Total production 656,738 hl
Average yield per hectare 6,900 kgs
Maximum permitted yield per hectare 12,000 kgs
A very good *sortie* was followed by generally unfavourable climatic conditions. The flowering was long, some *coulure* was evident and *millerandage* was widespread, especially amongst Chardonnay vines. Frequent bursts of hail and stormy weather induced attacks of grey rot early in the summer, while temperatures were generally cool, ensuring a late harvest. Quality was average and the year was not declared a vintage.

1964

Vineyard area in production 13,646 ha
Total production 814,548 hl
Average yield per hectare 8,895 kgs
Maximum permitted yield per hectare 10,000 kgs
A fine spring prompted an early flowering, followed by a hot and dry summer, with some welcome rain at the end of August. The grapes were ripe and healthy and produced high quality Champagnes. Generally declared a vintage, the wines are big bodied, with a certain roundness, richer and plumper than the 1966s, yet not lacking in finesse.

1963

Vineyard area in production 12,942 ha
Total production 759,575 hl
Average yield per hectare 9,000 kgs
Maximum permitted yield per hectare 9,000 kgs
Very average blending quality wines. Not declared a vintage.

1962

Vineyard area in production 12,463 ha
Total production 528,007 hl
Average yield per hectare 6,400 kgs
After a cool start and a slow-growing summer season, September brought some much needed sun, ripening the vines beautifully and transforming an average quality crop into one of excellent vintage potential. Wines of high extract, suppleness and distinction.

1961

Vineyard area in production 12,033 ha
Total production 574,262 hl

Average yield per hectare 7,160 kgs
A poor start to the year, but the climate picked up through the ripening months and yielded a rich harvest which produced deeply flavoured wines, lower in alcohol than 1959, but with more acidity.

1960

Vineyard area in production 11,873 ha
Total production 750,426 hl
Average yield per hectare 9,485 kgs
A large quantity of useful blending wines, although not quite of vintage quality.

1959 A large quantity of full-bodied, high alcohol Champagne comparable in quality to the 1947 and 1976. Long-lasting wines, low in acidity but extremely rich in extract. Universally declared a vintage.

1958 Despite rampant mildew, a quantity of fair blending quality wine was produced. Not declared a vintage.

1957 Spring frosts decimated the yield resulting in a feeble total of 168,000 hectolitres. Average blending quality. Not declared a vintage.

1956 Mediocre wines, above average in quantity. Not declared a vintage.

1955 A large harvest of very elegant wines, marked by their fine acidity. Declared a vintage.

1954 A good-sized harvest of useful blending quality wines which developed better than expected. Not declared a vintage.

1953 A good-sized harvest of excellent vintage quality wines. Fuller in body and higher in alcohol than the 1955 or 1952, these Champagnes are long-lived and noted for their deft balance of fruit.

1952 A good-sized harvest of exquisitely balanced wines. Firm, fine wines of great style and quality, widely declared a vintage. The Pol Roger 1952 Cuvée, disgorged in 1977 for Queen Elizabeth's Silver Jubilee, was twenty-five years later beautifully balanced and quite remarkable for its complexity and freshness.

1951 A small harvest of poor, acid wines. Not declared a vintage, although a non-commercial *cuvée* of Clos des Goisses 1951, opened in 1983, displayed extraordinary vitality and richness.

1950 A large harvest of fair quality wines. Declared a vintage by some producers.

1949 An average-sized harvest of classic, vintage quality wines, long-living and with more acidity than the 1947s.

1948 Slightly above normal quantity of very fair quality wines. Generally not declared a vintage, although one or two producers did.

1947 Big, rich, long-living, almost over-generous wines which have developed great complexity. Widely declared a vintage.

1946 Poor harvest of mediocre wines. Not declared a vintage.

1945 A normal size harvest of big, strong, virile wines; although lacking a certain suppleness, many have turned out to be all time greats.

1944 A normal size crop of fair quality, but not declared a vintage.

1943 A normal size crop of classic vintage quality. Wines of great finesse.

1942 A normal size crop of very good quality wines. Declared as a vintage by many, but not by all.

1941 A normal size crop of varying quality, from fair to very good. Declared a vintage by some.

1940 Difficult war-time conditions wrought extremely variable quality on a harvest which might have been generally good. Not declared a vintage.

1939 An average size harvest of good blending quality.

1938 A very large harvest of fair quality wines. Declared as a vintage by one or two producers, but not generally.

1937 A normal size crop of richly flavoured vintage quality wines.

1936 Poor harvest of rather neutral wines which were destined for the blending pot.

1935 A large crop of good to very good quality, but overshadowed by the two previous years. Not declared generally, although I believe one or two producers did.

1934 Good-sized crop of vintage quality wines, fine and harmonious in style.

1933 A small quantity of good quality wines, although quite variable. Declared a vintage by most.

1932 A small crop of mediocre wines.

1931 Above average in quantity, below average in quality.

1930 Normal-sized crop of generally poor wines.

1929 A large harvest of classic vintage quality wines, harmonious Champagnes deftly rich in fruit and extract.

1928 A good size crop of classic vintage quality wines. Generally believed to be better and longer-lived than the superb 1929, this vintage is often quoted as the best this century.

1927 A small quantity of poor quality wines. Not declared a vintage.

1926 Below average quantity of very good vintage quality.

1925 Average-sized crop of poor quality. Not declared a vintage.

1924 Average-sized crop of poor quality wines, low in sugar content. Not declared a vintage.

1923 A small quantity of excellent vintage quality wines.

1922 Large crop of mediocre quality. Although some producers were reported to have shipped this year as a vintage, it was not generally declared.

1921 A small crop of great vintage quality. Rich yet elegant wines, universally declared. Some normally disgorged 1921s were still good in the early 1980s.

1920 Small-sized crop of vintage quality, declared by several shippers.

1919 An average quantity of fine vintage quality, combining the classic qualities of richness, acidity and firmness. Declared by most.

1918 Small-sized crop of thin wines. Not declared.

1917 Small-sized crop of reasonable quality, some were quite good and a few shippers declared it a vintage.

1916 Small-sized crop of very poor wines. Not declared.

1915 A large crop of fine vintage quality. Widely declared.

1914 An average quantity of elegant vintage quality, harvested under war-time conditions and paid for with French lives, including those of more than twenty child pickers.

1913 Small crop of blending quality. Although a few did declare, this was generally considered to be a non-vintage year.

1912 An average quantity of light-weight wines good for blending. Not declared.

1911 A small crop of classic vintage quality wines, capable of great longevity.

1910 A dismal year. Not declared, although one producer was reported to have shipped a vintage.

1909 Small-sized crop of good blending quality wines. A few did declare, but generally not a vintage.

1908 Terrible mildew – a disaster.

1907 Heavy rain prior to the harvest reduced a potentially good quality harvest to useful blending wines. Not declared.

1906 Normal-sized crop of good vintage quality.

1905 Small crop of generally poor quality, although those who avoided mildew managed to produce some good wines and at least one shipper declared it a vintage.

1904 A big crop of exceptionally fine vintage quality wines. Elegant Champagnes widely declared.

1903 Normal-sized crop of average quality. Not declared.

1902 Small crop of mediocre quality, although one house apparently declared it a vintage.

1901 A large crop of important blending quality wines. Not declared.

1900 A large crop of great vintage quality, well constructed and full of extract. Universally declared.

Appendix II The CIVC: its Purposes and Powers

The decree-law of 28 September 1935 called for a special commission to be set up whose aims should be to assure the respect of local custom and tradition, the observation of which is necessary in order to preserve the quality of Champagne.

Accordingly the Commission de Châlons (so named because it was based in Châlons, the administrative centre on the eastern limits of viticultural Champagne) was set up. Not very effective, it was abolished by the decree of 20 November 1940 which required the Vichy government to replace the commission with the Bureau de Répartition du Vinicole de Champagne. The Bureau's life was ephemeral indeed, for not quite five months later it too was replaced, this time by the still functioning Comité Interprofessionnel du Vin de Champagne, or CIVC. The CIVC's success in the years to follow can be attributed to the very real power given to it by the German forces occupying Champagne at the time. This was the fruition of brave action by certain natives of Champagne: they argued that it would be to the Germans' benefit if the Champagne trade had the power to handle its own day-to-day problems without having to bother the authorities (see Chapter 1).

Power at the summit is held by the government commissioner, who is nominated by the minister of agriculture and whose role is that of arbiter and conciliator. He presides over meetings and represents, officially, the organisation in all circumstances. Beneath him are two presidents: the president of the *négociants* and the president of the growers, who form a permanent commission and who are the principal moving force behind the CIVC.

Supporting the commissioner and the two presidents is the consultative commission (the ConCom) or the 'think-tank' of the CIVC which is comprised of six growers (including their president) and six *négociants* (including their president). The effort, efficiency and penetration of the consultative commission is dependent upon the ten surrounding specialist committees.

The powers, functions and duties of the CIVC as laid out in Article 8 of the law of 12 April 1941 are:

1 To establish the balance of production levels and market growth potential.
2 To organise, check and direct production and distribution on home or foreign markets of wine produced in the delimited Champagne region and to ensure maintenance of tradition and quality.
3 To organise and discipline the relationships between the various professions concerned.
4 To intervene with general measures when the market is unbalanced in order to protect the future stability of prices for both production and consumption.
5 To study and propose the prices and methods of payment applicable to exchanges between the growers and *négociants* and similarly the remuneration of the various intermediaries.
6 To establish general conditions for export markets and to effect a check on the quality of export products at various stages of distribution.
7 To preside over the establishment of professional and technical literature.
8 To establish every year its own financial budget. The CIVC is authorised to raise taxes of a fiscal nature with its jurisdiction to cover the running costs of the organisation. Actual current taxes are levied on producers – based upon the number of sales of AOC Champagne – and levied upon the growers as a royalty – based on the volume of their AOC Champagne harvest.

The CIVC is one of the most active and powerful of all the interprofessional organisations throughout the wine regions of France. It organises the fight against the usurpation of Champagne in other countries; it suggests future modifications of statutory Champagne regulations; it undertakes much research into both traditional and modern techniques, with up-to-date laboratories and experimental field stations; it publicises information on better vine-growing and wine-making and gives practical technical assistance when needed. In the commercial field it establishes statistics; studies export markets; forms commercial agreements; grants certificates of origin and generally informs and publicises on issues concerning Champagne both in France and abroad.

Appendix III AOC and EEC Regulations

Like all wines produced in Common Market countries, Champagne is controlled and restricted first and foremost by EEC regulations (the last two numbers indicate the year of their enactment). These can only be superseded when local or national laws, decrees and regulations impose tighter conditions. Where Champagne regulations do not cover certain areas of wine law, EEC regulations come into force. Both domestic and EEC regulatory controls of Champagne's Viti-Viniculture are included below.

Delimitation

Legal delimitation of the Champagne region first came into effect with the passing of the law of 5 August 1908, which was a modification of the definition set three years earlier. The decree of 17 December 1908 listing the communes within viticultural Champagne was amended several times: by the law of 10 February 1911, the decree of 7 June 1911, the law of 6 May 1919 and the law of 22 July 1927. A list of the communes included is given in Appendix IV.

Permitted grape varieties

Article 5 of the amended law of 22 July 1927 referred to above covers permitted grape varieties in the making of Champagne. It includes Pinot Noir, Pinot Meunier, Chardonnay, Pinot Blanc, Arbanne and Petit Meslier and initially set a period of eighteen years for the phasing out of the Gamay, although amendments and individual concessions have meant that small parcels of this vine still exist today.

Permitted rootstock varieties

These are restricted to twenty-eight varieties as listed under EEC regulation 1388/70.

Density, training and pruning of vines

A decree of 17 January 1978 replaced the decree of 13 January 1938 which controls and specifies the various systems of viticulture.

Maximum yield per hectare

A limit of 50 hectolitres per hectare (equal to 7,500 kilograms per hectare) was imposed by the decree-law of 28 September 1935, although this may be modified on an annual basis (according to Article 159 of the *Code du Vin*) up to a ceiling of 13,000 kilograms, as expressed by decree number 74–872 of 19 October 1974.

Presshouse yields

The decree-law of 28 September 1935 restricts the right of appellation to the first 100 litres of juice extracted from every 150 kilograms of grapes for both Champagne and Coteaux Champenois.

Minimum alcoholic potential of the must

Prior to the 1979 vintage a minimum was set for both Champagne and Coteaux Champenois of 7.5% before any enrichment, and 9% after chaptalisation, by EEC regulation 817/70, modified by 338/79. These limits formed the basis upon which upward annual modifications have been made since 1979.

Minimum alcoholic strength at time of sale

The minimum total alcoholic strengths were set for Coteaux Champenois and non-vintage Champagnes by EEC regulation 3389/79 and for vintage Champagnes by the decree of 17 October 1952. The minimum total alcoholic strength for Coteaux Champenois was 9%, for non-vintage Champagne (including that from *liqueur de tirage* and the potential of the *liqueur d'expédition*) 10% and for vintage Champagnes (also including the above) 11%. Since and including the 1979 vintage the maximum has been set at 13% for all Champagne and at 12% for Coteaux Champenois.

Chaptalisation

Three limitations have been imposed:
1 A maximum increase of 2.5% alcohol by EEC regulation 337/79, which corresponds to a sugar limit of 4.5 kilograms per hectolitre.
2 The maximum addition of sugar is controlled by annual ministerial decree which has never been above 4.25 kilograms per hectolitre for white and rosé wine and 4.5 kilograms per hectolitre for red.
3 The amount of chaptalisation is restricted by Article 422 of the *Code Général des Impôts* (tax laws), which limits the total amount of sugar used to 300 kilograms for every hectare in production. At 4.25 kilograms per hectolitre, this would impose a 'chaptalisable' limit of 70.58 hectolitres of must per hectare (an effective yield of 1058.7 kilograms per hectolitre). If the yield per hectare was, say, 13,000 kilograms or 86.66 hectolitres, and all of it required chaptalising, the maximum level of sugar permitted would thus be 3.46 kilograms per hectolitre (86.66 × 3.46 equalling approximately 300 kilograms per hectare). Until 1980 the restriction was 200 kilograms.

Liqueur de tirage

The quantity and quality of ingredients used are controlled by EEC regulation 2893/74.

Liqueur d'expédition

The quantity and quality of ingredients are controlled by EEC regulation 2893/74.

Strength of *mousse*

A minimum pressure of 3.5 atmospheres (3 atmospheres for bottles less than 25 cl) is controlled by EEC regulation 817/70. A maximum pressure of 6 atmospheres is also indirectly controlled by EEC regulation 2893/74, prohibiting the *liqueur de tirage* from raising the alcoholic level by more than 1.5%. Pressures are measured at 20°C.

Crémant

In the regulations of *Le Statut Viti-Vinicole de la Champagne*, a traditional *crémant* is said historically to be a gentle *mousse* derived from a *liqueur de tirage* of 16 grams of sugar per litre, yielding approximately 3.6 atmospheres.

Sweetness levels

The terms brut, sec, demi-sec, etc. relate to specific residual sugar levels measured in grams per litre and set by EEC regulation 2893/74.

Pink Champagne produced by blending

The decree-law of 17 June 1938 requires the use of 'red Champagne', that is to say red wine which conforms to all the standards of Champagne (yield, alcohol level, etc.), not Coteaux Champenois. Under this decree-law, producers of pink Champagne must notify the local tax receipts office two hours prior to the blending operation.

Vin Originaire de la Champagne Viticole

This was the early name given for still wines of the region, as established by the law of 22 July 1927. The decree-law of 28 December 1935 defined the appellation as applicable to wines produced in excess of 50 hectolitres per hectare or wines which do not reach the alcoholic strength laid down for Champagne. The appellation was changed to Vin Nature de la Champagne in 1953 and changed again to Coteaux Champenois in 1974 (see following entry).

Coteaux Champenois

The law of 12 December 1973 redefining Champagne rendered the term Vin Nature de la Champagne obsolete and on 21 August 1974 a decree instituted the name Coteaux Champenois.

Vin de rebêche

The production of *vin de rebêche* (wine produced in excess of 100 litres of juice per 150 kilograms of grapes) is optional when making Champagne, but compulsory when pressing and vinifying still wine (now called Coteaux Champenois), by Article 3 of the decree-law of 28 September 1935. This obligatory amount fluctuates between 5–8% (in proportion to the volume of Coteaux Champenois produced) according to annual directives.

Rosé des Riceys

A wine of historical repute, relatively recently recognised by the decree of 8 December 1947, since replaced by the decree of 2 February 1971. Producers are compelled by this last decree to extract a further 12% of *vin de rebêche* from the total volume of Rosé des Riceys produced.

Ratafia

Controlled by the decree of 31 January 1930.

Eaux-de-vie

Wine-based and *marc*-based brandies are covered by the decree of 23 February 1942, modified in 1946, 1948, 1951, 1955 and 1962.

Obligatory analysis and organoleptic examination

The decree of 26 May 1964 (EEC regulation 817/70) and the decree of 19 October 1974 require that Champagne, like all quality wines produced in Common Market countries, should undergo analytical and tasting examination. These tests are organised by the CIVC under the auspices of the INAO. Producers of wines failing to pass have one month in which to appeal for another examination. Should the wine fail a second time, the producer may demand a tasting from a regional panel. Wines which fail are not allowed to be sold as Champagne.

Labelling

Champagne is unique among quality wines produced in Common Market countries in that it need not mention the terms Appellation d'Origine Contrôlée or Appellation Contrôlée on the label (all other AOC wines must print one of these terms above, below or alongside the wine-name). The tax authorities and the INAO initially took the view that the name Champagne itself was so synonymous with the image of quality that no further reference was necessary. This was endorsed by Article 12 of EEC regulation 817/70.

Obligatory label information

The name 'Champagne' (which should be easily noticed).
The name of the producer or his registered brand name.
The town or location of the producer or owner of the brand name.
The CIVC matriculation number.
The capacity of the bottle.

Optional label information

Grand Cru is only allowed for wines from 100%-rated growths.
Premier Cru is only allowed for wines from 90–100%-rated growths, and strictly speaking only for wines from growths which were rated 90–100% in

the échelle des crus which was in force on 1 July 1952, according to Article 467 of *Le Statut Viti-Vinicole de la Champagne*.

The words 'Clos', 'Château', 'Domaine', 'Mont', 'Côte' and 'Moulin' may be used provided they stem from an agricultural existence which is accurately described by such terms.

The name of a single-site vineyard is permitted if the wine is exclusively from that named plot of land.

The terms brut, sec, demi-sec, etc. must relate to specific residual sugar levels measured in grams per litre.

Forbidden terms

All confusing or ambiguous terms are prohibited, but some are expressly banned, for example, the word 'nature' (which has been forbidden since 12 December 1973); the use of *près* (near) to indicate proximity to a better-known place or growth (the two examples of this prohibited term which are given in *Le Statut Viti-Viniocole de la Champagne* are 'Près Reims' and 'Près Épernay', both of which are in fact widely used); the reference to any specific geographical entity other than 'Champagne' or a single-site vineyard, thus it is not permitted to use 'Montagne de Reims', 'Côtes de Blancs', 'Vallée de la Marne'; etc; the term Cru Classé (although both Grand Cru and Premier Cru are allowed).

Legislation relating to the above labelling information was embodied in the laws of 6 May 1919 and 20 March 1934 and the decrees of 21 August 1928, 29 June 1936, 1 July 1952 and 17 October 1952 and EEC regulations 2893/74 and 817/70.

The cork

The name 'Champagne' must be branded onto that part of the cork which is actually inserted into the bottle, as specified in Article 156 of the *Code du Vin*. All Champagnes sold under one vintage must have the specified year branded on the cork, according to the decree of 17 October 1952.

The capsule

Since 1 January 1972 the foil, or metalised-plastic capsule, which covers the bottle-neck must be applied in such a way that in order to get at the cork, the capsule must be destroyed.

Appendix IV The Delimitation of the Champagne Viticultural Region

The present delimitation of the viticultural region of Champagne is based on a law passed on 6 May 1919, which was subsequently modified by the law of 22 July 1927 and later amendments. The law of 1919 was born out of the struggle and violence surrounding attempts to delimit the region between 1908 and 1911 (see Chapter 1). This region extends across five *départements*, each of which is listed below with the specific *arrondissements* and *communes* permitted to produce Champagne.

Marne *département*

All *communes* within the *arrondissements* of Reims, Épernay and Châlons-sur-Marne (with the exception of Sainte-Marie-à-Py and Somme-Suippe) and, within the *arrondissement* of Vitry-le-François: all *communes* within the *canton* of Vitry-le-François; the *communes* of Bassu, Bassuet, Chagny, Doucey, Outrepont, Rosay, Vanault-le-Châtel, Vanault-les-Dames, Vavray-le-Grand and Vavray-le-Petit in the *canton* of Heiltz-le-Maurupt; and the *communes* of Arrigny, Arzillières, Encollemont, Giffaumont and Nuisement-aux-Bois in the *canton* of Saint-Rémy-en-Bouzemont.

Aisne *département*

Within the *arrondissement* of Château-Thierry: the *communes* of Condé-en-Brie, Saint-Agnan, Barzy-sur-Marne, Baulne, Celles-les-Condé, La Chapelle-Monthodon, Chartève, Connigis, Courboin, Courte-Mont-Varennes, Crezancy, Saint-Eugène, Jaulgonne, Mézy-Moulins, Monthurel, Montigny-les-Condé, Montlevon, Pargny-la-Dhuys, Passy-sur-Marne, Reuilly-Sauvigny and Trélou in the *canton* of Condé-en-Brie; the *communes* of Château-Thierry, Azy, Blesmes, Bonneil, Brasles, Chierry, Essômes, Étampes, Fossoy, Gland, Mont-Saint-Père, Nesles, Nogentel and Verdilly in the *canton* of Château-Thierry; and the *communes* of Charly, Bézy-le-Guery, Chézy-sur-Marne, Crouttes, Domptin, Montreuil-aux-Lions, Nogent-l'Artaud, Pavant, Romeny, Saulchery and Villiers-Saint-Denis in the *canton* of Charly. Within the *arrondissement* of Soissons: the *communes* of Braine, Acy, Augy, Barbonval, Blanzy-les-Fismes, Brenelle, Chassemy, Ciry-Salsogne, Courcelles, Couvrelles, Cys-la-Commune, Dhuysel, Glennes, Longueval, Merval, Saint-Mard, Paârs, Perles, Presles-et-Boves, Revillon, Sermoise, Serval, Vasseny, Vaux-Cère, Vauxtin,

Vieil-Arcy and Villers-en-Prayères in the *canton* of Braine; and the *communes* of Vailly, Bucy-le-Long, Celles-sur-Aisne, Chavonne, Chivres, Condé-sur-Aisne, Missy-sur-Aisne, Soupir and Sancy in the *canton* of Vailly.

Aube *département*

Within the *arrondissement* of Troyes: the *communes* of Montgueux and Sainte-Savine in the *canton* of Troyes-Ouest; the *communes* of Avirey-Lingey, Bagneux-la-Fosse, Balnot-sur-Laignes, Beauvoir, Bragelogne, Channes and les Riceys in the *canton* of les Riceys; the *communes* of Celles-sur-Ource, Courteron, Gyé-sur-Seine, Mussy-sur-Seine, Neuville-sur-Seine, Plaines-Saint-Lange, Polisot and Polisy in the *canton* of Mussy-sur-Seine; the *communes* of Bar-sur-Seine, Buxeil, Merrey-sur-Arce and Ville-sur-Arce in the *canton* of Bar-sur-Seine; and the *communes* of Bertignolles, Buxière-sur-Arce, Chacenay, Chervey, Cunfin, Éguilly-sous-Bois, Essoyes, Fontette, Landreville, Loches-sur-Ource, Noé-les-Mallets, Saint-Usage, Verpillières, Vitry-le-Croisé and Viviers-sur-Artaud in the *canton* of Essoyes. Within the *arrondissement* of Nogent-sur-Seine: the *communes* of Villenauxe-la-Grande and Villeneuve-au-Châtelot in the *canton* of Villenauxe-la-Grande; and the *commune* of Marcilly-le-Hayer in the *canton* of Marcilly-le-Hayer. Within the *arrondissement* of Bar-sur-Aube: the *communes* of Ailleville, Arconville, Arrentières, Arsonval, Baroville, Bar-sur-Aube, Bergères, Champignol, Couvignon, Colombé-le-Sec, Engente, Fontaine, Jaucourt, Lignol-le-Château, Montier-en-l'Isle, Proverville, Rouvres-les-Vignes, Urville and Voigny in the *canton* of Bar-sur-Aube; the *communes* of Argançon, Bligny, Dolancourt, Fravaux, Meurville, Spoy and Tragny in the *canton* of Vendeuvre; the *communes* of Colombé-la-Fosse and Saulcy in the *canton* of Soulaines; and the *communes* of Brienne-le-Château, Épagne, Précy-Saint-Martin and Saint-Léger-sous-Brienne in the *canton* of Brienne-le-Château.

Haute-Marne *département*

The *communes* of Argentolles and Rizaucourt.

Seine-et-Marne *département*

The *communes* of Citry, Méry-sur-Marne, Nanteuil-sur-Marne, Saâcy-sur-Marne and Saint Aulde.

Appendix V The Échelle des Crus: Forty Years of Change

The current échelle des crus is a modified version of the échelle imposed in 1945, which stemmed from the échelle of 1944 and was based upon the delimitation of 1919. A full explanation of how the échelle des crus system works is given in Chapter 3. Many changes have occurred during the forty years between its inception and the current rating, and although most of these modifications were included in the formative years of the échelle, the table below (drawn from statistics available from 1969) reveals that the process of change is on-going. In particular it is interesting to note that: the last two major shake-ups were in 1971 and 1985; some wines which are now grand cru and premier cru, formerly were not (five grands crus and seven premiers crus in 1985 alone); there has been a methodical move to push the base up from its 1945 level of 70% to the current minimum of 80%; and there has been a noticeable trend in recent years to raise the échelle for white grapes, a back-door *prime* or premium for the much sought after Chardonnay.

Cru (in alphabetical order)	Current échelle (%)	1945 échelle (%)	Notable changes
Allemant (b)	84	–	a) 1984
Allemant (w)	87	–	a) 1984
Ambonnay	100	100	
Areis-le-Ponsart	82	–	a) 1985
Aubilly	82	–	a) 1985
Avenay	93	93	
Avize	100	100	
Aÿ-Champagne	100	100	
Barbonne-Fayel (b)	85	–	a) Prior to 1969 b) From 82% in 1971, from **84%** in 1985
Barbonne-Fayel (w)	87	–	a) Prior to 1969
Baslieux-sous-Châtillon	84	81	b) From 81% in 1971, from 83% in 1979
Bassu	85	–	a) 1982
Bassuet	85	–	a) 1982
Baye	85	85	
Beaumont-sur-Vesle	100	100	
Beaunay	85	85	
Belval-sous-Châtillon	84	81	b) From 81% in 1971, from 83% in 1979
Bergères-les-Vertus (b)	90	90	
Bergères-les-Vertus (w)	95	93	b) From 93% in 1972
Bergères-sous-Montmirail	82	–	a) 1985
Berru	84	–	a) Prior to 1969 b) From 82% in 1971
Bethon (b)	84	–	a) Prior to 1969 b) From 82% in 1971

Key

(b) Black grapes only
(w) White grapes only

a) First specific mention in the échelle des crus
b) Upgraded in échelle

Cru (in alphabetical order)	Current échelle (%)	1945 échelle (%)	Notable changes
Bethon (w)	87	–	a) Prior to 1969 b) From 85% in 1984
Bezannes	90	–	a) 1985
Billy-le-Grand	95	–	b) From 90% in 1974
Binson-Orquigny	86	83	b) From 83% in 1971, from 85% in 1975
Bisseuil	95	90	a) Prior to 1969 b) From 90% prior to 1969, from 93% in 1985
Bligny	83	81	b) From 81% in 1971
Bouilly	86	86	
Bouleuse	82	–	a) Prior to 1969 b) From 80% in 1971
Boursault	84	80	b) From 81% in 1971
Bouzy	100	100	
Branscourt	86	84	b) From 84% prior to 1969
Breuil (le)	83	81	b) From 81% in 1971
Brimont	83	–	a) Prior to 1969 b) From 81% in 1971
Brouillet	86	85	b) Prior to 1969
Broussy-le-Grand	84	–	a) 1985
Broyes (b)	85	–	a) Prior to 1969
Broyes (w)	87	–	a) Prior to 1969 b) From 85% in 1984
Brugny-Vaudancourt	86	86	
Cauroy-lès-Hermonville	83	81	b) From 81% in 1971
Celle-sous-Chantemerle (b)	85	–	a) Prior to 1969 b) From 81% in 1974, from 84% in 1985
Celle-sous-Chantemerle (w)	87	–	b) From 85% in 1984
Cernay-les-Reims	85	–	a) Prior to 1969
Cerseuil	84	–	a) Prior to 1969 b) From 82% in 1971
Châlons-sur-Vesle	84	–	a) Prior to 1969 b) From 82% in 1971
Chambrécy	83	79	b) From 81% in 1981
Chamery	90	88	b) From 88% in 1985
Champillon	93	93	
Champlat-Boujacourt	83	81	b) From 81% in 1971
Champvoisy	84	82	b) From 82% in 1971
Chantemerle (b)	85	–	a) 1984
Chantemerle (w)	87	–	a) 1984
Châtillon-sur-Marne	86	82	b) From 82% in 1971, from 84% in 1976
Chaumuzy	83	80	b) From 81% in 1971

Cru (in alphabetical order)	Current échelle (%)	1945 échelle (%)	Notable changes
Chavot-Courcourt (b)	88	87	b) From 87% in 1985
Chavot-Courcourt (w)	88	88	
Chenay	84	82	b) From 82% in 1971
Chigny-les-Roses (b)	94	94	
Chigny-les-Roses (w)	94	86	b) From 86% in 1972
Chouilly (b)	95	90	b) From 90% in 1985
Chouilly (w)	100	93	b) From 93% prior to 1969, from 95% in 1985
Coizard-Joches	85	85	
Coligny (b)	87	85	b) From 85% in 1985
Coligny (w)	90	85	b) From 85% in 1985
Congy	85	85	
Cormicy	83	81	b) From 81% in 1971
Cormoyeux	85	83	b) From 83% in 1971
Coulommes-la-Montagne	89	89	
Courcelles-Sapicourt	83	–	a) Prior to 1969 b) From 80% in 1971, from 82% in 1985
Courjeonnet	85	85	
Courmas	87	86	b) From 86% prior to 1969
Courtagnon	82	–	a) Prior to 1969 b) From 80% in 1971
Courthiézy	83	81	b) From 81% in 1971
Courville	82	–	a) 1985
Cramant	100	100	
Crugny	86	86	
Cuchery	84	80	b) From 81% in 1971, from 83% in 1979
Cuis (b)	90	90	
Cuis (w)	95	93	b) From 93% prior to 1969
Cuisles	86	82	b) From 82% in 1971, from 84% in 1976
Cumières	93	90	b) From 90% in 1985
Damery (b)	89	85	b) From 85% in 1970, from 86% in 1985
Damery (w)	89	86	b) From 86% in 1985
Dizy	95	95	
Dormans (Try, Vassy, Vassieux, Chavenay)	83	81	b) From 81% in 1971
Écueil	90	90	
Épernay	88	88	
Étoges	85	85	
Étrechy (b)	87	–	a) Prior to 1969

Key

(b) Black grapes only   a) First specific mention in the échelle des crus

(w) White grapes only   b) Upgraded in échelle

Cru (in alphabetical order)	Current échelle (%)	1945 échelle (%)	Notable changes
Étrechy (w)	90	–	b) Prior to 1969
Faverolles	86	86	
Fèrebrianges	85	85	
Festigny	84	81	b) From 81% in 1971, from 83% in 1976
Fleury-la-Rivière (b)	85	83	b) From 83% prior to 1969
Fleury-la-Rivière (w)	85	83	b) From 83% prior to 1969
Fontaine-Denis (b)	84	–	a) Prior to 1969
Fontaine-Denis (w)	87	–	a) Prior to 1969
Germigny	85	85	
Givry-les-Loisy	85	85	
Grauves (b)	90	90	
Grauves (w)	95	93	b) From 93% in 1972
Gueux	85	85	
Hautvillers	93	90	b) From 90% in 1985
Hermonville	84	82	b) From 82% in 1971
Hourges	86	86	
Igny-Comblizy	83	80	b) From 81% in 1971
Janvry	85	84	b) From 84% prior to 1969
Jonchery-sur-Vesle	84	–	a) 1985
Jonquery	84	81	b) From 82% in 1972
Jouy-les-Reims	90	89	b) From 89% in 1985
Lagery	86	85	b) From 85% prior to 1969
Leuvrigny	84	82	b) From 82% in 1971
Lhéry	86	85	b) From 85% in 1985
Loisy-en-Brie	85	85	
Louvois	100	100	
Ludes (b)	94	94	
Ludes (w)	94	86	
Mailly-Champagne (b)	100	100	
Mailly-Champagne (w)	100	86	b) From 86% in 1972
Mancy (b)	88	86	b) From 86% in 1985
Mancy (w)	88	88	
Mardeuil	84	82	b) From 82% in 1971
Mareuil-le-Port	84	82	b) From 82% in 1971
Mareuil-sur-Aÿ	99	98	b) From 98% in 1985
Marfaux	84	81	b) From 82% in 1971
Merfy	84	82	b) From 82% in 1971
Méry-Prémecy	82	–	a) Prior to 1969 b) From 80% in 1970
Mesneux	90	90	
Mesnil-le-Hutier	84	82	b) From 82% in 1971
Mesnil-sur-Oger (le)	100	99	b) From 99% in 1985
Mondement	84	–	a) 1985

Cru (in alphabetical order)	Current échelle (%)	1945 échelle (%)	Notable changes
Montbré	94	–	a) Prior to 1969
Montgenost (b)	84	–	a) 1984
Montgenost (w)	87	–	a) 1984
Monthelon	88	88	
Montigny-sous-Châtillon	86	83	b) From 83% in 1971, from 85% in 1976
Montigny-sur-Vesle	84	–	a) 1985
Morangis	84	84	
Moslins	84	–	a) Prior to 1969 b) From 82% in 1971
Moussy	88	88	
Mutigny	93	93	
Nanteuil-la-forêt	82	–	a) 1985
Nesle-le-Repons	84	80	b) From 81% in 1971, from 83% in 1978
Neuville-aux-Larris	84	81	b) From 81% in 1971, from 83% in 1978
Nogent l'Abbesse	87	85	b) From 85% prior to 1969
Oeuilly	84	81	b) From 81% in 1971, from 83% in 1979
Oger	100	99	b) From 99% in 1985
Oiry	100	99	b) From 99% in 1985
Olizy-Violaine	84	82	b) From 82% in 1971
Orbais l'Abbaye	82	–	a) 1985
Ormes	85	–	a) Prior to 1969 b) From 80% in 1971, from 82% in 1985
Oyes	85	–	a) Prior to 1969
Pargny-les-Reims	90	89	b) From 89% in 1985
Passy-Grigny	84	82	b) From 82% in 1971
Pévy	84	81	b) From 81% in 1971, from 83% in 1985
Pierry	90	90	
Poilly	83	81	b) From 81% in 1971
Port-à-Binson	84	–	a) Prior to 1969 b) From 82% in 1971
Pouillon	84	82	b) From 82% in 1971
Pourcy	84	82	b) From 82% in 1971
Prouilly	84	82	b) From 82% in 1971
Puisieulx	100	100	
Reims	88	88	
Reuil	86	83	b) From 83% in 1971, from 85% in 1976

Key

(b) Black grapes only   a) First specific mention in the échelle des crus

(w) White grapes only   b) Upgraded in échelle

Cru (in alphabetical order)	Current échelle (%)	1945 échelle (%)	Notable changes
Rilly-la-Montagne	94	94	
Romery	85	83	b) From 83% in 1971
Romigny	82	–	a) 1985
Rosnay	83	81	b) From 81% in 1971
Sacy	90	90	
Sainte-Euphraise	86	86	
Sainte-Gemme	84	82	b) From 82% in 1971
Saint-Gilles	82	–	a) 1985
Saint-Lumier	85	–	a) 1982
Saint-Martin d'Ablois	86	86	
Saint-Thierry	87	87	
Sarcy	83	81	b) From 81% in 1971
Saudoy (b)	85	–	a) Prior to 1969 b) From 82% in 1971, from 84% in 1985
Saudoy (w)	87	–	a) Prior to 1969
Savigny-sur-Ardre	86	87	
Selles	84	–	a) 1985
Sermiers	89	88	b) From 88% in 1985
Serzy et Prin	86	86	
Sézanne (b)	85	–	a) Prior to 1969 b) From 82% in 1971, from 84% in 1985
Sézanne (w)	87	–	a) Prior to 1969
Sillery	100	100	
Soilly	83	81	b) From 81% in 1971
Soulières	85	85	
Taissy	94	–	a) Prior to 1969
Talus-Saint-Prix	85	85	
Tauxières	99	99	
Thil	84	82	b) From 82% in 1971
Tours-sur-Marne (b)	100	100	
Tours-sur-Marne (w)	90	90	
Tramery (b)	86	85	b) From 85% prior to 1969
Tramery (w)	86	86	
Trépail	95	90	b) From 90% in 1973
Treslon	86	86	
Trigny	84	80	b) From 82% in 1971
Trois-Puits	94	–	a) Prior to 1969
Troissy	84	81	b) From 81% in 1971 from 83% in 1979
Unchair	86	86	
Vandeuil	86	86	
Vandières	86	82	b) From 83% in 1971, from 85% in 1976

Cru (in alphabetical order)	Current échelle (%)	1945 échelle (%)	Notable changes
Vauciennes	84	80	b) From 81% in 1971
Vaudemanges	95	90	b) From 90% in 1973
Venteuil	89	85	b) From 85% in 1970, from 87% in 1985
Verneuil	86	82	b) From 82% in 1971, from 84% in 1976
Vert-Toulon	85	85	
Vertus	95	93	b) From 93% in 1972
Verzenay (b)	100	100	
Verzenay (w)	100	86	b) From 86% in 1972
Verzy (b)	100	99	b) From 99% in 1985
Verzy (w)	100	86	b) From 86% in 1972, from 99% in 1985
Villedommange	90	90	
Ville-en-Tardenois	82	79	b) From 79% in 1971, from 81% in 1985
Villeneuve-Renneville	95	–	a) Prior to 1969 b) From 93% in 1985
Villers-Allerand	90	90	
Villers-aux-Noeuds	90	–	a) 1985
Villers-Franqueux	84	82	b) From 82% in 1971
Villers-Marmery	95	90	b) From 90% in 1973
Villers-sous-Châtillon	86	83	b) From 83% in 1971, from 85% in 1976
Villevenard	85	85	
Vinay	86	86	
Vincelles	86	83	b) From 83% in 1971, from 85% in 1976
Vindey (b)	85	–	a) Prior to 1969 b) From 84% in 1985
Vindey (w)	87	–	a) Prior to 1969
Vitry-en-Perthois	85	–	a) 1982
Voipreux	95	–	a) 1985
Vrigny	89	89	
MARNE *département* (all other growths)	80	75	b) From 75% in 1971
AISNE *département*			
All growths within the canton of Condé-en-Brie except the three below	83	75	b) From 81% in 1971
Barzy-sur-Marne	85	75	b) From 82% in 1971, from 84% in 1985
Passy-sur-Marne	85	82	b) From 82% in 1971, from 84% in 1985
Trélou-sur-Marne	85	82	b) From 82% in 1971, from 84% in 1985
AUBE *département*			
All growths except the two below	80	70	b) From 75% in 1971
Villenauxe-la-Grande (b)	85	—	a) 1985
Villenauxe-la-Grande (w)	87	—	a) 1985

Appendix VI Nineteenth-century Classifications

Whatever the wine region, classifications old and new always arouse a certain curiosity amongst wine lovers. Are they consistent, from century to century, author to author? Why have some wines declined and others risen? Indeed, they probably pose more questions than they answer, but that is a part of their fascination.

While Champagne does not have a famous classification like that of Bordeaux in 1855, two nineteenth-century writers, André Jullien and Cyrus Redding, did make studies of its wines and vineyards and their scales of quality make for useful comparisons with those of today.

André Jullien *Topography of All Known Vineyards* (1825)

André Jullien (1766–1832) was a French wine merchant based in Paris who regularly visited most of the vineyard areas of Europe. He was a person with a profound knowledge of viticulture and winemaking and a meticulous man who made written notes about everything he saw and all the wines he tasted during his trips. Most of the information included in *Topographie de tous vignobles connus* published in Paris in 1816 is of special value due to its obviously original content. The quotations below are from the abridged English translation *Topography of All Known Vineyards* published in London in 1824 for use by importers as a buyer's guide (original quotations in italics, author's comments in brackets).

Red wines

Class I VERZY, VERZENAY, MAILLY, ST BASLE (part of Verzy): *produce wines of good colour, body and spirit, much finesse, sève and bouquet*; BOUZY: *all of the above qualities plus delicacy*; LE CLOS DE ST THIERRY (not Château-Thierry, but a vineyard near Château-St-Thierry at the foot of Massif de St Thierry north-west of Reims)
Class II HAUTVILLERS, MAREUIL, DISY [sic], PIERRY, ÉPERNAY: *More celebrated for whites than reds*; TAISSY, LUDES, CHIGNY, RILLY, VILLER AMAND [sic]: *furnish wines partaking all the qualities of first class* (sic); CUMIÈRES: *Reputed for red wines more fine and delicate than those of the montagne, but less body.*
Class III VILLEDEMANGE [sic], ÉCUEIL, CHAMENY: *Very good quality, keep 10 to 12 years*; ST THIERRY (the commune where the clos or walled vineyard of the Class I rated Clos de St Thierry is situated); IRIGNY, CHENA [sic]: *produce much sought after*

reds, deep colour, very pleasant flavour; AVENAY, CHAMPILLON, DAMERY: *Good reds but inferior to those above.*
Class IV VERTUS: *Good colour, body and spirit, very good flavour, not firm in first year, but gains much by age*; MARDEUIL, MONTHELON, MOUSSY, VINAY, CHAVEAU [sic], MANCY: *More delicate, more agreeable and forward than those of Vertus*; CHAMERY, PARGNY, VANTEUIL [sic], REUIL, FLEURY-LA-RIVIÈRE: *similar to Monthelon.*

White wines

Class I SILLERY: *produce most esteemed wines, Sillery itself being on a plain and contains but few vines, they grow on the side of Verzenay, which is contiguous; it is there where the best wines called Sillery are produced*; AY: *Furnishes the best vins mousseux, fine spiritous, sparkling and of beautiful bouquet, lighter and more moelleux than those of Sillery*; MAREUIL: *produces wines not different from Ay and pass in commerce as vins d'Ay*; HAUTVILLERS: *Formerly equalled or surpassed Ay, but vineyards not cultivated with the same care*; PIERRY: *Drier, keep longer than Ay, distinguished by a marked taste of pierre à fusil*; DEZY [sic]: *Same as Ay*; ÉPERNAY: *Inferior to Ay except for some called 'du Closet' which are equal.*
Class II CRAMANT, AVISE [sic], OGER, LES MENIL [sic]: *In general planted with white grapes which succeed there better than red. The wines are sweet, very fine, light and agreeable and, when mixed with Ay, furnish vins mousseux possessing all their qualities. This mixture being necessary in hot years when the black grapes are less apt to mousse.*
Class III and **Class IV** (These two classes are rather ambiguous; André Jullien refers not to actual village names, but sloping hills and sun exposure, with insufficient geographical references.)
Class V CHOUILLY, MONTHELON, GRAUVES, MANCY, MOLINS [sic], MAUGRIMAUD, BEAUMONT, VILLERS AUX NOEUDS: *Light and agreeable but weak, keep one year.*

Cyrus Redding *A History and Description of Modern Wines* (1833)

Cyrus Redding (1785–1870) was a successful author who developed a love of wine in Paris between 1814 and 1819, where he was sent as correspondent for *The Examiner*, then remained as editor of *Galinani's Messenger*. He spent much of his time visiting vineyards in France and Italy. The quotations below are from *A History and Description of Modern*

Wines, published in London in 1833, the first book in English to deal exclusively with contemporary wines. (Original quotations in italics, author's comments in brackets; prices are per hectolitre.)

Red wines

Class I CLOS ST THIERRY: *which mingles the best qualities of Burgundy with those of Champagne*; BOUZY (150FF) *Approach in bouquet the best wines of Burgundy*; VERZENAY (130FF), ST BASLE (130FF), MAILLY (130FF), VERZY (130FF): *produce wines held in considerable repute.*

Class II CUMIÈRES (50FF), CHIGNY, LUDES, VILLERS ALLERAND, HAUTVILLERS (50FF).

Class III DAMERY, VERTUS, CUIS, MONTHELON, MANCY, CHAVOST, MOUSSY, VINAY, ST MARTIN D'ABLOIS, MARDEUIL (40FF–60FF): *Inferior to those made on the lands of Reims, fetch only middling prices*; TERRES DE ST THIERRY (30FF–60FF, some ordinary sorts 20FF), ÉCUEIL (22FF–30FF): *Common wines*; VILLERS ALLERAND, AVENAY, VILLEDOMMANGE (25FF–30FF), CHAMPILLON.

White wines

Class I SILLERY: *A still wine with dry taste, fine amber colour, rich body and delicious bouquet*; BOUZY (150FF); AMBONNAY (150FF); AY (130FF): *An effervescing wine, ranks next*; MAREUIL (110FF): *Nearly equals it*; PIERRY (130FF–150FF in a plentiful year, 180FF–200FF in a medium year, and 200FF–250FF in a year of scarcity): *gives a drier wine, which will keep longer than those of Ay*; DIZY (110FF): *follows next*; ÉPERNAY: *part inferior and part equal to those of Ay, the wines called Closet may rank with any grown in Ay.*

Class II HAUTVILLERS: *formerly equal to any wine in Champagne*; CRAMANT (100FF–200FF), AVIZE [sic – 100FF–200FF], OGER (100FF–200FF), MENIL [sic] (100FF–200FF): *are all made with white grapes, are excellent and often mingled with the wines of Ay to their great advantage.*

Class III CHOUILLY (60FF–100FF), MONTHELON, GRAUVES, MANCY, BEAUMONT AND OTHER PLACES NEAR REIMS: *Inferior wines, the best being tolerable.*

Wines priced but not classified by Cyrus Redding

ST MENEHOULD (15FF); VITRY (20FF); CHÂLONS (12FF); MAREUIL (40FF/red); NORROIS (25FF–30FF/red); TARDENOIS (25FF–30FF): *All other wines of the river are common, and fetch in the market, on the average, only 25FF–40FF*; *The rest of the wines from the mountain district are ordinary wines, bringing only some 30FF to 40FF and some only 15FF–20FF*; *The second class wines of* ... AMBONNAY, LUDES, CHIGNY, RILLY, VILLERS-ALLERAND and TROIS-PUITS (all 50FF): ... *some are of tolerable quality and are mostly sold to foreigners*; MAREUIL LE PORT, LEUVRIGNY, CROISSY, VERNEUIL, DORMANS (all 22FF–30FF) *common wines.*

Appendix VII Annual Production 1969–85: Yields *v*. Limits

The decree-law of 28 September 1935 limited the yield permitted for the production of Champagne to 50 hl/ha or 7,500 kgs/ha. This maximum, however, made proviso for an annual modification to the yield and the one-off limits which resulted were, with the exception of vagaries of climate, set higher and higher. With the advent of modern technology this rising yield was natural enough, reflecting the improved viticultural conditions experienced elsewhere in France. But in the early 1970s there was growing concern that higher yields might be detrimental to the quality image of Champagne and a ceiling was set, beyond which it would be impossible to classify the wine as Champagne. This ceiling is called the *Plafond Limité de Classement* or PLC for short. Decree number 74–872 of the law of 19 October 1974 set the PLC for Champagne at 13,000 kgs per hectare.

Annual Official Limits and Average Yields, 1969–85

(in thousands of kilograms per hectare)

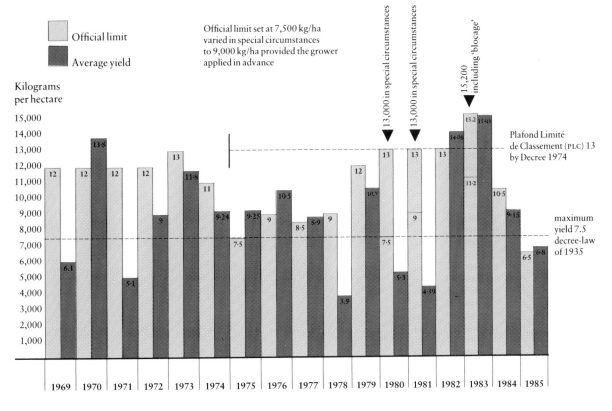

Harvest years

Appendix VIII Global Sales: 1969–85

Millions of Bottles

Year	Total sales	*Négociants'* total sales	*Récoltants'* total sales	French market	Export market
1985	195.4	134.4	61.0	122.6	72.8
1984	188.0	128.2	59.8	119.1	62.7
1983	159.5	104.6	54.9	109.8	49.7
1982	146.5	94.0	52.5	102.6	43.9
1981	159.0	104.4	54.6	109.4	49.6
1980	176.5	115.6	60.9	121.4	55.0
1979	184.1	120.6	63.2	128.4	55.8
1978	185.9	126.6	59.3	131.9	54.6
1977	170.2	116.8	53.5	124.5	45.7
1976	153.5	106.3	47.2	115.6	37.2
1975	122.2	81.3	40.9	93.9	28.2
1974	105.5	72.3	33.2	75.6	29.9
1973	124.7	90.0	34.7	80.5	44.2
1972	123.1	88.7	34.4	83.4	39.7
1971	116.4	84.0	32.5	82.4	34.0
1970	102.2	75.5	26.7	71.2	31.0
1969	94.0	70.2	23.7	67.0	26.9

Appendix IX Export Performance 1979–85

Millions of Bottles

Country	1985	1984	1983	1982	1981	1981	1980	1979
Britain	15.4	11.9	10.0	7.7	7.9	8.5	8.5	9.2
United States	14.2	12.8	9.7	7.1	7.9	7.1	7.1	7.8
West Germany	8.5	7.4	5.3	3.7	4.5	5.3	5.3	5.2
Switzerland	6.2	5.3	3.7	3.3	3.8	3.5	3.5	3.2
Italy	5.8	4.8	3.8	4.5	6.7	8.6	8.6	8.2
Belgium	4.6	4.9	4.1	3.7	3.8	5.9	5.9	6.7
Australia	2.0	1.8	0.8	0.8	0.8	0.7	0.7	0.6
Canada	1.7	1.5	1.0	1.1	1.2	1.0	1.0	1.0
Holland	1.4	1.3	1.2	0.8	0.8	1.3	1.3	1.3

Per Capita Consumption (1983)

Country	Bottles per capita	Country	Bottles per capita
United States	0.05	Italy	0.07
Britain	0.18	Belgium	0.41
West Germany	0.09	Holland	0.09
Switzerland	0.58	Canada	0.04

But Guadeloupe, with imports for 1983 at 0.8 million bottles and a population of only 334 thousand, consumes more per capita than any of the big markets – no less than 2.4 bottles a head.

Appendix X Annual Fixed Prices for Grapes 1969–85

Key to column headings

A Price per kilo of grapes for 100% échelle de cru.
B *Prime* or premium Chardonnay and Pinot Noir.
C Special *prime* (1984 – for grapes from Avize, Bergères-les-Vertus, Chouilly, Cramant, le Mesnil-sur-Oger, Oger and Vertus; 1978 – Pinot Meunier; 1973 – an exceptional *prime* uniform for all crus and *cépages*)
D Price for pressing per *pièce* (until 1982), or per hectolitre (from 1983), of *cuvée* or *taille* excluding *débourbage*
E Price for pressing per *pièce* (until 1982), or per hectolitre (from 1983), of *cuvée* or *taille* excluding *débourbage*

F Price for pressing per *pièce* (until 1982), or per hectolitre (from 1983), of *rebêche*
G *Courtier*'s* or broker's commission for a *pièce* (until 1982), or per hectolitre (from 1983), of *vin clair*
H *Courtier*'s per cent commission for transactions in bottle.

* There exists in Champagne a network of *courtiers* whose major function is to act as broker between the growers and the *négociants*.

French Francs

Year	A	B	C	D	E	F	G	H
1985	20.60	1.20	0.80	120	115	120	27.65*	
1984	16.10	1.00	1.00	113	108	113	22.25†	1
1983	14.20	0.90	–	105	100	105	25.50	1
1982	17.51	1.00	–	185	170	185	60.00	1
1981	16.00	1.00	–	160	148	160	55.00	1
1980	12.75	0.75	–	135	125	135	44.00	1
1979	10.91	0.65	–	110	102	113	37.20	1
1978	8.86	0.55	0.10	100	93	103	30.30	1
1977	7.53	0.45	–	86	80	88	24.20	1
1976	6.78	0.40	–	77	72	79	22.00	1
1975	5.53	0.32	–	67	62	69	18.20	1
1974	7.37	0.45	–	57	53	59	25.00	1
1973	6.37	0.45	1.00	49	46	51	25.00	1
1972	5.33	0.37	0.50	40	37	42	18.35	1
1971	4.66	0.35	–	33	29.70	35.20	16.14	1
1970	4.27	0.25	–	30	27	32	14.55	1
1969	4.14	0.25	–	27	24	29	14.45	1

* This is the price fixed at *co-opérative* presshouses, it was 34.55 elsewhere.
† This is the price fixed at *co-opérative* presshouses, it was 22.75 francs elsewhere.

Price per kilo of grapes (1950–68) in francs

1968	3.95	1967	3.75	1966	3.10	1965	2.91
1964	2.88	1963	2.85	1962	2.80	1961	2.70
1960	2.60*	1959	2.45	1958	2.30	1957	1.95
1956	1.32	1955	1.29	1954	1.23	1953	1.45
1952	1.40	1951	1.40	1950	1.40		

* The New Franc was introduced in 1960 (100 Old Francs equalling 1 New Franc), but the term 'New' was dropped in 1963.

Glossary

Abbreviations

AOC Appellation d'Origine Contrôlée
AR Appellation Réglementée
BOB Buyer's Own Brand
CIVC Comité Interprofessionnel du Vin de Champagne
CM Co-opérative-manipulant
CO₂ Carbon dioxide
CRD Capsule Représentative de Droits
DGI Direction Générale des Impôts
EEC European Economic Community
H₂CO₃ Carbonic gas
INAO Institut National des Appellations d'Origine des Vins et Eaux-de-Vie
MA Marque auxiliaire

NM Négociant-manipulant
NV Non-vintage
pH Potential hydrogen-ion concentration
PLC Plafond Limité de Classement
QWPSR Quality Wine Produced in a Specified Region
RD Récemment dégorgé
RM Récoltant-manipulant
SGV Syndicat Général des Vignerons
SO₂ Sulphur dioxide
VDQS Vin Délimité de Qualité Supérieure

Italicised words cross-refer to other entries in the Glossary.
(Fr.) indicates a French term.
(Ch.) Champagne dialect.

À la glace (Fr.) A system of *dégorgement* involving the immersion of bottle necks (containing the sediment) in a freezing brine.

À la volée (Fr.) Manual *dégorgement* resulting in an audible crack whence the name is derived.

Acetaldehyde The principal aldehyde in all wines, but found in much greater quantities in sherry. In unfortified wines, a large amount of acetaldehyde is undesirable, unstable, halfway to complete *oxidation* and evokes a *sherry-like* smell. Safe but higher levels than normal are found in Champagnes fermented or aged in wood.

Acidity Essential for the life and vitality of all wines, particularly Champagne. Relatively high degrees are required to carry the flavour through the tactile sensation of the *mousse*.

Aerobic In the presence of air.

Aftertaste The flavour and *aroma* left in the mouth after the wine has been swallowed. See *finish* for distinction.

Aggressive The opposite of *soft* and *smooth*. Young Champagnes can appear aggressive, but may *round* out with a little time in bottle. The younger the Champagne, the more sugar is added (via the *liqueur d'expédition*) to counter its aggressivity.

Agrafe (Fr.) An inverted U-shaped metal clip once used to secure the first corks during *prise de mousse*, but rarely encountered since the advent of *crown caps*. Some *Coteaux Champenois* are offered for sale with corks secured by agrafes.

Aigne (Ch.) A *marc* of grapes.

Alcohol In wine terms, this is ethyl alcohol; a colourless flammable liquid.

Ampelidaceae The botanical family to which jungle-creepers, ornamental ivies and all winemaking vines belong.

Ampelography The study of the vine.

Anaerobic In the absence of air.

Anthocyanins Various colouring pigments found in the skins of black grapes.

Anti-oxidant Any chemical which prevents grapes, must or wine from oxidising, *ascorbic acid* or *sulphur dioxide* for example.

Appellation d'Origine Contrôlée or AOC (Fr.) A quality control system accounting for some 20–25% of France's wine output. AOC was the first national wine regime and conforms to EEC QWPSR standards.

Appellation Réglementée or AR (Fr.) A quality control system similar to AOC but applicable to certain *eaux-de-vie*.

Appley Often applied to young wines, particularly those from northern wine regions, where the *malic* acidity (which is the main acid type found in apples) evokes a raw appley smell and a *tart*, *green* flavour. Champagnes which are appley have not undergone *malo-lactic fermentation* and are far too young to drink.

Are (Fr.) One-hundredth of a *hectare*.

Aroma This should really be confined to the *fresh* and fruity smells reminiscent of grapes, rather than the more winey or bottle-mature *complexities* of *bouquet*; but it is not always possible to use this word in its purest form, hence *aroma* and *bouquet* may be read as synonymous.

Arrondissement (Fr.) A sub-division of a *département*, roughly on a par with the area covered by a district council in the UK or a county in the USA.

Ascorbic Acid Commonly known as vitamin C and used in winemaking as an *anti-oxidant*.

Aseptic A characteristic of a substance which can kill bacteria, *sorbic acid* or *sulphur dioxide* for example.

Assemblage (Fr.) A blend of base wines to create the final *cuvée*. Depending on what the Champagne is to be, *vintage* or *non-vintage*, *blanc de blancs* or *rosé*, etc, this may mean blending wines of different grape varieties, various villages and several years.

Atmospheres A measure of atmospheric pressure: 1 atmosphere = 15 pounds per square inch.

Autolysis Enzymatic breakdown of yeast cells normally seen as a potential danger, as it increases the possibility of bacterial spoilage, but in the production of Champagne it is an essential biochemical process, taking place during the *prise de mousse* and effectively giving the wine its true 'Champagne flavour'.

Bagnolets (Fr.) The white linen bonnets traditionally worn by women in the vineyards during the harvest are now rarely seen.

Bague Carré (Fr.) A squared-off glass rim around the neck of a Champagne bottle onto which the *agrafe* is fixed.

Bague Couronne (Fr.) An exaggerated lip on the neck of a Champagne bottle is necessary if a crown-cap is to be used for the *prise de mousse*.

Balance Refers to the harmonious relationship between *acids*, *alcohol*, *fruit*, *tannin* and other natural elements.

Balle-sente (Ch.) A lazy *vigneron* who wanders from vine to vine.

Barbottin (Ch.) A drink made from hot sugary water and *eau-de-vie de marc*.

Bêche or bêche plate (Fr.) A sharp metal spade used to cut up the *marc*, before pressing out the *taille* and *rebêche*.

Belemnite chalk or **Belemnita quadrata** A Campanian chalk found on the slopes of the Montagne de Reims and Côte des Blancs.

Biscuity A desirable aspect of *bouquet* found in some Champagnes, derived from a well-matured, slightly increased *acetaldehyde* content. This may have developed through an extended bottle age or by certain vinification methods: cask-fermentation or cask-ageing for example.

Bite A very definite qualification of *grip*. Usually a desirable characteristic, but an unpleasant *bite* is possible.

Bitterness (1) An unpleasant aspect of a poorly made wine. (2) An expected characteristic of an as yet undeveloped concentration of flavours which should, with maturity, become *rich* and delicious. An *edge* of bitterness may be due to raw *tannin*.

Blanc de blancs (Fr.) A white wine made exclusively from white grapes. In Champagne this means a pure *Chardonnay* wine.

Blanc de Noirs (Fr.) A white wine made exclusively from black grapes. In Champagne this means a pure *Pinot* wine, *Pinot Noir* or *Pinot Meunier*.

Blind tasting An objective tasting of wines, the identity of which is unknown to the taster.

Blocage (Fr.) A stock of unclassified wines held in reserve until times of shortage when, upon ministerial decree, the wines will be granted full AOC Champagne status.

Bloom Yeast and bacteria adhering to the grape's *pruina* create a coating most noticeable on black varieties.

Blowsy An overblown and exaggerated fruity *aroma* which should not be a characteristic of a classic Champagne.

Bobillon (Ch.) A small cask.

Body The *extract* of fruit and alcoholic strength which together give an impression of *weight* in the mouth.

Botrytis A generic term for rot.

Bouchage (Fr.) To insert the cork in the bottle, now an automated operation.

Boucher (Fr.) The person responsible for inserting the corks.

Bouchon couronne (Fr.) A crown-cap or beer-bottle top.

Bouchon de liège (Fr.) A cork stopper. In Champagne this usually measures 32 mm in diameter by 48 mm long before it is pounded into its easily recognisable mushroom shape prior to the *ficelage*.

Bouchon d'expédition (Fr.) The permanent cork used after the *prise de mousse* and *dégorgement*.

Bouchon de tirage (Fr.) The temporary closure, either a cork or crown-cap, used to seal the bottle for the *prise de mousse*.

Boues de ville (Fr.) Literally the town's rubbish, this is ordinary domestic trash which has been sifted, processed and allowed to decompose before being deposited in large piles throughout the region. It is spread on the vineyards and used as a fertiliser.

Bouillage (Fr.) The initial, extremely vigorous, stage of fermentation, literally and aptly translated as 'boiling'.

Bouquet This should really be applied to the combination of smells directly attributable to a wine's maturity in bottle – thus *aroma* for grape and *bouquet* for bottle. But it is not always possible to use these words in their purest form, hence *aroma* and *bouquet* may be read as synonymous.

Bouvreu (Ch.) Bunches of grapes which are unripe at the time of harvest because of a late *sortie* – a good omen for the next vintage.

Breathing Term used to describe the interaction between a wine and the air after a bottle has been opened and before it is drunk.

Brut (Fr.) A Champagne with between 0 and 15 grams per litre of sugar (obtained through the addition of the *liqueur d'expédition*).

Brut Absolut, Brut Intégral, Brut Non Dosage, Brut Zéro (Fr.) All Champagnes which have not received a *dosage* of sugar through the *liqueur d'expédition*.

Buyer's Own Brand or **BOB** A brand name that belongs to the wholesale buyer, usually a supermarket or restaurant, not the producer.

Canton (Fr.) A district within an *arrondissement*.

Capsule Représentative de Droits or **CRD** (Fr.) The foil or metalised-plastic capsule which by law must be attached in such a way that the cork cannot be removed without breaking this seal.

Carbon dioxide or **CO₂** This is naturally produced in the fermentation process, when the sugar is converted into almost equal parts of carbon dioxide and *alcohol*. The CO_2 produced during the fermentation of a still wine is allowed to escape, although a tiny amount normally remains dissolved in the wine as carbonic gas (H_2CO_3), giving it life and vitality. During Champagne's *prise de mousse* the gas is prevented from escaping, thus the wine becomes sparkling. When retaining carbonic gas during the production of a wine, as in the *prise de mousse* for example, the pressure exerted affects the fermentation process. A reduced growth of yeast causes an increased yield of alcohol per gram of sugar and a higher ester content has also been noted.

Cave (Fr.) A below-ground cellar, as opposed to a *cellier*, which is an above-ground store.

Caviste (Fr.) A cellarworker.

Cellier (Fr.) An above-ground storage or warehousing premises.

Cendres noires (Fr.) *Lignites*.

Centrifuge Before *clarification* (and sometimes before *fermentation*), wines are often subjected to so-called centrifugal force to remove the majority of suspended matter which may cloud up a wine.

Chaptalisation (Fr.) Sugar added to grape *must* to raise a wine's alcoholic potential.

Chardonnay A vine producing white grapes, it is one of the region's three major varieties, the cultivation of which is favoured by growers on the *Côte des Blancs*.

Charm A subjective term: if a wine charms, it appeals without blatantly attracting in an obvious fashion.

Chaufferettes Paraffin burners used to heat the vineyards as a protection against frost-damage.

Cheesy A characteristic element in the *bouquet* of very old Champagnes and some unfiltered still wines. It is probably caused by the production during fermentation of a very small amount of butyric acid, which may later develop into ethyl butyrate, an ester. Butyric acid is responsible for the smell of rancid butter and smelly feet.

Chef de caves (Fr.) A cellarmaster.

Cheville (Fr.) A term commonly used to describe the straight tube-like shape of an old Champagne cork which has lost its capacity to swell once removed from the bottle. The opposite of *juponne*.

Chewy An extreme qualification of *meaty*.

Chlorosis A vine disorder caused by mineral imbalance (too much active lime, not enough iron or magnesium), often called green-sickness.

Citrus When mature, a fine *blanc de blancs* Champagne can achieve a zesty, citrusy character. When used by this author, 'citrusy' indicates aromas and flavours of far greater complexity than mere *lemony* can suggest.

Clarification, clarify To remove all suspended matter which may cloud a wine or grape *must*. See also *fining*.

Classic, classy Both subjective words to convey an obvious impression of quality. These terms are applied to wines which not only portray the correct characteristics for their type and origin, but possess the *finesse* and *style* indicative of top-quality wines.

Clean A straightforward term applied to any wine devoid of any unwanted or unnatural *undertones* of *aroma* and flavour.

Clone In a viticultural sense, intensive selection can, within varietal limitations, produce a vine to suit specific conditions: to increase yield maybe, or to resist certain diseases or local climatic conditions, etc. Identical clones of this one vine can then be replicated an infinite number of times by microbiogenetic techniques. See also *localised clone*.

Closed Refers to the *nose* or *palate* of a wine which fails to open or show much character. It also implies that the wine has some qualities, even if they are 'hidden' – these should open up as the wine develops in bottle.

Cloying Applies to the sickly and sticky character of a poor sweet wine, where the *finish* is heavy and often unclean.

Club de Viticulteurs Champenois (Fr.) Approximately fifty growers belong to this select organisation established in 1971 to market *Spécial Club* Champagnes.

Coarse A term which should be applied to a 'rough and ready' wine, not necessarily unpleasant, but certainly not fine.

Code du Vin (Fr.) The statute book of French wine laws for all regions and types of products.

Collage (Fr.) The act of *fining*.

Colporteur (Fr.) A vineyard worker who loads the baskets of grapes on to a lorry or trailer for the journey to the presshouse.

Comité Interprofessionnel du Vin de Champagne or **CIVC** (Fr.) The semi-governmental interprofessional body which regulates the Champagne industry.

Commercial A diplomatic way for experts to say 'I don't like this, but I expect the masses will'! A commercial wine is blended to a widely acceptable formula; at its worst it may be bland and inoffensive, at its best it is probably fruity, quaffable and uncomplicated.

Complete Refers to a satisfaction in the mouth that the wine has everything: *fruit, tannin, acidity, depth, length*, etc.

Complexity An overworked word which refers to many different nuances of smell or taste. Great wines in their youth may have a certain *complexity*, but it is only with *maturity* in bottle that a wine will eventually achieve full potential in terms of *complexity*.

Co-opérative-manipulant (Fr.) A co-opérative which produces and markets Champagne under its own label.

Corked Correctly used, the term applies to the cause, a penicillin infection inside the cork.

Correct A wine with all the correct characteristics for its type and origin. Not necessarily an exciting wine, but one that cannot be faulted.

Coteaux Champenois (Fr.) Red, white and rosé still wines produced in Champagne.

Côte des Blancs Spur of gently rolling hills south of Épernay, planted almost exclusively with *Chardonnay* vines.

Coulure (Fr.) A disorder of the vine usually caused by sudden warmth at the flowering, which diverts the sap from the clusters to wood growth. The neglected clusters do not develop and tiny, unripe, bullet-hard berries are encountered at harvest-time. This can be similar in appearance to *millerandage*, but the two disorders are quite different.

Coupage (Fr.) To cut: sometimes deemed synonymous with the *assemblage* or blending of a Champagne, but this is only correct in the case of pink Champagne, where the white wine is literally cut with red to make the required colour. See *assemblage*.

Coupe (Fr.) A shallow, saucer-shaped glass totally unsuited for any type of wine, especially Champagne, retaining neither *nose* nor *mousse*.

Courtier (Fr.) A broker – when discussing wine, it is assumed that a courtier is a wine broker.

Cramant Not to be confused with *crémant*, a style of Champagne, Cramant is a village on the *Côte des Blancs* renowned for its production of superb *Chardonnay* grapes.

Crayères (Fr.) Chalk-pits dug out in Gallo-Roman times to provide building material for the city of Reims. In the eighteenth and nineteenth centuries various Champagne houses connected many of these pits by a network of tunnels, developing a sophisticated cellarage system in which they could store their wines under ideal conditions. The temperature inside these *crayères* is between 10° and 11°C, with an annual fluctuation of less than 1.5°C.

Crecelle (Fr.) A mechanical riddler designed to replace the *remueur*.

Crémant (Fr.) Traditionally ascribed to a Champagne with a gentler *mousse* than normal.

Crisp A *clean* wine, with good *acidity* showing on the *finish*, yielding a *fresh* and *clean* taste.

Crochet de dégorger (Fr.) A special knife with a curved blade used to remove the *agrafe* in *dégorgement à la volée*.

Crown-cap The common beer-bottle cap now widely used as the *temporary closure* for the *prise de mousse*.

Cru (Fr.) Literally a growth, in Champagne the term usually refers to a commune like Cramant or Bouzy for example.

Cryptogamic Fungus-based: a cryptogamic disease is a fungus-based disease like *grey rot*.

Cuve (Fr.) A vat or tank.

Cuve close (Fr.) or **Charmat Method** Bulk production method of making inexpensive sparkling wine through a *second fermentation* in tank, invented by Eugène Charmat in 1907.

Cuvée (Fr.) (1) Originally the wine of one *cuve* or vat, but now refers to a specific blend or product which, in current commercial terms, will be from several vats. (2) The first 2,050 litres of *must* pressed from a 4,000-kilo *marc* of grapes. See also *vin de cuvée*.

Cuvée de prestige (Fr.) Most houses have their prestige or de luxe *cuvées*, the two most famous being Moët & Chandon's Dom Pérignon and Louis Roederer's Cristal.

Débourbage (Fr.) The cleaning or purging of the *must*, immediately after pressing, prior to fermentation.

Débourrement (Fr.) The budding of the vine.

Dedaine (Ch.) *Eau-de-vie de marc.*

Dégorgement (Fr.) The act of removing or disgorging the sediment created by the *prise de mousse* from a bottle of Champagne after *remuage*.

Dégustation (Fr.) A tasting; in a wine context, obviously a wine tasting.

Delicate Describes the quieter characteristics of quality which give a wine *charm*.

Demi-muid A wooden cask with a capacity of 600 litres.

Demi Sec (Fr.) A Champagne with between 33 and 50 grams per litre of sugar (obtained through the addition of the *liqueur d'expédition*).

Département (Fr.) An administrative sub-division of France, roughly on a par with a county in the UK or a state in the USA.

Déplacements (Fr.) The stacking, unstacking and restacking of bottles resting *sur lattes*. During these operations the bottles are disturbed, thus preventing the lees from forming sticky layers. In modern establishments where the wines are stacked in pallets, this is achieved by transporting pallets by fork-lift trucks.

Depth Refers first to a wine's depth of flavour and secondly to its depth of interest.

Deuxième taille The last 205 litres of *must* pressed from a *marc* of grapes. See also *vin de taille*.

Direction Générale des Impôts or **DGI** The tax mark stamped onto the very top of a bottle of Champagne's foil capsule.

Dirty Applies to any wine with an unpleasant off-taste or off-smell, probably the result of poor or non-existent filtration, or through bad vinification or bottling techniques.

Distinctive A wine with a positive character. All *fine* wines are distinctive to one degree or another, but not all distinctive wines are necessarily *fine*.

Dosage (Fr.) Sugar added to Champagne, particularly youthful Champagne, by way of the *liqueur d'expédition* after *dégorgement* and prior to sale.

Doux (Fr.) A Champagne with in excess of 50 grams per litre of sugar (obtained through the addition of the *liqueur d'expédition*, usually with addition of grape spirit) – very rare.

Downy Mildew A *cryptogamic* disorder of the vine, also referred to variously as *False Mildew*, *Peronospora* and *Plasmopara*.

Earthy A drying impression in the mouth which brings back vivid childhood memories of eating dirt! Some minor Champagnes, particularly if pure *Pinot Meunier*, have an earthy *varietal* character which is both honest and enjoyable, but the finest quality Champagnes should be as *clean* as a whistle.

Easy Refers to a simple enjoyable quality in a wine, probably *soft* and not too expensive.

Eau-de-vie (Fr.) Literally 'water of life', specifically a grape-derived spirit.

Eau-de-vie de marc (Fr.) A brandy produced from the spent *marc*.

Eau-de-vie de vin (Fr.) A brandy produced from wine.

Échelle des crus (Fr.) The *crus* or villages of Champagne are classified on a percentage basis, from 80 to 100%. See *grand cru* and *premier cru*.

Elegant A subjective term applied to wines that one may describe as *stylish* or as possessing *finesse*.

Épinettes (Fr.) Special secateurs used to cut grape clusters from the vine during the harvest.

Épluchage (Fr.) Sorting the grapes in the vineyard between the picking operation and transporting to the presshouse.

Esters Sweet-smelling compounds that contribute to the *aroma* and *bouquet* of a wine, formed during *fermentation* and throughout the process of *maturation*.

Euvitis A sub-genus of *Vitis* belonging to the botanical family *Ampelidaceae* and containing the species *Vitis vinifera* which contains all the classic winemaking varieties of *vine*.

Extract The sugar-free soluble solids which literally give body to a wine. This term covers everything from proteins and vitamins to *tannins*, calcium and iron.

Extra Sec (Fr.) A Champagne with between 12 and 20 grams per litre of sugar (obtained through the addition of the *liqueur d'expédition*).

Falaises, Les (Fr.) This is the hilly area of the *Montagne de Reims* and *Côte des Blancs* which rises from the plains of Champagne and upon which most of the region's vineyards are found.

False Mildew A *cryptogamic* disorder of the vine, also referred to variously as *Downy Mildew*, *Peronospora* and *Plasmopara*.

Farmyardy A term used by many people to describe a wine, quite often *Chardonnay*- or *Pinot*-based, which has *matured* through its initial *freshness* of fruit, past the desired stage of *roundness* and the pleasing phase when it acquires certain *vegetal undertones*, to the point where it is definitely pongy. The wine is still healthy and drinkable – for some, it is at the very *peak* of perfection. Unfiltered wines run the risk of becoming prematurely farmyardy unless produced with fastidious care and attention.

Fat A wine full in *body* and *extract*.

Fécondation (Fr.) Pollination of the vine.

Fermage (Fr.) Payment to a *vigneron* in cash, as distinct from *métayage* (payment in grapes).

Fermentation The biochemical process by which enzymes secreted by yeast cells convert sugar molecules into almost equal parts of *alcohol* and *carbonic gas*.

Ficelage (Fr.) To secure the *permanent cork* with a wire muzzle.

Fine Marne (Fr.) An *eau-de-vie* produced from *Coteaux Champenois*.

Finesse That elusive, indescribable quality separating a fine wine from those of lesser quality.

Fining The *clarification* of a wine after *fermentation* has ceased. In Champagne, this is usually achieved with gelatine to attract cloudy matter in the wine into tiny clusters or colloids which drop to the bottom of the vat to form the *lees*.

Finish The quality and enjoyment of a wine's *aftertaste*.

Firm Refers to a certain amount of *grip*. A firm wine is a wine of good constitution, held up with a certain amount of *tannin* and *acidity*.

Flabby The opposite of *crisp*, referring to a wine lacking in *acidity* and consequently dull, weak and *short*.

Flat (1) A sparkling wine which has lost all of its *mousse*. (2) A term which is interchangeable with *flabby*, especially when referring to a lack of *acidity* on the *finish*.

Fleshy Refers to a wine with plenty of fruit and *extract* and infers a certain underlying *firmness*.

Fleuillaison (Fr.) The first appearance of foliage on the vine, normally in early April in Champagne.

Flocculent A flaky *lees*, difficult to settle and inclined to cloud up a wine.

Floraison (Fr.) The flowering of the vine, normally between late May and early July in Champagne.

Foudre (Fr.) A large wooden cask or vat.

Foule, En (Fr.) Literally 'in a crowd', *en foule* is the rather haphazard effect created when *ungrafted* vines are cultivated by various methods of layering. See also *provignage*.

Fresh Wines which are *clean* and still vital with youth.

Full Usually refers to *body*, eg., full-bodied. But a wine can be light in *body* yet full in flavour.

Fut (Fr.) The standard wooden cask in Champagne has a capacity of 205 litres and is called a *fut* when empty. See *pièce*.

Gelatine Traditionally used in Champagne for *fining*.

Genus The botanical family *Ampelidaceae* has ten genera, one of which, *Vitis*, through the sub-genus *Euvitis*, contains the species *Vitis vinifera* to which all the famous varieties of winemaking vines belong, including Champagne's *Chardonnay*, *Pinot Noir* and *Pinot Meunier*.

Glace, À la (Fr.) A system of *dégorgement* involving the immersion of bottle necks (containing the sediment) into a freezing brine.

Goût de terroir (Fr.) Literally a 'taste of earth', the French term for *earthy*.

Graft The joint between the *rootstock* (of a *phylloxera*-resistant vine) and the *scion* (of the *producer* vine).

Grand cru (Fr.) Literally 'great growth', in Champagne specifically referring to one of seventeen villages with a 100% rating in the *échelle des crus*.

Grand mousseux Strong in effervescence with an internal pressure of approximately 6 *atmospheres*, as opposed to a *crémant* which is a gently sparkling 3.5 *atmospheres*.

Grande Marque (Fr.) Literally a 'great brand' or 'famous name', in Champagne also a term applied to houses belonging to the Syndicat de Grandes Marques de Champagne.

Grappillage (Fr.) A tradition preserved by some growers three weeks after the harvest, whereby the young and the poor are encouraged to help themselves to any bunches which might have been missed or unripe during the vintage.

Grapy Can be applied to the *aroma* and flavour of a wine which is reminiscent of grapes rather than overtly winy. An unsuitable characteristic in Champagne, it would be distinctly welcome in *Coteaux Champenois*.

Green Young and tart, as in Vinho Verde. It can be either a derogatory term, or simply an indication of youthful wine which might well improve.

Green sickness *Chlorosis* of the vine.

Grip is applied to a *firm* wine with a positive finish. A wine showing *grip* on the *finish* indicates a certain *bite* of acidity and, if red, *tannin*.

Gueule à rebêche (Ch.) A *vigneron* whose face is always red owing to his continually drinking *vin de rebêche*.

Guérite A receptacle, often cut out of an old cask, which is used to catch the *temporary cork* and the sediment during *dégorgement* when performed manually *à la volée*.

Gyrasols (Sp.) or **gyropalettes** (Fr.) Pallets that replicate the effects of *remuage* and which may be operated manually or by computer. A Catalonian invention, these pallets each contain approximately 560 bottles of Champagne which have undergone the *prise de mousse*.

Habillage (Fr.) Labelling the bottle and dressing it with foil.

Harsh A more derogatory form of *coarse*.

Hautvillers (Ch.) 'The cuckolds of Hautvillers.'

Hectare (Fr.) An area of land equal to 2.4711 acres.

Hectolitre (Fr.) Liquid measure of 100 litres, equal to 22.01 Imperial gallons or 19.43 US gallons.

Hollow A wine which appears to lack any real flavour in the mouth compared to the promise shown on the *nose*.

Hordon (Ch.) A group of grape pickers.

Hydrogen sulphide Elemental sulphur remaining from rot control sprays applied to the vines can occasionally reduce into hydrogen sulphide, a compound with a characteristic rotten-egg smell.

Institut National des Appellations d'Origine des Vins et Eaux-de-Vie or **INAO** The body responsible for administering AOC regulations.

Juponne (Fr.) *Il juponne* describes the mushrooming effect on the base of a youthful Champagne cork when it expands upon extraction. The opposite of *cheville*.

Lattes, Sur (Fr.) *Lattes* are thin planks, slats or lathes on which bottles are stacked horizontally (*sur lattes*) during the *prise de mousse*.

Lees The sediment which accumulates in the bottom of a vat during the *fermentation*, *racking* and *fining* of a wine.

Lemony With some bottle age, *blanc de blancs* Champagnes can acquire a zest and a tang reminiscent of lemons.

Length A wine which has length indicates that the flavour *lingers* in the mouth a long time after swallowing.

Levurage (Fr.) The addition of yeast, usually used to indicate the addition of yeast through the *liqueur de tirage*.

Lie (Fr.) *Lees*: *sur lie* refers to a wine kept in contact with its *lees*.

Liège et agrafe (Fr.) The cork and clasp combination which was commonly used as the *temporary closure* during the *prise de mousse* before the *crown-cap*.

Lignite The 'brown coal' of Germany: a brown carbonaceous material which is at an intermediary stage between peat and coal.

Lingering Normally applied to the *finish* of a wine – an *aftertaste* which literally lingers.

Liqueur de tirage (Fr.) The bottling liqueur: wine, yeast and sugar added to still Champagne to induce the *prise de mousse*.

Liqueur d'expédition (Fr.) A liqueur of wine and sugar added to Champagne after *dégorgement*. This smooths out the *aggressive organoleptic* effect of a youthful effervescing wine which is naturally high in *acidity*. The older the wine, the lower the *dosage* of *liqueur d'expédition*.

Localised clone A variant of a vine variety which is peculiar to a specific *terroir*.

Long Refers to a persistent taste which remains in the mouth after the wine has been swallowed. See also *short*.

Longevity Potentially long-lived wines may owe their longevity to a significant content of one or more of the following: *tannin*, *acidity*, *alcohol* and *sugar*.

Macération carbonique (Fr.) or **maceration style** Generic terms which group together several similar methods of initially vinifying wine under the pressure of CO_2.

Maie (Fr.) The receptacle part of a traditional Champagne press.

Malic A more precise term for *appley*.

Malo-lactic fermentation Conversion of the hard *malic acid* into the soft lactic *acid*.

Marc (Fr.) (1) The capacity of a traditional Champagne press, i.e., 4,000 kilos. (2) The residue of skins, pips and stalks after pressing.

Mardeuil (Ch.) 'If he's from Mardeuil, he must be a terrific salesman!'

Marque (Fr.) A brand or make.

Marque d'acheteur (Fr.) A *Buyer's Own Brand* or BOB is a brand name which belongs to the wholesale buyer, usually a supermarket or a restaurant, not the producer.

Marque auxiliaire or **MA** A second or, literally, auxiliary brand.

Mature, maturity The term refers to a wine's development in bottle, as opposed to *ripe*, which is a state of maturity of the grape itself.

Meaty This suggests a wine so rich in *body* and *extract* that the drinker feels that he can almost *chew* it. *Tannin* also plays a role in a meaty wine.

Mellow *Round* and at its *peak* or *maturity*.

Mercaptans Methyl and ethyl *alcohols* can react with *hydrogen sulphide* to form *mercaptans*: foul-smelling compounds which can be difficult for the winemaker to remove and thus ruin a wine.

Mesnil-sur-Oger (Ch.) 'The bigheads of Mesnil.'

Métayage (Fr.) Payment to a *vigneron* in grapes, as distinct from *fermage* (payment in cash).

Méthode Champenoise (Fr.) The establishment of the Champagne Method was a gradual accumulation over two hundred years of various practices which enhanced the unsophisticated *rural method*: the development, utilisation and application of a *liqueur de tirage*, *remuage*, *pupitre*, *dégorgement* and *liqueur d'expédition*.

Since 1985 the term *Méthode Champenoise* has been officially banned by the EEC for all wines other than Champagne (whose producers never use the term anyway). This was a step backwards for the consumer who, after the ban's eight-year transitional period, will be deprived of the one essential piece of information required to separate premium non-Champagne sparkling wine from inferior products.

Micraster A chalk common to the plains, but also encroaches upon the *Falaises*, particularly in villages along the northern edge of the *Montagne de Reims*.

Mildew A *cryptogamic* disorder. *True Mildew* is *oidium*.

Millerandage The effect of cold or rainy weather at the time of flowering, resulting in imperfect fertilisation, causing grape clusters to contain partly developed berries with no seeds amongst perfectly healthy berries.

Millésime (Fr.) The year of vintage.

Millésimé (Fr.) The wine of one year, in other words a vintage Champagne.

Mise en masse (Fr.) Stacking bottles in large piles *sur pointes* after *remuage*.

Moelleux (Fr.) Literally soft or mellow, this term is usually seen on the label of medium-sweet wines.

Mono cru Wine of a single commune, Champagne Salon for example.

Montagne de Reims Hilly outcrop between Reims and Épernay, planted mostly with *Pinot Noir* vines on vineyards which are higher and steeper than those of the *Côte des Blancs*.

Montre (Fr.) The emergence of embryo bunches of grapes, the size of which is the first indication of the potential size of a harvest. Also called *sortie*.

Mousse (Fr.) The effervescence of a sparkling wine, which is deceiving in a glass and can best be judged in the mouth. The same wine may appear to be *flat* in one glass and vigorous in another owing to the microscopic differences of surface, which could in turn be due to either manufacture or the washing up! The bubbles should be small and persistent, with the strength of effervescence dependent on the style of wine.

Mousseux (Fr.) Sparkling, foaming, frothy, etc.

Mout (Fr.) *Must.*

Mouton (Fr.) The lid of a traditional Champagne press which comes down on the *marc* contained by the *maie*.

Muselet de fil de fer (Fr.) The wire muzzle used to secure the *permanent cork* during the *ficelage*.

Must The freshly pressed, unfermented juice of grapes.

Muted *Reticent* on the *nose*.

Négociant (Fr.) Trader or merchant.

Négociant-manipulant or **NM** (Fr.) A Champagne house – a firm which makes and sells Champagne.

Négociant-non-manipulant (Fr.) A merchant who sells Champagne under his own name, but does not actually make it.

Nematodes Damage to vines caused by these microscopic root-worms was first identified in California in 1930. *Nematodes* are very difficult to treat effectively or permanently and it is often easier to select a *nematode*-resistant *rootstock* in badly affected areas.

Node The swellings from which buds emerge, which are located at intervals along a mature shoot, are called nodes.

Non-vintage or **NV** Theoretically a blended wine made from two or more years, but usually based upon one – the last – and in the instance of *récoltant-manipulant* Champagnes, it may well be 100% of the last saleable vintage. Non-vintage Champagnes must have at least one year in bottle and cannot be bottled before January of the year following the harvest.

Nose The smell or odour of a wine, encompassing both *aroma* and *bouquet*.

Nouaison (Fr.) The setting of the grapes which usually takes place from June onwards.

Nutgalls Swellings found on the leaves of certain oak trees which provide Champagne's traditional source of tannin used to instigate the electrolytic process of *fining* with *gelatine*.

Oenology The chemistry of wine and winemaking.

Oidium or **Oidium Tuckery** A *cryptogamic* disorder of the vine, also called *Powdery Mildew*, *True Mildew* and *Uncinula Necator*.

Openknit An open and enjoyable *nose* or *palate*, usually a modest wine, not capable of much development.

Opulent Suggestive of a rather luxurious *varietal aroma*, very *rich*, but not quite *blowsy*.

Organoleptic Affecting a bodily organ or sense, usually taste and smell.

Osmotic pressure When two solutions are separated by a semi-permeable membrane, water will leave the weaker solution in an endeavour to equalise the differing strengths of the solutions. In vinous terms this is most usually encountered when yeast cells are expected to work on a *must* containing too much sugar. Since water accounts for 65% of a yeast cell, osmotic pressure causes the water to escape through its semi-permeable exterior membrane, the cell caves in (*plasmolysis*) as it dries up and eventually it dies.

Ouillage (Fr.) Topping-up of casks or vats.

Ouverture des vendanges (Fr.) An announcement by the CIVC giving the opening dates of the *vintage*, before which the grapes are not allowed to be harvested. The dates differ from year to year in line with the general climatic conditions, the viticultural progress of the vine and the *ripening* pattern of the grapes. Variances on a local communal scale are often taken into consideration, with specific dates being set for particular villages or districts.

Overtone A dominating element of *nose* and *palate* and often one that is not directly attributable to the grape or wine.

Oxidised An ambiguous term. From the moment the grapes are pressed or crushed, oxidation sets in. It is an essential element of the fermentation operation and is the process by which wine matures in bottle. All wine is therefore oxidised to a certain extent. What is generally meant when the term *oxidised* is used as a condemnation is that the wine is in a prematurely advanced stage of oxidation. Such a wine would have a noticeable *sherry-like* odour.

Palate The flavour or taste of a wine.

Pannier de mannequin (Fr.) Oval-shaped baskets traditionally used for transporting grapes from the vineyard to the presshouse.

Peak The so-called peak in the *maturity* of a wine is subject to the consumer's point of appreciation. Those liking *fresher*, *crisper* wines will perceive an earlier peak (in the same wine) than 'golden oldy' drinkers. As a rule of thumb which applies to all extremes of taste, a wine will remain at its peak for as long as it took to reach it.

Pear-drop The *aroma* of ethyl-acetate which is produced in higher than normal quantities by various intensive *macération carbonique* techniques of vinification.

Pelles (Fr.) Blunt wooden instruments used for the *retroussage*.

Permanent cork The cork used to seal a Champagne bottle after *dégorgement*.

Peronospora A *cryptogamic* disorder of the vine also known as *Downy Mildew*, *False Mildew* and *Plasmopara*.

Pétillant A wine with enough residual carbonic gas to create a light sparkle.

Petiole The stem of a leaf.

Petiolar sinus The space between the lobes at the junction of the *petiole* and the leaf.

Photosynthesis The most important biological process of the vine, by which certain carbohydrates are synthesised from CO_2 and water by chlorophyllous cells in the presence of light, oxygen being the by-product.

Phylloxera vasterix World-wide vine louse which spread from America to virtually every commercial viticultural region in the late nineteenth century, causing vines to be *grafted* to *phylloxera*-resistant American *rootstocks*.

Pièce (Fr.) A standard Champagne measure of 205 litres. When a Champagne cask is empty it is called a *fut*, when full a *pièce*.

Pinot Meunier A vine producing black grapes; the widest planted of the region's three major varieties. Poor cousin of the *Pinot Noir*, its cultivation is desirable in frost-prone areas of the *Vallée de la Marne*.

Pinot Noir A vine producing the classic black grape of Champagne and the variety favoured by growers on the *Montagne de Reims*.

Piquant Usually applied to a pleasing white wine with a positive underlying fruit and *acidity*.

Plafond Limité de Classement or **PLC** The theoretical ceiling of yield, above which the wines should be sent for distillation.

Plaque (Fr.) The metal cap which prevents the *permanent cork* from being severed by the wire muzzle which secures it to the bottle.

Plasmolysis The caving in of a yeast cell due to *osmotic pressure*.

Plasmopara A cryptogamic disorder of the vine also known as *Downy Mildew*, *False Mildew* and *Peronospora*.

Pleurs (Fr.) Tears which weep from the pruning wounds when the sap rises.

Poignetage (Fr.) Physical shaking of the bottles during the *déplacement* operations.

Pointes, Sur (Fr.) Wines which are *mise en masse* are stacked *sur pointes* in large piles after *remuage*, ie., the 'point' or cork of an inverted bottle is lodged in the *punt* of the bottle beneath.

Pomponne (Fr.) A flute-shaped glass without a stem or base, merely a glass knob which prevents it from being put down. The *pomponne* was popularised in the eighteenth century by aristocratic ladies on long coach journeys who, during the course of such bumpy rides, found little practical use for a glass with a base.

Porteur (Fr.) One who receives baskets of grapes harvested by a picker and then passes them on to the *colporteur*.

Potential hydrogen-ion concentration or **pH** A measure of the active acidity/alkalinity of a liquid. It does not give any indication of the *quantity* of acidity present in a wine, but neither does the human palate. The pH measurement is more closely associated with the acidity *organoleptically* perceived in wine. In the scale from 0 to 14 pH, 0 is extremely acid, 7 is neutral and 14 is extremely alkaline. Wine is normally around 3.5 pH, although Champagne is nearer 3 pH (the *cuvée* averages 2.85 pH and the *taille* 3.1 to 3.3 pH, but the pH tends to rise slightly during *fermentation*). It is important to remember the *higher* the pH, the *lower* the acidity.

Pourriture (Fr.) A generic term for rot.

Powdery Mildew A *cryptogamic* disorder of the vine, also called *True Mildew*, *Oidium*, *Oidium Tuckery* and *Uncinula Necator*.

Premier cru (Fr.) Literally a 'first growth', in Champagne specifically referring to villages rated between 90% and 99% in the *échelle des crus*.

Première taille (Fr.) The first 410 litres of grape juice following the *cuvée* when pressing a 4,000 kilo *marc* of grapes. See also *vin de taille*.

Pressurage (Fr.) The act of pressing (grapes).

Prise de mousse (Fr.) During the *second fermentation*, the *liqueur de tirage* is converted into almost equal quantities of *alcohol* and *carbonic gas*. When a bottle of Champagne is opened, the *carbonic gas* escapes from the wine in the form of bubbles creating the *mousse*, thus this whole process is encapsulated in the French term *prise de mousse* or 'capturing the sparkle'.

Producer vine Vines in commercial vineyards are usually *grafted* onto a *rootstock* for resistance against *phylloxera*, but the grapes produced are characteristic of the producer vine, varieties of *Vitis vinifera* like Champagne's classic *Chardonnay*, *Pinot Noir* or *Pinot Meunier*.

Provignage (Fr.) A method of propagating vines growing *en foule* by layering. In Champagne, prior to the advent of *grafting* onto *rootstocks* in the wake of *phylloxera*, two systems of layering were in common use: *provignage à l'avance* and *provignage à l'écart*.

Provignage à l'avance (Fr.) A system of layering whereby the vine advances forward by one shoot a year.

Provignage à l'écart (Fr.) A system of layering whereby the vine advances forwards and outwards by two shoots a year.

Pruina Waxy substance on the surface of grapes to which yeast and bacteria adhere to form a *bloom*.

Punt The indentation at the base of a bottle, which helps spread the internal pressure over a greater surface area and thus reduce strain on the bottle's structure. It is also useful when storing wines, the cork of one bottle neatly nestling in the *punt* of another.

Pupi-matic (Fr.) An automatic *pupitre*.

Pupitre (Fr.) Two rectangular boards hinged together at the top to form an inverted V shape. Each board contains 60 holes cut at an angle of 45° in which Champagne bottles, having endured the *prise de mousse*, undergo *remuage*.

Quality Wine Produced in a Specified Region or **QWPSR** The EEC standard which quality control systems like AOC must achieve.

Race The liveliness and vitality of a wine, often attributed to the type of soil on which the vines grow.

Racking This is an operation which entails draining the wine off its lees into a fresh cask or vat. The term derives from the different levels (or racks) from which the wine is run from one container to another.

Raffles (Fr.) Grape stalks.

Ratafia (Fr.) A sweet apéritif made by adding pure grape spirit to fresh grape juice, thereby preventing any chance of *fermentation*.

Rebêche (Fr.) The juice extracted after the *taille* but before *surpressage*, i.e., in excess of 2,666 litres per 4,000 kilos of grapes, but not exceeding 3,076 litres.

Récemment Dégorgé or **RD** (Fr.) Literally refers to a wine which has been recently disgorged, but usually indicates that a late-released vintage Champagne has been kept under ideal conditions in the producer's cellars and has only just been disgorged. The use of the initials RD on a label is reserved by Bollinger, having registered it as a trade mark.

Récoltant-Manipulant or **RM** (Fr.) A grower who produces and sells his own Champagne.

Réglementation de vendange (Fr.) Last-minute regulations affecting a harvest issued by the CIVC.

Remplissage (Fr.) Topping up the bottles after *dégorgement* usually, but not necessarily, with *liqueur d'expédition*.

Remuage (Fr.) The riddling of Champagne bottles after the *prise de mousse* encourages the sediment to slide down to the base of the *temporary closure*.

Remueur (Fr.) A *caviste* skilled in the art of *remuage*; also called a *manipulateur*.

Rendement (Fr.) The yield of vines usually expressed in kilos or *hectolitres* per *hectare*.

Reserve wines Still wines from previous vintages, preserved in casks, vats or bottles of various sizes (Bollinger uses magnums for example) are blended with the wines of one principal year to produce a balanced *non-vintage* Champagne.

Reticent Suggests that the wine is holding back on its *nose* or *palate*, perhaps through youth, and may well develop with a little more *maturity*.

Retroussage (Fr.) Breaking-up the *marc* after pressing and shovelling it into the centre of the *maie* for re-pressing.

Rich A *balanced* wealth of fruit and *depth* on the *palate* and *finish*.

Ripe Refers to a wine with the *richness* that only ripe grapes can give. It is the ripeness of grapes, rather than the *maturity* of wine.

Robust A milder form of *aggressive*, which may often be applied to a *mature* product, i.e., the wine is robust by nature, not *aggressive* through youth.

Rootstock Since the spread of *phylloxera vasterix* in the nineteenth century, the majority of vines in most commercial vineyards have been *grafted* onto *phylloxera*-resistant *rootstock*. Not detracting from this basic fact, the development and selection of rootstock varieties (which are crosses between two or more, usually American, species of vine) has become very sophisticated owing to the fact that a rootstock should not only induce a level of resistance to *phylloxera*, but the choice made must suit the prevailing conditions of soil and climate and can affect when the vine flowers, when its grapes ripen, the quality and quantity of those grapes and other characteristics.

Round A wine which, through *maturity* in bottle, has rounded off all its edges of *tannin*, *acidity*, *extract*, etc.

Rural method The first and very basic commercial method of producing a sparkling wine which entailed the bottling of a wine before its *fermentation* had completely finished, thus creating a naturally effervescent wine. Without a *liqueur de tirage* it is not possible to guarantee a consistent degree of effervescence and, as the rural method does not employ *dégorgement*, the sediment tends to cloud the wine. The monks at the Abbey of St Hilaire were the first to utilise the rural method in 1531 when they produced Vin de Blanquette and it was still the only method available when Dom Pérignon made his reputation at Hautvillers.

Sans-année (Fr.) Literally 'without year', this term is the French equivalent of *non-vintage*. See also *non-vintage*.

Scion That part of the *graft* which belongs to the fruit and leaf-bearing *producer vine*, as opposed to the stock, which belongs to the root-producing *rootstock*.

Sec (Fr.) A Champagne with between 17 and 23 grams per litre of sugar (obtained through the addition of the *liqueur d'expédition*).

Séchoir (Fr.) A small, narrow press designed to extract the *rebêche* out of the seemingly dry residue of *marc* which has already provided 2,666 litres of juice from 4,000 kilos of grapes.

Second fermentation A second and separate *fermentation* which creates the *prise de mousse* by the addition of a *liqueur de tirage*.

Sève (Fr.) Literally meaning sap, a French tasting term used to indicate a wine with a healthy vigour.

Sharp This applies to *acidity*, whereas *bitterness* applies to *tannin*. An immature wine might be sharp, but, if used by professional tasters, the term is usually a derogatory one.

Sherry-like Undesirable in low strength or unfortified wines, refers to the odour in an advanced state of *oxidised* wine.

Short Refers to a wine which may have a good *nose* and initial flavour, but which falls short on the *finish*, the taste quickly disappearing after the wine has been swallowed. See also *long*.

Sinus The space between the lobes of a leaf.

Skin-contact The maceration of grape skins in *must* or *fermenting* wine can extract varying amounts of colouring pigments, *tannin* and various aromatic compounds.

Smooth The opposite of *aggressive* and more extreme than *round*.

Soft Interchangeable with *smooth*, although it usually refers to the fruit on the *palate*, whereas *smooth* is more often applied to the *finish*. Soft is very desirable, but 'extremely soft' may be derogatory, inferring a weak and *flabby* wine.

Solid Interchangeable with *firm*.

Solumology The science of soil and, in the context of wine, the relation between specific soil types and vine varieties.

Sommelier (Fr.) A wine waiter.

Sortie (Fr.) The emergence of embryo bunches of grapes, the size of which is the first indication of the potential size of a harvest. Also called *montre*.

Sous marque (Fr.) Another *marque* under which wines, usually second rate in quality, are offloaded.

Spécial Club (Fr.) A skittle-shaped bottle and special labelling in which a *récoltant-manipulant* belonging to the *Club de Viticulteurs Champenois* may sell his *cuvée de prestige*.

Statut Viti-Vinicole de la Champagne (Fr.) A catalogue of laws, decrees, decree-laws and other regulations, both domestic and EEC, which effectively control the production of Champagne.

Stock That part of the *graft* which belongs to the root-producing *rootstock*, as opposed to the fruit and leaf-bearing *producer vine*.

Stylish Wines possessing all the subjective qualities of *charm*, *elegance* and *finesse*. A wine might have the 'style' of a certain region or type, but a wine is either *stylish* or it is not. It defies definition.

Sub-genus The botanical family *Ampelidaceae* has ten genera, but only one of these, *Vitis*, is important to winemakers. Of the two sub-genera belonging to *Vitis*, *Muscadinae* and *Euvitis*, it is the latter which contains *Vitis vinifera*, the species responsible for all the famous winemaking varieties of vine, including Champagne's classic *Chardonnay*, *Pinot Noir* and *Pinot Meunier*.

Sulphur dioxide or SO_2 An *antioxidant* with *aseptic* qualities used in the production of wine. It should not be noticeable in the finished product, but for various reasons a whiff may be detected on recently bottled wines. However, a good swirl in the glass or a vigorous decanting should remove this odour and with a few months in bottle it should disappear naturally. The acrid smell of sulphur in a wine should, if detected, tingle the *nose* and be akin to the relatively *clean* smell of an extinguished match. If it has a rotten-egg *aroma* it means that the sulphur has reduced to *hydrogen sulphide* and the wine may well have formed *mercaptans*. *Mercaptans* cannot be removed except by intensive industrial methods which are ruinous to the quality of the wine. The chemical symbol SO_2 is commonly adopted for *sulphur dioxide*.

Supple Indicates a wine easy to drink, not necessarily *soft*, but suggesting more ease than simply *round* does. With age the *tannin* in wine becomes supple.

Surpressage (Fr.) Any juice extracted after the *rebêche*, defined by the *Code du Vin* as anything in excess of 3,076 litres per *marc* of 4,000 kilos of grapes.

Taille (Fr.) The 615 litres of grape juice following the *cuvée*, which is broken down into the *première taille* and the *deuxième taille*. See also *vin de taille*.

Tailler (Fr.) To prune.

Tannin Generic term for various polyphenols found naturally in wine from the skin, pips and stalks, sometimes added during the fining process, and which may also be picked up from wooden casks.

Tart Refers to a noticeable acidity, coming somewhere between *sharp* and *piquant*.

Tartrate crystals Sometimes produced when wines have encountered low temperatures which precipitate the formation of *tartrates* forming a crystalline deposit in the bottle. A fine deposit of glittering crystals can also be deposited on the base of a cork when it has been soaked in a solution of meta-bisulphite. Both are harmless.

Temporary cork or **Temporary closure** The closure used to seal a Champagne bottle for the *prise de mousse*, usually a *crown-cap*, corks for the temporary closure being a thing of the past for all but a few *cuvées de prestige*.

Terroir (Fr.) Literally 'soil', but in a viticultural sense referring to the complete growing environment, which also includes altitude, aspect, climate and any other factors which may affect the life of a vine.

Tête de cuvée (Fr.) The first flow of juice during the pressing, the cream of the *cuvée*. It is the easiest to extract and the highest in quality with the best *balance* of *acids*, sugars and minerals.

Thin A wine lacking in *body*, fruit and other properties.

Third leaf Refers to a vine which has yielded foliage for the third time, is therefore three years old and, consequently, legally entitled to produce grapes for AOC Champagne.

Tight A *firm* wine of good *extract* and possibly significant *tannin* which seems to be tensioned like a wound spring waiting to be released. Its potential is far more obvious than *reticent* or *closed* wines.

Toasty The smell of toast is a *varietal* characteristic of wines made from *Chardonnay* grapes.

Transvasage (Fr.) In Champagne this refers to the decanting under pressure of a wine bottle-fermented in one size of bottle and rebottling in another. This operation is often considered necessary for very small and very large bottles which are not economical sizes for a truly commercial production and are also awkward for a *remueur* to manipulate. It is, however, contrary to the ideals of *Méthode Champenoise*.

True Mildew A *cryptogamic* disorder of the vine, also called *Powdery Mildew*, *Oidium*, *Oidium Tuckery* and *Uncinula Necator*.

Typical An over-used and less than honest form of *honest*.

Uncinula Necator A *cryptogamic* disorder of the vine, also called *False Mildew*, *Powdery Mildew*, *Oidium* and *Oidium Tuckery*.

Undertone Subtle and supporting, not dominating like an *overtone*. In a fine wine a strong and simple *overtone* of youth can evolve into a delicate *undertone* with *maturity*, adding to a vast array of other nuances that give it *complexity*.

Ungrafted vines Vines which grow on their own roots, rather than being *grafted* onto American *rootstock*.

Up-front Suggests an attractive, simple quality immediately recognised, which says it all. The wine may initially be interesting, but there would be no further development and the last glass would say nothing more than the first.

Vallée de la Marne The river Marne flows through Châlons-sur-Marne. Épernay and Château-Thierry, thus cutting into the heart of Champagne country, separating the *Montagne de Reims* north of the river from the *Côte des Blancs* south. The predominant vine variety planted on the banks of the Marne and in its hinterland is the hardy *Pinot Meunier*.

Varietal The characteristics portrayed in a wine that are directly attributable to and indicative of the varieties of grape from which it is made.

Vegetal A term applied to wines of a certain *maturity*, often *Chardonnay* or *Pinot*-based, which are well *rounded* and have taken on a *bouquet* pleasingly reminiscent of vegetation rather than fruit. It comes after *rounded* and before *farmyardy*.

Vendange (Fr.) The harvest.

Vendangeur (Fr.) The harvester or picker.

Vendangoir (Fr.) A purpose-built structure to house and feed the *vendangeurs* at harvest time.

Véraison (Fr.) The ripening process of grapes which in Champagne normally begins in August.

Vertus (Ch.) 'Where there are none!'

Verzenay (Ch.) 'The one and only!'

Vieillessement sur lattes (Fr.) The ageing of wines stacked *sur lattes*.

Vieillessement sur pointes (Fr.) The ageing of wines stacked *sur pointes*.

Vieux vignes (Fr.) Literally 'old vines', this term usually refers to *ungrafted* vines growing *en foule*.

Vigne Mère (Fr.) The mother vine from which *rootstock* is cut.

Vigneron (Fr.) A vinegrower or a vineyard worker.

Vignoble (Fr.) Vineyard.

Vin clair (Fr.) A wine which has cleared, usually after *racking* and *fining*.

Vin de cuvée (Fr.) The first 2,050 litres of *must* pressed from a 4,000 kilo *marc* of grapes corresponds to 200 litres of *vin de cuvée*, after loss through *débourbage*, *fermentation* and *fining*.

Vin de détour (Fr.) A wine made from grapes rejected at the *épluchage* – not commercialised, it is kept for domestic consumption only.

Vin de garde (Fr.) A wine capable of significant improvement if allowed to age.

Vin Délimité de Qualité Supérieure or **VDQS** A quality control system below AOC, but above *Vin de table* and *Vin de pays*.

Vin de pays (Fr.) Literally a country wine, a step up from *vin de table*, but a step below *VDQS*.

Vin de rebêche (Fr.) Wine made from the *rebêche*, i.e., that which is extracted after the *taille* but before *surpressage*.

Vin de table (Fr.) The lowest category of wine produced in France, it is not allowed to mention either a grape variety or a geographic area of production on the label and is probably a blend of wines made from various grapes grown in numerous areas.

Vin de taille (Fr.) The 615 litres of grape juice called the *taille* (that which follows the *cuvée*) corresponds to 600 litres of *vin de taille*. This is broken down into the *première taille* (the first 410 litres of juice or 400 litres of wine) and the *deuxième taille* (the remaining 205 litres of juice or 200 litres of wine).

Vin pierre (Fr.) Commonly called winestone, this is an argol crust deposited after *fermentation* by a wine of high tartaric acid content.

Vine Commercial vines are members of the same botanical family, *Ampelidaceae*, as jungle creepers and ornamental ivies. See also *genus*.

Viniculture All operations, commencing in the presshouse, that may be utilised in the production and maturation of wine.

Vintage (1) A wine of one year. (2) Synonymous with harvest.

Viticole (Fr.) Delimited viticultural area under vine.

Viticulture The science and practice of cultivating the vine up to and including the harvest.

Vitis One of ten *genera* belonging to the botanical family *Ampelidaceae*.

Vitis vinifera All varieties of vines producing classic winemaking grapes belong to the species *Vitis vinifera*.

Volée, À la (Fr.) Manual *dégorgement* resulting in an audible crack from whence the name is derived.

Warmth Suggestive of a good-flavoured red wine with a high alcoholic content.

Watery An extreme qualification of *thin*.

Weight, weighty Refers to the *body* of a wine.

Yeasty Not a complimentary term for most wines, it is, however, a desirable characteristic when found on the *nose* of a young Champagne.

Yield Refers either to the size of harvest (e.g., kilograms per *hectare*) or the quantity of juice extracted during pressing (e.g., *hectolitres* per *hectare*).

Zing, zingy, zip, zippy Terms all indicative of something refreshing, lively and vital, resulting from a high balance of *ripe* fruit *acidity*.

Bibliography

ARLOTT, John, *Krug, House of Champagne*, London, 1976

BERGEOT, Paul, *Champagne: la coupe est pleine*, Paris, 1980

CARTER, Youngman, *Drinking Champagne & Brandy*, London, 1968

CHIMAY, Jacqueline de, *The Life and Times of Madame Veuve Clicquot-Ponsardin*, Reims, 1961

DOVAZ, Michel, *L'Encyclopédie des vins de Champagne*, Paris, 1983

DUMAY, Raymond (ed.), *Le Vin de Champagne*, Paris, 1977

DUIJKER, Hubrecht, *The Wines of the Loire, Alsace and Champagne* (English translation), London, 1983

FENTON MW, Colin, *Salon le Mesnil*, Reims, 1981

FORBES, Patrick, *Champagne: The Wine, the Land and the People*, London, 1967

FORBES, Patrick, *The Story of the Maison Moët & Chandon*, London, 1972

GARCIA, André, *Grandes Marques & Maisons de Champagne*, Reims, 1982

HENDERSON, Alexander, *History of Ancient and Modern Wines*, London, 1824

HENRIOT, Joseph, *Champagne Charlie*, Paris, 1982

JULLIEN, André, *Topography of All Known Vineyards*, London, 1824

KRUG, Henri and Rémi, *L'Art du Champagne*, Paris, 1979

LALLEMAND (ed.), *Champagne Wine of France*, CIVC, Paris, 1968

MACCULLOCH, J., *Remarks on the Art of Winemaking*, London, 1921

MCDOUALL, Robin and BUSH, Sheila, *Recipes from a Château in Champagne*, London, 1982

MAGE, Michel, *Le Champagne*, Paris, 1982

MELE, Pietro Francesco, *Moët & Chandon – Impressions of France*, Rome, undated

RAY, Cyril, *Bollinger*, London, 1971

REDDING, Cyrus, *A History and Description of Modern Wines*, London, 1833

REDDING, Cyrus, *French Wines and Vineyards*, London, 1860

SDE, designed and produced by, *Piper-Heidsieck*, Paris, 1982

SDE, designed and produced by, *G. H. Mumm et Cie*, undated

SIMON, André, *History of the Wine Trade in England*, London, 1905

SIMON, André, *The History of Champagne*, London, 1962

THUDICHUM, John Luis William, *A Treatise on the Origin, Nature, and Varieties of Wine*, London, 1872

TOMES, Robert, *The Champagne Country*, New York, 1867

TOVEY, Charles, *Wine and Wine Countries*, London, 1862

TOVEY, Charles, *Champagne, its History, Manufacture, Properties, etc*, London, 1870

TOVEY, Charles, *Wine Revelations*, London, 1880

VANDYKE PRICE, Pamela, *Guide to the Wines of Champagne*, London, 1979

VANDYKE PRICE, Pamela, *The Wines of Champagne*, London, 1984

VEUVE CLICQUOT-PONSARDIN, 'One quality... the very finest', Reims, 1971

VIZETELLY, Ernest, *The Wines of France*, London, 1908

VIZETELLY, Henry, *Wines of the World*, London, 1875

VIZETELLY, Henry, *A History of Champagne*, London, 1882

VOGÜÉ, Count Bertrand de, *Madame Clicquot: Her Peaceful Conquest of Russia*, Reims, 1982

Technical literature consulted:

Bulletin Trimestriel d'Information, CIVC, quarterly publication

Les Expéditions de Champagne, CIVC, annual publication

Le Statut Viti-Vinicole de la Champagne, CIVC, Épernay, 1982 and subsequent updates

Le Vigneron Champenois, L'Association Viticole Champenois, monthly publication

Les Vins et Eaux-de-Vie d'appellation d'origine, Décrets et Arrêtés de Définition, INAO, Paris, 1976 and subsequent updates

Réglementation de la Taille pour les Appellations 'Champagne' et 'Coteaux Champenois', edited by CIVC, 1979

Résumé du Cours d'Oenologie Champenoise, Paul Francot, École de Viticulture et d'Oenologie d'Avize, undated, believed late 1940s

Index